JOURNEY THROUGH
Britain & Ireland

Rob Neillands • Ross Finlay • Roger Thomas • Terence Sheehy

FRASER STEWART

Contents ~ England

Contents ~ Scotland

Contents ~ Wales

Contents ~ Ireland

Endpapers: The timeless countryside of Upper
Slaughter, Gloucestershire

Title page: Cranborne Manor in Dorset

Title verso/Introduction: The falls at Glenariff,
County Antrim

Contents page: England: The River Cam at
                    Cambridge
                    Scotland: The palace of Linlithgow,
                    West Lothian
                    Wales: Harlech Castle seen amid the
                    rugged countryside of Gwynedd
                    Ireland: Atlantic Drive, County
                    Donegal
England opener: The rooftops of Ludlow,
Shropshire

This edition published by
Fraser Stewart Book Wholesale Ltd.
Abbey Chambers
4 Highbridge Street
Waltham Abbey
Essex EN9 1DQ

Produced by Marshall Cavendish Books
(a division of Marshall Cavendish Partworks Ltd.)
119 Wardour Street
London W1V 3TD

© Marshall Cavendish 1987, 1991, 1992

ISBN 1 85435 544 9

Printed in Italy

Introduction

Britain and Ireland, taken together, boast an unparalleled variety of scenery and attractions. Within these relatively tiny, overcrowded islands there are mountain ranges – the Cairngorms of Scotland, the high peaks of the Lake District, Snowdonia in Wales – of true grandeur. On a smaller scale there are the picturebook villages, each with a stream, a pub and a green, which characterise England but whose counterparts exist in Wales, Ireland and Scotland too.

Beautiful beaches, where you need not see a soul exist in the west of Ireland, in contrast to the crowded shores, donkey rides and 'kiss me quick' hats of England's popular holiday destinations. Others may prefer to spend their holidays on the bonnie banks of Scotland's freshwater lochs, famed in song and sparkling with a brilliance matched only by the tumbling waterfalls of Wales, that land of castles, wizardry and male voice choirs.

Fine walking country, wild and rugged in some parts of Britain and Ireland, but in others a gentle progress along ancient drove roads, through silent forests or on smooth, green downlands is open to all who wish to explore these beautiful islands on foot. Motorists will find mile upon mile of uncrowded, well-surfaced roads exist to speed them on their way from region to region.

'Journey Through Britain and Ireland' is a celebration in words and pictures of all that is good in four glorious countries – England, Scotland, Wales and Ireland – written especially for those people who like to seek out the interesting corners whether at home or abroad. All four countries are split up into regions just the right size for touring, each with its own colour location map.

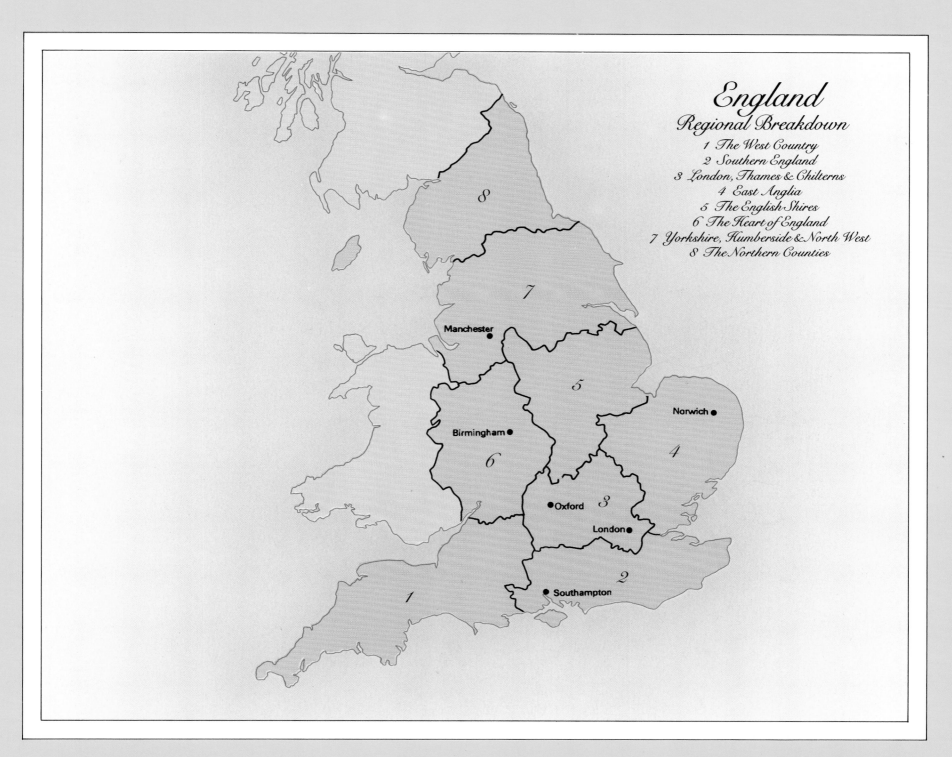

England

Regional Breakdown

1 The West Country
2 Southern England
3 London, Thames & Chilterns
4 East Anglia
5 The English Shires
6 The Heart of England
7 Yorkshire, Humberside & North West
8 The Northern Counties

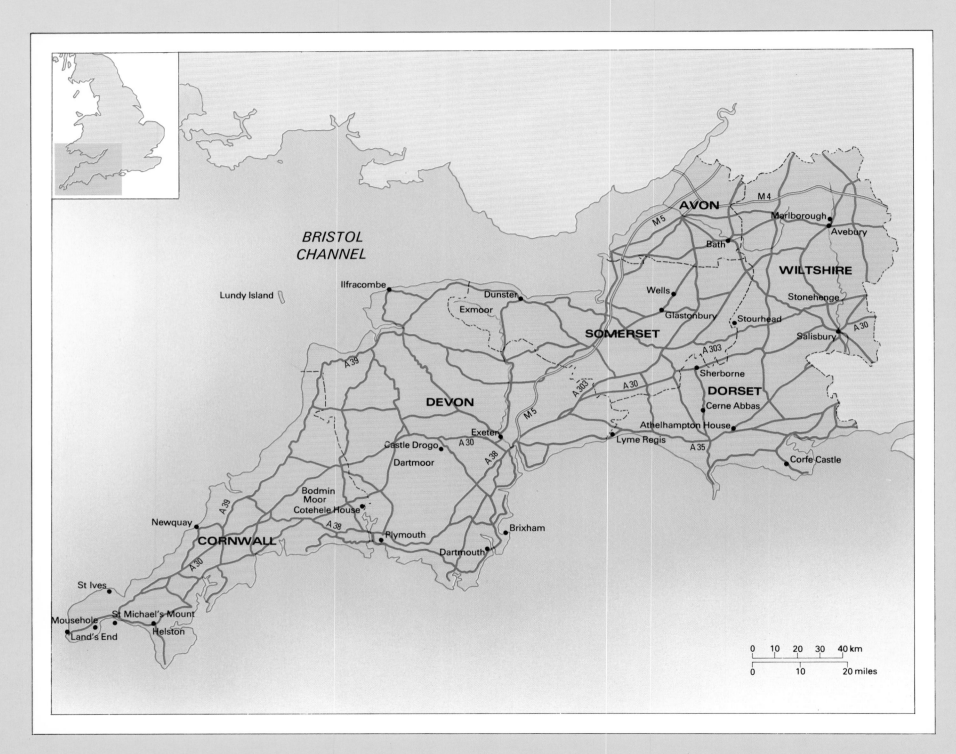

BRISTOL
CHANNEL

Lundy Island

Ilfracombe
Dunster
Exmoor

AVON
M 4
Marlborough
M 5
Avebury
Bath
WILTSHIRE

Wells
Stonehenge
Glastonbury
Stourhead
SOMERSET
Salisbury
A 303
A 30
A 303
A 30
Sherborne
DORSET
DEVON
Cerne Abbas
A 39
M 5
Exeter
Athelhampton House
Castle Drogo
A 30
Lyme Regis
A 35
Dartmoor
A 38
Corfe Castle

Bodmin
Moor
Cotehele House
Brixham
Newquay
A 38
Plymouth
CORNWALL
A 39
Dartmouth
A 30
St Ives
A 30
Mousehole
St Michael's Mount
Land's End
Helston

0   10   20   30   40 km

0   10   20 miles

The West Country

The sweep of beach and the white chalk cliffs of Durdle Door, on the west coast of Dorset

RUNNING OUT INTO the Atlantic at Land's End, the West Country encapsulates much of the beauty and variety that is England. Even though they combine into a delightful whole, the counties of the West Country are distinctly different. Indeed, the true natives of Cornwall regard those of the British nation who live across the Tamar as 'foreigners', and say so at length. Cornwall is a county of small villages, a fey country, somewhat Celtic, with historic industries, like the mining of tin that dates back to Roman times. Devon is a maritime county, with the smack of the sea about it, the home of Drake and Raleigh, a wide, beautiful county, occupied in the centre by the vast wastes of Dartmoor.

Somerset is the rich cider county of England, a land awash with cream and honey, less known than Devon and Cornwall but not a place to miss. Among the local gems one can list the county town of Taunton and the pilgrim centre of Glastonbury.

The Dorset coastline is a beautiful, indented place, full of coves and bays and historic ports, with Lyme Regis as the Queen of them all. Inland, Corfe Castle, now in ruins, dominates the village below, an echo of the glory that is gone, while just to the north in the new county of Avon, Bath, that glorious Georgian city, continues to draw the crowds.

Finally, heading east, the traveller comes to windy Wiltshire, filled in the centre by Salisbury Plain, littered with historic churches and cathedrals, and the hilltop relics of the Iron Age.

ATHLEHAMPTON HOUSE
Dorset

Athlehampton House is yet another of those magnificent survivals from England's medieval past. Built for the Marlyn family in the 15th century, and much enlarged in the 16th, the Hall has a fine timbered roof, oriel windows with plenty of heraldic glass, and such intriguing features as hidden cupboards, secret stairways, and a Tudor chamber. The outside is equally attractive, for the house is surrounded by courtyards and walled gardens and is almost encircled by the river which acts as a moat. The stable block is thatched and the ten acres of garden contain a late-medieval dovecote. The last Marlyn died at the end of the 16th century, but subsequent owners have kept this house and the surrounding lands in the most beautiful condition, and not a lot has changed since this lovely house was built five centuries ago. The house is open to visitors on certain days.

🚗 *ATHLEHAMPTON lies off the A35, 5 miles north-east of Dorchester.*

A view through the gate across the garden to Athlehampton House

AVEBURY
Wiltshire

Avebury lies at the western end of the Ridgeway Path, a fittingly ancient terminal for this ancient trackway.

The village of Avebury is quite small, barely a hamlet, but although it is not as well known as Stonehenge, it contains the largest and most striking array of solitary *menhirs* (standing stones) and stone circles in Britain, dating from the Bronze Age. These encircle the village in serried ranks, most still standing, some sunken in the grass, the total effect very impressive. A short walk south from the centre brings the traveller to Silbury Hill, a pudding-basin shaped prehistoric burial mound set by the A4 road. This too dates from the Bronze Age, about 1500 years BC and is beautifully shaped.

🚗 *AVEBURY lies off the A4, 8 miles west of Marlborough.*

BATH
Avon

The city of Bath is one of the historic glories of England, and it has been so since Roman times. When the Romans built their first city here, as a spa, they called it *Aquae Sulis*, The Waters of the Sun, and Bath is still a spa, and never more beautiful than when seen from the south as the sun goes down in the evening, for the light then casts a deep red glow over the golden Cotswold stone.

The Bath we see today is a Georgian city, built during the 18th and early 19th centuries by three architects, the brothers Wood and William Pultney, urged on by that elegant man of fashion, Beau Nash, who made Bath a centre of society and the Queen of English Spas. The present city reflects that gracious age and, for a detail, note the passages

Soft Cotswold stone and fine Georgian

architecture combine to form this attractive curving terrace of houses in Bath

and alleys off the main streets, just wide enough to permit the passage of a sedan chair. Grander sights in Bath include the magnificent sweep of The Royal Crescent, elegant Pulteney Street, or the splendid views from Pulteney Bridge, which rivals anything they have in Venice. One unique attraction in Bath is the Pump Rooms, built in 1785 and made famous by the works of Jane Austen. They are still open, close to the town centre and just the place for morning coffee or afternoon tea, taken to the tunes of a string ensemble.

Bath is a place to stroll about in, full of splendid sights and interesting museums. Do not neglect to visit the Bath Museum of Costume in the Assembly Rooms, where one exhibition is devoted to a history of knickers, or the American Museum in Britain at Claverton, four miles to the south-east. That, plus the Abbey and the Roman Baths, will take up at least three days of your time.

BATH lies on the M4 motorway, 80 miles west of London.

BODMIN MOOR
Cornwall

Cornwall is more famous for its coast than its hinterland, and there are no wild inland places here to match those of Dartmoor or Exmoor in Devon, but Bodmin Moor, which lies between Bodmin town and Launceston, and is straddled by the A30 trunk road, is a pretty, attractive alternative. Bodmin Moor owes much of its fame to Daphne du Maurier's *Jamaica Inn*, which is set on the moor, while an even more legendary spot is the Dozmary Pool, set on a bleak spot of the moor and said to be the place into which King Arthur's magic sword 'Excalibur' was thrown as the King lay dying.

Like the other Western moors,

Bodmin is an open, treeless place, well scoured by the ceaseless Atlantic winds, with great views on offer from such heights as Brown Willy (1375 ft) or Rough Tor (1312 ft).

Bodmin, on the western side of the moor, is the county town, although many other Cornish towns are now much larger. It is the ideal centre for exploring Bodmin Moor and has two fascinating museums, one on the Great Western Railway Company, and the other on the history of the county's regiment, the Duke of Cornwall's Light Infantry.

BODMIN lies 22 miles west of Launceston on the A30 across Bodmin Moor.

BRIXHAM
Devon

Brixham lies at the southern end of Torbay, on that long sweep of coastline which is now known as the English Riviera, and runs south to Brixham, through Paignton from Torquay. The centrepiece of Brixham is the harbour, a sunny spot, full of fishing boats and offshore trawlers surrounded by serried ranks of pastel-washed houses.

Brixham, in spite of having a prosperous foothold in the tourist trade, is still very much a fishing port, with a considerable fleet still in residence. Another noted resident in the harbour is a replica of *The Golden Hind*, the ship in which Sir Francis Drake sailed round the world. HMS *Bellerophon* put in here in 1815, carrying Napoleon to exile in St Helena. In 1688, William of Orange landed here to start The Glorious Revolution which removed James II from the throne, and in the little church, a 19th-century vicar, Henry Lyle, wrote that seafarer's hymn *Abide with Me*. The little winding streets of

Brixham are full of evocative spots, but wherever you go you will never be far from the sight of the sea, the smell of salt and the high cries of the herring gulls. Do not leave without visiting the Fishermen's Museum, the Aquarium, and the National Coastguard Museum, all of which are close to the harbour.

🚗 BRIXHAM lies 12 miles from Torquay on the A3022.

CASTLE DROGO
Devon

Visitors from abroad who travel through England soon become attracted by the blissful spectacle of the English country house. Often seen through trees, at the head of a long driveway, or across a copse-dappled parkland, they are relics of a now bygone and more gracious age, beautiful to look at, ruinous to maintain. Many have passed into the hands of the National Trust, but far too many have fallen into decay or simply disappeared.

Castle Drogo is probably the last country house that will ever be built in the old, grand manner and is therefore worth visiting. It was built between 1911 and 1930 by the famous architect Sir Edward Lutyens for his client, Julius Drew, a grocer. Even Drew's wealth could not sustain it and it passed to the National Trust in 1974.

As befits the long tradition of English country houses, Castle Drogo is a huge building, built in granite and occupying a commanding site overlooking a vast open countryside. However, as a basically modern building it also contains all the best of modern comforts, and visitors can admire the best that money could buy and good taste command, in furniture and paintings. The castle is open during the summer months only, and

The Renaissance splendour of Castle Drogo is an illusion, for this fine house was built in the present century

should not be missed on any journey through this part of England.

🚗 CASTLE DROGO is at Chagford which lies off the A382, 3 miles west of Moretonhampstead.

CERNE ABBAS
Dorset

Cerne Abbas is a pretty village, built of the most beautiful soft stone. It was once a centre for the leather trade and had a famous Benedictine abbey, parts of which can still be seen. In the village itself stands the Church of St Mary, a mainly 15th- and 16th-century building in local stone, which is one of the loveliest religious buildings in the country. This fine church was carefully restored and cleaned in the 1960s and the 13th-century church and the fine tower are now again quite splendid.

Attractive though Cerne Abbas is, visitors are drawn here not so much by any love of architecture but by the sight of that immense and rather startling hill figure, the Cerne Abbas Giant, a (very) naked figure of a man, 180 ft tall, cut out of the turf on the hillside, north of the village. The Cerne Giant bears a club and is therefore held by some to be a representation of the pagan god Hercules, and to date from the Romano-British era, AD 300-400. Others feel that it is a much earlier fertility symbol. Whatever the origins of this unique hill figure, it is still regarded as a considerable and most unusual attraction, well worth a diversion.

🚗 CERNE ABBAS is on the A37, 9 miles north of Dorchester.

CORFE CASTLE
Dorset

The Isle of Purbeck, south of Poole in Dorset, is often said by its admirers to be one of the loveliest parts of England. In the centre of this island, which is really rather more a peninsula formed by the great inlet of Poole Harbour to the north, lies the medieval town of Corfe, overlooked from the green ridge above by the spectacular ruins of a once mighty castle.

Corfe itself is a quaint, rambling little town, full of those leaning photogenic houses, but the eye is drawn inevitably to the castle walls above, which are best seen from the Arne road on the north side or from the Kingston one to the south.

William the Conqueror laid the foundations of the present castle but it was rebuilt and extended several times in the next few centuries. King John used it as a prison and it was here that he starved to death a number of captured French knights who disputed his claim to the English throne. Corfe remained a Royal castle up to the time of the Civil War, when it was held for King Charles during a siege, and only captured by treachery. After the castle fell, Cromwell ordered it to be 'slighted' or made indefensible, a fate which overtook many castles, and the walls were breached with gunpowder.

What remains is still an evocative reminder of a violent era of English history, though very beautiful to look on.

🚗 CORFE lies 5 miles east of Swanage on the A351.

COTEHELE HOUSE
Cornwall

This medieval manor house, built between 1485 and 1539, is generally regarded as the finest example of its kind in England.

It is not very large, but it is well preserved and very beautiful. From 1485 until 1947 it stayed in the hands of one family, the Mount-Edgecumbs, but they then presented it to the National Trust, ending a connection that began when Richard Edgecumb, the local lord, raised his tenants to fight for Henry Tudor against Richard III. The chapel of the manor contains a clock from this period, dating from 1489, while the house holds the results of nearly 500 years of discreet collecting, with a fine display of armour, furniture and tapestries. The park and grounds cover nearly 1000 acres, a considerable estate, and this too is beautiful, with rose gardens, ponds and a dovecote set into the natural beauty of the green Cornish landscape. Down on the banks of the River Tamar stands the manorial mill and cider press.

🚗 COTEHELE HOUSE lies at St Dominik, 2 miles west of the village of Calstock, north of Saltash.

DARTMOOR
Devon

Dartmoor occupies most of Central Devon, and plays an equally prominent part in the English concourse. On this bleak and lonely moor, Conan Doyle set his *Hound of the Baskervilles*. At Princeton, in the heart of this desolation, stands Dartmoor prison, built to house captured French soldiers during the Napoleonic Wars, and still in use. When the mists come stealing in across the moors, this is a fearsome place.

When the sun shines, which is quite often, Dartmoor sparkles, a place of subtle colours, purple heather, flaring gorse, and everywhere the tinkle of streams, with sheep and Dartmoor ponies cropping the short grass. Dartmoor is the largest stretch of open country in the south of England, and is a wonderful place for walkers, campers and horse-riders, even though much of it is reserved all or part of the time for military training and exercises. It lies at well over the 1000 ft mark and is well supplied with dramatic rocky outcrops known as tors, which add much beauty and

The Cerne Abbas Giant still strides across this green Dorset hillside, high above the town

Dartmoor, that vast, wild expanse of rock, heather and bog

terest to this otherwise open landscape. Places to visit on the moor include Two Bridges, which lies close to Princeton in the centre, Postbridge on the B3212, Moretonhampstead, a very pleasant little town and, of course, Widecombe-in-the-Moor, east of Two Bridges, which still holds that Fair which Uncle Tom Cobbley and All were so keen to visit.

🚗 *DARTMOOR lies north of the A38, between Newton Abbot and Plymouth.*

DARTMOUTH
Devon

The Dart is one of the most glorious rivers in the West of England, and is never lovelier than at Dartmouth, where it broadens into a wide estuary before the sea. Here the river is overlooked and guarded by two great castles, one on either bank, which were built to defend the shipping sheltering in the green estuary which sweeps upstream almost to Totnes, crammed with sailing craft all along the way. The Royal Naval College, where officers are trained for the Royal Navy, has been at Dartmouth since 1863, and provides just one of the many links which join pretty, busy Dartmouth to England's strong maritime tradition.

Most visitors to Dartmouth find enough to do just wandering about the streets, admiring the Elizabethan houses near the quay, or the Jacobean houses along the Butterwalk, but there are boat trips to sea or to Totnes, fishing in the river or offshore, and a whole host of things to see and do here, many of them inevitably connected with sailing, for this is a great centre for West Country yachtsmen, and a popular port for visiting yachts, from across the Channel or even the broad Atlantic. Do not leave without trying a boat trip,

which is the best way to view the town, or getting a good view over the harbour from the walls of Dartmouth Castle, built in the late 15th century and still in a superb state of preservation.

🚗 *DARTMOUTH lies on the B3207, 30 miles east of Plymouth.*

DUNSTER
Somerset

Set on the north-east side of Exmoor, little Dunster is a splendid town, full of romantic medieval echoes. The Luttrell Arms is a fine old hostelry, much restored as late as the 17th century. The famous Yarn Market is at least a hundred years earlier, and recalls the fact that little Dunster was an important centre for the cloth trade. The Church of St George, England's patron saint, contains all the true glories of an English parish church, a fine 15th-century roof, a magnificent rood-screen, brasses, flags, monuments, gleaming brass, tall vases full of flowers — all quite outstanding.

The glory of this lovely town however, is Dunster Castle, the ancient home of the Luttrell family who have lived here since 1376. Seen from the town, the castle looks like everyone's idea of a medieval fortress, but over the centuries the Luttrells have gradually changed it into a comfortable country home. They held Dunster for the King for five months in 1646, and the wall suffered severely from the ceaseless cannonades, but the interior is still intact and reflects the richness of English style from the 17th to the 19th century. The castle is now owned by the National Trust and is open to visitors on most days in summer, and like the town itself, should not be missed.

🚗 *DUNSTER lies 3 miles south of Minehead, off the A396.*

The Druids at Stonehenge

Dusk at Stonehenge, that unique stone circle and Druid temple

The stone circle called Stonehenge near Amesbury was erected by Bronze Age people about 4000 years ago. It is either a solar observatory or more probably a temple, and it was in that latter role that it attracted the attention of the Druids in the years before the Romans came, and their interest continues even today. Curious though it may seem, it is typical of England that a Druidic order still exists — the Ancient Order of Druid Hermetists. They assemble at Stonehenge on Midsummer's Eve and keep a

vigil there throughout the night to watch the dawn break over the Sun Stone, and then hold a service on the old pagan altar where, in prehistoric times, a sacrificial victim was executed as the sun's first rays touched the stone.

Even today, mercifully without the blood letting, and in spite of the presence of too many less-than-decorous spectators, the Midsummer Druidic ceremony at Stonehenge is a unique, almost eerie spectacle. The Druids are robed in white, and wear hoods

decorated with various designs. Bearing banners and sprigs of holly or mistletoe, they circle the stones to sing their hymns and listen to ancient, pre-Christian incantations.

The cult of the Druids has deep roots, which go far back into the dark ages, when it may — who really knows — have had links with the cult of Mithras, or with all those now long-forgotten religions that gave meaning to the life of prehistoric Man. Typically, it is here in England that their cult survives, revived each year.

EXETER
Devon

Although this city suffered considerably during air attacks in the early years of World War II, and rather more severely from developers in the years since, Exeter still retains a number of historic sights, and is a place with considerable charm.

The setting helps; Exeter stands on the River Exe, at the point where it begins to widen into a broad estuary of sand and mud flats which lead down to the sea at Exmouth. Setting this aside though, Exeter is an old city dating back to Roman times. The splendid cathedral, first erected in the pre-Conquest days of 1050, was rebuilt in the next century, then largely pulled down and rebuilt yet again in the 14th century, during the golden age of Gothic architecture, of which this is a magnificent example. The interior is quite glorious, with superb 13th-century vaulting and soaring columns in Purbeck marble. Outside, visitors marvel at the carvings on the West Front, while two original pieces of work are the 14th-century Bishop's Throne which slots together without the use of nails, and a very fine 15th-century clock. There is modern work here too, notably in the Chapter House.

Strolling about Exeter, especially in the parts around the cathedral, is always enjoyable, for the Cathedral Close is full of old buildings, and the High Street contains a 14th-century Guild Hall which is said to be the oldest in England — a claim disputed by some — which somehow escaped destruction during the air raids of 1940-42. Down by the quay visitors will enjoy seeing the Customs House, built in 1681, and a tour of the fascinating Maritime Museum, a superb collection of ships and yachts from the age of sail or the early days

Oare Church, in the centre of Doone Valley, by Exmoor, where Lorna was killed by evil Carver Doone

as the book describes. In Oare Church, which stands on a little hill beside the road, the locals will show you the window through which the wicked Carver Doone shot Lorna as she was marrying the hero, John Ridd; R.J. Blackmore knew this church well, for his grandfather was the vicar.

The Doone Valley is pleasant farming country, steep-sided, full of little hamlets and traversed by a sparkling river, quite a delightful spot in the summer sunshine.

◆ *THE DOONE VALLEY lies 9 miles west of Minehead, south of the A39.*

GLASTONBURY
Somerset

Glastonbury is much more than a town; it is a legend, and a place of pilgrimage. There is something about Glastonbury that takes the visitor back to another age, for this is a haunting, memorable spot, like nowhere else in the broad kingdom — the place of King Arthur and the Glastonbury Thorn.

To the visiting eye, the most striking part of the town is the remarkable setting at the foot of the steep Glastonbury Tor, and the fine array of old buildings, especially that ancient inn, The George and Pilgrims, which has been welcoming devout pilgrims for centuries.

Such sights apart, it is the legends that draw people to Glastonbury. Legend has it that Joseph of Aramathea came here and buried the Holy Grail, the cup Christ used at the Last Supper, under the Tor. A great abbey flourished on this story, and on the belief that King Arthur — 'the once and future King', and his Queen Guinevere are buried here. The abbey grew to great size and wealth during

of steam, many of them afloat. This unique Museum is a must in any visit to the fine cathedral city of Exeter.

◆ *EXETER lies just off the M5 motorway, 170 miles from London.*

EXMOOR
Somerset

Next to the wilds of Dartmoor, Exmoor is the largest expanse of open country in the West of England, a high, breezy place, very green, often shrouded in rain or mist. Much of the Moor lies in Somerset, abutting the border with Devon, with Exford as the central village, and plenty of little roads fanning out from there into some remote parts of this beautiful, empty landscape.

On the northern edge, close to the sea, lies Porlock, from which the 'Person from Porlock' came to interrupt Coleridge during the writing of *Kubla Khan*, which was therefore never finished. A little to the west of Porlock, a minor road off the A39 leads down to Oare and the so-called Doone Valley, the setting for R.J. Blackmore's famous romance, *Lorna Doone*. The story is fiction but the Doones really existed and were a band of 17th-century thieves, exactly

Looming high above the old town and abbey, Glastonbury Tor

the Middle Ages before it was totally destroyed by the orders of Henry VIII in 1539, when the King's Commissioners hanged the last Abbot of Glastonbury at his own gate.

Legends laid aside, this is a beautiful spot, evocative of the past. Do not leave without climbing to the top of the tor, for the fine views.

🚗 *GLASTONBURY lies 20 miles east of Bridgwater on the A39.*

HELSTON
Cornwall

Unlike most of the places featured in this area, Helston is quite a large town. It lies on the main A394 road between Truro and Penzance, and is famous for its Floral Day celebrations which take place each year on 6 May, a relic of some pagan rite of welcome to the spring. The whole day is devoted to music and dance, and the noontide dance is particularly memorable, for the townsfolk; the men in full morning dress, pick up the tune of the Floral Dance and dance in and out of the houses.

That annual excitement apart, Helston is an interesting historic town at any time of the year. A mining centre, it has a Charter dating back to 1305 and the craft shops and stalls along Meneage Street are full of interest, as is the Monday cattle market. The Guildhall dates from 1576, and the 16th-century Angel Hotel was once the town house of the politician Sidney Godolphin. Helston is the ideal spot to stay in while touring the Lizard Peninsula. There is a bar now across Helston river, which forms a vast pool, Loe Pool, below the town, while to the north and west lies beautiful wild country, dotted with old tin mines, which should not be entered. Other sights to see hereabouts include the Seal Sanctuary at Gweek, the Camborne School of Mines Museum on the A3047 and, if you must visit a mine, you can explore the Poldark Mine at nearby Wendron, which has the old machinery in operation, as well as a bookshop and museum.

🚗 *HELSTON lies 13 miles east of Penzance on the A394.*

ILFRACOMBE
Devon

Ilfracombe lies on the north coast of Devon, and looks out across the Bristol Channel to the green and misty coastline of Wales. The harbour is, as always in these West Country ports, the principal place of interest, and it was once a centre for coastal cruise ships, plying across the Bristol Channel to ports around the shore. These have all gone except for the one to Lundy Island, but Ilfracombe is still a pleasant place and an excellent base for touring this attractive coast east to Lynton and Lynmouth, and up onto the wastes of Exmoor, west to the vast sands of Woolacombe in Morte Bay. There is an Iron Age fort on Hillsborough which overlooks the harbour, an interesting town museum, and a Tropical Wildlife Zoo in Bicclescombe Park. The town beaches are plentiful, if rather small, some of sand, some of shingle, but all have rock pools to paddle in, and sheltered sun-traps to doze away the day.

🚗 *ILFRACOMBE is 13 miles north of Barnstaple on the A361.*

LAND'S END
Cornwall

From the high breezy cliffs of Land's End, pounded by the full fetch of the Atlantic waves, the visitor to Britain looks out towards America, 3000 miles away or more. This is the most Western point in England, and although it is naturally very crowded with visitors in summer, it is here, far more than elsewhere in Britain, that you really appreciate that Britain is an island.

Those who manage to visit this spot in winter, when the westerley gales come roaring in from the Atlantic, will find the seascapes and spray quite awesome to behold. Out to sea, the tall spire of the Longships Lighthouse blinks a warning to passing ships, in spite of which they regularly come to grief here. The islands far out on the horizon are the Scillies.

Close by is a host of attractive little villages, along the coast or tucked away just inland, like Sennan or St Just, while Penzance is just a few miles away.

🚗 *LAND'S END lies 10 miles west of Penzance on the A30.*

LUNDY ISLAND
Devon

Lundy Island lies well out in the Bristol Channel, off Hartland Point, and can only be reached either by helicopter or on a twice-weekly boat service from Ilfracombe or Bideford.

It now belongs to the National Trust, though the properties here have been converted into holiday homes for let by The Landmark Trust, which devotes itself to the preservation of old buildings of all kinds. About 40 people live on Lundy all year, and amenities on shore include one pub, The Marisco Tavern, a one-man brewery, a small shop and a lot of sheep. The principal residents are seabirds and it is Lundy's reputation as a centre for birdwatching that draws the visitors throughout the year.

It was once a refuge for pirates, and can still be a wild spot in winter when the great gales come booming up the Channel from the Atlantic, but in Spring and Summer Lundy is delightful, full of birdsong, mellow with sunlight, a great curtain of sea-pinks sweeping down the slopes of the western cliffs towards the blue sea far below. It is not the easiest place to get to but those who make the effort find Lundy the perfect island, and tend to return there again and again.

LUNDY lies off Hartland Point on the north coast of Devon, and is best reached from there by helicopter. The flight time from Hartland Point is 7 minutes.

LYME REGIS
Dorset

Lyme Regis is a beautiful place, very historic, very photogenic. The suffix 'Regis', 'the King's town', was granted by King Edward I, 'The Hammer of the Scots', in the middle of the 13th century, and that famous curving breakwater, 'the Cobb', which has featured in such novels as Jane Austen's *Persuasion* and John Fowles's *The French Lieutenant's Woman* was built to protect the harbour in the 14th century, and is still intact today. In later centuries Lyme Regis saw the first sea fights against the Spanish Armada (1588) and in 1685 the Duke of Monmouth landed here to start that ill-fated rebellion that led to his execution — history is everywhere in this little Dorset port.

Lyme Regis today is a very pretty spot, set in a wide bay, and the chalk cliffs hereabouts are noted for fossils, many examples of which can be seen in the town museum. Best of all though, just sit somewhere on the beach and watch the boats, or tread the path of the fictional heroines and walk out on the Cobb for a fine view back into the town.

LYME REGIS lies 25 miles west of Dorchester by the A35.

MARLBOROUGH
Wiltshire

Marlborough is an old coaching town, a way-station on the road from London to Bath. It still looks like a stage-stop, for the broad High Street which leads west to the precincts of Marlborough College, one of England's most famous public schools, is still lined with old coaching inns. If Mr Pickwick and his friends were to be seen strolling by, no one would be a bit surprised!

In fact, Marlborough pre-dates coaching days of the 18th and early 19th centuries by many hundreds of years, in spite of all that central Georgian architecture. The Bath Road it lies on was a Roman military road, there was a Norman castle in the place where the College now stands, and legend has it that King

The elegant facade of Marlborough College

Arthur's wizard, Merlin, is buried hereabouts. A fire in the 16th century destroyed the medieval town.

MARLBOROUGH lies 16 miles east of Calne, on the A4.

MOUSEHOLE
Cornwall

Mousehole could only be a Cornish village — and they pronounce it 'Muzzle' locally, by the way — quaint, picturesque, busy, and looking out to sea, in this case across the sweep of Mounts Bay and the open sea towards Lizard Point. Until quite recently, Mousehole was a prosperous village, and a great centre for the pilchard fleet, but this excellent fish has now vanished from these Western waters and the village depends increasingly on tourism. Fortunately, they come in droves, for Mousehole is attractive, with pastel-painted houses, built in Cornish granite, and a pretty harbour full of small boats in a crescent-shaped cove.

Mousehole has long been an artists' centre, certainly since the 18th century, and they still flock here, drawn by that clear Atlantic light, the con-

a great open bay, Newquay is an elegant town, full of fine hotels, and the principal seaside resort in Cornwall. Until the end of the last century there was nothing here but a few fishermen's huts, so the growth of Newquay has matched that of holidaymaking in the West Country and has grown by leaps and bounds over the last 50 years. The town has become well established in recent years as a surfing centre, and when great waves sweep in from the Atlantic, and 'the surf is up', the sea offshore is full of weaving surfboards — a wonderful, exciting spectacle.

The coastline is a diverse mixture of cliffs, beaches and bays, but one particularly memorable sight lies five miles to the north beyond Walingale Bay at Bedruthan Steps. There is a fine sandy beach here, dominated by a line of vast rocks which culminate in a line of 200 ft-high offshore stacks. One of these greatly resembles the profile of Good Queen Bess.

NEWQUAY lies 17 miles north of Truro, on the A3075.

PLYMOUTH
Devon

Plymouth is a fine old English city, a great place to remember those fighting seamen of Elizabethan England who sailed from here to thrash the galleons of Phillip II's Spanish Armada. Those stormy times and the city's maritime connection can be best evoked up on Plymouth Hoe, where there is still a bowling green. It was here that a messenger interrupted Sir Francis Drake with the news that the Spanish Fleet had just entered the English Channel, but Drake was unperturbed. 'There is time to finish this game and beat the Spaniards too,' he said, and proceeded to do both.

From the Hoe the visitor can look across Plymouth Sound to Drake's Island, and there are sure to be one or two ships of the Home Fleet slipping in or out of Devonport, for this is still a great naval base.

As such, it was flattened by aerial bombardment during World War II, and much of what the visitor sees today, off the Hoe at least, has been constructed since the 1950s. Look about though, and there are still some historic sights to see. Around the Barbican there are old houses and narrow streets leading down to the Mayflower Steps from which the Pilgrim Fathers embarked for the New World in 1620. From the Citadel on the Hoe there are great views out to sea, to the Eddystone lighthouse and the green heights of Mountbatten, while those who want to see more of Plymouth's maritime connection may be able to visit the Naval Dockyard; Britons only in here though, I'm afraid.

PLYMOUTH lies 75 miles west of Exeter on the A38.

ST IVES
Cornwall

St Ives is the picture-postcard town of Cornwall, a necessary stop on any journey through this delightful and very different English county. Until about 100 years ago, this was a fishing port, thriving on vast catches of pilchards, but when this trade declined, the town took on a fresh lease of life as an artists' and tourists' centre. Among those who have painted scenes hereabouts were Sickert and Whistler, as well as the potter Bernard Leach, and the sculptor, Barbara Hepworth, and her house, now a museum, is one of the sights of the town. It is not hard to see why artists flock here, for the town is nothing if not picturesque, all narrow cobbled streets, winding lanes and

leaning pale-washed houses. The street names are another minor fascination and owe their origin to the constant visits of John Wesley, the father of Methodism; Virgin Street, Teetotal Street, and Salubrious Street, are just a few of them, although they all contain a pub or two today.

A day could be spent wandering about the harbour, casting an eye over the artists working at their easels. There are fine examples of local artists' work in the popular Penwith Gallery, while those who like more fresh air and walking on their holiday will find plenty of sandy beaches and sheltered coves for bathing.

ST IVES lies 13 miles north-east of Penzance, on the B3311.

ST MICHAEL'S MOUNT
Cornwall

No visit to Cornwall would be complete without a visit to the little island of St Michael's Mount, which can be reached along a causeway at low tide, or by boat. St Michael's Mount lies in Mounts Bay, just off Penzance. The island is topped by a splendid castle, which although much restored, dates back in part to the 11th century. Legend has it that St Michael's Mount was once a haven for the wandering Celtic saints, or even that it is all that remains of the lost Kingdom of Lyonesse, much written about in the legends of King Arthur and his Knights, which has long since sunk beneath the stormy waters of the Atlantic. The castle is a National Trust property, open to visitors on most days in summer and well worth a visit. The monastery chapel dates from the 14th century, and the halls now contain a fine collection of armour, paintings and furniture, while from the battlements and walkways

trasting colours of the sea, the boats and the serried cottages along the quay. Apart from its own very strong attractions, Mousehole is a good centre for touring Western Cornwall, ideal for fishing trips or walks, or simply sitting about in the sun, watching the crowds go by.

MOUSEHOLE lies 3 miles south of Penzance, off the B3315.

NEWQUAY
Cornwall

Set on the north coast of Cornwall, overlooking a wide, sandy beach and

The castle-topped island of St Michael's Mount seen from Marazion

the visitor can get beautiful views across the bay and along the Cornish coast by Marazion.

🚗 *ST MICHAEL'S MOUNT lies ¼ mile offshore near Penzance.*

SALISBURY
Wiltshire

Those who know England's fine old cathedral cities well, rate Salisbury among the finest of them all. As English towns go, this is not an old city, dating only from the 13th century, but in spite of the traffic which crowds the streets today, it remains a beautiful place, with the great spire of Salisbury Cathedral as the crowning glory. Before visiting that vast and magnificent building, take time to look about the town which is full of fine architecture and pleasant shops. The Guildhall of the Shoemakers is 17th century, that of the Joiners' Guild a hundred years earlier. The Old George Inn is old indeed, and was serving ale as long ago as 1320. Salisbury is full of such places, on and over the old bridges which span the Avon, bringing the visitor past the bookshops and out onto the green by the Cathedral, where the Cathedral Close provides the most splendid setting for the great church.

The spire of Salisbury Cathedral is 424 ft high. Built quickly between 1220 and 1258, the structure is unique among English Cathedrals for the purity of the style which is entirely Early English Gothic.

🚗 *SALISBURY lies 25 miles northwest of Southampton along the A36.*

SHERBORNE
Dorset

The buildings of Sherborne are this little town's greatest and most enduring attraction, and what fine buildings they are. Sherborne is a medieval market town, with an ancient public school for boys dating from 1550, two castles, a fine abbey church, and a host of other buildings solidly built of stone.

The castle to the east of Sherborne was built by the Abbot, Bishop Roger in 1107. Note it carefully, for it was one of the first concentric castles ever built in England. Sir Walter Raleigh lived here, but the castle was one of those which Cromwell knocked about a bit in the Civil War, and is therefore now more of a romantic ruin than the one Sir Walter knew. He built Sherborne Castle, and this still stands.

On any day in summer, Sherborne appears as one of those dreamy little English towns, so right here, so hard to imagine anywhere else. There is a timeless air about it, and in the detail of the buildings, many signs of an historic past; a Saxon doorway; the great bell in the Church of St Mary, donated by Cardinal Wolsey; the brasses, effigies and stained glass.

Sherborne is one of the great little towns of England and must not be missed during any journey through this part of the island kingdom.

🚗 *SHERBORNE lies 5 miles east of Yeovil on the A30.*

STONEHENGE
Wiltshire

Stonehenge is remarkable. At first sight, seen from a car when rushing past down the main road, this famous site looks much smaller than it appears on any photograph, but if you stop and look closer, the effect is most impressive.

Excavated by the antiquarian John Aubrey in the 17th century, Stonehenge today is seen distinctly, much as it was in prehistoric times, as a circle of standing or arched stones, all of great size and weight. No one

The newly restored West front of Wells Cathedral

really knows what it is, or how the great cross-members were manoeuvred into place; perhaps it was a temple or an observatory. Certainly the main axis is in line with the Sun's path on 21 June, the longest day of the year, a fact which has drawn Druids and Sunworshippers in recent years to a Solstice Festival. The stones came from as far away as Wales, again no one knows how, and estimates have it that Stonehenge was erected between 1900 and 1300 BC, a considerable time span for any work.

🚗 *STONEHENGE lies 3 miles west of Amesbury off the A303.*

STOURHEAD
Wiltshire

Stourhead is now a National Trust property. This house and the beautiful gardens which surround it is the pearl of their extensive collection, and draws visitors by the thousand throughout the year. The house was built in the 1720s in the Palladian style, and although it was badly damaged by fire in 1902, enough remains to provide the gardens with a splendid backdrop. The house itself contains an extensive collection of Chippendale furniture and splendid 17th- and 18th-century paintings.

The glory of Stourhead though, lies in the gardens. They were laid out by the owner of Stourhead, Henry Hoare, between 1741 and 1750, in the Italian style, with water and shrubberies interspersed with grottoes and little temples. In the late spring, when the azaleas and rhododendrons are in full bloom, the sight and scent is quite stunning, especially when viewed

from across the ornamental lake at evening time. Allow several hours to explore Stourhead, and do not leave before dropping down to the village of Stourton, or into the nearby town of Mere.

🚗 *STOURHEAD lies 3 miles north of Mere, off the A303.*

WELLS
Somerset

Wells is the smallest cathedral city in England, but a perfect gem. It was once chiefly noted as a dairy farming centre, producing some notable cheeses, but today it is the setting and the architecture which draw the summer visitors, and as in all these ancient English cities, the visitor would be well advised to park the car and enjoy the sights quietly, on foot.

The Cathedral is so magnificent that you will need to build up to it, or all else will pall. Look at the City Arms public house, once the town gaol, and the leaning houses around the church of St Cuthbert before you go on to inspect the vast and recently restored West Front of the Cathedral.

Wells is an ancient bishopric, dating back to AD 909. The Gothic Cathedral dates from between the 12th and 14th centuries and is a glorious example of that soaring style. The great array of sculptured figures at the West Front is best viewed through binoculars as are the actions of the 14th-century astronomic clock where knights appear to tilt with each other every hour. Inside, the Cathedral is equally magnificent and interesting, with stained glass and fine vaulting. After an hour or so here, cross the green to the Bishop's Palace, where the swans floating on the moat are wise enough to ring a bell at mealtimes. Wells deserves a day or two's stay.

🚗 *WELLS is 5 miles north of Glastonbury on the A39.*

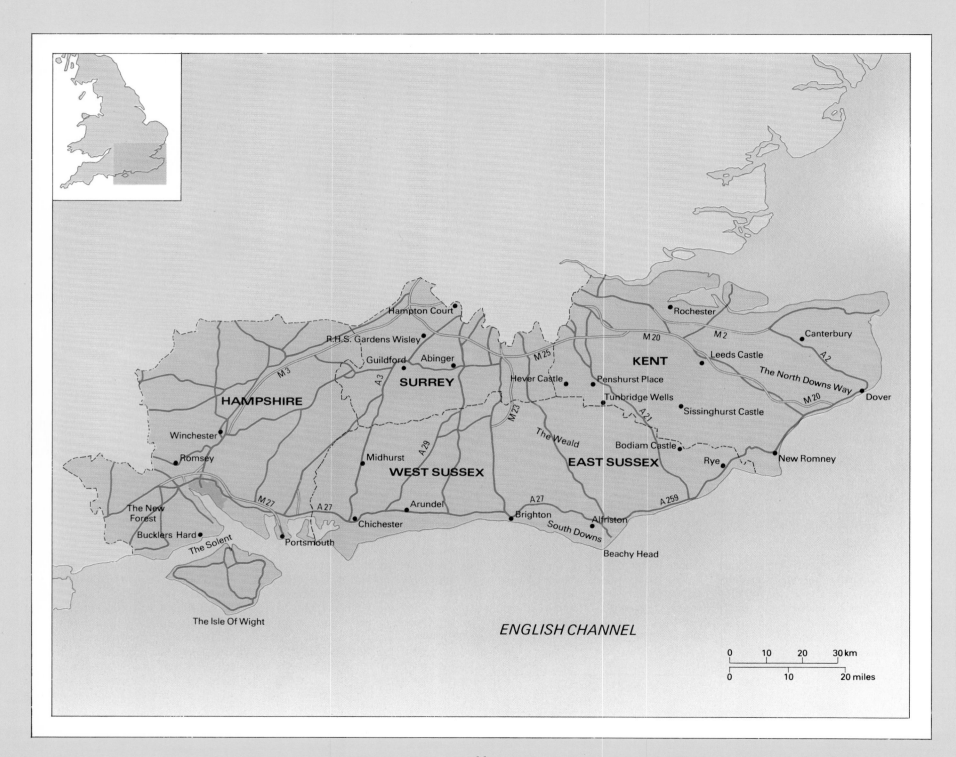

Hampton Court

R.H.S. Gardens Wisley

Rochester

Canterbury

M 20

M 2

KENT

Leeds Castle

Guildford

Abinger

A 2

SURREY

The North Downs Way

M 3

A 3

M 25

Hever Castle

Penshurst Place

HAMPSHIRE

Tunbridge Wells

M 20

Dover

M 23

Sissinghurst Castle

A 21

Winchester

The Weald

Bodiam Castle

Romsey

Midhurst

A 29

WEST SUSSEX

EAST SUSSEX

Rye

New Romney

The New
Forest

M 27

A 27

Arundel

A 27

A 259

Bucklers Hard

Chichester

Brighton

Alfriston

The Solent

Portsmouth

South Downs

Beachy Head

The Isle Of Wight

ENGLISH CHANNEL

| 0 | 10 | 20 | 30 km |

| 0 | 10 | 20 miles |

Southern England

A shimmering stretch of the River Wey as it wends its way through Guildford in Surrey

ALTHOUGH THE TITLE is usually reserved for the orchard-crowded parts of Kent, the term 'The Garden of England' could just as easily be applied to all the counties which make up the south-east corner of Britain.

This is the part of England which civilised man has inhabited in an unbroken chain for well over 2000 years, and the mark of man has been almost invariably benign. Even the New Forest owes its state and existence to William the Conqueror, and those who travel across the South country will marvel continually at the constant beauty of the English garden, whether it lies outside a suburban villa, beneath the walls of a castle or a country house, or in the careful cultivation of a public park. There are the great gardens of England, like those owned by the Royal Horticultural Society at Wisley, or the Savill Garden by Windsor Great Park. There are the historic gardens like those at Hever Castle, or the classic ones like those created at Sissinghurst by Vita Sackville-West. Above all though, there are the glorious, infinitely varied garden created by millions of ordinary folk.

The traveller passing across the South of England would be well advised to wander, keeping off the motorways and main roads, exploring instead along those little lanes that seam this well-tended countryside. Chalk provides the sub-strata, rearing into view along the North and South Downs, in rounded open hills, making a bed for trout streams.

The beautiful thatched, timber-framed Clergy house at Alfriston

ABINGER
Surrey

Abinger, and the adjoining hamlet of Abinger Hammer, is one of those delightful English villages. It lies in woodland, below the south slopes of the North Downs, and was once an industrial centre, noted for the smelting of iron ore by the 'hammer pound' method, which gave Abinger Hammer its name. The local iron industry flourished hereabouts until long after the Civil War, but the only traces of such industry here today are the village smithy and the village clock, where the hours are still marked by a working model of a smith striking a bell. The village green has a pair of stocks and a whipping post, and the setting, old red houses set against the green woods, is never less than delightful.

🚗 *ABINGER lies 5 miles north of Dorking.*

ALFRISTON
East Sussex

Alfriston is a jewel of the Downs. Once, like so many of these little villages close to the shore, it was a seaport, and a smuggling centre. The smugglers would gather to divide their spoils at The Star Inn, which still stands in the narrow High Street of the village, and is one of the oldest inns in the county. The Parish Church stands a little apart, on a small hill by the river, and is known as 'The Cathedral of the Downs', not least because it is far too large for any possible congregation. The Clergy House, thatched and half-timbered, was built in 1380, and the stone cross in the Market Place is the only one in Sussex outside Chichester, which gives some idea of how important this village once was.

🚗 *ALFRISTON lies 3 miles north of Seaford by the B2108.*

ARUNDEL
West Sussex

Arundel is most famous for its castle and the family which live here. The castle was built to defend a gap in the South Downs and has been a home for centuries of the Dukes of Norfolk, Earls of Surrey, and Earl Marshals of England. The best view of Arundel is from the south across the River Arun, which is still tidal here. Across the Arun the town and castle march together, a splendid sight in the clear light of a summer day.

Lyrical though one can wax about it, it has to be said that the present Arundel is not all that ancient. Cromwell's artillery smashed the place in the 1640s, and it was not rebuilt until the 1780s, and only fully restored at the end of the last century. It still looks magnificent.

The town contains many old houses and two fine churches, the parish church which dates from the 14th century, and the 19th-century Roman Catholic Church of St Philip Nevi, which contains the tombs and memorials of the Fitz-Alan Howards, Dukes of Norfolk, and England's premier Catholic family. There is a Heritage Centre in the High Street and at least one splendid inn, inevitably called the Norfolk Arms.

🚗 *ARUNDEL lies 12 miles east of Chichester on the A27.*

BEACHY HEAD
East Sussex

Beachy Head is a splendid spot, a great jutting headland in the chalk cliffs which march along the Saxon Shore, with great views along the South Downs to the west, out to sea, or east to Pevensey Bay, where the Conqueror landed in 1066, even to the matching headland at Dungeness. Below the sheer cliff, lies Beachy Head lighthouse, and from Birling Gap, a little to the west, a narrow road slices up into the Downs, cutting the route of the South Downs Way, which begins on Beachy Head and runs for 80 miles across Sussex. Below this headland lies the town of Eastbourne, one of the South Coast's more elegant seaside resorts.

🚗 *BEACHY HEAD is 3 miles south west of Eastbourne off the B2103.*

BODIAM CASTLE
East Sussex

Seen across the vast expanse of lily-pads that now fill the moat, Bodiam Castle is the archetype of every sand-castle, a fine example of a 14th-century fortress, and is in an excellent state of preservation. Historical detail apart, Bodiam is a romantic place, an evocation of the Age of Chivalry.

Stay a little away though, and do not linger inside the walls, for the interior of Bodiam is no more, and those splendid walls contain an empty shell. Cromwell passed this way and his men sacked the castle before putting it to the torch. That incident apart, Bodiam, although built in 1385, never saw action. It is now being gradually restored to its original glory and rests in the secure hands of the National Trust.

🚗 *BODIAM CASTLE lies off the A229, 3 miles south of Hawkhurst.*

BRIGHTON
East Sussex

Brighton is Britain's most famous seaside town, a lung for London and an attractive little Regency town in its own right. It has a two piers, one in urgent need of restoration, a long

Moated Bodiam Castle is a splendid example of a 14th-century fortress

pebble beach, well covered with bathers throughout the summer, and a vast quantity of hotels along the front, and above the arches of the Marine Parade. One of the great attractions of modern Brighton is 'The Lanes', a narrow, winding network of alleyways, full of antique shops, bistros and boutiques, and part of the old fishing and farming village of Brightlingstone, which stood here before the Prince Regent and his friends made Brighton fashionable between 1780 and 1820. Their town still reeks of the Regency, with the amazing cupolas of the Royal Pavilion as a centrepiece, but today most visitors to Brighton go there for the good food, the bracing air, and the great variety of nightlife available in this lively and attractive seaside town.

It is hard to say why the Prince Regent commissioned his friend, the architect John Nash, to design and construct the Royal Pavilion. Even today, when we are used to the unusual, it looks odd and not a little out of place; what people must have thought in 1820 when this onion-domed pleasure palace was finally complete, hardly bears thinking about, but it appears that opinions were sharply divided. Queen Victoria, surprisingly enough, liked it, although she transported its furniture and treasures to Windsor but most arbiters of taste, then and since, have laughed at it — and why not — for the Royal Pavilion was built for the Prince Regent's amusement. The Prince loved the fantasy world of the Thousand Nights, and this Arabian, or Chinese, or purely baroque extravaganza, has been amusing visitors ever since, although the poor Prince Regent died in 1827, and only enjoyed it for a very short time.

🚗 *BRIGHTON lies 60 miles from London by the A23.*

BUCKLERS HARD
Hampshire

Bucklers Hard may not look up to it today, but in the great days of sail, many of the 'Wooden Walls of England', the ships of Nelson's navy, slid into the water here. It lies on the tidal waters of the River Beaulieu, and among the famous ships launched here was HMS *Agamemnon*, Nelson's favourite flagship.

The village street slopes down to the shore between widespread 18th-century houses, and at the top stands the Maritime Museum, full of information on ships and the sea, with diagrams and models illustrating the former history of Bucklers Hard. Not far away lies Beaulieu Abbey, a popular tourist centre and home of the Montagues, which has a very popular motor museum, a monorail and park.

🚗 *BUCKLERS HARD lies 10 miles south of Lyndhurst on the B3058.*

CANTERBURY
Kent

Canterbury is a magnificent town, certainly one of the finest cathedral cities in England, but if one must choose a place to focus on, then it must be the great cathedral, scene of the famous martyrdom of Thomas Becket, burial place of Edward of Woodstock, called the Black Prince, home church of the Anglican Community, premier see of the Church of England — quite magnificent.

The first Christian Cathedral was built here as long ago as 597 by St Augustine, but the present Cathedral was built under the guidance of a Burgundian master mason, William of Sens. Work began soon after the Conquest and was almost complete by 1170 when four knights of Henry II's household burst into the nave and

The rich colours of a modern tapestry inside Chichester Cathedral

slaughtered Archbishop Thomas before the High Altar. The Canterbury Pilgrimage began within months, and though much reduced, still continues, made most famous in the 14th century in the works of Chaucer.

The town is still walled, full of fine buildings worth exploring, but days can be spent in the Cathedral alone, seeing the tomb of Henry IV, or that of the Black Prince, attending Evensong, or just marvelling at the beauty of this great church.

🚗 *CANTERBURY lies 16 miles north-west of Dover on the A2.*

CHICHESTER
West Sussex

Chichester is one of those towns which is very old everywhere, but older in parts. If the overall impression is uniformly attractive, this is because the town is basically Georgian, and built for the most part in that pleasant and comfortable style. On the other hand, there was a Roman camp here — any town with

'Chester' as a suffix has Roman roots — and a fine Roman villa can be viewed nearby at Fishbourne. The Saxons called it Cissa's Ceaster (Cissa's Camp). The Normans built the cathedral and the walls were built up over the centuries from around AD 250. The centre of the town is marked by a well-preserved 15th-century market cross, from which four main streets fan out across the city.

Chichester Cathedral is the only one in Sussex, and the only one in Britain with a separate 'madeleine' or bell tower. The spire was one of the shore marks for sailors making their careful way round the sandbanks and shoals of Chichester Harbour, that vast estuary that lies just to the south, and the church, now well restored, is full of fine memorials and tombs. As a place to visit, or a touring centre for the rich variety of the surrounding coast and countryside, Chichester today is hard to beat.

🚗 *CHICHESTER lies 15 miles east of Portsmouth on the A27 road.*

DOVER
Kent

Dover is the gateway to England, a rather busy, traffic-jammed town, set in a hollow of the famous white cliffs. A traveller would need a lot of imagination to visualise much of romance in Dover today, unless he or she were wise enough to walk up, out of the town, to the great castle which stands high on the cliffs above.

The castle was built by the Normans during the 12th century, but it stands on Roman foundations and a Roman lighthouse remains within the walls. The castle was garrisoned by troops during World War II, was defended by Hubert de Burgh in the 13th century when the French ravaged the lands round about, and it has seen plenty of action down the centuries. The oldest part is Peverell's Tower, but all the walls are intact, the keep still stands, and the whole castle is well worth a visit, both for itself and for the magnificent views across the Channel to the distant land of France, which can be clearly seen from the ramparts.

 DOVER lies 15 miles south of Canterbury on the A2.

GUILDFORD
Surrey

Guildford is the capital of the county of Surrey, and it looks it today, still an old city but with two recent embellishments such as a capital city should have; the new cathedral on the hill, and the ever-expanding buildings of the University of Surrey, just to the south.

The town dates back to pre-Conquest days, and is listed in Domesday Book, but it really grew up in medieval times as a staging point on the road to the south coast ports. Most of the castle has gone, though the grounds remain as a public park, but the chief attraction of the town is the steep High Street, marked at the centre by the great clock jutting from the belfry of the Guildhall. Observant visitors, walking down here, will note the historic 'Angel Inn', a coaching centre complete with gallery and cobbled yard, the Abbot's Hospital almshouses, founded in 1619, and Guildford House, which dates from 1660 and is a fine example of Restoration architecture. Guildford today is a busy, traffic-crammed town, but those who park the car and walk about with their eyes open will find a great deal of interest.

 GUILDFORD lies 32 miles southwest of London on the A3.

HEVER CASTLE
Kent

History oozes from the stones of Hever Castle, but that apart, it's beautiful, an enchanted and enchanting place. It stands on the banks of the Eden, a winding little river, and was once a proper fortress with battlements and towers. In 1462 the castle came into the hands of the Bullens — or Boleyns — and one of their descendants, Lady Anne Boleyn, was married to Henry VIII and became the mother of Elizabeth I of England, before the King had her executed. The King courted Anne in the grounds of Hever, and it remains a romantic spot, much improved by the Astors, who bought Hever in 1903 and lived there until quite recently. The castle can now be visited, and the gardens are quite delightful, the whole area evocative of the more gracious — if sometimes more dangerous — age of the Tudors.

 HEVER CASTLE lies 3 miles south of the village of Edenbridge, off the B2026.

Anne Boleyn, second wife of Henry VIII, was courted here at Hever Castle

The Isle of Wight

A short voyage across the yacht-crowded waters of the Solent brings the traveller to the Isle of Wight and a different, if very English world. The Isle of Wight is a little place, just 23 miles long by 13 miles wide, but that small area packs in a great deal of beauty and charm.

The coastline, and most particularly the Solent, are the major attractions for visitors, but the hinterland lying behind the coast is very beautiful, rolling, intensely farmed, and full of little villages. Carisbrooke, a mile south of Newport, is dominated by a great castle where Charles I was held prisoner before his trial and execution, and there are marvellous views from the castle walls.

Back on the coast, most visitors begin with a visit to famous Cowes, which is divided into East and West by the River Medina. Cowes is the home of yachting, the base for the Royal Yacht Squadron, one of the world's most exclusive clubs. There are yachts here all the year round, but the place really comes alive during Cowes Week in August when, so it is said, you can walk across the Solent, stepping from boat to boat!

To the west of Cowes lies Alum Bay, a geological marvel with a multi-coloured sandstone strata — green yellow, grey and brown — set among the chalk. Here, too, at the very tip of the island, stands the Needles, tall fingers of rock projecting from the sea. To the east lies the Nab Tower, one of a series of sea defenses built to project the Solent and the Naval base in Portsmouth Harbour.

Although the coastline is beautiful and studded with fine towns, there is history too. This was a Roman base called Vectis, and it was here, at Osborne House near Cowes, that Queen Victoria, the 'grandmother of the Royal houses of Europe', died in 1901. To those who take the trouble to go there and look about, the Isle of Wight can be a constant fascination.

Carisbrooke Castle on the Isle of Wight was once a prison

Osborne House was a favourite residence of Queen Victoria

LEEDS CASTLE
Kent

This splendid pile, set in a lake, beautifully preserved, is said with good reason to be the finest castle in all England. It straddles three islands and has a very long history, for the first fortress on the site is attributed to Ethelbert, King of Kent, as long ago as AD 857! Another, later fortress belonged to Edward I, who gave it to his wife, Eleanor of Castile, and Henry V who gave it to *his* wife, Catherine de Valois — the name 'Leeds' is a corruption of the name 'Ladies Castle'. Other ladies who lived here included Catherine of Aragon and, as a prisoner, Elizabeth Tudor.

The present castle was built by that mighty monarch, Henry VIII, who transformed the grim medieval fortress into a palace fit for a King. The Banqueting Hall is vast, the Chapel mangificent, the gardens beautiful — but the setting is superb. Swans and waterfowl cruise the moat, and the castle is surrounded by 400 acres of deer park and gardens. The castle serves as a Conference Centre, but is open on most days in Summer.

LEEDS CASTLE lies off the A20, near Maidstone.

MIDHURST
West Sussex

Midhurst is one of those places better known locally than anywhere outside a 20 mile radius, a place that people stumble upon, although few places can muster so much mellow English charm. The Angel Inn and the 15th-century Spread Eagle Hotel are just two of this little market town's attractive pubs, and the whole place is a picture, with leaning medieval houses and a number of narrow flower-fringed alleyways. The ruins of Cowdray Park, a house built by

Shakespeare's patron, the Earl of Southampton, stands just on the northern outskirts. It dates from 1520, was burned down in 1793, and is one of those places where Queen Elizabeth I definitely slept during the Royal Progress of 1591, three years after the Armada.

The Cowdray Museum is worth a visit, and the polo matches at Cowdray are still popular events.
MIDHURST lies 12 miles north of Chichester on the A286.

THE NEW FOREST
Hampshire

It is typical of England that the 'New' Forest should be 1000 years old, and was not 'new' in any accepted sense of the word, when the Conqueror came to claim it and put the animals and people who lived there under the fierce rule of the Forest Laws; woe to any man who harmed the King's deer, 'for he loved them as if he were their father'. Hunting was the great recreation of the medieval monarch, and this New Forest, large as it is, is but a fragment of those vast hunting demesnes which once covered much of England. Lyndhurst is the centre of the present forest, and visitors here can see the famous New Forest ponies cropping the grass by the roadside, visit the new Butterfly Museum, or enjoy a drink in one of the old inns. Near Minstead, a stone pillar set in the woods marks the spot where the second Norman king, the unpopular William Rufus, was killed by an arrow while hunting. The New Forest still covers more than 100,000 acres, and is still a beautiful place, and a paradise for wildlife. Even today, deer lurk in the thickets, but the sound of the King's Hunt has long since passed away.
LYNDHURST lies 7 miles west of Southampton, on the A35.

Deer and ponies still roam the dense, green thickets of the New Forest in Hampshire

THE NORTH DOWNS WAY
Surrey

The North Downs Way is one of England's oldest footpaths, running along the old track that led pilgrims from Winchester to Canterbury, and at the same time one of the country's newest designated long-distance footpaths, a fine, long, rural ramble that is never better than here, along the crest of the North Downs, between Box Hill, that smooth chalk promontory, and Westerham to the east.

From Box Hill, which lies a little to the north and east of Dorking, the visitor can enjoy vast views across the flat headland of Surrey, across the plain where aircraft rise and descend over Gatwick, even as far as those southern neighbours, the South Downs, which lie in Sussex by the sea. These Downs are chalk, but well wooded over the short grass, and although people ski down the face of Box Hill in winter, most of the North Downs Way threads a path through shady woods, down into busy little towns, like Reigate or Redhill, picking its way carefully through suburbia, as it heads east into Kent.

🚗 *BOX HILL lies 2 miles north of Dorking off the A24.*

ORCHARDS AND OAST HOUSES
Kent

Kent has often been called 'The Garden of England' and it is certainly a beautiful and fruitful county, noted for orchards and the growing of hops. The orchards have changed a lot in recent years and are now smaller and less varied than they used to be, but they still present a glorious picture in the late Spring, when they float on a great white sea of blossom, which flows for mile upon mile across the countryside.

In other parts the tall poles which support the hop-vines stand in serried ranks; it is these hops which give bite to the good English ale. In these hop-fields stand curious houses, white walled and beautiful, with unusual pointed, sloping roofs. These are the oast houses, where the hops are dried before the malting, and those funnel-roofs permit the air to circulate below, whatever the direction of the wind, apart from adding a rare and attractive touch in this beautiful garden of England.

🚗 *ORCHARDS and hopfields with oast houses can be found in all parts of Kent, but especially in the Weald, south of the M20.*

PENSHURST PLACE
Kent

Those who may never have heard of Penshurst will call it to mind more readily as the birthplace of that 'very parfit' Knight, Sir Philip Sidney, the Elizabethan soldier poet who died most gallantly in the Battle of Zutphen in 1586. His father, William Sidney, was the first lord of Pen-

Penshurst is one of the finest country houses in England, the birthplace of Sir Philip Sidney the Elizabethan poet

shurst, and the Sidney family have lived there ever since. The present owner, the Viscount de l'Isle, won the V.C. during World War II, and is clearly a chip off the great old block.

Penshurst still retains most of the agreeable medieval features, including the Baron's Hall, which has great beams and a Minstrels' Gallery, while in the dining room, the table is permanently set to display a magnificent collection of Rockingham china. In the crypt the family maintains a fine collection of armour and weapons, while other attractions in-

It is still the Sidney family home

clude a toy museum, and the beautiful Tudor gardens.

🚗 *PENSHURST lies 3 miles west of Tonbridge, on the B2176.*

PORTSMOUTH
Hampshire

Portsmouth has always been a Naval town, one of the bases for the British Home Fleet, and proud of it. Those who sail out of here on a cross-Channel ferry do so through lines of warships, while in the centre of the dockyard the flagship of Lord Nelson lies at rest, though still in commission, an office for the local Admiral. H.M.S. *Victory* looks much as she did when Lord Nelson sailed her into battle off Cape Trafalgar. The spot where he fell, struck down by a marksman from the fighting tops of the French Warship *Redoubtable*, is marked by a brass plaque, and the place where he died, below decks, is now a Naval shrine. His most famous memorial lies all about though, in the fine ships and stout traditions of the Royal Navy, whose reputation he established on secure and still enduring foundations.

Portsmouth town was severely damaged by bombing in World War II, but visitors can see Charles Dickens' birthplace in Commercial Road, The Royal Marines Museum at Eastney Barracks, or the D-Day Museum at Southsea, as well as the Sally-Port and the remains of the old fortifications.

🚗 *PORTSMOUTH lies on the A3, 17 miles south of Petersfield.*

ROCHESTER
Kent

Dickens is the author who put Rochester on the map, and the citizens repay his effort today by dressing up in period costume for their annual one-week Dickens Festival which takes place in the week after the Spring Bank Holiday. The town features in many of his books under various names and guises, in *The Pickwick Papers*, *Edwin Drood*, and *Great Expectations*, and Eastgate House in the High Street is now a museum full of Dickens' memorabilia. That apart, Rochester is not the most attractive of towns, at least not visually, but it does have a number of fascinating corners. Rochester Castle, built to guard the

Nelson's flagship at Trafalgar, H.M.S. *Victory*, in Portsmouth dockyard

Medway, is a magnificent example of a square towered Norman fortress, and dates from the reign of Henry I in the early years of the 12th century. The Cathedral Church is also magnificent, and the Cathedral Library contains a fine collection of very early manuscripts and books. Put all this together, and a day exploring Rochester and the Medway makes the perfect day out from London.

🚗 *ROCHESTER lies 25 miles east of London on the A2.*

THE ROMNEY, HYTHE AND DYMCHURCH RAILWAY
Kent

There is something quintessentially British about the Romney, Hythe and Dymchurch Railway. It looks like a giant's toy, but it is in fact a busy, popular and useful little railway, the only link across the Romney Marsh to the point of Dungeness. It runs for a total length of just over 13 miles, and travellers can get on or alight at a number of little stations along the way. The line is open throughout the summer months, when it provides the perfect way to see the hidden sights of Romney Marsh, and engines can be inspected at other times in their sheds at New Romney.

🚗 *NEW ROMNEY lies on the A259, south-east of Folkestone.*

ROMSEY
Hampshire

Romsey owes its existence to the founding of Romsey Abbey, and grew up around it down the centuries into the pleasant country town we see today. The foundations of the old Saxon abbey, circa AD 1000, can be seen through a trapdoor in the nave, but the present building is entirely 12th century, a magnificent example

Romsey Abbey was founded by the Saxons in about 1000 AD, but the abbey-church is Norman

of Norman craft and energy, but one which retains a number of relics or touches from the Anglo Saxon period. The cross, or rood, behind the altar is Saxon, as is a Crucifixion in the South Aisle. Nearby lies the grave of Lord Louis Mountbatten of Burma, who lived at Broadlands nearby, and was buried here after being murdered by the I.R.A. in 1979.

Broadlands itself is one of the finest examples of a Palladian House in England, once the home of the Palmerston family and still the home of the Mountbattens. It can be visited on most days in summer. The town of Romsey is also very pleasant, full of fine architecture and small, specialist shops.

🚗 *ROMSEY lies 11 miles south-west of Winchester on the A31.*

ROYAL HORTICULTURAL SOCIETY GARDENS
Surrey

The English are a nation of gardeners. Visitors from abroad never cease to marvel at the sight of so many flower-filled plots, and the poet who wrote that 'all England is a garden' was simply offering a well-phrased statement of the obvious. There are gardens in England of every shape and size, but if any one place can claim much of the credit for the *quality* of English gardens, it must be the Royal Horticultural Society's gardens at Wisley. Here, many new varieties of fruit, flower and vegetable are impartially tested, while established varities are improved and cross-bred. The alpine garden and the rock

garden are quite outstanding, but apart from being a useful and indeed, a fascinating place, Wisley is beautiful, full of glorious flowers throughout the year, an essential stop on any journey through England for lovers or admirers of the English garden.

🚗 *THE R.H.S. GARDENS lie on the A3 near Ripley, 7 miles north of Guildford.*

RYE
East Sussex

Rye is one of the Cinque Ports, a group of seven — not five — towns, which held favoured charters from the Kings of England in return for supplying ships for the Royal Navy in times of peril, and transport for the

The Rock Garden at Wisley, studded with pools and planted with many rare species, is a colourful spectacle

Kings' armies during any campaigns in France. From this arose a small string of ancient South Coast towns, of which Rye is perhaps the most attractive and surprising.

The first surprise is that Rye does not actually lie on the sea; not any more. That withdrew centuries ago, so present-day Rye lies on a hill two miles from Rye Bay, though linked to the sea by a tidal channel. It is a beautiful little town, full of steep streets. The Mermaid Inn was first built in 1330, but a French raiding party destroyed Rye in 1332, and the inn was not rebuilt until 1420. The church of St Mary is very large and very magnificent, often called the Church of Earl Sussex. The nearby Ypres Tower, which contains the Town Museum, dates from 1250, when it was part of an Augustinian priory. There is a lot to see in Rye, but most people will be happy just to gaze at the views across the flats to the sparkling sea, or climb up cobbled Mermaid Street, taking photographs on the way.

RYE lies 12 miles east of Hastings, on the A259.

THE SAVILL GARDEN
Surrey

The Savill Garden is part of Windsor Great Park and lies half-hidden at the end of a lane in Egham, the village which lies on the hill above Runnymede, on the South Bank of the River Thames. Like the R.H.S. Gardens at Wisley, Savill Garden is devoted to the cultivation and improvement of rare plant species, but also produces bulbs and seeds for the Royal Parks and gardens. The water garden, the trees and flowering shrubs here are a glorious sight, especially in the early spring, and like the R.H.S. Gardens, the Savill Garden should not be missed by any garden-lover travelling through this party of the country.

🚗 *EGHAM lies 3 miles south-west of Staines, off the A3.*

SISSINGHURST CASTLE
Kent

Sissinghurst Castle is quite an old place, and in its time has served as a fortress and a prison. Thousands of French soldiers were incarcerated here during the Seven Years War, and they called it a *chateau*, as people still do. The old manor, much neglected, was in ruins by the 1930s, when it was purchased by Sir Harold Nicolson, the critic and historian, and his wife Vita Sackville-West. The Sissinghurst which compels visitors today is almost entirely their creation. Together they restored the house, while Vita created the wonderful and varied gardens, some of which are said to be the finest in England. There is a herb garden, a cottage garden, even a famous 'white' garden where all other colours are banished. The house and gardens now belong to the National Trust, and can be visited in summer.

🚗 *SISSINGHURST CASTLE lies 1 mile east of the village, on the A262, north of Cranbrook.*

THE SOLENT
Hampshire

The Solent, that narrow stretch of water which divides Hampshire from the Isle of Wight, is a fascinating and famous water. Henry V's fleet lay here, before sailing for France in 1415, so did the D-Day forces, 500 years later. The great trans-Atlantic liners came, and still come up here, borne on 40 ft tides to dock at Southampton, and throughout the year these waters are alive with all kinds of shipping, tankers from Fawley refinery, cross-Channel ferries for Brittany and Spain, and, all the time, all manner of yachts and sailing craft, not least during that great yachting festival, Cowes Week, one of the great sporting and social occasions of the English season. On the Hampshire shore, Lymington is typical of the little ports and yachting resorts which line the shores of the Solent, a place where the water groans under the keels of a thousand craft, the pubs are alive with sailing talk, and the main sound of a summer evening is the musical clatter of halyards against metal masts.

🚗 *LYMINGTON lies 10 miles south of Lyndhurst on the A337.*

THE SOUTH DOWNS
Sussex

Ask any lover of the South Country to list his or her favourite areas, and the South Downs will surely fall in the first three. Green, bare, windswept, rolling, they are the southern backdrop for Sussex, and look appealing from any viewpoint. Once they rested under the sea, and were smoothed and shaped by the last Ice Age; today they shelter a score of pretty places — Alfriston, Willingdon, with the Long Man, a famous hill figure, Ditchling Beacon, a well-known viewpoint, Steyning...... the list is almost endless. Here and there the bare crest of the Downs is marked by great copses or clumps of trees crowning the green hills like arboreal coronets, and from anywhere on the top the views across the county to the north, or down to the blue Channel to the south, are never less than superb, a summer paradise.

Although there are extensions and outcrops, the main part of the South Downs runs from west of Eastbourne to a point above South Harting in Hampshire, an 80 mile ridge of open

A typical view of the South Downs of Sussex, green, rolling, very English

The famous Pantiles of Tunbridge Wells, which visitors would follow down to the waters of the spa

grassland and sheep pasture, spanned by yet another famous and popular footpath, The South Downs Way, which begins at Eastbourne and is clearly waymarked all the way west. ➤ *THE SOUTH DOWNS lie just north of the Channel Coast between the A259 and the A27 and A283 roads.*

TUNBRIDGE WELLS
Kent

Tunbridge Wells or, to give it its full title, Royal Tunbridge Wells, is one of the classic English spa towns, and therefore a very elegant place, set firmly in the style of the Regency period, around the beginning of the 19th century. Tunbridge Wells is not an old town, certainly not as English towns go, for most of the buildings date from the 18th and 19th centuries, especially those which line the famous Pantiles, an elegant, Italianate collonade of shops and houses. It takes its name from the fact that it was once a tiled walkway leading visitors to the mineral springs, and the waters, chanced upon by Lord North in the early 17th century, can still be drunk here. To modern visitors, Tunbridge Wells presents the air of a quiet, restful town, the sort of place favoured by retired military gentlemen.

➤ *ROYAL TUNBRIDGE WELLS lies 6 miles south of Tonbridge, on the A26.*

WINCHESTER
Hampshire

Winchester is really a medieval city, and was once a Saxon capital, the focal point of the kingdom before the Conquest, and a departure point in later years for travellers on the Old Pilgrim Road to the Shrine of St Thomas at Canterbury. They left from the old church at St Cross, just south of the city, and at St Cross pilgrims can still receive a 'dole' of ale and bread before departing.

The centre of Winchester is dominated by a huge statue of King Alfred, the great monarch of the Saxons, but the town abounds in fine sights. The Norman castle has mostly been destroyed, although the Great Hall where Sir Walter Raleigh was tried, still stands. The High Street is medieval, the Town Museum, St John the Baptist's Church, and the Museum of the Royal Greenjackets, one of the great English infantry regiments, is well worth seeing. The top half of the High Street has been pedestrianised, and contains some fine shops, and plenty of cafés and pubs. For a good view over the town, climb St Giles Hill, a public park which offers broad vistas over the attractive and ancient Hampshire city.

Winchester Cathedral is one of the glories of the South, a large, magnificent church, beloved by the townspeople, still filled each Sunday by a considerable congregation. The present building dates from the post-Conquest years; it was started in 1079 and completed in 1093, although this basic structure was improved and embellished later on in the 14th century by William of Wykeham, who also founded the famous boys school which lies just across the green. The Cathedral is best remembered for the Shrine of St Swithin, that rainy-day saint, but the Cathedral cloisters, nave and garth are full of memorials to famous men and women, Earl Wavell, Izaak Walton, author of *The Compleat Angler* and of course, Jane Austen, who lived in Winchester for much of her life. The present building is full of interest, with much Norman work, a marvellous font in Tournai marble, and a host of battle flags and brasses glowing against the old whitestone walls.

➤ *WINCHESTER lies 12 miles north-east of Southampton on the A33.*

BEDFORDSHIRE

Elstow

OXFORDSHIRE

Blenheim Palace

A 40

Godstow

Oxford

Thame

Abingdon

Dorchester

M 40

White Horse
Vale

Ewelme

The Ridgeway
Path

Streatley

Goring

Henley-on-Thames

BERKSHIRE

Newbury

M 4

BUCKINGHAMSHIRE

A 41

Whipsnade Zoo

The Chiltern Hills

West
Wycombe

Fingest

Turville Valley

Marlow

Penn Street

Beconskot Model Village

Jordans Village

Cookham

Cliveden House

Windsor

Savill Garden Egham

HERTFORDSHIRE

St Albans

Hertford

Hatfield House

M 25

Grand Union
Canal

M 1

A 5

A 1 (M)

INNER
LONDON

Syon Park

GREATER
LONDON

0   10   20   30 km

0   10   20 miles

30

The bright lights of London's Piccadilly Circus in the heart of theatreland

*E*NGLAND IS A country of contrasts. Few regions illustrate this fact more clearly than this one, which is composed of London, the country's ancient capital, and two distinct and diverse tracts of country which lie a short distance to the west, the long and winding valley of the River Thames, which leads up to Oxford, and a little to the north, the hidden valleys of the beautiful Chiltern Hills.

The Romans built London, choosing to establish a city at the first fordable point on the tidal reaches of the Thames, the spot still marked by the long arch of London Bridge. Subsequent conquerors and colonisers, Danes, Normans, the Plantagenet kings, all found in London a worthy site for their capital. William the Conqueror began the Tower of London to overawe the City, and from that first beginning the present London grew, spreading along the then green Thames to Westminster.

One of this city's ancient jewels is the River Thames, but here in London the Thames is tidal, busy, even commercial, although now so clean and free from pollution that salmon swim upstream to the end of the tidal river at Teddington, where the Thames Valley begins. Visitors can follow this valley all the way upstream, past Hampton Court, a gem of Tudor architecture, to Runnymede, where President Kennedy of the U.S.A. is commemorated, and the English barons forced King John to sign the Magna Carta in 1215, to the Queen's castle at Windsor, and the traditional halls and cloisters of Eton College, that great public school.

ABINGDON
Oxfordshire

Abingdon was once a Berkshire town, but was transferred to Oxfordshire in the county boundary changes of the 1970s. Not much else has changed however, and Abingdon is still a bustling, prosperous Thames-side market town, with good shopping and some impressive public buildings. There are two splendid churches, St Nicholas which dates from the late 11th century and retains a typical Late Norman doorway, and the Parish Church of St Helen, much larger and endowed with a remarkable painted vault in the nave, dating from the 1390s. The most striking secular building is the Town Hall, built in the baroque style between 1678 and 1682. It is said, with some justification, to be the finest town hall in England.

Two other worthwhile places for any visitor's list are the Abingdon Museum and the County Hall. The Museum is actually housed in the County Hall, itself an ancient building containing a wide and varied range of arms, paintings, displays, tools and artifacts from Saxon times to the present day.

Those who have a low boredom threshold for architecture or museums will enjoy riverside walks from here, along the banks of the Thames, or car tours along the valley or up into the Berkshire Downs.

ABINGDON lies 7 miles south of Oxford.

BEKONSCOT MODEL VILLAGE
Buckinghamshire

This model village, of knee-high houses, is the chief tourist attraction of this pleasant little town. Set out in the shape of a modern village, this is Lilliput indeed. There are lakes and

The awesome facade of Blenheim Palace in Oxfordshire

rivers, sailing ships and steamers, railway stations and a track with busy locomotives tugging trains about, and a hand-carved population of 1200 tiny people. The detail is quite remarkable and visitors to Britain can find a whole range of very English activities displayed in this quaint little village. It is open daily from Easter to early October.

THE MODEL VILLAGE is at Beaconsfield on the M40 motorway, 25 miles west of London.

BLENHEIM PALACE
Oxfordshire

Blenheim Palace at Woodstock is a stop on that popular tourist route that leads from Oxford to Stratford, but however crowded it may be in summer, it is not a place to miss.

It was built in the Royal manor of Woodstock, in the first quarter of the 18th century, a gift of Queen Anne and the nation to their great General, John Churchill, Duke of Marlborough, who beat the armies of Louis XIV in a series of brilliant campaigns. It is named after Blenheim, his most famous victory in 1704, and held by a quit-rent. Every year, on the anniversary of the Battle of Blenheim, the present Duke must present the Sovereign with a pennon, being the fleur-de-Lys of France. If he forgets, the property reverts to the Crown.

Blenheim is vast, covering three acres, and the park extends across the lake for another 2500 acres — a great estate indeed. It was built by Sir John Vanburgh, who was also a playwright, and took years to complete, is decorated in the baroque style, and although still lived in by the Dukes, house and park are open to visitors.

Sir Winston Churchill was born here, and a visit to his grave, in the nearby village of Bladon, usually forms part of any visit to Blenheim Palace. Do not leave this attractive spot without an hour's walk around the streets of Woodstock, to see The Bear Hotel and the Country Museum in the High Street, or buy a pair of gloves, the local speciality.

WOODSTOCK lies 10 miles north of Oxford on the A34.

THE CHILTERN HILLS
Buckinghamshire

The Chiltern Hills, though green and gentle, are best imagined as a clenched fist resting on the flat surface of the Oxford Plain, the knuckles representing the steep, wooded slopes of the escarpment, the back of the hand sloping away gently to the east. From out on the plain this long escarpment lies like a cloud across the horizon, dark, even a trifle menacing, and indeed this was once a dangerous place, full of highwaymen and outlaws.

Today it lies in the commuter country, close to London, and is a peaceful place, designated as an Area of Outstanding Natural Beauty, full of beech trees and long, dry valleys, well sprinkled with attractive villages and little towns. These hills lie within 30 miles of London, and cover a total area of some 400 square miles of farm and forest. This is a place to wander about in, perhaps by car, preferably on foot. There are nearly 2000 miles of waymarked footpaths, and the escarpment is spanned by one of England's most historic trails, the Ridgeway, which begins at Ivinghoe Beacon and runs south across the Thames to Avebury in Wiltshire, 80 miles of wonderful walking with superb views in all directions.

THE CHILTERN HILLS run from Goring in the Thames Valley to a point near Hitchin, Herts.

CLIVEDEN HOUSE & GARDEN
Buckinghamshire

Although there has been a country house on the site since the 17th century when the first Cliveden was built by George Villiers, the second Duke of Buckingham and a close friend of his frequent guest, Charles II, this present building is Victorian and owes its position in present memory to the American Astors. Between the Wars this was the centre for the Cliveden Set, who were said to favour Hitler, and certainly had considerably powerful political influence, not least in the person of Nancy Astor, a prominent personality who was Britain's first woman M.P. After the last War the building was handed over to the National Trust and then loaned until recently to Stanford University.

The house remains magnificent, a tribute to the power of the Victorian age and the wealth and good taste of the Astors. The gardens, which are open to the public, offer great sweeping views over the Thames Valley and the Chiltern Hills, and contain many interesting corners, not least the sword-shaped flowerbed where George Villiers fought and killed the husband of his mistress, the Countess of Shrewsbury, and Canning's Oak, under which the great 19th-century statesman would rest from his cares. It was here, during a play called *The Masque of Alfred*, that the anthem *Rule Britannia* was played for the first time at the end of the 18th century.

CLIVEDEN at Taplow, lies beside the B476, north of Maidenhead.

COOKHAM
Berkshire

Cookham is quite the most delightful village, a jewel beside the River Thames. See the beautiful little church by the river before heading up the High Street, past the ancient Tarry Stone that marked the start line for the village sports. One essential stop is the Stanley Spencer Gallery, which contains work by the late Sir Stanley Spencer (R.A.), who was born in Cookham and immortalised this village in his work between the two World Wars.

Opposite lies a famous pub, Bel and the Dragon, which has a fine restaurant and dates from the 15th century. This short, curving High Street is full of good, traditional pubs and restaurants, and leads out to the wide, green expanse of Cookham Moor, from which a footpath leads back to the river by the bridge. While here notice Mr Turk's boatyard, for Mr Turk occupies an unusual post, that of the Royal Swan-Upper, and is

Tall trees throw a reflection across the water gardens of Cliveden House

responsible for marking and protecting the Queen's swans on the river.

Look up from the bridge, towards the Buckinghamshire shore and you will see the towers of historic Cliveden House, once the home of the Astors and one of England's great country houses. Today it is an hotel, leased from the National Trust.

🚗 *COOKHAM is 7 miles south of High Wycombe.*

DORCHESTER
Oxfordshire

Dorchester is an attractive village, with a wide main street curving through the centre, and lined with thatched-roof cottages and antique shops, while The George is one of the most ancient and famous coaching inns in England.

However, the real glory of this place lies in the abbey, once the centre for a cathedral city founded by a missionary, St Birinius, who preached the gospel to the pagan tribes of the Thames Valley. His shrine still lies within the abbey, which is itself a shrine to the energy and good works of an American lady, Miss Edith Stedman. She came here on holiday, found the Abbey in ruins, and almost single-handed raised the money for its present restoration.

Inside there are medieval wall paintings, a magnificent Jesse window tracing the descent of Jesus, the shrine of St Birinius, and a fierce statue of a long-dead Crusading Knight. The churchyard is beautiful, and if you examine the Abbey fabric closely, you will find a most unusual corbel on the outer face of the tower. Here, carved into stone, the cheerful face of Miss Stedman looks down on her work, a part of this building she has done so much to preserve.

🚗 *DORCHESTER lies on the A423, 10 miles east of Oxford.*

A fine view of Dorchester Abbey from the gatehouse showing the well-preserved Norman tower

ELSTOW
Bedfordshire

Elstow is chiefly remembered for its associations with the preacher John Bunyan, author of *The Pilgrim's Progress*, who was born here in 1628. The cottage where he spent that part of his life when not in prison for his preaching, has long since vanished, but the Old Moot Hall where Bunyan would lead his followers in prayer is a magnificent red-brick, half-timbered Tudor building, and the ground floor once contained a market.

The Church of Sts Mary and Helen, where Bunyan was baptised, is basically Norman, although it contains much later work and many 16th-century monuments and brasses. Elstow Place, just to the south of the church, includes parts of the old Norman nunnery founded in the days of the Conquest, which held a two-day fair which became so notorious for merrymaking and general disorder that Bunyan used it as the model for 'Vanity Fair' in his *Pilgrim's Progress*, and Thackeray took it as the title for a novel.

🚗 *ELSTOW is on the A418, just south of Bedford.*

EWELME
Oxfordshire

Ewelme is not the easiest place to find, tucked away into a fold of the hills somewhere north-east of Wallingford, but those who take the trouble to find it will have discovered a perfect gem, a place which contains all that is best among English villages.

Beside the quiet main street, wide watercress beds ripple and sparkle in the sun. At the centre, set off by these tinkling streams, stands a fine group of buildings, all dating from the 15th century, each a marvel to behold.

There is the Church of St Mary, a glory in Gothic, built by William de la Pole, Duke of Suffolk in the 1450s. His wife Margaret was the grand-daughter of Geoffrey Chaucer, author of *The Canterbury Tales*, and her tomb in the church, by that of her father Thomas, is blazon bedecked and quite splendid, as is the contemporary wooden font cover. In the churchyard note the tomb of Jerome

K. Jerome, author of *Three Men in a Boat*, and see that the 'K' stands for 'Klapka'.

A few steps down from the church lead into the courtyard of the almshouses, endowed by the Suffolks for '13 poore men', who must say a daily prayer for the Duke's soul, as they still do, while a little further away, lies another Suffolk foundation, the little brick-built grammar school, founded in 1437 and still serving as the oldest church school in England. Ewelme is a beautiful historic village, full of quiet little corners, perfect on a summer's day.

🚗 *EWELME lies 5 miles south of Dorchester off the A423.*

FINGEST
Buckinghamshire

There is no prettier place in England than Fingest in the spring, when the almond blossom is draped like deep pink snow on the trees in the old churchyard.

Fingest is a very old village, dating back to Saxon times and mentioned in that great account book of the Norman Conquest, *The Domesday Book*, when it was referred to as 'Tinghyrst'. The pale yellow tower of the present Norman church merely tops off a basically Saxon building, for although the first church rector was not appointed until 1217, the demesne of Tinghyrst — or Fingest — once belonged to Edward the Confessor. Fingest is a real country village, set at the centre of a steep-sided Chiltern valley. Those who come to see the church will enjoy a drink or a meal at The Chequers, where the way to your table leads through the gleaming brass and appetising aromas of the kitchen.

🚗 *FINGEST lies 5 miles north-west of Marlow, off a minor country road, the B482.*

Swan-Upping

Even though they are wild, every swan in England has an owner. Ever since the swan, that graceful bird which so enhances England's rivers, was first introduced into Britain some time in the 12th century, it has been regarded as a royal bird, and in the beginning all swans belonged to the monarch with fearful penalties for anyone killing or injuring one.

Elizabeth I made two exceptions to this rule and granted the right to own swans to two ancient livery companies of the City of London, the Vintners and the Dyers.

Ever since that time, on or about the first Monday in July, the ceremony of 'Swan-Upping' or marking, takes place along the River Thames to maintain the Royal prerogative and establish the ownership of every swan on the river between London Bridge and Henley. The number of cygnets caught and marked has declined in recent years, but in the course of a week's swan-upping some 500 cygnets are usually found and identified.

The procession of boats, rowing steadily upstream, is a colourful, romantic sight. First comes the Queen's Swan Master, in the royal livery of scarlet, his skiff and the one which follows flying the Royal Standard.

Then come four more skiffs, two bearing the Swan Master of the Vintners and his staff in green, two for the Dyers Company in blue. The rowers are wearing striped, vari-coloured jerseys and the whole spectacle makes the most beautiful picture. Each cygnet is caught and noted; those which belong to the monarch are left like their parents, unmarked, but those belonging to the Dyers carry a nick on one side of their bill and those belonging to the Vintners carry it on both sides. The whole Swan-Upping process lasts up to a week, providing a delightful spectacle.

The Queen's Swan Master on the Thames at Marlow

Set at the foot of Streatley Hill, the Bull Inn looks down the main street to the bridge across the Thames just below

GORING AND STREATLEY
Oxfordshire and Berkshire

These twin Thames-side villages occupy both banks of the Thames, at a part of the valley known as the Goring Gap, where the river has forced its way through the chalk escarpment and flows on east, leaving the Chiltern Hills to the north and the much more open Berkshire Downs to the south and west.

By any yardstick this is a beauty spot. The river tumbles in white water and is fringed with colourful flowerbeds, and usually filled with river craft and cruisers, and the villages are full of good country pubs,

notably The Miller of Mansfield in Goring, which is a popular stop for walkers on the Ridgeway footpath. The Church of St Thomas, just across the street, is basically Norman, dating from 1125.

Across the bridge, enjoying marvellous river vistas on the way, the visitor arrives in Streatley. Here, one riverside pub-hotel, The Swan, is sure to catch the eye, while a drink at The Bull will refresh the walker before he or she sets out to climb the stiff slopes of Streatley hill, where the effort of reaching the top is rewarded by magnificent views over the Thames Valley. Other attractions nearby include Basildon House, and

The Childe-Beale Wildlife Trust, close to the river.

GORING and Streatley are on the A329, 9 miles north-west of Reading.

GRAND UNION CANAL
Cassiobury Park, Watford

The Grand Union Canal is a great waterway, a relic of that period in English history known as the Industrial Revolution, but still very much in use, especially by cabin cruisers and holidaying narrowboats. It was built at the end of the 18th century to link the industrial Midlands to the port of London, and

much of it lies deep in the countryside, or cuts through the industrial suburbs of our major towns.

The planned route across Hertfordshire cut through the estate of the then Earl of Essex at Cassiobury, and he only permitted the canal through his land on condition that he received both a large fee and the free erection of a splendid bridge across the water, which can still be seen and crossed by Grove Mill, in what is now a public park, full of trees, flowers and waterfalls, a favourite spot for picnics and weekend excursions in this part of the country.

WATFORD lies on the M25 motorway, north and west of London.

HAMPTON COURT
Middlesex

Few places evoke the might and grandeur of Tudor England so much as Cardinal Wolsey's great red-brick palace by the Thames at Hampton. Wolsey, a worldly and ambitious cleric, who rose to be Chancellor of England, built this palace at the height of his power in 1514-15, but it so aroused the envy of Henry VIII that Wolsey was obliged to present it to his sovereign, an act of generosity that did not prevent his fall from Royal favour a few months later. Henry enlarged the Palace still further and it was later beautified still more by Sir Christopher Wren.

Today, after the first impact of this rich red building has been absorbed, visitors will find plenty of interest in the house and grounds. There are magnificent State Rooms, a vast kitchen, an ancient vine which still produces grapes, and in the garden, a riot of flowers, a knot garden, and the maze made famous by Jerome K. Jerome in that classic River Thames tale, *Three Men in a Boat*, where to-

Heraldic supporters carved in stone line the bridge at Hampton Court

The 16th-century chapel of Hampton Court, where Wolsey preached

day's visitors can still become gloriously lost. Look out for the ghost of Jane Seymour.

🚗 *HAMPTON COURT lies on the A308 road, south-west of London.*

HATFIELD HOUSE
Hertfordshire

Hatfield House is one of the great houses of England, a splendid 17th-century palace still lived in by the Cecils, who are directly descended from Robert Cecil, first Earl of Salisbury, Counsellor to Queen Elizabeth I and James I. The previous palace to stand on this site was built in 1497 for yet another royal adviser, Bishop Morton, he who invented the stratagem of 'Morton's Fork' to extract high taxes from the nobility. (If you are shabby and live simply, you must have money saved; if you dress well and live extravagantly, you must have money to spare — either way, some must come to Our Lord the King.)

In 1607, Salisbury engaged the architect Robert Lyminge to rebuild the palace and he created the present exquisite building in the Elizabethan style with Jacobean overtones. The building took four years to complete and the size is still impressive, with a long facade and square towers on each corner. Inside it contains fine furniture, tapestries and paintings and a fine collection of Elizabeth I

Friday Street in the centre of Henley is full of overhanging late medieval houses

memorabilia. The gardens are beautiful and there is a park.
🚗 *HATFIELD HOUSE lies off the A1000 on the outskirts of Hatfield.*

HENLEY-ON-THAMES
Oxfordshire

Although it is a sizeable town, Henley enjoys the feel and calm of a rather pleasant village. Much of this is due to the town's position on the banks of the River Thames, in a leafy part of the Thames Valley, a peaceful spot which is only seriously disturbed once a year, in early July when Henley is the setting for the Royal Regatta and becomes a mecca for rowing folk the world over.

They have rowed at Henley for nearly 150 years. Indeed, the first Oxford and Cambridge Boat Race took place here in 1829, when the Cambridge crew wore the pink later made famous by Henley's Leander Club.

The first full regatta took place in 1839 and the event gained the Royal title under the patronage of Prince Albert, husband of Queen Victoria, in 1851, and has flourished ever since. Henley, during Regatta week, displays the England of a mostly bygone age; clean-cut young men, pretty girls in summer dresses and hats, old rowing Blues in blazers, lobster for lunch and strawberries for tea in a line of marquees along the river. Some people even go there to watch the rowing.

Out of the Season, Henley remains a pleasant town, with fine churches, good pubs, a number of nice tea shops and restaurants, and at any time of the year, that glorious Thames-side setting.
🚗 *HENLEY-ON-THAMES lies 6 miles from Maidenhead on the A423.*

HERTFORD
Hertfordshire

Little, quaint, red-brick Hertford is the county town of Hertfordshire, although it is now much smaller than many other towns in this county. It is a pleasant place to visit, although many of the old attractions have long since vanished, including no less than five splendid medieval churches. One place worth seeing is the 17th-century Quaker Meeting House, the oldest Quaker Meeting House still in use. Not much remains of Hertford Castle by the River Lea, except the gatehouse, but the central charm of this little town remains intact, and is best seen down the old side streets or in the many ancient inns, such as The Salisbury Arms, which was serving English ale as long ago as 1425.
🚗 *HERTFORD lies 20 miles north of London, off the A10.*

JORDANS
Buckinghamshire

Jordans village is, by any yardstick, a most curious place, a living reminder that many places in England retain strong links with some event in the distant past. On first sight, Jordans today looks like many other pleasant English villages, but then look closer.

The story of Jordans dates back to 1671 when a local farmer sold to the Society of Friends, the Quakers, a plot of land on which to build a Meeting House — the asking price was £4. The Meeting House was first built in 1681 during a time of religious persecution of the Quakers, whose chief spokesman was a local preacher, William Penn.

Jordans became a centre for the Quakers, and they still run this village and assemble in the Meeting House, a small, oak-panelled chapel, surrounded by a green, studded with small tombstones.

William Penn was buried here in 1718, under the usual plain Quaker headstone, and this spot, linked as it is with Pennsylvania, attracts thousands of Transatlantic visitors every year, who should also take time to see the Mayflower Barn further up the hill, which was built from the timbers of the ship which took the Pilgrim Fathers to America.

JORDANS lies a mile east of Beaconsfield, off the A40 road.

LONDON
Covent Garden

Until quite recently, Covent Garden was best known as a centre for the fruit and vegetable trade, a place where the narrow streets filled up with produce-laden trucks each evening, and trading went on for most of the night.

Now the market has moved and Covent Garden has been transformed into one of London's liveliest and most fascinating places, full of little shops, cafés, restaurants and boutiques, a place where street performers gather to entertain the crowds, the perfect spot to see the city people at play on a warm Summer evening.

While you are there though, look up and look about you, for the square, or *Piazza*, is an architectural gem. Much of it dates from the 17th century, when this square, in a then rural part of London, was laid out by the fourth Earl of Bedford and his famous architect, Inigo Jones. Above the modern cafés and shop fronts, Covent Garden has an elegant facade, so study closely such places as the Church of St Paul, built by Inigo Jones in 1633, or the most famous landmark of all, the Corinthian portico of The Royal Opera House, a stage for world-class performances, and a social centre for London society, who love to gather in the elegant crush bar.

COVENT GARDEN lies half-a-mile east of Trafalgar Square.

The old hall, once the centre of Covent Garden Market

LONDON
Hyde Park Corner

Hyde Park Corner is one of the focal points of this sprawling city, a busy, traffic-filled maelstrom, which offers much of interest to those with an observant eye. It lies at a junction of two famous parks, Hyde Park to the north, Green Park to the east, at the foot of Park Lane, sandwiched between the sweep of Piccadilly and the elegant shops of Knightsbridge.

As befits such a splendid setting, Hyde Park Corner contains some notable memorials, mostly of a military nature, not least Apsley House on the north side of the square.

This was built by Robert Adam in the 1770s, and later purchased by the 'Iron Duke', the Duke of Wellington, victor of Waterloo, when, because of his eminence in public affairs, it became known as No. 1, London. It is now a musuem, full of Wellington memorabilia.

That apart, there are fine memorials to the Machine Gun Corps of the Great War, and a particularly splendid one to the Royal Artillery, a magnificent, evocative and tragic creation. Visit Hyde Park Corner at around 10 o'clock on any weekday morning, and watch the Queen's Life Guard ride past to mount guard at St James's Palace, a colourful spectacle.

HYDE PARK CORNER lies half-a-mile west of Piccadilly Circus.

LONDON
The River Thames

Poets have eulogised the Thames at London for centuries, and those visitors who stand on Westminster Bridge and look up or down stream will find it easy to see why. The river sets off the city, the city puts the river in a timeless frame. Look west, upstream, to the Victorian Gothic of

the Houses of Parliament, to the half-hidden roofs of Lambeth Palace on the South Bank, the London home of the Archbishop of Canterbury, or to the clean and glittering pinnacles of Westminster Abbey. Upstream lies the City where tall skyscrapers somehow fail to overawe St Paul's Cathedral, or the delicate tracery of a dozen Wren churches, all best seen from the river, perhaps when on a trip downstream, past the concrete temples of the National Theatre, past the brooding walls of the Tower, under bridge after bridge, to the elegant little suburb and great palace at Greenwich, now the home of the National Maritime Museum. This River Thames has been the Londoner's highway for centuries and there is no finer way to see the City and town, than from the deck of a cruiser, sailing down towards the sea.
WESTMINSTER BRIDGE lies by the Houses of Parliament.

LONDON
St James's Park

St James's Park is the oldest Royal Park in London, dating from the time when Henry VIII seized the monastic lands and established this Park as the garden of his new palace of St James, which he was building for his new Queen and second wife, Anne Bolyn. Then the park was stocked with deer and other game, and visitors today still love to stand on the bridge which spans the lake to feed the pigeons or marvel at the flocks of colourful waterfowl which thrive here in the heart of the city. Even pelicans live on the lake and can be seen preening themselves in the rocks by the Horse Guards parade, a former tilt yard for

Tower Bridge from the Pool of London, a reminder that this was once a major port

The spires and pinnacles of the Whitehall/Westminster skyline seen from the bridge in St James's Park

the Palace of Whitehall. St James's Park is marked to the north by The Mall, a broad ceremonial way that leads from the Admiralty Arch to Buckingham Palace. Down this road distinguished visitors progress in carriages to the Sovereign's principal home, and every year, after the Ceremony of the Trooping of the Colour, which marks the Queen's Birthday, Her Majesty leads her Regiments of Foot Guards between cheering crowds.

At other times St James's is a quiet, restful spot, popular with Londoners at all times, but especially in Spring when the grass is carpeted with great swathes of Spring flowers.
🚗 *ST JAMES'S PARK lies half-a-mile south of Piccadilly.*

LONDON
Westminster Abbey

Westminster Abbey is one of the great historic shrines of the English people, the place where their kings and queens have come for their coronation these last thousand years.

It was built in the years leading up to the Norman Conquest by the last Saxon King, Edward the Confessor, and extensively rebuilt in the present Early English style by King Henry III in the 1250s. The outside, now cleared of London grime, is a glorious sight, and the inside, equally impressive but very different, is full of little corners to attract the curious. What a wealth of fame lies here! At the entrance lies the tomb of the

Unknown Soldier, the prototype for similar memorials all over the world, and among a host of tombs and plaques to the famous, visitors may notice one to Major Andre, executed by the Americans for conspiring with the traitor Benedict Arnold. Poets' Corner contains the literati of the last several centuries.

As always in England, look about you and notice the detail. See the helm of Henry V dented on the field of Agincourt, notice the banners and stalls in the choir, see the cloisters and do not leave without visiting St Margaret's Church on the Green, a popular place for Society weddings.
🚗 *WESTMINSTER ABBEY lies near the Thames, close to the Houses of Parliament.*

MARLOW
Buckinghamshire

Marlow is a riverside town, cool, elegant, largely Georgian. It is best appreciated from the south, across the bridge that leads over the river from Bisham (pronounced Bizzam) on the Berkshire side. This fine suspension bridge was built by Teirney Clarke, who also built the much larger span that links Buda with Pest, and the southern arch frames the parish church of All Saints perfectly. From the bridge visitors can watch the waters sweeping over Marlow Weir, or look down on the gardens of the Compleat Angler Hotel, one of England's most famous hostelries. Tea on the lawns here is one of the great pleasures of a summer Sunday.

Marlow High Street is wide, full of good shops built into the ground floors of mostly Georgian buildings, so look up to see a good many fine examples of this graceful, comfortable period. At the top of the High Street, an obelisk marks the miles to Bath on the 'gout track', the way taken by stagecoaches bearing gout-stricken victims to the curative waters of Bath. West Street contains the house where the poet Shelley lived with his wife, Mary, while he wrote *The Revolt of Islam*, and she wrote the much more famous *Frankenstein*.

🚗 *MARLOW lies on the A308, 9 miles west of Maidenhead.*

NEWBURY
Berkshire

Newbury is one of England's more delightful market towns, sleepy enough today but once the scene of dramatic events, for two battles were fought here during the long years of the English Civil War (1642-1648), and those who leave their cars and

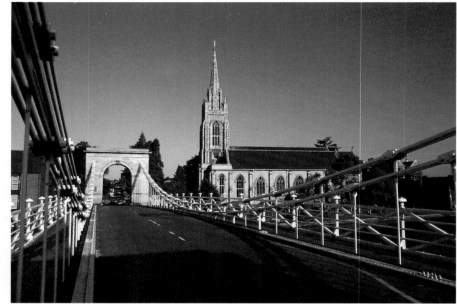

St Helens Church at Marlow, viewed across the suspension bridge

walk about the town will find plenty of interesting sights. The Town Museum, set in the Old Cloth Hall, is a fine Jacobean building, and a reminder that this was the home of Jack Winchcombe, called 'Jack o' Newbury', who is said to have won a huge sum of money by betting that he could take wool from the sheep's back in the morning and have it made into a coat by nightfall.

Jack Winchcombe was certainly rich enough to entertain Henry VIII and Catherine of Aragon, to pay for the restoration of St Nicolas Church in the town centre, and establish an almshouse. That apart, Newbury has good pubs, and pleasant walks along the reedy River Kennet, or by the banks of the interesting Kennet and Avon Canal, a fine stroll on a summer evening. Two miles to the north lie the remains of Donnington Castle, a medieval fortress largely destroyed in the Civil War.

🚗 *NEWBURY lies on the M4 motorway, 17 miles west of Reading.*

OXFORD
Oxfordshire

Oxford has been described as both a 'city of dreaming spires' and 'an organised waste of time'. Visitors must make up their own minds.

The expression 'Town and Gown' is said to set out the two broad divisions in Oxford society, and the same might be said for the town itself. Part of it is modern, commercialised, even industrial, while the Oxford of students and visitors is tranquil, academic, and an attractive architectural treasure house. This side of the city is best seen on foot, by strolling along the 'Broad' or the 'High', to look almost anywhere around the Carfax where these two meet. Note the now re-carved heads of the Roman Emperors outside the Sheldonian Theatre, and pop into Blackwell's Bookshop to buy a map or a guide to the numerous and varied colleges of the University; Keble, red-

brick and very Victorian; Merton College, where the famous Mob Quad is the oldest in Oxford; St John's, which has a magnificent garden; Christchurch, founded by Cardinal Wolsey in the 16th century and said to be the grandest, overtopped by a huge bell tower; or, my personal favourite, Magdalen, down by the river, a timeless, beautiful place with quiet cloisters, smooth green lawns, a pleasing blaze of flowers against the old stone buildings, even a deer park.

If one must choose a central jewel in Oxford, it would probably be the buildings, quad, and collections of the Bodleian Library.

The buildings are masterpieces of their time and date from the Late Medieval and Jacobean period, and the best of all is generally conceded to be that pure example of the 15th-century Perpendicular which houses the Divinity School, although some

put up a strong case for the Radcliffe Camera in the beautiful proportions of Radcliffe Square. There is so much to enjoy here that there may seem no need to step inside, but the collections are no less remarkable.

The Bodleian is one of the largest libraries in the world, with over three million books. One splendid room, Duke Humphrey's Library, contains the manuscript collection donated originally by Humphrey, Duke of Gloucester, youngest brother of Henry V. This library was completed in 1490, but virtually destroyed in the Reformation when the collection was dispersed..The present collection, and indeed the whole library, owes its existence to the Elizabethan Knight, Sir Thomas Bodley (1545-1613) who made the refurbishing and restocking of this library his lifetime's work. Another noted collection is the Radcliffe Science Library. Duke Humphrey's Library and part of the

Oxford's dreaming spires (*left*), seen from the air and (above) a typical college quadrangle

New Bodleian are open to the public.

Oxford has an atmosphere all its own, and is not a place to rush round in a few hours. There is a great deal to see, enjoy and appreciate, so spend a few days here and see the place properly.

OXFORD lies 40 miles south-west of London on the M40 motorway.

PENN STREET
Buckinghamshire

The village of Penn Street has two main claims to your attention, quite apart from its beauty. The first is its historic links with the family of William Penn the Quaker. This family founded the State of Pennsylvania in the United States, and were considerable landowners hereabouts, with numerous memorials in the area, at Penn Street, Penn, and the Quaker village of Jordans, two miles to the west of Chalfont St Giles.

The second, and perhaps more compelling reason to visit Penn Street, is the famous pub, The Hit and Miss (please note, not Hit *or* Miss). This stands across the road from the village green, and provides the village cricketers with ample amounts of sustenance during the long hours of the summer cricket matches. To sit out here, pint in hand, listening to the crack of bat on ball, and the rustle of clapping from the crowd, is to feel very much at home, and in England.

PENN STREET is 3 miles north west of Beaconsfield on the B474.

THE RIDGEWAY PATH
Berkshire/Wiltshire

The Ridgeway is one of Britain's oldest long-distance footpaths, and it follows an even longer, older route,

The romanesque abbey-church of St Albans

for travellers have been walking along this green road since prehistoric times. North of the Thames, much of this modern creation follows the Icknield Way, an Iron Age route along the valley, under the loom of the Chiltern beeches, but heading south and west from Streatley it becomes the open, breezy Ridgeway proper, a splendid walk across the wind-tousled grass of the Downs.

If the path seems far too wide for any footpath, this is because this route was originally a drove road, down which sheep and cattle were driven to market. From the top there are good views to quaint little villages

tucked below the hills in steep little valleys. The path leads past the site of old roman villas, past Wayland's Smithy, an Iron Age site, past the cooling towers of Harwell, and brings the walker after two or three days down to the end of the Path at Avebury in Wiltshire.

THE RIDGEWAY PATH runs from Berkshire to Wiltshire.

ST ALBANS
Hertfordshire

St Albans deserves much more consideration than it usually gets. This is a very old town, and it stands on the

ruins of a Roman city, *Verulamium*, and part of this can still be seen in a park just outside the centre of the modern town.

Queen Bodicea of the Iceni tribe, led her warriors to destroy Verulamium in AD 61, and it did not really recover until the 4th century AD, when the first abbey church was built here to enhance the shrine of St Alban, England's proto-martyr, a Roman citizen martyred on the hill here in AD 209. This church became the most famous and important abbey in England, and it eventually produced the country's only Pope, Nicolas Brakespear, who was enthroned as Adrian IV in 1155. In subsequent centuries, St Albans saw a great deal of strife, and was the scene of two bloody battles during the Wars of the Roses in 1455 and 1461.

Today it is a crowded, busy market town, best visited on a weekday. Sights to see include the great abbey church, with the shrine of St Alban, the Roman ruins and theatre down by the little River Ver, which gave its name to the original town, the clock tower, and the City Museum on the Hatfield road, while a walk down Holywell Hill is always interesting.

ST ALBANS lies 20 miles north of London on the A5183.

SYON PARK
Middlesex

Syon House, and the great park which surrounds it, lies on the western outskirts of London, close to the old Bath Road. This is one of several great houses, built close to the Thames, on the outskirts of London Town, which date from the 18th century and were designed as palaces for the provincial nobility, in this case for the Dukes of Northumberland, during their attendance at Court for the London Season.

This conservatory at Syon House is the centrepiece to beautiful gardens

Syon House rests on the foundations of a monastery, founded in 1415, the year of the Battle of Agincourt. Though now encased in Portland stone, much of the exterior dates from this period, but the interior was designed and furnished by Robert Adam in the 1760s. The glory of Syon is the garden, laid out in the 18th century by a famous English landscape gardener, Capability Brown, and this has been enhanced and embellished down the centuries to present a most beautiful and varied scene throughout the year.

SYON HOUSE lies off the A4 road, 3 miles west of Central London. Nearest Underground Station: Brentford or Osterley.

THAME
Oxfordshire

Thame is an historic town, the central jewel in that flat Oxfordshire plain that spreads out beneath the Chiltern escarpment, and runs north and west to Oxford. It is a pleasant market town, full of pubs, coaching inns and antique shops, set on either side of an extra wide High Street. Thame has produced a good number of famous sons from both the town itself and from the pupils educated at the grammar school; not least John Hampden, that patriot who defied King Charles I in Parliament and raised a regiment of local men to serve in the Parliamentary army. Hampden was killed nearby in the Battle of Chalgrove Field in 1643. Other students who went on to leave their mark on English history were the cavalier poet Edmund Waller, John Milton, Dr Fell — he of the old nursery rhyme ('I do not like thee, Dr Fell, The reason why I cannot tell......') and Anthony Wood, an Oxford antiquarian of the 17th century.

Perhaps it is the spirit of these people which gives Thame such a graceful, timeless air; certainly it seems to have slipped a little out of the 20th century and is all the better for it. As points of interest for a stroll about the town, do not miss the grammar school, built in 1569, or the little Church of St Mary the Virgin, built in the 13th century and vast — a perfect example of the English medieval church.

THAME lies on the B4011, 10 miles south of Aylesbury.

THE TROUT PUB
Oxfordshire

The Trout at Godstow is one of those pubs that poets and visitors will rave about. It stands beside the Thames on the northern outskirts of Oxford, and was once part of the fabric of Godstow Abbey, when Henry II of England kept his most beguiling mistress, Rosamund Clifford, 'Fair Rosamund', back in the 12th century.

The Trout has been an inn for hundreds of years, and has long been a particular favourite with the University students, who walk out here in the evening or at weekends to drink a pint on the terrace by the river, and put the world to rights.

On a summer's day The Trout is a perfect picture, a long stone building with flowers in pots, flagged floors without and within, and great trout finning quietly in the clear waters of the river, feeding well on bread tossed in by the patrons.

THE TROUT at Godstow lies off the A34 road from Oxford to Stratford, on the outskirts of the city.

THE TURVILLE VALLEY
Buckinghamshire

Hidden away though it is, in one of those deep folds of the Chiltern Hills a little north of Marlow, the Turville

The squire played cards inside the golden ball on West Wycombe's church

Valley is not difficult to find. The first sight to strike the eye is Turville windmill, a beautifully restored white-painted smock-mill high on the crest of the hill. This is now a private home, not open to the public, but if it looks familiar that is because it was the inventor's home in the movie *Chitty-Chitty-Bang-Bang*. Climb up for a closer look before turning to gaze down on the valley and villages below; Fingest, Turville itself full of fine flint-stone cottages, and little Skirmett. At any time of the year this is a delightful spot, so try it in spring, when the bluebells form a deep carpet in the woods, in summer when every field and hedgerow is bursting with blossom, or in autumn when the fall colours of the beechwoods are a glory to behold, or even in the depths of winter, when the air crackles with frost and the holly berries are red.

THE TURVILLE VALLEY lies north-west of Marlow.

WEST WYCOMBE
Buckinghamshire

West Wycombe lies a little to the west of the much larger town of High Wycombe, and a good deal further away in time and beauty. It is worth noting that this entire village belongs to the National Trust, that excellent organisation which aims to preserve the best in Britain.

Architectural attractions apart, West Wycombe has some curious places and tales to attract the visitor. Note the great golden ball atop St Lawrence's Church. Inside that sphere, the rakish Sir Francis Dashwood used to play cards with his friends in the 18th century. Further up the road lie the Hellfire Caves, where, so it is said, Sir Francis and his friends held unspeakable orgies, which seems unlikely since the 'caves' are actually tunnels left when excavating chalk for a roadway.

The present home of the Dashwood family is West Wycombe park, also owned by the National Trust, and a fascinating example of an English country home. It was built by the first Sir Francis in 1700, and he was devoted to classical architecture; each facade presents a different style to view, Doric, Palladian, Greek and Italian. The gardens are quite outstanding, and the interior, decorated in the style of the 1750s, is a mixture of neo-classical and baroque. West Wycombe is a beautiful village, now spared much of the heavy traffic that used to pour west along the A40, and worth a full day's visit.

WEST WYCOMBE lies on the A40, a mile west of High Wycombe.

WHIPSNADE ZOO
Bedfordshire

Whipsnade was the first open zoo in the world, the first place where wild animals were kept in enclosures rather than cages. It is a strange sight to see wallabies hopping about on a green English hillside, or take a train ride through the White Rhino park, but the overall effect is pleasing to both animals and visitors. Whipsnade is famous for its success in breeding and conservation, and the 2000 birds and mammals who live there seem content with their lot.

The Zoo was opened in 1931 as the country home of the Royal Zoological Society, which also owns London Zoo in Regents Park. It covers 500 acres and contains, apart from the safari railway, a dolphinarium, and all kinds of deer, birds and beasts, the perfect place for a Sunday afternoon in the English countryside.

WHIPSNADE ZOO lies at Dunstable, 5 miles west of the M1 motorway, on the B4540.

WHITE HORSE VALE
Oxfordshire

No one really knows how long the great white horse has been running on White Horse Hill, but although it has been attributed to King Alfred in the 9th century it was probably there long before the Romans came to these islands, 2000 years ago, and is certainly the oldest of several white horses cut into the Southern hills. The Vale of the White Horse was once part of Berkshire, and the Horse still runs across part of the Berkshire Downs, even if this part of the country was transferred to Oxfordshire in the 1970s.

The White Horse itself is large, elongated, dramatic, cut out of the turf and so revealed in the chalk, stark against the green of the hill, and although a minor road leads up close to the Horse, the best view can be obtained from further out in the Vale, at Uffington, which lies four miles to the north. The famous Ridgeway long-distance footpath runs just to one side of the White Horse.

THE VALE of the White Horse lies to the west of Wantage.

WINDSOR CASTLE
Berkshire

Windsor Castle is a splendid sight, especially if seen from the river far below, or at evening time from the spur-road which runs into Windsor from the nearby M4 motorway.

William the Conqueror built the first 'motte-and-bailey' (hill and wall) castle here in 1067, as one of the defenses of London, and it served that purpose until the end of the Great Civil War in 1648. Much of the castle which visitors see and relish today owes its existence in the present form to the Hanovarian George III, who loved to visit Windsor, as his descen-

The great sweep of the Long Walk seen from the Staines road provides the perfect foreground to this view of Windsor Castle

dants of what is now the House of Windsor still do. Her Majesty Queen Elizabeth II still spends most weekends at Windsor and holds a house-party during Royal Ascot week.

Visitors will enjoy exploring old Windsor, seeing the daily march-past of the Guard, and visiting the magnificent St George's Chapel, a splendid example of English Gothic, which is the home of the Order of the Garter, Europe's most ancient Order of Chivalry. The helms, banners, and name plates of the Knights may be inspected in the choir, in a building full of the tombs of English Kings. Other attractions here include the famous Royal Dolls' House and, when Her Majesty is not in residence, the State Apartments.

🚗 *WINDSOR lies 20 miles west of London, off the M4 motorway.*

WINDSOR GREAT PARK
Berkshire

Half hidden behind the old streets and ancient buildings of this medieval town, Windsor Great Park is magnificent, a vast expanse of farmland and forest, great trees and small copses, full of deer and other wildlife, haunted by a famous ghost.

Windsor Great Park, large as it is, is but a remnant of a once great hun-ting forest that spanned much of Royal Berkshire, and as such it remains part of the Royal demense. Much of it is open to the public though, and there is no finer view of Windsor Castle than that from the bottom of the Long Walk, where it crosses the A308 between Windsor and Staines. Come here in Ascot Week and watch the Queen and her guests jingle past as the carriage procession makes its way down the Long Walk to the racecourse, while on any summer weekend you may find Her Majesty out riding here, early in the morning. If you should do so, smile, bow, remove your hat and say 'Good morning, Ma'am'. Her Majesty never gives autographs.

One part of the park which should not be missed by any lover of flowers is the Savill Garden, on the eastern side near Egham, begun in 1931 and now a riot of flowering shrubs, trees and plants.

As to that ghost, some claim to have seen it. Herne the Hunter poached the King's Deer and was flayed alive for it. He hunts the forest still, on cloudy, moonlit nights, his skin flying from his shoulders, a set of antlers nailed to his brow...... or so it is said.

🚗 *WINDSOR GREAT PARK begins a mile south of Windsor town centre.*

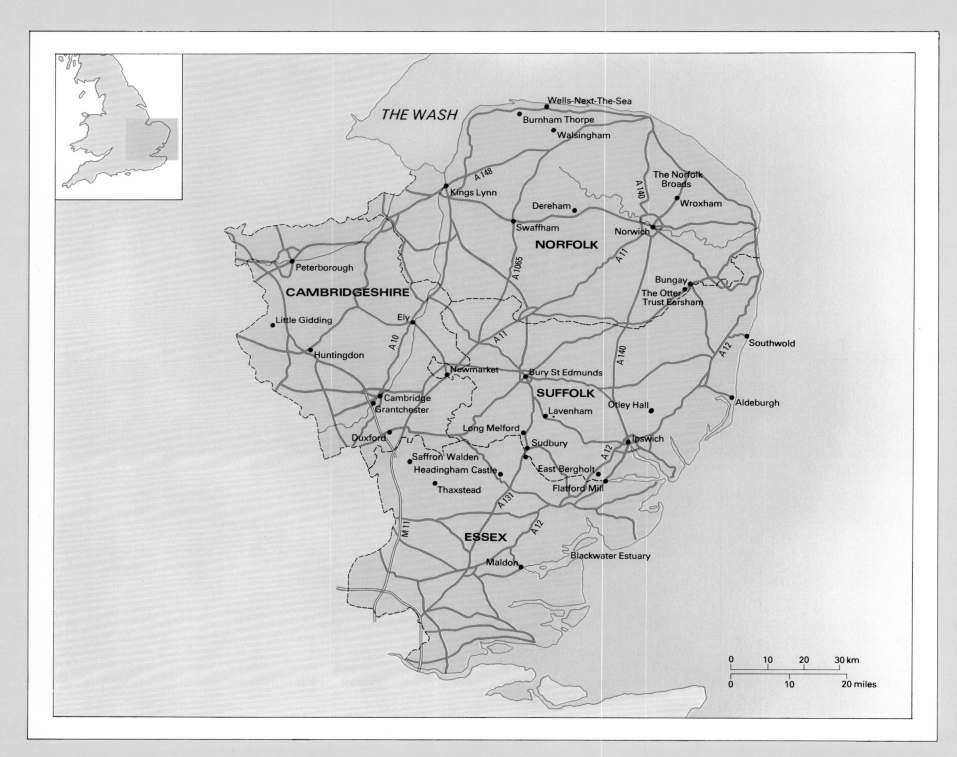

THE WASH

Wells-Next-The-Sea
Burnham Thorpe
Walsingham

The Norfolk
Broads
Wroxham

A 148
Kings Lynn
Dereham
Swaffham
Norwich

NORFOLK

A 1065

A 11

Peterborough

CAMBRIDGESHIRE

Bungay
The Otter
Trust Earsham

Little Gidding
Ely

A 10
A 11
A 140

Southwold

Huntingdon

Newmarket
Bury St Edmunds

SUFFOLK

Otley Hall

Aldeburgh

Cambridge
Grantchester
Lavenham

Long Melford

Duxford
Sudbury
Ipswich

A 12

Saffron Walden
Headingham Castle
East Bergholt

Thaxstead
Flatford Mill

A 131

M 11

A 12

ESSEX

Blackwater Estuary

Maldon

0   10   20   30 km

0   10   20 miles

East Anglia

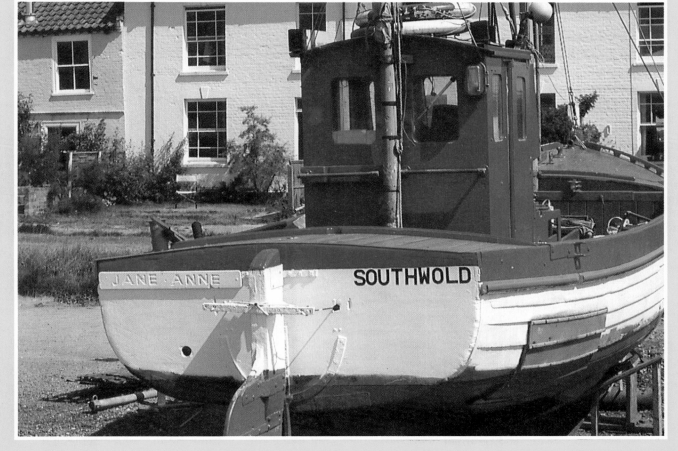

There is always that salty tang of the sea in the air wherever you happen to be in East Anglia. The sky reflects the steely tints of the North Sea, never far away

THE NORTH SEA shaped East Anglia. A chill, cold, often hostile sea, it pounds the East Anglian coast, piles up the shingle between the groynes along the beaches, hollows out the little creeks where the yachtsmen come to moor and shelter, and creeps in twice a day to remind the people how much of their lives is dictated by the regular flooding of the main. Nine centuries ago this sea road from the North brought the Vikings, those Jutes and Angles who first raided around the coast, then came to settle here and give their names to the present counties. East Anglia is the land of the Angles; Suffolk, the South Folk; Norfolk, the North Folk — and in many of the little towns and villages, even the local dialect recalls that far-off invasion.

East Anglia is a very diverse region, and although the change is gradual, no two counties are alike. By and large, the area is low-lying and needs protection from the sea, which from time to time eludes all man's inventions and bursts in to flood across the county. Here there are vast bulbfields reminiscent of Holland, fen country around Ely and east of Norwich in the Norfolk Broads. Cambridgeshire, famous for its old cities and University town, is flat farming country, full of slow rivers, while Norfolk is a sweep of curving coastline, little ports and towns.

In Suffolk and parts of Essex the land is less striking, but no less beautiful, for here the visitor will find the Constable country, so well remembered from a host of prints and paintings.

ALDEBURGH
Suffolk

Aldeburgh is a quiet seaside town for much of the year until it bursts into life in June, during the two weeks of the Aldeburgh Festival, founded many years ago by the town's most famous resident, Sir Benjamin Brittan, who came to live here in 1948. The story for one of his most famous operas, *Peter Grimes*, was taken from a tale written by the poet George Cramble, who lived in the town and wrote a series of stories centred on the Suffolk coast. The long beach is overlooked by a Martello tower, one of hundreds built to defend England during the Napoleonic Wars. The Moot Hall by the shore dates from the 16th century, when the town was an active centre for the coastal trade.

Many of the Festival events take place in The Maltings at Snape, a few miles inland which, apart from the Festival, holds musical events and concerts throughout the year.

🚗 *ALDEBURGH lies 30 miles north-east of Ipswich on the A1094.*

THE BLACKWATER ESTUARY
Essex

The Blackwater is one of those slow, tidal Essex rivers, with high mud-banks, ambling east against the surge and out into the sea near Maldon. From here it widens steadily out into the North Sea, and the Blackwater offers the perfect haven for yachtsmen, with shelter from the north-easterly gales when they sweep down from Norway, and plenty of tidal waters for coasting yachts and dingheys. From Maldon sailors cruise up the Blackwater to Mersea Island, to Brightlingsea, even up the River Cole to Colchester or out towards the Wallet and the sandbanks of Gunfleet — a lovely spot to sample the cruising

waters or the east coast of Britain.

🚗 *THE BLACKWATER estuary runs east from Maldon to Sales Point and Mersea Island.*

BUNGAY
Suffolk

Bungay has a longer continuous history than most English towns, as is indicated in the Saxon titles of Reeve and Feoffees instead of the more usual Mayor and Counsellors. Bungay Castle, which stands in ruins off the High Street, was once a mighty fortress with a high keep and a strong curtain wall, but very little now remains, even though many of the castle stones can be seen in the town's older buildings. The Butter Cross in the market dates from 1688, and please note the weather vane topped by the effigy of Black Shuck, the devil dog, or hell-hound of East Anglia. Bungay lies on the River Waveney and is an attractive town with easy access to the coastlines of Norfolk and Suffolk.

🚗 *BUNGAY lies on the A143, 6 miles west of Beccles.*

BURNHAM THORPE
Norfolk

Here, in this little Norfolk village, Horatio, Viscount Nelson was born. His father was the vicar here, so Horatio grew up with the sea not far away, and returned here throughout his life. As Burnham Thorpe's — if not England's — most famous son, he is commemorated in Burnham in both the church and in Nelson Hall next door. The church lectern was made from the wood of his flagship HMS *Victory* on which he died in the Battle of Trafalgar, and both the church and Hall are full of Nelson memorabilia. It seems a quiet little place to be the birthplace of someone who spent his life in battle, but it is a pretty spot,

just right for the home of a sailor, returned from the sea.

🚗 *BURNHAM THORPE lies 1 mile south-east of Burnham Market.*

BURY ST EDMUNDS
Suffolk

Bury St Edmunds is a very fine, very old town, and the ideal centre for touring East Anglia. It takes its name from St Edmund, King of the East Angles, who was martyred here by the invading Danes in AD 869. His body was enshrined in a monastery here about AD 900, and Bury St Edmunds was a centre of pilgrimage throughout the Middle Ages. King Canute was just one of the abbey patrons. The Barons of England met here in 1214 to draw up the terms of Magna Carta, and though the abbey suffered from riot and the inevitable consequences of the Reformation, the Abbey Gate is still intact and quite magnificent. Down in the town, which is laid out in the grid-pattern of a medieval *bastide*, St Mary's Church contains the tomb of Mary Tudor, and Bury Moyses Hall on Cornhill is a fine 12th-century building, now a museum. As a place to relax in, or a touring centre for visits out to Suffolk or Norfolk, few towns could be more suitable than beautiful Bury St Edmunds.

🚗 *BURY ST EDMUNDS lies 25 miles east of Cambridge on the A45.*

CAMBRIDGE
Cambridgeshire

Cambridge is a beautiful city, rich in history, architecture and scholarship. The Romans were here of course, and built the first town astride the River

Punts on the 'backs' at Cambridge on the River Cam

The soaring Gothic columns and magnificent stained glass windows of Kings College Chapel, Cambridge

vous for centuries and stroll down to the riverside to the 'Backs' to watch — or join — the young people punting on the river, a peaceful sight on a warm summer evening in this most delightful university city.

🚗 *CAMBRIDGE lies off the M11, 15 miles north of Saffron Walden.*

DEREHAM
Norfolk

Dereham was said by the novelist George Borrow to be '......the pattern for an English market town', but then he was a local lad and probably biased. That said, it is a very attractive place with much fine architecture in that attractive Georgian style, and a particularly interesting church, St Nicolas, built from the 12th to the 16th centuries in a mixture of Norman and Perpendicular styles, which works rather well. It was once a pilgrim church, for it contains the shrine of St Withburga, an obscure Saxon saint, who founded an abbey here in the 17th century. Her empty tomb now contains a spring which fills the churchyard well. William Cowper, that most English of poets, was born in Dereham and he was buried in St Nicolas Church, under a fine monument by John Flaxman.

🚗 *EAST DEREHAM lies off the A47, 16 miles west of Norwich.*

DUXFORD
Cambridgeshire

During World War II, Duxford aerodrome was a front line fighter airfield, home base for the famous Duxford Wing which fought off the German air force day after day during the Battle of Britain. How fitting therefore, that this airfield should now contain the aircraft exhibits of the Imperial War Museum, housing them here on the concrete standings,

Cam. William the Conqueror built a castle here just after the Conquest, and some time in the next century the monks of Ely established a school which was the foundation of the present University. Since that time Cambridge has grown in both reputation and beauty, but not much in size, for it is really a small place, easy to explore on foot. Indeed it is so congested with traffic that anything else is impossible.

Visitors can wander at will around the college grounds, except during certain weeks in April and May when the colleges are closed to the public while the students sit their end of year examinations. See Clare College, or the beautiful Kings College Chapel, begun by Henry VII, or Christs College in St Andrews Street, where Milton wrote *Lycidas* under the mulberry trees. The first college, Peterhouse, was founded by the Bishop of Ely in 1281, while Corpus Christi, one of the most renowned, was endowed by the townspeople in 1352, or take a look at the more modern colleges of Robinson or Churchill, founded as recently as the 1960s. There is so much to see and do in Cambridge that a whole book would hardly suffice, but for a diversion, why not visit the Scott Polar Institute in Lensfield Road, a museum to Captain Robert F. Scott and his ill-fated expedition. Two essential acts in Cambridge are to take a drink in the Blue Boar pub, a student rendez-

and in the World War I hangars. There are over 70 aircraft in the collection, from both world wars to Concorde, including Spitfires, Hurricanes, a B17 Flying Fortress, Mustang and a German Junkers 52. On a summer day, when they stand on the peri-track, their propellers sniffing at the sky, those long ago air battles seem only yesterday.

🚗 *DUXFORD lies off the M11 motorway, 5 miles south of Cambridge.*

ELY
Cambridgeshire

There is something romantic about Ely, something immediately evocative of the past. It might be the clear, rain-washed air of the Fens, it might be the countless rows of Georgian buildings, or more probably the soaring front of the cathedral. Whatever the cause, the atmosphere of Ely is gentle and sublime. The cathedral is, of course, both famous and magnificent. It was begun on the orders of William the Conqueror in the years after the Conquest, but not finally completed until the end of the 14th century, for the work was delayed when the tower collapsed into the nave in 1322. When completed though, the cathedral became the crowning jewel of the Fen country, with a marvellous octagonal tower and a Lady Chapel which is probably the finest in all England. Kings School is also marvellous, as is Ely Porta, the gateway to the medieval monastery and the old buildings beside the river. Those who visit Cambridge without diverting north to Ely, are missing a great deal.

🚗 *ELY lies 17 miles north of Cambridge by the A10.*

FLATFORD MILL
East Bergholt, Suffolk

John Constable made Flatford Mill famous, but it was always a beautiful place and it still is. Constable must have known the Stour Valley in which it stands from childhood, for his father was a miller and Flatford was just one of the mills the family owned along the river. Indeed, Constable claimed that his childhood home, among this beautiful, lush countryside, provided the scenes that made him an artist, and one of the present delights of exploring this 'Constable Country' is spotting the places he immortalised in his paintings. 'The Cornfield' can be identified along the lane from Flatford to East Bergholt, and indeed very little has changed at all since he wandered hereabouts with paint and easel. Flatford Mill is now owned by the National Trust and occupied by the Field Studies Council, who run courses here on the local wildlife and, of course, on painting.

🚗 *FLATFORD MILL lies 1 mile south of East Bergholt, by a minor road.*

GRANTCHESTER
Cambridgeshire

Rupert Brooke made Grantchester famous through his poetry, but this pretty village on the River Cam has been a popular place with the Cambridge student community for centuries, who come here along the river by punt on summer evenings during term time. The village is rather as Brooke described it, although the church clock will repay a look, as well as the Saxon brickwork.

🚗 *GRANTCHESTER lies 3 miles south of Cambridge off the A10.*

HEADINGHAM CASTLE
Halstead, Essex

Unlike most of England's Norman castles which were destroyed by time or battered into rubble by Cromwell, Headingham Castle is in a remarkable state of preservation. It was built in the middle of the 12th century by the De Vere's, Earls of Oxford, and they held the castle for the next 500 years, when they served successive kings as soldiers and admirals. The castle is surrounded by a moat, like all the best castles, and a bridge leads across the water to the *enciente*, and the keep which soars up for 100 ft and gives great views over the countryside. The second floor of the keep contains the Great Hall, which has a

Flatford Mill, once owned by John Constable's father, now belongs to the National Trust

circular wooden gallery and relics of the original plaster. A splendid evocative place, Headingham Castle should not be missed by any lover of castles.

HEADINGHAM CASTLE lies 5 miles north of Halstead, off the A604.

HUNTINGDON
Cambridgeshire

Not many people know it, but Huntingdon produced one of the great men of English history, one of the founders of our modern Parliamentary system of government, Oliver Cromwell, the Lord Protector. He was born in a house in the High Street here in 1599. During the Civil War both Cromwell and King Charles held the town in turn, neither doing the place any damage, but it is its native son whom Huntingdon remembers today.

There is a Cromwell Museum in Market Square, a Norman building which was a school in Cromwell's day. Both he and Samuel Pepys, the diarist of Charles II's time, were educated here, and it contains a great many artifacts and memorabilia, including Cromwell's death mask. Not a place to be rushed by those people who have seen what remains of Cromwell's work in other parts of the country.

HUNTINGDON lies on the A141, 17 miles north-west of Cambridge.

IPSWICH
Suffolk

When visiting any English county, do not neglect to visit the county town. It did not rise to that position by accident and is sure to be full of fine sights and historic reminders.

Ipswich, the county town of East Suffolk, used to be a sea-port. It lies

This Customs House by the quay is just one example of Kings Lynn's fine architecture

at least ten miles from the North Sea, but it looks like a port, with a line of sea-captains' houses and quays along the River Orwell.

As a port it has been busy since Roman times, although it really developed under the Normans, and was an important town under the Plantagenets and Tudors. Do not miss St Mary Elms Cottages, built in 1467, or two Tudor houses, the Ancient House and Christchurch House, which now contains work by Gainsborough and Constable as well as much fine furniture from Tudor times to Victorian. That apart, Ipswich is a place to wander about, along winding medieval streets and quays, sniffing the sea breezes that blow in from the coast, or popping in and out of the town's old churches — a delightful spot.

🚗 *IPSWICH lies on the A12, at the head of the Orwell estuary.*

KINGS LYNN
Norfolk

However many places have to be missed on a journey through East Anglia, spare some time to visit the exquisite town of Kings Lynn. It was established as a port long before the Conquest, but it flourished under the Normans and continued to grow in wealth and beauty between the 14th and 19th centuries, until today it is a treasure house of English domestic architecture. The Guildhall, built in 1421, overlooks the Market Place and contains the town treasure, which includes charters from King Canute and King John. St George's Guildhall is the largest surviving Guildhall in England, and is now a theatre; but these are just the central gems, for all Kings Lynn is a treasure house where medieval streets curve down to old quays, lined with merchants' houses. From Lynn a narrow channel leads

The 15th-century Guildhall in the centre of Lavenham, finest of the East Anglian wool towns

out to The Wash, where visitors still search for King John's treasure. It was from here that Captain Vancouver, a local man, sailed in 1780 to explore the west coast of Canada, and Lynn, as the locals call it, remains much as he left it — a beautiful place and one of the finest towns in all England.

🚗 *KINGS LYNN lies on The Wash, 11 miles north of Downham Market.*

LAVENHAM
Suffolk

Although the centre of the English wool trade was the Cotswolds, the sheep of Suffolk paid their dues to the Exchequer and provided the profits which enhanced the East Anglian wool towns, like pretty medieval Lavenham. The streets wobble about the town centre, lined on either side with those leaning half-timbered 15th-century houses which are so pleasing to the eye, and lead to the market place with its 15th-century Woolstaplers Hall and the equally lovely Corpus Christi Guildhall flanked by Tudor shops, many with their original windows. Close your eyes to the traffic here in the centre and it is not hard to imagine this town in the reign of Richard II. During his reign the parish church, with its high, dramatic tower, 140 ft tall, was finally completed. It contains many fine brasses, carved stalls and excellent stained glass. To get an even deeper look at the Lavenham of days gone by, visit the museum in the Corpus Christi Guildhall, which now contains exhibits charting 700 years of the cloth trade.

🚗 *LAVENHAM lies 10 miles south of Bury St Edmunds on the A1141.*

LITTLE GIDDING
Cambridgeshire

Like a number of places in Cambridgeshire, Little Gidding has a long history and a strong literary connection which endures to the present day. The history goes back to 1625

Georgian pepper-pot towers crown the front of Long Melford Hall

when a religious community established itself here, founded by Nicolas Farrar, as a place of refuge from the world's strife. Even Charles I found Little Gidding restful. The literary connection accrues to T. S. Eliot, who found his inspiration for one of his four quartets, *Little Gidding* in the life and works of Farrar. Lovers of Eliot come here in great numbers to see the church and cottages, and breathe a little of that tranquil air.

LITTLE GIDDING lies on the B660, 5 miles north-west of Huntingdon.

LONG MELFORD
Suffolk

Like Lavenham a little to the east, Long Melford is a wool town and therefore beautiful, not least along the splendid straggling high street which is lined with antique shops and Georgian houses, leading to the green behind which stands the 15th-century Church of the Holy Trinity, which the local people claim with pride to be the finest, lightest and most attractive church in Suffolk, which is saying a great deal. Nearly 100 high windows contribute to the airy feel of the building which is built in the Perpendicular Gothic style and dates from 1450.

Near the green lies Long Melford Hall, an early-Elizabethan manor house with Georgian additions which include pepperpot towers. This was a hunting lodge for the abbots of Bury St Edmunds, and after it passed into the hands of William Cordell, a counsellor of Henry VIII, it became one of the few places in England where Elizabeth I definitely spent the night during the Royal Progress through Suffolk in 1588. Since 1786 it has been the home of the Parker family, who open the house and gardens to visitors throughout the summer.

LONG MELFORD lies on the A134, 10 miles south of Bury St Edmunds.

MALDON
Essex

Little Maldon, once a Roman seaport, lies at the head of the Blackwater estuary, a pretty place, full of old buildings and popular today with yachtsmen. The town is commemorated from the 10th century in an Anglo Saxon epic poem, *The Battle of Maldon*, and was the first town in Essex to gain a charter from the Norman kings in 1171. It continued to serve as a busy seaport throughout the Middle Ages and this period has left the town with such places as the Moot Hall, built in 1450, and still used by the Council, the old leper hospital, the Hospital of St Giles, the Blue Boar Inn which is early 16th century, and the Church of All Saints. Maldon is a lovely spot, the ideal place to spend a weekend away from London, loud with the cry of gulls, where the air is full of the salty tang of the sea.

MALDON lies 10 miles east of Colchester on the A414.

NEWMARKET
Cambridgeshire

It could probably be said, with a considerable degree of accuracy, that Newmarket is the horseracing capital of the world. Certainly it has antiquity on its side, for it was the Scots nobles of James I who introduced horseracing to England in about 1605, and they found the springy turf of Newmarket ideal for these contests.

Charles II adored horseracing, and made Newmarket his second home. The Rowley Mile course at Newmarket is named after the King's

The Royal Arcade in Norwich is an excellent shopping centre

hack, Old Rowley, and indeed was the King's nick-name. The town was well established as a training and racing centre by the end of the 17th century and has remained that way ever since. The Jockey Club maintains its headquarters in the High Street, racing stables are everywhere, and the normal sound early in the morning is the clip-clop of hooves as the strings move out to the gallops. As a result of all this, there are good pubs, fine restaurants, and a generally pleasant country air about the place.

NEWMARKET lies 15 miles west of Bury St Edmunds on the A11.

NORWICH
Norfolk

Norwich — a very fine city. That's what the tourist board claims and few would disagree with that firm statement. It is an old place with Saxon roots, a Norman castle, a magnificent cathedral, and a pub for every other day of the year.

Like many of England's older cities, it is clogged by the motor car, and really must be seen on foot, so be sure to explore the Haymarket, stepping into the glorious church of St Peter Mancroft, then on to see Charing Cross, a medieval merchant's house, and for an historic over-view of the city, stop for a tour of the Bridewell Museum. The city is full of good architecture from almost every period, but the houses which line cobble-stoned Elm Hill are certainly among the most picturesque.

Norwich Castle is a must, and especially so now it contains the County Museum. It was built in the 12th century, and then became the city jail, which kept it intact until 1887. It has recently been fully restored and is now a very splendid castle indeed, with a museum and art collection.

Norwich Cathedral is one of the finest in England, the pride of this fine city. It was begun in 1096, and with many later additions and alterations is a magnificent building with a notable interior.

The vault of the nave is studded with ceiling bosses, and the Bishop's Throne is said to pre-date the Conquest. Outside the cathedral two sights to see are the grave of Nurse Edith Cavell, shot by the Germans in 1915, and the Erpingham Gate which contains a carving of old Sir Thomas Erpingham who fought at Agincourt and features in Shakespeare's *Henry V*. Explore Norwich thoroughly — it really is a fine city.

NORWICH lies 19 miles east of Great Yarmouth on the A47.

OTLEY HALL
Suffolk

If the Georgian style is the most attractive form of urban dwelling, the medieval manor house fills the same proud position out in the countryside.

Otley Hall, nine miles north of Ipswich, is a perfect example of this attractive genre. It was built in the latter part of the 15th century and today remains in superb condition and is a splendid example of English domestic architecture. It has a moat, tall pointed chimneys, dull-red herringbone brickwork, oak beams, wall paintings, pargetting and panelling — in short the lot. It was built by the Gosnold family, who lived in it until the mid-18th century, during which time one member of the family, Bartholomew Gosnold, a sea-captain, crossed the Atlantic to discover Cape Cod and found Martha's Vineyard. The manor house is open to visitors throughout the summer and is well worth a visit.

OTLEY lies 9 miles north of Ipswich, off the B1079.

The Norfolk Broads

For all its concentration on agriculture, East Anglia is a great holiday region, containing in the flat country between Norwich and the North Sea fishing port of Great Yarmouth, an attraction which is unique to England; the Norfolk Broads.

This area of fen and marsh, lined by thick reed beds, dates back to the Middle Ages, when the local commoners exercised their rights to cut turfs from any 'turbury' or turfland. Because of extensive turf cutting, broad channels were created and then flooded by the sea and the overspill of such local tidal rivers as the Yare, Waveney, Buse and Ant. The main flooding occurred at the end of the 13th century and by the 16th century the present Broads had already come into existence, a haunt of heron, and the booming bittern, full of duck, a paradise for wildlife.

Today the Norfolk Broads are a water-lover's haven, full of boats in summer, with most of the action centred around the inland port of Wroxham, where the rows and rows of cabin cruisers can be seen each summer, tied up, waiting for their crews or chugging out into the stream, but not just modern cruisers; there are sailing dinghies and sailboards and small yachts, even from time to time a stately Norfolk wherry, beating against the tide with her mass of high tan-coloured sails.

Today, although much eroded and under the ever-present threats of silting up and man-made pollution, the Broads remain a unique part of the English landscape, and are well worth a visit at any time of year.

As one of the largest remaining wetlands in England, they are full of rare plants and provide a habitat for many rare resident and migrant birds, so that those who love natural history will find the Norfolk Broads an experience as well as a playground.

A yacht cuts its way across Hornsey Mere, behind the reed beds, under the high blue sky

THE OTTER TRUST
Earsham, Suffolk

Over the last few decades, that endearing creature, the otter, has become one of the world's most threatened species. Here, in a conservation centre near Bungay in Suffolk, the otter is being conserved, bred and re-introduced to the wild. The centre is devoted to the conservation of otters from all parts of the world, but particular attention is paid to British otters. The otters are kept in large natural enclosures, each with a stream for them to play in. Otters apart, there are three large lakes with great numbers of waterfowl, and a wood full of muntjac deer. An attractive and useful place which will attract all visitors passing through Suffolk.

EARSHAM lies 2 miles west of Bungay off the A143.

PETERBOROUGH
Cambridgeshire

Peterborough is a neglected cathedral city, which is a great pity, for it has a lot to offer the dedicated traveller with a sense of history. It is now a noted centre for heavy engineering with an excellent shopping centre, and has been a prosperous place since Norman times. In spite of much modern development on the outskirts, those who penetrate to the city centre will find the old 17th-century market place quite delightful, while Priestgate contains many fine old houses. The glory of the town though, is Peterborough Cathedral, which may not rank with the other cathedrals of Britain, but is still the most impressive Romanesque building in Britain, and will please any lover of the Romanesque style.

Architecture apart, it is full of history. The long-suffering Catherine

Pargetting (patterns pressed into plaster) is a feature on a number of buildings in Saffron Walden

of Aragon, wife of Henry VIII, is buried here, as was Mary, Queen of Scots after her execution at Fotheringhay, before her body was removed to Westminster Abbey. The bulk of the cathedral dates from the 12th century, but the West Front is 13th century, as is the nave and much of the decoration comes from the High Medieval period.

PETERBOROUGH lies 35 miles north of Cambridge, off the A1.

SAFFRON WALDEN
Essex

To those who love that classic domestic architecture which dates back to Tudor and medieval times, the town of Saffron Walden is a necessary visit, for the town contains an almost unique collection of beautiful buildings. Besides, the name itself is attractive, and dates back to the 14th century when the saffron crocus grew in quantity hereabouts.

On a small rise above the common, stands the ruin of a castle built by one of the Conqueror's comrades, Geoffrey de Mandeville, in about the year 1100. That, inevitably, was destroyed by Cromwell, who quartered himself at the Old Sun Inn in the town centre during the siege. The church of St Mary is the largest in Essex and is built in that soaring Perpendicular

Gothic, a triumph of verticality, and the vault and interior carvings are equally magnificent.

After visiting the town, go out a mile to the west, to Audley End House. This was once a Benedictine monastery, dissolved and destroyed at the Dissolution, and the ruins sold to Sir Thomas Audley who built the first house here before the estate passed to Lord Howard de Walden. This house in turn was largely pulled down at the start of the 18th century when Sir John Vanburgh, the architect of Blenheim Palace was in charge of the work. Alterations continued for most of the century and the result is the Audley End House of today, a mixture of styles reflecting the work of various masters; John Vanburgh, Robert Adam, and gardens of course by Capability Brown. Much smaller today than in its Jacobean heyday, Audley End House remains magnificent, full of paintings and fine furniture.

SAFFRON WALDEN lies 1 mile east of the M11, north of Bishop's Stortford.

SOUTHWOLD
Suffolk

An attractive, elegant Victorian town set on a cliff top over a shingle beach, Southwold has always been a busy fishing port. For the last 100 years or so it has also been a popular seaside resort, but still maintains a life of its own outside that supplied by the summer visitors.

There are fishermen's cottages, fine old streets, good pubs, notably the Sole Bay Inn, and a church dedicated to St Edmund, that popular East Anglian saint, with a good example of Perpendicular architecture. One feature of the church is a manikin, Southwold Jack, which dates back to the 15th century and strikes the bell of the church clock. The town museum, which contains relics of the Anglo-Dutch naval battle of Sole Bay of 1672, is an interesting place, but the chief attraction of Southwold lies in strolling about the old streets and taking the air along the beach.

SOUTHWOLD lies 16 miles south of Lowestoft, off the A12.

SUDBURY
Suffolk

Although Suffolk is best known among art lovers for the 'Constable Country', it produced at least one other famous English painter, Thomas Gainsborough, who was

Southwold's elegant houses face the green

born in Sudbury in the elegant house in what is now Gainsborough Street, which contains the Gainsborough Museum. The contents include work by this artist and also by Constable, much 15th-century furniture, and Gainsborough memorabilia.

Sudbury itself is one of those market towns which look so right in the green parts of the English countryside. It is an ancient town, full of fine buildings and contains one good example of a medieval church, the 14th-century St Gregory's, where the church treasury contains a curious relic of another of Sudbury's sons, Simon Sudbury, a local cleric who

rose to be Archbishop of Canterbury under Richard II. During the Peasants' Revolt in 1381 he was seized by the rioters and beheaded on Tower Hill, but his skull somehow found its way back to Sudbury and can be seen in St Gregory's Church.

SUDBURY lies 23 miles west of Ipswich on the A1071.

SWAFFHAM
Norfolk

Swaffham, with a population of about 4000, is rather more a large village than a town, but it is still a busy, thriving and beautiful town of the

18th century, and as such, well worth a visit. The market square is actually a triangle, and lined with fine buildings looking out at an unusual Palladian style market cross under a cupola and set on columns. The parish church pre-dates most of the town and was built in the 15th century. It is a splendid Perpendicular building with a notable hammerbeam roof. Of the attractive Georgian style which dominates the rest of the town, two of the finest examples are the old School House and the Assembly Rooms, both worth inspection.

SWAFFHAM lies on the A47 road, 28 miles west of Norwich.

THAXTED
Essex

Although the country's steel and cutlery trade is commonly supposed to reside in Sheffield, Thaxted craftsmen have been producing fine English cutlery since the Middle Ages. In 1380 no less than 89 cutlers or blacksmiths were working in the town, and they built the Guildhall in Town Street to house the Cutlers Guild just ten years later. As a result of this industry, which thrived until the 16th century, Thaxted is a rather splendid town, topped off by the soaring spire of the town church, St John's, an excellent medieval church, decorated with gargoyles and glass. Between here and the Guildhall the streets are lined with 15th-century houses.

THAXTED lies 9 miles southeast of Saffron Walden.

WALSINGHAM
Norfolk

Walsingham is a haunting spot, for centuries the site and objective of the most famous and popular of all the English pilgrimages, to the shrine of Our Lady of Walsingham. Henry VIII came here before he ordered its destruction; Sir Walter Raleigh lamented the glory that was gone. Not much remains to see today, although a fresh shrine has been established by the Catholics. The Walsingham Abbey grounds contain the former site of Our Lady of Walsingham, with the remains of the Augustinian priory and the old gatehouse. The present shrine of Our Lady is in Holt Road nearby, but the medieval pilgrimage can be recalled at the small 14th-century Slipper Chapel at Little Walsingham, two miles to the south, where pilgrims would wash their feet before walking

Pilgrims still visit the shrine of Our Lady of Walsingham

barefoot to Walsingham. You can still do that today, and many do.

WALSINGHAM lies on the B1105 road, 4 miles south of Wells-next-the-Sea.

WELLS-NEXT-THE-SEA
Norfolk

Wells is a delightful, old fashioned Norfolk fishing port, famous for whelks and silvery sprats. It is quite large, full of flint-stone houses set around the Green, with a main street running down to the quay. A wide beach runs off beside the harbour wall, backed by pine trees. Many of the houses are Georgian and a surprising number seem to be pubs. It is still a port for small coasting craft, and is at one end of a little narrow-gauge railway which runs inland to Walsingham.

WELLS-NEXT-THE-SEA lies on the A149, 4 miles east of Burnham Market.

WROXHAM
Norfolk

What Wroxham is, hardly matters. It is a centre for that magical place, the Norfolk Broads. That fact cannot escape even the passing eye in Wroxham, for the little town is a miniature Venice, completely surrounded by water, and the surface groans with pleasure craft, cruisers, yachts and motor boats. This town is the place where holidaymakers equip their craft for a holiday on the Broads, and it is a hive of activity in summer, a busy, noisy spot, full of colour. Wroxham Barns, built in the 18th century, contain a unique display of rural crafts, a museum and such working exhibits as a wood carver and a potter.

WROXHAM lies 9 miles from Norwich on the A1151.

Mam Tor ▲

Eyam

Chatsworth House

DERBYSHIRE

Hartington

Tissington

The Tramway
Museum Crich

Thorseby Hall

NOTTINGHAMSHIRE

Newark Castle
Southwell

A 1

A 631

A 57

A 15

A 46

Lincoln

LINCOLNSHIRE

A 158

A 16

Louth

Boston Stump

M1

A 46

A 17

Nottingham

A 52

Grimsthorpe Castle

Bourne

Spalding

Melton Mowbray

Ashby-De-La-Zouch

Crowland Abbey

Bosworth Field

Oakham

Burghley House

A 47

M 69

Rockingham Castle

Deene Park
Oundle

Broughton
House

Naseby

NORTHAMPTONSHIRE

Higham Ferrers

Althop House

Northampton

The Waterways
Museum Stoke Bruerne

0   10   20   30 km

0   10   20 miles

62

The English Shires

This peaceful scene at Foxton Locks, Leicestershire, typifies the scenery to be found within the English Shires, much of it unchanged for centuries

WITH THE CERTAIN exception of the Derbyshire Peak District, the English Shires have somehow slipped through the tourist net. Despite the fact that they have a great deal to offer the traveller, in the shape of fine towns and a beautiful countryside well laced with history and splendid country houses, this, the very heart and heartland of England, is all too often overlooked.

What links these counties together is the life on the land, which to a very great extent has gone on unchanged for centuries. These are the hunting shires of England, which come alive each autumn to the clip-clop of hooves on cobble-stones, the high cries of the hounds and the long drawn-out wail of the horn — and whatever you may think of hun-

ting the fox, few can deny that the sight of the hunt in full cry, thundering across the fields in red coats and a spattering of mud, is a thrilling and memorable spectacle.

Within all this farming country, tucked into the patchwork of field and copse and forest, lies the Derbyshire Peak District, one of the glories of the English countryside. Visitors here will catch a touch of the old pagan past of England in such ceremonies as the Tissington Well Dressing, or recall the tragedy of the Great Plague in nearby Eyam, where the population elected to stay in their village and die when the plague came, rather than scatter and carry the plague about the country; a quiet, very English sort of courage.

ALTHORP HOUSE
Northamptonshire

This splendid house is owned by the Spencers — the Princess of Wales' family. It was built by Sir John Spencer in 1508, rebuilt by Henry Holland in 1790, and redecorated from top to bottom as recently as 1982. It is still the home of the present Earl and Countess Spencer but open to visitors throughout the summer. Apart from the curiosity of seeing inside the home of the country's future Queen, there is a magnificent art collection, with many works by Reynolds and Gainsborough, excellent French and English porcelain, and some rare items of furniture. The park is very fine and the nearby village most attractive.

ALTHORP lies near Harlestone, 6 miles north-west of Northampton on the A428.

ASHBY-DE-LA-ZOUCH
Leicestershire

Most people remember Ashby-de-la-Zouch from Sir Walter Scott's novel *Ivanhoe*, where it appears as the site of the famous tournament where the mysterious knight first makes his appearance and overthrows the Templars. Ashby today is a quiet, rather pleasant little town with many Georgian buildings and little evidence of the Middle Ages, except the ruins of Ashby-de-la-Zouch Castle, which dates from the early days of the 12th century and was later extended and strengthened by Lord Hastings before he was executed for treason by Richard III. During the Civil War the garrison held this castle for the king for over a year, but after they surrendered, with all the honours of war, the Parliamentary army 'slighted' the walls, and reduced the castle to its present ruined condition.

The ruins of the Norman Castle are all that remain of the fortifications of Ashby-de-la-Zouch

ASHBY-DE-LA-ZOUCH lies 20 miles north-west of Leicester on the A50.

BOSTON STUMP
Lincolnshire

Standing out above the roof tops of this old port and market town, the tall tower — or stump — of St Botolph's Church is a landmark for miles around. At 272 ft high the top offers marvellous views to those strong enough to plod up the 365 steps, one for every day of the year, which lead out onto the roof. The Stump is an airy church, well furnished and full of interest, as is the little town which surrounds it. Boston, on the edge of the Wash, gained its charter from King John in 1204, and was a major port for the cloth trade throughout the Middle Ages before the harbour began to silt up and the balance of trade switched to the West Coast ports. It was from here in 1612 that a group of Puritans sailed for America and founded the great city of Boston in Massachusetts. Around the town today visitors can inspect many

The tall tower of St Botolph's Church, better known as Boston Stump

16th and 17th-century houses, the 15th-century Guildhall (now a museum) and the local theatre which occupies the half-timbered Shodfriars Hall in South Street.

🚗 *BOSTON lies 25 miles north of Spalding on the A16 and 34 miles north west of King's Lynn.*

BOSWORTH FIELD
Leicestershire

On the banks of the Ashby Canal, close to the town of Market Bosworth, lies Bosworth Field, where in 1485 Richard III, the last Plantagenet King of England, was killed, '......fighting valiantly in the press of his enemies'. His crown was retrieved from a thorn bush and placed on the head of Henry Tudor, and a new dynasty came to the throne of England. The battlefield is marked today by a Battlefield Visitor Centre with exhibitions and models, a film theatre where the Olivier version of Shakespeare's *Richard III* is often shown, and the main features of the battle can be followed on the waymarked Battlefield Trail. A bookshop and cafeteria complete the amenities, and the whole area is well planned and well worth a visit. Richard III has been greatly maligned, not least by Shakespeare, so it is worth remembering that on the evening of the battle a chronicler of York wrote in the city journal, 'This day was our good King Richard slain, to the great sadness of this city.'

🚗 *THE BATTLEFIELD lies near Sutton Cheney, 2 miles south of Market Bosworth, off the A447.*

BOURNE
Lincolnshire

Bourne is a place of legend in the Fen Country, the birthplace of that Saxon warlord, Hereward the Wake, who retreated into the Fens after Hastings and fought off the Normans for years — or so it is said. In fact, the evidence for Hereward's existence is slight, and the evidence for his connection with the De Wake family who built the Norman castle here and founded the Abbey in 1138 is virtually non-existent. Inevitably, Bourne Abbey was destroyed by Henry VIII, the Great Vandal, but the Abbey Church survived as the parish church, and still stands. Note Red Hall in South Street, where lived the Digby family, executed for their share in the Gunpowder Plot of 1605. The Red Hall eventually became the home of the local station master, and is now a museum with some fine Elizabethan furniture.

🚗 *BOURNE lies 12 miles west of Spalding on the A151.*

BROUGHTON HOUSE
Kettering, Northants

This splendid Tudor mansion began its existence as a monastery. The central parts date back to the mid-1450s and were gradually enwrapped in a Tudor building, spread over seven courtyards and completed in 1695 with an addition in the style of Louis XIV's palace at Versailles, which looks both unusual and attractive. The house now contains some priceless works of art, including paintings by the Spanish masters, El Greco, (who was actually Greek), Murillo and Caracci. There is a notable private collection of arms and armour, a coach house, excellent 17th and 18th-century furniture in both the English and French styles, fine ceilings and, to top it all, the most beautiful gardens. 'House' is hardly the word for it — Broughton is really a palace.

🚗 *BROUGHTON lies 3 miles north of Kettering off the A43.*

BURGHLEY HOUSE
Stamford, Lincolnshire

Burghley was built by Elizabeth I's great counsellor, William Cecil, Lord Burghley, and completed in 1598, only three years before the Queen died. The house was badly damaged by Cromwell's forces during the Civil War, but a great deal remains of the Elizabethan building, including the Great Hall. The beautifully proportioned State Apartments contain fine furniture, paintings, silver and tapestries, while the ceiling of the Great Hall is itself a masterpiece. Verrio painted the Heaven Room in 1694 and the gardens are the creation of Capability Brown, who laid them out between 1760 and 1780. The park is open throughout the summer and in early September is the site of the famous Burghley Horse Trials.

BURGHLEY HOUSE lies on the B1443, 1 mile south-east of Stamford.

CHATSWORTH HOUSE & GARDENS
Derbyshire

Chatsworth House, gardens, and collections are just simply magnificent. Chatsworth is more like a palace than a country house and has been the home of the Dukes of Devonshire since the 17th century. The present house stands on the site of a Tudor mansion and is built entirely from local materials, grit-stone, marble and black-stone, all from nearby quarries. The house is full of treasures, furniture, paintings by Poussin, Rembrandt and Reynolds, and some exquisite porcelain, but the park and gardens really draw the crowds. The famous arboretum contains trees from all parts of the world,

Chatsworth House in autumn shades

the Grand Cascade is the largest of many waterfalls and the Emperor Fountain, built to commemorate the visit of Tzar Nicolas I can throw a jet of water nearly 300 ft into the air. The gardeners at Chatsworth are clearly devoted to their work, for with its shrubs, roses, trees and floral beds, the garden is a picture.

🚗 *CHATSWORTH lies 3 miles from Bakewell on the A619.*

CROWLAND ABBEY
Lincolnshire

Crowland Abbey, or what remains of it, lies in the Fen Country of Lincolnshire, just on the border with Cambridgeshire. The original abbey was founded in the 8th century, and destroyed by the Vikings in AD 870. The then abbot's skull, still marked by a sword blow, is displayed in a glass case on the north wall of the Abbey Church. Constant raids and the eventual passing of Crowland into the Danelaw, virtually extinguished the Celtic abbey and the present one dates from the 12th century, after which Crowland grew in prosperity up to just before the Dissolution, when one of the abbots was Henry VII's chancellor, Bishop Morton of 'Morton's Fork' fame.

Henry VIII's commissioners destroyed most of the abbey in 1538 and what remained was damaged still further during the Civil War. What can be seen today is still attractive; the north aisle of the church and the West Front set off by the arch of the Norman abbey.

🚗 *CROWLAND lies 10 miles south of Spalding on the A1073.*

DEENE PARK
Northamptonshire

Deene is a tiny village with a population hovering around the hundred mark, set in a leafy valley in the limestone northern part of the county. The great attraction hereabouts is Deene Park, a classic house in that beautiful light-coloured Welden stone, owned for several centuries by the Brundells, one of whose ancestors led the Charge of the Light Brigade at Balaclava during the Crimean War. Sir Robert Brudenell bought Deene Park in 1514 and it is a fine building with Tudor roots, a deer park with a large lake and extensive gardens, full of flowerbeds and shrubs, all in all a delightful spot.

🚗 *DEENE lies 8 miles north-east of Corby on the A43.*

EYAM
Derbyshire

Eyam is a beautiful Derbyshire village with a sad but historic past. During the time when the Great Plague was sweeping London in 1665, a local tailor received a contaminated consignment of cloth from the city. The bubonic plague swept through the village and although flight into the surrounding countryside would have saved lives, it would also have risked spreading the disease throughout the country. Led by their vicar, the villagers of Eyam decided to stay put. Within a year 259 of the 350 villagers were dead and their graves can be seen around the village in little clumps. The six 17th-century plague cottages where the victims were housed still stand, and the tragedy is commemorated with a procession on the last Sunday in August. Other sights nearby are Monpessons Well, named after that gallant vicar, and on a nearby hill a Celtic preaching cross. Today Eyam is a pretty spot and a pleasant place for the visitor to wander about.

🚗 *EYAM lies off the A623, 10 miles west of Chesterfield.*

The graves of the Hancock family, Eyam plague victims

67

Well-dressing in Derbyshire

Though well dressing is not entirely restricted to Derbyshire, it is seen at its best in a handful of villages which lie deep in the folding valleys and hills of the Peak District, at Tideswell, Tissington, Barlow, Wirksworth and Youlgrave.

Although the origin of this custom is almost certainly pagan, the ceremony has been Christian since the Middle Ages, and is said to be a direct link with the Black Death, when a supply of unpolluted water was essential to the survival of small communities.

Those who have never seen the beautiful pictures and patterns which the villagers form by each well, pressing flower petals into flat trays of wet mud, will be amazed at the detail, and the artistry, for these 'portraits in petals' illustrating religious themes or scenes from the Bible are works of art indeed.

The well dressing takes place on Ascension Day each year, and the villagers compete to make their well, or wells, the most beautiful in the district. Tissington has five wells, and each is covered with a large wooden frame, filled with wet clay and then carefully decorated.

At 11 o'clock on the morning of Ascension (the Thursday before White Sunday — now the Spring Bank Holiday weekend) a procession led by the clergy, will visit and bless each well.

Derbyshire well dressing, seen here at Tideswell

GRIMSTHORPE CASTLE
Lincolnshire

Grimsthorpe is a dramatic place and it has seen dramatic events, not least in 1541 when Henry VIII chose a tournament at Grimsthorpe as the place to accuse his wife Catherine Howard of adultery. Poor Catherine lost her head, and their host, the Duke of Suffolk, was covered with understandable confusion. That scene was preceded by some rapid rebuilding to house the court, and only one tower dates from the original 13th-century building.

In the early 18th century, Vanburgh, the architect of Blenheim, was asked to undertake the conversion of Grimsthorpe into a palace, but although he died long before the work was completed, Grimsthorpe is certainly the greatest country house in Lincolnshire. The Great Hall is magnificent, and the castle contains such interesting relics as the suit Charles I wore for his portrait by Van Dyke, and some fine paintings, (including Van Dyke's) and much beautiful furniture.

🚗 *GRIMSTHORPE lies west of Bourne on the A151.*

HARTINGTON
Derbyshire

Hartington is the classic little village of the Peak District, a good touring centre for the entire area and an attractive place in its own right. Places to visit include the Charles Cotton Inn, named for Izaak Walton's famous fishing companion, and the local Stilton cheese factory, which has that delicious, tangy cheese for sale in attractive little pots. The Market Place is enhanced by a wide green and a duck pond, and is surrounded by pretty houses and cottages. Close by, and a favourite excursion for visitors to Hartington, lies the beautiful Dovedale, marking the boundary between the Derbyshire and the Staffordshire Peaks.

There are good pubs and cafés, a youth hostel and a small hotel, all the necessities to make a visit to Hartington worthwhile.

🚗 *HARTINGTON lies off the A515, 10 miles north of Ashbourne.*

HIGHAM FERRARS
Northamptonshire

The Market Square, composed of beautiful stone houses grouped around the early 19th-century Town Hall, provides the central gem of Higham Ferrars. Today it is a pleasant, busy market town, but it has deep historic roots. Close to St Mary's parish church stands the medieval Bede House and Chantry. In the Lady Chapel of St Mary's the East Window commemorates Henry Chichele, who was born in Higham Ferrars and rose to become Archbishop of Canterbury in 1413.

🚗 *HIGHAM FERRARS lies 10 miles east of Northampton, on the A45.*

LINCOLN
Lincolnshire

Few cities in England can compare with Lincoln, a place where the setting and the architecture have conspired to create a town of rare beauty and a distinctly different atmosphere. Lincoln reeks of history; the Romans came this way and travellers still enter the city under the Roman Newport arch. Inside, the streets are lined with old houses, some dating back to Norman times, leading on to the half-timbered Tudor buildings and shops that stand on the medieval bridge over the river. Above all this, and visible for miles across the flat surrounding countryside, stands Lin-

High on a hill above the city stands Lincoln Cathedral

later, dating from the 14th century, while the keep, or Lucy Tower, was built about 1130. The castle was a royal prison, and the old cells and even iron fetters can still be seen, notably in the prison chapel.

🚗 *LINCOLN lies 16 miles north-east of Newark on the A46.*

THE LINCOLNSHIRE BULB FIELDS
Spalding

The flat fen country around Spalding and Holbeach in the south of Lincolnshire is the centre for one of England's most prosperous and attractive rural industries — the growing of tulips and daffodils. Springfields at Spalding is the centre for this activity, and in the springtime the fields around both towns are a multi-coloured carpet as the flowers come into bloom. In May, Spalding holds a Flower Festival when flower-decked floats parade through the streets to mark the end of the bulb season and the start of the summer, when roses and bedding plants make their colourful contribution to the local landscape.

🚗 *SPALDING lies 20 miles south of Boston on the A16.*

LOUTH
Lincolnshire

Louth is the capital of the Lincolnshire Wolds, a broad strip of country lying across the north-east corner of the country, designated an Area of Outstanding Natural Beauty, and crossed by one of Britain's most popular footpaths, the Viking Way. Louth stands on the eastern side of the Wolds, and is the main market centre for the district, being once second only to Lincoln. Today, Louth is a dreamy little place, mostly Georgian but topped by the splendid Church of St James, which has a 140 ft spire and is definitely one of the most beautiful churches in England, built between 1450 and 1515. The great Cistercian Abbey, which once provided the town with wool for the

coln Cathedral and Castle set on the hilltop which rises above the city. Lincoln Cathedral is one of the largest in England, floodlit at night like a great stone ship. The first cathedral here was built in 1092, but this was destroyed by an earthquake in 1186 and the present building was not finally completed until 1280. It con-

tains all the glories of the English Gothic, and the interior is noted for the carved choir stalls, the 13th-century glass, the Angel Choir and the large collection of medieval brasses.

The castle, a fearsome pile, was built by William the Conqueror in 1076, although the gatehouse is much

The medieval home of Aaron the Jew in the historic heart of Lincoln

thriving local cloth trade — that Lincoln Green so popular with Robin Hood — was destroyed at the Dissolution when many of the monks were hanged in the town square for refusing to obey the Royal Commissioners. As a touring centre for the Wolds, Louth is quite ideal and not far away lies the long, curving attraction of the Lincolnshire Coast.

LOUTH lies 27 miles east of Lincoln on the A157.

MAM TOR
Derbyshire

Derbyshire is a county best known for its superb countryside, which must rank among the most attractive in England, with jumbled dales, steep hillsides lined with drystone walls, rushing streams, grit-stone rock faces, and the endless tugging of the wind. In a county which abounds in great views, one stands out above the rest. Mam Tor is a lofty, windy spot on the B6061 road, crowned at the very top by the relic of an Iron Age hill fort. Above here, the hang-gliders swoop and hover, and lesser mortals can look out across Castleton far below in the valley to Edale, and the southern end of the Pennines. Castleton lies in the so-called White Peak, a limestone region riddled with vast underground caves.

MAM TOR lies 1 mile west of Castleton on the B6061.

MELTON MOWBRAY
Leicestershire

Melton Mowbray is yet another of those old, traditional market towns, a centre for the local countryside and country people. It is particularly famous for the quality of its local pork pies which are said to contain 'everything but the squeal' of the pig, and for the manufacture of Stilton cheese. Both products can be purchased in the town and their history is recorded in the Carnegie Museum. Melton Mowbray is also one of the great hunting towns, the home of the famous Quorn Hunt, and the clip-clop of hooves is almost as common a sound here as the roar of traffic. The town has a fine parish church, with every shade of Gothic, and a very busy open air market. In the surrounding countryside lies the beautiful Vale of Belvoir, another famous hunting region, well worth exploring, but do not fail to spend a day in Melton Mowbray, a town well equipped with old ruins, fine shops and interesting sights.

MELTON MOWBRAY lies 15 miles north-east of Leicester on the A607.

NASEBY
Northamptonshire

The Battle of Naseby in 1645 effectively settled the outcome of the English Civil War, for here Cromwell's New Model Army shattered King Charles' Cavaliers, and destroyed the King's power for ever. The Battle and Farm Museum contains a miniature layout of the battle as well as farm tools and implements, while the battlefield itself is marked with an obelisk. This is best visited after hearing the commentary on the battle in the museum.

THE BATTLEFIELD lies off the B4036, 20 miles north-east of Daventry.

NEWARK CASTLE
Nottinghamshire

Newark has been voted one of the most historic towns in the country, but it is still very far from a tourist trap, in spite of having a fine castle, a popular racecourse and a great many

Despite damage during the Civil War, Newark Castle is spectacular

old buildings.

St Mary Magdalene Church, in the market place, has a tall spire, many curious gargoyles, and a notable brass of 1349. There are a great many fine old pubs, notably the Saracen's Head and the Clinton Arms, both frequented in their time by Sir Walter Scott. The houses in Kirkgate are even older, being Tudor, while Newark Castle is older still.

The castle was built to secure the Great North Road in the 12th century, and severely damaged during the Civil War when it was besieged by Parliament. The walls and towers

are still intact though, and the 12th-century chapel can be visited. An attractive town, quite unspoiled, Newark is one of the places which must find a place in the itinerary of a visit to the Midlands.

🚗 NEWARK lies 8 miles east of Southwell.

NORTHAMPTON
Northamptonshire

No visitor to Northamptonshire can ignore the county town, once a centre for the shoe trade and very historic under the usual modern trappings. King John gave Northampton Castle to the Barons as a pledge for keeping Magna Carta, though Charles II, who disliked the inhabitants' Parliamentary attitudes, had it and the town walls pulled down at the end of the 17th century. During the Wars of the Roses, a battle took place here in 1460, when the Lancastrians were defeated and Henry VI taken prisoner. At nearby Hardingstone travellers can inspect one of the few remaining Eleanor crosses erected across England by Edward I to mark the places where the body of his beloved wife, Eleanor of Castile, rested on its way from Nottinghamshire to London. There is another, even finer, near Geddington. Back in the town, St Peter's Church is Norman, and All Saints Church early medieval. The town museum includes an exhibition of leathercraft and the shoe trade, and the shopping is excellent.

🚗 NORTHAMPTON lies 4 miles east of the M1, off Junction 15 by the A43.

NOTTINGHAM
Nottinghamshire

The old city of Nottingham is said to have the prettiest girls in England and it may well be true. That apart, it is a most attractive town. Any visit might begin with a drink at the famous Trip to Jerusalem Inn by the castle, from which Crusaders set out for the Holy Land. The castle itself was destroyed in the Civil War, but 'The Trip' is still in business and is said to be the oldest inn in England, dating from 1189.

Horseshoes paid as toll fees in the Banqueting Hall of Oakham Castle

Close by stands the statue of Nottingham's most famous son, Robin Hood, who warred for justice with the notorious Sheriff, while for something a little more accurate than those legends of the past, visitors might take in the Museum of Costume at Castlegate which displays among other items a 200 year old collection of underwear.

The old houses of the lace-makers, off the Lace Market, are very attractive, as are the shops surrounding the great central market area where Nottingham's famous Goose Fair is held every October.

Today Nottingham is famous for bicycles, and for good pubs, and is a most attractive city for visitors and residents alike.

🚗 NOTTINGHAM lies 50 miles north-east of Birmingham.

OAKHAM
Leicestershire

Oakham was once the county town of the now-vanished but well-remembered little county of Rutland, which Leicestershire absorbed in the 1970s. Oakham is a very fine town, with a famous public school, Uppingham, an excellent county museum and a number of historic and attractive inns. One somewhat different local attraction at Oakham is the Rutland Farm Park, where rare breeds of sheep and cattle are collected, conserved and bred, and can be seen cropping the grass under the trees. Oakham Castle is Norman and visitors should note the numerous horse-shoes which adorn the walls of the Banqueting Hall. These were paid over as a toll fee by any baron who

A detail from the exquisite foliage carving on a window in the Chapter House at Southwell Minster

passed a night in the castle. Other sights include the old market square, Oakham School, and not far away, the vast sweep of Rutland Water, a reservoir as big as Lake Windermere, ideal for sailing, fishing or birdwatching.

🚗 *OAKHAM lies 11 miles west of Stanford on the A606.*

OUNDLE
Northamptonshire

Oundle is a very fine little town, a beautiful spot, and rightly designated as a Conservation Area. The stone buildings which make it so attractive include those of the public school.

The White Lion Inn dates from 1641 just before the Civil War, while much of the Talbot Inn was built with stones filched from the ruins of near-by Fotheringhay Castle, where Mary, Queen of Scots was executed. Needless to say, the Queen's ghost is said to haunt the inn. The parish church is early medieval with fine glass and brasses, and the almshouses were endowed in 1611.

🚗 *OUNDLE lies 8 miles east of Corby on the A427.*

ROCKINGHAM CASTLE
Northamptonshire

If Rockingham looks familiar to the visitor that may be because it swept to worldwide fame as Arnscote Castle in the TV series *By the Sword Divided*. Descriptions may therefore be superfluous, for it is clearly a beautiful place. William the Conqueror built the first castle here, and the present building has been the home of the Watson family since 1530. Their house is basically Elizabethan, but the outer walls are Norman and encircle such medieval relics as a tilt yard, a 16th-century yew hedge and fine rose gardens. The interior has a good collection of Rockingham china, excellent paintings and a notable connection with Charles Dickens. The castle is open in summer and should certainly be included during any visit to this part of the country.

🚗 *ROCKINGHAM lies 10 miles north-east of Market Harborough on the A6003.*

SOUTHWELL
Nottinghamshire

Southwell is a splendid place, overlooked and beautified by the soaring magnificence of Southwell Minster. This was built by the Normans and only elevated to cathedral status as recently as 1884. The brass lectern in the Minster is all that remains of the contents of the nearby abbey at Newstead, largely destroyed at the Dissolution, but even James I remarked that the Minster, which survived this unhappy time, was ......the finest kirk in England'.

Byron entertained his ladies at the Saracen's Head Inn, and it was here that Charles I surrendered himself to the Scots in 1646. Mostly though, it is the great Minster which attracts the visitors today and rightly so, for it is most decidedly a splendid, evocative building.

🚗 *SOUTHWELL lies 8 miles west of Newark on the A612.*

THORSEBY HALL
Worksop, Nottinghamshire

Thorseby Hall isn't as old as it looks. It appears to be a Tudor building but actually dates from 1864, and is the result of a Neo-Tudor enthusiasm which swept through England. It has a hammer-beam roof, an intriguing clock collection, various state apartments, and over 200 rooms; no one is quite sure exactly how many, but that is one estimate. The park is equally vast, covering over 12,000 acres. In the 1800s the house was the home of Lady Mary Montagu, a writer and traveller who pioneered the concept of innoculation against smallpox.

🚗 *THORSEBY lies 7 miles south-east of Worksop off the A616.*

A statue of Robin Hood rears from the shrubbery at Thorseby Hall

TISSINGTON
Derbyshire

Set in the heart of the Derbyshire Peak District, little Tissington is a popular spot with visitors, and especially with that increasing number of travellers who arrive there on foot or bicycle down the Tissington Trail, which follows the route of the old railway from Buxton and is therefore very level, a boon to hikers and cyclists. The centre of Tissington is marked with a green, around which stand solidly built cottages backed by the village church and a fine Jacobean manor house.

Tissington is one of those villages where well-dressing is still practised on Ascension Day. The custom is said to date back to the time of the Black Death. The village wells are decorated with pictures made by pressing flower petals into frames filled with a layer of soft mud and moss. The effects are both lifelike and artistic, depicting religious or historic scenes — an attractive custom from the distant past.

🚗 *TISSINGTON lies 6 miles north of Ashbourne, off the A515.*

THE TRAMWAY MUSEUM
Derbyshire

The Tramway Museum at Crich contains the national collection of trams, some of which are still working, on a mile or so of track within the museum grounds. There are about 40 various vehicles, ranging from an 1874 horsedrawn tram from Sheffield to that city's last tram which carried its last passenger as recently as 1960. The Museum and Tram Sheds can be visited throughout the year, and provide the perfect place to visit on a rainy day. Other sights within the park are a monument to the Sherwood Foresters Regiment and a display devoted to the history of the Derbyshire lead mines.

🚗 *CRICH lies 5 miles south of Matlock on the B5035.*

THE WATERWAYS MUSEUM
Stoke Bruerne, Northamptonshire

This museum, set beside the Grand Union Canal, is one of the finest small museums in the country, devoted to recreating the life, times and history of the 200-year span of the Canal Age, before it was first threatened and then destroyed by the coming of the railways. There are narrow boats and all manner of interesting curios and artifacts. Ideal for children.

🚗 *STOKE BRUERNE lies off the A43 road, 3 miles east of Towcester.*

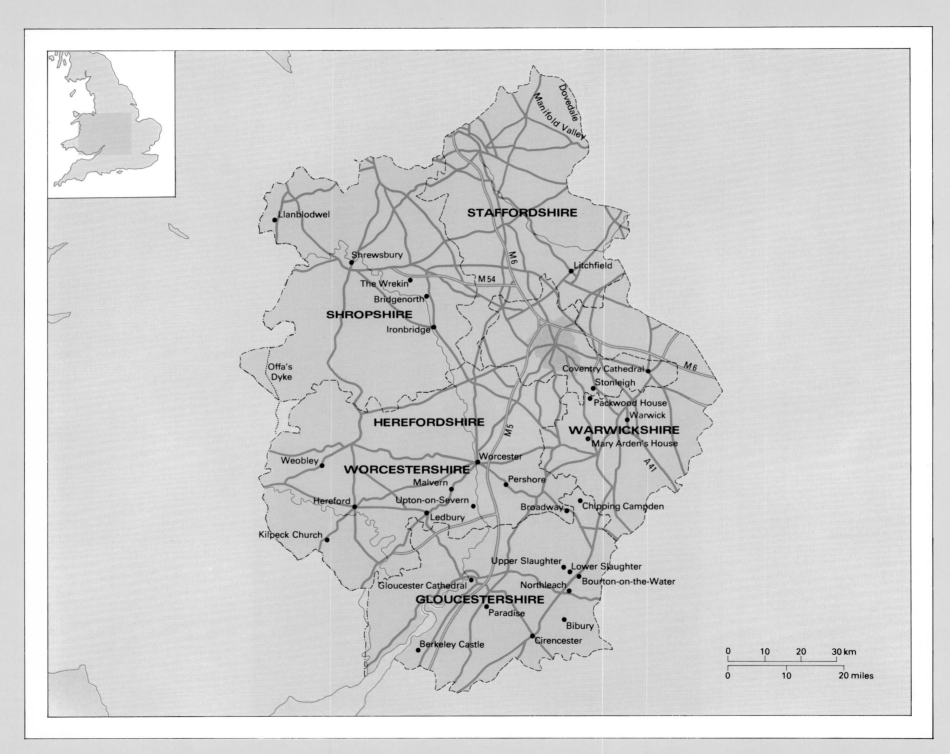

STAFFORDSHIRE

Dovedale

Manifold Valley

Llanblodwel

Shrewsbury

M 6

M 54

Litchfield

The Wrekin

Bridgenorth

SHROPSHIRE

Ironbridge

Offa's
Dyke

Coventry Cathedral

M 6

Stonleigh

Packwood House

Warwick

HEREFORDSHIRE

WARWICKSHIRE

M 5

A 41

Mary Arden's House

Weobley

Worcester

WORCESTERSHIRE

Malvern

Pershore

Hereford

Upton-on-Severn

Broadway

Chipping Campden

Ledbury

Kilpeck Church

Upper Slaughter

Lower Slaughter

Bourton-on-the-Water

Gloucester Cathedral

Northleach

GLOUCESTERSHIRE

Paradise

Bibury

Berkeley Castle

Cirencester

0	10	20	30 km
0		10	20 miles

74

The Heart of England

Set in a garden full of trim hedges, the home of Shakespeare's mother, Mary Arden, is an excellent example of a yeoman's dwelling

RUNNING ACROSS FROM the green and gold country of the Cotswold hills to the Marches of Wales, this part of England offers extremes. In the beginning, among those small, stone-built Cotswold villages, each tucked away in the valley, the air is soft, the landscapes gentle. The Cotswolds are almost archetypal England, a place which people visiting for the first time find very beautiful and somehow familiar. Places like the Slaughters, Bibury, Bourton-on-the-Water, or the glorious town of Chipping Campden are quite unmatched for beauty. Many of these Cotswold towns grew to wealth and prominence during the Middle Ages, when the wealth of England grew on the sheep's back. The country flourished by selling wool to the cloth

looms of Flanders, and from the profits of this trade the burghers endowed their home towns with fine houses and magnificent churches.

Move west, out of these sheltering hills and the land changes, becomes more open, and the sky lifts, offering great sweeping views across the fruit orchards of the Vale of Evesham and across the hills to that old embattled frontier, the Welsh Marches. In this part of England, historical provincial cities have seen their share of strife, and record the events of more jarring days in their great castles, old walls, fine cathedrals — Berkeley Castle and Warwick are but two well-preserved examples of the medieval fortress — while few cathedrals in England can compete with Gloucester, Worcester or Hereford.

BERKELEY CASTLE
Gloucestershire

Even those who love castles cannot claim that Berkeley Castle is beautiful. But then it was not built for beauty but for utility and defence in times of war, and that original purpose shows. The walls are 14 ft thick, the Keep is Norman, the Great Hall dates from the 14th century, as do the kitchens. The castle is best remembered as the place where King Edward II was tormented, starved and finally murdered with a red-hot poker. Today, this castle, which has been a seat of the Berkeley family for over 700 years, is still in magnificent condition. The state apartments are full of armour, weapons, banners and paintings, while the terrace gardens and deer park are well worth seeing, as is the mainly Georgian Berkeley town itself, where, in the Norman Parish Church many of the Berkeleys lie in their tombs.

BERKELEY lies 20 miles north of Bristol off the A38.

BIBURY
Gloucestershire

Bibury is almost too pretty. It straggles up a hill above the River Coln, where a trout hatchery attests to the purity of the water, and is one of those places which gentrification has hardly touched. The cottages on Arlington row were hailed as just perfect by William Morris a century ago, and they still look right today. The Church of St Mary is basically Saxon, and Arlington Mill dates from around the 1650s. Bibury is not one of those places with one overriding attraction. Rather it is a place which looks just right in its setting and pleases all the senses with a fine touch all its own.

BIBURY lies on the A433 8 miles north-east of Cirencester.

BOURTON-ON-THE-WATER
Gloucestershire

Bourton-on-the-Water sounds as beautiful as it is. This is a large Cotswold village, full of attractions and popular with tourists. The River Windrush flows right through the village and is spanned at regular intervals by low bridges. The village is full of fine Georgian houses, there are various museums, curio shops, antique shops and a famous model village, also a fascinating aviary containing species of birds from all over the world — but do not let this modern touristic covering put you off, Bourton-on-the-Water.

BOURTON-ON-THE-WATER lies on the A429 3 miles south of Stow-on-the-Wold.

BRIDGNORTH
Shropshire

Like so many of these Shropshire towns, Bridgnorth stands looking out across the River Severn, keeping a wary eye on the Welsh. It is, of course, medieval, and has not grown much, or changed a lot since Tudor times, so it remains full of old houses, narrow streets, all clustered within what remains of the old ramparts. There are in fact two parts to the town, High and Low, one on the ridge, the other by the river, linked by a cliff railway and a series of steep steps hacked out in the limestone. It has been compared to one of those Tuscan *roccas* so common on the hilltops of Italy, and there are distinct similarities, even to the leaning tower of the ruined 12th-century castle and the warren of little streets. As one of the least-known towns in one of England's least-known counties, Bridgnorth is well worth a diversion.

BRIDGNORTH lies 20 miles south-east of Shrewsbury, on the A458, west of Wolverhampton

BROADWAY
Worcestershire

Broadway has been called the Show-Village of England, a place the tourist books like to present as typical of all English villages. If this were so, it would be no bad thing for Broadway is very attractive, but it can stand on its own as a fine example of a Cotswold village, and of traditional English country architecture. It is built in that soft yellow and white Cotswold stone that mellows so attractively, and with a setting of smooth lawns, cropped hedges and trees, the whole place is a picture. The High Street runs up from the wide Green where the Broadway Hotel and the famous Lygon Arms compete for attention, rising steadily to Fish Hill, where the ancient Fish Inn looks a little out of its depth. Carry on climbing, and you will arrive by Broadway Tower, a folly built in 1800 by the Earl of Coventry. From here you can see the spires of Worcester Cathedral, 20 miles away, but the best place to be on any warm summer evening is down in Broadway itself, enjoying the quiet corners of this pretty English village.

BROADWAY lies on the A44, 5 miles south-east of Evesham.

CHIPPING CAMPDEN
Gloucestershire

Chipping Campden is a wool town, one of those places that grew to prosperity off the sheep's back, for Cotswold wool was the main export of medieval England, a source of the country's riches. It is as a reminder of

A row of cottages built in Cotswold stone stand beside the mill stream at Arlington Row in Bibury

this fact that the Lord Chancellor of England sits on the Woolsack to this very day. Chipping Campden is a glorious town, full of fine buildings. The Woolstaple Hall was built in 1380, and parts of the Town Hall are even earlier. In the High Street stands the much photographed 17th-century Market Hall, a magnificent building, as is the medieval church, dedicated to St James and built by William Grevel 'the flower of all the wool merchants of all England', according to his memorial. This church is full of fascinating corners, glass, brasses, tombs, a wonderful find for any lover of the medieval world, but the same might be said of the whole town. Not much has changed here since the first Queen Elizabeth sat on the throne, and it remains a gem of old England, the perfect example of a market town.

🚗 *CHIPPING CAMPDEN lies 10 miles north of Stow on the Wold, by the A424 and A44 roads.*

CIRENCESTER
Gloucestershire

Unlike many of the other towns hereabouts, which grew up in the Middle Ages, Cirencester is Roman. Known then as *Corinium*, it was the second city of the country after London, and recent excavations have revealed just how extensive the Roman city was. The Roman walls still encircled the town in the Middle Ages, but the success of the wool trade can be seen here as elsewhere, most notably as always, in the magnificent 15th-century parish church of St John the Baptist, which is rightly regarded as one of the most perfect Perpendicular style churches in England. It is useless to describe St John's, for words are just inadequate; it has to be seen. Do not leave Cirencester without visiting the Corinium Museum, and Cirencester

Park, which is now open to the public and set off by the great house built by Earl Bathurst in 1718.

🚗 *CIRENCESTER is 19 miles southeast of Gloucester.*

COVENTRY CATHEDRAL
Warwickshire

There is not much left of the old Saxon city of Coventry, where Lady Godiva rode through the streets on a white horse to spare the citizens from her husband's rapacious tax gatherers; the German bombers saw to that. On the night of 14 November 1940, Coventry endured one of the most sustained air attacks of the War and most of the city was totally destroyed, including the magnificent medieval Gothic Cathedral.

Modern Coventry is simply not attractive, but Sir Basil Spence's Cathedral, begun in 1954 and consecrated in 1962, is a modern marvel, and must be seen. The ruins of the old Cathedral act as a stepping stone to the new one, which is built in concrete and full of works of art. The porch contains a statue of St Michael by Epstein, the tapestry of Christ behind the High Altar is the largest in the world and was woven in France, the baptistry window is by John Piper and is a riot of colours, while the Chapel of Christ in Gethsemane contains a magnificent mosaic by Sykes. Perhaps the most effective memorial is a little iron cross forged from nails found twisted by fire in the ashes of the old Cathedral.

🚗 *COVENTRY lies 12 miles north of Warwick on the A46.*

DOVEDALE
Staffordshire

Though chiefly connected with Derbyshire, the Peak District laps over into Staffordshire, where Dovedale is

A view of Dovedale from Thors Cave, high above the river

78

one of the most beautiful of the dales. Dovedale is a lovely valley and the whole of it, from Hartingdon down to the stepping stones near Thrope, is a well-famed beauty spot, and rightly so. Two places to visit are Thors Cave and Weltonmill. Tors Cave is a strange place, the entrance alone being 60 ft high, set 200 ft or more above the river. The Dove actually marks the boundary between Derbyshire and Staffordshire, and is a famous fishing river, the happy hunting ground of Izaak Walton and his boon companion Charles Cotton. At any time of the year this deep little valley, with its river rushing fast along its bed, is one of the great natural attractions of this little-known county.

🚗 *DOVEDALE lies east of the A515 between Ashbourne and Hartington.*

GLOUCESTER CATHEDRAL
Gloucestershire

Gloucester is an industrial city today, but it does have one attraction that makes a visit here more than worthwhile; the great Gothic Cathedral, full of memorials, evocative of England's colourful history.

The cathedral towers over the workaday city and is dominated in its turn by a soaring Perpendicular tower, which was erected in the mid-15th century. The cathedral nave is Norman, and stands on the site of a Saxon abbey with a 14th-century trancept, a 15th-century Lady Chapel and medieval cloisters to top off the work. The interior glows with colour as light streams through the huge 72 ft-high East Window — the largest stained glass window in Britain — and illuminates the old battle flags, stonework, brasses and tombs. Most notable of these is the 14th-century tomb of Edward II who was

The aisles of Gloucester Cathedral, lined with fine stained glass windows

murdered in nearby Berkeley Castle. Gloucester Cathedral is one of the centres for the tri-annual Three Choirs Festival.

🚗 *GLOUCESTER lies 9 miles west of Cheltenham, on the A40, or M5 motorway.*

HEREFORD
Herefordshire

Hereford is an unusual market town, for while many are attractive, if a touch bucolic, Hereford has a long connection with the arts. Garrick the playwright was born here; Kemble and Sarah Siddon came to play here; and the town is one of the founder cities for the famous Three Choirs Festival, which dates back to 1720.

Going back even further, Hereford is a Border town, a bastion on the Marches of Wales. Parts of the old walls still remain, there are many attractive half-timbered houses to beautify the old streets and the cathedral is said by cathedral lovers to be one of the finest in the kingdom. It is a very early Norman building, with a 14th-century central tower, and full of all the best cathedral features, including stained glass, brasses, tombs, fine vaulting, chantry chapels, the lot. There is also a notable chained library and a very old map of the world. Hereford is also a good centre for touring north along the Marches, or south to the Severn Valley.

🚗 *HEREFORD lies 13 miles south of Leominster on the A49.*

IRONBRIDGE
Shropshire

Perched on limestone cliffs above the River Severn, the gorge spanned by that famous iron bridge that gives the town its name, this town set the benchmark for the Industrial Revolution that transformed England from a largely agricultural community into an industrial society. Today, the town is a great centre for the study of

A view of Ironbridge where the Industrial Revolution really began

industrial archaeology, with several museums recording the history and development of the local iron industry. After visiting there though, remember to go closer for a look at the great iron bridge itself. It was made in 1777, the first bridge built in iron in England. Now take an even closer look and you will see that while the metal is iron, the method was carpentry — note the joints of the beams, the slotting of the cross-members, exactly as used on wooden bridges. The bridge still arches high above the river, a magnificent sight. Not far away, in the suburb of Coalbrookdale, the ironmaster Abraham Darby first discovered how to smelt iron with coking coal, and although this is probably the birthplace of the Industrial Revolution,

it remains quite a pretty place, with a number of half-timbered houses. England's history is by no means all medieval, as Ironbridge proves.

🚗 *IRONBRIDGE lies 6 miles south of Telford on the A4169.*

KILPECK CHURCH
Herefordshire

Kilpeck Church is most attractive, one of the best preserved Norman churches in England. There is a huge Norman font and some magnificent Norman carving on the south door. It stands beside the remains of a Norman motte, and probably dates from about 1135. The style which we call Norman is known on the Continent as Romanesque, and there are distinct similarities between the rich carvings

Rich Romanesque carvings decorate the doorway of Kilpeck Church

at Kilpeck and those found on the great pilgrimage churches of south-west France, on the famous Road to Compostela, tempting speculation that the master-mason who worked at Kilpeck had followed that road to the Shrine of St James at Santiago de Compostela in Galicia.

KILPECK lies 6 miles south-west of Hereford, off the A465.

LEDBURY
Herefordshire

Set beneath the bare green slope of the Malvern Hills, Ledbury is a very attractive market town which contains a considerable number of those pleasing black and white half-timbered houses seen in this part of England. Two worth noting are the Old Market House, which has been hoisted onto wooden pillars in the High Street, and the much restored Grammar School in Church Lane, where a museum charts the development of Ledbury from Anglo-Saxon times. Those who like visiting old churches will enjoy the medieval Church of St Michael and All Angels, though the spire dates from as recently as the 1730s. The interior contains a good number of brasses from the 14th to the 19th centuries.

LEDBURY lies 8 miles south of Malvern on the A449.

LICHFIELD
Staffordshire

Lichfield is best known to the world as the birthplace of that 18th-century writer and sage, Dr Samuel Johnson, who was born here in 1709. His birthplace is now a museum and his statue stands in the market place. The town dates back to Roman times, although it is the Georgian facades that strike the eye most pleasantly today, as well as the fine cathedral

Three tall spires set off the rooftops of St Chad's Cathedral built between 1195 and 1235

dedicated to that little-known cleric, St Chad, Bishop of Mercia about AD 660. The pilgrimage to his shrine raised the money for this huge three-spired cathedral. It was built between 1195 and 1235 and can be seen for miles, but the west front repays closer inspection for it is covered with statues and carvings. The Lady Chapel contains some fine 16th-century glass and the Cathedral treasury holds St Chad's Gospels, a rare collection of early Gospels. Taken all in all, Lichfield is one of those towns that all true travellers should visit.

🚗 *LICHFIELD lies 20 miles south of Stafford on the A51.*

LLANBLODWEL
Shropshire

Llanblodwel sounds very Welsh, but it is an English town, one of those graceful little places on the eastern side of the Marches. It goes back to the early days of the 12th century, when the Normans first arrived at this far frontier, and built the Church of St Michael the Archangel, which after 800 years has evolved into an amazing mixture of architectural styles, with a bit of this and a bit of that, a Norman doorway, a detached bell tower built in the last century, a spire set on top like a witch's hat, a marvellous carved south porch. There is a medieval bridge over the river, and a 16th-century inn.

🚗 *LLANBLODWEL lies off the A495, 4 miles south of Oswestry.*

MALVERN
Worcestershire

The two boroughs of Malvern, Great Malvern and Malvern Link lie on the side of the Malvern Hills, a curious,

A view of the green and winding Manifold Valley, one of the less well-known beauty spots of Derbyshire

high, nine-mile long ridge that dominates the countryside round about. In the last century Malvern developed into a spa, thanks to the purity and abundance of Malvern Water, which is still bottled here today. This era has left Malvern with a fine collection of hotels, and it now acts as a tourist centre, lying as it does in some splendid countryside, with first-class walks on the hills above. Great Malvern also contains a marvellous relic in the shape of the Priory Church founded during the reign of William the Conqueror, much of which survives. The carving on the choir pews shows the labours of the seasons, the stained glass is magnificent, and the building practically unique. For this and all the other reasons given here, Malvern should not be missed on any journey through this region of England.

🚗 *GREAT MALVERN lies 10 miles south of Worcester, on the A449.*

THE MANIFOLD VALLEY
Staffordshire

The River Manifold is a tributary of the River Dove, running into the larger river through the Staffordshire Peak. It rises, like the Dove, close to the Traveller's Rest Inn on the Buxton Road near Leek, and the upper reaches of this river are quite spectacular, the river cutting a deep gorge in the gritstone rock, and after winding down a deep limestone valley, the Manifold suddenly narrows at Eaton Hill and finally flows into the Dover near Ilam. Sights to see on the way include Darfor Bridge and the place where the river vanishes underground for a while near the Redhurst Swallets, only to reappear in the grounds of Ilam Hall, a National Trust property where the river's reappearance can be seen. The name Manifold refers to the meander-

An inside view of Mary Arden's house at Wilmcote

ing way it winds across the country — there is no industrial connection.

🚗 *THE MANIFOLD VALLEY and river can best be viewed near Hulme End, north of the A523.*

MARY ARDEN'S HOUSE
Warwickshire

No tour of Warwickshire would be complete without some reference to the county's most famous son, William Shakespeare of Stratford-on-Avon. Indeed, memorials and reminders of Shakespeare abound in the county, but Wilmcote was the home of his mother, Mary Arden, and her house can still be visited. It is a rather fine half-timbered building of the classic Tudor style, so she was clearly a lady of property; her father was in fact a wealthy yeoman. She married John Shakespeare of Stratford in 1557, and moved into town, but her house at Wilmcote is now a Shakespeare Museum.

🚗 *WILMCOTE lies off the A34, 3 miles north-west of Stratford.*

NORTHLEACH
Gloucestershire

The Cotswolds are full of attractive villages, many of them well established on the tourist trail, but little Northleach has been overlooked. It lies in the valley of the River Leach, just north of the A40 road, and is noted in particular for the Church of Sts Peter and Paul, a very large 15th-century building, built, like so many of these impressive Cotswold churches, from the profits of the local wool trade. The west tower is lofty, and the porch is full of statues is lofty, and the porch is full of statues and delicate tracery. Inside there is a remarkable brass to John Fortey, who built the clerestory in the Chancel, and an equally remarkable font. All in all, this church contains some of the finest elements of English Gothic.

🚗 *NORTHLEACH is 10 miles north east of Circencester on the A429.*

OFFA'S DYKE
Herefordshire

No county can really lay claim to Offa's Dyke, a vast ditch and earthwork constructed in the 8th century by command of King Offa of Mercia. It runs for nearly 200 miles along the Marches of Wales, from the Dee in the North to the banks of the River Wye near Chepstow.

It cannot have been Offa's intention to defend this land, and the opinion of modern historians is that he had it built to mark the frontier between his kingdom and the Welsh. The Dyke today provides the basic route for the Offa's Dyke Footpath, a 168-mile journey over countless stiles, a challenge indeed to the fit, well-equipped hill walker.

🚗 *OFFA'S DYKE can be followed from various points along the Welsh border, notably near Hay-on-Wye.*

Morris Dancing

Morris Dancing is a uniquely English custom. It dates back certainly to the early medieval period, but the origin of this custom is probably pagan, when the people danced to celebrate the start of spring or to ensure the fertility of their crops. It has to be said also that while Morris Dancing is often done for the delight of visitors and tourists, it is part of a genuine local folklore, and the people would still dance whether there were visitors to watch or not.

Morris Dancing can be found in Yorkshire, in the Midlands or many parts of the West Country, often in a distinctly different local form, or with additions and embellishments unique to a particular village. The Cotswolds, however, maintain a regional form of this dance, the almost classic 'Cotswold-Morris' which can be seen at its best on any summer Bank Holiday Monday, in the village of Bampton.

Cotswold-Morris Dancers are all men, and the Bampton team starts dancing soon after daybreak, and continues to dance throughout the day, although with frequent pauses for rest and refreshment in the various local pubs. The dance ends officially with tea on the Vicarage lawn, but if the dancers are still in the mood, as they always are, it then continues well into the evening. The music is provided by fiddle, accordian or tambourine, helped out by the Morris bells lashed to every dancer's leg below the knee, and while every dancer is dressed in white, some have their faces black, which gives rise to the theory that the word 'Morris' is a version of 'Moorish', which seems somewhat unlikely in this typically English setting.

Morris dancing by the Compden Morris Men at Chipping Camden in the Cotswolds

Fine 18th-century wrought-ironwork enhances this balcony in a home in Bridge Street, Pershore

PERSHORE
Worcestershire

Pershore is not one of those towns that many English people think about or tourists visit, and this is passing strange because it has a lot to offer. It lies on the River Avon on the western edge of the Vale of Evesham, so the setting alone is very beautiful. Penetrate to the centre and you will discover an almost intact 18th-century Georgian town, with a square and High Street lined with row after row of elegant buildings, most pleasing to the eye. Pershore Abbey, which was the reason that the town grew up here, was destroyed during the Reformation, but the Abbey Church was preserved to serve the parish, as it still does. From here it is just a short step to the delicate foot-bridge across the river, which gives visitors a fine view of the old houses on the banks. On any journey into Wales, a diversion through Pershore could be most rewarding, as trips off the too-well-trodden track usually are.

PERSHORE l.es 6 miles west of Evesham on the A44.

SHREWSBURY
Shropshire

Set on a great winding loop of the River Severn, one of the Border fortresses guarding the Welsh Marches in days gone by, Shrewsbury has somehow managed to preserve all that is best of the old town through much recent reconstruction — in short, it still looks right.

It takes the visitor a day or two to get to grips with Shrewsbury, for it is a narrow, tightly-knitted town, a place of narrow streets and old houses, with ruins and churches. The castle is Norman and the gateway is still exactly as it was 500 years ago,

PACKWOOD HOUSE
Warwickshire

Packwood House is an elegant Tudor manor house built about 1550, and much expanded about 100 years later. Pleasant though it is, Packwood's main attraction for visitors is the garden, and the reason it came to be constructed. When the Civil War broke out in 1642, the then owner of Packwood, John Fetterston, could not decide between King and Parliament, so he decided most wisely to stay at home. He collected sundials, of which several still remain in the grounds, and was an expert at topiary, so during the long years of the War he clipped and trimmed the yew trees of Packwood to represent the Sermon on the Mount. The house contains needlework and tapestry, but the gardens should not be missed.

PACKWOOD HOUSE lies at Lapworth, near Knole, off the A34 south of Birmingham.

PARADISE
Gloucestershire

It would be a very world-weary traveller indeed, who could resist visiting a village called Paradise. It is really little more than a hamlet, lying just off the A46 road, north of Stroud, and it had no name until King Charles stumbled upon it during the Civil War. On hearing that this beautiful little place had no name, he told them to 'call it Paradise'. The setting by the little River Slad is quite delightful, and it makes a pleasant stop on the way to the Benedictine Abbey at Prinknash, which may be visited, together with its working pottery and craft shop.

PARADISE lies off the A46, 3 miles north of Painswick.

even if the rest has been over-restored. St Mary's Church is also Norman, with plenty of later additions including some fine glass, and there are plenty of monastic buildings around the town, though Shrewsbury School dates from the 16th century, after the Reformation. The whole town is worth exploring, from the banks of the Severn to the castle up above, as a splendid relic of the High Middle Age, and a very fine city of today.

🚗 *SHREWSBURY lies 11 miles west of Wellington by the A5.*

THE SLAUGHTERS
Gloucestershire

The twin villages of Upper and Lower Slaughter, set beside the little River Eye, in a green fold of the Cotswolds, are quite delightful. This is a place of mellow Cotswold stone, of ivy-draped drystone walls, of birdsong and the tinkle of water in the brook, everything an English village — or villages — should be. The two villages are a mile or so apart, and most of the buildings date from the 16th or 17th centuries. There is a fine 16th-century dovecote in the grounds of the Manor Hotel in Lower Slaughter, while the Church of St Mary contains many memorials to the local squires, the Whitmores. The centrepiece of this village is The Square, which has lots of old cottages and the old corn mill which still retains the water wheel, and there are more of these attractive golden stone houses on the banks of the Eye.

Upper Slaughter, as the name implies, stands on a hill. The remains of a Norman motte and bailey (hill and ditch) castle still stand behind Home Farm, but the name 'Slaughter' has nothing to do with any medieval massacre. It is from the Saxon 'sloutre' — which gives us 'Slough' —

A view across the green and stream into the centre of Lower Slaughter, one of the most attractive Cotswold villages

a muddy place, and it can get very muddy indeed hereabouts, especially during the winter months.

🚗 *THE SLAUGHTERS lie 3 miles west of Stow on the Wold, off the A436.*

STONLEIGH
Warwickshire

Stonleigh can rightly claim to be one of the loveliest villages in Warwickshire, that country of lovely villages. It is not very large, but what there is, is choice, from the Tudor almshouses to the 14th-century bridges over the river, and the solid Norman church. The village has belonged for centuries to the Leighs of Stonleigh Abbey. Alice Leigh built the almshouses here in 1594, two years before she married Robert Dudley. She lived on until well into the next century, supported the Royalists during the Civil War and was made a Duchess by Charles I in 1645. Stonleigh is a place to wander about in, crossing the River Sowe by

Sowe Bridge, looking at yet more of those beautiful black and white houses.

🚗 *STONLEIGH lies 3 miles east of Kenilworth, off the A46.*

UPTON-ON-SEVERN
Worcestershire

Upton-on-Severn is not very large but it has a long and fascinating history, and a good range of architecture. It lies on the west bank of the River Severn, overlooked by the green Malvern hills on one side, and by Bredon Hill on the other. It is now an important boating centre for the Severn valley, with a large marina and plenty of moorings. A number of good riverside pubs and a series of coaching inns line the main street. Clearly, despite its present obscurity, little Upton was once a place of importance. It was a strategic centre during the Civil War and the Upton Heritage Centre, in the old tower known as the Pepperpot, recounts the story of those Cavalier-v-Roundhead

battles fought on this soil long ago.

🚗 *UPTON-ON-SEVERN is on the A4101, 12 miles south of Worcester.*

WARWICK
Warwickshire

By any standards, Warwick is a splendid place. It may look like just another pretty market town, but Warwick is more than it seems, for this is, or was, the home of the mighty Nevilles, Earls of Warwick, makers and breakers of kings.

There is so much to see here that it is hard to know where to start, but the castle must dominate any visit, and is clearly the glory of the town. Parts of it date from AD 900, but most of the present buildings were erected during the jarring days of the 14th and 15th centuries. Caesar's Tower and Guy's Tower overlooking the Avon, are filled with treasures, armour, paintings, tapestries, furniture, the collections of that great series of families, Beauchamp, Neville and Dudley, who held the earldom of Warwick and their symbol, the bear and ragged staff, can be seen everywhere in the town. In Warwick Castle, Piers Gaveston was tried and condemned, and here Warwick the Kingmaker pondered on who to support during the Wars of the Roses. If this is too much, then visit a still surviving relic at the Lord Leycester Hospital, now a home for old soldiers and endowed by Robert Dudley, Earl of Leicester and favourite of Queen Elizabeth I. Pass on from there to explore the streets of this historic town, to see especially the Beauchamp Chapel in the Church of St Mary, which contains the tomb of its founder, Richard Beauchamp, Constable of France to Henry VI, and those of many other Earls.

🚗 *WARWICK lies 8 miles north of Stratford-on-Avon by the A46.*

The Wrekin, a round green bump of a hill crowned by an Iron Age fort

WEOBLEY
Herefordshire

Weobley — pronounced Webley — is one of the famous black and white villages which are not uncommon in this region of England. It can be said though, that Weobley is one of the finest, a place where striking timber-framed houses fan out from the main street, and in the narrow byways beneath the sharp spire of the church. A local man, Ben Tomkins, is credited with breeding those black and white Hereford cattle back in the 18th century, perhaps to match the architecture. The Church of Sts Peter and Paul dates from the 14th century, and contains among other memorabilia, a fine statue of Colonel John Birch, a Cromwellian officer who regularly fell out with Cromwell and was imprisoned on countless occasions. Weobley is a place that can be found only in England, and then only on the March of Wales, and it alone would make a trip there worthwhile.

WEOBLEY lies on the A4112, 12 miles north-west of Hereford.

WORCESTER
Worcestershire

Worcester is a very fine, very historic city on the River Severn. It has been an important place since Celtic times, and seen a lot of strife down the centuries, yet somehow preserved some fine buildings, and a rather peaceful air. The town is built on both banks of the river, and as the Severn is one of England's less predictable streams, the city gets flooded from time to time. One place unravaged by fire or flood, is Worcester Cathedral. Parts of this date from the 7th century, but it has been added to, or rebuilt, many times, and the pleasing whole we have today is on that account rather remarkable. It took 200 years to complete the Nave, which contains the tomb of King John, who loved the place so much that he wanted to be buried here rather than at Westminster or the Plantagenet mausoleum at Fontevraud. The old Bishop's Palace at Hartleberry contains the County Museum, and has an impressive collection of gypsy caravans.

WORCESTER lies 12 miles north-west of Pershore, on the A44.

THE WREKIN
Shropshire

The Wrekin is a beautiful hill, very distinctive, lying a little to the south of Wellington. On the summit, stand the smooth grass ramparts of an Iron Age hill fort and those who plod to the top will be rewarded with wonderful views over a broad band of country, and looking south, see the high, green and russet ridge of Wenlock Edge. The hill fort was probably the marshalling place for the warlike Cornovi tribe of Britons who lived here on the wild march for centuries before the Romans came to Britain, 2000 years ago.

THE WREKIN is just south of Wellington, which is north west of Telford on the A442.

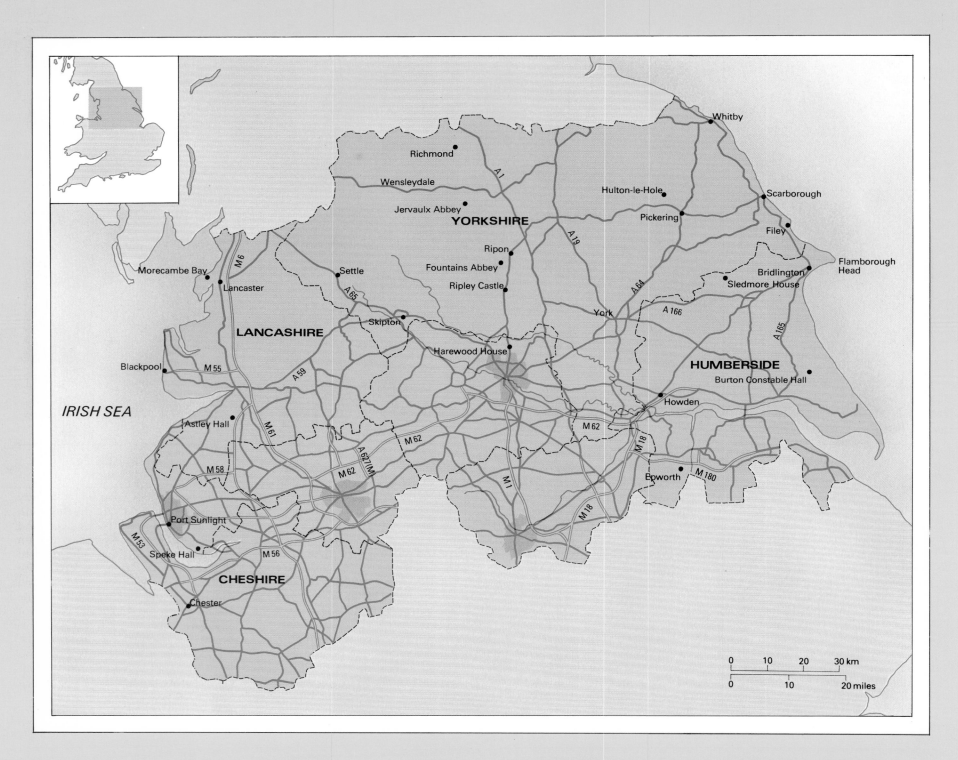

IRISH SEA

LANCASHIRE

YORKSHIRE

HUMBERSIDE

CHESHIRE

Whitby
Richmond
Wensleydale
Hulton-le-Hole
Scarborough
Jervaulx Abbey
Pickering
Filey
Ripon
Fountains Abbey
Bridlington
Flamborough Head
Ripley Castle
Sledmore House
Morecambe Bay
Settle
Lancaster
York
A 166
Skipton
A 165
Harewood House
Blackpool
Burton Constable Hall
Astley Hall
Howden
Port Sunlight
Epworth
Speke Hall
Chester

M 6
A 65
A 1
A 19
A 64
M 55
A 59
M 61
M 62
A 627(M)
M 62
M 58
M 62
M 1
M 18
M 18
M 180
M 53
M 56

0   10   20   30 km
0   10   20 miles

Yorkshire, Humberside & North west

Sheep crop the grass on Lewisham Moor in Yorkshire, a patchwork of green fields stretching as far as the eye can see

YORKSHIRE IS, WITHOUT DOUBT, one of the finest of all the English counties; for it combines a striking mixture of neat farms, green dales, high hills, tumbling waterfalls, open wind-swept moorlands, an attractive coastline and a benevolent climate with ancient cities, strong castles, soaring cathedrals, and the usual pleasing pattern of small villages, little market towns, and here and there among the green valleys, the jumbled old stone litter of some ancient ruined abbey.

Not only the abbeys have passed, but Yorkshire itself has also changed, with the ancient 'Ridings', North, South and West now changed into sub-divisions and newly-created counties, South, West and North

Yorkshire which with Humberside now blankets the old county which was, in its day, the largest county in England and held, in the City of York, the second town of the Kingdom. All that may have been swept away in the county reorganisation of the 1970s, but nothing else has changed and Yorkshire remains magnificent, a beautiful, varied county.

Yorkshire is the traveller's county whether you ride about by car or bicycle, or on one of the famous railway lines like the Settle to Carlisle or the North Yorkshire Moors Railway.

Next door Lancashire is an underrated county, best known perhaps for Blackpool, the Jewel of the North, with its Golden Mile, its 518 ft tower, its Victorian-style entertainment and ultra-modern facilities.

Blackpool's colourful illuminations

ASTLEY HALL
Lancashire

Astley Hall is a curious place, to say the least. It was built, or rather begun, in Elizabethan times, so that the basic structure is Tudor. This classic, central core is however totally overshadowed by the 17th-century additions of the great many-windowed bays which flank the main building, so that at first sight, Astley Hall glitters with the reflections from the glass.

Once inside, visitors can inspect the great bed, called Cromwell's Bed, because the Lord Protector is said to have slept in it before the Battle of Preston. Note the extensive dining table in the Long Gallery.

🚗 *ASTLEY HALL is in Park Road, Chorley — Chorley lies just south of Preston on the A6.*

BLACKPOOL
Lancashire

England has two great and vastly popular seaside towns, Brighton in the South and, on the coast of industrial Lancashire, Blackpool.

Of the two, Blackpool is the larger, the more colourful, the less elegant, but the most fun, and as a seaside town in the best sense of the word, offers all the elements of the English seaside holiday. There are donkeys on the sands, bandstands, dancing in the Tower ballroom where the organ plays, all the sweetshops and stalls sell Blackpool rock, the illuminations are famous and draw the crowds by the coach-load every year, and the famous Blackpool Tower looms over it all, a landmark for miles around.

Out of season, Blackpool is much quieter, and then the conference season begins, attracting vast numbers of more serious folk to enjoy the sights before summer comes again, but those who enjoy a little fun but prefer the quiet life can always play golf around Lytham St Anne's or just take a walk along the beach early in the day before the tourists arrive.

🚗 *BLACKPOOL lies 15 miles west of Preston on the A583.*

BRIDLINGTON
Humberside

Bridlington, set in the sheltered southern side of Flamborough Head, is first and foremost a fishing port and only incidentally a tourist centre, although the fishing has declined and the tourist trade flourishes. Like a number of the old Yorkshire towns, it was once a pilgrimage centre, and had a famous Priory, founded in 1114 and greatly extended throughout the Middle Ages. John of Bridlington, the local saint, was canonised in 1401, and although the Priory went the way of most monastic buildings in 1538, the Priory Church is now the Parish Church of St Mary, still a glorious building, though over-restored by the Victorians. The Priory Gatehouse now contains a museum, but those who have no love of history or architecture will find plenty of interesting walks around the old fishing port, on the sandy beaches or down by the harbour.

🚗 *BRIDLINGTON lies 20 miles south of Scarborough on the A165.*

BURTON CONSTABLE HALL
Humberside

The masters of their craft worked to beautify Burton Constable Hall and make it the place we see today. They were helped by the Tudor mansion on

The rows at Chester, black and white 'magpie' style architecture

Chester and are a unique feature of English architecture. Legend has it that the 'Rows' dates back to 1485, the year of Bosworth Field, but those which remain today are from the later Tudor and Stuart periods. They are a most unusual sight, running down Eastgate, Bridge Street and Watergate; clearly they are designed to provide good, covered shopping in the rainy north-west, but since they are both functional and especially attractive, one can only wonder why they have not appeared in other English cities. As it is they remain unique to Chester and this is one reason for visiting this elegant provincial city.

The cathedral dates back to the immediate post-Conquest period and stands on the site of a Saxon shrine. It began life in 1092 as the church of a Benedictine community, although it has been greatly enlarged and beautified down the centuries. The Treasury contains a fine collection of medieval manuscripts, while the nave has superb 14th and 15th-century stonework, including the gargoyle known as 'The Chester Imp'. Things to see in the countryside round about include Little Moreton Hall, perhaps the finest Tudor style mansion in Britain.

CHESTER lies 17 miles south of Liverpool.

which it is based; this was built in 1570 and then altered by Robert Adam and Wyatt in the 1750s. They added another storey to the eastern side, and balanced this with the central block and pediment, while retaining the Tudor minstrel gallery and adding a Georgian dining room to the interior. The grounds and park were in the hands of Capability Brown, who cannot have visualised the attraction which exists there today — there is also a zoo and a model

railway. Burton Constable is a fine house, and provides an interesting visit during the summer when it is open to visitors.

BURTON CONSTABLE HALL lies 1 mile north of Sproatley, off the B1238, east of Kingston-upon-Hull.

CHESTER
Cheshire

Chester is an ancient city dating back to Roman times, when it was founded

as *Deva*, a base for the XXth Legion. It stands on a strategic site on the River Dee, close to the March of Wales, and remains an important commercial city, with several sights to attract the attention of the passing traveller, not least the Roman remains, the cathedral, the encircling city wall which provides the ideal route around the city and, of course, the famous 'Rows'. The Rows is a series of multi-storey shops and houses which line the main streets of

EPWORTH
Humberside

Epworth really ought to be a famous spot, even though it is just a pretty little place tucked away in Humberside's countryside west of Doncaster. As it is, Epworth is hardly known outside the Methodist community, for John Wesley, the founder of Methodism, was born here in 1710, three years after his brother Charles, the author of some stirring hymns.

In fact, the building which claims to be Wesley's birthplace is actually the one built to replace the Wesley home which was burned down by a mob some years after John Wesley was born — and the motive was political not religious. It was the family home for several years, and is today a Wesley Museum, full of memorabilia and open during the summer months.

🚗 *EPWORTH lies 2 miles south of the M180 motorway, west of Doncaster.*

FILEY
North Yorkshire

Filey is one of the most popular seaside resorts of the Yorkshire coast, and blessed with a beautiful natural setting. The sands are wide, safe and gently shelving, well supplied with cliffs, caves and rockpools where crabs lurk to be chased out by small children armed with shrimping nets. There is something almost Edwardian about Filey, a place evocative of those childhood seaside holidays in times gone by, with walks along the cliffs, putting greens, golf links, concert parties and bandstands.

Old Filey, the fishing quarter of the town that existed here long before tourism was invented, is a quaint place, full of old houses and little courtyards called 'yards'. Charlotte Brontë often stayed in Cliff House in Bell Street, which is now a restaurant, and she mentions Filey frequently in *Jane Eyre*.

🚗 *FILEY lies 10 miles south of Scarborough off the A165.*

FLAMBOROUGH HEAD
Humberside

Flamborough is one of the great sea promontories of England, a vast, soaring cliff, rising up out of the grey

Flamborough Head lies in the sea like a piece of a giant's jigsaw puzzle

stormy waters of the North Sea. This is the place to go when an easterly gale is sweeping in across the sea from Norway and great waves send the spray soaring high into the air in sheets of foam. On less dramatic days there are seabirds by the thousand, an old lighthouse, and Flamborough Church, basically Norman. Andrew Marvell was the rector here.

🚗 *FLAMBOROUGH HEAD lies 17 miles south of Scarborough.*

FOUNTAINS ABBEY
North Yorkshire

In its heyday, during the 15th century, Fountains was the richest Cistercian abbey in England. The Cistercians preferred these quiet, remote locations for their monasteries and the community worked hard to transform this bleak valley into fertile farming country. The abbey dates from 1150, and although much was destroyed or carried away at the Dissolution, a considerable amount remains, notably the secular buildings, kitchens, dormitories and cellars, as well as the nave of the Abbey Church and the Chapel of the Nine Altars. The ruins and the gardens were landscaped in the last century and there is no more beautiful spot in Yorkshire when the sun is setting and the gardens are filled with the song of the birds and the sound of rippling water. Fountains Hall nearby, was built with dressed stone filched from these ruins.

🚗 *FOUNTAINS ABBEY lies 4 miles south of Ripon on the B6269.*

GARSDALE
Lancashire

Garsdale lies in that part of Lancashire which juts up into Cumbria and belongs more to those dales more commonly found in Yorkshire. It is a quiet, beautiful place, where the steep sides of the surrounding fells fall almost sheer to the valley floor where a rushing beck tumbles down towards the River Eden further to the west. This is a place to park the car and climb up some steep, winding footpath to the breezy fells.

🚗 *GARSDALE lies west of Garsdale Head on the A684.*

HAREWOOD HOUSE
West Yorkshire

Lying just off the main road between Leeds and Harrogate, Harewood House is just one of those great country houses which do so much to enhance the Yorkshire landscape. It stands in the middle of a vast park, and was built between 1759 and 1771 by a local builder, Richard Carr, although Robert Adam was charged with the interior decoration. Harewood House remains the finest example in Britain of the Adam style. The present Earl of Harewood has added a tropical aviary by the lake to an already long list of attractions which include a fine silver collection, a tea service once belonging to Marie Antoinette, and some magnificent Italian paintings. Harewood House is open daily in the summer and on a number of days during the winter months.

🚗 *HAREWOOD village lies 5 miles south of Wetherby on the A659.*

THE HERRIOT COUNTRY
North Yorkshire

When James Herriot wrote his first book, *All Creatures Great and Small*, he can have had no idea what it would do to much of Yorkshire, transforming Swaledale and a large

The magnificent gallery inside Harewood House

part of the county between Coverdale and the North Yorkshire Moors into 'The Herriot Country'. According to the author his fictional village of Darrowby is a combination of Thirsk, Richmond and Middleham — and a lot of imagination.

Even so, the Herriot Country does exist, and can be visited, and travellers will find it by wandering about along Swaledale, across the Vale of York to Middleham, north and west of York and south even as far as Selby, across dales and moorlands, a delightful and (with the books beside you) an evocative journey.

🚗 *THE HERRIOT COUNTRY all lies within 50 miles of York, to the west and north.*

HOWDEN
Humberside

Howden isn't very big but it has two features which make it outstanding. The first is the Horse Fair which Dickens wrote about, which is still one of the largest in the country. The second, and a more constant attraction, is the Church of St Peter in the centre, which seems far too large and magnificent for any possible congregation. The main part is medieval, with a fine 14th-century west front, but the interior woodwork is modern and bears here and there the mouse emblem of Robert Thompson. St Peter's is a very fine English church, topped by a bell tower.

🚗 *HOWDEN lies 4 miles north of Goole on the A614.*

HUTTON-LE-HOLE
North Yorkshire

Hutton-le-Hole is a small, straggling village, lying a little to the north of the A170 and acting as a gateway to the Cleveland Hills and the North

Yorkshire Moors. The houses lie on green banks on either side of Hatton Beck which plunges through this valley from the high moorland to the north, past Roseland Abbey which lies five miles away. Hutton was listed in the Domesday Book but most of the present village dates from the 17th and 18th centuries. The Rydale Folk Museum, next to the Crown Inn, is well worth a visit, for although small it presents a comprehensive picture of Yorkshire village life.

There are several pleasant pubs and a wide green, ideal for picnics beside the stream, while the other villages round about provide good objectives for walks or car excursions.

🚗 *HUTTON-LE-HOLE lies north of Kirkby-Moorside, off the A170, 7 miles north-west of Pickering.*

JERVAULX ABBEY
North Yorkshire

Jervaulx is one of the great ruins of Yorkshire, an example — and a terrible one — of all that was lost when Henry VIII smote the monastic orders in the 16th century. Jervaulx was founded in 1155 and rose to become one of the most important Northern abbeys, a place of work, worship and learning unrivalled in the country, and noted for the quality of the sheep farming. The King's Commissioners were particularly brutal at Jervaulx, sacking the abbey, dispersing the monks and encouraging local people to level the buildings and carry away the stones.

🚗 *JERVAULX ABBEY lies 2 miles south of East Witton on the A6108.*

LANCASTER
Lancashire

Ask a hundred people to name six historic English cities and the chances

A quiet moment at popular Morecambe Bay

are that not one will mention Lancaster, and yet few places can match this historic county town for relics of the past. The Romans had a marching camp here and the town has remained an important trading centre ever since, but the historic heart of the town is the great castle built by the Normans, rebuilt by John of Gaunt and still in service during the reign of Elizabeth I.

Unlike other English castles, Lancaster has little romance. This one was built for war and oppression, and it shows in every stone. It records, in various collections, the savage laws of England since Magna Carta, and displays include instruments of torture, branding irons, the old gallows, the cells, and the prisoners' chapel.

LANCASTER lies 22 miles north of Preston off the M6.

MORECAMBE BAY
Lancashire

Morecambe Bay is one of the wonders of the North West, a vast area, drained twice a day by a huge tidal range which reveals mile after mile of sand flat and shallows, the sea flooding back to reflect the slow descent of the western sun in the evening.

The bay is surrounded by the attractive coastline of Lancashire and Cumbria, reaching from Morecambe itself all the way north and west to Grange-over-Sands and Walney Island on the tip of the Furness peninsula. The bay is fed by several rivers, the Kent and the Duddon in particular, which widen into estuaries as they pour into the bay. It is possible to walk across the sands between Grange and Morecambe, but the sands are dangerous, the tides rapid and this walk should only be made with an experienced local guide.

MORECAMBE lies 29 miles north of Blackpool.

Horn-blowing ceremonies

Yorkshire retains a number of ancient ceremonies, enshrined for all time in the customs of the county.

Two which can be seen regularly, and often every day for at least part of the year, are the Horn-blowing Ceremonies of Ripon and Bainbridge.

The horn-blowing in Ripon goes back well into the Middle Ages, to the time when the chief lay-officer of the city was known not as the Mayor but as the Wakeman. Among the Wakeman's daily tasks was to sound a horn at dusk as a signal to close the town gates and announce that the city had passed into his care for the night.

This custom continues to this day and can be observed every evening at 9 o'clock in the Market Square, when a horn-blower, wearing a tri-corn hat, sounds the horn four times, from each corner of the central obelisk. This ceremony is also recorded in the city motto 'Except the Lord keep ye Cittie, ye wakeman waketh in vain'.

The horn-blowing at Bainbridge, which takes place every evening in winter between Holyrood (27 September) and the evening of Shrove Tuesday, dates back to Norman times, when the forests hereabouts were the hunting grounds of the Lords of Middleham. The original intention was that the sound of the horn would draw benighted travellers through the outlaw-infested woods to the shelter of the city, and the sound can be heard up to three miles away.

Horn blowing at Ripon, Yorkshire

PICKERING
North Yorkshire

The railway station is, for most visitors anyway, the most important part of Pickering. Not that the town is unattractive, far from it, for it is a busy place and a market town for the surrounding district. Not much remains of the castle except some fragments of the old walls and keep, but many kings stayed here during the Middle Ages including King John and Richard II. The Parish Church is Norman and certainly well worth looking at, for it contains a remarkable array of wall paintings showing the lives of the apostles and dating from 1450. They are so fresh because they were covered during Puritan times and only uncovered again 100 years ago.

Having seen all that, and explored Pickering's excellent shops, there remains the railway station. This is quite old — at least 150 years — and is the terminal for that wonderful train ride across the countryside, the North Yorkshire Moors Railway, a picturesque journey on a train pulled by steam! No visitor should visit Pickering, or indeed Yorkshire, without enjoying a day out on this excellent little railroad, and spending a little time either before or after the journey looking at the engines or wandering around the bookshop and information centre.

PICKERING lies 25 miles north of York on the A170.

PORT SUNLIGHT
Lancashire

Those who think that 'New Towns' are a post-World War II idea, should take a look at Port Sunlight, a garden village on the banks of the River Mersey, built to house the employees

The lush greenery around Richmond, seen from the hilltop castle

of the local Unilever soap factory. This is no collection of grim tenements, but an architectural storehouse of styles. Nearly all the buildings are now under Conservation Orders and the Lady Lever Gallery in the centre contains a unique collection of works by the Pre-Raphaelites, and Wedgwood, as well as ceramics, tapestries, furniture and needlework. The over-riding impression though, is of a pleasant place to live, after the day's work is done.

🚗 *PORT SUNLIGHT lies south-west of Manchester on the banks of the River Mersey.*

RICHMOND
North Yorkshire

Those who journey through England hoping to find some splendid little-known places, will chance upon Richmond with delight. This is probably the most attractive town in Yorkshire, enhanced by the great ruins of the castle which stand on the hilltop above the town. It was built in 1071 and legend has it that King Arthur sleeps somewhere beneath it. Certainly the views from the ramparts are fabulous, looking out over the town below and Swaledale.

Richmond is seamed with little wandering alleyways, called *wynds*, and has the largest market square in Britain, attractive walks by the River Swale, and a great abundance of medieval architecture. Do not leave without visiting the museum of the local regiment, the Green Howards, or the Grey Friars Church.

🚗 *RICHMOND lies 3 miles north of Catterick.*

RIPLEY CASTLE
North Yorkshire

Set in a deer park, with lakes and walled gardens, is this ideal kind of English manor house, built on medieval foundations and still retaining part of the old walls before the more modern, Tudor and Jacobean additions.

The castle has been owned by the Ingelby family for nearly 700 years and is now open to the public regularly throughout the summer. The library is beautiful and the Knight's Chamber contains a fine collection of armour worn by the family during the Civil War. This chamber also contains a Priest's Hole built into the fabric to hide fleeing Jesuits in 1544 and only discovered in 1964. There are family portraits, fine furniture, beautiful panelling, and all one could wish to see in an historic house that is also a family home.

🚗 *RIPLEY CASTLE lies 7 miles north-east of Harrogate on the A61.*

RIPON
North Yorkshire

Ripon is a rather stark city, less cluttered than many of the older English towns. Old it certainly is, for St Wilfrid founded the great cathedral here in about AD 670, and parts of that building can be seen under the crypt of the 12th-century building. Ripon Cathedral is particularly interesting because it contains all the main periods of Gothic architecture on a Saxon foundation, and it all blends together most successfully.

Apart from the cathedral there are old houses round the market square, where the Town Crier or Wakeman can be heard every evening, sounding his horn. There are also pleasant walks along the banks of the River Skell.

🚗 *RIPON lies 26 miles north of Leeds on the A61.*

SCARBOROUGH
North Yorkshire

Scarborough is one of those towns with some claim to the title of the 'Queen of English seaside resorts'. The town lies around the wide bay and is protected by a Norman castle.

Donkey rides are still popular on Scarborough's sands

Its present role as a seaside resort and spa town dates back to the 1620s when mineral springs were discovered, but the town really developed in the last century when many of the great hotels were built on the cliffs and behind the harbour.

The castle, which catches every eye, was built by Henry II, but it was besieged regularly thereafter, constantly damaged and as constantly rebuilt. Down in the town, St Mary's Church is medieval, but St Martin's-on-the-Hill is last century Gothic, a shrine to the Pre-Raphaelites, with work by William Morris, Burne-Jones, Rossetti and Ford Madox Brown.

🚗 *SCARBOROUGH lies 20 miles east of Pickering on the A170.*

THE SETTLE TO CARLISLE RAILWAY
Yorkshire

The Settle to Carlisle Railway is a marvellous train ride, taking the traveller across some beautifully scenic parts of Yorkshire, into the Pennines and out into Cumbria. The ride actually begins in Leeds, from where the line goes north-west to Keighley and Skipton before the true trip begins at Settle. From here the track continues north and west across the wild moor, through Blea Moor Tunnel which is 2649 yards long, over Dent Head Viaduct to Dent, then through Garsdale and out into Cumbria.

All along the way the views are quite superb.

🚗 *SETTLE lies 12 miles north of Skipton on the A65.*

SKIPTON
North Yorkshire

Set in the heart of the Yorkshire Dales, Skipton is one of those perfect

Skipton Canal basin is filled with a variety of craft

little country towns, with all the traditional elements intact, a castle, an old church, a weekly market. The town centres on a wide main street, down which sheep were driven in years gone by. Nearby, in Chapel Street, is the 13th-century High Corn Mill, now a museum, well restored and still producing working grindstones and waterwheels.

Skipton Castle, near the parish Church, is protected on one side by the sheer rock wall. The bulk of the castle dates from 1310-15, when it was built by the Clifford family, who lived here until the 1950s. In the Civil War they held this castle for King Charles, but after his execution the walls and towers were blown up — or 'slighted' — to make the castle useless as a stronghold.

SKIPTON lies 26 miles northwest of Leeds.

SLEDMERE HOUSE
North Yorkshire

Sledmere is the Yorkshire home of the Sykes family and a magnificent example of the Georgian country house. It was built in 1751 and enlarged in 1758, gutted by fire in 1911 but rebuilt to the original designs after World War I. It is still lived in by the Sykes family, and much of it is open to visitors, which is a good thing as there is a lot to see including Chippendale and Sheraton furniture, paintings, porcelain and plenty of statues as well as a finely tiled Turkish Bath.

SLEDMERE HOUSE lies at Driffield, 16 miles from Bridlington.

SPEKE HALL
Lancashire

Speke is better known today as the location of Liverpool's local airport, but those wishing for a flight would do well to leave a little earlier and spend an hour or so looking over the attractions of Speke Hall. Speke is a Tudor mansion and has all the attractive Tudor features, with lots of half-timbering, four wings surrounding a central courtyard, a massive Great Hall, and some excellent panelling and carving. The courtyard contains two very ancient yew trees, while the interior has an unusual collection of Victorian household artifacts, William Morris wallpaper and some fine tapestries.

🚗 *SPEKE HALL lies in Merseyside, 8 miles south of Liverpool on the A561.*

WENSLEYDALE
North Yorkshire

Wensleydale in the Yorkshire Dales National Park is among the most enchanting of all the Yorkshire dales and the one to visit if time is pressing, for it contains some beautiful villages and the great natural attraction of that famous waterfall, Aysgarth Force.

Wensleydale is a green and graceful place, and the calm valley of the River Use, which flows through here into the Yorkshire Ouse. Just to the south at the eastern end lies Middleham Castle. Leyburn is the only town of any size and there are some beautiful villages. Wensley itself has a fine church with some excellent brasses, while nearby Bolton Castle was built by the Scropes in the reign of Richard II.

Aysgarth is very central, especially for walkers, and two essential sights here are the Force and the church which stands nearby. This done, climb the sides of the dale, up onto one of the small rocky escarpments and just enjoy the views which are among the best in Yorkshire.

🚗 *WENSLEY lies 20 miles north of Ripon on the A6108.*

The Shambles, one of York's picturesque shopping streets

WHITBY
North Yorkshire

This is the place where Captain Cook started his sailing career and some items of Cook memorabilia can be seen at the Whitby Literary and Philosophical Society Museum in Pannett Park. Whitby is a lovely little fishing port on the River Esk and there was a town here in Saxon days. Whitby Abbey was founded by the Saxons long before the Norman Conquest.

Today, Whitby is still a fishing port and a popular centre for visitors who use Whitby as a touring base.

🚗 *WHITBY is on the coast, 45 miles north east of York.*

YORK
North Yorkshire

If the North of England can be said to have a capital, York is the city which would command that title. Indeed, York was, and still is, the second city of the Island Kingdom. In many ways it is more interesting, historically, than London, for it has retained more of the feel of a capital city, and contains, even today, a host of historical artifacts; Jorvik, for example, recalls the capital of the Danelaw, when the Vikings ruled at least half of England. York was an outpost of Denmark until 944, and the very street names recall that connection — the Shambles, Walingate, Micklegate,

Whip-ma-Whop-ma Gate, where thieves were flogged — no one could visit York and doubt that this was once a very important city of the Kingdom, as indeed it still is today.

York is not a place to rush through in a day or two; it has a host of places to slow the traveller down, from the famous Minster to the modern Railway Museum, which opened in 1975 and is the finest in Western Europe. Half a day at least must be allowed for this museum alone, and then there are the marvellous parish churches, the shops and markets, the medieval Merchant Adventurers' Hall in Fossgate which dates from 1360, and as an introduction to the County of Yorkshire, the Yorkshire Museum in Museum Street. A full weekend, or better still, a week, is the minimum time necessary for a real visit to York.

The Cathedral Church of St Peter is one of the largest English cathedrals. The present Minster has now been restored after years of work, and a sudden fire in 1984. The present building dates from the 1250s, but it stands on the site of a much earlier church built by Bishop Paulinus about AD 625.

York Minster is simply magnificent, a poem in stone. It celebrates the glory of Gothic architecture, and in the West window, the end of the Wars of the Roses; examine the glass closely, for those alternating emblems of that long Plantagenet conflict can be seen. Earlier work includes the 13th-century Five Sisters window, the Chapter House of the monks, and a marvellous medieval vault.

Restoration work carried out in the 1970s and 1980s has ensured the survival of York Minster for centuries to come, and revealed the Roman roots of the ancient City of York itself.

🚗 *YORK MINSTER dominates the City of York, which lies 26 miles south of Leeds.*

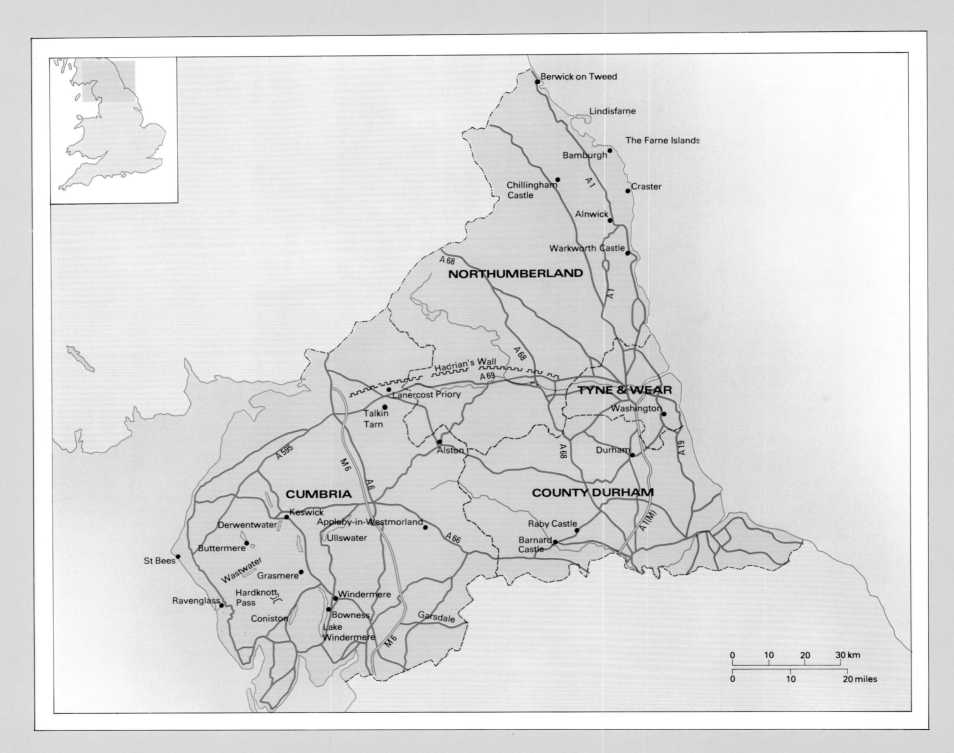

Berwick on Tweed

Lindisfarne

The Farne Islands

Bamburgh

Chillingham
Castle

Craster

A1

Alnwick

Warkworth Castle

A 68

NORTHUMBERLAND

A1

A 68

Hadrian's Wall

A 69

Lanercost Priory

TYNE & WEAR

Talkin
Tarn

Washington

A595

M 6

Alston

A 68

Durham

A 19

CUMBRIA

A 6

COUNTY DURHAM

Keswick

Derwentwater

Appleby-in-Westmorland

Raby Castle

Buttermere

Ullswater

A 66

Barnard
Castle

A1(M)

St Bees

Wastwater

Grasmere

Ravenglass

Hardknott
Pass

Windermere

Coniston

Bowness
Lake
Windermere

Garsdale

M 6

0	10	20	30 km
0		10	20 miles

The Northern Counties

An evening view across Derwentwater from Friars Crag in the Lake District

THESE SPLENDID NORTHERN counties lie around the Scottish March and between them straddle the Pennines. Northumberland and Cumbria are the northern buttresses of England, and the traveller who wanders about here, along those narrow, high-banked roads, will soon find plenty of evidence of a not far distant warlike past.

Across the neck of land between Newcastle and Bowness lies Hadrian's Wall, that great 1st century fortification built to keep the warlike Picts in their place. The old kingdom of Northumbria, which now, as a tourist zone includes Northumberland, Durham and Tyne and Wear, is studded with fine castles, like mighty Bamburgh or splen-

did Alnwick, where the Percys have lived for over 700 years.

A little to the north and a 'must' on any traveller's itinerary, lies Lindisfarne, the Holy Island, which is in fact only a part-time island for a long curving causeway links this historic spot (where St Cuthbert and his monks brought Christianity to the pagans), to the mainland a mile away, while further out to sea the Farne Islands lie flat against the ocean, loud with the shrieks and cries of seabirds.

Across the Pennines, between the Eden Valley and the coast of the Irish Sea lies the famous Lake District of England, a beautiful spot with hills and lakes and little towns, a mecca for climbers and walkers, a place of poets and a popular haunt of holidaymakers.

Alnwick Castle, border fortress and ancestral home of the Percys still guards the road south from Scotland

ALNWICK
Northumberland

Alnwick (pronounced Annick) is one of the greater border towns of England, built during centuries of war and the home of the Percy family, who have lived and ruled in Northumberland for over 600 years, Harry Hotspur being one of the most famous of that warlike line and the one immortalised by Shakespeare in *Henry IV*.

Alnwick is still a fine medieval town, full of narrow streets with antique names, Bondgate, Narrowgate, Bailiffgate and so on. There is a curious pub known locally as the 'Dirty Bottles', which is said to be haunted, and many interesting tombs in the Church of St Michael. Looking about the town it is interesting to note how many buildings bear the stiff-tailed lion emblem of the Percy's. Only one of the town gates is still standing but this, luckily, is the 14th-century Hotspur Tower, and the past is still fairly intact in the streets around the market.

Unlike all too many English castles, Alnwick is still inhabited, and by the family who built it, the Percys. The Percys first came to Alnwick Castle in 1309, and their first task was to strengthen it against the Scots. The process of building and alteration has never stopped and over the centuries Alnwick has been transformed from a breezy medieval fortress into a great country home. Robert Adam restored it, but most of it is still outwardly a 14th-century castle, topped by a series of figures along the battlements, which look like living people when seen from far off across the water meadows down by the River Aln, which was the original idea. In the last century the interior of the castle was converted into the style of the Italian Renaissance, which is still quite pleasing and very effective. Much of the castle is open to visitors in summer, when the guardroom, keep and library can all be visited. The walls are furnished with works by the Italian masters, Titian, Tintoretto and so on; the family coach rests in the stables and a museum of the Royal Northumberland Fusiliers is well worth seeing. All in all, a place which is full of history and interest for the visitor.

ALNWICK *is 30 miles south east of Berwick-upon Tweed.*

ALSTON
Cumbria

Alston is a quaint, sturdy little town, the highest market town in England. Built of grey stone, it's a place that seems to topple about in all directions, with no street staying on the level for long. Alston has no major sight to compel the visitor's attention; the attraction is all in the setting and in seeing a town which retains a strong independent and very English air. The railway station is worth inspection, as are the old churches, and the roofs of the solid stone houses, but that apart, Alston is a good touring centre, west to Weardale and Durham, north to the Border across the moor, or south towards Melmerby, where at Melmerby Fell there is a famous view across the vast valley to the west, even to the distant fells of the Lake District.

ALSTON *lies 20 miles south-east of Brampton by the A689.*

APPLEBY-IN-WESTMORLAND
Cumbria

Before the English counties were regrouped in the 1970s, an act that many people still regret, Appleby was the capital of the historic and

The Moot Hall of Appleby-in-Westmorland, seen from the castle gates

beautiful county of Westmorland. It lies on the River Eden, a sparkling stream, and has long been the centre for a famous Horse Fair held on the second Tuesday and Wednesday in June. It is dominated by Appleby Castle, still a private home, where the grounds contain a centre for the Conservation of Rare Breeds. This castle and the town which runs down the hill from the gatehouse belonged to the Clifford family, and Lady Anne Clifford restored both to their present state after Cromwell sacked the place during the Civil War. At the foot of the High Street, which is lined with old inns and houses, stands the parish church, a splendid example of a medieval Gothic building. Little Appleby offers good walks along the River Eden and into the Western Pennines and is, taken all together, a

most attractive example of an English market town.

APPLEBY-IN-WESTMORLAND *lies on the A66, 21 miles south-east of Penrith.*

BAMBURGH
Northumberland

Bamburgh is dominated by the great formidable pile of Bamburgh Castle, one of the mightiest castles in England, which in one form or another has guarded this shore and held the border against the Scots these thousand years or more. From the ramparts visitors can see out to the Farne Islands, now a famous bird sanctuary, to Lindisfarne, inland to the Cheviot Hills, north to Berwick. Bamburgh was once the capital of the Kingdom of Northumbria, in the days of the Saxons, and, later, a great fief for the Percy's, that noble family which still lives in Alnwick. The castle looks at its best when seen from the shore, but is impressive inside, with narrow passages, crenellated walls and a magnificent medieval King's Hall. The castle is open to visitors in summer.

The village at its foot, all that remains of the old town, is the birthplace of the heroine Grace Darling, who rowed out one stormy night to rescue the sailors from the ship wrecked on the Longship's Rock. Grace is buried in the churchyard, and the village contains a small museum dedicated to her exploits and the lifeboat service.

BAMBURGH *lies on the B1342 30 miles south of Berwick-on-Tweed.*

BARNARD CASTLE
County Durham

Barnard Castle is a rather lush little town on the River Tees, overlooked, as the name implies, by the now ruined walls of a medieval castle; what town around here could have survived without one? A Norman, Guy de Baliol, began the castle shortly after the Conquest, and his nephew, Barnard, gave his name to the town which grew up around it; his son John founded Baliol College, Oxford, while *his* son, John, became King of the Scots in 1292. Much later, Barnard Castle, town and fortress, came into the possession of Richard III. Of the fortress which he must have visited, only the keep and part of the walls remain, but the town is full of interest, with a sweeping 15th-century bridge and a great deal of attractive 17th and 18th-century architecture. The Church of St Mary, situated in the Market Place, is basically Norman though much restored by the Victorians. The Bowes Museum, a little to the west of Barnard Castle is really superb.

BARNARD CASTLE lies 6 miles south-west of Raby Castle.

BERWICK ON TWEED
Northumberland

Berwick is a fortress city, built and rebuilt against the Scots. The last rebuilding, by Queen Elizabeth I, was practically unnecessary, as her successor, James I of England and VI of Scotland, united the two kingdoms with the result that the Elizabethan walls of Berwick are still intact.

Today, Berwick is an attractive little town, straddling the Tweed and overlooking the small harbour which is still full of fishing boats.

The sparkling Tweed is spanned by three bridges and the town, not surprisingly, is a centre for salmon fising. Lovers of fortifications will enjoy walking along the walls, or visiting the old barracks, designed by John Vanburgh, the architect of Blenheim Palace, which is the oldest example of

military barracks in Britain. In previous centuries, and for a long time afterwards, troops were simply billeted on the local population. The museum of the local regiment, the King's Own Scottish Borderers, is also well worth a look for those who enjoy militaria.

BERWICK is on the A1 road, 46 miles north of Alnwick.

BUTTERMERE
Cumbria

Buttermere is one of the most beautiful, wildest and least touristic lakes in Lakeland, a place which draws the visitor again and again, with the ceaseless attraction of its views, which lie vast and varied on every side. If one must choose, the view across the lake to Haystacks from Buttermere village will take some beating. The Buttermere fells rise up to the north-east, Red Pike and High Stile are open to the south and west, making this lake — or mere — the perfect starting point for walkers who enjoy trekking in the high fells.

By that spit of land which is all that prevents Buttermere joining up with Crummock Water, lies the tiny village of Buttermere. Another nearby attraction is Scale Force waterfall, which curves down for 120 ft between the rocks, the highest waterfall in the Lake District.

Buttermere is peaceful and beautiful at any time of the year, but perhaps most of all in autumn, when the fall colours tint the leaves and the bracken on the fells. Those who don't want to walk on the fells or around the lake can view all this from the B5289 road which runs along the eastern shore and is well supplied with parking places.

BUTTERMERE lies on the B5289, 20 miles south-west of Keswick.

The small church, or chapel, in Buttermere village

CHILLINGHAM CASTLE
Northumberland

By now it must be obvious that Northumberland is a land of castles. This county is full of them, topping every hillside, guarding fords and road junctions, each a relic of the long centuries of Border strife. At Chillingham Castle however, the attraction is even more interesting and yet still alive. The white cattle of Chillingham have been there since prehistoric times. The present animals are directly descended from a herd of wild white oxen which once roamed the great forest which covered Northumberland in the past. The present herd is quite small, only 40 beasts, but some trick of genetics evades inbreeding and under the protection of the Chillingham Wild Cattle Association, they continue to thrive. The cattle really are wild and

can be dangerous to approach on foot, but they remain a rare survival from a far-off age, and long may they continue to live here.

CHILLINGHAM CASTLE lies 2 miles east of Wooler off the A697.

CONISTON
Cumbria

Coniston draws visitors from all over the world. Those who like the high fells will be attracted by the loom of that famous peak, The Old Man of Coniston, which any able-bodied walker can reach by following the footpath signs from the village centre. Two miles to the north-east lies the gem-like little lake of Tarn Hows, one of the most photographed lakes of Lakeland. Coniston Water itself lies only a short walk from the village.

Coniston Water is just over five miles long and perhaps best known in

Low cloud can mark the top of Coniston Old Man, even on a summer's day, and snow often lingers on the summit

recent years as a centre for various attempts on the world waterspeed record. Sir Malcolm Campbell set up a record here in 1939 and his son Donald was killed here during another attempt in 1967. Although other boats using the lake are restricted to 10 mph, it is still used for waterspeed record attempts when the speed rule is temporarily waived.

Such events apart, Coniston is also noted as the home of the Victorian writer John Ruskin, who lived at Brantwood on the eastern shore from 1871 to 1900. His house is much as he left it and open to the public. Ruskin was buried in Coniston village and the Ruskin Museum in the village centre contains many other Ruskin memorabilia, including the pall which covered his body.

It is possible to cruise on the lake, notably on the steam yacht *Gondola*, built in 1859 and beautifully restored by the National Trust.

CONISTON lies 5 miles from Hawkshead on the B5285.

CRASTER
Northumberland

Craster is a fishing port, famous for well-smoked kippers. In itself it is only a little place, a couple of streets full of fishermen's cottages, a small harbour, and the rich tang of the sea, but the coastline here is very beautiful.

A mile to the north, a half-hour stroll across the springy turf, lies the great gaunt pile of Dunstanburgh Castle, its foundations resting on the wave-washed rocks, a marvellous sight in the early morning as it looms up out of the sea mist. Needless to say, it is haunted, by Sir Guy who roams the Great Hall seeking his lost lady. Dunstanburgh is the largest of all the Border castles, and was built in 1313 by the Earl of Lancaster, later passing to John of Gaunt. During the Wars of the Roses it was under constant siege, and by the mid-16th century it was as we see it today, in ruins. It remains a wonderful sight; Turner painted it several times and no one should pass this way without seeing it.

CRASTER lies 6 miles east of Alnwick.

DERWENTWATER
Cumbria

People will argue about which is the finest of the lakes of the Lake District, but all would concede that Derwentwater takes some beating. The name has a Scandinavian root and is said to mean, 'the lake of the river which is fringed by oak trees', as indeed it is. Derwentwater is the widest lake, one-and-a-half-miles across, three miles long and 72 ft deep at the deepest point. Elsewhere it shallows to less than 18 ft, so it freezes during most winters and therefore attracts skaters by the score. There are five islands on the lake plus one odd one known as Floating Island, which is composed of weeds and sunken vegetation and only pops up now and again, propelled to the surface by marsh gas.

The lake can be viewed from many parts around the shore and is encircled by various roads but to enjoy it, as well as see it, take a cruise on one of the launches which ply from Keswick. It is possible to get off at one of the landing stages around the shore, go for a walk and pick up another boat later on or from another stage — a good way to pass the day.

DERWENTWATER runs south from Keswick to the Jaws of Borrowdale.

DURHAM
County Durham

Durham is a splendid town, set above the River Wear, one of the undebatable glories of the North. It is an old town, founded by the monks who fled from Lindisfarne, and by the early years of the 11th century there was a castle and cathedral here, protecting the shrine of St Cuthbert. The present city, although still small and unlikely to expand because of its siting, is one of the most delightful little cities in England, crowned by the great soaring Romanesque cathedral. The river cutting past the cliffs is littered with punts and rowing boats in summer; the narrow streets are filled with visitors from all over the world, and students from the University give the town a youthful, lively air.

Just off Palace Green stands Durham Castle, built by William the Conqueror to nail down the north. This was the residence of those formidable clerics, the Prince-Bishops of Durham, who founded the University. The castle is full of interesting relics, most notably the 13th-century Great Hall, hung with banners and lined with armour. The Keep was refashioned in the last century and is now a dormitory for students, but much of this great castle is as it was during the Middle Ages and, with the cathedral, it provides a fine central core to this lovely old and interesting town.

The present Durham Cathedral stands on the site of the former Saxon cathedral, and being built by the Normans in 40 years from 1093, is basically Romanesque, or as the English call it, Norman, although there are many overtones of the later Gothic style.

The site is spectacular and the best view of the cathedral is the one which displays this to the full, the view from the opposite bank of the River Wear to the great building high up on the cliff. Inside the effect is still overwhelming, with a soaring vault above the thin ribbed columns, and a number of later, elegant chapels, notably the 12th-century Galilee Chapel. The Nine Altars Chapel was added a century later and the Central Tower, which gives tremendous views over the town below and the countryside round about, was rebuilt at the end of the 15th century. Three essential and rare attractions at Durham Cathedral are the Sanctuary Knocker on the North Door which, if he could grasp it, gave protection to the fleeing criminal (sanctuary rights were abolished in 1540); the painted wooden coffin of St Cuthbert, carried here by the monks of Lindisfarne nearly a thousand years ago; and in a chapel off the nave, a bullet-riddled cross which once topped the Butte de Warlicourt on the Battlefield of the Somme, a height captured by the Durham Light Infantry in the Autumn of 1916.

DURHAM lies 20 miles south-east of Sunderland, just off the A1 (M) motorway.

THE FARNE ISLANDS
Northumberland

The Farne Islands are easier to see than to reach, but those who are able to make the journey across the tumbled waters of the North Sea will not regret the trip, for these islands which now belong to the National Trust are one of the country's most important seabird sanctuaries, a migrant stop in the spring and autumn and a place full of breeding colonies for gulls and terns. Seen from Lindisfarne or Bam-

Dove Cottage is now part of the Wordsworth Museum

burgh they look like nothing more than a litter of flat, grey rocks on the silver face of the sea, but when the easterly gales sweep down from Norway, the Farnes become a fearsome spot and many ships have come to grief on the Longships Reef.

Visiting is not permitted during the breeding season in the late spring, but otherwise there are boat trips out to the Farnes from the little port of Seahouses. Getting ashore on the Farnes is a tricky business and depends on the tides and sea-state, but the trip there is still well worth while.

SEAHOUSES lies 3 miles south of Bamburgh on the B1340.

GRASMERE
Cumbria

No visitor to the Lake District gets away without visiting Grasmere or, to be more exact, Dove Cottage, where Wordsworth lived from 1799 until 1808, during which time he wrote most of his more famous poems. Wordsworth loved Grasmere and the Lake District and made it famous, but people would go there anyway for it is a beautiful spot. The mere at Grasmere lies in the valley and reflects the shape and colours of the surrounding woods and fells. A main road divides the village from Dove Cottage, and while Wordsworth's home and the newly opened Grasmere & Wordsworth Museum have to be seen, the village itself is well worth wandering around, especially the Church of St Oswald which dates from the 13th century.

GRASMERE lies 3 miles north of Ambleside on the A591.

A view over Grasmere in the early spring, when snow still lies on the top of the nearby fells

Lakeland sports

Those who seek visible evidence that the Lake District of Cumbria is a place apart need do no more than visit a Lake District Summer Show. These are held throughout the summer in many different parts of the Lakes and have all the usual trappings of an English agricultural show, plus some unique local events.

There are stands and sideshows, pony club events, horse jumping and parades of cattle and livestock, but while all this is going on, the eye is caught and the attention held by the local people competing in some distinctly local attractions; fell-running and Cumberland and Westmorland wrestling.

Fell-running requires the stamina of a marathon runner with the nerve and ability of a mountain goat, for the competition, if simple, is never less than demanding; just spring up some 2000 ft or so to the top of the nearest fell — or maybe two — and then run back to the finish, over rocks and scree, along steep sheep tracks with the risk of a broken ankle at every stride. This is a sport you must be born to, and the winner is usually a local lad.

The wrestling is said to date back to Viking times and is now an exclusively Cumbrian affair which looks like a simple trial of strength but actually calls for considerable skill. The wrestlers face each other in a small arena, grasp their hands behind each other's backs and try to topple their rival over, while breaking his hold, and the one who comes out on top is the winner. It may sound simple, but it is not for the feeble and no Lakeland Show can be without a contest between the local strong men.

Local men test their strength in a bout of Westmorland wrestling

HADRIAN'S WALL
Northumberland

The great Roman Wall, built against the Picts who then lived in Scotland, by the Roman Emperor Hadrian in the decade from AD 120, runs for 72 miles from Bowness-on-Solway in the West, right across the narrow neck of Northern land to Wallsend on the River Tyne. It is undoubtedly one of the finest artifacts in England, and one of the most splendid examples of the energy of the Roman Empire still standing in Western Europe. The Wall is in an excellent state of preservation and recent excavations have revealed more of the way-stations and garrison camps which once supported the Wall itself. When completed the Wall was 15 ft high, 10 ft wide, and protected by a steep ditch.

It was built to mark and guard the northern-most boundary of the Roman Empire, and was garrisoned for nearly 300 years until the legions were withdrawn in the early years of the 5th century AD. The Wall can be viewed, running along the crest to the North, at many points along the B6318 west of Newcastle, and one particular excavation which has a museum, is the remains of the Roman fort at Housesteads.

Housesteads stands to guard one of the more vulnerable places, and since the foundations are intact, the visitor can see just how large and strong these Roman forts could be.

HADRIAN'S WALL lies west of Newcastle-on-Tyne, close to the B6318.

HARDKNOTT PASS
Cumbria

The Hardknott Pass is one of the most dramatic parts of Cumbria. It runs east-west along and astride the

Hadrian's Wall stretches along what was once the northernmost boundary of the Roman Empire

narrow, intensely winding road which leads from the western coast at Ravenglass, beginning at Eskdale and climbing over and down to little Langdale through its eastern extension, the almost equally famous and spectacular Wrynose Pass. This road, small as it is, is very ancient, following the path of a prehistoric track and a later Roman road. On the top of the pass, at 1290 ft, stands the ruin of a Roman fort, but the real attractions are scenic rather than historic. This road can become very crowded indeed in summer, and should only be attempted by motorists with strong nerves and good brakes, especially if heading towards the west.

THE HARDKNOTT PASS lies east of Eskdale, above Boot village.

KESWICK
Cumbria

Overlooked by one of the magnificent peaks of the region, Skiddaw, Keswick is the 'capital' of the Northern Lakes and therefore ideally situated at the northern end of Derwentwater and the foot of Skiddaw. Once a mining town and a market for the people who lived and farmed on the local fells, it is now devoted to tourism. Attractions in the town include the Keswick Railway Museum and the church-like Moot Hall which stands in the very centre of the town. Sights round about include the prehistoric Castlerigg Stone Circle, dating from circa 1400 BC, which lies to the east, and the Friars Crag Nature Walk. That apart, no one visits Keswick without taking the long walk up towards the peak of Skiddaw where, according to the poem, the beacon flared to "......wake the burghers of Carlisle" when the Spanish Armada was sighted in 1588. Skiddaw is topped by snow even in summer, and if the day is clear the views from the top are quite outstanding.

🚗 *KESWICK lies 27 miles west of Penrith on the A66.*

LANERCOST PRIORY
Cumbria

Not much remains of the once vast priory of Lanercost, but what there is should provide an interesting visit, and the setting itself is beautiful. It lies some five miles north-east of Brampton, and was founded in 1169 for the Augustinian priors by a local lord, Robert de Valibus. Most of the priory was destroyed in the Reformation, when the community was dispersed, but the priory church, in the local dull red sandstone, was retained to serve as the parish church, which it still does, attracting a considerable congregation every Sunday and a host of visitors throughout the summer months. In the ruins of the priory, behind the church, note the 13th-century cross in the Celtic fashion, as well as the much later Tudor bridge which spans the river nearby. The Roman Wall passes close by and can be seen at Banks.

🚗 *LANERCOST lies 5 miles north of Brampton, on a minor road off the A69.*

LINDISFARNE
Northumberland

Lindisfarne, the Holy Island, lies across a causeway from the coast of Northumberland, and is cut off by the tide twice a day. The original monkish settlement here was made by Celtic monks from Iona, led by St Cuthbert, but the Vikings drove them out eventually, and the present priory, though in ruins, dates from the 11th century and was built by the Benedictines.

Lindisfarne is a magic spot, a

Lindisfarne Castle, high on a spur of rock

paradise for birdwatchers, historians and all lovers of the rare quiet places, though it can get very crowded indeed in high summer. The church was once part of the priory, and contains replicas of the Lindisfarne Gospels, as well as many memorials and stained glass. From the lower end of the churchyard, Lindisfarne Castle stands framed in a raised window arch, high on a spur of dolerite rock, a wonderful sight.

The castle, which is now in the hands of the National Trust, was built in the 16th century, mostly from stone filched from the abbey after the monks were dispersed by the Reformation. In its time it served as a border fortress, barracks and coastguard station.

At the turn of the century, the ruined castle was restored by the architect Edwin Lutyens, and the result is this splendid castle of the present day. From the upper battery there are vast views to Bamburgh, Berwick or the Farne Islands, far out to sea, while just across the valley lies the unique walled garden created by Lutyens' collaborator, Gertrude Jekyll. From up there, with birds circling overhead and seals cavorting in the waves offshore, Lindisfarne, the Holy Island, is a marvellous sight.

🦢 *LINDISFARNE lies offshore, 16 miles south of Berwick.*

RABY CASTLE
County Durham

Raby Castle is a famous pile and still topped by nine crenellated towers. It is regarded as one of the largest and best preserved castles in the North of of England. There was a fortification here in the time of King Canute, but the present castle was begun by the Nevilles in the 12th century and remained in their hands until 1569 when the last Neville was executed for attempting to put Mary, Queen of Scots, on the throne of Elizabeth I. The Great Hall of Raby Castle was built to seat 700 knights. In 1626 Raby was sold to Sir Henry Vane and his descendants live here to this day, having carried out alterations from time to time. In the 18th and 19th centuries it became a country seat, and therefore displays a range of periods in both architecture and decoration. The Neville Gate and the towers are 13th century, the gardens are 18th and 19th, with trim yew trees and a spread of oaks, while the interior is Victorian. The castle is open to visitors on most days during summer.

🚗 *RABY CASTLE lies 1 mile north of Staindrop, and 9 miles south of Bishop Auckland on the A688.*

RAVENGLASS
Cumbria

Ravenglass, which is now reduced to little more than a single street of old houses with one good hostelry, The Pennington Arms, was once a famous place and a major port. When the Romans came to subdue this part of Britain, Ravenglass was their port, and it remained important until the middle of the last century, served by the Ravenglass and Eskdale Railway which brought ore down to the quay here and is still running tourist trains

Ullswater, most attractive of the lakes, winds its way north from Glenridding to Pooley Bridge

ULLSWATER
Cumbria

Ullswater is the most varied of the lakes. Others may be a little larger or more dramatic, but none has as much to offer the visitor. Ullswater is a winding lake, over seven-and-a-half miles long, and nearly a mile wide at its broadest point, running north from Glenridding and Patterdale to Pooley Bridge. It can be viewed and enjoyed from the A592 road which runs along the western shore, or better still, from the deck of one of the many boats which cruise about the water from Pooley Bridge down to Glenridding and back again throughout the summer. A good place to start any visit to Ullswater is in the straggling little village of Glenridding, reached from the south over the Kirkstone Pass, from where the road falls past the little lake at Brotherswater down to the big lake by Patterdale.

🚗 *ULLSWATER lies 20 miles north of Windermere on the A592.*

WARKWORTH CASTLE
Northumberland

Warkworth is another very splendid example of a Border fortress. It was built originally by Henry, son of King David I of Scotland, and that should not be too surprising for many Scots kings held land in England. Henry was made Earl of Northumberland in 1139, but dispossessed in 1157 when Henry II gave the castle to Roger de Stuteville, whose family built much of the present castle before it passed to the Percys in the 14th century.

Much still remains. The Grey Mare's Tail is a fine tower, pierced by cross-bow loopholes, the Lion's Tower still guards the entrance, and the Keep has been transformed into a house, although it is still reminiscent

into the fells. Sights in the town include the harbour, the famous 'gullery' where seabirds nest in spring, Muncaster Castle just up the hill, and the Railway Museum in the station. The High Street is full of fine old houses and little shops.

🚗 *RAVENGLASS lies on the west coast of Cumbria, 23 miles south of Whitehaven.*

ST BEES
Cumbria

St Bees is a straggling little coastal village of whitewashed houses, set beneath the jutting promontory of St Bees Head, one of the great viewpoints on the West Cumbrian coast. The town is chiefly noted for the public school there, but there is also a fine beach and a host of seabirds nest on the high cliffs of St Bees Head. A little to the north lies Whitehaven, once a coal and iron-ore centre, and to the east lies the old town of Egremont.

🚗 *ST BEES lies 4 miles south of Whitehaven on the B5345.*

TALKIN TARN
Cumbria

Talkin Tarn is a most attractive little lake, set a mile or so south of the small market town of Brampton. As is often the case in Cumbria, the setting is the reason for going there, and the setting for Talkin Tarn is quite superb. There are good walks around the shore, a delightful hotel for lunch or dinner, even a golf course, but most people will be quite content to sit under the trees and just gaze out across the waters of the lake.

Brampton, a mile to the north, is a pleasant, unassuming town, a popular place with ramblers and cycle-tourers, convenient for those who wish to explore the western end of Hadrian's Wall.

🚗 *TALKIN TARN lies a mile south of Brampton on the B6413.*

of the Middle Ages. A tour of the castle can take in the guardroom, the pantry, the Great Hall which Shakespeare featured as the home of Harry Hotspur in *Henry IV: Part 1*; visitors can also see the castle chapel which looks out across the tumbled waters of the North Sea towards Coquet Island.

🚗 *WARKWORTH lies 10 miles south of Alnwick on the A1068.*

WASHINGTON
Tyne & Wear

Washington is little known outside the district, and deserves to be more famous than it is, for Washington Old Hall, a Jacobean residence which lies just on the outskirts of the village, was the ancestral home of George Washington, first President of the United States.

The Washingtons arrived here in 1183, although they lost the manor of Washington in 1376 and dispersed throughout the kingdom, which accounts for the fact that various other parts of Britain lay claim to the patriotic founder of the U.S.A. The house, which is open to the public during the summer months, contains a fine collection of 17th-century furniture and much Washington memorabilia.

🚗 *WASHINGTON lies 5 miles west of Sunderland on the A1231.*

WASTWATER AND WASTWATER SCREES
Cumbria

Few places in the Lake District are as fine and memorable as Wastwater, and the Lake District is full of memorable places which remain fixed in the mind's eye. To see this long, dramatic lake at its best, go to the south-western end. From there the lake and the steep, dark screes which plummet down to the water along the south-eastern shore are quite overwhelming, while through the gap in the hills to the north one can see the central fells and the distant peak of Great Gable.

Wastwater is three miles long and at 258 ft, the deepest lake in England. The Screes peak at the 2000 ft mark, and although they look practically sheer at a distance, they lie back quite a bit if you cross the lake and take the footpath which runs along the south-eastern shore. At the head of the valley (a favourite spot for hill-walkers) lies The Wasdale Head Inn, where the Will Ritson Bar commemorates a man who claimed to be the biggest liar in England. Wasdale, the valley which contains Wastwater, is a beautiful spot, but tends to be empty of people even in the height of summer.

🚗 *WASDALE lies 15 miles north-east of Ravenglass, off the A595.*

WINDERMERE
Cumbria

To say Windermere 'Lake' is tautological, for a mere *is* a lake, but we refer here to the lake (or mere), not the town on its banks. Windermere is England's largest lake; ten and a half miles long, a mile wide, over 200 ft deep. These waters are cold and clear and contain a rare fish, the *char*, a popular local delicacy, and it is the lake which draws most visitors to this popular spot in the Lake District. They come to swim, paddle, sail, row, windsurf or cruise, and in summer time certainly, the surface of Windermere must creak under the weight of passing craft.

Steamers run up and down the lake from Bowness to Ambleside and south to Lakeside, but other visitors stay closer to the centre around Bowness and simply take the guided

A view of Windermere from the shore by Bowness

tour across to Belle Isle, a 38 acre island just offshore with the only truly round house in England on it. A ferry cuts across the lake, taking visitors to the opposite bank for a visit to Beatrix Potter's home at Hill Top Farm at Near Sawrey, and other roads circle the shore and offer views down towards the lake. At Brockhole, south west of the town, is the National Park Centre.

🚗 *WINDERMERE runs south and north of Bowness, 14 miles west of Kendal.*

WINDERMERE AND BOWNESS
Cumbria

The twin towns of Windermere and Bowness, the one on the hill and the other by the lake shore, have now expanded and thereby combined into a whole. Windermere, a mile from the lake, really began to develop after the railway arrived in 1847, when it became popular with rich Northern mill owners and industrialists who came here to build country houses, many of which have now become hotels. Today, Windermere is very much a tourist town, quite large, quite attractive, full of restaurants, cafés and hotels, with good walks and great views.

Bowness, down by the shore, is much older and is said to date back to Viking times. St Martin's Church dates from the late 15th century and the churchyard contains the mass grave of 47 people who drowned when a ferry sank in 1635; the first mention of a cross-lake ferry from Bowness is made as early as 1454. Attractions here, apart from the lake itself, include the Windermere Steamboat Museum, and the Model Railway Exhibition (Railrama) in Fallbarrow Road.

In spite of the inevitable influx of tourists, this centre of Bowness and Windermere is still one of the best places to start any tour of the Lake District, by steamer, car, or on foot.

🚗 *WINDERMERE and Bowness lie 14 miles west of Kendal.*

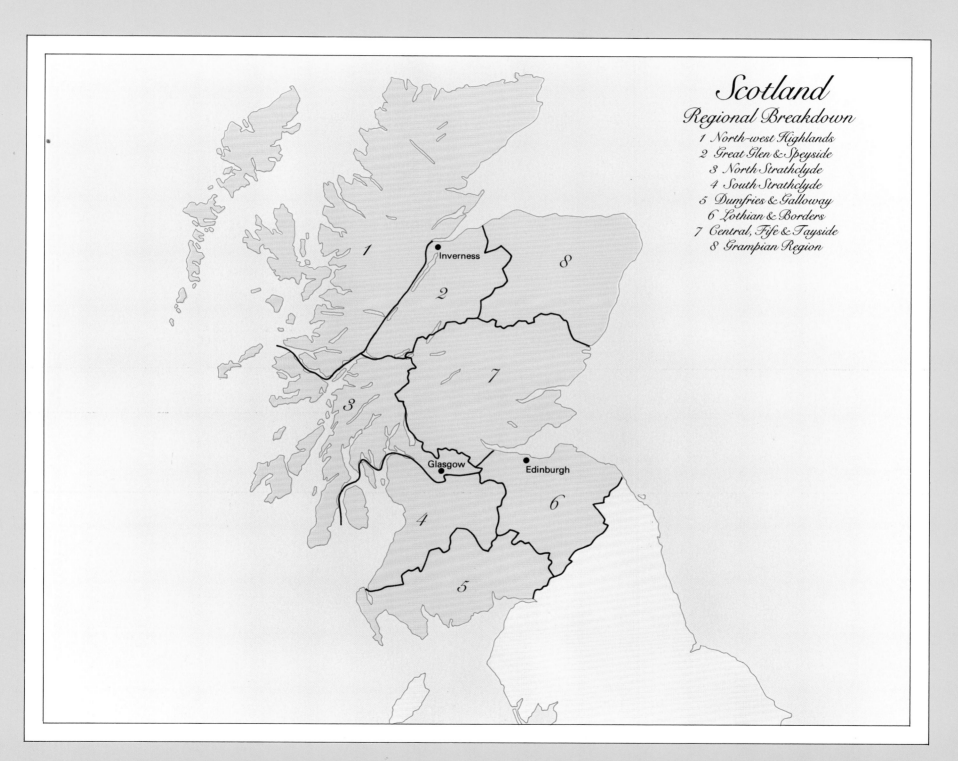

Scotland

Regional Breakdown

1 *North-west Highlands*
2 *Great Glen & Speyside*
3 *North Strathclyde*
4 *South Strathclyde*
5 *Dumfries & Galloway*
6 *Lothian & Borders*
7 *Central, Fife & Tayside*
8 *Grampian Region*

Inverness

Glasgow

Edinburgh

John o'Groats

Durness

Lybster

A 838

A 836

NORTH WEST HIGHLANDS

A 897

Inverpolly

A 837

Golspie

North Minch

Mellon Udrigle

Ullapool

Kyle of Sutherland

Dornoch

Harris Beaches

Inverewe Garden

Corrieshalloch Gorge

A 835

Leverburgh

Rodel

Gairloch

Black Isle

Dun Carloway

Callanish
Standing Stones

Kilmuir

Quiraing

Beinn Eighe ▲

Strathpeffer

Torridon

A 890

Portree

Applecross

Raasay

Plockton

SKYE

Lochalsh Woodland Garden

Eilean Donan Castle

Glenelg

Glen Affric

Elgol

A 87

Clan Donald Centre

Mallaig

Morar

Arisaig

Glenfinnan

Castle Tioram

Ardnamurchan

Strontian

0   10   20   30   40 km

0   10   20   30 miles

114

North-west Highlands

The evening sun illuminates the waters at Glenelg on the Sound of Sleat, reached by the hairpinned pass of Mam Ratagan

*B*EYOND THE GREAT GLEN Fault which slashes through Scotland from Loch Linnhe to the Beauly Firth there are land and sea-scapes of mesmerising variety.

In Caithness there is a lowland landscape beyond the Highlands. The Black Isle is rolling farm and forest land. And on the faraway island beaches of Lewis and Harris, white-tipped Atlantic breakers spill onto gold and silver sands from a turquoise sea.

There are spectacular fresh-water lochs like Shiel and Morar, Affric and Maree. And although the almost eccentrically indented west coast twists and turns past holiday villages at Gairloch and Plockton, Arisaig and Ullapool, it is a working coastline too.

Kinlochbervie, for instance, may be the remotest fishing port in mainland Britain, tucked away at the side of a Sutherland sea-loch; but the landings there are worth £10 million per year.

Tens of thousands of acres of magnificent mountain scenery are pro-tected by the Nature Conservancy Council and the National Trust for Scotland. Prehistoric settlements survive as brochs and duns and stan-ding stones. The influence of the Vikings is clear from place-names like Laxford and Lybster, Valtos and Seilebost.

Clan history comes alive in castles like Dunvegan and Eilean Donan. And this is the country where the fugitive Bonnie Prince Charlie was sheltered after the Jacobite cause was finally lost at Culloden.

APPLECROSS
Ross and Cromarty

On the shore of an exposed, west-facing bay looking out to the island hills of Raasay and the Cuillin peaks of Skye, Applecross village is approached from the east by the lonely and imposing Pass of the Cattle. Hairpin bends on the way to the summit at 2053 ft are loomed over by towering cliffs and rock terraces.

From the north, another single-track road offers spreading views over old crofting settlements to Raasay and its satellite island of Rona.

Southwards, scattered hamlets are beautifully situated at the edge of rocky bays. An intriguing footpath leads through a fringe of woodland to the old village of Coillegillie, a less familiar viewpoint across the Inner Sound to Raasay and Skye.

THE PASS OF THE CATTLE leaves the A896 north of Kishorn; the North Applecross road leaves it south of Shieldaig.

ARDNAMURCHAN
Lochaber

This long and hilly peninsula, mostly occupied by sheep farms and deer forests, ends at mainland Britain's 'farthest west'. The lighthouse on Ardnamurchan Point provides a series of stunning Hebridean views.

Beside the narrow south-coast road, otters frisk in the rocky bays and seals bob up offshore. Minor roads turn north towards the sandy beaches at Sanna, Portuairk and Kilmory.

Near the village of Kilchoan, the ancient monument of Mingary Castle stands on a bluff above the sea. It was in this fortress of the MacIans of Ardnamurchan, in the 1490s, that James IV received the chiefs of the Hebri-

The mountainous Beinn Eighe National Nature Reserve is rich in wildlife

dean clans when, after years of rebellion and punitive expeditions, they were finally forced to acknowledge their allegiance to the Crown.

B8007, the road through Ardnamurchan, turns off the A861 at Salen.

ARISAIG
Lochaber

At the head of Loch nan Ceall, where a flurry of reefs and skerries almost blocks the way to the open sea, Arisaig is famous for its island views, to the abrupt silhouette of Eigg and the grander mountains of Rum and Skye.

There are pleasant walks and drives: for instance, past Camas an-T Salainn — Salt Bay — where stores for the village used to be landed from a beached supply ship.

South-east of Arisaig is Loch nan Uamh. Bonnie Prince Charlie landed here to start the 1745 Jacobite Rising, intended to put his father on the British throne. And this is where, at a place marked by a memorial cairn the dispirited Prince sailed away in September 1746, the last glimmer of hope for a Stuart restoration snuffed out for ever.

ARISAIG is on the A830, 38 miles west of Fort William.

BEINN EIGHE
Ross and Cromarty

Established in 1951, Britain's first National Nature Reserve includes several summits of the Beinn Eighe range and an important fragment of the old Caledonian Pine Forest.

A visitor centre explains the geology and wildlife of the area. There are red and roe deer on the reserve, as well as pine martens and occasional wildcats.

Two nature trails start from a lochside birchwood. The one-mile trail reaches 356 ft, with superb views to the beautifully proportioned peak of Slioch — the Spearhead — across Loch Maree, and to the site of a 17th-century charcoal ironworks.

The four-mile Mountain Trail is a stiffer climb. In clear weather, more than 30 major summits can be identified from its 1800-ft viewpoint.

🚗 *THE BEINN EIGHE reserve visitor centre is at Aultroy, on the A832 half a mile north-west of Kinlochewe.*

BLACK ISLE
Ross and Cromarty

Neither black nor an island, this undulating peninsula edged in part with precipitous cliffs mixes farmland and forest with old-established coastal towns and villages.

Rosemarkie's Groam House Museum displays an intricately carved 8th-century Pictish stone. Nearby Fortrose, headquarters of a busy sailing club, was once the ecclesiastical centre of the province of Ross, and the ruins of its great cathedral still stand.

The two towns are linked — or separated — by a fine sea-shore golf course on Chanonry Point.

Cromarty was the birthplace of the 19th-century stonemason, geologist, journalist, author and editor Hugh Miller, and his cottage home is maintained as a museum by the National Trust for Scotland.

The Black Isle is well-known for its walks. More than 20 have been laid out, taking in countryside as different as the mudflats of Udale Bay, pine and larch plantations at Blackstand, an old railway line half-lost in beechwoods near Avoch, the Fairy Glen at Rosemarkie, the fossil beds at Eathie where Hugh Miller studied,

A shroud of mystery 4000 years old covers the 14 standing stones at Callanish

and the clifftops of the South Sutor where derelict gun emplacements watch over the entrance to the Cromarty Firth, once an anchorage of the Home Fleet.

🚗 *THE MAIN access to the Black Isle from the south is by the Kessock Bridge, on the A9 bypassing Inverness.*

CALLANISH STANDING STONES
Western Isles

On a promontory overlooking Loch Roag in Lewis, 13 stones, up to 12 ft high, are arranged in a circle around a taller central megalith. An incomplete double avenue extends to the north, while shorter single lines face east and west.

The Callanish stones stand higher than they did before encroaching peat was dug away in the 1850s, as it was from several other circles within a three-mile radius, all around Loch Roag.

Speculation about their likely astronomical purpose continues. They are no longer considered 'false men' turned to stone by some magic spell. But they are still enveloped in a

mystery which stretches back something like 4000 years.

🚗 *CALLANISH is on the A858, 15 miles west of Stornoway.*

CASTLE TIORAM
Lochaber

The 13th-century 'dry castle' has an impressive setting, on the summit of a rocky islet in beautiful Loch Moidart, with the larger, wooded Eilean Shona immediately to the north. At low tide, the castle can be approached on foot over a sand and gravel spit.

Tioram was the impregnable

The spectacular Falls of Measach at Corrieshalloch Gorge

stronghold of the MacDonalds of Clanranald. But in 1715 the clan chief joined the Jacobite Rising and had the castle set in flames so that, if the Jacobites were defeated, it would never fall into the hands of his traditional enemies, the Campbells.

🚗 *CASTLE TIORAM is 3 miles north of Acharacle, reached by a side-road off the A861.*

CLAN DONALD CENTRE
Skye and Lochalsh

The summer car-ferry from Mallaig to Armadale on Skye has its island terminal at Armadale Bay on the Sleat peninsula, less rugged than the mountain country to the north, and often referred to as 'the garden of Skye'.

Overlooking the bay are the wooded grounds of Armadale Castle. The present building was erected in 1815 for the chief of the MacDonalds of Sleat, but the estate is now in the hands of the Clan Donald Lands Trust.

Part of the square-towered Gothic castle, and its restored stables block, house the Clan Donald Centre, with information on all aspects of the history, genealogy, ancestral territory and world-wide connections of Scotland's largest clan.

🚗 *ARMADALE CASTLE is on the A851, 1 mile north of the ferry terminal.*

CORRIESHALLOCH GORGE
Ross and Cromarty

The most spectacular box canyon in the Highlands is on National Trust for Scotland property at Braemore. A mile long and 200 ft deep, the wooded and precipitous gorge is a copybook habitat for ferns, wildflowers and mosses which relish damp and shadowy conditions.

It is fed by the river which tumbles over the plunging Falls of Measach. Both gorge and waterfall can be seen from a viewing platform and from a handsome Victorian suspension footbridge. This was built, almost as a whimsy, by Sir John Fowler, one of the designers of the Forth Bridge, who was also laird of Braemore.

🚗 *CORRIESHALLOCH GORGE is on the A835, 20 miles north-west of Garve.*

DORNOCH
Sutherland

Once the county town of Sutherland and seat of the bishops of Caithness, Dornoch has many historical connections. Its 13th-century cathedral has been remodelled as the parish church. The turreted Bishop's Palace is now a hotel. The Victorian jail is a museum. And there is a memorial stone to Janet Horn, the last witch executed in Scotland after due process of law, in the year 1722.

But Dornoch is also a pre-eminent golfing resort. The Old Course of Royal Dornoch Golf Club is one of the most highly regarded in the world.

It is on splendid links-land turf, bounded by the extensive beaches which stretch for miles, north and west of the hook-shaped Dornoch Point.

🚗 *DORNOCH is on the A949, 11 miles east of Bonar Bridge.*

DUN CARLOWAY
Western Isles

Not far from the standing stones of Callanish in Lewis, the ruined drystone tower of Dun Carloway is a well-preserved example of a broch — a circular, double-walled Iron Age dwelling of something like beehive shape.

Eilean Donan Castle was built to defend western mainland Scotland against the Vikings

Its hollow walls were immensely strong, and included several rooms and galleries within them. For security, the entrance was kept both low and narrow, so that intruders could approach only one at a time, and at a crouch.

Maintained as an ancient monument since 1887, Dun Carloway is a fine viewpoint over the rumpled country of rock-outcrops and lochans east of Loch Roag.

🚗 *DUN CARLOWAY is on the A858, 20 miles west of Stornoway.*

DURNESS
Sutherland

This crofting settlement among limestone fields alive with summer wildflowers is flanked by sandy beaches and cliffs where thousands of sea-birds make their nests.

East of the village at Smoo there is a famous triple-chambered sea-cave. To the north-west, beyond a craft village whose visitor centre displays the work of potters and jewellers, bookbinders and candlemakers, the dune-backed sands of Balnakiel Bay face the highest sea-cliffs in Britain, towards Cape Wrath.

The ruined church of Balnakiel dates from 1619. It was paid for in part by one Donald McLeod, to ensure his burial in hallowed ground, despite the 18 killings on his conscience.

Also commemorated here is the 18th-century Gaelic bard Rob Donn Mackay, who farmed Balnakiel on behalf of his clan chief, Lord Reay.

🚗 *DURNESS is on the A838, 30 miles west of Tongue.*

EILEAN DONAN CASTLE
Skye and Lochalsh

Set in a dramatic situation on a rocky islet at the junction of Loch Duich and Loch Alsh, with tidal waters, mountains and forests all around, Eilean Donan was built about 1230 as part of Alexander II's defence of the western mainland against the Vikings.

Later, it became the property of the Mackenzie Earls of Seaforth. One of them was heavily involved in the half-cocked Jacobite Rising of 1719, when government warships bombarded the fortress into a smouldering ruin.

After a £250,000 restoration, which started in 1912 and finished 20 years later, Eilean Donan is open to the public as a faithful reproduction of the 18th-century castle.

🚗 *EILEAN DONAN CASTLE is at Dornie on the A87, 8 miles east of Kyle of Lochalsh.*

ELGOL
Skye and Lochalsh

Beginning high up on the peninsula of Strathaird, the scattered crofting village of Elgol sweeps down towards a shingle beach, past one of the most overwhelming viewpoints on Skye — north and north-west over Loch Scavaig to the saw-toothed peaks of the Black Cuillin.

Westwards across the sea-loch is the island of Soay, where Gavin Maxwell ran a shark fishery — and wrote *Harpoon at a Venture* — before becoming involved with otters and starting a series of best-sellers with *Ring of Bright Water*.

On the roadless coast south of Elgol is the cave where Bonnie Prince Charlie hid, in July 1746, before being rowed in an open boat across the 18 miles to the mainland near Mallaig, on a night of storm-force winds and rain-lashed seas.

🚗 *ELGOL is on the A881, 14 miles south-west of Broadford.*

GAIRLOCH
Ross and Cromarty

Golden sands, sea-angling, trout-fishing in hill and moorland lochs, small-boat sailing, and golf on a coastal course where a despairing glance after a duffed shot may give a consoling sight of the mountain peaks of Torridon — this is the mixture at Gairloch, a holiday resort and at the same time a fishing port with its own small but active harbour.

On the very attractive southern shore of Loch Gairloch there are wooded and deeply-indented bays, before the road follows the coast round past the windblown sands of Opinan to a panoramic viewpoint over Skye and Applecross, above yet another beach at Red Point.

Gairloch Heritage Museum displays farming, fishing and household appliances, to give a fine impression of a West Highland way of life in generations not long gone by.

🚗 *GAIRLOCH is on the A832, 44 miles west of Garve.*

GLEN AFFRIC
Inverness

Once on the route of the great cattle-drives from Skye, Glen Affric owes much of its present appearance to foresters and hydro-electric engineers.

There are modern spruce plantations on most of the hillsides, but an area of the old Caledonian Pine Forest is encouraged to regenerate. And although Loch Affric itself and the lower Loch Benevean feed the hydro-electric power station at Fasnakyle, this activity is very unobtrusive.

Forest walks lead to the Dog Falls in the Affric gorge, and through pine and birchwoods above the river which joins the lochs. One footpath here leads to an impressive viewpoint over the whole lovely glen, the forests and the deer-stalking mountainsides.

🚗 *THE ROAD to Glen Affric starts at Cannich on the A831. 17 miles south-west of Beauly.*

GLENELG
Skye and Lochalsh

Reached by the hairpinned pass of Mam Ratagan, Glenelg is a village on the Sound of Sleat, linked by a summer car-ferry with Kylerhea on Skye.

Near the shore is the substantial ruin of the army barracks erected after the abortive Jacobite Rising of 1719. A largely ineffective garrison was stationed here until the 1770s.

Many of the building stones for the barracks were pilfered from two Pictish brochs in nearby Glen Beag, but Dun Telve in particular remains an impressive sight.

Southwards, the road skirts a forest plantation above Sandaig — Gavin Maxwell's 'Camusfearna' — on the way to the even remoter villages of Arnisdale and Corran, facing the forbidding mountain country known as the Rough Bounds of Knoydart across Loch Hourn.

🚗 *THE MAM RATAGAN road starts at Shiel Bridge on the A87.*

GLENFINNAN
Lochaber

On a truly dramatic site, silhouetted against the towering mountains which stretch away down Loch Shiel, the tall Glenfinnan monument is where, in August 1745, Prince Charles Edward Stuart ordered his standard raised — the opening act of the final Jacobite Rising.

The battlemented stone tower was built in 1815 by MacDonald of Glenaladale, one of whose predecessors had been the Prince's host. Beside it is a white rose bush, originally a sprig of the very same bush from which Charles plucked his 'white cockade' — the Jacobite emblem.

The monument is owned by the National Trust for Scotland, whose visitor centre outlines the history of the Rising and the activities of the fighting clans.

🚗 *GLENFINNAN is on the A830, 17 miles west of Fort William.*

GOLSPIE
Sutherland

This trim little town grew up from a handful of turfed huts when tenants evicted from their inland holdings in the Sutherland clearances of the early 19th century came to settle by the sea.

Ironically, Golspie is dominated, from the summit of Ben Bhraggie, by a giant statue of the 1st Duke of Sutherland, in whose name the clearances were made. The Sutherlands' ornate Dunrobin Castle is just north of the village.

St Andrew's church of 1619 has a notable 'laird's loft' for the landowning family. There are attractive walks in the gorge of the Golspie Burn and through hillside pinewoods.

A long sandy beach stretches in front of a testing links golf course. And beyond it, hidden behind grassy bankings, is a first-class kart-racing circuit.

GOLSPIE is on the A9, 22 miles north-east of Bonar Bridge.

HARRIS BEACHES
Western Isles

Although the east coast of Harris is a series of rocky bays, the west coast has a succession of some of the finest beaches in Europe. At Luskentyre by the mouth of the Laxford River, Seilebost, Nisabost, Traigh Iar — the 'west beach' — and Scarista, breakers roll in from the Atlantic, over beaches backed by dunes and grassy banks.

The extensive sands of Scarista have been used as a landing ground by light planes, and the smooth turf behind them is where the annual Harris sheep-dog trials are held. More peacefully, most of the beaches are within strolling distance of ancient chambered cairns and standing stones.

THE HARRIS BEACHES are beside the A859 Tarbert to Leverburgh road.

The Glenfinnan Monument occupies a breathtaking lochside site where the Stuart standard was raised in 1745

INVEREWE GARDEN
Ross and Cromarty

In 1862, when Osgood Mackenzie became the owner of this bare sandstone peninsula at the head of the Loch Ewe, there was not only an almost complete absence of plant-life apart from heather and crowberries, but also an almost complete absence of soil.

He imported tons of it, planted pine-tree windbreaks and in the fullness of time created a splendid garden of exotic plants, shrubs and trees, sheltered from the salt-laden winds.

Now owned by the National Trust for Scotland, the 26 acres of Inverewe house something like 2500 different species — a subtropical garden level in latitude with Greenland.

🚗 *INVEREWE GARDEN is on the A832, half a mile north of Poolewe.*

INVERPOLLY
Ross and Cromarty

This is one of the largest National Nature Reserves in Britain — more than 26,000 acres, all but uninhabited, of primeval mountains, remote lochs with birch-studded islands, tumbling rivers and a stretch of sea-coast at Enard Bay.

The highest peak is Cul Mor at 2876 ft, but the most bizarre — seen clearly from the road along Loch Lurgainn on the south side of the reserve — is Stac Polly, with a fantastic series of towers, pinnacles and rock-flakes forming its summit ridge.

The main public access to the reserve is at Knockan on the eastern boundary. There is a visitor centre and a fascinating waymarked trail which points out the geological curiosities of the Knockan Cliff.

🚗 *KNOCKAN is on the A835, 11 miles north of Ullapool.*

Angling in Scotland

A glance at even a small-scale map of the North-west Highlands and the Western Isles makes it clear why this is such a fine area for trout and salmon anglers. There are innumerable major lochs and rivers, burns and scattered hill lochans.

Parts of islands like North Uist and Benbecula, for example, seem to be almost as much water as land. On Lewis, fishing estates like Grimersta and Garynahine include complete river systems and chains of lochs.

On the mainland, Loch Maree is not only spectacularly beautiful, with its surrounding mountains and scatter of wooded islands; it is also world-famous for its sea-trout.

Flowing north into the Pentland Firth there are substantial salmon rivers like the Halladale and the Thurso. Others — like the Helmsdale, where the first salmon of the year in Scotland is often landed — flow into the Moray Firth.

In the far north, some places on the map — like Forsinard and Altnaharra — have angling hotels as very nearly the main reason for being there at all.

Some fishing waters are

controlled by private estates or hotels — Scourie Hotel in Sutherland has rights on more than 200 lochs; some by public bodies like the Forestry Commission; and others by angling associations.

The finances of the sport are equally varied. Many hotels offer their guests fishing at no extra charge; and bank fishing on some lochs is available for as little as £1 per rod per day.

But there are some much more rarefied estates, on which the cost of a single week's salmon fishing and accommodation can be over £1000 — for an acceptable individual prepared to wait anything up to two years for the privilege.

Left Young anglers at Stornoway
Below Fishing fleet in the harbour at Kyle of Lochalsh

JOHN O'GROATS
Caithness

John o'Groats — named after the 15th-century ferryman Jan de Groot — is often publicised as the most northerly point on the British mainland, although that superlative really belongs to Dunnet Head, a few miles away along the northern coast.

North of the village itself, the hotel and pier at the very end of the road have a fine view to the deserted island of Stroma and, beyond it, to Orkney. A summer-time ferry runs to Burwick on the Orkney island of South Ronaldsay. Boats also sail along the coast past the precipitous rocky inlets called geos to Duncansby Head, which with its lighthouse can also be reached by car. But the boats continue southwards 'round the corner' past the sea-bird colonies on the cliffs to where jagged sandstone stacks rise offshore.

🚗 *JOHN O'GROATS is on the A9, 14 miles north of Wick.*

Stac Polly seen across Loch Lurgainn in the stunning Inverpolly Nature Reserve

KYLE OF SUTHERLAND
Sutherland

The hillsides around this narrow tidal waterway fed by the Rivers Oykel and Shin are clothed in conifer plantations. One forest walk goes through pine, spruce and larch at Carbisdale, the only castle built in Britain this century. Another makes for the salmon-leap waterfalls in the gorge of the Shin.

There are old watermills in the area, Victorian ice-houses built to ease the transport of salmon, and many prehistoric sites.

Lairg, north of the Falls of Shin, is a famous livestock trading centre. In August it hosts the biggest one-day sheep sale in Europe.

🚗 *KYLE OF SUTHERLAND is on the A836, immediately north-west of Bonar Bridge.*

LEVERBURGH
Western Isles

Until 1923 this village on the Sound of Harris was known as Obbe — from the Gaelic word *ob*, which indicated the tidal creek immediately back from the shore.

In that year the millionaire industrialist Lord Leverhulme decided to transform Obbe into a major Hebridean fishing port, re-naming it after himself.

The great project to build new roads and houses, a modern pier and processing sheds was put under way; but Leverhulme died in 1925 and the whole scheme was abandoned.

Now the main attraction for visitors to Leverburgh is a modern craft centre with a museum which tells the story of a more enduring local industry — Harris tweed.

🚗 *LEVERBURGH is on the A859, 19 miles south-west of Tarbert.*

KILMUIR
Skye and Lochalsh

The old churchyard at Kilmuir in the north of Skye, with its extensive seaward views to the Western Isles, is a place of pilgrimage for people from all over the world. They come to visit the grave, marked by a stately Celtic cross, of Flora MacDonald, who, with the connivance of her father — an army officer but also a Jacobite sympathiser — arranged the famous escape of Bonnie Prince Charlie from the island of Benbecula, when troops were closing in on his hiding place. This is the story told in the famous *Skye Boat Song.*

Also at Kilmuir, a group of old thatched houses is now a folk museum — one is a typical croft cottage, another a weaving shed, the third displays a collection of documents, while the fourth is laid out as a blacksmith's forge.

🚗 *KILMUIR is on the A855, 6 miles north of Uig.*

LOCHALSH WOODLAND GARDEN
Skye and Lochalsh

Planted around 1890, Lochalsh House grounds are maintained by the National Trust for Scotland as a specialised woodland garden. The original tree cover of beech and oak, larch and several kinds of pine combines with the garden's location above a rocky shore to provide habitats for a great variety of birds.

Winding footpaths meander through the woodlands, which also contain exotic shrubs from Asia and the Pacific, and are currently being redeveloped.

A visitor centre in the old coach house stands close to a viewpoint above the coastline, looking through the narrows of the Sound of Sleat.

LOCHALSH WOODLAND GARDEN is off the A87, 3 miles east of Kyle of Lochalsh.

LYBSTER
Caithness

Viking settlers gave this substantial Caithness village its name — 'the homestead on the hill'. From an early 19th-century coaching inn, a side-road dips down to an extensive harbour, separate from the village itself, in a fold of the rumpled coastline at the mouth of the Reisgill Burn.

Last century, Lybster was for a time the third biggest fishing port in Scotland. It supported a thriving community of fishermen, fish-curers, coopers and general labourers.

When the herring shoals went farther north, business slumped dramatically. But the harbour has recently been improved again, and Lybster still maintains its own small fishing fleet.

LYBSTER is on the A9, 13 miles south of Wick.

Mallaig's crowded waters bob with fishing boats and ferries jostling to take visitors to the Isles

Mallaig kippers — a local delicacy

MALLAIG
Lochaber

The opening in 1901 of the Mallaig extension of the West Highland Railway transformed this previously tiny hamlet on a rocky coast into a ferry terminal and busy fishing port.

A hill road progresses to Mallaigvaig, providing an eagle's-eye view across the Sound of Sleat to Skye. And a rougher continuation opens up to walkers the rarely-seen vista of the hill-country of Knoydart across the mouth of Loch Nevis.

Major ferry destinations from Mallaig include Armadale on Skye; the islands of Rum, Eigg, Muck and Canna; and — through the Sound of Sleat — Kyle of Lochalsh.

Small boats operate regular but occasional services to Inverie and Tarbet, places with no road connections on the mountainous Loch Nevis shores.

🚗 *MALLAIG is on the A830, 46 miles west of Fort William.*

MELLON UDRIGLE
Ross and Cromarty

This hamlet on an inlet of Gruinard Bay has a curiously mixed Gaelic and Norse name, meaning 'Idrigill's little hill'. Its beautiful silver beach is backed by dunes which were badly threatened by erosion until taken in hand

Morar's dazzling white sands and freshwater loch attract many visitors

— as part of a national environmental project of the 1970s — by the children of a Midlothian school.

Mellon Udrigle, with a handful of cottages looking across shell-sand turf and a burn trickling along the edge of the sands, is one of the pleasantest picnic places in Wester Ross, facing the outstanding peaks of Coigach beyond the scattering of islands in the mouth of Loch Broom.

🚗 *MELLON UDRIGLE is 3 miles north of Laide on the A832.*

MORAR
Lochaber

The village of Morar backs onto a curving estuary with magnificent white sands rising on both sides. A remarkably short stretch of non-tidal river links it with the freshwater Loch Morar, which is 12 miles long, rarely more than a mile and a half wide, and by any standard one of the most beautiful lochs in Scotland.

At the west end there is a cluster of attractively wooded islands. An exhilarating footpath follows the north shore to Swordale, off which phenomenal soundings of more than 1000 ft have been recorded. And there have been, as at Loch Ness, persistent stories of some unidentified creature occasionally surfacing from those almost impenetrable depths.

🚗 *MORAR is on the A830, 3 miles south of Mallaig.*

PLOCKTON
Ross and Cromarty

This spectacularly located village spreads along a main bay and some narrower rocky inlets on the shore of Loch Carron, a popular small-boat sailing ground.

Plockton was settled by early 19th-century smallholders evicted from the hill grazings which were then more profitably rented out to sheep-farmers. After a time as a boat

building centre, it is now a highly regarded holiday resort.

One very pleasant walk is through the woodland fringe around the head of the village bay, towards the Victorian Duncraig Castle with its towering backdrop of rugged crags and buttresses. Another is along the edge of the hill above Harbour Street, with the back gardens of the houses falling steeply away below.

🚗 *PLOCKTON is 7 miles north-east of Kyle of Lochalsh.*

PORTREE
Skye and Lochalsh

Although it is principally the administrative, business and shopping centre of Skye, Portree also has a broad harbour area. Overlooked by tiers of colour-washed houses, shops and hotels, the harbour is only a tiny part of a larger sea-loch dominated by soaring outer cliffs.

Immediately above the fishing boat

quay, wooded crags rise to a level sports field where the Skye Games are held every summer.

Bonnie Prince Charlie and Flora MacDonald parted for the last time in Portree, but the inn where they said goodbye has been replaced by a modern hotel.

In fact, the oldest occupied building in Portree dates only from 1810 — Meall House, the tourist information centre, which originally served as the jail!

 *PORTREE is on the A856, 35 miles from the ferry terminal at Kyleakin.*

QUIRAING
Skye and Lochalsh

Running for miles north of Portree, and forming the central spine of the huge Trotternish peninsula, is an escarpment of basalt cliffs. Here and there, ancient landslips have eroded into a series of separated rock pinnacles and grass-topped towers.

One of the most majestic of these areas, reached by a hairpinned minor road which clambers up the escarpment itself, is the Quiraing, which can be explored by an access path along the foot of cliffs and scree-runs.

It is not only a place of outstanding scenery and widespread views, but also a natural garden of rare alpine flowers.

 *THE QUIRAING is on the minor road between Staffin and Uig.*

RAASAY
Skye and Lochalsh

This long, narrow, green and remarkably varied island has all kinds of hill, moorland and forest walks with close-up views to the mountains of Skye and Applecross.

Ruined Brochel Castle, in golden eagle country on the north-east coast,

was the stronghold of the MacLeod lairds until they moved to Raasay House, where Dr Johnson was famously entertained in 1773. Fearns on the south-east coast is at the start of a walk by birchwoods to the fine waterfall at Hallaig.

Derelict remains survive of the ironstone mine workings of World War I. The incongruous 'workers-row' village of Inverarish was built — with armed sentry-posts — for the German prisoners who made up most of the labour force.

 *THE CAR-FERRY terminal for Raasay is at Sconser on Skye, on the A850, 12 miles south of Portree.*

RODEL
Western Isles

At the south-eastern tip of Harris, this village is overlooked by the most notable church in the Hebrides. St Clement's, with its square, battlemented tower, was built in 1528 by Alexander MacLeod of Dunvegan, 8th chief of the clan. His lavishly carved tomb is the main feature of a carefully preserved ancient monument.

The MacLeods' hereditary standard-bearers used to be buried here too — all in the same stone coffin in the chancel. Whenever one of them was laid to rest, his predecessor's bones were still there, and had to be pushed down through a grating to make way for the new arrival.

 *RODEL is on the A859, 3 miles south-east of Leverburgh.*

STRATHPEFFER
Ross and Cromarty

In Victorian and Edwardian times, this dignified village of stone-built villas, boarding-houses and hotels — all in streets which to this day have no names — was the most northerly

One of Scotland's finest mountains, the quartzite topped Liathach ridge is part of the Torridon estate

spa in Britain. A fashionable clientèle came to 'take the waters' of its sulphur and chalybeate springs, or recline in all manner of therapeutic baths.

All that has passed, but Strathpeffer is still very much a holiday resort, offering golf, angling, hill and woodland walks.

A large Bavarian-style hotel overlooks the attractive village square. The pump room and spa pavilion have been restored, and although the Strathpeffer branch line is long since closed, the Highland Railway station of 1885, with its elegant glass canopy, has been turned into a craft and visitor centre.

🖂 *STRATHPEFFER is on the A834, 4 miles west of Dingwall.*

STRONTIAN
Lochaber

This modern village and the older crofting settlements in the valley of the Strontian River are all on Crown property, bought in 1920 to guarantee land to returned ex-servicemen.

North-east of the village, the Strontian Glen nature trail passes through an oakwood reserve to a high moorland around old lead mines, worked at intervals since 1722.

Other disused mines can be seen from the narrow and twisting hill road which goes over a pass with wide-ranging views of the forests and mountainsides around Loch Shiel, to the remote village, built by the Forestry Commission, at Polloch.

🖂 *STRONTIAN is on the A861, 14 miles west of Corran Ferry.*

TORRIDON
Ross and Cromarty

Along the north side of Glen Torridon and the sea-loch to the west, the National Trust for Scotland's 16,000-acre estate of the same name includes all seven summits of the quartzite-topped Liathach ridge — a riot of steep rock terraces, skyline pinnacles and menacing screes — and the sandstone peaks of Beinn Alligin, soaring up from the shore of Upper Loch Torridon.

There are beautifully located villages along the lochside: Torridon itself, beyond the NTS visitor centre and red-deer museum; Alligin and Wester Alligin with their majestic views across the water to Beinn Shieldaig and Beinn Damh; and Diabaig, where the road plunges down to a bay circled by a wild rocky amphitheatre.

🖂 *THE TORRIDON road turns off the A896, 10 miles south-west of Kinlochewe.*

ULLAPOOL
Ross and Cromarty

Curiously located where a triangle of level ground sweeps out into Loch Broom from an otherwise hilly coast, Ullapool was one of the settlements created in the 1780s by the British Fisheries Society.

The modern village, where whitewashed hotels, shops and houses face an inner bay, still earns much of its living, directly or indirectly, from the sea. It is the car-ferry port for Stornoway in Lewis; and freezer ships from Eastern Europe buy up the catches of fishing boats operating in the Minch.

Old-style Ullapool fishing is recalled in the excellent Loch Broom Museum, housed in one of the town's original buildings.

There is recreational sailing here too, as well as sea-angling and cruises to sea-bird and seal colonies. Nearby, too, is the Inverpolly Nature Reserve.

🖂 *ULLAPOOL is on the A835, 32 miles north-west of Garve.*

Ullapool is a popular resort and traditional fishing port, famous for white fish. It also attracts sea anglers

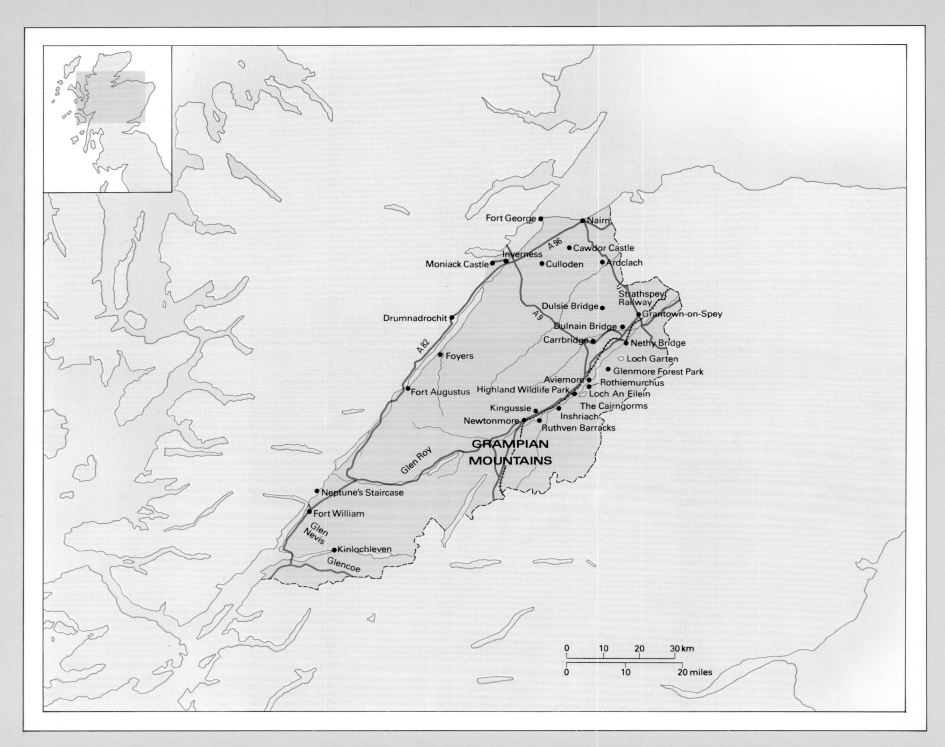

Fort George
Nairn
A 96
Cawdor Castle
Inverness
Moniack Castle
Culloden
Ardclach
Strathspey
Railway
Dulsie Bridge
Grantown-on-Spey
Drumnadrochit
A 9
Dulnain Bridge
Carrbridge
Nethy Bridge
A 82
Loch Garten
Foyers
Glenmore Forest Park
Aviemore
Rothiemurchus
Fort Augustus
Highland Wildlife Park
Loch An Eilein
Kingussie
The Cairngorms
Newtonmore
Inshriach
Ruthven Barracks
GRAMPIAN
MOUNTAINS
Glen Roy
Neptune's Staircase
Fort William
Glen
Nevis
Kinlochleven
Glencoe

0   10   20   30 km

0   10   20 miles

Great Glen & Speyside

One of Scotland's best-known historic sites, Glencoe is a tremendous deep-cut glen amid glorious mountain scenery. Once the scene of a hideous massacre, the glen is now a place of tranquillity

MOUNTAINS AND FORESTS, together with lochs and river valleys following the general north-east/south-west lie of the land, make up this varied and beautiful area of the Central Highlands — which has coastal lowlands around Nairn and Inverness.

The Great Glen can be traced almost ruler-straight on any map of Scotland. Britain's highest mountains are here — Ben Nevis and the Cairngorms. And in the middle valley of the Spey there is a busy all-year-round holiday area where resort attractions are only a few minutes away from birch and pinewood walks, nature trails, castles, fortresses and faint reminders of old Highland industries long since stilled.

There are many unexpected places, like the little upland 'lake district' among the grass and heather moors south of Inverness; the road ablaze with golden flowers of broom and gorse that leads to Dores; the low-key road junction in Fort William which points the way to the majestic Nevis gorge; and the lonely glen where an eerie landscape once believed to be the work of giants finally revealed its secrets to the 19th-century eye of science.

In the high Cairngorms there are nesting birds known to lowland ornithologists only from illustrations in books. And ospreys, which shunned Scotland for many of their generations, are re-establishing themselves in the Highlands from an original single nest in the Abernethy pine forest.

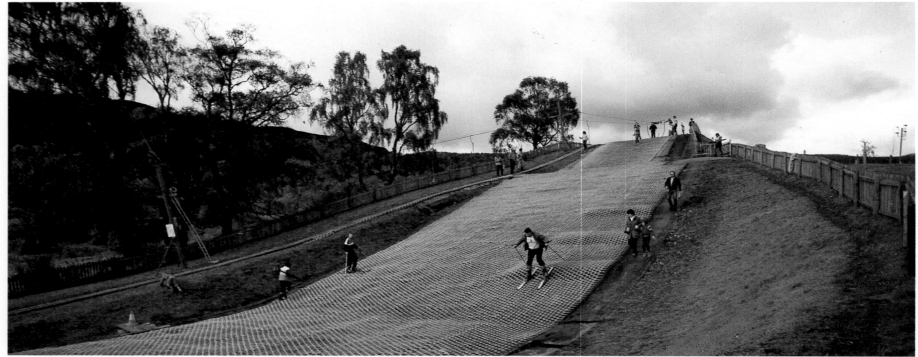

The Aviemore ski centre is popular all year round as both expert skiers and beginners can take advantage of the dry practice slopes

ARDCLACH
Nairn

This is a very attractive parish of farm and forest land split by the wandering course of the River Findhorn. The old church of 1626 is oddly located, on a fan of low-lying ground where hills rise from a sweeping bend on the river.

In the early years, that caused a problem, because the sound of the church bell — not just a call to Sunday service, but also the traditional warning that cattle-raiders had been seen — carried only a short distance. So a separate bell tower was built on the hillside above.

Later, the bell tower was where parishioners who had offended against church rules were sometimes detained. It is now an ancient monument.

🚗 *ARDCLACH is reached by a side-road off the A939, 1½ miles north of Ferness.*

AVIEMORE
Badenoch and Strathspey

In the 18th century, Aviemore was a tiny settlement round an inn on the military road through the Spey Valley. The railway arrived in mid-Victorian times, and a modest village-style holiday resort developed.

Then in 1966 the multi-million pound Aviemore Centre was opened, swamping the older village with a modern resort of hotels, chalets, restaurants, shops, a theatre, cinema, swimming pool, ice rink, sauna and dry ski slope.

Aviemore is an all-year-round resort, since it is also the main accommodation centre for the Cairngorm ski slopes, on the mountains which soar up from the pine forests across the Spey and provide it with a memorable eastward view.

While the open Cairngorm slopes are used for the downhill runs, many of the forest tracks are signposted for cross-country skiers.

Immediately above Aviemore, peregrine falcons nest on the rock-face of Craigellachie. There is another Craigellachie more than 30 miles away in the lower course of the Spey. The two cliffs marked the eastern and western limits of the territory of Clan Grant, who used 'Stand fast, Craigellachie!' as their battle-cry.

A nature trail is laid out through the Craigellachie birchwoods, where the tiny Loch Puladdern is stocked with brown and rainbow trout.

🚗 *AVIEMORE is on the A9, 30 miles south-east of Inverness.*

CARRBRIDGE
Badenoch and Strathspey

Now bypassed by the main Aviemore to Inverness road, this is a village holiday resort with a golf course, pony-trekking and a substantial interest in the Cairngorm ski-ing.

Built in 1717, the original Bridge of Carr survives as a beautifully proportioned arch across the River Dulnain.

The imaginative Landmark Visitor Centre is set in 30 acres of old-established pine forest. It has a multi-screen audio-visual show in a modern theatre overlooking a lochan.

Outside in the pinewoods, other attractions include an adventure playground and mile-long woodland maze, a contemporary sculpture park, a conventional nature trail and another on stilts at tree-top level, from which roe deer, red squirrels,

A solitary cairn at windswept Culloden stands as an eerie reminder of the last bloody battle for supremacy fought on British soil

goldcrests and crossbills can sometimes be seen.

🚗 *CARRBRIDGE is on the B9150, 6 miles north of Aviemore.*

CAWDOR CASTLE
Nairn

Not simply a museum-piece, but also the home of the Earl of Cawdor, this splendid castle with its crow-stepped gables and turreted central keep stands among lawns and gardens, backed by mellow oak and beechwoods cut by tumbling burns.

In Shakespeare's play, Macbeth was Thane of Cawdor, and his castle was where King Duncan was murdered. But the present Cawdor Castle post-dates *Macbeth* by many generations: the keep is known to have been built in 1454.

However, part of the castle is cer-tainly older, and there is a family tradition that the builder was in-structed in a dream to place it beside a hawthorn tree.

This sounds a typical legendary tale; except that, as well as the elegant sitting rooms, the kitchens and the dungeons shown to the public, there is also, deep in the heart of the castle, a tiny chamber where, even to this day, a tiny fragment of an ancient and dessicated hawthorn can still be seen.

🚗 *CAWDOR is on the B9090, 5 miles south-west of Nairn.*

CULLODEN
Inverness

The last great pitched battle on British soil was fought on 16 April 1746, when the Duke of Cumberland's government army routed the Jacobite forces on Culloden Moor.

From the outnumbered Jacobites' point of view, the place, the time and the set-piece style of the battle could not have been more ineptly chosen.

Open moorland facing a better-equipped enemy was hopeless terrain for the Highlanders' favourite tactic of a fearsome, claymores-drawn charge; their attack was intended to be at night, but was delayed so long that it had to be postponed till daylight; once the battle started, Cumberland's far superior artillery poured withering cannon and mortar fire on the opposing ranks; he also had the advantage in cavalry; when the Jacobites finally charged, the movement was unco-ordinated, and the well-trained government troops, including those from non-Jacobite Scottish regiments, held their line.

Prince Charles, who had taken bad advice, retreated from the field. But Cumberland, son of King George II against whom the Rising was directed, started a reign of terror.

The murders and lootings which followed Culloden explain why, although he was greeted back in Lon-don with Handel's specially-composed *Hail, the Conquering Hero Comes*, he is still known in many parts of Scotland as 'the Butcher'.

The battlefield is now owned by the National Trust for Scotland. A visitor centre explains the course of the whole 'Forty-Five Rising. There are memorials and clan burial grounds. And the modern road cuts across the opposing armies' lines, as they were on the day when the Highlands changed for ever.

🚗 *CULLODEN MOOR is on the B9006, 4 miles east of Inverness.*

DRUMNADROCHIT
Inverness

Lying back from Urquhart Bay on Loch Ness, this is a low-set village with forest plantations, farms and isolated houses climbing the steep hillside to the north.

Urquhart Castle, a ruin overlooking the bay, was destroyed after the early Jacobite Rising of 1689. This is where many sightings have been reported of whatever it may be that is called the Loch Ness Monster. The comprehensive Loch Ness Monster Exhibition, with photographic, sonar and other records, is in the village.

Beside the main road south is a memorial to John Cobb, who was the holder of the world land speed record in 1952, when he was killed on Loch Ness trying to set a new water speed record in his boat *Crusader*.

DRUMNADROCHIT is on the A82, 14 miles south of Inverness.

DULNAIN BRIDGE
Badenoch and Strathspey

About a mile upstream from where the River Dulnain meets the Spey, overlooked by woodlands and hill farms, this 18th-century bridge and the village clustered round it used to mark the boundary between the counties of Inverness and Moray.

Dulnain Bridge is a small but individual holiday resort. Many visitors come for the Dulnain's 12 miles of salmon and trout-fishing.

On the south side of the bridge, a side-road runs through the spread-out crofting settlement of Skye of Curr, where the Speyside Heather Garden Centre displays more than 200 cultivated varieties of Scotland's best-known wildflower.

DULNAIN BRIDGE is on the A95, 3 miles south-west of Grantown-on-Spey.

DULSIE BRIDGE
Nairn

The military road of the 1750s from Deeside to Fort George on the Moray Firth was designed by Major Caulfield, successor to General Wade as the great road-builder in the Highlands. Caulfield was responsible for several routes — including this one — mistakenly marked on the map as 'Wade roads'.

When it came to crossing the River Findhorn at Dulsie, Caulfield encountered a ravine with rock pools and birchwoods. He built a sturdy but picturesque little high-level bridge which survives to the present day.

Nearby, a side-road follows the Findhorn upstream towards the heavily eroded valley, flanked by heathery grouse moors.

DULSIE BRIDGE is reached from a crossroads on the B9007, 14 miles north of Carrbridge.

FORT AUGUSTUS
Inverness

This forestry, angling and sailing centre at the head of Loch Ness is on the Great Glen Fault, which provides the deep trough-like structure of Loch Ness and also accommodates the Caledonian Canal. A Great Glen Exhibition has been established at the main-road canal bridge.

St Benedict's Abbey, open to visitors, stands in beautifully wooded grounds, between the canal and the River Tarff. The original building here was the Hanoverian fort which gave the village its name. It remained in government hands until 1867. Nine years later it was gifted to the Benedictine Order.

Ben Nevis rises majestically beyond the ruins of Inverlochy Castle

Within four more years a monastery, chapel, boarding school and guesthouse had been created from renovated military buildings. The cloisters were new, of fine grey granite with decorated Gothic windows overlooking the lawn which covers the original flagstone courtyard of the fort.

The Abbey remains one of the finest groups of integrated buildings in the Highlands.

FORT AUGUSTUS is on the A82, 33 miles north of Fort William.

FORT GEORGE
Inverness

In the aftermath of Culloden, the government constructed one of the most formidable 18th-century fortresses in Europe on a promontory which matches Chanonry Point in the Black Isle to form the narrows of the Moray Firth.

Fort George is the biggest fort in Britain, but by the time it was completed in the 1760s there was no longer any Jacobite threat to test its

complex landward defences or the gun emplacements on its massive bastions.

In fact, Fort George has never heard a shot fired in anger, but it is still garrisoned. The parts classified as an ancient monument are open to the public, as is the regimental museum of the Queen's Own Highlanders, and there are impressive views from the mile-long rampart walk, especially to the cliffs of the Black Isle.

 *FORT GEORGE is on the B9006, 8 miles west of Nairn.*

FORT WILLIAM
Lochaber

Built on a spectacular site — partly on a hillside rising directly from Loch Linnhe, and partly on flatter ground at the mouth of the River Lochy with the great bulk of Ben Nevis looming behind — Fort William is the business and communications centre of Lochaber.

The fort which gave it its English name — and its Gaelic name, which means 'the garrison' — was built in 1690 during the reign of William III. Almost all trace of it was swept away in Victorian times. An older fortress which survives as an ancient monument is the 13th-century Inverlochy Castle.

Several Jacobite relics are displayed in the West Highland Museum, including a famous 'secret portrait' of Bonnie Prince Charlie. This is a tray painted with apparently random coloured daubs. But when a reflecting cylinder is put in place on it, a portrait of the Prince suddenly appears.

FORT WILLIAM is on the A82, south of its junction with the A830 Mallaig road.

FOYERS
Inverness

This attractively suited village, built on a Wade road of the 1730s, is on a steeply-rising forested hillside above Loch Ness. Plunging down a dramatic rocky gorge, the Falls of Foyers were harnessed in the 1890s to

The tranquil atmosphere of St Benedict's Abbey is well-preserved and enjoyed by many visitors to Fort Augustus

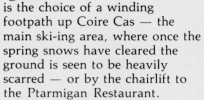

The Cairngorms

Although they extend over both Highland and Grampian Regions, the Cairngorms — for non-climbers — are more easily approached from their western side above the Spey Valley. The 'ski road' from Glenmore climbs high above the tree line, well up the bare hill slopes.

Beyond the final car park there

The spectacular snow-capped peaks and the gentler grassy slopes of the Cairngorm Mountains attract climbers

is the choice of a winding footpath up Coire Cas — the main ski-ing area, where once the spring snows have cleared the ground is seen to be heavily scarred — or by the chairlift to the Ptarmigan Restaurant.

From the Ptarmigan, which is already among the frost-shattered granite rocks characteristic of the Cairngorm plateau, it is only a short walk to the 4084-ft summit of Cairn Gorm itself.

'Plateau' is a fairly mild word for this high-level landscape, the most extensive area of mountains in Britain over 3000 ft; and 'summit' is also misleading, since the actual tops of the Cairngorms have nothing to offer climbers.

The rolling tableland is interrupted by sudden corries gouged out by the last of the glaciers, and it is there that the steepest slopes occur — colossal descents of rock and scree to the glacial lochs far below.

Birds never seen in lowland Britain nest here — ptarmigan, snow bunting and dotterel. Heather fades out by 4000 ft, hardy rushes and grasses take over, and alpine plants are mostly restricted to the corries.

It is important to remember that this *is* the highest mountain plateau in Britain. Even on a fine summer day there is a stiff temperature drop compared with the valleys, and the wind-chill factor must always be taken into account. The plateau is no place for a casual, ill-equipped stroll at any time of year, as walkers have often found to their cost.

provide hydro-electric power for a pioneering aluminium factory built near the lochside.

The factory closed in 1967, although its Victorian buildings remain. But hydro-electricity is still of major importance at Foyers, which is now the site of a pumped-storage generating scheme.

Narrow wooded pathways, and a railed-off belvedere, give excellent views of the falls. There are forest walks to the north. And this is another place where sightings of the Loch Ness Monster have been reported.

FOYERS is on the B852, 11 miles north-east of Fort Augustus.

GLEN NEVIS
Lochaber

In the middle of Fort William, an unobtrusive bridge over the River Nevis marks the entrance to one of the most magnificent mountain scenes in Scotland. The north-bank road leads to the so-called 'tourist path' up Ben Nevis — a real mountain trek to the summit plateau at over 4400 ft, and not to be tackled lightly.

South of the river, another road forms the first section of the 95-mile West Highland Way towards the outskirts of Glasgow; passes Glen Nevis House, the Jacobite headquarters during the siege of Fort William in 1746; crosses the river at the lower Nevis falls and finishes at a car park from which a spectacular footpath continues.

It threads its way to where the mountains jam even closer together to form the precipitous birch and pine-clad slopes of the Nevis gorge. Above the gorge, a waterfall dashes down a hanging valley beside the climbers' hut at Steall.

THE GLEN NEVIS road turns east off the A82 in Fort William.

GLEN ROY
Lochaber

From a Nature Conservancy viewpoint halfway up this narrow valley north of Glen Spean, the famous 'parallel roads' are clearly seen. These wide grassy ledges circle the heathery hillsides at three different levels — about 1149 ft, 1068 ft and 857 ft.

It was only in Victorian times that the puzzle of how they were created was finally solved.

The 'roads' are actually the ancient shorelines of the glacier lake which filled Glen Roy during the Ice Age, and the three levels show how movements of the main glacier in Glen Spean allowed the lake to drop.

GLEN ROY is entered from Roybridge on the A86, 3 miles east of Spean Bridge.

GLENCOE
Lochaber

This tremendous deep-cut glen with its almost overwhelming mountain scenery is well-known to anyone with the faintest interest in Highland history.

The National Trust for Scotland's 14,000-acre Glencoe estate includes most of the south-side peaks and ridges, as well as the northern mountain wall.

In the wooded lower part of the glen there is an NTS visitor centre, a folk museum and a beautiful forest walk to a lochan overlooked by ranks of Corsican pines.

But Glencoe is best remembered for the massacre of February 1692, when a company of government troops billeted on the MacDonalds of Glencoe were ordered to wipe out the entire population of the glen.

Because their chief had been delayed in taking the compulsory oath of allegiance to William III, the MacDonalds could be technically regarded as rebels.

In fact, thanks partly to veiled warnings from some of the soldiers, many of them escaped into the snowy mountain passes. But an annual memorial service at the MacDonald

Backpacks and stout hiking boots are essential for those determined to scale the heights of Glencoe

The indoor collection at Kingussie Folk Museum includes this scene of a blacksmith at work

monument beside the Bridge of Coe is only one long-standing reminder of an offence that shocked the country — the execrated crime of 'murder under trust'.

GLENCOE is on the A82, 15 miles south of Fort William.

GLENMORE FOREST PARK
Badenoch and Strathspey

Bought by the Forestry Commission in 1923, this one-time estate of the Dukes of Gordon is one of Scotland's most beautifully located forest areas, between the heather-purple corries of the Cairngorms and the River Spey. The plantations are mainly of Scots pine and Sitka spruce, while the park also contains open mountainside.

It begins with plantations round three sides of Loch Morlich, more than 1000 ft above sea level and a popular — if chilly — sailing, canoeing, windsurfing and angling water.

There are waymarked walks in the conifer plantations, more substantial trekking routes on the ridges and through the hill passes.

Glenmore Lodge, at the entrance to the glaciated Pass of Ryvoan, is the National Outdoor Training Centre; courses are run here in outdoor sports and mountain rescue.

Visits can be arranged to the high-level grazings of Scotland's only reindeer herd, established from Lapland stock in 1952.

Lower down, the forest itself is the home of black grouse, capercaillie and the curious crossbill, whose beak is designed to winkle into pine cones for the seeds which are its staple diet.

GLENMORE FOREST PARK is 5 miles east of Aviemore.

GRANTOWN-ON-SPEY
Badenoch and Strathspey

Named after the Grant family who, in the 1760s, began to lease out house-building sites on a barren moorland near their castle, this is a carefully planned little town centred on a handsome square of 18th and 19th-century houses, shops, hotels and public buildings.

Although Grantown had a brief but successful foray into the linen trade, it began to flourish as a holiday resort after the railway came through in the 1860s.

There is excellent salmon and trout fishing on the local beats of the River Spey; a fine golf course, an outdoor curling pond first used in 1865, and other sports facilities; and very pleasant walking on the pine-needled footpaths of the Anagach Wood, the Free Church Wood and the Ladies Garden Wood.

Grantown is also well placed, of course, for the Cairngorm ski slopes.

GRANTOWN-ON-SPEY is on the A95, 14 miles north-east of Aviemore.

HIGHLAND WILDLIFE PARK
Badenoch and Strathspey

Established in 1972 over 250 acres of heathery moorland dotted with birches, in the foothills of the Monadhliath' this park has a collection not only of animals and birds currently living in Scotland in the wild, but also of others whose native strain died out hundreds or even thousands of years ago.

A 200-acre drive-through area is home to red and roe deer, Highland cattle and a herd of bison built up from a few animals sent from a breeding colony in a Polish forest.

There are smaller enclosures for

wildcats, pine martens, foxes, lynx and bears, and the park maintains its own wolf pack.

Birds range from eagles and snowy owls in the collection to snipe and lapwing which come here naturally to nest.

THE HIGHLAND WILDLIFE PARK is on the B9152, 8 miles southwest of Aviemore.

INSHRIACH
Badenoch and Strathspey

Forestry Commission conifer plantations occupy most of the one-time moorland of this small district east of the Spey. A picnic site above the rapids and rock pools of Feshiebridge is the start of a short walk to a viewpoint over the forest towards the Cairngorms.

A mile to the south is the airstrip from which the Cairngorm Gliding Club take advantage of the rising air currents of the mountain edge.

Established in 1938, the Inshriach Nursery attracts visitors from all over the world. It has a collection of more than 600 alpine and Himalayan plants.

INSHRIACH is on the B970, 4 miles south of Aviemore.

INVERNESS
Inverness

The Highland capital is a place whose history goes back a very long way. There is a record that in 565 St Columba came to visit King Brude of the Picts, and the vitrified fort on the summit of Craig Phadrig — culminating point of a fine forest walk — may have been the hilltop stronghold of the Pictish kings.

Modern Inverness has a pleasant situation, spread along both sides of the sweeping River Ness. There are several footbridges, including a series which link the wooded Ness Islands to pathways on both banks.

Directly above the river, Inverness Castle is an imposing pink-sandstone building erected as the court house in 1834. Its immediate predecessor on the site was blown up by the Jacobites, in a spectacularly mismanaged explosion in 1746. In front of the castle, a statue of Flora MacDonald gazes westward across the river, forest and mountain view.

Other notable buildings in Inverness include the ornate Victorian Gothic town house; St Andrew's Cathedral and, beside it, the modern Eden Court Theatre incorporating the original bishop's residence; the clock tower which is all that remains of the fort built in the 1650s by Cromwell's troops; and the restored, late 16th-century Abertarff House, headquarters of the Gaelic association, *An Comunn Gaidhealach.*

Out of doors, Inverness has good salmon and sea-trout fishing on the Ness. There are two golf courses, extensive parks and sports grounds. And from the Caledonian Canal basin, cruises leave for Loch Ness.

INVERNESS is where the A9 and the A82 meet the A96.

KINGUSSIE
Badenoch and Strathspey

Often called the capital of Badenoch, Kingussie was no more than a few houses round a church until 1799, when the Duke of Gordon advertised leases of ground. In the years which followed, it developed into a neatly laid-out little town of traditional stone-built houses.

The Highland Folk Museum transferred to Kingussie in 1944. Set

Twinkling lights along the River Ness illuminate the castle above

In summertime, the cool, clear waters of Loch an Eilein are framed by deep green forests of larch and pine

in six acres, it includes indoor and outdoor collections, as well as complete buildings like a Lewis 'black house'.

Kingussie has a testing golf course, designed by Harry Vardon, in the birchwood hills which rise to the north. Above it, and a wide-ranging view-point over the Spey Valley to the Cairngorms, is the craggy 1581-ft summit of Creag Bheag.

KINGUSSIE is on the A86, 11 miles south-west of Aviemore.

KINLOCHLEVEN
Lochaber

This industrial village in the dominating mountain landscape at the head of Loch Leven was built in Edwardian times to serve an aluminium factory. The classic *Children of the Dead End* by Patrick MacGill describes the harsh, wild life of the 'navvies' who worked on the dams and tunnels of the factory's hydro-electric scheme.

The West Highland Way comes into Kinlochleven from the south-east, down a steep birchwood glen on the old Devil's Staircase military road from Glencoe. It passes the penstock — where the water from the Blackwater Reservoir is fed into the huge pipes which supply the factory's turbines.

North-west of the village, the Way zig-zags up towards its final mountain crossing to Fort William.

KINLOCHLEVEN is on the B863, 7 miles east of Glencoe village.

LOCH AN EILEIN
Badenoch and Strathspey

In the heart of the superb Rothiemurchus pinewoods, with their scattered larch and pine and undergrowth of juniper, Loch an Eilein is on the edge of the 100 square-mile Cairngorms

National Nature Reserve.

A nature trail round the loch passes through the territory of roe deer, red squirrel and wildcat. Birds resident here range from the bulky caper-caillie, with its bubbling and cork-popping call, to the tiny goldcrest.

Many species of wild duck feed on the loch. On the island which gives it its name there is a ruined 15th-century castle. Ospreys were last recorded nesting on the castle ruins in 1899; now their place has been taken by jackdaws.

🚗 *LOCH AN EILEIN is off the B970, 2½ miles south of Aviemore.*

LOCH GARTEN
Badenoch and Strathspey

A few years after they left Loch an Eilein, ospreys were lost to Scotland for almost half a century. Then, in 1954, a pair returned to Loch Garten, among the pines of Abernethy Forest. There has been a nest here ever since, in a reserve of the Royal Society for the Protection of Birds.

From the time the ospreys arrive in April until they leave again in August, their nest is in clear view from the visitor centre. And in the lochs of the Spey Valley, the adult birds will sometimes be seen, swooping down on pike or trout.

🚗 *LOCH GARTEN is off the B970, 2 miles east of Boat of Garten.*

MONIACK CASTLE
Inverness

In latitudes and temperatures where grapes cannot be grown outdoors, many private houses and stately homes in the Highlands nevertheless manage to produce their own wine — from elder flowers and rowan berries, and the sap of the silver birch.

Only at white-towered Moniack Castle, a 16th-century Fraser proper-ty among the fields and woodlands between Inverness and Beauly, is this done on a commercial scale. Highland Wineries were established there in 1979, and are open to the public to demonstrate a wine-making tradition handed down through many generations.

🚗 *MONIACK CASTLE is off the A862, 7 miles west of Inverness.*

Nairn boasts some of the most magnificent sandy beaches in Scotland

NAIRN
Nairn

James VI of Scotland was referring to Nairn when, having also become James I of England, he boasted that in his Scottish kingdom there was a town so long that the people at either end of it could not understand one another's conversation.

Size had nothing to do with it, but for many years Nairn was right on the boundary between Gaelic and English speakers.

The modern town is built on both banks of the River Nairn, with sandy beaches extending east and west. Its one-time fishing harbour is now mainly given over to yachts and dinghies.

The old Fishertown — once a prosperous exporter of salted herring — survives in neat rows of restored cottages, and has its own museum to recall the days when Nairn was one of the most important centres of the Moray Firth fishing.

Nairn is a well-known and championship-standard golfing resort, with links courses backed by gorse and pine. There are footpaths along both banks of the wooded riverside, and a heritage trail round the town's most notable buildings.

🚗 *NAIRN is on the A96, 16 miles north-east of Inverness.*

NEPTUNE'S STAIRCASE
Lochaber

Notorious as probably the most lackadaisical construction job ever tackled in the Highlands, Thomas Telford's flight of eight locks at the southern entrance to the Caledonian Canal was started in 1805 and not completed until six years later. Even then, the contractor's masonry work was so poorly done that — together with other problems elsewhere — it delayed the official opening of the canal until 1822.

Soon christened Neptune's Staircase, these locks nevertheless remain the most impressive piece of canal design in Scotland, above a sea-loch and in full view of Ben Nevis across the water.

NEPTUNE'S STAIRCASE is at Banavie on the A830, 3 miles north of Fort William.

NETHY BRIDGE
Badenoch and Strathspey

Now a quiet holiday village within easy reach of the Cairngorms and the Speyside pinewoods, and with its own golf course nearby, Nethy Bridge shows few signs of the furious industrial activity which overtook it in the 18th century.

On the rocky banks of the River Nethy which cascades through the village is the site of a charcoal-fired iron furnace, in short-lived production from 1729.

Charcoal was made in the local forests, and the iron-ore was carried by pony-trains from a remote mine in the hills 15 miles to the east. Timber was also floated to the Spey, where great rafts of it were navigated down-river to the boat-building yards on the Moray Firth.

NETHY BRIDGE is on the B970, 5 miles south of Grantown-on-Spey.

NEWTONMORE
Badenoch and Strathspey

This is the heart of Macpherson country, and the first clan museum in Scotland was opened here in 1952. The Macphersons' March is a feature of Newtonmore Highland Games, every year on the first weekend in August.

The long, stone-built village began to grow up in the early 19th century,

populated partly by farmers who had been forced out of Glen Banchor to make way for sheep.

Pony-trekking was introduced to the Highlands here. There is angling on the Spey, its tributaries and lochans in the hills. Newtonmore has a beautifully situated riverside golf course. But the biggest cheers here are for shinty: Newtonmore's team has been the most consistently successful in the history of this essentially Highlanders' sport.

NEWTONMORE is on the A86, 14 miles south-west of Aviemore.

ROTHIEMURCHUS
Badenoch and Strathspey

This famous estate, owned since 1580 by the Grants of Rothiemurchus, extends from the east bank of the Spey to the 4248-ft summit of Braeriach on the Cairngorm plateau.

Its facilities include the Moormore picnic area in heathery pinewood beside the tumbling River Luineag, the outflow from Loch Morlich; a rainbow-trout fishery; low-level walks among pine and birchwoods; and hill-walkers' rights-of-way through the pass of the Lairig Ghru towards Deeside, and into the huge corrie of Loch Einich, a glacial valley encircled by prodigious rock buttresses and scree-runs.

There is a visitor centre at Inverdruie, once the headquarters of those characters who built and floated the timber-rafts down the Spey.

INVERDRUIE visitor centre is on the B970, 1 mile south-east of Aviemore.

RUTHVEN BARRACKS
Badenoch and Strathspey

In 1719 the hilltop site of an old castle overlooking an important Spey crossing was chosen as the location of a

new government fort. The Jacobites besieged it in 1745, but got no change out of the formidable Sergeant Molloy, who held them off with a defensive force of only a dozen men.

The Jacobites returned the following year, and this time burned the barracks out. That was no good omen for them, because it was back at Ruthven — which is now a floodlit ancient monument — that Bonnie Prince Charlie, after the defeat at Culloden, formally disbanded the last-ever Jacobite army.

RUTHVEN BARRACKS are on the B970, 1 mile south-east of Kingussie.

STRATHSPEY RAILWAY
Badenoch and Strathspey

Until 1863, Boat of Garten was simply the location of a chain-ferry across the Spey. Then the Inverness and Perth Junction Railway arrived, and a fair-sized village grew up.

The railway closed in 1968. Exactly ten years later, the volunteer-run Strathspey Railway began scheduled summer services on five miles of restored line through pine and birchwood to Aviemore Speyside.

Many of its furnishings arrived here after ending their useful life on main-line routes — the station buildings from Dalnaspidal, the footbridge from Longmorn, the turntable from Kyle of Lochalsh.

The Strathspey Railway has a comprehensive stock of steam and diesel locomotives, carriages and wagons; and there are plans to extend it down-river to Grantown-on-Spey.

BOAT OF GARTEN is 6 miles north-east of Aviemore.

Eerily silhouetted against a darkening sky, the grim ruins of Ruthven Barracks

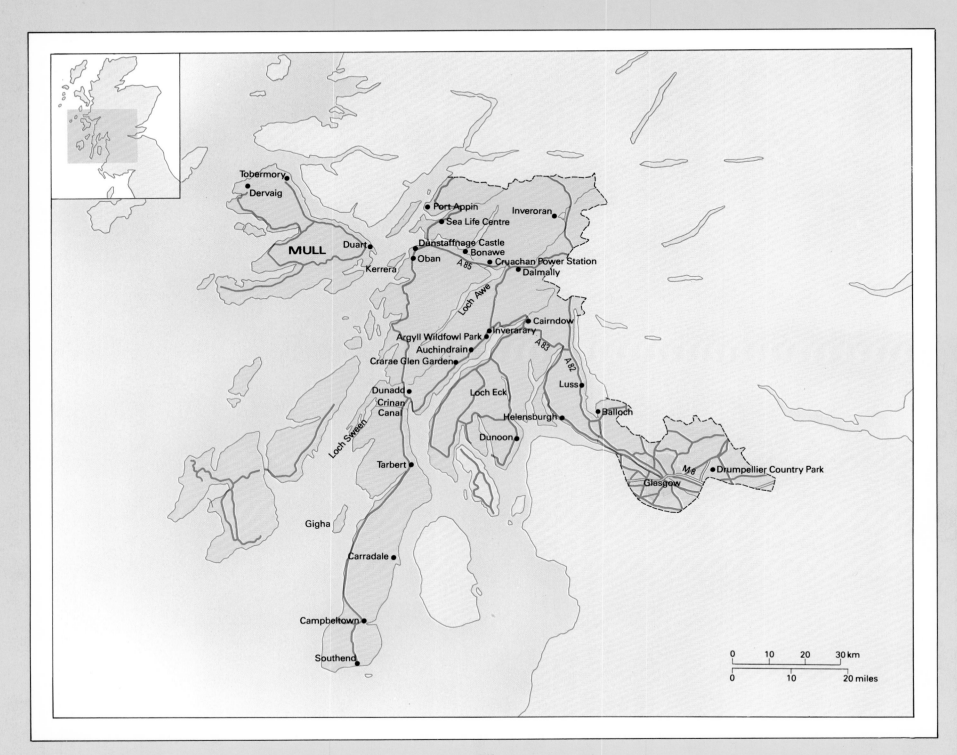

Tobermory
Dervaig

Port Appin
Inveroran
Sea Life Centre

MULL Duart
Dunstaffnage Castle
Bonawe
Oban Cruachan Power Station
A 85 Dalmally
Kerrera

Loch Awe

Cairndow
Argyll Wildfowl Park Inverarary
Auchindrain A 83
Crarae Glen Garden A 82

Luss
Loch Eck

Dunadd Balloch
Crinan Helensburgh
Canal

Dunoon

Loch Sween

Tarbert M 8 Drumpellier Country Park

Glasgow

Gigha

Carradale

Campbeltown

Southend

0   10   20   30 km

0   10   20 miles

North Strathclyde

Dunollie Castle, a hill-top ruin above Oban's sweeping Ganavan Sands, was the home of the Mac Dougall chiefs until the mid 18th century

WHEN SCOTTISH LOCAL government boundaries were re-drawn in 1975, Strathclyde became the country's most important Region — a vast area containing half of Scotland's population, and spreading from the Lowther Hills of the Southern Uplands to some of the Inner Hebrides.

The northern part of Strathclyde therefore stretches from the city of Glasgow to the Atlantic coast and beyond. It includes industrial areas, the museums and galleries for which Glasgow has become world-famous, part of Loch Lomond, great tracts of mountain and forest and lochside in Cowal, and a scattering of islands off the west coast — Islay and Jura, Colonsay, Coll and Tiree, Iona and Mull.

There are forest walks, nature trails and compact, rock-climbers' mountain ranges like the 'Arrochar Alps' between Loch Lomond and Loch Fyne. And the 'great gardens of Argyll' justify the name.

Famous castles are to be seen here, like the ones whose fire-beacons used to flash messages of war and peace along the Sound of Mull, and the ancestral homes still lived in by the Campbells and the Macleans.

But there are many relics of the hazy centuries well before the upsurge of the clans. This is also the country of Dalriada, the first settlement made by the Scots when they arrived from Ireland. They crowned their kings on a hilltop fortress overlooking a fertile valley whose cairns and standing stones played a significant part in ancient societies.

ARGYLL WILDFOWL PARK
Argyll and Bute

Established in 1984, in 55 acres of forest, open ground and pebble beach on the shore of Loch Fyne, this unusual nature park has expanded far beyond the limit suggested by its title. In scattered ponds it has a collection of well-known wildfowl species, as well as rarer breeds like Fulvous Tree Ducks and Lesser Magellan Geese.

But the plantation is now home to roe deer, wildcats and even wallabies; and one section is entirely given over to owls. The total number of bird and animal species in the park is now well over 100. With its forest, shore and nearby grazing land, it also attracts passing birds which temporarily 'join' the collection.

🚗 *ARGYLL WILDFOWL PARK is on the A83, 1½ miles south-west of Inveraray.*

AUCHINDRAIN
Argyll and Bute

This partly open-air museum is unique. Auchindrain was the last farming settlement in the whole of Scotland to persevere with the old multiple-tenancy system — its 4000 acres, mostly hill grazing for sheep and cattle, were farmed as a unit, not by a single family, but by several families living in the same group of cottages. That arrangement came to an end only in 1935, long after it had been given up elsewhere.

Some of the 18th- and 19th-century cottages are furnished from different periods in Auchindrain's history. And the six arable fields which remain at the 30-acre heart of the old farm, protected from the advancing ranks of conifers, are steadily being reclaimed.

🚗 *AUCHINDRAIN is on the A83, 5 miles south-west of Inveraray.*

BALLOCH
Dumbarton

Built on both banks of the River Leven, where it leaves Loch Lomond, Balloch is the start of many of the cruises on the loch, and there are boatyards and dozens of moorings. A wildlife park occupies part of the Cameron estate on the west bank, while Balloch Castle Country Park rising from the east bank is the headquarters of a countryside ranger service.

It is the land around an early 19th-century hilltop castle, set above sweeping lawns. The park has a tree trail with several rareties, a keep-fit trail, informal woodland walks and a quiet walled garden.

A much older castle survives only as a grassy mound near the loch. It was the seat of the Earls of Lennox, who transferred around 1390 to a more secure location on the offshore island of Inchmurrin.

🚗 *BALLOCH is off the A82, 3 miles north of Dumbarton.*

BONAWE
Argyll and Bute

The most famous, and by far the best-restored, of Scotland's 18th-century charcoal ironworks is in a truly incongruous setting, looking out to the mountains flanking a lovely sea-loch.

Auchindrain's old whitewashed farming cottages are now part of a unique museum complex

English industrialists founded the Lorn Furnace above Loch Etive in 1753, shipping in the ore from Furness in Lancashire. They built a self-contained village around the works, which were out-dated almost before they went into production, because charcoal-fired furnaces which needed close-by woodlands were being replaced by coke-fired operations nearer the coalfields.

Bonawe produced cannonballs and shot as well as pig-iron during more than 120 years of operation. Unused for over a century, its buildings now house a fascinating exhibition of the industry's techniques and favoured locations.

🚗 BONAWE is immediately north of Taynuilt on the A85.

CAIRNDOW
Argyll and Bute

An old coaching village long since bypassed by the modern main road, Cairndow shelters below steep, sheep-grazed hills near the head of Loch Fyne. On a fine day, green hills, blue sky and white cottages reflect pleasantly in the loch.

John Keats, the poet, stayed at the village inn during an energetic walking tour when he came over the stiff climb of the Rest and be Thankful from Loch Long.

The white-walled octagonal church has a square tower and some curious headstones in the graveyard that surrounds it.

Nearby is Strone woodland garden, laid out along both banks of the Kinglass Water. There are masses of springtime daffodils, a fine collection of rhododendrons and azaleas, and, at 200 ft, one of the trees in the spectacular pinetum is the tallest in Britain.

🚗 CAIRNDOW is off the A83, 12 miles north-west of Arrochar.

The island of Davaar lies in the mouth of Campbeltown Loch

CAMPBELTOWN
Argyll and Bute

Originally on the territory of the MacDonalds, this town at the head of an east-facing sea-loch took its modern name in 1667, after it had come into the hands of their rivals, the Campbell Earls of Argyll.

Campbeltown was a great fishing and whisky-distilling centre, as the local museum shows; but the 32 distilleries that were once on record have dwindled to two.

In the mouth of Campbeltown Loch is the hilly, lighthouse island of Davaar, reached at low water by a walk along the edge of a shingle bank. In 1887 a local man called Archibald MacKinnon painted a dream-inspired Crucifixion scene on an inner wall. He went back to renew the colours 47 years later, and the painting is still kept freshened up.

There is a fine golf course on the links of Machrihanish, due west of Campbeltown, behind the dunes of a three-and-a-half mile Atlantic beach.

🚗 CAMPBELTOWN is on the A83, 52 miles south of Tarbert.

CARRADALE
Argyll and Bute

A link with the faraway Viking past, Carradale is a fishing and holiday village on the coast of Kintyre, with almost mile-long sands at the head of a south-facing bay, and a river winding down a narrow farmland valley between forested hills.

There is a golf course, sailing and windsurfing in the main bay, and many smaller bays down unobtrusive side-roads. Salmon and trout-anglers fish the river, and forest walks lead to viewpoints over Kilbrannan Sound to the mountains of Arran.

Roe and fallow deer browse in the plantations, there is a herd of wild

Cabin cruisers follow the route taken by Queen Victoria's royal barge in 1847 on the Crinan Canal

goats on Carradale Point, and this is the hunting ground of kestrel, buzzard, hen harrier and golden eagle.
● *CARRADALE is on the B879, 23 miles south of Tarbert.*

CRARAE GLEN GARDEN
Argyll and Bute

First planted around 1912 on both sides of a handsome glen, down which a burn tumbles on its way to Loch Fyne, this is a garden where tall sheltering trees protect a glorious variety of flowering shrubs. Many were brought from the Himalayas in the garden's earliest years.

Run by a charitable trust, Crarae has a brilliant display of rhododendrons in spring and early summer. But its magnolias and other later-flowering shrubs keep the garden bright and lively right through until the autumn. Much of the tree cover has been thinned so as to re-open the splendid views over the loch.
● *CRARAE GLEN GARDEN is on the A83, 11 miles south-west of Inveraray.*

CRINAN CANAL
Argyll and Bute

Although work started in 1794 on the nine-mile waterway from Ardrishaig to Crinan, it was 23 years later that the Crinan Canal was satisfactorily completed.

After Queen Victoria's voyage to Crinan in 1847, when her lavishly furnished barge was drawn along by three horses, the canal was publicised as part of the 'Royal Route'.

It has 15 locks and seven swing bridges — two of which, Miller's Bridge and Bellanoch, are in particularly fine settings. The towpath,

Dervaig Church has an unusual, Irish-style pencil tower

in stretches doubling as a public road, makes an excellent walk, especially towards the west end, where it passes the wooded cliffs around Crinan, with magnificent views over a sea-loch to the Poltalloch hills.

Crinan itself is an attractive but bewilderingly scattered village with a busy canal basin. At Crinan Harbour — separate from the canal — a network of forest walks leads to high-level viewpoints over the Sound of Jura.

ARDRISHAIG is on the A83, 1½ miles south of Lochgilphead; Crinan is on the B841, 7 miles west of Lochgilphead.

CRUACHAN POWER STATION
Argyll and Bute

Ben Cruachan is Scotland's 'hollow mountain'. Deep within it, in an excavated chamber big enough to accommodate a seven-storey block of flats, is the machine hall of a pumped-storage hydro-electric generating scheme opened in 1965.

Water is piped from a reservoir in a corrie high on the mountain slopes. During the day, that water turns the generating turbines. At off-peak periods, the turbines are reversed so that water from Loch Awe is pumped back up to the reservoir.

There is a very informative visitor centre on the lochside, from which minibus tours are arranged along the road-tunnel right into the heart of the mountain.

CRUACHAN power station is on the A85, 6 miles west of Dalmally.

DALMALLY
Argyll and Bute

Although it grew up around a mid-Victorian railway station, this is a village in several separated parts. It is surrounded by hills and glens, and is

bounded to the north by the lower reaches of the River Orchy, a good angling water whose pebbly banks are popular for picnics.

Dalmally has a busy livestock market and a shinty field. Its parish church is on a rise of ground where two channels of the Orchy have created an often unnoticed island.

A narrow road climbs from the station to Monument Hill — named after the impressive memorial to one of Gaeldom's most famous poets, Duncan Ban MacIntyre — and opens up a majestic view to Ben Cruachan and the tangle of islands in Loch Awe.

DALMALLY is on the A85, 11 miles west of Tyndrum.

DERVAIG
Argyll and Bute

At the very end of the 18th century, 26 matching houses were built near the head of Loch Cuin in the north-west of Mull, and they still form the major part of the village of Dervaig.

Overlooking the tidal mouth of the River Bellart, which flows into the sea-loch, Kilmore parish church is highly unusual. The original church of 1755 was dismantled early this century, and the architect of its replacement included a round, pencil-tower belfry in a style he had often seen in Ireland.

Anglers fish the Bellart for salmon and sea-trout. Dervaig also attracts many visitors to its Old Byre Heritage Centre, where the history of the area is documented and explained.

At the enterprising Mull Little Theatre, whose audiences are limited to intimate gatherings of around 40 people, visitors can enjoy a variety of live entertainment throughout the year.

DERVAIG is on the B8073, 6 miles south-west of Tobermory.

DRUMPELLIER COUNTRY PARK
Monklands

Referred to in charters from as early as the 12th century, Drumpellier was handed over in 1919 to Coatbridge town council. It includes woodlands of beech and oak, ash and sycamore and rhododendron thickets; lawns and a pair of lochs; two nature trails and pathways along the banks of the old Monkland Canal.

There is a very good visitor centre on the north shore of Lochend Loch, which is stocked with trout and is also the nesting-place of mallards, coots and moorhens. The most notable birds here, though, are the mute and whooper swans.

🚗 *DRUMPELLIER COUNTRY PARK visitor centre is 2 miles north-west of Coatbridge town centre.*

DUART
Argyll and Bute

The two castles which face each other across Duart Bay on Mull could hardly be more different; but both are still owned and occupied by the families which had them built, and both are open to the public.

Duart Castle itself, a 14th-century fortress dominating the entrance to the Sound of Mull, is the home of the 27th chief of the Macleans of Duart and Morvern. The Macleans were a powerful clan, and displays in the castle show how they figured in many important Highland and island affairs.

Torosay is the work of two notable Victorian architects. David Bryce designed the castle in the 1850s with familiar 'baronial' flourishes, and Sir Robert Lorimer laid out the gardens with their balustraded lawns and Italian-style statue walk.

Between Torosay and the ferry-

Pipe bands create a colourful spectacle in the streets of Dunoon

terminal village of Craignure there is a narrow-gauge railway whose leisurely schedule allows plenty of time for photography.

🚗 *TOROSAY CASTLE is off the A849, 1 mile south of Craignure; Duart Castle is on a side-road which leaves the A849 south of Torosay.*

DUNADD
Argyll and Bute

The grass-topped rock outcrop of Dunadd, with its naturally fortified summit, stands above the reclaimed farmlands of Crinan Moss, once a marshy inlet of the sea. Carvings near the summit are traditionally connected with the crowning of the monarchs of the Celtic kingdom of Dalriada, founded at the beginning of the 6th century AD.

Dalriada grew in strength and territory until, in 843, it absorbed the kingdom of the Picts; and that marked the beginning of a country recognisably like modern Scotland.

Although the capital then moved elsewhere, Dunadd remains a notably atmospheric site. And it looks over the Kilmartin valley, whose standing stones, cairns and mysterious carvings go back to the time of Dunadd's own earliest history as a Dark Age hill-fort in the second millenium BC.

🚗 *DUNADD is off the A816, 4 miles north of Lochgilphead.*

DUNOON
Argyll and Bute

In the early 19th century, as steamships began to operate on the Firth of Clyde, Dunoon and its satellite village of Kirn grew up as favourite places for Glasgow people to have weekend and holiday homes.

Dunoon is still a significant holiday resort, with a long promenade of sea-facing villas and hotels linking it with Kirn. Every year it plays host to the Cowal Highland Games, where no fewer than 150 pipe bands can be seen marching in line ahead and the whole town celebrates.

Above the pier, in the hillside park which occupies the site of the old Dunoon Castle, is a statue to a local girl called Mary Campbell — Robert Burns's 'Highland Mary'. They were about to marry and emigrate to the West Indies, but Mary suddenly took ill and died. Burns decided, after all, to stay with his own folk in Scotland.

🚗 *DUNOON is on the A815, across the Firth of Clyde from the east-side car-ferry terminal at Gourock.*

Scottish forests

Britain's first forest park was established in Argyll in 1935, but extensive woods of birch and pine were growing here thousands of years before that — the birch an excellent self-propagator, the pine eventually the first conifer to be cultivated in plantations.

Millions of acres of the old Caledonian Forest were sacrificed to farming — whether by the clearing of land for the plough, or by the grazing of sheep, or by the practice of burning the moorland to encourage new grass to grow.

Foresters tend to be sceptical that other popular explanations for the disappearance of the original woodlands — deliberate

Forestry plantations at Dalchork

destruction of the hiding-places of wolves and human bandits, or colossal storms, or natural fires — can have had much large-scale, long-term effect.

Now there are modern commercial plantations — mostly of spruce and larch, Scots and Lodgepole pine — in many parts of north Strathclyde, but especially on the hills and lochsides of Argyll; even on the rugged island of Jura. They provide nature trails and picnic places, bridle paths, viewpoints and holiday villages.

But areas of older forests survive, and there are some real showpieces. Above Kilmun on the Holy Loch, for instance, the Commission maintains an arboretum, with steep and winding pathways through plots of forest and ornamental trees, and many flowering shrubs.

And at Glen Nant, a Forest Nature Reserve encloses an old woodland harvested on the coppice system for almost 120 years, to provide charcoal for the ironworks at Bonawe on Loch Etive, themselves a splendidly restored and informative ancient monument.

Woodland for all to enjoy at Galloway Forest Park

DUNSTAFFNAGE CASTLE
Argyll and Bute

More than 20 generations of Campbells have been hereditary Captains of Dunstaffnage, but this strategically-placed castle guarding the entrance to Loch Etive was begun in the 13th century by their predecessors, the MacDougall Lords of Lorn.

Dunstaffnage was garrisoned, attacked and defended in many wars, from the time of the Jacobites — Flora MacDonald was briefly held prisoner here after it was discovered how she had helped Bonnie Prince Charlie, but she was gently treated.

Since 1958 the curtain-walled castle, which from the open sea stands on the summit of a rocky outcrop, but on the other side has lawns rising from a sheltered bay, has been looked after as an ancient monument.

DUNSTAFFNAGE CASTLE is signposted from Dunbeg, on the A85, 2 miles north-east of Oban.

GIGHA
Argyll and Bute

In the days of the Norsemen, Gigha was named Gudey — 'the Good Island'. It is the most southerly of the Inner Hebrides, famous for the sheltered sub-tropical gardens of Achamore House.

Established in 1945, the gardens feature a dazzling display of rhododendrons, as well as trees and other flowering shrubs from South America and Australasia. In 1962 the plant collection was presented to the National Trust for Scotland; but the grounds — although open to visitors — remain in private hands.

Otherwise, Gigha is a fertile dairy-farming island, with a single village at Ardminish, fine sandy beaches backed by springy machair turf, fishing lochs, yacht anchorages and many ancient standing stones.

🚗 *GIGHA is reached by car-ferry from Tayinloan, on the A83, 19 miles south of Tarbert.*

GLASGOW
City of Glasgow

Although it was one of the power-houses of the Industrial Revolution, Glasgow has developed into a city with more than 70 public parks and some of the finest art galleries in Britain.

In the whole of Scotland, the place which attracts more visitors than any other — a million of them in a year — is the Burrell Gallery set in the 361 acres of woodlands, lawns, nature trails and grazing land of Pollok Park.

The magnificent 8000-piece collection of paintings, tapestries, ceramics, stonework, stained glass and silverware was presented to the city by the ship-owning millionaire Sir William Burrell.

But 'the Burrell' is not the only important building in the park. The 18th-century Palladian mansion of Pollok House is a museum showing off elegant plasterwork, furniture and furnishings, and one of Britain's finest collections of Spanish art.

Other major collections are housed in the Art Gallery and Museum in Kelvingrove Park, and in the People's Palace — which concentrates on the city's own social and industrial history — on Glasgow Green.

A monument nearby celebrates the spot where, in the course of a Sunday-morning stroll in the year 1765, James Watt — mulling over his ideas about steam engines — was struck by the notion of the fundamental improvement which transformed them into reliable and economical power-sources, and made the In-

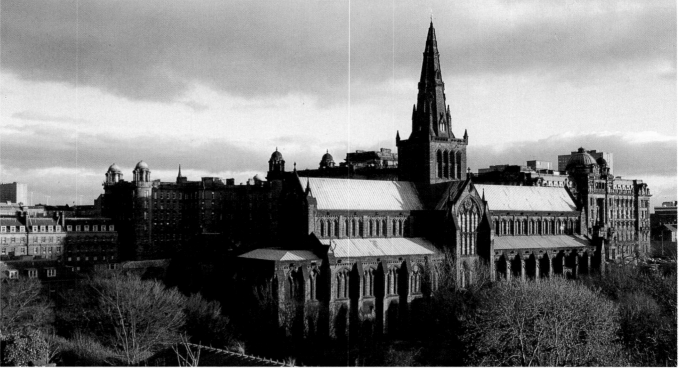

Glasgow Cathedral is pre-Reformation Gothic

dustrial Revolution a possibility.

Much of Glasgow is Victorian, like the Italian Renaissance-style City Chambers, where guided tours show off beautiful ceilings, mosaic floors and the superb staircase with its alabaster pillars, Numidian and Carrara marble.

Glasgow was also the native city of the architect Charles Rennie Mackintosh, many of whose buildings — like the School of Art — attract worldwide attention. His own house, with its original scheme of furnishings, has been reconstructed in the tower of Glasgow University's Hunterian Art Gallery.

Away from art and architecture, Glasgow is also the home of Scottish Opera, Scottish Ballet and two full-scale symphony orchestras.

🚗 *GLASGOW is 45 miles west of Edinburgh.*

The Venetian-style Templeton factory on Glasgow Green

Hill House, Helensburgh, is a delight, both outside and in, for lovers of Rennie Mackintosh's *art nouveau* style

HELENSBURGH
Dumbarton

One of several towns on the Firth of Clyde which expanded after the railway arrived from Glasgow, Helensburgh was founded some years earlier — in 1776 — by Sir James Colquhoun, who named it after his wife.

On the promenade there is a monument to Henry Bell, whose *Comet* of 1812 was the world's first sea-going steamship. His wife kept the family financially afloat by running a fine hotel.

Helensburgh was the birthplace of television pioneer John Logie Baird. One of his original 'televisors' is preserved in the local library.

But the showpiece of the town is the Edwardian villa called Hill House, designed by Charles Rennie Mackin-

tosh. Now owned by the National Trust for Scotland, it retains the furniture and furnishings of Mackintosh's *art nouveau* style.

🚗 *HELENSBURGH is on the A814, 8 miles north-west of Dumbarton.*

INVERARAY
Argyll and Bute

The northern aspect of this elegant little town is a line of whitewashed Georgian buildings and archways facing Loch Fyne.

Originally, the town stood near Inveraray Castle, home of the Dukes of Argyll who head the senior branch of Clan Campbell.

But in 1743, when the 3rd Duke decided to have a much grander castle built, the old town was cleared away and the present one was created, vir-

tually all of a piece.

The castle has an extensive collection of portraits and tapestries on show; and its armoury hall displays something like 1300 broadswords, muskets and pikes.

Memories of a later style of war are revived in a nearby museum. In the 1940s, Inveraray was the training centre for the Combined Operations unit which planned and rehearsed the assault landing techniques put into practice on the coasts of Norway, Italy, North Africa and Normandy.

In the town itself, the Bell Tower is not only an excellent viewpoint over the loch; it also has a ten-bell peal regarded as the finest in Scotland, installed as the Campbell war memorial.

🚗 *INVERARAY is on the A83, 22 miles west of Arrochar.*

INVERORAN
Argyll and Bute

Now little more than a lonely hotel patronised by walkers, mountaineers and anglers, this was once an overnight stance for man and beast on the busy cattle-drovers' route from Fort William; and the military road to the fort there was built through Inveroran in the 1750s.

The West Highland Way approaches it from the south-east over the winding viewpoint pass of the Mam Carraigh, and continues north by a remote, exposed route to Glencoe with tremendous views west to the outstanding peaks and corries of the Black Mount range, and east over the almost trackless lochside peat mosses of Rannoch Moor.

🚗 *INVERORAN is on the A8005, 3 miles north-west of Bridge of Orchy.*

KERRERA
Argyll and Bute

The long island of Kerrera which shelters the harbour and anchorages of Oban Bay is much more than simply a windbreak; it is also an exhilarating place for walkers.

On the coast of the narrow Sound of Kerrera is the area still called the King's Field, where Alexander II died in 1249 during an expedition round the West Highland castles.

The ruins of the 16th-century MacDougall stronghold of Gylen stand on a rocky peninsula on the south coast. Nearby, an old drove road — once part of the complicated route by which cattle from Mull were driven to the mainland markets — leads back across the heart of the island to the ferry.

⛴ *THE KERRERA ferry is reached by taking the Gallanach road from the centre of Oban.*

Shades of autumn in the Younger Botanic Garden, south of Loch Eck

conifer plantations, rocky cliffs and lateral glens of open grazing land, this narrow and gently winding loch is one of the most striking inland waters in Scotland.

Sailing, canoeing and angling are all encouraged. The main road along the east shore has water's-edge parking and picnic places. A walking route follows the west shore, and there are — as in the rest of the Argyll Forest Park — others to viewpoints all over the forested hills.

Just south of the loch, the superb Younger Botanic Garden features a Wellingtonia avenue planted in the 1860s, more than 250 species of rhododendron and one of the best collections of Asiatic conifers in the country.

🚗 *LOCH ECK is on the A815, north of Dunoon.*

LOCH SWEEN
Argyll and Bute

This sea-loch penetrating deep into the hills of Knapdale, where it begins among the labyrinth of forested inlets, takes its name from what is probably the oldest stone-built castle on the Scottish mainland. Castle Sween was begun in the 12th century, but has been in ruins since its final besieging in 1647.

There are three villages round the loch. Tayvallich is an attractive sailing centre with a more than semi-circular bay. Achnamara is a forestry settlement on one of the long upper inlets. And Kilmory Knap, looking out towards the island peaks of Jura, has the roofed-over ruin of a 12th-century chapel with a notable collection of carved and decorated gravestones dating back over 1000 years.

🚗 *LOCH SWEEN is south of Crinan, reached by the B8025 from Bellanoch.*

LOCH AWE
Argyll and Bute

From the scree-slopes of the Pass of Brander to the village of Ford, the 27 miles of Loch Awe are surrounded by very fine mountain and forest scenery.

Inverliever Forest, on the western side, has miles of walks, picnic places and viewpoints. A famous name by the water's edge there is New York — a long-since abandoned 18th-century hamlet.

Well-known fishing hotels at Taychreggan and Portsonachan face each other across the narrowest stretch of the loch. They were originally built as inns at either side of the main ferry crossing.

Several notable buildings have Campbell connections. The ruined island stronghold of Innischonnel Castle was where the ancestors of the Duke of Argyll established themselves in the 12th century, long before making the move to Inveraray.

Kilchurn Castle, a dramatically situated ancient monument on a marshy peninsula towered over by Ben Cruachan, was built in the 15th century by the Campbells of Glenorchy, later Earls of Breadalbane, before they too moved elsewhere.

On a smaller scale, St Conan's Kirk on the outskirts of Lochawe village, built between 1881 and 1930, was designed by Walter Campbell of Innischonain to have an almost eccentric variety of architectural styles and details.

🚗 *THE A85 reaches the north shore of Loch Awe 1 mile west of Dalmally.*

LOCH ECK
Argyll and Bute

The steep hillsides around Loch Eck are mostly owned by the Forestry Commission; but in its mixture of

McCaig's Tower, set high on a hill above Oban, is perhaps the town's best-known feature

LUSS
Dumbarton

Although the Colquhouns have been lairds of Luss on Loch Lomondside for nearly 800 years, the present village of attractive single-storey cottages dates only from the middle of the 19th century.

Luss has a shingle beach, a pier for the Loch Lomond cruises and a splendid view northwards to the 3192-ft Ben Lomond. Its dignified parish church was built in 1875 in memory of one of the lairds, who was drowned in a winter storm.

A narrow road climbs into Glen Luss, opening up a panoramic view of the wooded islands which crowd the southern end of the loch.

LUSS is on the A82, 8 miles north of Balloch.

OBAN
Argyll and Bute

Holiday resort, railhead, yacht anchorage, fishing harbour, ferry terminal for half a dozen islands — Oban is a place of constant comings and goings. Its Victorian houses climb from the shore of a bay, and it is a town with many walks on ridges and wooded hills.

McCaig's Tower is the classic high-level viewpoint — a massive, turn-of-the-century round tower in Argyll granite with arched window openings. In daytime, it provides breathtaking views over Kerrera to the mountains of Mull and Morvern; later, the attraction is the other way round, as the tower is floodlit against the evening sky.

Another favoured view is from Pulpit Hill, the wooded crag which rises south of the bay.

Northwards, the shore road to Ganavan Sands passes below the hilltop ruin of Dunollie Castle, the home until the mid-18th century of the MacDougall chiefs, whose modern home is nearby.

🚗 *OBAN is at the junction of the A85 from Dalmally and the A816 from Lochgilphead.*

PORT APPIN
Argyll and Bute

Although steamer calls are a thing of the past, Port Appin still has a passenger ferry to the north end of the island of Lismore.

From the wooded ridge above the cottages which lead to the jetty, there is a wide-ranging view over Lismore and the skerries north of it to the rugged hills of Kingairloch. A very fine coastal walk circles the ridge.

North of the village is the restored and spectacularly located island tower of Castle Stalker, once a royal hunting resort and a stronghold of the Stewarts.

🚗 *PORT APPIN is reached by a side-road off the A828, 22 miles north of Oban*

SEA LIFE CENTRE
Argyll and Bute

Outdoor activities around the village of Barcaldine include forest walks, trout fishing in a hill reservoir, sailing and sea-angling in Loch Creran. The loch is also the base of a commercial fish-farm, whose owners in 1979 established the Sea Life Centre in a pinewood beside a rocky bay.

It has indoor display tanks of fish as different in character and appearance as rays and eels. Herring show off their compulsion to swim in shoals. And twice a day there is a flurry of elegant activity as the seals cavort around while waiting to be fed in their outdoor pool.

🚗 *THE SEA LIFE CENTRE is on the A828, 10 miles north of Oban.*

SOUTHEND
Argyll and Bute

This is the last village in Kintyre, with excellent beaches and a fine golf course. On the rock of Dunaverty is the site of a castle taken by the Covenanting army in 1647, when everyone in it was slaughtered.

In a far gentler context, the traditional first landing place in Scotland of the crusading St Columba, when he came over as a missionary from Ireland in 563, was below the cliffs at Keil Point.

Away to the west, a convoluted hill road climbs to the pass known simply as 'The Gap', then plunges down towards the Mull of Kintyre lighthouse, with an impressive over-the-sea view to Rathlin Island and the Antrim coast.

🚗 *SOUTHEND is on the B842, 9 miles south of Campbeltown.*

TARBERT
Argyll and Bute

As it does elsewhere, this name describes a narrow isthmus over which a boat can be manhandled. At the end of the 11th century, tradition insists that Magnus Barefoot craftily ordered his men to haul his galley across the neck of land which connects the peninsula of Kintyre to the rest of the Scottish mainland, and

was thus able to claim Kintyre as Norse territory, within the terms of a treaty which gave the Vikings all the land they could sail a boat round.

After they were driven out of Scotland in 1263, Tarbert continued to be a significant place. Robert the Bruce extended an existing castle here in the 1320s, and the castle ruin still overlooks the sheltered bay.

It was this deep-set bay which caused the present village to be built around it. Tarbert was an ideal harbour for the 19th-century herring fishing in Loch Fyne.

There is less fishing now than there used to be, but Tarbert remains very popular with yachtsmen.

TARBERT is on the A83, 14 miles south of Lochgilphead.

TOBERMORY
Argyll and Bute

This waterside town, where colour-washed houses backed by wooded hills face a natural harbour, never reached the heights of prosperity its creators expected. Tobermory was established at the end of the 1780s by the British Fisheries Society; but once the railways reached the mainland fishing ports, the east coast of Mull was inconveniently far from the markets.

It remains the only town, rather than village, on the whole of Mull, with products ranging from pottery to malt whisky, and it is a famous yachting harbour — the finishing point of a summer race from the Clyde which regularly attracts more than 200 crews.

There are invigorating coastal walks on each side of the bay, the one to the south-east heading into the Forestry Commission's Aros Park. Speculation continues about a Spanish Armada galleon known to have sunk in the bay; but recent research has proved that the treasure-ship it was once believed to be actually reached home safely.

TOBERMORY is on the A848, 21 miles north-west of the ferry terminal at Craignure.

Southend (*left*) is a popular holiday destination
The colour-washed houses of Tobermory (*right*)

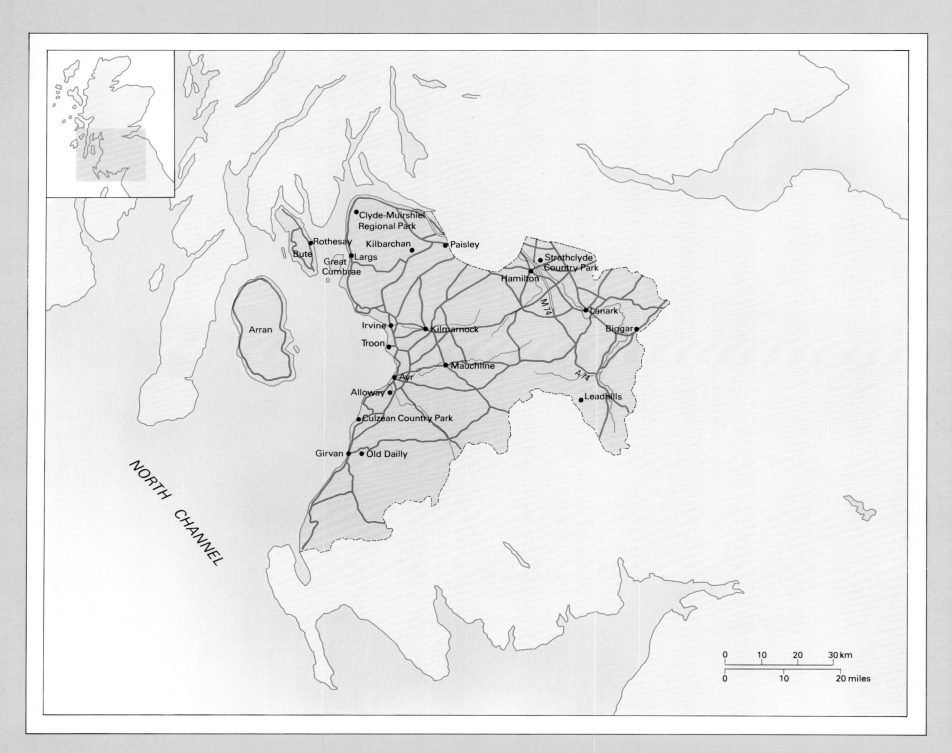

Clyde-Muirshiel
Regional Park

Rothesay
Bute
Great
Cumbrae
Largs
Kilbarchan
Paisley
Strathclyde
Country Park
Hamilton
M 74
Lanark
Biggar
Arran
Irvine
Kilmarnock
Troon
Mauchline
A 74
Ayr
Alloway
Leadhills
Culzean Country Park
Girvan
Old Dailly

NORTH CHANNEL

0   10   20   30 km

0   10   20 miles

The streets of Lanark come alive once a year at the time of the Lanimer Week celebrations. Pipe bands create a blaze of colour in this thoroughly Scottish spectacle

LANDSCAPES IN SOUTH STRATHCLYDE are at extremes. There are towns in the industrial belt and — not far away — high, heathery grouse moors. Through the heart of Ayrshire, rich farmland sweeps south to meet up with the forested hills of Carrick. And the gentle, dairy-herd country on some of the islands in the Firth of Clyde contrasts with the massive rock of Ailsa Craig and the granite peaks of Arran.

For generations, the Ayrshire coast and the islands have been places where people go to relax. And this process shows no signs of slackening off. The golf courses on the coastal links regularly play host to the Open Championship. Watersports of all kinds are enjoyed here, on a coast which has marinas, island cruising grounds and sailing schools.

Arran is a splendid centre for hill-walking and rock-climbing. Major recreational areas run from privately-owned woodland estates to a 30,000-acre Regional Park.

This is a country of long memories. Robert Burns's appeal to Scots world-wide has never faded. The Covenanters — stern defenders of the Presbyterian faith in the religious civil wars of the 17th century — are remembered in towns and villages, churches, memorials and the lonely places where, with guards posted against the arrival of government troops whose mission was to hunt them down, they held their services out of doors.

ALLOWAY
Kyle and Carrick

Robert Burns was born here, in what is now a leafy suburb of the town of Ayr, in the house his father built — a thatched-roofed, whitewashed cottage on the edge of his market garden.

Sold off for a time as an inn, the house was later rescued; it and the museum built alongside it are open to the public, showing some of Burns's belongings, paintings and original manuscripts.

The ruined 16th-century Alloway Kirk is much as it was when Burns described how Tam o'Shanter stumbled on the witches and warlocks revelling there.

The furious chase which followed came to its climax at the old single-arch bridge over the River Doon, still preserved. Overlooking the bridge are the gardens of the Burns Monument completed in 1823.

Nearby, the Land o'Burns Centre is an ambitious exhibition of his life and works, and of the Burns Country named after him, with an audio-visual theatre, other displays and an extensive bookshop.

ALLOWAY is on the B7024, south of Ayr.

ARRAN
Cunninghame

With its jagged-outline granite mountains, Arran is like an only-just miniature Skye deposited by accident in the Firth of Clyde. The north-eastern quarter of the island is made up of a series of spectacular peaks and ridges, corries and glens which provide excellent rock-climbing, scrambling and hill-walking as well as the backdrop to some dramatic views.

This is uncompromising mountain country at a substantial height. Goat Fell is the highest point at 2866 ft, and although there is a 'tourist path' to the summit, a jigsaw-puzzle of curving saddles opens up an area best left to experienced ridge-walkers.

But there is a much milder Arran too. Brodick, at the foot of Goat Fell, is the main ferry port on Arran, and its principal holiday resort, with sandy beaches which families have enjoyed for generations.

To the north of the village is the Isle of Arran Heritage Museum, created from a collection of 18th-century croft buildings. A fine golf course — one of seven on the island — is laid out around the tidal lagoons of the Glenrosa Water.

Other sports for which Arran provides facilities include bowls and tennis; riding and pony-trekking; sailing, windsurfing and diving; sea-angling as well as salmon and trout-fishing on the rivers — the Machrie, the Rosa, the Sannox, the Cloy and the oddly-named Sliddery.

Away from the north-eastern mountains, Arran has footpaths through forest plantations and around the southern moorlands where standing stones, cairns and vitrified forts point to a pre-history reaching back to Neolithic times.

Round its 56-mile coast road there are a dozen holiday villages from Lochranza at the north-west corner where whitewashed houses and a ruined castle look over a sea-loch, and a summer car-ferry runs to Claonaig in Kintyre, to Kildonan in the south-east with its view to the rocky lighthouse island of Pladda and — farther away — to the massive 'granite haystack' of Ailsa Craig.

Whiting Bay is a modern village with a walk to a 200-ft waterfall in Glenashdale, and, at Kingscross, the

In the heart of Burns's country are these beautifully-kept gardens and the bridge at Alloway

place from which Robert the Bruce set sail in 1307 to start his guerilla war to wrest back control of Scotland from the English.

Lamlash is the administrative centre of the island, looking out over a sheltered anchorage where the Viking fleet gathered before being defeated, across the Firth, at the Battle of Largs in 1263.

Some of the Vikings with time on their hands carved messages still to be seen on the walls of caves on the 1030-ft Holy Island which holds off the easterly wind. The island can be visited from Lamlash.

The showpiece of Arran is Brodick Castle, whose earliest part dates from the 14th century, although it was completed in its present-day form in the 1840s.

For generations one of the homes of the Dukes of Hamilton, the castle — with its woodlands and the gardens with their extensive collection of flowering shrubs from China, Burma, Tibet, South America, Australia and New Zealand — is now owned by the National Trust for Scotland.

ARDROSSAN on the Ayrshire coast is the departure point for the main Arran car-ferry.

AYR
Kyle and Carrick

Recognised as a royal burgh in the early 13th century, Ayr is a town with two distinct aspects.

One is to the sea. More than two miles of esplanades and fine sandy beaches stretch southwards from the mouth of the River Ayr, passing the headquarters of two sailing clubs. North of the river is the harbour area.

But Ayr is also a county town, the focus of the administrative, trading, business, sporting and social life of central Ayrshire's inland villages, farms and landed estates.

Either by purchase or by gift, Ayr has gathered into public ownership a remarkable number of parks, gardens, sports grounds and other open spaces.

There are three 18-hole golf courses actually inside the town, as well as major parks at Belleisle, Craigie and Rozelle. The last of these has nature trails, a handsome Georgian mansion used for exhibitions, an art gallery and a sculpture garden. The Dam Park is the venue, every August, for Scotland's largest flower show.

The old racecourse is now given over to sports fields, while the present-day racecourse, home of the Ayr Gold Cup and the Scottish Grand National, is the busiest and most important centre of Flat and National Hunt racing in the country.

Robert Burns was baptised in the Auld Kirk of Ayr, and the town, naturally, keeps his memory alive. Burns Statue Square should be one of the architectural features of the place, but some of the modern buildings sadly let it down.

In the High Street, the Tam o'Shanter Museum is given over to Burns displays. In Burns's day the building was a brewery, and one of the farmers who supplied it with malted grain was none other than Douglas Graham of Shanter — the original of the ballad's hero Tam.

AYR is 32 miles south-west of Glasgow.

BIGGAR
Clydesdale

In 1451, James II granted Biggar its burgh charter, and the right to hold weekly markets. Over the years, it developed into a pleasant, spacious market town on the edge of the hill-country between the Clyde and the Tweed.

The Tam o'Shanter Museum, one of Ayr's most popular attractions, is dedicated to the local poet, Robert Burns

A taste of bygone days is preserved at Biggar

Biggar people are remarkably keen on preserving the past, and have created their own Museum Trust.

It runs the Gladstone Court Museum — a splendid re-creation, using the original shop-fronts, of the grocer's, chemist's, ironmonger's, bootmaker's and so on which used to serve the town; a Heritage Centre in the mid-Victorian Moat Park Church; and Greenhill, a historic farmhouse re-erected in a riverside park to provide an exhibition on the Covenanters.

Even the gasworks, which closed in the 1970s after being at work for more than 130 years, is now an out-station of the Royal Scottish Museum in Edinburgh.

BIGGAR is on the A702, 29 miles south of Edinburgh.

BUTE
Argyll and Bute

After Arran, this is the biggest of the islands in the Firth of Clyde; but it is very different in appearance. The appeal of Bute is not in mountains, but in a fine variety of low hills, rolling farmland, open moorlands and attractive woods.

Rothesay, the island town, has been one of the favourite Clyde Coast holiday resorts since the days when the steamers began operating.

Here and in other parts of the island there are facilities for golf, bowling, tennis, fishing, diving, swimming and pony-trekking. Rothesay Bay and Kames Bay, to the north, are good sailing centres.

Rothesay is a mainly Victorian town which was built round its extensive bay.

There are walks to the north-west in the Skeoch Wood, and again to the north-east in Bogany Wood, which is planted on the side of Canada Hill — so-called because it was from here

that the people left behind had their last glimpse of the sailing-ships taking emigrants to a new life in North America.

In happier days, Canada Hill remains an excellent viewpoint over the Firth of Clyde and the mainland hills. Rothesay's golf course, designed by the great James Braid, sweeps towards the summit. The motorist's way to it is up through the hairpin bends of the well-named Serpentine Road.

The Bute Museum on Rothesay's Chapelhill has comprehensive displays on the island's history, archaeology and wildlife.

Nearby is the most imposing historic building on Bute — the partly

Pony-trekking is popular along Bute's pebbly shores

restored 13th-century Rothesay Castle, standing behind a moat in the very centre of the town.

For over a century it was one of the regular residences of the Scottish kings. In 1398, Robert III created his eldest son Duke of Rothesay. As the present-day heir to the throne, Prince Charles retains that as his principal Scottish title.

Following the main coast road round the foot of Canada Hill — through Craigmore and Orcadia, past the gardens and glasshouses of Ardencraig, and beyond the village of

Ascog whose churchyard contains only a single grave — leads to the unexpected sight of Kerrycroy, a hamlet at the entrance to the grounds of Mountstuart, the mid-Victorian mansion of the 6th Marquess of Bute.

The 2nd Marchioness had Kerrycroy built in the style of a typical English estate village, complete with half-timbered cottages round a maypole.

There is another holiday resort village at Kilchattan Bay on the south-east coast. Sandy bays are strung along the west coast at Dunagoil, Stravanan, Scalpsie and Ettrick.

And the depression which runs diagonally across the centre of Bute

accommodates a line of open waterways — the Kirk Dam, Loch Fad and Loch Quien — which point directly at the mountain peaks of Arran, only one of many superb views on this beautiful and varied island.

⛴ *THE CAR-FERRY TO ROTHESAY sails from Wemyss Bay on the A78. A smaller car-ferry to Rhubodach at the north end of the island leaves from Colintraive on the A886.*

CLYDE-MUIRSHIEL REGIONAL PARK
Inverclyde / Renfrew / Cunninghame

Covering 30,000 acres in public and

private ownership — lochs, glens, woodlands, high sheep farms and grouse moors — this 'park' is left mostly in its entirely natural state.

There are four major access points, each with its own information centre and each with a quite different appeal.

Cornalees Bridge is on the outflow from the Loch Thom scheme of reservoirs and 'cuts' — or open channels — which supplied water to the houses, mills and factories of Greenock from 1827 until the cuts were made redundant in 1971.

Now the area is a preserved industrial monument; but there is also a great deal of wildlife interest around the moorland tracks which follow the cuts to high-level viewpoints over the Firth of Clyde.

Muirshiel is an old estate in the lonely headwaters of the River Calder. Surrounded by grouse moors, it has woodland trails and a series of rocky waterfalls.

Lower down, Castle Semple Loch has been turned into a recreational area for rowers, dinghy-sailors, canoeists and coarse anglers who fish for pike, perch and roach.

At one time a part of Castle Semple Loch, Aird Meadow was then drained in an effort to transform it into arable land; but it has now gone back to marsh, and is a reserve of the Royal Society for the Protection of Birds.

There are ground-level observation hides on the edge of scrubby woodland and a visitor centre with a first-floor viewing area over a habitat which attracts more than 100 species of resident and migrant wildfowl.

🚗 *CORNALEES BRIDGE is 3 miles east of Inverkip on the A78. Muirshiel is 4 miles north-west of Lochwinnoch on the B786. Castle Semple Loch and Aird Meadow are immediately east of Lochwinnoch.*

CULZEAN COUNTRY PARK
Kyle and Carrick

If Clyde-Muirshiel is left largely in its natural state, Culzean is a park of an entirely different character. It is a one-time private estate on which generations of landowners lavished attention: more than 500 acres of woodlands and shoreline centred on a glorious Adam castle on a clifftop overlooking the Firth of Clyde.

Culzean Castle, built in the second half of the 18th century for the Earls of Cassillis, was offered to the National Trust for Scotland in 1945 by their successor as head of the Kennedy family, the 5th Marquess of Ailsa.

The Trust still owns the castle, while the grounds form a Country Park managed by it for various local authorities.

Guided tours of the castle show off its impeccable furnishings and spectacular architectural details, like the superb oval staircase and the round drawing room high above the sea.

Many of the original plans of the castle, and information on the running of the estate through the years, are on show in the Park Centre which has been created by the restoration of Robert Adam's stylish but practical Home Farm complex.

Reminders of the spacious days when Culzean was a genuinely stately home are ornamental features in the grounds like the Orangery, the Camellia House, the Fountain Court, the swan pond, aviary and walled garden.

But there are many purpose-built features too: a bath house and ice house, the estate's own gas house, a fire pond, pathways originally in-

Red deer, although a rare species, can still be spotted at Culzean

tended for gamekeepers and laundrymaids hurrying about their work.

The beautiful and varied woodlands are criss-crossed by footpaths. Others follow the clifftops and descend to secluded beaches. And a series of sea-caves bite deep into the sandstone cliffs.

CULZEAN is on the A719, 13 miles south-west of Ayr.

GIRVAN
Kyle and Carrick

Looking directly out across the Firth of Clyde to the huge, isolated rock of Ailsa Craig, Girvan is a holiday resort with a long sandy beach, sports facilities and entertainments.

But it is also a fishing port with an attractive riverside harbour where gulls racket around as catches are being landed.

Ten miles offshore, Ailsa Craig appears from this angle to be virtually sheer-sided. But Girvan boat-hirers take parties to the island.

Only lighthouse-keepers occupy it now, but there is plenty to see from the steep, zig-zag path which starts from the derelict gas-works beside the lighthouse, passes a small ruined castle and then climbs dizzily above it to the 1110-ft summit.

The 360-degree view is magnificent, taking in the coast of Ireland, Kintyre and the Galloway Hills, and the island peaks of Arran and Jura.

Bird-watchers will also be impressed by the traffic of gannets around their fishing grounds in the Firth from the thousands of nests on the southern and western cliffs of Ailsa Craig itself.

GIRVAN is on the A77, 22 miles south of Ayr.

GREAT CUMBRAE
Cunninghame

This is an island to which generations of holidaymakers have returned year after year. The inland hills are partly given over to sheep and dairy-farming, while the 11-mile coast road passes a Marine Biological Station open to the public, the massive lava dyke known as the Lion Rock, the National Water Sports Training Centre and — on the west coast facing across the Firth of Clyde to the island of Bute — red-sandstone inlets where shelduck gather, and a beautiful beach at Fintray Bay.

An 'inner circle' road leads to the Glaid Stone, Cumbrae's highest point at 415 ft, below which stretches a well laid-out golf course.

The only town on the island is Millport, spreading for two miles round a semi-circular bay with a cluster of rocky points and islets. The Garrison, originally built by the captain of an 18th-century revenue cutter, houses the Museum of the Cumbraes.

One of many pleasant walks is along the ridge of the Farland Hills which shelter Millport from the easterly winds — especially on a clear evening when, beyond the lights of the town and of the yachts and cruisers anchored in the bay, the sun sets over the mountain peaks of Arran.

THE CAR-FERRY for Cumbrae sails from Largs on the A78.

HAMILTON
Hamilton

This sprawling town above the south bank of the Clyde is a place with a very long history, mentioned under its original name of Cadzow in accounts of events in the 6th century.

Robert the Bruce gave the lands of Cadzow to the Hamilton family, and a royal charter of 1445 later changed the town's name to theirs.

On the outskirts is the extraordinary mausoleum completed in 1854 for the 10th Duke of Hamilton. Guided tours allow demonstrations of the remarkably long-lasting echo inside its towering dome.

In its historic core, Hamilton retains some other impressive buildings. Hamilton Museum was originally a 17th-century coaching inn.

Nearby, a Victorian riding school has been transformed into a museum

A thriving fishing industry means that Girvan does not have to depend on tourism alone for its income

Robert Burns

Burns had a love life of almost unravellable complications. In mellow reflection on his passions, he wrote some of the world's gentlest and longest-enduring love songs.

After his first book of poems was published in 1786, he took the sophisticated literary society of Edinburgh by storm. But one glowing review contained the millstone-round-the-neck phrase 'heaven-sent ploughman'.

Burns was in fact a well-educated and well-read tenant farmer; a lively conversationalist with a quick if often outrageous turn of speech and actions.

Memories of literary conversations fade quickly. Raffish behaviour can hardly establish a long-term reputation. Love songs are not entirely the

It says a great deal about Lowland Scots that the towering personality they recognise above all others is not a politician or a general or an industrialist — but a poet.

Robert Burns, dead almost 200 years, retains an enthusiastic and affectionate following, not only in Scotland but also in every continent where Scots have settled.

The anniversary of his birth in 1759 — 25 January — is celebrated all over the world in traditional-style Burns Suppers; and that date is referred to in Scotland, as a matter of course, as Burns Night.

Robert Burns was born in this whitewashed cottage in Alloway (*above*). He and his wife Jean rented a room in this house at Mauchline (*below*), now a museum

stuff of immortality.

But Burns was also a liberal, crusader and annihilating satirist. *Holy Willie's Prayer* and *Address to the Deil* savaged the ultra-conservatives in the 18th-century Scottish church as no amount of pamphlet-writing or speechifying could have done. Away from disputations, he created in *Tam O'Shanter* the fastest-moving and most uproarious of Scottish ballads.

Burns was in tune with the early ideals of the French Revolution. And part of his lasting appeal is that, in poems like *A Man's a Man for A' That*, he delivered some of the most powerful declarations of equality ever written.

It sums him up that, in every Burns Supper throughout the world, although one toast is 'To the Lassies', the main speaker of the evening proposes his 'Immortal Memory'.

of the Cameronians — the locally-raised regiment formed from the ranks of the Covenanters after the Glorious Revolution of 1688 ended their half-century of relentless persecution.

East of the town there is a country park split by the winding and thickly-wooded Avon Gorge. On one side of the river is the ruin of the Hamiltons' old stronghold of Cadzow Castle.

On the other side is Chatelherault, a restored 18th-century hunting lodge in the grand style. The Dukes of Hamilton are also the Dukes of Chatelherault in France.

🚗 *HAMILTON is off the M74, south-east of Glasgow.*

IRVINE
Cunninghame

As one of Scotland's New Towns, Irvine has its fair share of industrial development, bypass roads and up-to-date recreational facilities — both indoors and outdoors, notably at the multi-million pound Magnum Centre and the Beach Park around it.

But Irvine also pays great attention to the past. The old harbour area on the river is being rebuilt as the Scottish Maritime Museum; and Irvine Burns Club is one of the most important in the world, with an irreplaceable collection of documents, paintings, and rare first editions.

The club has also been closely involved with the restoration of the Glasgow Vennel, the street where Burns's efforts as a young man to make a trade out of flax-dressing were frustrated by the 'scoundrel of the first water' his partner turned out to be, and by 'the drunken carelessness of my partner's wife', who started a fire which gutted the shop during her New Year carousings in 1782.

Dean Castle Country Park, Kilmarnock, lies amid a 200-acre estate

However, it was in Irvine that Burns was first advised to think about publishing his poems, and here that he discovered the works of Robert Fergusson, whom he regarded for the rest of his life as his poetic mentor.

🚗 *IRVINE is 11 miles north of Ayr.*

KILBARCHAN
Renfrew

In 1723 the Bryden family built themselves a cottage in the heart of this weavers' village; and the same house, still with the Brydens' initials carved on the lintel, is carefully preserved as a museum, not simply of the long-since abandoned handloom-weaving trade, but also of the furniture, furnishings, clothes and domestic equipment of generations gone by.

The Weaver's Cottage is now in the hands of the National Trust for Scotland, and a working loom has been re-installed in the ground-floor workshop where generations of Brydens, Brodies and Christies bent to their shuttles.

🚗 *KILBARCHAN is off the A761, 5 miles west of Paisley.*

KILMARNOCK
Kilmarnock and Loudoun

Always a rival to Ayr, Kilmarnock is the industrial centre of what used to be the county of Ayrshire, and the home of one of the world's best-known brands of Scotch whisky.

The town played a very important part in the life of Robert Burns, because in 1786 the local printer John Wilson produced the first — 'Kilmarnock' — edition of his *Poems, Chiefly in the Scottish Dialect.*

Wilson's printing shop has gone, but its site is marked by a plaque in the town's shopping centre.

There is a Burns Memorial in the

Kay Park, but Kilmarnock is better known for the Dean Castle Country Park — 200 acres of woods and farmland where the Fenwick and Craufurdland Waters meet. It is centred on the basically 14th-century castle of the Boyd family, which features collections of musical instruments and tapestries, and a well-presented medieval armoury.

🚗 *KILMARNOCK is off the A77, 21 miles south of Glasgow.*

LARGS
Cunninghame

One of the most significant encounters in Scottish history took place at Largs in 1263. Alexander III, having failed in negotiations with the Vikings, defeated their battle fleet here. They gave up control of all the Hebrides, holding on for a few years more only to Orkney and Shetland.

With enthusiastic Norwegian help, Largs celebrates the occasion every September with a Viking Festival of sports, parades, bonfires and music.

Largs is a well-equipped holiday resort on the Firth of Clyde, with facilities for all kinds of sports from windsurfing to golf. The most prominent of its open spaces is Douglas Park, which begins among formal gardens in the town itself and sweeps uphill to a magnificent viewpoint over the Firth and its islands.

Back down among the shoppers and visitors, a little lane off the main street leads to the sole remaining aisle of the old parish church.

Maintained as an ancient monument, the Skelmorlie Aisle contains the Renaissance-style tomb built in 1636 for the Montgomeries of Skelmorlie, and its barrel-vaulted ceiling retains the original painted scenes, emblems and Zodiacal signs.

South of the town, Kelburn Castle is the home of the Earl of Glasgow, whose family have been here since the 12th century. Its extensive grounds, on both sides of the fine ravine where the Kel Burn cascades over waterfalls, are now a Country Centre, with winding paths through woodlands of beech and ash, oak, sycamore, chestnut, birch and spruce.

🚗 *LARGS is on the A78, 30 miles north of Ayr.*

LANARK
Clydesdale

At the foot of the busy High Street, Lanark Cross is the focus of interest in this market town in the heart of Covenanter country. Its history goes back to a royal charter, now lost but believed to have been signed by David II at Lanark Castle in 1140.

William Wallace, Bruce's predecessor in the independence wars of the 13th and 14th centuries, had a house near the Cross. And this is where the Lanimer Week celebrations come to an end with the crowning of the Lanimer Queen.

To the east, Lanark Moor is the town's historic common land. The racecourse here has, sadly, been given up for regular events; but the moor is still parkland, with woods, a loch and an excellent golf course.

A side-road in the town leads to what is probably Scotland's grandest industrial monument — the village of New Lanark, established in the 1780s where the water-power of the River Clyde would turn the machinery of its cotton mills.

Although the last mill closed in 1968, a massive restoration programme has preserved New Lanark as it was in the heyday of Robert

Although a lived-in village New Lanark remains as it was in the time of Robert Owen

Owen's pioneering social experiments; but it is still a lived-in village, and no moribund museum.

From Caithness Row at the east of the village, a nature trail leads up to the wide and rocky Falls of Clyde. Although a hydro-electric power scheme taps most of the water before it tumbles over the Falls, on a few days every year their full majestic flow is restored.

🚗 *LANARK is 14 miles south-east of Hamilton.*

LEADHILLS
Clydesdale

In the 16th century, James V had some sceptical French guests served with 'fruit' from the seemingly barren Lowther Hills — dishes heaped with gold coins.

But the later riches of the Lowthers came from the mineral which gave the remote village of Leadhills its name. It is still lived in, although the last of the mine-workings closed in 1928.

There are memorials to John Taylor, whom the lively upland air allowed to survive until the ripe age of 137, and to William Symington, designer in 1788 of the world's first steamboat engine. And the library of the Leadhills Miners' Reading Society still serves subscribers today, after more than 240 years.

🚗 *LEADHILLS is on the B797, 6 miles south of Abington.*

MAUCHLINE
Cumnock and Doon Valley

This is one of the important stops on the Burns Heritage Trail — the town where many of the characters lambasted in his most famous satires were all too clearly identifiable, but where he also made influential friends, many of whom are buried in

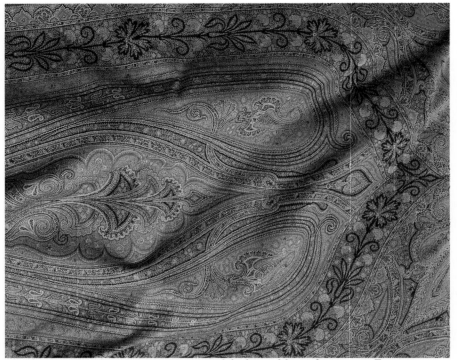

The famous Paisley pattern captivated fashionable 19th-century Europeans

the parish churchyard.

The two-storey stone-and-slate house where Burns and his wife Jean Armour first rented a room has been turned into an attractively laid-out museum, and not just on the Burns theme. There are displays on the town's most famous industries — the old Mauchline box-ware much prized by collectors, and the still-in-production curling-stone factory.

To the north, the ornate red-sandstone tower of the National Burns Memorial is a viewpoint over the fields of Mossgiel where the brothers Robert and Gilbert Burns struggled through some difficult years as tenant farmers, and where the poet, one harvest-time, encountered the 'wee, sleekit, cowrin, tim'rous beastie' which figures in *To a Mouse*.

🚗 *MAUCHLINE is on the A76, 8 miles south of Kilmarnock.*

OLD DAILLY
Kyle and Carrick

Time has passed this village by; but it has left the mellowed and well-kept ruin of the original parish church, with its notable Covenanter memorials.

To the east lies the historic estate of Bargany, whose beautiful woodland gardens, around an ornamental lake and down a narrow glen, are open to the public most of the year.

In the hills above Old Dailly, guided tours can be arranged of the astonishing Penkill Castle, lavishly rebuilt and refurnished in Victorian times with paintings, tapestries, murals and architectural details contributed by the Pre-Raphaelite artists who were friends of the laird.

🚗 *OLD DAILLY is on the B734, 3 miles east of Girvan.*

PAISLEY
Renfrew

In 1163 Walter FitzAlan was given a charter to establish a priory near the banks of the White Cart Water. It was soon elevated to the status of an abbey; and through all the changing years Paisley Abbey — now a charge of the Church of Scotland — has remained the dignified centre of the town.

Walter FitzAlan was also David I's hereditary High Steward of Scotland. His successors changed their surname to Stewart and eventually to Stuart.

This was the line which produced the monarchs of Scotland and, later, of the United Kingdom, from Robert II — grandson of Robert the Bruce — to that James VII of Scotland and II of England who abandoned his throne in 1688.

All but one of the original line of High Stewards are buried in the Abbey, which has memorials, wood-carving and stained glass windows of the highest order. And the long years over which it achieved its present form are shown by the progression of architectural styles, from the Romanesque onwards.

The Museum and Art Galleries in the High Street display hundreds of 'Paisley pattern' shawls — based on Kashmiri designs — which were the height of European fashion for much of the 19th century.

Behind the Museum, the Coats Observatory — concerned with satellite weather reports, seismological recordings and general astronomical work — has regular guided tours.

Rising to the south of the town, the road to the 1000-acre Gleniffer Country Park — with its walks, picnic areas and wide-ranging views — was used in Edwardian times as a test hill for the pioneering Arrol-Johnston

All manner of sports and leisure pursuits are practised in the Strathclyde Country Park

cars, and again in the 1920s for the thousands of Beardmore taxis which Paisley sent to the cab-ranks of London and other British cities.

PAISLEY is on the A737, west of Glasgow.

STRATHCLYDE COUNTRY PARK
Motherwell/Hamilton

Occupying the riverside ground between the towns of Motherwell and Hamilton, this recreational area centres on a 200-acre artificial lake beside the Clyde, used for training and competitions in sailing, rowing and canoeing.

On land, there are three main sports pavilions serving football, rugby, hockey and cricket pitches; a golf course; nature trails and other walks to locations like the excavated bath-house built by the Romans.

STRATHCLYDE COUNTRY PARK is reached from Junctions 4 and 5 on the M74.

TROON
Kyle and Carrick

Of all the resorts on the Ayrshire coast, where most things take second place to golf, Troon devotes more space to it than any other. The town is ringed by no fewer than five 18-hole courses and has played host to several Open Championships.

One local hotel has a 'real' — rather than lawn — tennis court; there is an archery club; a riding academy teaches equitation in the classic style; and an extensive marina occupies the old inner harbour, on the curving promontory that reminded the early settlers who gave the place its name of the shape of a nose — for which their word was 'trwyn'.

TROON is on the A759, 6 miles north of Ayr.

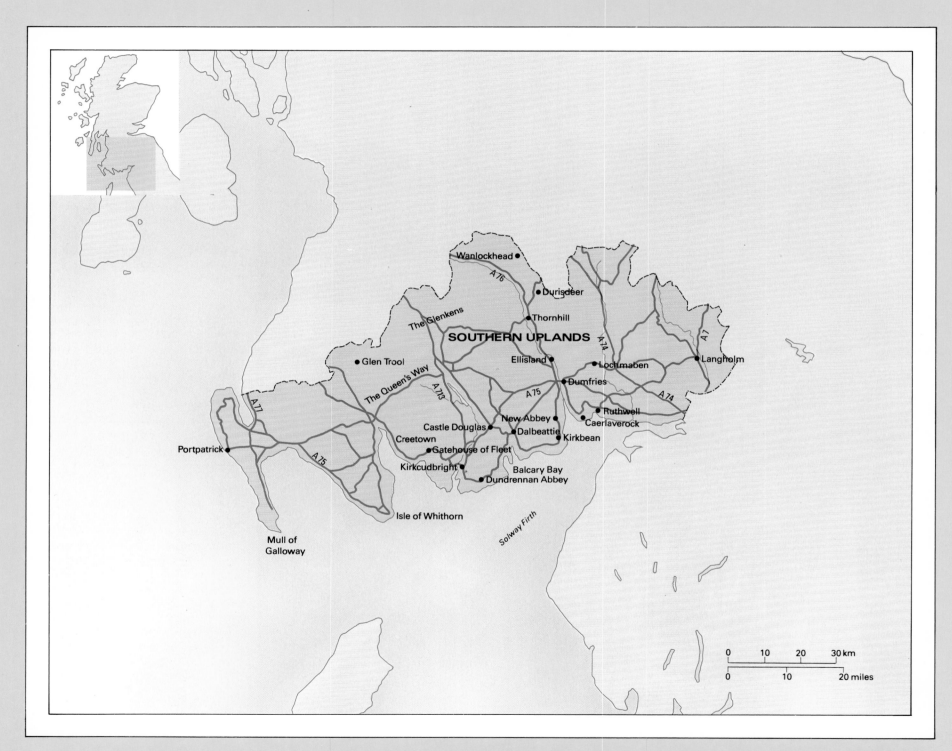

Wanlockhead ●

● Durisdeer

A 76

The Glenkens

● Thornhill

SOUTHERN UPLANDS

A 74

A 7

● Glen Trool

Ellisland ●

● Lochmaben

● Langholm

The Queen's Way

A 713

● Dumfries

A 75

A 74

A 77

New Abbey ●

● Ruthwell

Castle Douglas ●

Dalbeattie ●

Caerlaverock

Creetown

● Kirkbean

Portpatrick ●

● Gatehouse of Fleet

A 75

Balcary Bay

Kirkcudbright ●

● Dundrennan Abbey

Isle of Whithorn

Solway Firth

Mull of
Galloway

| 0 | 10 | 20 | 30 km |

| 0 | 10 | 20 miles |

Dumfries & Galloway

High above Loch Trool stands Bruce's Stone, facing the spot where Robert the Bruce defeated the English at Glen Trool

SCOTLAND'S WESTERN BORDER with England is formed by the unobtrusive meanders of the little River Sark, which flows into the head of the Solway Firth. As the Firth progresses and widens, it passes beautiful river estuaries on its way to the daunting cliffs of the Mull of Galloway, where sea-birds wheel around a wave-lashed lighthouse point.

Inland, there are richly farmed parishes with well-wooded estates, notable castles, fine gardens and busy market towns. But on The Moors of Wigtownshire, lowland dairy farms give way to bare peat-mosses where bog-cotton shivers in the breeze.

Galloway Forest Park covers 240 square miles of plantations, lochs and unexpectedly rugged hills; it also has a network of forest trails.

Galloway was the scene of Robert the Bruce's early victories against the occupying English armies. Mary, Queen of Scots spent her last night in Scotland at Dundrennan Abbey, on her way to exile.

Paul Jones, first Commander of the United States Navy, was born a gardener's son at Arbigland. Thomas Telford, the founding father of British civil engineering, was brought up in Glendinning.

And Dumfries is the last resting-place of Robert Burns, who in his later years moved from Ayrshire to be a farmer and revenue-officer in the district where his writings were as various as the stirring *Scots Wha Hae* and the rollicking *Tam o'Shanter*.

171

BALCARY BAY
Stewartry

One of the smaller inlets in the extensive tidal stretch of Auchencairn Bay, Balcary is one of the most timelessly beautiful places on the Solway Coast. A very old-established stake-net fishery still traps salmon when the tide recedes, and there is a fine view to the one-time smugglers' outpost on Hestan Island, a mile or so offshore.

But the smugglers were active on the mainland too. Balcary Bay Hotel has a bar converted from secret cellars excavated by the smuggling company who built the house in the first place.

A bracing walk leads uphill from the bay, starting on farmland then skimming along the top of sea-bird cliffs before turning round Balcary Point for a view of the Cumberland hills across the wider Solway Firth.

Here, it passes above the natural rock formation called Adam's Chair, from which lantern signals used to be given to contraband ships approaching secretly at night.
BALCARY BAY is 2 miles south-east of Auchencairn on the A711.

CAERLAVEROCK
Nithsdale

On its eastern side, the estuary of the River Nith turns along the ragged inlets and extensive salt-marshes of the Merse, a lonely and atmospheric part of the coast. Behind the Merse, stands one of the most striking castles in Scotland — the red-sandstone ruin of Caerlaverock.

The first castle here was built in the late 13th century, to the elegant triangular plan followed by its successors, with curtain walls between sturdy towers.

Protected by a surrounding earthwork and a moat, Caerlaverock

Caerlaverock Castle, a handsome ruin, once suffered a 13-week siege

was the stronghold of the Maxwell family. In 1640 Robert Maxwell, the 1st Earl of Nithsdale, held the castle for Charles I, but had to surrender it after a 13-week siege by the Covenanters. They partly dismantled it, for the last — but not by any means the first time in its turbulent career.

Beyond the castle, a National Nature Reserve and a Wildfowl Trust reserve cover almost 14,000 acres of salt-marsh and farmland, the winter roost of thousands of pinkfoot and greylag geese, and most of the population of barnacle geese from Spitzbergen.
CAERLAVEROCK is off the B725, 8 miles south-east of Dumfries.

CASTLE DOUGLAS
Stewartry

Originally, this was a village called Carlingwark, sharing its name with the loch on its southern boundary. But in 1792, raised to the status of a burgh, its name was changed to honour the landowner Sir William Douglas.

Castle Douglas grew into a well-planned town which has a famous market for Ayrshire and Galloway cattle. Carlingwark Loch is one of its major recreational features; dinghies sail among wooded islets, and there is a public park on the banks.

Beyond the south-west corner of the loch, the grounds of Threave

House are the National Trust for Scotland's School of Practical Gardening, open to visitors along with a woodland nature trail.

The Trust also owns Threave Wildfowl Refuge, bounded by the River Dee. This is a noted winter roost for migratory ducks and geese.

One of the islands in the Dee is the site of Threave Castle, the ruined but still purposeful four-storey fortress of the Black Douglases, reached by a short boat trip from the east bank.

It was built at the end of the 14th century with double protection against a surprise attack; although the castle is on the edge of its island, a right-angled moat ensures that it is surrounded on all sides by water.

Reached only by boat, Threave Castle is surrounded by a deep, lily-filled moat

Like Caerlaverock, its last military engagement was a successful siege by the Covenanters in 1640.

CASTLE DOUGLAS *is on the A75, 18 miles south-west of Dumfries.*

CREETOWN
Wigtown

Granite from the quarries near this village at the head of Wigtown Bay was used to build the Thames Embankment in London and the Mersey Docks in Liverpool. Nowadays, on a smaller scale, craft-workers here create jewellery from gold, silver and semi-precious stones, as well as from unusual kinds of wood.

The astonishing Gem Rock Museum houses a unique collection of minerals and gemstones. Among hundreds of these on display are rose quartz, malachite and jade; a massive amethyst geode; a 200 million year-old droplet of water encased in a South American agate; and a remarkable group of apparently dull-hued stones which come to brilliant multi-coloured life under ultra-violet light.

CREETOWN *is on the A75, 7 miles south-east of Newton Stewart.*

DALBEATTIE
Stewartry

Most of Dalbeattie — houses, churches, the square-towered town hall and the inevitable Queen Victoria Jubilee fountain — is built of granite. And it was the opening in the late 18th century of the huge quarry on Craignair Hill across the River Urr which sparked off the growth of this pleasant town with its variety of parks and open spaces.

Dalbeattie's own port on the Urr could take only shallow-draught vessels; so an old smuggling harbour called Boglescreek, a few miles down the winding course of the river, was enlarged to become the village of Palnackie. For generations, it sent locally-owned ships with cargoes of Dalbeattie granite, not only to British sea-port cities, but also to Scandinavia, Belgium and Portugal.

Down the other bank of the river, beyond the entrance to the trails in Solway Forest, the non-identical twin villages of Kippford and Rockcliffe, linked by a maze of beautiful viewpoint paths, face the almost excessively tidal estuary of the Urr.

Kippford has a long row of former quarrymen's, boatbuilders' and fishermen's cottages, and is the headquarters of the Solway Yacht Club.

Rockcliffe's villas among well-tended gardens look out over the sands and rocky outcrops which made it a favourite 19th-century bathing resort.

🚗 *DALBEATTIE is on the A711, 14 miles south-west of Dumfries.*

DUMFRIES
Nithsdale

Built along both sides of the winding River Nith, Dumfries was created a royal burgh as early as 1186, and it remains the largest town in Dumfries and Galloway.

Many historic events have been recorded here. In 1306 Robert the Bruce killed Sir John Comyn, representative of the English King Edward I, in the Greyfriars church, and committed himself to the independence war which ended in victory eight long years later.

Dumfries was only passively involved in the Jacobite Risings — because this was no Jacobite town. Bonnie Prince Charlie occupied it for three days in December 1745; but at that time, despite its up-river situation, Dumfries was far more in-

The Globe Inn, Dumfries, is full of Burns memorabilia

terested in developing its sea-going trade.

This was one of the reasons why Robert Burns moved to Dumfries in 1791: to devote himself wholeheartedly to his flourishing Excise career, as well as to the writing of the hundreds of songs which were the great creative output of his later years.

His second residence in the town showed how he was prospering — a solid, two-storey house in local sandstone.

In the summer of 1796, however, Burns took seriously ill. A doctor friend gave the fatal advice to try a sea-bathing cure in the Solway, which simply accelerated the condition.

He died at home in Dumfries, on 21 July. Two army regiments and a procession of thousands of mourners accompanied him to his last resting-place in St Michael's churchyard.

The Burns House, where his wife Jean outlived him by no fewer than 38 years, is now a well cared-for museum.

The main Dumfries Museum, however, is a larger and very well equipped one on higher ground. It began life as an 18th-century windmill, and the top of the old windmill tower houses a camera obscura, which still gives an intriguing outlook over activity down in the town.

🚗 *DUMFRIES is on the A75, 25 miles west of Gretna.*

DUNDRENNAN ABBEY
Stewartry

Very little is known of this substantial but out-of-the-way Cistercian house from its founding in 1142 until the May evening in 1568 when it finally entered the mainstream of Scottish history.

Mary, Queen of Scots, having abdicated her throne, spent her last night on Scottish soil here. Next morning, she took a ship across the Solway Firth from the little natural

harbour now called Port Mary.

But exile in Queen Elizabeth's England was no safer for the woman who was, after all, next in succession to *that* throne. Elizabeth had her cousin held under house arrest for 19 years, and then ordered her execution.

Dundrennan is now a gracious ancient monument. Major parts of the cloister, the chapter-house and the abbey church are still standing. Among its many memorials is a mystery not mentioned in any surviving records — the carving of an unidentified abbot, quite clearly stabbed to death.

🚗 *DUNDRENNAN is on the A711, 12 miles south-west of Dalbeattie.*

DURISDEER
Nithsdale

There are traces of ancient earth-works on the Lowther Hills above the tiny village of Durisdeer, and the line of an 18th-century coaching road can be followed through a pass to the north-east, on the same route up the rounded, heathery, sheep-grazed slopes.

The parish church, standing back from a noisy rookery, was probably built — according to a sundial above the south door — in 1699.

It attracts particular interest because of the mausoleum, completed a few years later, for the 2nd Duke and Duchess of Queensberry. A Dutch sculptor created this 'exuberant monument' in black and white marble.

🚗 *DURISDEER is off the A702, 6 miles north of Thornhill.*

ELLISLAND
Nithsdale

This is the farm, by the banks of the Nith, where Robert Burns settled

when he first moved from Ayrshire to Dumfries-shire. He took it over in March 1788, and found out all too soon that the land was virtually exhausted.

Once he started with the Excise — in September 1789 — he had the triple task of riding all over the county on official business, continuing to write, and overseeing work on the farm.

He left Ellisland after three and a half hard years; but it was here that he composed the magnificent ballad *Tam o'Shanter*, set in the Alloway of his boyhood.

His wife said that he wrote the entire poem in a single day, walking by the riverside, acting all the parts, and roaring with laughter as his imagination took hilarious wing.

ELLISLAND is off the A76, 6 miles north-west of Dumfries.

GATEHOUSE OF FLEET
Stewartry

Within a one-mile radius of the bridge over the River Fleet at Gatehouse there is enough to keep any enquiring visitor happily occupied for weeks.

This fascinating little town was laid out towards the end of the 18th century as a centre for cotton-milling. Many buildings from its heyday survive — not only elegant Georgian houses, but also others long since converted from their original use: as a mill, perhaps, a tannery, a brass-foundry, a soap-works or a brewery.

It was the landowner James Murray of Cally who engineered the expansion of the town. The old Cally estate parkland is now mostly in the hands of the Forestry Commission.

Fleet Forest Nursery has operated here since 1936, raising millions of

Cardoness Castle stands on high ground at Gatehouse of Fleet

Bruce's Stone stands high above Loch Trool in Galloway Forest Park

conifer seedlings; but there are trails through broad-leaved woodland.

Robert Burns, inevitably, came this way. It was in the Murray Arms at Gatehouse, following a long and drizzly moorland ride, that he put on paper the words of the song *Scots Wha Hae* — his stirring version of Robert the Bruce's address to his army before the Battle of Bannockburn.

The part-restored 15th-century Cardoness Castle stands on a hilltop above the Creetown road. For generations, the McCullochs of Cardoness were notorious for their hair-trigger tempers. The murder of a neighbour gave one of them the distinction of being almost the last man to submit to the attentions of the 'maiden' — the euphemistic name for the old Scottish guillotine.

🚗 *GATEHOUSE OF FLEET is 14 miles south-west of Castle Douglas.*

Irish pilgrims were drawn to St Ninian's shrine at Whithorn

GLEN TROOL
Wigtown

In the heart of the Galloway Forest Park, this is a valley which becomes progressively more dramatic until, around Loch Trool, towering hillsides and rugged heathery crags signal the start of the hill-walkers' tracks to the Merrick — at 2764 ft the highest point in Galloway — and the harshly-named, remote upland features like the Rig of the Jarkness and the Murder Hole of Loch Neldricken.

The start of the glen is at the rocky Falls of Minnoch, where forest trails meander through larch and spruce.

There are more than conifer plantations at the head of Loch Trool: the Buchan and Gairland Burns cascade through protected oakwoods.

High above the loch, the finest easily accessible viewpoint is the commemorative Bruce's Stone. Another trail across the hillside opposite shows where an English force, one day in 1307, was ambushed by a barrage of tumbling boulders, behind which Bruce's men rampaged down the hill to clinch the battle known as the Steps of Trool.

🚗 *GLEN TROOL is north-east of Bargrennan on the A714.*

THE GLENKENS
Stewartry

This is the name of the valley where, among lochs and forested hills, the Water of Deugh joins the Water of Ken and the united river combines with the Dee.

Carsphairn, the highest village, had the misfortune to be on the estates of Sir Robert Grierson, whose enthusiastic persecution of Covenanters centred on his own tenants.

There are Covenanter memories too at St John's Town of Dalry, a

The Solway Smugglers

Many things combined to make the Solway Coast the main centre of Scotland's flourishing 18th and 19th-century smuggling trade.

It was within overnight sailing distance of the Isle of Man, where cargoes could be landed quite legally from foreign ports without any duty being paid — and then, quite illegally, trans-shipped to secret mainland harbours, with which the Solway was remarkably well supplied.

This began as a small-scale operation. But then, in 1707, the Union of Parliaments brought Scotland, England and Wales under one central government which at first created, and then greatly increased, the duty payable on imports of wines, spirits, salt, tobacco, lace and other luxury fabrics.

Smuggling activity on the Solway followed suit. Natural sea-caves and specially extended farmhouse cellars were turned into contraband stores. Individual smuggling companies were set up, with their own shareholders, carefully-kept accounts, pony-trains for overland transport, and a network of middle-men in the cities.

It was only in 1822 that the government turned its full attention towards stamping out the illegal trade.

Money was poured into the revenue service — for coastguard stations, patrol boats and greatly increased manpower. New laws brought in much stricter penalties. Within the decade, smuggling had been virtually wiped out.

It has left one highly popular song — not, oddly enough, about the smugglers, but about their pursuers.

When Robert Burns, to help boost his meagre income from farming and from his notoriously tight-fisted Edinburgh publisher, took up his post as a revenue officer, one of the incidents in which he was involved was the capture of an armed smuggling ship, grounded near the mouth of the River Sark.

While waiting impatiently for reinforcements before boarding the ship, he composed a lively song which is still performed in concerts all over Scotland — *The Deil's Awa' wi' the Exciseman.*

bright and attractive hillside village which has its own lively summer street fair; at nearby Balmaclellan, where the 18th-century stonemason Robert Paterson, who travelled the country keeping Covenanter memorials in good condition, gave Sir Walter Scott the idea for 'Old Mortality'; and across the Water of Ken at New Galloway, a trim little town which was once the smallest of Scotland's royal burghs.

The chain of lochs in the Glenkens — Kendoon, Carsfad, Earlstoun and Ken — are all part of the ingenious Galloway hydro-electric scheme opened in 1936.

Its layout and operation are explained in guided tours of the main Tongland power station, nearer the mouth of the Dee, which also has a 29-pool salmon ladder tackled by as many as 4000 fish per year, on their way to the spawning grounds.

THE MAIN ROAD through the Glenkens is the A713 from Ayr to Castle Douglas.

ISLE OF WHITHORN
Wigtown

The first cargo attracted to this little landing-place on the Solway were Irish pilgrims on their way to St Ninian's shrine at Whithorn. A ruined chapel on the island, built specially for them, dates from the 12th century.

As the inland town of Whithorn increased in importance, 'the Isle' was designated as its port. Later, it was the scene of hair-raising escapades in the heyday of the Solway smugglers.

The tidal bar which linked the island to the mainland eventually had houses and a main street built along it. The grassy Isle, with its tiny rock-flanked bays, has become a very attractive, natural public park, centred on an old tide-signalling tower.

The rugged coastline around the Solway is full of caves

Although there are still some fishing boats at Isle of Whithorn, it is now better known as a holiday resort with a flourishing sailing club.

🚗 *ISLE OF WHITHORN is on the A750, 14 miles south of Wigtown.*

KIRKBEAN
Nithsdale

On the edge of the Solwayside farmlands, this is a neatly laid out village where a lane leads over a burn to the parish church built in 1776.

That was a significant date in Kirkbean, as elsewhere: when the American War of Independence broke out, a local sea captain who had emigrated to Virginia was already the 'father' of the fledgling United States Navy.

Although he has gone down in history as Paul Jones, he was born John Paul, son of the gardener on the nearby Arbigland estate.

The church has a memorial font donated in his honour by officers and men of the modern U.S. Navy; and his boyhood home — a cottage at Arbigland — has been visited by many famous Americans.

Not many of them, perhaps, knew that after the war, having failed in his efforts to set up a fur-trading company, he accepted a pressing invitation from Catherine the Great and became a Rear-Admiral in the Russian Black Sea Fleet.

The modern gardens of Arbigland are open to the public for part of the year, sheltering in woodlands back from the secluded Solway shore.

🚗 *KIRKBEAN is on the A710, 12 miles south of Dumfries.*

KIRKCUDBRIGHT
Stewartry

Under both his names, Paul Jones paid separate official visits to the

Kirkbean is an attractive village on the edge of farmland. Nearby is the birthplace of Paul Jones

spacious county town.

The first was when — as John Paul — he stood trial on a vague and quickly-dismissed charge of killing a seaman.

The other was when, commanding a United States warship, he landed a raiding party to try to kidnap the Earl of Selkirk from his estate outside the town.

Jones had a plan — which turned out successfully — to exchange Americans held prisoner in Britain for hostages taken during his coastal raids; but the Earl of Selkirk, away

from home at the time, was not to be one of them.

Paul Jones's Point on St Mary's Isle is a reminder of that bold attempt; just as the bay called Manxman's Lake recalls the contraband cargoes landed from the Isle of Man.

Robert Burns visited Kirkcudbright too, and it was here that he composed the Selkirk Grace with which every Burns Supper begins.

However, this was an important place long before their time. Its name is a corruption of 'the Kirk of (Saint) Cuthbert', established in the 9th

century.

Much of the town is 18th and 19th-century, but its most notable building is the ruined MacLellan's Castle, completed in 1582 and now an ancient monument standing in gardens near the riverside harbour.

The fine Georgian-style Broughton House contains the library and picture collection bequeathed to the town, like the house itself, by the painter Edward Hornel. One of the leaders of Kirkcudbright's artists' colony, he died in 1933.

A gallery beside the harbour shows

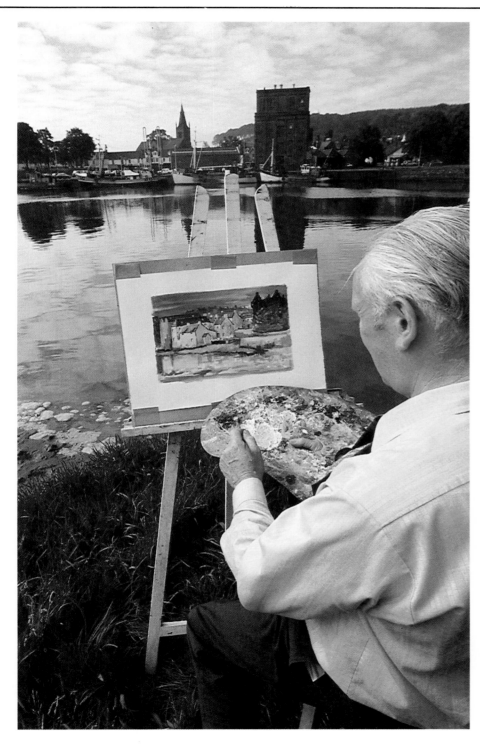

Kirkcudbright, on the Dee estuary, is an artist's haven

that the town's long-standing artistic tradition continues.

🚗 *KIRKCUDBRIGHT is on the A711, 10 miles south-west of Castle Douglas.*

LANGHOLM
Annandale and Eskdale

Located in a valley where, within a quarter of a mile, the Ewes and the Wauchope Waters both join the Border Esk, Langholm is a place with an abundance of riverside walks. Others contour the hills through gentle woodland.

Whita Hill rises steeply to the east. The monument on its 1162-ft summit is a glorious viewpoint — in clear weather, to as far away as the hazy silhouette of the Isle of Man. And an exuberant charge up Whita Hill is one of the features of Langholm's famous Common Riding.

Horses are important around Langholm. So is rugby. And so is the trout and salmon angling on the Esk, the Ewes and the Wauchope.

This has been a significant textile town for something like 200 years. And one local company weaves the most expensive pure-wool suitings in the world.

Langholm also has an extra-terrestrial connection. Its burgh charter dates from the 1620s, but the town took a very long time about deciding who should be dignified by being created its first freeman.

Eventually, in 1972, the choice fell, not on a Langholm man, but on a descendant of Langholm men — Neil Armstrong, the first astronaut to walk on the moon.

🚗 *LANGHOLM is on the A7, 23 miles south of Hawick.*

LOCHMABEN
Annandale and Eskdale

At the head of the main street in Lochmaben there is a statue of Robert the Bruce; and the Latin motto of the little town is *E nobis Liberator Rex* — 'from us is sprung the liberator King.'

His exact birthplace is uncertain, but the Bruce connection with Lochmaben started in 1124, when David I made a grant of lands in Annandale to the Norman family then called de Brus. However, it was only around 1200 that they built a castle in Lochmaben, which survives as a grassy mound on the golf course.

Thanks to its status as the headquarters of the Warden of the Western Marches, Lochmaben suffered badly in the interminable border wars after Robert the Bruce's time. But there were other violent clashes between two great rival families — the Johnstones and the Maxwells — for the wardenship itself.

In 1593 a party of Johnstones had the upper hand in a skirmish at Lochmaben. The Maxwells fled for sanctuary to the parish church, which the Johnstones promptly burned down around them. More Maxwells gathered to have a final showdown with their enemies. By the River Dryfe, east of the town, in the last great family battle, the Maxwells were heavily defeated.

Clan warfare was certainly not confined to the Highlands.

Partly because of the attention it received during these years, the second Lochmaben Castle is little more than a fragmentary ruin on a peninsula at the south end of Castle Loch.

This very attractive heart-shaped loch — one of a remarkable number in and around Lochmaben — is fringed by woodland and forms the centrepiece of a carefully managed nature reserve. There is a dinghy club, and anglers come for the coarse fishing.

Lochmaben is also the home water of that rarest of Scottish freshwater fish, the vendace — still not quite extinct, although a rumoured conservation project has a discreet veil of silence drawn around it.

🔹 *LOCHMABEN is on the A709, 10 miles north-east of Dumfries.*

MULL OF GALLOWAY
Wigtown

The 'Land's End' of Galloway is a spectacular headland ringed with sea-bird cliffs plunging down towards the circling currents where the Solway Firth meets the Irish Sea.

Lichens, wildflowers, close-cropped grazing land and intrusive veins of other rocks streaked through the Mull's basic sandstone all combine to make it an unexpectedly colourful if often windswept place.

Mull of Galloway lighthouse, completed in 1830, is a phenomenal viewpoint. On a fine day, the view extends from the Isle of Man and the Antrim coast to the Inner Hebridean peaks of Jura.

A network of loop roads means that several different routes can be chosen to and from the Mull. They pass through the old smuggling village of Drummore on Luce Bay; the higher-set village of Kirkmaiden with its viewpoint church; and Port Logan, where the wind-driven sea dashes into an exposed west-facing bay.

Before 1800, the laird of Logan had a tidal fish pond built, stocked with cod to provide a regular supply of fish for the mansion house kitchens; but the fish soon became pets, and their successors can still be seen enjoying their hand-feeding today.

The weather in this part of

Galloway is surprisingly mild. With walled and wooded areas to divert the wind, many sub-tropical plants can be grown out of doors. Logan Botanic Garden is one of the most famous in Scotland, with dazzling displays of Southern Hemisphere trees and flowering shrubs.

🔹 *MULL OF GALLOWAY lighthouse is 5 miles south of Drummore on the A716.*

NEW ABBEY
Nithsdale

The important point about this intriguing and attractive village, which follows a winding main street beyond a bridge over the burn known as the New Abbey Pow, is that its abbey was 'new' only in the context of the 13th century.

It was endowed after her husband's death in 1268 by Devorgilla, widow of the enormously wealthy landowner John Balliol, and herself the descendant of Scottish kings.

For the 21 years that she survived him, Devorgilla kept constantly by her a little ivory and silver casket which contained her husband's embalmed heart. It was buried with her,

when she was laid at rest beside him, before the altar of what its Cistercian monks — who had come from the 'old' abbey at Dundrennan — gave its present name of Sweetheart Abbey.

Only the precinct wall and the abbey kirk, a handsome if ruined building of red sandstone with pointed Gothic arches, remain as an ancient monument; but New Abbey has several other features of note.

The whitewashed 18th-century corn mill, in commercial production until World War II, has been restored and is now open to the public.

And the Victorian mansion-house

The lonely sentinel of Mull of Galloway lighthouse is a stunning viewpoint

of Shambellie, one of David Bryce's Scottish Baronial designs with tower and turrets and skyline crow-stepped gables, has become the Museum of Costume, combining an extensive private collection with other displays from the stock of the Royal Scottish Museum in Edinburgh.

NEW ABBEY is on the A710, 6 miles south of Dumfries.

PORTPATRICK
Wigtown

Named for St Patrick, this very pleasantly situated village has crescents of colour-washed houses half-circling a harbour set in an otherwise cliff-bound coast, with villas and hotels in spacious grounds rising above.

Until mid-Victorian times, it was the ferry-port for the short sea crossing to Donaghadee in Ireland, made redundant only by the development of the rival port of Stranraer. Portpatrick used to have both town and harbour stations.

Colonel Street and Barrack Street recall that this was where troops embarked for postings in Ireland; and some buildings date from the harbour extension work started in the 1820s.

Present-day Portpatrick is a colourful and well equipped holiday resort. A flight of steps up the North Cliff marks the start of the 212-mile coast-to-coast Southern Upland Way, which begins as a familiar village walk alongside the high-level golf course, before heading north-east across Wigtownshire towards Glen Trool.

PORTPATRICK is on the A77, 8 miles south-west of Stranraer.

Portpatrick is a pleasant and lively holiday village encircling a harbour, once the crossing point to Ireland

181

THE QUEEN'S WAY
Wigtown and Stewartry

This stretch of road through the Galloway Forest Park was named by the Forestry Commission at the time of the Queen's silver jubilee in 1978.

It passes a memorial to another of Robert the Bruce's early victories — this time at the skirmish of Moss Raploch in 1307; the very informative Galloway Deer Museum, which also includes displays on the geology and botany of the Park, as well as modern stained-glass windows on wildlife themes; a hillside red deer enclosure and a similar wild goat park; and the start of the summer-only Raiders Road forest drive alongside the Black Water of Dee, on a route followed by 18th-century cattle rustlers hurrying back from raids on Solway estates.

The finest scenery on the Queen's Way is at Talnotry, where forested hills rise sharply to a monument in honour of Alexander Murray, a locally-born shepherd's son who became one of the most notable Oriental linguists in early 19th-century Europe.

There are fine waterfalls at Talnotry, and a stiff four-mile forest trail which rises to extensive hilltop viewpoints and the site of old lead and nickel mines beside an abandoned 17th-century coaching road.

🚗 *THE QUEEN'S WAY is part of the A712, west of New Galloway.*

RUTHWELL
Nithsdale

In farmlands a mile back from the Solway, this neat village of 18th and 19th-century cottages is notable because of the activities of a remarkable parish minister, the Reverend Dr. Henry Duncan, who served here from 1799.

He was a man of many parts —

The richly-carved Ruthwell Cross made the village famous

Ruthwell's banking museum commemorates the world's first savings bank, set up here in 1810

preacher, writer, editor, antiquarian, enthusiastic curler, philanthropist and pioneering banker.

It was in Ruthwell that he started the world's first savings bank, in a cottage which is now a banking museum.

And it was Dr. Duncan who rescued from disregarded decay one of the finest Dark Age sculptures in Europe, the magnificent 7th-century Ruthwell Cross, with its four faces of intricately carved Biblical scenes. It is now installed in a specially constructed apse in the parish church.

🚗 *RUTHWELL is off the B724, 7 miles west of Annan.*

THORNHILL
Nithsdale

The first village on this site, on a gentle rise of ground above the River Nith, was built in 1664 as the burgh of New Dalgarno. But Thornhill took its place in the late 18th century, built to plans approved by the Duke of Queensberry. It is a very pleasant little town, with a wide main street centred on a Queensberry monument.

In 1810 the Queensberry title was merged with that of Buccleuch, and the present Duke of Buccleuch's Dumfries-shire home is the superb 17th-century Drumlanrig Castle upstream from Thornhill, in wooded parkland near the river. It was built for the 1st Duke of Queensberry, who eccentrically spent only one night in it, then continued to live elsewhere.

On display are the castle's oak panelled state rooms, and very valuable collections of furniture and paintings.

🚗 *THORNHILL is on the A76, 14 miles north-west of Dumfries.*

WANLOCKHEAD
Nithsdale

This is the highest village in Scotland — an old lead-mining settlement almost 1400 ft up in the bleak landscape of the Lowther Hills. Gold used to be panned in the Wanlock Burn, hence the street name Goldscaur Row.

A mining museum in Goldscaur Row has a visitor trail which includes the walk-in Lochnell Mine.

Among the indoor displays is a model of the Leadhills Light Railway, which crossed the highest standard-gauge summit in Britain at 1498 ft between Wanlockhead and Leadhills. Part of the old track-bed, closed in 1938, is being rebuilt as an enthusiast-run narrow gauge line.

🚗 *WANLOCKHEAD is on the B797, 6 miles north-east of Mennock.*

The area around Wanlockhead has been mined since Roman times and the remains of old mine workings can be seen

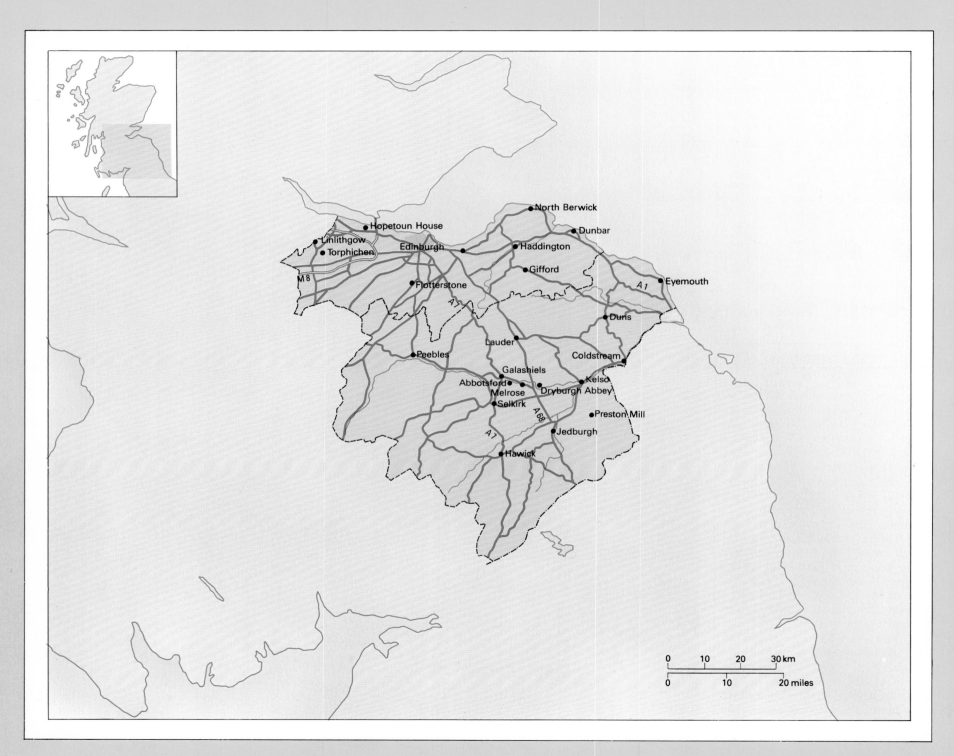

North Berwick

Dunbar

Hopetoun House

Linlithgow
Torphichen
Edinburgh
Haddington

Gifford

Eyemouth

M8

Flotterstone

A1

A7

Duns

Lauder

Coldstream

Peebles

Galashiels

Kelso

Abbotsford
Melrose
Dryburgh Abbey
Selkirk

A68

Preston Mill

A7

Jedburgh

Hawick

0   10   20   30 km

0   10   20 miles

Lothian & Borders

The ruins of Dryburgh Abbey, stark against the evening sky, stand on a tongue of land reaching out into the beautiful River Tweed

WHILE EDINBURGH IS the historic capital of Scotland — the Festival City with a Royal palace, a spectacularly located castle, elegant Georgian terraces, allusions to literary personalities at almost every corner — it also has a spreading hinterland.

Stately homes and fishing harbours, inland gardens and a multitude of beautifully conserved estate villages of the 18th and 19th centuries make sure that any visitor is seriously embarrassed for choice.

In the south, Lothian Region rises to a boundary of rounded hill ranges — the Pentlands, the Moorfoots and the Lammermuirs. Beyond them is the Border country, fought over by generations of armies.

Now, this is an area of quiet and reflective river valleys, most of whose waters eventually congregate into the Tweed, sturdily independent towns, mellow ruined abbeys and some prodigious mansions.

One man is the common link here, not simply because of the ballads and novels with which he kept his early 19th-century readers enthralled, and not simply because in his travels as a Sheriff he was well known personally to mighty landlords and poorer folk alike.

In his straightforwardness and honesty, his punishing work schedule and intimate knowledge of his native land, Sir Walter Scott was a man of whom nobody who met him had an ill word to say.

It is a lasting tribute to him that this part of Scotland is still referred to, without affectation, as the Scott Country.

ABBOTSFORD
Ettrick and Lauderdale

Sir Walter Scott had good historic grounds for changing the inelegant name of the farm he bought in 1812 from Cartleyhole to Abbotsford: the house looked over meadows to the Tweed, where the monks of Melrose Abbey once crossed it by a ford.

It was here that — in between relentless spells of writing the best-selling and influential *Waverley* novels — he lived the life of a Border laird; latterly in the present mansion of Abbotsford, which was completed in 1824. And it was here in 1832 that in his last illness he had his bed taken to a riverside room through whose open windows would come the sound of the murmuring waters of the Tweed.

Since then, Abbotsford has always been lived in by his direct descendants. Much of it is open to the public, with his splendid 9000-volume library and remarkable collection of relics of famous and diverse characters like Robert Burns, Flora MacDonald, Rob Roy MacGregor, Napoleon and Charles Edward Stuart.

🚗 *ABBOTSFORD is on the B6360, 2 miles west of Melrose.*

COLDSTREAM
Berwickshire

For almost 1000 years, Coldstream has been a major border crossing between Scotland and England, beside a ford replaced in 1776 by John Smeaton's bridge across the Tweed.

The old toll-house on the Scottish side of the bridge was the scene of many a clandestine marriage between English couples, often just ahead of outraged parents racing from the south.

The town gave its name to the

Sir Walter Scott spent many happy years on his estate at Abbotsford

Coldstream Guards, and there is a regimental collection in the museum in the market square. The regiment has the distinction of being the oldest corps in continuous existence in the British Army.

Nearby, a long-dismantled Cistercian priory has left behind little more than the name of Abbey Road, the Nuns' Walk along the bank of the Tweed, and the Penitents' Walk up the side of the tributary River Leet.

Outside Coldstream, the Leet flows through the Hirsel estate of the Douglas-Homes. The estate is open to the public all through the year, with a fine exhibition centre, riverside walks and meandering footpaths through the rhododendron plantations in Dundock Wood.

🚗 *COLDSTREAM is on the A698, 9 miles north-east of Kelso.*

DRYBURGH ABBEY
Ettrick and Lauderdale

One of the most beautiful stretches of the River Tweed is at the sweeping double-back bend where, on a tongue of land now laid out with fields and lawns and specimen trees, the ruins of the Premonstratensians' 12th-century Dryburgh Abbey stand.

Dryburgh was farther off the beaten track than the other great Border abbeys, but like them it suffered drastically in the incessant 14th to 16th-century cross-border raids. It was finally left in ruins in 1544.

And yet, a remarkable amount of Dryburgh remains to be looked after as an ancient monument — cloister, transepts, chapter-house and the 15th-century rose window high in the refectory wall.

Sir Walter Scott, who had a family claim to the right of burial here, lies in the north transept. Nearby is the grave of the World War I commander Earl Haig of Bemersyde, the ancestral estate bought back for him by public subscription in 1921.

🚗 *DRYBURGH is across the Tweed from St Boswells on the A68.*

DUNBAR
East Lothian

Weather records prove that this is one of the sunniest resorts in Scotland, and it takes full advantage of that, with two 18-hole golf courses, other sports facilities and a fine clifftop trail, part of the John Muir Country Park which extends along eight and a half miles of fascinating coastline towards the dunes, woodlands, rocks and saltmarshes of Belhaven Bay and the estuary of the River Tyne.

John Muir was a powerful advocate of the National Park movement in the United States, and the house in the High Street where he was born in 1838 is now a museum.

Dunbar's fishing fleet is based on the New or Victoria Harbour of 1842, in a splendid situation overlooked by the red-sandstone ruin of Dunbar Castle, now a nesting place for sea birds.

A town trail points out many of the Georgian and earlier buildings at the heart of this dignified old burgh.

DUNBAR is on the A1087, 6 miles east of East Linton.

DUNS
Berwickshire

The site of an ancient hill fort on Duns Law gave this market town and administrative centre its name: here, as in the Highlands and Islands, 'dun' was the Celtic word for just such a fortification.

A footpath to the 714-ft summit, where a Covenanter army gathered in 1639, opens up a wide-spreading view over the rich farmlands of the Merse of Berwickshire to the Cheviot Hills on the southern horizon.

The Jim Clark Room in Newtown Street displays more than 100 trophies won during his career by one of the world's most highly respected Grand Prix drivers.

Manderston, 'the finest Edwardian country house in Britain', is just outside the town. The mansion with its lavish furnishings, extravagantly equipped stables and even a marble dairy is open regularly in the summer. And the Biscuit Tin Museum is a clue to the business on which the family fortunes were founded.

DUNS is on the A6105, 16 miles west of Berwick.

Besides a fine collection of books, Scott's library contains relics of eminent historical figures

EDINBURGH
City of Edinburgh

Princes Street in Edinburgh may have some ill-advised modern shop frontages, but it remains one of the most impressively located city-centre streets in Europe, dominated by the great basalt cliffs on which Edinburgh Castle stands.

Every year, the castle esplanade is the scene of the Military Tattoo, one of the most atmospheric events of the Edinburgh International Festival, especially when, the sky being dark, a lone piper is spotlighted on a high balcony.

Downhill to the east of the castle, the Royal Mile is extravagantly historic; and at almost every step there are buildings steeped in literary memories — like Lady Stair's House with its displays on Burns, Scott and Stevenson.

The Royal Mile finishes at the Palace of Holyroodhouse, the Queen's official residence in Scotland. Around and above the Palace stretches Holyrood Park, whose name may conjure up gracious Lowland landscaping, but is in fact all sweeping grassy swards, steep footpaths and rugged cliffs leading up to the spectacular viewpoint summit of the old volcano called Arthur's Seat.

The prosperous legal, banking, mercantile, literary and philosophical centre which Edinburgh became in the 18th century far outgrew its original setting around the Royal Mile. One of the most graceful city layouts in the world is the New Town begun in the 1770s — all unselfconsciously elegant Georgian terraces and crescents; and a second New Town was started in the 1820s.

Away from the centre, with its museums, art galleries, concert halls, memorials and formal gardens, Edinburgh is no kind of homogeneous city

(above) **Built on volcanic rock, Edinburgh Castle dominates the city** *(left)* **The magnificent gates to the Palace of Holyroodhouse**

— rather a collection of loosely connected villages.

The old weavers' village of Duddingston has a bird sanctuary round its loch, and the oldest pub in Scotland.

Dean Village is an astonishingly carefully restored place, established in the 12th century by millers and bakers and tanners, but now almost entirely residential in its half-secret location by the Water of Leith.

And Cramond, with its narrow anchorage at the mouth of the River Almond, where the white-walled, red-roofed houses were once the home of oyster fishermen, has been settled since Roman times. It was a port for the materials that went into the building of Antonine's Wall, the northern frontier of the Roman Empire. Roman ships based here were the first to sail right round Britain.

🚗 EDINBURGH is 45 miles east of Glasgow.

EYEMOUTH
Berwickshire

There have been North Sea fishermen based on this historic little town since the 12th century. Trawlers and shellfish boats still operate from John Smeaton's shrewdly designed harbour of 1768, at the rocky mouth of the Eye Water.

In 1597, Eyemouth was declared a free port. This led to one unexpected development: especially in the 18th century, it became a highly organised smuggling centre. Gunsgreen House, still overlooking the river from the east bank, was built with secret storage chambers and underground passages all around it.

After the smuggling days, Eyemouth men went back full-time to fishing, and this was the scene of the greatest fishing-fleet disaster in Scottish waters: on 14 October 1881, no fewer than 23 boats and 129 fishermen were lost in a furious storm.

Near the quay where catches are auctioned, the Eyemouth Museum has extensive displays on the place itself, its fishing and the marine wildlife of the coast; and there is an almost million-stitch tapestry.

🚗 EYEMOUTH is on the B6355, 8 miles north of Berwick.

FLOTTERSTONE
Midlothian

The Pentland Hills rise directly from the south-western suburbs of Edinburgh, extending for miles, with many individual grassy summits, gentle passes, quiet valleys and a network of pathways.

One of the main access points is at Flotterstone, the start of a tarmac road which can be used by walkers as it curls into a Highland-looking glen to service the reservoirs at Glencorse and Loganlea.

The hill immediately west of Flotterstone was the scene in 1666 of the Battle of Rullion Green, in which government troops — after a first rebuff — heavily defeated an outnumbered force of Covenanters.

This was the subject of Robert Louis Stevenson's first-ever published work. His booklet called *The Pentland Rising* was dated exactly 200 years after the event.

🚗 FLOTTERSTONE is on the A702, 4 miles south of Fairmilehead.

GALASHIELS
Ettrick and Lauderdale

This substantial town with an often abbreviated name, at the foot of the valley of the Gala Water just before it flows into the Tweed, grew up as a textile centre. It was the Gala weavers who, by forming themselves into a trade corporation, created the basis of a textile *industry*, where only small, individual producers had existed before.

That was in 1777. Textiles in Galashiels reached their peak in late-Victorian times, when the names of almost 30 mills and dyeworks were recorded. Their numbers have been drastically reduced, and Galashiels has been forced to diversify. But its Nether Mill is still the largest producer of woollen tartan cloth in the world, with more than 700 patterns in stock.

Nether Mill also has an exhibition on the woollen industry, which merges into another one on the history of the town.

The war memorial in Galashiels picks up that theme. It includes a fine statue, by a local sculptor, of an armed, mounted and ready-for-action Border reiver.

🚗 GALASHIELS is on the A7, 3 miles west of Melrose.

GIFFORD
East Lothian

Three villages along the northern fringe of the Lammermuir Hills are among the architectural showpieces of East Lothian. Gifford is the biggest of them, dating from the 17th century but laid out to a largely Georgian and Victorian plan.

The remarkable tapestry of almost a million stitches in the Eyemouth Museum, sited near the quay

The architect of its parish church, built in 1710, obviously had Dutch as well as Scottish designs in mind; and a memorial here recalls that the Reverend John Witherspoon, who signed the American Declaration of Independence, was a son of the Gifford manse.

A reconstructed market cross and the elegant town house with its Victorian clock tower face an avenue of limes which leads to the ornamental gates of Yester House.

A few miles to the north-east, Garvald is an attractively tucked away tangle of red-stone and pantile-roofed cottages in the valley of the Papana Water. Above it is the modern Cistercian Abbey of Nunraw.

Stenton is a beautifully preserved 18th and early 19th-century village, with an earlier dovecot tower and the re-erected scales on which bartered goods were weighed.

In 1819 a hill burn south of Stenton was dammed to create the narrow and winding mile-long Pressmennan Lake, where a Forestry Commission trail now runs through shady plantations of spruce, oak and larch.

GIFFORD is on the B6355, 11 miles south-west of Dunbar.

Common Ridings

One thing more than any other which shows the local spirit of the Border towns is the Common Ridings — that tradition of riding round the town's boundaries to check that there had been no encroachments on its common land.

Every festival has its leading personalities — the Melrosian and the Festival Queen at Melrose; the Cornet and his Lass at Peebles, Hawick and Lauder; the Braw Lad and the Braw Lass at Galashiels; the Reiver and his Lass at Duns.

Early on the Friday of Selkirk Common Riding almost the whole town joins in procession to sing *Hail, Smiling Morn*; one of Jedburgh's songs echoes the town's old authentic battle-cry *Jethart's Here!*

Not all the battles and skirmishes recalled in the ceremonies were Scottish victories. James IV's disastrous defeat in 1513 at Flodden in Northumberland still stirs the emotions.

In Coldstream Civic Week there is a ride-out across the border so that the Coldstreamer can lay a wreath on the Flodden memorial.

And Selkirk Common Riding has one heart-stopping moment: the Standard Bearer, re-enacting the traditional way in which the sole survivor of the 80 Selkirk men who went to fight at Flodden — too struck down by emotion to speak — brought back the news of the overwhelming defeat, 'casts the colours' in the market place. Other standards are then cast down to honour the dead of later wars.

But these festivals are, above all, exuberant celebrations.

They feature parades and processions, firework displays, music and dancing, sports and even — at Kelso — a raft race down the Tweed.

The annual raft race down the Tweed begins at Kelso where a fine bridge by John Rennie spans the river

HADDINGTON
East Lothian

Very few places in Scotland are as wholeheartedly devoted to architectural conservation as Haddington, the business and administrative centre of East Lothian, and once the county town of what was originally called Haddingtonshire.

This explains the presence of elegant town mansions built for county families, the banks and public buildings.

The early 17th-century Haddington House is the headquarters of the enthusiastic trust which co-ordinates many of the town's projects. Its wall-ed garden is laid out in contemporary Scottish style, featuring a laburnum walk and sunken flower beds.

Within strolling distance are the largely restored, basically 14th-century St Mary's Church; an 18th-century dovecot which houses an exhibition on the history of the town; and an elegant red-sandstone footbridge over the gentle River Tyne to the new but appropriately designed houses in the ancient suburb of Nungate.

There is a museum in the Georgian heart of the town devoted to the writer Thomas Carlyle and his locally-born wife Jane Welsh. And among the colour-washed house fron-tages there are many intriguing smaller details — like the recurring motif of a goat. Haddington's coat of arms has the puzzling combination of a goat with a bunch of grapes.

HADDINGTON is off the A1, 10 miles west of Dunbar.

HAWICK
Roxburgh

Largest of the Border towns, Hawick is centred on a narrow but busy High Street in which the oldest building is the Tower Hotel, once the town house of the Douglas and then the Scott families, but converted into a coaching inn during the 1770s.

Among its notable guests have been William and Dorothy Wordsworth, whom Sir Walter Scott brought here in 1803 when he was escorting them on part of a Border tour.

Hawick has three main preoccupations: its busy woollen industry which sends cashmere, Shetland and lambswool knitwear, as well as tweeds and tartans, all over the world; sales of livestock from the well-farmed valleys and upland grazings nearby; and — like the Border towns — an almost overwhelming interest in rugby.

The town is built along both banks of the Teviot, and features a 107-acre riverside park around the mansion-house of Wilton Lodge.

Here, there are walled gardens and walks, a local-history museum and the re-erected market cross, and a memorial to one of Hawick's most famous sportsmen, the international motorcycle racer Jimmy Guthrie — killed in 1937 in an accident while competing, like Jim Clark a generation later, in an event in Germany.

HAWICK is on the A7, 23 miles north of Langholm.

HOPETOUN HOUSE
West Lothian

Although it looks like a single part of a grand architectural and landscape plan, this majestic mansion house in wooded parkland above the Firth of Forth — home of the Marquess of Linlithgow — is actually one house grafted onto another.

Between 1599 and 1603 Sir William Bruce was the architect of what is now the central part of the house. William Adam began adding to the masterly work with substantial wings on either side; he was still engaged on it at the time of his death in 1748, and the interior decoration was finished by his sons Robert and John — 19

Court Street in the former county town of Haddington is a tribute to sensitive architectural conservation

years later.

Hopetoun has lavishly furnished state rooms with beautiful Adam plasterwork, wood-carvings, tapestries and portraits.

In the north-wing pavilion there is an exhibition on 'Horse and Man in Lowland Scotland'. And the tour of the main house includes a visit to the Roof Observatory, which is actually a high-level viewpoint over the estate woodlands to the two Forth Bridges.

A very attractive nature trail looks down from yew hedges to a red deer park bounded on the north by the estuary of the Forth, and finishes along a lime avenue back towards the grand old house.

◆ *HOPETOUN HOUSE is reached from South Queensferry, off the A90 north-west of Edinburgh.*

JEDBURGH
Roxburgh

Since it is on one of the main cross-border roads, this historic town with a finely restored centre has been visited by many famous travellers: Bonnie Prince Charlie in 1745; Robert Burns in 1787, when he was made a freeman of the burgh and charmed its ladies; and Sir Walter Scott, who made his first courtroom appearance as a lawyer here in 1793.

But the visitor who made the greatest impression was Mary, Queen of Scots. She spent some time in 1566 living in a fortified mansion-house which is now a notably well-furnished museum among gardens overlooking the Jed Water.

Jedburgh's splendid ruined abbey was founded in 1118. Like the other great religious houses in the Borders, it never recovered from the notorious 'Rough Wooing' of the 1540s.

This was the invasion whose unsuccessful purpose was to force the Scots to allow the infant Queen Mary to be betrothed to Henry VIII's son and heir, thus eventually uniting both kingdoms under a Tudor monarch.

Instead, in 1603, they were united under Mary's son James, when the succession fell to the Stuarts.

In the higher part of the town, Jedburgh Castle is misleadingly named. The original castle changed hands so many times in the border wars that in 1409 the Scots exasperatedly demolished it.

The present building — now a comprehensive but highly unusual museum — may have battlemented curtain walls, a dummy portcullis and ornamental towers; but it was built in the 1820s to serve as a prison.

◆ *JEDBURGH is on the A68, 12 miles north of the border at Carter Bar.*

KELSO
Roxburgh

This is another Border town which grew up beside a 12th-century abbey. Kelso Abbey, on a curve of the Tweed just after it is joined by the Teviot, was the most substantial religious house in the Borders; but it was another victim of the Rough Wooing, and what the English left standing was further reduced at the time of the Reformation in 1560.

Kelso's central square is one of the great Georgian townscapes of the Borders. Livestock sales used to be held there, but they have moved across John Rennie's five-arched bridge of 1803 to Springwood Park on the far bank of the Tweed, which is also the site of the famous Border Union agricultural show.

There is a racecourse outside the town. The Tweed and, to a lesser extent, the Teviot are well-known salmon rivers. Rugby is the favourite game, but Kelso cricket club has been in operation since 1821.

The priory at Jedburgh was founded for the Augustinian Canons in 1118 and made an abbey in 1147

A short distance up-river from Kelso, the Tweed curves past the parkland of Floors Castle, home of the Duke of Roxburghe. William Adam's original restrained Georgian mansion was almost swamped by the unbridled ornamentation — and massive new wings — added by William Playfair in Victorian times.

This is the largest inhabited house in Scotland, with a window for every day in the year. Guided tours show off some of the rooms and their fine collection of portraits. The gardens are open at the same times as the castle, and the grounds are a favourite venue for horse-driving trials.

KELSO *is on the A698, 10 miles north-east of Jedburgh.*

LAUDER
Ettrick and Lauderdale

This ancient burgh at the heart of Lauderdale has been involved in many historic events. In 1483, for instance, James III's courtiers, exasperated by the King's reliance on low-born advisers, insisted that six of them be hanged from the old Lauder bridge.

Lauder Tolbooth on its island site is a constantly rebuilt version of the 1318 original. The parish church of 1673 is a curious design, to a Greek-cross plan, surmounted by an octagonal steeple.

The Southern Upland Way crosses the main road here and passes through the grounds of Thirlestane Castle, built for Mary, Queen of Scots' private secretary Maitland of Lethington and extended in Restoration style for his descendant the 1st Duke of Lauderdale.

After massive renovations, the castle, whose decorated plasterwork ceilings have few equals in Europe, is open to the public. Part of it is now the Border Country Life Museum.

LAUDER *is on the A68, 27 miles south-east of Edinburgh.*

LINLITHGOW
West Lothian

Motorists on the M9 have one of the most striking views of the old county town of West Lothian, where a royal palace of the Stuarts looks down over lawns to Linlithgow Loch, and behind it stands the imposing, mostly 15th-century St Michael's parish church with its modern sculptured spire.

Edward I of England fortified this site as his headquarters during the winter campaign of 1301/2. But work on the present palace started in 1425, during the reign of James I.

Many other Stuart personalities were closely involved with Linlithgow. James V and his daughter Mary, Queen of Scots were born here; Charles I spent a single night in the palace; and Bonnie Prince Charlie passed through during the last Jacobite Rising which tried to put the Stuarts back on the throne.

Ironically, much of the building was destroyed in a fire started while the Duke of Cumberland's troops were in occupation in 1746. Now it is partly restored, and is a very impressive ancient monument.

Thanks to its royal connections and its status as the county town, Linlithgow has a fine centre, with many 17th to 19th-century buildings in the East and West High Streets.

North-east of the town is the House of the Binns, home of the Dalyells and now owned by the National Trust for Scotland. It contains many relics of Sir Thomas Dalyell, Charles II's commander-in-chief in the ferocious campaign against the Covenanters.

In the hills to the south of Linlithgow, Beecraigs County Park includes more than 700 acres of

Linlithgow Palace, the ruined birthplace of Mary, Queen of Scots

woodlands crossed by footpaths and bridleways, a good visitor centre and a trout lake formed from a redundant reservoir.

🚗 *LINLITHGOW is off the M9, 17 miles west of Edinburgh.*

MELROSE
Ettrick and Lauderdale

High above the beautifully placed Tweed-side town of Melrose are the three rounded summits of the Eildon Hills. Eildon Hill North was settled, 2000 years ago, by a tribe known to the Romans as the Selgovae, whose vast circular earthwork, enclosing the sites of nearly 300 turf houses, can still be traced round the summit today.

The Romans took over the same hilltop for a signal station, watching over the road to their major settlement of Trimontium — 'the three mountains'. Much later, as Newstead, this was the home of the masons who built Melrose Abbey, which was established by Cistercian monks in the 1140s.

Robert the Bruce's heart is believed to be buried in the Abbey; he was one of several kings who endowed the religious house with extensive lands and possessions.

Now, its power and influence long since gone, it stands in stately ruins as a very fine ancient monument.

Next to it, in the National Trust for Scotland's Priorwood Gardens, old strains of apples which the monk-gardeners and even the Romans knew have been re-established, and flowers are prepared for autumn drying.

Melrose is a great rugby town, and it was at the local club's Greenyards ground in 1883 that the seven-a-side game was first played.

The Southern Upland Way crosses the Tweed by Melrose's suspension footbridge of 1826. And the Eildon Walk heads steeply up towards the hilltop where families of the Selgovae, then watchful Roman legionaries, looked out.

🚗 *MELROSE is 3 miles north-west of Newton St Boswells on the A68.*

NORTH BERWICK
East Lothian

On the outer limit of the Firth of Forth, this holiday resort has long sandy beaches, a yachting harbour and two golf courses on splendid links that stretch to east and west.

Rising immediately to the south is the outstanding viewpoint of North Berwick Law.

Even more spectacular, out in the mouth of the Firth, is the massive, mile-round Bass Rock. Boat trips are run from North Berwick to this towering, cliff-bound outcrop where a lighthouse stands on a terrace below the slanting upper grasslands. Thousands of gannets, gulls and kittiwakes wheel around.

The 7th-century St Baldred is believed to have had his hermit's cell here, and there is a ruined chapel dedicated to him.

In the 1690s, four resourceful men held the island fortress — by that time a state prison — in the Jacobite interest for longer than any other place in Britain.

East of North Berwick, Tantallon Castle is a ruined clifftop stronghold forming an impressive foreground to a view of the Bass.

West of the town there is a coastal nature trail among the woods and sea-buckthorn of Yellowcraig.

🚗 *NORTH BERWICK is on the A198, 12 miles north-west of Dunbar.*

Despite the depradations of the English, Melrose Abbey retains some fine decorative work and sculpture

The former county town of Peebles, with Mercat Cross — a 12ft high octagonal column dating back to 1320 — in the foreground

PEEBLES
Tweeddale

Forest trails on the hills of Glentress to the east, a golf course on the open hillside to the west, parks and riverside walks along the River Tweed which runs through the town, rounded hills and valleys stretching away to the south — all these features combine to give Peebles a setting of great variety and charm.

It is an old-established county town, a royal burgh after the granting of a charter by David I in the 12th century.

Dignified frontages of 17th to 19th-century buildings line the lively High Street; and tucked away in Cross Road is the protected ruin of the Cross Kirk of 1261.

Peebles is within easy reach of several notable buildings open to the public, up and down Tweeddale.

West of the town, poised dramatically above a narrow and wooded stretch of the river, Neidpath Castle is a fortified 14th-century tower remodelled as more of a family home 300 years later.

Farther up-river, the parish church of Stobo is in authentic Norman style. Nearby, the extensively wooded Dawyck estate is an out-station of the Royal Botanic Garden in Edinburgh.

Downstream from Peebles, Traquair House dates in part from 1107 and is said to be the oldest inhabited house in Scotland. It has many mementoes of the Stuart kings to whom its lairds were related, and of the tragic Mary, Queen of Scots who stayed here with Darnley in 1566.

Traquair is famous for its Bear Gates, which are not to be opened until another Stuart takes the throne.

In an altogether different context, it is also known for Traquair Ale, still produced in small quantities in the estate's own 18th-century brewhouse.

PEEBLES is at the junction of the A72 and the A703, 23 miles south of Edinburgh.

PRESTON MILL
East Lothian

One of the smallest properties of the National Trust for Scotland — but also one of the most attractive in its fabric, its immediate surroundings and the authenticity of its restoration — is this sole-surviving example of the meal-mills of the lower River Tyne.

Preston Mill dates mainly from the 17th century, although there have been millers here for something like 800 years.

With its seemingly random out-buildings, the grain-drying kiln with its wind-directional vane, and all the

Millers have worked in the idyllic setting of Preston Mill, the last mill on the lower River Tyne, for about 800 years

roofs covered in East Lothian's favourite red pantiles, Preston Mill is a photographers' and artists' delight.
🚗 *PRESTON MILL is on the B1407, north-east of East Linton.*

SELKIRK
Ettrick and Lauderdale

Higher set than the other Border towns, Selkirk is on a hillside above the textile mills along the Ettrick Water. It was often the base of the Scottish kings, on their way to the royal hunting reserve of Ettrick Forest.

In the upper part of the town is the Market Place, with its statue of Sir Walter Scott. He was here many times in real life — as one of the Sheriffs of Selkirkshire — hearing cases in the now-disappeared Tolbooth on whose site his statue stands, and after 1803 in the Court-room beside it, where mementoes of him are retained.

On the west side of the square, Halliwell's Close leads to a restored 18th-century house which is partly a local-history museum and partly a museum of vintage ironmongery.

Farther up the Ettrick Water, among fields and sweeping woodlands, Bowhill House is the mostly 19th-century Border home of the Duke of Buccleuch. It is open in summer to show its grandly furnished state rooms and valuable collection of paintings.

Two attractive and informative woodland trails meander through the grounds, past ornamental lochs and along the banks of the Ettrick's major tributary, the Yarrow Water.
🚗 *SELKIRK is on the A7, 7 miles south of Galashiels.*

TORPHICHEN
West Lothian

The Knights of the medieval Order of St John chose this location for the preceptory which became their Scottish headquarters — and the heart of a sanctuary area. Its central tower and transepts remain as an ancient monument, and the rebuilt nave is a parish church.

On the summit of Cairnpapple Hill, south-east of the village, there is a remarkable ceremonial and burial site, first used around 4000 years ago. A dome now protects the excavated site, and allows some of the early graves to be displayed.

One element in Cairnpapple's mystic appeal must have been that, in clear conditions, the view extends all the way across Central Scotland, literally from sea to sea.
🚗 *TORPHICHEN is on the B792, 2 miles north of Bathgate.*

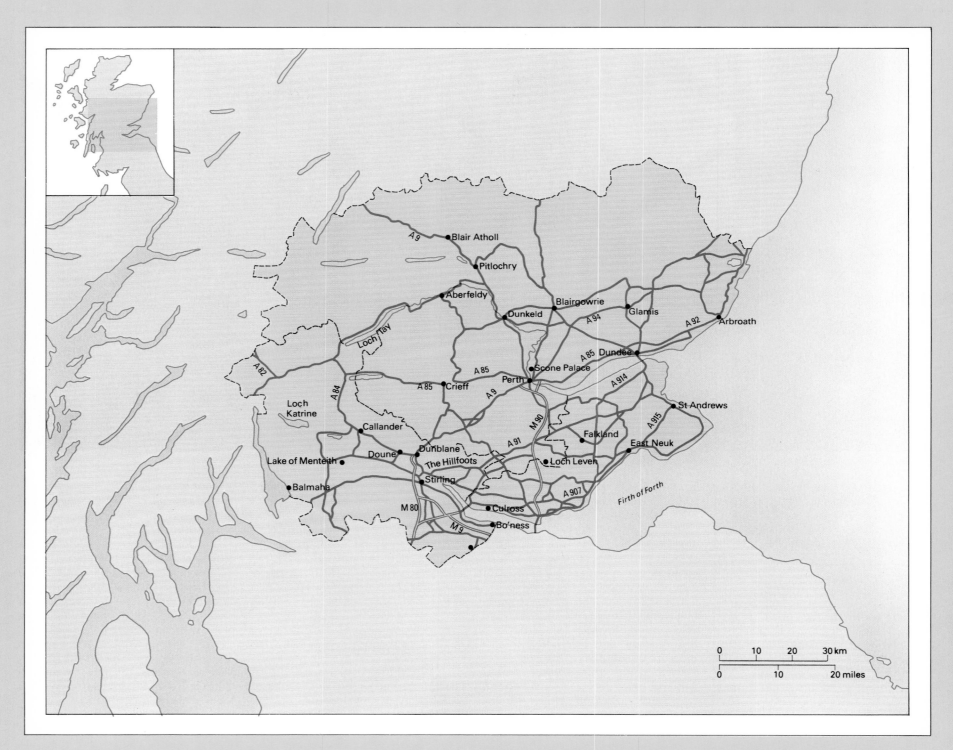

Blair Atholl

Pitlochry

Aberfeldy

Dunkeld

Blairgowrie

Glamis

Arbroath

Loch Tay

A 9

A 94

A 92

A 82

A 85

A 85

Scone Palace

A 85 Dundee

Crieff

Perth

A 9

A 914

Loch
Katrine

A 84

St Andrews

Callander

M 90

Falkland

A 915

East Neuk

Doune

Dunblane

A 91

Lake of Menteith

The Hillfoots

Loch Leven

Balmaha

Stirling

A 907

Firth of Forth

M 80

Culross

Bo'ness

M 9

0   10   20   30 km

0   10   20 miles

Central, Fife & Tayside

Walter Scott's ballad *The Lady of the Lake* was inspired by Loch Katrine, a fact which draws many visitors. Summer cruises can be taken on a turn-of-the-century steamer named after the great man

IF THERE WERE A prize for the most boring name handed out to any of Scotland's new Regions in the local government reorganisation of 1975, it would have to go to Central. The name conjures up visions of ...... nothing very alluring.

And yet, this is the area which includes places like the Trossachs — the lochsides, mountains and forests where Sir Walter Scott set many of his romances, and Rob Roy MacGregor was a real-life outlaw; almost the whole of the eastern side of Loch Lomond, with its oakwoods and offshore islands; historic cathedrals, monuments, battlefields, full-scale mountains and miles of hill and forest walks.

In that same reshuffle of boundaries and names, the old 'Kingdom' of Fife fought an impressive battle to remain separate and complete.

This massive peninsula between the estuaries of the Forth and the Tay is far from being — in a King of Scotland's one-time jibe — 'a beggar's mantle with a fringe of gold'. The fringe is certainly still there, in the string of beautifully restored little coastal towns and sandy beaches; but the interior of Fife has its own fair share of the spirit of conserving the attractive and historic fabric of the past.

Tayside is mostly the former counties of Perth, Angus and Kinross. The miles upon miles of arable farms in Strathmore and the Carse of Gowrie, separated by the rounded Sidlaw Hills, are balanced by coastal towns, cliffs and inland mountain glens.

ABERFELDY
Perth and Kinross

Coming here in 1787, Robert Burns was delighted by a walk through the wooded ravine around the Moness Falls on the outskirts of the town, and wrote the still-popular song called *The Birks of Aberfeldy*.

The birks (or birches) and many other trees still flourish, and the glen now has a beautiful nature trail.

Aberfeldy lies in the valley of the River Tay, with sweeping hills to north and south. Beside General Wade's bridge of 1733 is the Black Watch memorial; the famous regiment was raised here in 1739, and its original duty was to keep watch on the Jacobite clans.

To the north-west of Aberfeldy, the sturdy 16th-century Castle Menzies is being restored by the Clan Menzies Society. On either side of the town are the colourful shrub and woodland gardens at Bolfracks and Cluny House. And, off the Grandtully road, the 16th-century St Mary's church is preserved as an ancient monument because of its intricately painted ceiling.

🚗 *ABERFELDY is on the A827, 23 miles north of Crieff.*

ARBROATH
Angus

The most significant building in this independent-minded fishing town is the ruined 12th-century Abbey, where the Declaration of Arbroath was composed in 1320.

Six years after Bruce's victory at Bannockburn had reasserted Scotland's independence, there were still innumerable nuisances and border raids. The Declaration, written in clerical Latin, was addressed to Pope John XXII in an effort to have him convince the English that the war

Arbroath smokies, a popular national dish

was over. Even then, the formal peace treaty was not signed until 1328.

Nowadays, the town's most famous product is the 'Arbroath smokie'. Haddock bought at the quayside fish market are put into curing sheds, and then sold all over Scotland.

There is a breezy clifftop nature trail to the north-east; and a comprehensive local museum is contained in a notable building — the early 19th-century Signal Tower from which communication was maintained in pre-radio times with Bell Rock Lighthouse 11 miles out to sea.

🚗 *ARBROATH is on the A92, 16 miles north-east of Dundee.*

BALMAHA
Stirling

This gorgeously situated Loch Lomondside village, with its boatyard, yacht and dinghy moorings, is sheltered from the north by the descending summits of Conic Hill. They mark the edge of the Highland Boundary Fault.

Inchcailloch, the island immediately opposite Balmaha, has a beautiful Nature Conservancy trail through hilly oak and alder woodlands — browsed by fallow deer — which were once commercially cropped. There is also the site of a 13th-century church and burial ground.

On the mainland, pathways climb through larch and spruce plantations to glorious viewpoints on Conic Hill, down which the West Highland Way approaches Balmaha before continuing up the lochside to Rowardennan at the foot of Ben Lomond.

Balmaha is also the starting point for the regular passenger-carrying island mailboat run.

🚗 *BALMAHA is on the B837, 3½ miles west of Drymen.*

BLAIR ATHOLL
Perth and Kinross

This is the village at the gates of Blair Castle, the dignified white-towered home, surrounded by wooded parkland, of the Duke of Atholl. The oldest part of the castle dates from 1270, and no fewer than 32 of its apartments are open to visitors, from supremely elegant state rooms to the passageway called the Fourth Duke's Corridor.

The Duke of Atholl is the only person in Europe to be allowed a private army — a privilege granted by Queen Victoria. One of the great events at Blair Castle is the Atholl Highlanders' annual inspection and parade.

Blair Atholl has a local museum and a working old-style corn mill.

Three miles west, the Clan Donnachaidh Museum is devoted to the families of Robertson, Reid and Duncan. It is at the foot of the steeply wooded glen where paths and footbridges show off the triple cascades of the Falls of Bruar.

🚗 *BLAIR ATHOLL is off the A9, 7 miles north of Pitlochry.*

BLAIRGOWRIE
Perth and Kinross

On opposite banks of the rushing River Ericht, Blairgowrie and Rattray combine to form a single town which, thanks to the hundreds of acres of soft-fruit farms around it, is no less than 'raspberry capital of the world'.

The soft-fruit industry started in the 1890s. Before that, the waters of the Ericht powered a series of now-abandoned flax and jute mills.

One point on the river is still known as Cargill's Leap, after a hair-raising escape from pursuing soldiers by one of the most famous of all the Covenanting preachers, the Rattray-born Reverend Donald Cargill.

Blair Castle is the 13th-century stronghold of the Duke of Atholl. Within its handsome walls are displays of china, weaponry and Jacobite relics

South of the town, the suburb of Rosemount is the home of Blairgowrie Golf Club, whose courses set among heather banks, pines and birchwoods are among the finest inland layouts in Scotland.

To the west, Ardblair Castle, home of the Blair-Oliphant family descended from Bonnie Prince Charlie's aide-de-camp, is open on certain days to display its Jacobite relics.

🚗 *BLAIRGOWRIE is on the A93, 16 miles north of Perth.*

BO'NESS
Falkirk

Built on rising ground on the south side of the Firth of Forth, this once heavily industrialised town has long since given up its fuller name of Borrowstounness; the old shipyards, whaling dock, salt-pans, coal-mines and potteries have also gone, along with a flourishing trade in pit-props imported from the Baltic.

Handsomely situated above the town, and noted for its ornamented walls and ceilings, the old mansion-house of Kinneil — once a seat of the Dukes of Hamilton — is preserved in an attractive public park with fine views across the Forth to the hills of Fife.

A Roman fort built as part of the Antonine Wall has been uncovered in the Kinneil grounds, and the old stables block has been turned into an excellent local-history museum.

On the shore of the Forth, the volunteer-run Bo'ness and Kinneil Railway offers steam-hauled services on summer weekends.

🚗 *BO'NESS is on the A706, 3 miles north of Linlithgow.*

CALLANDER
Stirling

There are traces of a remoter past in and around Callander — a Roman fort, and the grassy mound by the meadows of the River Teith named

Culross Palace was the first property bought by the National Trust for Scotland

after the 6th-century St Kessog; but the centre of this attractively laid-out town still follows a plan devised in 1739.

Ancaster Square remains the heart of the plan, with many original houses. A great deal of Callander, though, is 19th-century, built to cater for tourists come to thrill at the district where Sir Walter Scott set so many of his exciting ballads and novels.

Callander has a genuinely Highland backdrop. Behind it rise

steep wooded crags which, despite their forbidding appearance, have well-marked footpaths to dramatic summit viewpoints.

There are beautiful autumn beechwoods on the edge of the golf course. High above is another footpath, with spreading views over the Teith valley, to the rock-ledged Bracklinn Falls.

North-west of the town, the main road enters the Highlands proper at the narrow and thickly wooded Pass of Leny, where footpaths follow old

charcoal-burners' routes and skirt a deserted village, and there is a famous salmon-leap.

CALLANDER is on the A84, 16 miles north-west of Stirling.

CRIEFF
Perth and Kinross

This is another place where Lowlands and Highlands meet — a process which has not always been peaceful. In 1716 the Jacobite army left the town a smoking ruin. Bonnie Prince

Charlie, exactly 30 years later, held a war council here during his retreat to Culloden.

But there was normal commercial traffic too: Highland drovers used to bring thousands of cattle to Crieff market.

In mid-Victorian times, the town began to develop as a health and holiday resort. Now it has golf courses, parks, riverside paths like Lady Mary's Walk alongside the Earn, and footpaths climbing the hill called the Knock, where pinewoods, birch and rowan give way to heather moors with magnificent high-level views.

There are artists and craftsmen here too. Crieff produces glassware and pottery, crystal and paperweights on a considerable scale; and the oldest malt whisky distillery in Scotland operates from a quiet nearby glen.

🚗 *CRIEFF is on the A85, 17 miles west of Perth.*

CULROSS
Dunfermline

At the foot of a hill rising from the north shore of the Firth of Forth, Coo'ross is a place in an apparent time-warp. There are no television aerials or telephone poles, and many of its houses are intricate restorations of carelessly attractive 17th-century originals.

Culross once had famous coal mines under the sea, dozens of salt-pans on the shore, blacksmiths' shops and a harbour busy with Dutch and Baltic trade.

Back as ships' ballast from the Netherlands came loads of red-clay pantiles. Together with white-harled walls, outside stairways, crow-stepped gables, dormer windows, turrets and corbels, these have become the architectural mark of the little town.

Most notable of the buildings open to the public — one of several owned by the National Trust for Scotland — is Culross Palace, completed in 1611 for the wealthy merchant laird Sir George Bruce.

A Culross Trail explores all levels of the place, from the Georgian town house, up narrow lanes towards the high-set parish church built alongside the substantial ruin of a 13th-century Cistercian Abbey.

🚗 *CULROSS is off the A985, 7 miles west of Dunfermline.*

Dunblane has picturesque stone-built houses and an ancient cathedral

DOUNE
Stirling

One of Scotland's finest medieval castles stands above the winding and wooded banks of the River Teith on the outskirts of this little town once famous for the manufacture of the pistols which still appear on its coat of arms.

Doune Castle was built around 1380 as the stronghold of the Stuart Duke of Albany, taken over as a residence of the Stuart kings and queens, then given back to the original family, who became the Stuart Earls of Moray. The 20th Earl is the laird of Doune today.

The whole fabric of the castle was restored in the 1880s. Most of it is unfurnished; but rooms shown to visitors include the royal apartments and the dignified Lord's Hall with its heraldic screen displaying 20 coats of arms.

On the far side of the town, Doune Motor Museum is housed in rebuilt 19th-century farm buildings. It has the Earl's own collection as its base.

🚗 *DOUNE is on the A84, 8 miles north-west of Stirling.*

DUNBLANE
Stirling

Although a town in size, Dunblane is sometimes given the courtesy of being called a city, because of the cathedral which was built here beside the Allan Water early in the 12th century — on the site of a Celtic church established by St Blane himself about the year 600.

Carefully-restored buildings at the Cross which forms the heart of the town focus attention on the cathedral.

This is still the parish church, with much of the early stonework restored

Scotland's fourth largest city, Dundee's industrial sprawl covers the north bank of the Firth of Tay

at the turn of the century. The oldest surviving features of the building are a Norman tower and the marble-floored, oak-panelled Lady Chapel.

Buried in the choir are Margaret Drummond, mistress of James IV, and her two sisters. Political intrigue led to their being poisoned at a meal in 1502, to make sure that Margaret would never marry the King.

Now almost entirely surrounded by Dunblane, the little hamlet of Ramoyle, near the cathedral, was visited in Victorian times because of its mineral wells.

South of Dunblane, passing at first below the hillside golf course, the wooded and very attractive Darn Walk follows the river to Bridge of Allan, a town which developed more wholeheartedly as a spa.

DUNBLANE is on the A9, 5 miles north of Stirling.

DUNDEE
City of Dundee

This is an uncompromisingly industrial city on the north bank of the Firth of Tay, producing — as the local saying has it — 'jute, jam and journalists' in great quantities.

There are many modern factories on the outskirts, whereas in previous centuries the emphasis was on the woollen and linen trade, the docks and the whaling fleet.

From Edward I in 1296 to Cromwell's General Monck in 1651, Dundee attracted a disastrous number of besieging armies and fleets. Very few historic buildings survive, although the Old Steeple of the 15th-century parish church is one of the city's many museums, and the very well restored Claypotts Castle of a century later stands casually among

lawns and gardens at the side of a suburban road.

Dundee has an unexpectedly fine variety of public parks. Camperdown Park houses a golf museum; the Mills Observatory was built in 1935 in Balgay Park, specifically for public use; and the highest park is around Dundee Law, the 571-ft spectacular viewpoint summit of an old volcano.

Down in the harbour is the oldest British warship still afloat: the frigate *Unicorn* launched at Chatham in 1824 and now most impressively equipped as a privately-run naval museum.

DUNDEE is 21 miles north east of Perth.

DUNKELD
Perth and Kinross

The town and cathedral here — on a site where a monastery was establish-

ed in the 6th century and some masonry of its 848 replacement can still be seen — both suffered because of their all too accessible position on the main route into the Central Highlands.

In 1560 the Reformers badly damaged the cathedral, which had taken from 1318 to 1501 to reach completion; and in 1689 only three houses in the whole town survived the Battle of Dunkeld, a Pyrrhic victory by a Covenanting regiment over the Jacobites.

Several restorations in more recent years have preserved the remains of the cathedral, on its very pleasant site among wooded lawns above the River Tay. The National Trust for Scotland has painstakingly rebuilt the houses leading up to it — 17th- and 18th-century replacements for the town burned down in the battle.

The Tay here is a famous salmon river overlooked by steeply wooded hills. Thomas Telford's seven-arched bridge of 1808 crosses it to the Victorian village of Birnam, where what is claimed to be the last surviving oak of the Birnam Wood in Shakespeare's *Macbeth* is propped up beside the beautiful riverside Terrace Walk.

DUNKELD is off the A9, 15 miles north of Perth.

EAST NEUK
North-east Fife

The string of very attractive little harbour towns and holiday resorts along the coast from Largo Bay to Fife Ness occupy the district known unofficially as the East Neuk — or corner — of Fife.

Earlsferry takes its name from a traditional ferry-crossing over the Forth to the Lothian shore. A curving sandy bay links it with Elie, where the Lady's Tower above the low cliffs beyond the yachting harbour was where the imperious Lady Janet Anstruther used to bathe after sending a bellman round the town to warn the 18th-century commoners away.

St Monance has a handsomely restored 14th-century church, and a yard where fishing boats have been built for well over 200 years.

Along the High Street of Pittenweem there is a fine display of 16th to 18th-century architecture, notably in the 1588 Tolbooth and the stone-towered Kellie Lodging built two years later.

Narrow wynds lead down to the harbour, where the central fish-market of the East Neuk is overlooked by more elegant buildings restored, like so much hereabouts, by the National Trust for Scotland.

Last of the historic East Neuk burghs is Crail. A heritage trail takes

The Birthplace of Golf

Nobody knows for certain when or where golf was first played in Scotland; but there were several 15th-century Acts of Parliament by which the authorities tried — with no great success — to have men of fighting age stop spending time on golf which would have been better devoted to archery practice in preparation for yet another war with the English.

These prohibitions were difficult to enforce, because golf was a game with no social distinctions. It was not just the common people who played; Mary, Queen of Scots was a golfer, and so was James VI, who is on record in the royal accounts-book as having lost a wager on the result of a match with one of his earls.

Golf was at first essentially a coastal game, played on the links — literally, the sandy turf which linked the countryside with the sea-shore.

Many Scottish courses, like the most famous of them all, the Old Course at St Andrews in Fife, are still laid out in these same basic conditions.

The Old Course has no trees, no flowering shrubs, no lakes, no ornamental landscaping. It is simply an uncompromising stretch of very well maintained coastal turf, with ridges and hidden hollows, a burn meandering across it, massive greens and fearsome sand-filled bunkers with names like Coffin, Grave and Hell.

While golf has spread from Scotland all over the world, St Andrews remains the game's spiritual but watchful home.

When one of the American astronauts played what amounted to a bunker shot on the gravelly surface of the moon, the Royal and Ancient Golf Club of St Andrews sent him a congratulatory message, but at the same time pointed out that an infraction of the rules had been noted from 240,000 miles away.

The courses at Gleneagles Hotel attract golfers from all over the world

in its basically 12th-century church, the elegant Nethergate and Marketgate, and restored houses with carved 'marriage lintels' over the doors, recording the initials and often the marriage dates of the couples who first lived in them.

🚗 *THE EAST NEUK towns are on the A917 east of Leven.*

FALKLAND
North-east Fife

The glory of this little town at the foot of the rounded Lomond Hills is Falkland Palace, created in the time of the Stuart kings and still a royal property today, although the splendidly restored buildings and furnished state rooms are open to the public through the National Trust for Scotland.

Generations of Stuart monarchs and their courtiers, from the time of James II in the 14th century onwards, loved to hunt in the forests around Falkland, and the palace was a favourite royal residence.

James V's French stonemasons added to it in Renaissance style; but after the court moved to London in 1603, the palace gradually fell into decay, before a grand rebuilding programme was put under way in the 1880s.

In terms of meticulous restoration, the rest of Falkland matches its palace. Town mansions, shops, cottages, workshops and taverns of the 17th to 19th centuries occupy the central area, which was Scotland's first-ever specially designated Conservation Area.

🚗 *FALKLAND is on the A912, 5 miles north of Glenrothes.*

This recreated schoolroom is part of the fascinating Angus Folk Museum housed in Kirkwynd Cottages, Glamis

GLAMIS
Angus

The grandest building in Angus is Glamis Castle, home of the Earls of Strathmore since 1372, and famous for its literary connection with Macbeth, courtesy of William Shakespeare's tragic play. It is built of delicately-shaded red sandstone, with a roofline which is a riot of slim, slate-roofed corbelled towers.

The heart of the castle, with its 15-ft thick walls, pre-dates by many centuries the main building completed in 1687. It has valuable collections of furniture, tapestries and china; outside, there are formal gardens and a nature trail in the wooded parkland, and a hugely ornamented sundial on one of the lawns.

In the village of Glamis, the National Trust for Scotland looks after the 17th-century Kirkwynd Cottages, home of the extensive Angus Folk Collection; the last of Scotland's handloom linen-weavers can also be seen at work.

🚗 *GLAMIS is off the A94, 25 miles north-east of Perth.*

THE HILLFOOTS
Clackmannan

Laid out along the very foot of the Ochil Hills, five villages and towns here are noted for their mild weather, colourful gardens and well-restored houses.

Blairlogie is a compact village sheltering below crags and gorsebanks. Once a year, visitors crowd its narrow lanes when more than a dozen village gardens are open to view.

Alva's fortunes were founded at the very end of the 18th century when the first of several woollen mills was built. In the 1820s, Alva Burn was

tapped to provide water-power for the mills, and a spectacular footpath follows the pipeline, high above a precipitous ravine, up into the Ochils.

In Menstrie, the 16th-century castle has been ingeniously converted into flats and a public library: but it also houses the Nova Scotia Room. This commemorates the founding, in the reign of James VI and I, of the colony of Nova Scotia — New Scotland — in Canada.

Coats of arms are displayed of the baronetcies of Nova Scotia created in the hope that their holders would finance the colony's development. Sir William Alexander of Menstrie was the prime mover of the scheme.

At Tillicoultry, the Mill Glen nature trail climbs steeply past waterfalls to open moorland. And at Dollar, paths and footbridges in a wooded glen lead up to the fine viewpoint of Castle Campbell, a part-restored 15th to 17th-century fortress of the Campbell Earls of Argyll.

🚗 *THE HILLFOOTS road is the A91, north-east of Stirling.*

LAKE OF MENTEITH
Stirling

Although there are smaller, artificially created lakes elsewhere, this is the only stretch of natural inland water in Scotland which is not called a loch.

At Port of Menteith, the square-towered parish church, the white buildings of a lakeside hotel and the water's-edge screen of trees with the wooded Menteith Hills in the background are all reflected in the still waters.

Port of Menteith is an angling resort, and in hard winters curling matches are sometimes held on the ice.

A ferry runs to Inchmahome, largest of the lake's wooded islands.

This is a remarkably peaceful place, where the ruins of a 13th-century Augustinian priory are maintained as an ancient monument among well-trimmed lawns.

Inchmahome is most famous as the hideout — during an English invasion in 1547 — of the infant Mary, Queen of Scots. She was brought here secretly for a few days before being moved, for greater safety, across the Channel to France.

🚗 *THE LAKE OF MENTEITH is off the A81, 6 miles east of Aberfoyle.*

LOCH KATRINE
Stirling

Visitors started coming in great numbers to admire the rugged Highland scenery here after Sir Walter Scott's ballad *The Lady of the Lake* — the lake being Loch Katrine — was published in 1810. He used the district again as the setting for his best-selling novel *Rob Roy*.

The most spectacular approach to Loch Katrine is over the Duke's Road from Aberfoyle, originally built in 1820 by the Duke of Montrose to provide a carriage-route for tourists. It winds over a pass through birchwoods and forest plantations, then plunges down past Loch Achray to the turn-off for Loch Katrine itself.

The loch and its entire hilly catchment area are owned by Strathclyde Regional Council's water department, which provides a visitor centre where the public road ends at Trossachs Pier.

Summer cruises to Stronachlachar at the far end of the loch are run by the elegant little turn-of-the-century steamer *Sir Walter Scott*. Walkers and cyclists can reach there by using the private road past Rob Roy MacGregor's birthplace at Glengyle.

🚗 *TROSSACHS PIER is on the A821, 7 miles north of Aberfoyle.*

LOCH LEVEN
Perth and Kinross

Extending to nearly 4000 acres, with seven islands of varying sizes, Loch Leven is a famous trout fishery and National Nature Reserve. Geese, ducks and swans winter in their thousands here.

The Lomond Hills sweep up to the east, and part of Benarty Hill to the south is occupied by the Vane Farm reserve of the Royal Society for the Protection of Birds. Gliders, using the air-currents over the hills, soar from Portmoak on the south-eastern side.

Kinross on the west side of the loch is the old county town. A lochside park is the starting point of ferry trips to the wooded Castle Island.

The basically 14th-century island fortress is famous as the prison where Mary, Queen of Scots was forced to abdicate in favour of her infant son James VI.

In 1568 she made a daring escape, only to meet imprisonment and death in England.

KINROSS is off the M9, 13 miles north of Dunfermline.

LOCH TAY
Perth and Kinross

Surrounded by mountains, this 15-mile loch is fed from the west by the united waters of the Lochay and the Dochart, which tumbles into the village of Killin in a series of famous rapids and rocky falls.

The main road along the north side runs below the looming 3984-ft bulk of Ben Lawers, where the National Trust for Scotland has a visitor centre and a notable reserve of arctic and alpine wildflowers.

Eventually, the road skirts the plantations of Drummond Hill Forest, with their network of high-level viewpoint walks, and arrives at the beautifully located and arranged village of Kenmore, built by the Earls and Marquesses of Breadalbane as an ornament at the entrance to Taymouth Castle.

The inn at Kenmore, built in 1572, is the oldest in Scotland; this is where the ceremonial opening of the Tay salmon season is celebrated every January.

A minor road turns back from the foot of the loch, along the southern shore past the old mill village of Acharn and the smaller angling resort of Ardeonaig, as it makes its way through woodlands and fields back towards Killin.

THE MAIN ROAD along Loch Tay is the A827 from Killin to Kenmore.

PERTH
Perth and Kinross

Spreading out from a mostly Georgian centre, Perth is built on both banks of the Tay, with riverside parks at the North and South Inch which have been public property since the 14th century.

The North Inch has a golf course and sports fields, behind which are the modern Bell's Sports Centre and the historic 16th-century Balhousie Castle which acts as the Black Watch museum.

The house called Branklyn at the foot of Kinnoull Hill has probably the finest town garden in the country, now maintained by the National Trust for Scotland.

Substantial villas are set in wooded grounds on the slopes of Kinnoull Hill. Another public park on the highest level above cliffs overlooking

Perth is spread over both banks of the River Tay and contains some interesting and historic buildings

the lower Tay provides outstanding views and is crossed by a multitude of footpaths.

Down in the town centre, St John's Kirk was the scene on 11 May 1559 of the most significant sermon ever preached in Scotland.

Unerringly catching the mood of the time, John Knox's fiery address from the pulpit set ablaze the forces of Reformation.

PERTH is off the M90, 40 miles north of Edinburgh.

PITLOCHRY
Perth and Kinross

This is a beautifully situated holiday resort in the mountain and forest-flanked valley of the River Tummel, which was dammed as part of a hydro-electric scheme to create the attractive and gently winding Loch Faskally.

A fish ladder allowing salmon to make their way to the traditional spawning grounds upstream is included in the visitor centre at Pitlochry dam.

There is a modern Festival Theatre on the far bank of the Tummel. Pitlochry is an angling and golfing centre. There are forest walks by Loch Faskally and the smaller Loch Dunmore, and up to the viewpoint summit of Craigower. And beauty spots like the wooded ravine at the battlefield of Killiecrankie are within easy reach.

PITLOCHRY is off the A9, 26 miles north of Perth.

ST ANDREWS
North-east Fife

As well as being the home of golf — with no fewer than four 18-hole courses owned by a public trust on the world-famous links behind the two-mile West Sands — St Andrews

St Andrews has Scotland's oldest university, founded in 1411

has Scotland's oldest university, which was founded in 1411 and still spreads all over the town in a series of handsome colleges and quadrangles.

The ruined cathedral, dedicated to Scotland's patron saint, gave the town its name; by the time it was completed in 1318, it was the largest church ever to be built in Scotland.

St Andrews Castle, with the grisly Bottle Dungeon from which there was positively no escape, was built in the 12th century. It became the fortress of Cardinal Beaton, who had several Reformers burned at the stake before being himself assassinated in the castle in 1546.

Fortunately, there are many happier places in St Andrews — a neatly proportioned town plan, carefully restored buildings, the finest city gate in Scotland at the West Port, pleasant walks on the wooded Lade Braes above the Kinness Burn, a botanic garden, holiday facilities and the modern Byre Theatre, on the same site as the original theatre, which really did begin its working life as the cow-shed of a dairy farm.

🚗 *ST ANDREWS is on the A91, 10 miles east of Cupar.*

SCONE PALACE
Perth and Kinross

The present mansion-house here, completed in 1808 for the Earl of Mansfield, stands on the site of a 16th-century predecessor whose main gateway is still in place. But the historic significance of Scone goes far further back in time.

In the grounds is the site of an ancient capital of the Picts, and Scone was the place where the kings of Scotland were crowned, from the 9th century until Charles II's coronation in 1651.

The palace is splendidly furnished, with collections of paintings, china, ivory, clocks and needlework on display. Its grounds feature formal gardens and a very extensive pinetum.

🚗 *SCONE PALACE is on the A93, 2 miles north of Perth.*

STIRLING
Stirling

Even today, this is a town in an important location, on the main road and rail routes north. But its position was much more significant in earlier centuries, when its fortress on a huge, unscaleable crag faced west over the all but trackless marshes round the meanders of the River Forth, and all land traffic to the Highlands was forced to pass this way.

The present Stirling Castle was built by the Stuart kings, and it is open to the public as one of Scotland's most impressive ancient monuments.

The castle is supported by many other substantial buildings in 'the top of the town', which is currently being revitalised; high-level walks around the hill offer outstanding views.

On Abbey Craig across the Forth there is a Victorian monument, in the form of a 220-ft tower with display rooms, to Sir William Wallace, victor at the Battle of Stirling Bridge in 1297 over an invading English army.

Dramatically floodlit, like the castle itself, at night, it has an eagle's-eye view over no fewer than seven battlefields.

Most famous of these, south of the town, is Bannockburn, where the National Trust for Scotland has a major exhibition on the site of Robert the Bruce's final and decisive victory over Edward II in 1314, thereby guaranteeing Scotland's independence once and for all.

🚗 *STIRLING is off the M9, 26 miles north-east of Glasgow.*

Stirling Castle from the approach across the gardens. The castle houses the museum of the Argyll and Sutherland Highlanders

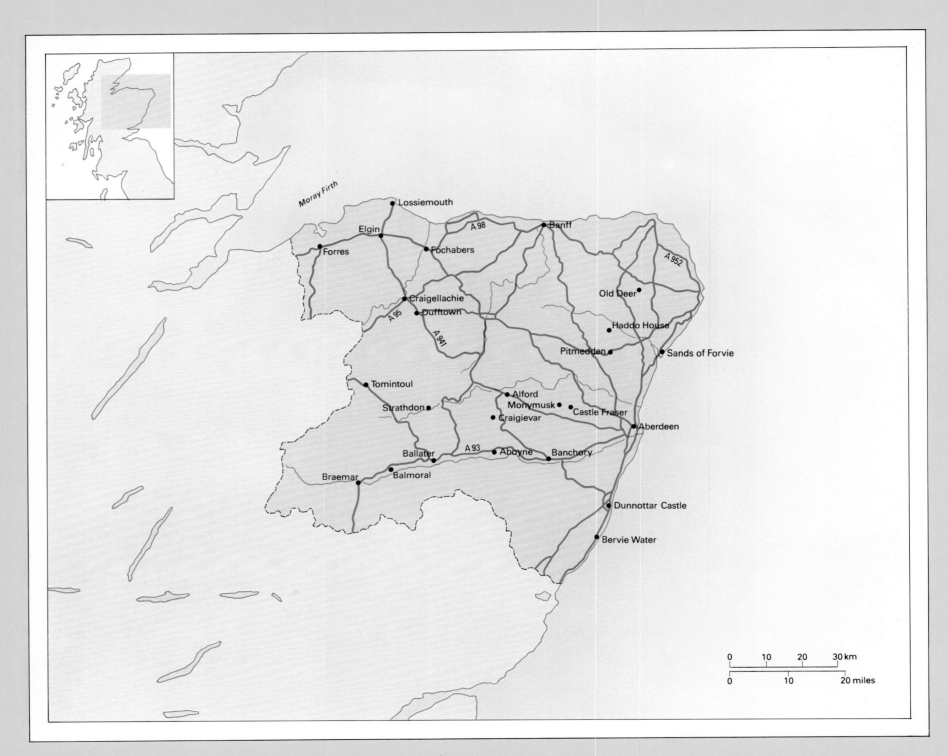

Moray Firth

Lossiemouth

A 98

Banff

Elgin

Forres

Fochabers

A 952

Craigellachie

Old Deer

A 95

Dufftown

Haddo House

A 941

Pitmedden

Sands of Forvie

Tomintoul

Alford

Monymusk

Strathdon

Castle Fraser

Craigievar

Aberdeen

A 93

Ballater

Aboyne

Banchory

Braemar

Balmoral

Dunnottar Castle

Bervie Water

0   10   20   30 km

0   10   20 miles

Grampian Region

Elgin's ruined 13th-century cathedral is its most famous building. It was burned out in the raid by the Earl of Buchan which was his reply to a sentence of excommunication

THIS NORTH-EASTERN corner of Scotland takes its name from a range of mountains which, in their turn, are a misprinted version of the Latin name *Mons Graupius*, a famous battle between the Romans and the Picts whose actual site is still in debate.

The heart of Grampian is undoubtedly Royal Deeside, where tourists and wealthy mansion-house builders took their cue from Queen Victoria and Prince Albert, the creators of Balmoral as the Royal Family's Scottish home.

But there had been castle-builders here generations before: not only the barons who raised fortresses like Kildrummy and Corgarff, but also the prosperous merchants and landowners who commissioned local ar-

chitects and masons to design some of Scotland's finest stately homes at places like Crathes, Castle Fraser and Craigievar.

There are rugged mountains inland, like Lochnagar with its towering cliffs; old-established pinewoods and newer plantations of spruce; lesser heathery summits crossed by winding hill roads like the Lecht, Cabrach and Cairn o'Mount, and many well-run, productive farms.

As a contrast, Grampian also includes the bustling city of Aberdeen and a well-settled coast where holiday resorts and fishing ports at Stonehaven, Peterhead, Fraserburgh, Banff and Macduff share the extensive sands, cliffs and headlands with active or retired fishing villages like Pennan and Gardenstown, Findochty, Burghead and Findhorn.

ABERDEEN
City of Aberdeen

Visitors to Aberdeen airport, where helicopters run all-day shuttle services to production platforms far out in the North Sea, may have the impression that this is little more than a modern oil city.

But the place the Vikings called *Apardion* has civic history going back to the early 12th century. Its extensive public parks can be traced to a charter signed in 1319 by Robert the Bruce, outlining the Freedom Lands of Aberdeen. And the fortunes made from the Baltic trade financed many of the city's fine public and private buildings.

Despite its not entirely undeserved reputation for north-east hard-headedness, Aberdeen is lavish in many unexpected ways. It may be the Granite City, for instance, but in summer it is also the City of Roses — on the first Rose Day in 1983, a quarter of a million rosebuds were handed out free.

Parks, gardens, golf courses and a two-mile beach make sure that Aberdeen has plenty of fresh air and elbow-room; but the historic centre is well worth exploring too.

St Nicholas Church in Union Street has a carillon of 48 bells, the largest in Britain. Wealthy merchants like Provost Ross and Provost Skene built themselves grand town houses which are now museums: Provost Ross's house in the Shiprow includes displays on Aberdeen's fishing and harbour trades, and on the National Trust for Scotland's properties all over Grampian.

Most of Aberdeen's university buildings are in Old Aberdeen, a copybook example of Georgian restoration. Notable earlier buildings there include St Machar's Cathedral and the original King's College of 1505.

Older still is the splendid Gothic-arched Brig o'Balgownie over the River Don, opened in 1329 and now one of Scotland's finest medieval structures still in everyday use.

ABERDEEN is 117 miles north of Edinburgh.

ABOYNE
Kincardine and Deeside

After being established in the 1670s, the village here became the focal point of the River Dee timber trade. Pinewood logs cut in the Forest of Glentanar were assembled at Aboyne into rafts which were floated downriver to Aberdeen.

Retaining its granite houses overlooking the green where Aboyne

Aberdeen was a thriving port by the 13th century. Today it is the largest oil field supply base in Scotland

Neo-classical Aberdeen: Union Street, built in the 1800s

Highland Games are held every year, the village was rebuilt and extended in mid-Victorian times by Sir William Cunliffe Brookes, a millionaire banker who became the proprietor of Glentanar estate, one of many incoming Royal Deeside lairds.

In and around Aboyne, there are facilities for golf and angling, waterskiing on Aboyne Loch and gliding on Dinnet Moor.

An informative visitor centre is provided at Braeloine in Glentanar, at the start of a network of very attractive riverside, farm and woodland walks.

🚗 *ABOYNE is 31 miles west of Aberdeen on the A93.*

ALFORD
Gordon

This market town is in the Howe of Alford, a low-lying area around the windings of the River Don where farms and wooded estates give way to forest plantations and rounded open hills.

The Grampian Transport Museum

is located here; undoubted star of its display is the Craigievar Express, a steam-powered tricycle built by a remarkable local postman, Andrew Lawson, and put on the roads in 1897.

Nearby, the redundant main line Alford station has been restored as a local railway museum. From it, a narrow-gauge railway runs regular leisurely services into the two country parks — Haughton House and Murray Park — which bound Alford to the north. Murray Park was presented to the people of Alford in 1935 by a highly-regarded north-east poet, Charles Murray.

In both parks there are nature trails through birch, conifer and mixed woodland where roe deer browse.

Provost Skene's 16th-century house on Flourmill Lane contains a folk museum

🚗 *ALFORD is 26 miles west of Aberdeen on the A944.*

BALLATER
Kincardine and Deeside

A town built of granite to a regular, rectangular plan, Ballater is on a fan of level ground in a bend of the River Dee. There are wooded hills all around — notably just behind the town at Craigendarroch, where footpaths climbing through birch, oak and pinewood lead to a summit viewpoint which opens up a splendid Deeside panorama.

As the idea of Royal Deeside gathered momentum, so the 18th-century settlement of Ballater grew in size and significance as a holiday resort.

The riverside land south-west of the town is laid out as an attractive golf course. There is angling on the rivers and on various nearby lochs.

A four-mile walk heads east along the track-bed of the old Deeside Railway to Cambus o'May. Another walk by the wooded riverside follows what was intended to be an extension of the railway westwards to Braemar; but Queen Victoria vetoed it, because the line would have brought the trains directly in sight of Balmoral.

🚗 *BALLATER is 42 miles west of Aberdeen on the A93.*

BALMORAL
Kincardine and Deeside

It was in 1847 that Queen Victoria and Prince Albert, having a fairly miserable late-summer holiday on an Inverness-shire estate where the rain battered down all day and the cloud-capped mountains were already sprinkled with snow, heard that the weather on Deeside was bright, sunny and dry.

For the next few years, they rented

Balmoral, on a bend in the River Dee between Ballater and Braemar; and in 1852 Prince Albert finally bought the whole Balmoral estate.

In 1853 building work started on the present granite castle with its 100-ft turreted tower. The Prince collaborated with Aberdeen architect William Smith on the detail design, and with the creation of new gardens as well as new houses for the staff, Balmoral was on its way to becoming what it still is today — a model but working estate of hill, forest and farmland.

It remains the Royal Family's private Scottish home; but the beautifully wooded grounds and gardens are open to visitors during most of May, June and July, and there is an exhibition in the ballroom.

Balmoral Estates have also co-operated with the Scottish Wildlife Trust in providing public access to a spectacular 6350-acre mountain reserve which includes the major summits of Lochnagar. The reserve's visitor centre is near Loch Muick, at the end of a minor road south-west of Ballater.

BALMORAL is 48 miles west of Aberdeen off the A93.

BANCHORY
Kincardine and Deeside

Golf, sea-trout and salmon fishing are among the attractions of this inland Deeside holiday resort, and Banchory is also an excellent centre for walking. There are wandering paths all around it, in natural woodlands and in Forestry Commission plantations of pine, spruce and larch.

An unexpected product of the district is lavender, and there are guided tours of the Ingasetter factory which distills it into perfumes.

About three miles down the valley of the Dee, Crathes Castle is one of

the grandest properties of the National Trust for Scotland. Although the castle itself was built towards the end of the 16th century, the Burnett lairds — originally de Burnards — who owned it until 1952 were granted the lands here by Robert the Bruce.

He appointed his supporter Alexander de Burnard a royal forester; and the hunting horn which, according to tradition, was presented as the badge of office still hangs in the High Hall of Crathes today.

There are nature trails in the well-wooded 595-acre Crathes grounds. But Crathes is more famous for its eight inter-linked gardens with their varying colour and landscape themes. Lawns and topiary-worked yew hedges planted in Queen Anne's time add to the attractions of one of north-east Scotland's finest open-to-the-public estates.

BANCHORY is 18 miles south west of Aberdeen on the A93.

BANFF
Banff and Buchan

A lively Preservation Society makes sure that the architectural heritage of this old county town is maintained. Houses, churches, inns and public buildings are mostly of the 17th and 18th centuries.

Duff House, outside the town, is a Georgian extravaganza designed by William Adam for the 1st Earl of Fife; but an icy row between them, over a structural fault, meant that the building was never completed according to its original plans.

The mansion-house is open to the public as an ancient monument; its grounds include a golf course by the River Deveron and a woodland walk

Balmoral Castle, bought and rebuilt by Prince Albert in the 1850s

The L-shaped tower house of Crathes Castle contains some outstanding examples of painted ceilings

famous of all the races to bring back the first high-value shipload of the new season's China tea.

Sir Francis Chichester came to Inverbervie in 1969 to unveil the striking Linton memorial.

🚗 *INVERBERVIE is on the A92, 10 miles south of Stonehaven.*

BRAEMAR
Kincardine and Deeside

The highest village on Royal Deeside, Braemar is a place whose story traditionally goes back to the 10th century, when Kenneth II is said to have brought his courtiers here on a deer-hunt, leaving the wooded hill which rises east of the village — Creag Choinnich, or Kenneth's Crag — named after him.

A much later hunting party was the occasion when the Earl of Mar raised the Jacobite standard to announce the start of the 1715 Rising.

Queen Victoria and Prince Albert came to the Braemar Gathering during their first holiday at Balmoral in 1848, and established it as the pre-eminent sporting and social event of the Deeside season — which, with the Royal Family always in attendance, it remains to the present day.

Rather more quietly, Robert Louis Stevenson brought his family here in the summer of 1881, renting a holiday cottage on the Glenshee road. He spent most of the days writing, and by the evening fireside would read aloud the latest completed chapters of *Treasure Island*.

In the valley, the historic 17th-century Braemar Castle is open to visitors during the summer. Higher up, there are magnificent views towards the Cairngorms from the birchwood and juniper reserve on the hillside of Morrone.

🚗 *BRAEMAR is 16 miles west of Ballater on the A93.*

up-river to the ravine crossed by the high-arched Bridge of Alvah.

Over the bridge, an old livestock-drovers' track leads through Montcoffer Wood back to Macduff, the rival town built opposite Banff on the far side of the river-mouth.

Unlike Banff's own harbour, Macduff's remains a busy and prosperous fishing port. Sea angling and water-skiing are also catered for at Macduff. There is a fine viewpoint in front of the high-set parish church, and a striking war memorial tower rises on another hilltop.

At Tarlair, an open-air swimming pool with attached boating lake is overlooked by an adventurously laid-out clifftop golf course.

🚗 *BANFF is 47 miles north west of Aberdeen.*

BERVIE WATER
Kincardine and Deeside

This unobtrusive river is formed from a number of streams draining the hillsides of Drumtochty Forest, and gathers more tiny tributaries as it flows through the farmlands of the Mearns in a series of sweeping curves which are themselves made up of innumerable smaller bends.

Robert Burns's father was a farmer's son hereabouts before moving to Edinburgh and latterly as a market gardener to Alloway. Several of Burns's relations are buried in the leafy churchyard at Glenbervie.

Downstream at Arbuthnott, one of Scotland's most notable rural churches — St Ternan's, based on a restored 13th-century chancel — stands above one of the Bervie Water's beautiful wooded curves.

In the churchyard there is a memorial to James Leslie Mitchell — otherwise the novelist Lewis Grassic Gibbon — whose *Sunset Song* trilogy, familiar from television, recalled the hard life earlier this century in the hill-farm country to the north.

The river reaches the sea at Inverbervie, birthplace of the great clipper-ship designer Hercules Linton. In 1872 his *Cutty Sark* won the most

Malt Whisky

Connoisseurs of whisky give classic status to the unblended 'single malts', whose brand names are also the geographical locations of the distilleries which produce them.

What gives each single malt whisky its characteristic and never-duplicated taste is not just the standard processes of barley-malting followed by mashing followed by fermenting, distilling and maturing. The pure water of Highland burns tumbling down peaty hillsides is simply not available anywhere else in the world — and every individual distillery has its own carefully guarded supply.

Six distilleries in Grampian have combined to offer visitor facilities and guided tours on the Malt Whisky Trail, where history, tradition, explanation of processes and a complimentary 'dram' are all part of the attraction.

Glenfiddich attracts over 90,000 visitors in a typical year; The Glenlivet — in a district which was originally a hotbed of illegal distilling — was granted that significant definite article in 1880; at Glenfarclas the Grants are the only malt whisky dynasty to have passed ownership on in an unbroken line from father to son, since the June day in 1870 when John Grant, while more concerned at that time with clipping sheep, noted almost as an afterthought in his diary that the first 320 gallons had been produced in his lately-acquired

The Glenfiddich Distillery pagodas — the name given to the pyramid-like roofs over the malt-drying kiln

A whisky connoisseur's paradise: the cellars at Glenfiddich Distillery

distillery.

At Tamdhu the visitor centre is in the station built for the distillery on a now-abandoned railway; Glen Grant is in the whisky town of Rothes, beside the angling waters of the Spey; and Strathisla at Keith has claims to being the oldest working distillery north of the Highland Line.

Old or new, and whether or not they actually continue to malt their own barley over peat fires, most distilleries retain that famous architectural feature which identifies them from miles away: the special roof over the malt-drying kiln which is always described as a pagoda.

CASTLE FRASER
Gordon

In 16th and 17th-century Aberdeenshire there were two families of architects and master masons — the Bells and the Leipers — who were both involved in the creation of the spectacular Castle Fraser, on the edge of the middle valley of the Don.

This is the largest of the National Trust for Scotland's Castles of Mar, a building extended from a smaller original in 1575, for a Fraser laird after whom the square Michael Tower is named.

Later additions up to 1636 gave the castle an ornamented roofline of remarkable elegance — delicate dormer windows, cornices, crow-stepped gables, corbelled turrets and a massive heraldic carving with a modest addition of the date 1617 plus 'I. Bel' — John Bell, the self-effacing master designer.

Inside the castle, there are appropriate furnishings, portraits and needlework to be admired; and the Round Tower is topped by a balustraded viewing platform looking out over the wooded parkland grounds.

🚗 *CASTLE FRASER is 3 miles south of Kemnay.*

CRAIGELLACHIE
Moray

Well-known to anglers for its salmon-beats on the River Spey, this is a whisky distillers' and coopers' village of Victorian granite, taking its name from the wooded cliff across the Spey which marked the traditional eastern boundary of the Clan Grant lands.

Across this stretch of water, the master bridge builder Thomas Telford built one of the most graceful bridges in Scotland.

With a 150-ft cast-iron span and four 'chess-piece' towers, his Craigellachie bridge was completed in 1815 and remains open to pedestrians — a fine industrial monument as well as an ornament to the landscape.

🚗 *CRAIGELLACHIE is 13 miles south of Elgin on the A941.*

CRAIGIEVAR
Gordon

Looking over its hillside parkland, midway between the valleys of the Dee and the Don, Craigievar is perhaps the most perfect 17th-century Scottish castle, in the ornamentation of its upper storeys and the uncluttered purity of its basic tower-like design.

There are no subsidiary wings or other buildings to divert the eye as it gazes up at the turreted skyline and balustraded rooftop platform.

Craigievar was almost certainly another masterpiece to the design of John Bell. It was completed in 1626 for William Forbes, one of Aberdeen's richest Baltic merchants, and remained a family home until it was bought by the National Trust for Scotland in 1963.

All the major rooms are open to visitors. Many have intricate moulded-plaster ceilings, and plaster is also used for the imposing Royal Arms over the fireplace in the medieval-style hall.

🚗 *CRAIGIEVAR is off the A980, 6 miles south of Alford.*

DUFFTOWN
Moray

In 1817 James Duff, 4th Earl of Fife, established a town on the hillside above the meeting of the Dullan Water and the River Fiddich.

Dufftown was therefore ideally situated in time and place to take advantage of the change in whisky

The outstanding ceiling in the Great Hall at Craigievar Castle

distilling from a largely illegal adventure to a substantial taxpaying industry which occurred a few years later; south-west of the town, the Dullan Water runs through Glen Rinnes, whose rounded hills had sheltered many an illicit whisky still.

Dufftown is now the heart of the malt whisky country, and Glenfiddich distillery's visitor centre is the busiest in Scotland.

But Dufftown's history goes back much further. The first church in the Kirktown of Mortlach is said to have been founded in the 6th century, and the present, much-restored church has old Pictish symbol stones on display.

From Mortlach, a footpath up the wooded Dullan valley makes for a delicate waterfall known as the Linen Apron, and the sturdy rock formation of the Giant's Chair.

North of the town, the basically 13th-century Balvenie Castle is open as an ancient monument; and the history of the area is summed up in a museum in the baronial clock tower in the square.

🚗 *DUFFTOWN is 18 miles south east of Elgin on the A941.*

DUNNOTTAR CASTLE
Kincardine and Deeside

Occupying the summit plateau of a prodigious cliff-bound rock, Dunnottar is an all but island fortress on the coast south of the holiday resort of Stonehaven.

A stronghold to be coveted by either side, it was attacked and defended heartily during all the English wars. The present castle was started in the 14th century by Sir William Keith, Earl Marischal of Scotland.

With defences which had been continually strengthened over the years, Dunnottar was the last place to hold out against Cromwell's army, surrendering with honours, after an eight-month siege, in May 1652.

The besiegers had expected to find, in the castle, the Regalia of Scotland — the crown, sceptre and sword of state; but in a magnificently daring escapade, they had already been smuggled out, and were safely hidden in the parish church of Kinneff, a few miles down the coast.

Kinneff's historic church is well restored, and has an exhibition on its most exciting episode.

Dunnottar itself was partly dismantled after the Jacobite Rising of 1715; but much of it was restored in an extensive private project started in 1925. It is open to visitors, still a place with massive defences, in a stunning location with wide-ranging North Sea views.

🚗 *DUNNOTTAR is 2 miles south of Stonehaven.*

ELGIN
Moray

This is the market town for the farms and estates in the Moray lowlands, with the River Lossie meandering along its original northern boundary.

Much of Elgin, like the Greek-pillared church in a widening of the High Street, was built in Georgian style. But the most famous building here is the ruined 13th-century cathedral.

In 1390 it was burned out in a raid by the Earl of Buchan, known with good reason as the 'Wolf of Badenoch'. This was his typical riposte to a well-deserved sentence of excommunication.

The cathedral was rebuilt; but it was brusquely treated after the Reformation. Now preserved as an ancient monument, it remains strikingly handsome even in decay.

Elgin Museum has a notable geological collection as well as displays on local regiments; and a meal-mill restored to working condition is open to visitors during the summer.

🚗 *ELGIN is 67 miles north west of Aberdeen.*

FOCHABERS
Moray

The conservation area at the heart of this 'planned' town on the east bank of the Spey is mostly Georgian, although there is also an impressive Victorian school.

Fochabers folk museum is noted for its collection of horse-drawn carriages. Across the Spey bridge to the west, Baxters of Speyside is a food-processing firm with a world-wide export trade, whose visitor centre includes the rebuilt Victorian shop from the High Street of Fochabers where the business started on a much more modest scale.

The Winding Walks in Speymouth Forest wander through a glen with rhododendrons, birches and mixed conifer plantations. A high-level viewpoint known as The Peeps looks down along the High Street, and over the wooded farmlands of lower Speyside.

🚗 *FOCHABERS is 9 miles south east of Elgin on the A96.*

FORRES
Moray

In Shakespeare's *Macbeth*, the second scene is in 'a camp near Forres', following on the famous opening when the witches chant through the thunder and lightning of an

The seemingly impregnable position of Dunnottar Castle forced Cromwell's army to besiege it

anonymous 'open place'. Traditionally, this is identified as the Hardmuir west of the town.

But Forres, built on both sides of the little Mosset Burn, has much more to offer than the brief encounter with great drama. It is a town of parks and gardens, where the wooded summits of the small-scale Cluny Hills have footpaths towards a viewpoint tower set up to commemorate Nelson's victory at Trafalgar.

One of Scotland's finest early sculptured monuments stands beside the Kinloss road. Sueno's Stone is a 20-ft pillar with detailed carvings of warriors in battle array.

Four miles west of Forres, the Brodies of Brodie — now in their 25th generation of chiefs — have been landowners since 1160. Their 16th-century Brodie Castle, with its collections of furniture, paintings and porcelain, is now the property of the National Trust for Scotland. There is a woodland walk in the grounds, skirting a four-acre ornamental lake.

South of Brodie Castle are the extensive forests and farmlands of the Earl of Moray's Darnaway estate. Guided tours are arranged in summer from the visitor centre at Tearie Farm, and include the basically 15th-century Darnaway Castle.

FORRES is 11 miles west of Elgin on the A96.

The Blue Drawing-room at Brodie Castle, showing the fine barrel-vaulted plasterwork ceiling

HADDO HOUSE
Gordon

Although Haddo House is still the centre of a privately-run estate, the mansion and its gardens are now owned by the National Trust for Scotland, and 180 acres of the wooded grounds make up a local-authority country park.

William Adam designed Haddo House in the 1730s for the 2nd Earl of Aberdeen. Its restrained Georgian style was altered in detail during a remodelling in the 1880s, when the Gothic chapel with its Burne-Jones stained-glass windows was added.

The main rooms, still furnished in distinguished style, are open to visitors. Haddo House Choral and Operatic Society, founded in 1945, continues to produce operas, concerts and plays in the late-Victorian maplewood hall.

The country park consists of lawns and grazing land, picnic areas in a sheltered rhododendron wood, enough broadleaved and conifer species to justify the Tree Trail, and other footpaths round an ornamental lake which is also a popular roost for wildfowl.

🚗 *HADDO HOUSE is 6 miles north east of Oldmeldrum.*

LOSSIEMOUTH
Moray

Until a few hundred years ago, there was not only no town at Lossiemouth — the mouth of the River Lossie was also some distance away. The sea-coast ran much closer to the county town of Elgin, which had its salt-water port at a place called Spynie.

But a massive sand and shingle bar built up, cutting Spynie off from the sea and creating a vast inland lagoon. In 1698 the town council of Elgin had to buy land for a new harbour at what is now Lossiemouth, and the town built up steadily around it.

The lagoon and its marshland fringe were drained for farmland in the 1880s, and the Spynie Canal built for the project still flows through Lossiemouth today.

An excellent museum near the harbour has comprehensive displays on Lossiemouth and its fishing industry through the years.

It also includes the re-created study of Lossiemouth's most famous son — Ramsay MacDonald, Britain's first Labour prime minister. A hillside memorial to him is a fine viewpoint over the old Seatown, the remains of the lagoon, the sand-dunes and beaches — reached by a long footbridge — on its seaward side, and the plantations of Lossie Forest stretching to the south-east.

West of the town there are more beaches, a picnic area and a fine golf course, which all have a grandstand view of the RAF planes on training flights from Lossiemouth aerodrome.

🚗 *LOSSIEMOUTH is 5 miles north of Elgin.*

MONYMUSK
Gordon

A little way back from the south bank of the Don, where the river finally shakes itself free of the hills and comes into lowland country, Monymusk is centred on a square of very attractively restored cottages around the village green. They were remodelled at the turn of the century by Sir Arthur Grant of Monymusk estate.

Towering above the cottages, however, is the real architectural glory of the village — the 12th-century Norman church of sandstone and granite, carefully restored in the 1930s and also given some good modern stained glass.

In the porch is a reminder that there was a religious house on this site long before the present one. The Monymusk Stone dates from the time of the Culdee priests of the earlier Celtic church which faded before the advance of the disciplines of Rome.

🚗 *MONYMUSK is on the B993, 10 miles east of Alford.*

OLD DEER
Banff and Buchan

Until the Reformation, this little grey-stone village at a double bend of the South Ugie Water was best known for the 13th-century abbey nearby. The buildings then fell into decay, and were almost completely destroyed by a Victorian landowner who ransacked them to build a family burial aisle.

The ruins have now been reinstated as an ancient monument, standing peacefully among riverside lawns.

Immediately east of Old Deer, Aden House was once the centre of an extensive farming estate. But the Russell lairds of Aden fell on hard

Haddo House, home of the Earls of Aberdeen, where concerts are regularly performed

times, and the last of them sold out in 1937.

In the 1970s, 220 acres around the now-ruined mansion were transformed into Aden Country Park, one of the showpieces of Buchan. The totally restored home-farm buildings include one of the finest estate-history displays in Scotland.

🚗 *OLD DEER is 2 miles west of Mintlaw.*

PITMEDDEN
Gordon

Although most of the National Trust for Scotland's properties in Grampian feature the castles and mansion-houses, at Pitmedden the principal attraction is the re-created 17th-century Great Garden, first laid out for Sir Alexander Seton.

Its centrepiece is the series of parterres with low boxwood hedges outlining patterns which are filled in with 40,000 flowers planted out every season. One of the designs shows Sir Alexander Seton's coat of arms; the others are based on drawings of the old gardens of Holyrood Palace in Edinburgh.

Elsewhere on the estate, restored farm buildings house a Museum of Farming Life. There are indoor displays of vintage farm equipment and outdoor collections of rare Scottish livestock breeds like the Rum pony, Soay and Boreray sheep from the far-out Atlantic rockstacks of St Kilda.

🚗 *PITMEDDEN is 5 miles east of Oldmeldrum.*

SANDS OF FORVIE
Gordon

Although there was a time when as many as 250 fishermen operated from Collieston, this colourful little village of cottages scattered round a tidal bay is now mostly a holiday resort.

To the south, the cliffs with their one-time smugglers' caves gradually give way to a shoreline of extensive sand-dunes. From here to the estuary of the River Ythan is the Sands of Forvie nature reserve. Terns and eiders in huge numbers come here to nest, and wild geese winter in their thousands.

From Collieston, a footpath leads through the lonely heathland in the centre of the reserve, passing the ruined church of the lost village of Forvie, which now lies under the sands.

🚗 *COLLIESTON is on the B9003, 22 miles north east of Aberdeen.*

STRATHDON
Gordon

At Cock Bridge, where the Lecht road from Tomintoul plummets out of the wild hill country above, the River Don is overlooked by the recently restored 16th-century Corgarff Castle, manned by troops till as late as the 1830s, in the government's efforts to stamp out the last traces of illicit whisky distilling.

Several miles down the winding and beautifully wooded course of the Don, Kildrummy Castle, like Corgarff, is an ancient monument, considered to be the finest of all the medieval fortresses in the north of Scotland, but partly dismantled after the Jacobite Rising of 1715.

The modern Kildrummy Castle, now a hotel, was built at the turn of the century. Between the two castles, the 'back den' is a series of water, shrub and alpine gardens.

Midway between Kildrummy and Corgarff, the village of Strathdon is where, every August, the Lonach Highlanders with shouldered pikes and in full Highland dress march round the mansion-houses of the district before the start of the Lonach Games in the riverside sports field.

🚗 *STRATHDON village is on the B973, 19 miles west of Alford.*

TOMINTOUL
Gordon

After a steep and winding climb from Cock Bridge, past the skiing grounds around its summit, the Lecht road continues to the highest village in the Highlands at Tomintoul.

This is a bright and airy, neatly laid-out place around a central square, still following the street-plan drawn up in 1776.

There is a local museum; a country walk explores the steeply wooded glen of the River Avon; and athletes congregate at Tomintoul in July for Scotland's highest Highland Games.

🚗 *TOMINTOUL is on the A939, 26 miles north-west of Ballater.*

The 17th-century gardens at Pitmedden were neglected until restored by the National Trust for Scotland

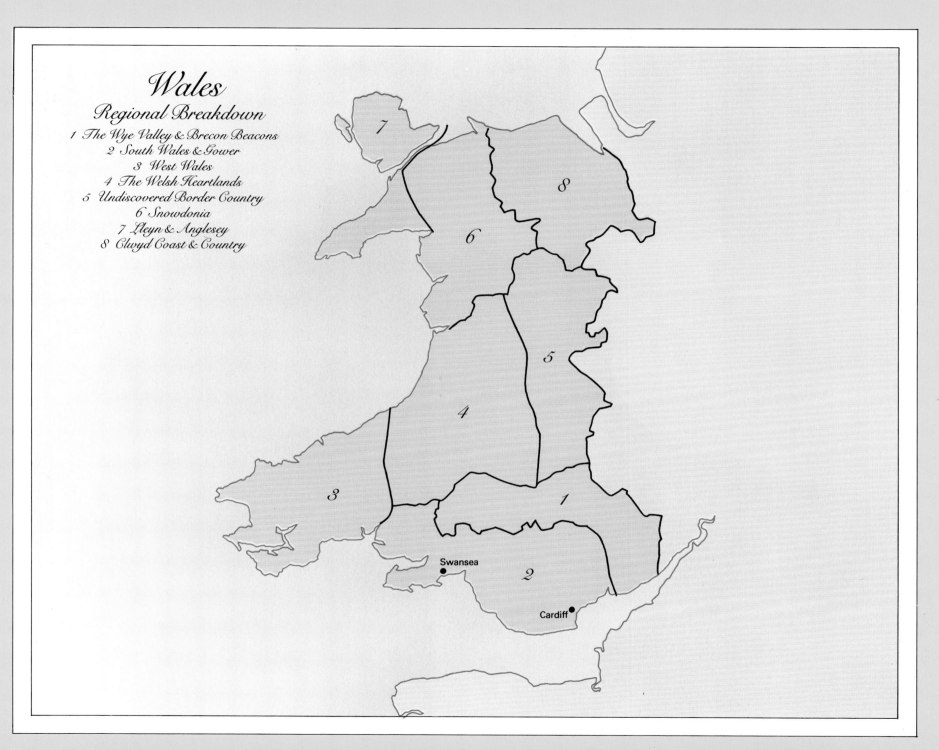

Wales

Regional Breakdown

1 The Wye Valley & Brecon Beacons
2 South Wales & Gower
3 West Wales
4 The Welsh Heartlands
5 Undiscovered Border Country
6 Snowdonia
7 Lleyn & Anglesey
8 Clwyd Coast & Country

Swansea

Cardiff

The Wye Valley & Brecon Beacons

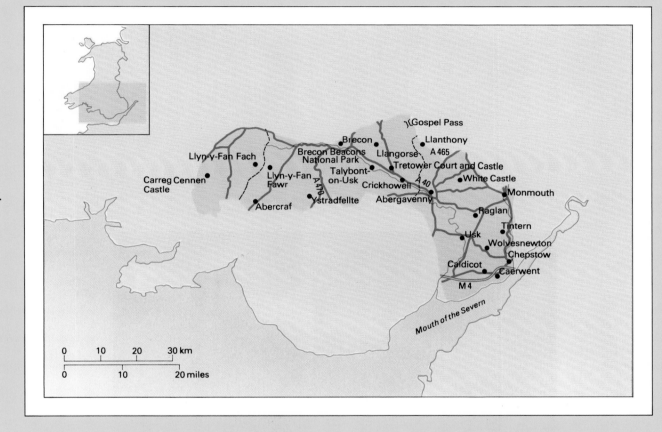

Left: Dramatic skies over one of Wales's most dramatic castles. Carreg Cennen, perched on a lonely outcrop in the brooding Black Mountain

(map labels: Gospel Pass, Llanthony, A 465, Brecon, Llangorse, Brecon Beacons National Park, Tretower Court and Castle, Llyn-y-Fan Fach, Talybont-on-Usk, White Castle, Carreg Cennen Castle, Llyn-y-Fan Fawr, A 470, Crickhowell, A 40, Monmouth, Ystradfellte, Abergavenny, Raglan, Abercraf, Tintern, Usk, Wolvesnewton, Chepstow, Caldicot, Caerwent, M 4, Mouth of the Severn)

0   10   20   30 km
0   10   20 miles

AS REPRESENTED ON the map, the Wye Valley north of the medieval gateway town of Chepstow does nothing more than define the line of the border between Wales and England. Closer acquaintance reveals a lovely, leafy vale, its riverbanks and wooded hillsides protected as an 'Area of Outstanding Natural Beauty'.

Few will quarrel with this official description. There is no better introduction to Wales than the drive north from Chepstow. Open meadowland soon narrows into the sinuous, shady confines of the Wye Valley. The valley opens out again at Monmouth into undulating, undisturbed border country, a patchwork of farmlands dotted with pretty towns and villages. The ebb and flow of Welsh history has washed across these strategic borderlands, leaving Roman remains and castles.

The busy market town of Abergavenny is another gateway, standing at the entrance to the Brecon Beacons National Park. The park — all 520 square miles of it — sweeps across much of southern Wales from the Black Mountains, which straddle the border, to the similarly named, but entirely separate Black Mountain in the far west.

The Beacons themselves occupy centre stage, their fresh and windy flanks rising to nearly 3000 ft at Pen-y-fan, South Wales's highest peak. Unlike the rocky mountains in the north of Wales, the Brecon Beacons ars smooth and green. A string of lakes and pockets of pine forest are dwarfed by big skies, huge views and unbroken horizons.

ABERCRAF
Powys

Two attractive places to visit are located next door to each other within the confines of the narrow, steep-sided Upper Tawe Valley near this village. The 40-acre Craig-y-Nos Country Park, by the banks of the river, is a pleasant, ornamental parkland of specimen trees, open meadowland, lake and pond.

It was designed as a 'pleasure ground' for the 19th-century opera singer, Madame Adelina Patti. The park was an accompaniment to her home, a rambling sham castle of monumental proportions which is now a home for the elderly.

The limestone outcrops in the hillside above the castle mark the entrance of the Dan-yr-Ogof caves. This showcave complex, which claims to be the largest in western Europe, contains no less than three separate systems open to the public. Guided tours in the main showcave just scratch the surface of a vast and labrynthine network of caves, discovered in 1912, which extends for miles into the mountain. A second entrance leads to the Cathedral Cavern, 160 ft long by 70 ft high. Further up the hillside is the architecturally fascinating 'Bone Cave', which tells the story of its occupation by man and beast from prehistoric times.
BOTH ATTRACTIONS are located on the A4067, 20 miles northeast of Swansea.

ABERGAVENNY
Gwent

This busy town, surrounded by farms and fields in the pastoral Vale of Usk, retains its long established links with the countryside. The farming community still comes to town every Tuesday for important livestock sales, held in the market place behind the bustling main street.

Abergavenny Castle, a scant ruin dating from the 12th century, overlooks green fields and meadows leading down to the Usk. Today, it seems unthinkable that this pleasant spot was the scene of a treacherous murder on the Christmas of 1176 when the infamous Norman lord William de Braose invited an unsuspecting group of Welsh noblemen to a banquet, killing them whilst unarmed.

Abergavenny's backdrop of rolling hills and mountains is a beautiful one, dominated by the distinctive shape of the 1955 ft Sugar Loaf.
ABERGAVENNY can be reached on the A4042 from Newport, the A40 from Raglan and the A465 'Heads of the Valleys' road from Merthyr.

BRECON
Powys

The narrow streets of this ancient market town are now thankfully by-passed by through traffic. Brecon's charter was granted in 1270, at which time it was ruled by its hilltop castle, now an intriguing ruin, partly incorporated into the Castle Hotel.

Brecon's Welsh name, *Aberhonddu* ('Mouth of the River Honddu'), reflects its location at the confluence of the Honddu and Usk. Twice-weekly markets, on Tuesdays and Fridays, perpetuate its strong links with the farming community and genuine, country town atmosphere. Brecon is also a natural centre for the Brecon Beacons National Park. The park's three main upland areas — the wild Black Mountain in the west, the central Beacons, and the borderland Black Mountains — are all within easy reach. The main headquarters for the park are in the town. And Pen-y-fan, its highest peak, dominates the horizon to the south.

Brecknock Museum displays a marvellous collection of Welsh love spoons, traditional symbols of betrothal intricately carved from single blocks of wood. The museum, housed in a classically designed building which was originally an assize court, preserves the Victorian courthouse intact, complete with prisoner's dock. A second museum, dedicated to the South Wales Borderers, contains a Zulu War Room which commemorates the regiment's heroic defence of Rorke's Drift in 1879.

The grand Church of St John, also known as Brecon Cathedral, really deserves its alternative title. This vast medieval church, which achieved cathedral status in 1923, serves a huge diocese extending as far as Swansea.
BRECON, at the junction of the A470 and A40, is 44 miles north of Cardiff.

BRECON BEACONS MOUNTAIN CENTRE
Powys

On a fine day, the views from the terraces of the Mountain Centre are magnificent. The centre, run by the National Park, is located at an altitude of 1100 ft on Mynydd Illtyd, an open common with panoramic vistas across to the high peaks of the Beacons.

Pen-y-fan, at 2907 ft the loftiest mountain in South Wales, dominates the skyline. Its unusual flat-topped summit crowns a mountain range which is quite unlike any other in Wales. Old red sandstone is the underlying rock, creating a largely

Brecon's market hall, open for business Tuesdays and Fridays

The smooth, green flanks of the Brecon Beacons spread themselves below a series of swooping crests

can be expected from a site which has witnessed so much history and been used as a home for so many centuries, it incorporates a wealth of architectural detail ranging from a Norman bedchamber to a Victorian housekeeper's room.

🚗 *CAERWENT is on the A48 between Chepstow and Newport, accessible from junctions 22 and 24 off the M4 motorway.*

CALDICOT
Gwent

Most visitors to Caldicot come by night, to enjoy the candlelit medieval banquets which are held within the walls of the castle. This is a pity, for this strangely unknown fortress only reveals its true size and splendour to daytime guests.

Caldicot Castle stands in a beautiful country park setting on the edge of an expanding town. Its solid round keep immediately catches the eye. This is the earliest stonework, probably put up by Humphrey de Bohun in the 13th century. Although a site of great antiquity, the castle is largely intact. The 14th-century Great Gatehouse, for example, still sees regular service as the venue for the nightly banquets of dubious 'medieval' authenticity.

The whole castle, snug within its walls, is full of interest. Medieval military architecture merges with Tudor-style half-timbered influences, the castle benefitting from a thorough yet sympathetic restoration in the last century.

Conspicuous amongst the exhibits in the castle museum is the huge figurehead rescued from the *Foudroyant*, Nelson's 'darling child' of a ship that was wrecked in 1897.

⚓ *CALDICOT, on the B4245, is 5 miles south-west of Chepstow, 6 miles east of Newport.*

treeless landscape which rises and falls in a series of gentle, rounded inclines, steep escarpments and razor-sharp ridges.

The Mountain Centre is a mine of information. Maps, models, exhibitions and films introduce visitors to the wealth of outdoor activities on offer in the 520-square-mile National Park,

🚗 *THE CENTRE, located on a minor upland road, is signposted off the A470 at Libanus, 4 miles south-west of Brecon.*

CAERWENT
Gwent

Sleepy Caerwent, skirted by the M4 motorway, is today no more than a village. In Roman times, it was firmly on the map as a large and important city, *Venta Silurum*, 'the market town of the Silures.'

Only by delving into its past can visitors understand the huge stretch of walls, still standing 17 ft high in places, which now defends nothing but green fields. *Venta Silurum* was

founded about A.D. 75 for the local hill tribe, the Silures, as part of the Romans' grand plan to subdue the natives. Quite what the Silures initially made of Roman civilization is anybody's guess, for their new home contained such novelties as public baths, a forum, temple and amphitheatre.

Penhow Castle, two miles to the west, is another history-laden site. Dating from the early 13th century, this fortified manor house claims to be Wales's oldest lived-in castle. As

CARREG CENNEN CASTLE
Dyfed

This castle invites superlatives. It has been variously described as 'the most theatrical of British castles' and an 'eagle's nest' fortress. Carreg Cennen, a lonely sentinel, crowns a limestone outcrop in the foothills of the remote Black Mountain. Its battlements are built into a sheer cliff which drops dizzily into the valley below. Weatherbeaten but unbowed, this castle is one of those rare historic sites which evokes the spirit of medieval Wales in an authentic, profound way.

The castle site is an ancient one. Roman coins have been found on the summit of this natural defensive position, which saw much bloody action during the troubled 13th century. A complicated series of fortifications cover the hilltop, which commands breathtaking — though windy — views of the unexplored western corner of the Brecon Beacons National Park. Below the surface, a narrow passageway, cut into the cliff face, leads to a cave beneath the foundations where prehistoric skeletons were unearthed. The mighty 'showpiece' castles of North Wales might be better known. Carreg Cennen is the one which lingers in the memory.

THE CASTLE is located near the village of Trapp, 3 miles south-east of Llandeilo.

CHEPSTOW
Gwent

Most motorists entering Wales by the Severn Bridge and M4 motorway sweep past this charming little town, unaware of its existence. This was not always possible. Chepstow is an historic gateway settlement which once controlled a strategic river crossing into Wales.

The Normans constructed a castle here, on slopes above a great bend in the River Wye. Theirs was no ordinary stronghold, for Chepstow was the first stone-built castle in Britain. Its sturdy walls, on a river cliff above the swirling, muddy-brown waters of the Wye, mark the end of crude earth-and-timber defences and the dawn of a new era in castle construction.

The castle was started shortly after William the Conquerer's victory at Hastings in 1066. Over the years — right up to the 17th century, in fact — Chepstow was improved and added to. As well as being an important first, this fascinating fortress is therefore one of the few sites which spells out in its stonework all the different periods of castle building.

The town of Chepstow grew up on the hillside around the castle, its narrow streets, medieval gate and remnants of town walls providing further evidence of a long history. North of the town, in open, glorious countryside, stands Chepstow Racecourse, the largest in Wales.

CHEPSTOW is located 1½ miles north of Junction 22 on the M4 motorway, directly after the Severn Bridge.

Left: Chepstow Castle, an architectural landmark as Britain's first stone-built fortress

CRICKHOWELL
Powys

The Welsh derivation of the town's name, *Crug Howell* ('Howell's Fort'), refers to the ancient Celtic stronghold on the flat-topped summit of Table Mountain, which looms above the rooftops. Crickhowell still has the air of an old coaching and market town. The Bear Hotel — an historic coaching inn — retains its cobbled courtyard and archway decorated with the words 'Post Horses'. Georgian streets lined with fashionable craft and clothes shops lead down to the River Usk, spanned by a picturesque 13-arched stone bridge.

The long, narrow bridge, put up in the 16th and 17th centuries, continues to carry traffic. St Edmund's Church, dating from the 14th century, is another historic landmark. The church's tall, needle-sharp spire and striking red-tiled roof make it easy to spot. Its porch contains a stone slab which laid down the marital law to 19th-century parishioners in no uncertain terms. Thirty categories of relation, to whom marriage is forbidden, are blacklisted, culminating in wife's sister's daughters!

�car CRICKHOWELL *is on the A40, 6 miles north-west of Abergavenny.*

THE GOSPEL PASS
Powys

Few roads make any serious attempts to venture into the largely uninhabited Black Mountains. The Gospel Pass, a bold exception, strikes out due south from Hay-on-Wye, gradually climbing into high country.

The road, a narrow one with airy, panoramic views around almost every bend, runs along the lower slopes of Hay Bluff, a massive shoulder of land rising to 2200 ft. From here, the thin grey strip of tarmac takes advantage of a slight break in the ridge, climbing to a summit of 1778 ft before plunging into the secluded Vale of Ewyas, past Capel-y-ffin, with its little chapel and monastery, to Llanthony Priory.

The Gospel Pass's narrowness and great scenic qualities can also create great traffic congestion, especially on busy summer weekends. At its peaceful best — try to come out-of-season, or at least during mid week in summer — a drive over the Gospel Pass is a stirring experience.

🚗 *THE GOSPEL PASS leads off the B4350 on the outskirts of Hay-on-Wye.*

HAY-ON-WYE
Powys

Anyone interested in books needs no introduction to this small town with a big reputation. At the last count, there were 14 major bookshops here, easily justifying Hay's claim to the title of 'second-hand book capital of the world'.

Businesses which previously sold groceries and hardware have been converted into bookshops. Films are no longer shown at Hay's cinema, the building now stocking a good portion of the million-odd books which are for sale in this town of only one thousand people.

Hay is a paradise for bibliophiles and browsers. Antiquarian books and prints are also sold, together with an excellent selection of new titles often at knock-down, bargain prices.

If visitors can tear themselves away from the miles of book-laden, groaning shelves, they will discover a delightfully unspoilt town of terraced stone cottages, steep streets and an old covered marketplace. The main part of the town is neatly contained between the River Wye, at its foot, and the ruined castle-cum-mansion on a perch above the rooftops.

🚗 *HAY, on the B4350, is accessible off the A438 north-east of Brecon.*

LLANDEILO
Dyfed

The lords of Dinefwr, the ancient rulers of South Wales, presided over their kingdom from Dinefwr Castle, now a romantic ruin veiled amongst trees and ivy on its rocks to the west of the town. The Tywi winds its way along the foot of both castle and town in a rich, green and fertile river valley on which Llandeilo depends for its livelihood.

Llandeilo is an olde-worlde collection of narrow, steep-sided streets lined with little businesses which serve the prosperous farmlands of the Vale of Tywi. From the south the town is approached by a beautifully designed, slender single-span bridge, its 145 ft arch said to be the longest in Wales. A deer herd, arboretum, woodland walks and formal gardens are all contained within the Gelli Aur Country Park, just over four miles south-west of Llandeilo.

🚗 *LLANDEILO, which can be reached on the A40 and A483, is about 22 miles north of Swansea.*

LLANDOVERY
Dyfed

George Borrow, the 19th-century traveller and writer whose classic book, *Wild Wales*, is still in print, described Llandovery as 'the pleasantest little town in which I have halted in the course of my wanderings'. He stayed at the Castle Hotel; those following in his footsteps might wish to know that the four-poster bed in which he slept is still there, in the rechristened 'Borrow Room'.

Llandovery, little changed since Borrow's visit over 100 years ago, continues to delight visitors. It has escaped the blight of modern development and remains a Welsh country town through and through. The ruined castle, a precarious grey shell on a steep earthen tump, overlooks the sheep pens where the weekly livestock markets are held. The town square, with its covered market place, cobbles and clocktower, is charming. And on a hill on the outskirts stands a large church, its presence signalled by a sturdy 13th-century tower, built on the site of a Roman camp.

🚗 *LLANDOVERY is on the A40, 20 miles west of Brecon at the junction with the A483 and A4069.*

LLANGORSE
Powys

Llangorse provides the setting for the largest natural lake in South Wales. The lake, fringed by reed beds and low-lying fields, fills one of the few stretches of flat land in the Brecon Beacons. On a still day, its waters — one mile long by half-a-mile wide — mirror the distinctive summit of Pen-y-fan, the highest peak in the Beacons.

Llangorse village, a short distance from the lake, is a pretty cluster of cottages which grew up around an ancient church and bridge. The Church of St Paulinus, Norman in design, retains part of its original roof. It is named after Paulinus, a 6th-century missionary and tutor to St David, Wales's patron saint, who founded a religious community here.

🚗 *LLANGORSE, on the B4560, is 6 miles east of Brecon.*

LLANTHONY
Gwent

Mountain-locked Llanthony, on the road to nowhere in particular, is not the kind of place visitors tend to stumble on by chance. The hamlet is hidden away in the remote Vale of Ewyas, deep in the Black Mountains.

Religious men in search of solitude founded a monastery here in the early 12th century. In the words of the peripatetic medieval chronicler, Giraldus Cambrensis (Gerald of Wales), no place was more 'truly calculated for religion' than Llanthony. The priory as it now stands, dating from 1175, forms the core of the hamlet. Although 800 years old, the original beauty of this red-stoned ruin survives, aided and abetted by timeless, unchanging surroundings. Its greatest glory is a magnificent avenue of pointed archways framing open hill-sheep country.

Llanthony has captivated many, though for the 19th-century poet, Walter Savage Landor, the outcome was unhappy. He bought the estate with grandiose plans to install himself as the model country gentleman. The locals, however, were unimpressed and Landor left under a cloud in 1813, never to return.

At one time in its history, part of the abandoned priory was used as a shooting box with a licence to sell drink. This explains Llanthony's unique 'pub in the priory' — a tiny hotel-cum-inn, built over the abbot's house, with a deserved reputation for good food and beer.

LLANTHONY can be reached by the B4423 north of Abergavenny or from Hay-on-Wye via the narrow Gospel Pass mountain road.

Llanthony's ruined priory, alone in the tranquil Vale of Ewyas

LLYN-Y-FAN FACH and LLYN-Y-FAN FAWR
Dyfed/Powys

Myth and legend surround this pair of isolated lakes, well and truly off-the-beaten-track in the wilderness of the Black Mountain. Of the two, Llyn-y-Fan Fach is the more accessible. The lake shelters beneath a near vertical escarpment which curves around the shoreline, forming a natural amphitheatre for its black waters.

This gloomily beautiful setting inspired the story of a Lady of the Lake who rose from the waters to marry a farmer. She, and the farm's entire herd of cattle, disappeared into the lake when the farmer struck her three times, though only in play.

The couple are said to have raised sons with remarkable healing powers. Whether by coincidence or not, the Physicians of Myddfai — a village five miles away and the only settlement of note near the lake — were famous, and much in demand, throughout medieval Wales.

Llyn-y-Fan Fach lies beneath the Carmarthen Van, at 2632 ft the highest point in the Black Mountain. A spectacular ridge walk runs through these boggy uplands from one lake to the other.

🚗 *THE LAKES should be approached via the hamlet of Llanddeusant, accessible off the A4069 Brynaman to Llangadog road. Park near the waterworks and follow the unmade track.*

MONMOUTH
Gwent

A statue of Charles Rolls, of Rolls-Royce fame, stands amongst traditional hotels and coaching inns in Monmouth's tightly-packed main square. Rolls, born at nearby Hendre, is not the only famous figure to have associations with this prosperous old country town. In 1387, Henry V was born in Monmouth Castle — now in ruins, alas, though his statue shares a place in the square with Rolls.

Admiral Lord Nelson's visit of 1802 is remembered at the local museum which contains, amongst other Nelson memorabilia, an outstanding model of his flagship, H.M.S. *Victory*. Place names such as Agincourt Square and Glendower Street reflect Monmouth's involvement in the mainstream of Welsh and English history. The Monnow Bridge is undoubtedly the town's most interesting historic landmark. This 13th-century fortified bridge gateway, the only one of its kind in Britain, still restricts access into the town, its narrow portal proving most effective against the modern motor car.

Nelson journeyed to the 840 ft high summit of The Kymin, one mile east of Monmouth, during his visit to admire the views and the Naval Temple, a monument erected in 1800 to commemorate British victories at sea.

🚗 *MONMOUTH stands at the junction of the A40 with the A466, just inside the Welsh border.*

RAGLAN
Gwent

All attention here centres on the castle. Raglan is one of Wales's most handsome — even elegant — ruined fortresses. Its grandeur is linked to its status as 'the last medieval castle', for by the time Raglan came to be constructed, castle builders could afford to pay more attention to decoration and less to defence.

This shapely castle belongs mainly to the early 15th century, a product more of social aspiration than military necessity. Sir William ap Thomas, an ambitious royal servant, began work here in 1431. His preoccupations, and those who succeeded him, are clearly evident in Raglan's stately tower and, most of all, the Great Hall, the former splendour of which is hinted at by its finely decorated windows, roof and vast fireplace.

For all its embellishment, Raglan was no weak-walled pushover. This extensive, moated fortress can pride itself in enduring the longest siege of the Civil War.

🚗 *RAGLAN is situated on the A40 about half-way between Monmouth and Abergavenny, and 12 miles north-east of Newport.*

TALYBONT-ON-USK
Powys

The place name of *Talybont* is a confusingly popular one in Wales. This particular Talybont is located amongst green farmlands on the side of forested slopes in the gentle Vale of Usk.

The river, some distance from the village, is somewhat usurped by a second waterway — the Monmouthshire and Brecon Canal — which flows right through Talybont supported by massive retaining walls. The canal was built between 1799 and 1812 to connect Brecon with Newport and the Severn estuary. Originally, it carried coal, wool and lime. Today, this scenic waterway, navigable for 33 miles through some of the loveliest countryside in the Brecon Beacons National Park, serves a different purpose. It is popular with holiday cruisers, many of which are invariably berthed along the towpath next to Talybont's excellent selection of pubs and inns.

🚗 *TALYBONT, on the B4558, is 6 miles south-east of Brecon and 7 miles north-west of Crickhowell.*

Tintern Abbey's soaring arches and sylvan setting have struck a chord with many artists and writers

TINTERN
Gwent

The thick woods and lazily-flowing waters in the Wye Valley between Monmouth and Chepstow have always inspired peace and contemplation. Tintern stands in a particularly tranquil spot. Here, in the 12th century, white-robed Cistercian monks founded a great religious house which was an active community until its dissolution in 1536.

In later centuries, the roofless abbey attracted artists and poets, including William Wordsworth who was inspired to pen his famous sonnet. This evocative, well-preserved ruin still retains much of its original grace and dignity. The abbey's majestic arches, walls and windows point skywards in complete harmony with its sheltered riverside setting.

Tintern itself is a small, scattered settlement in a part of the Wye Valley officially designated as being of 'Outstanding Natural Beauty'.

From the old railway station, now converted into a countryside information centre, waymarked walks lead through the woodlands. Most spectacular of all is the Wyndcliff walk and viewpoint high above the valley two miles to the south.

TINTERN is on the A466 5 miles north of Chepstow, 10 miles south of Monmouth.

TRETOWER COURT AND CASTLE
Powys

This is an interesting two-in-one historic site. A starkly simple round tower, unambiguously military in design and purpose, stands in meadows next to a substantial fortified manor house which must have been a comfortable residence in its time.

When the tower, or keep, was put up in the bellicose 12th century, life in Wales was full of threat. The court, in contrast, has all the home comforts of the more settled 14th and 15th centuries. A stone gatehouse leads to a grassy courtyard surrounded by rooms which contain superb examples of late-medieval craftsmanship in stone and wood (the woodwork and timber fittings in the hall and gallery are exceptional).

The court is also notable for its general state of preservation and similarity, in plan, to the colleges of Oxford and Cambridge. Tretower was the home of Henry Vaughan, the celebrated 17th-century metaphysical poet who is buried at nearby Llansantffraed Church.

TRETOWER is near the junction of the A40 and A479, 9 miles north-west of Abergavenny.

USK
Gwent

Usk takes its name from the mighty river that marks the western boundary of this compact little town located in quiet and rural border country. To the Romans, who built an important fortress here, it was known as *Burrium*. One thousand years later, the Normans arrived and founded a castle on the hill above the river. More substantial stone defences were built in later centuries, the 14th-century gatehouse now serving as a family house for a castle that is in private ownership and not normally open to the public.

Usk relies on its river for more than its name. The inns, tackle shops and fishing hotels ranged around the spacious town square benefit from the excellent salmon and trout waters.

USK stands at the junction of the A472 and A471 just off the A499, 9 miles north of Newport.

WHITE CASTLE
Gwent

This castle should not really be viewed in isolation. Together with two others — Grosmont and Skenfrith — it formed a triangle of strongholds which plugged a gap in a weak section of the troublesome border country between England and Wales.

The 'Three Castles of Gwent' were built in stone largely in the 13th and 14th centuries on foundations of earlier fortifications. White Castle, so called because of the white plaster which originally covered its walls, must have been a stunning sight indeed in its prime. The placid rural

The smooth, deep waters of the River Usk are rich in salmon and trout

235

retreat of Skenfrith in the once-bloody borderlands is noted for its powerful round tower and ring of curtain walls. French influences at Grosmont extend beyond the style of military architecture employed to the name itself, *gros mont* being a Gallic equivalent to 'big hill'.

THE 'THREE CASTLES' are within 5 miles of each other near the Wales/England border in the countryside to the north-east of Abergavenny.

WOLVESNEWTON
Gwent

This scattered hamlet, in peaceful rolling countryside between the Vales of Usk and Wye, is the home of the Model Farm Folk Collection and Craft Centre. The farm itself is a rather special one: it is dominated by a unique, cross-shaped barn, built by the Duke of Beaufort at the end of the 18th century.

This cruciform barn now houses a folk collection which reflects agricultural and domestic life over the last one hundred years or so, mainly from Queen Victoria's time to the coronation of Elizabeth II. The farm site also contains a mill gallery of changing exhibitions and craft workshops where the traditional skills of the potter and corn dolly maker can be seen.

WOLVESNEWTON, 10 miles north-west of Chepstow, can be reached from the east via Devauden on the B4293 and via Llangwm, on the B4235, from the west.

YSTRADFELLTE
Powys

This tiny hamlet — a church, whitewashed pub, post office and handful of houses — is better known than its size suggests. Its name is synonymous with the distinctive limestone scenery which occurs along the southern rim of the Brecon Beacons National Park.

Unlike the wide and open spaces in the rest of the park, the waterfall country around Ystradfellte consists of thickly wooded gorges carved deep into the landscape and riddled with caves and pot-holes. Just south of the hamlet, the River Mellte completely disappears for one-quarter of a mile as it is swallowed up by the gaping Porth-yr-Ogof cavern.

The river reappears only to tumble, a mile further on, down a series of spectacular waterfalls in a shady, steep-sided valley. The most famous waterfall of all is on the River Hepste, a tributary of the Mellte. This is Sgwd-yr-Eira ('The Spout of Snow'), which overhangs to such an extent that a footpath passes behind it.

YSTRADFELLTE is on a minor road off the A4059, approximately 12 miles north-west of Merthyr Tydfil.

The cascading River Mellte in Ystradfellte's 'waterfall country'

The Romans in Wales

The Romans' self-confident boast, 'Veni, Vidi, Vici' ('I came, I saw, I conquered') might have applied elsewhere in their empire. In Wales, victory was never unequivocal, conquest never complete.

Difficult highland terrain populated by non-cooperative, if not downright intransigent Celtic tribes created problems which they never encountered in the intensively Romanized south and east of Britain. Some kind of wary co-existence was eventually achieved — after all, the Romans remained in Wales for over 300 years — though Roman might was largely confined to the more manageable lowland areas of Wales.

The Romans invaded Britain in A.D. 43. Tentative expeditions into Wales, possibly inspired by the lure of Welsh gold, prepared the ground for an arrival in strength in A.D. 74. Those wishing to follow in the Romans' footsteps should start, as they did, at Caerleon, where a powerful base was constructed for the crack Second Augustan Legion.

At nearby Caerwent, they created a city which introduced Roman notions of civilization to the natives. They also set about building a network of roads which linked their two main bases at Caerleon and Chester with a series of lesser forts. And at Pumpsaint, deep in the hills, they found what they had been looking for — gold.

Tracking down traces of these ambitious empire builders can be a tantalising process. Their straight-as-a-dye, well engineered

road systems outlive them still. In some cases — across Gelligaer Common north of Caerphilly, for example — modern road builders have simply followed old Roman routes. In others, the original trackways remain, charting typically direct and uncompromising courses across inhospitable moorland. And, scattered throughout Wales, grassy hummocks and fragmentary remains indicate the existence of Roman outposts (*Y Gaer*, their fort near Brecon, is one such site).

The Roman hold on Wales, although never complete, left its mark — and brought its benefits. Their departure, at the end of the 4th century, left Wales unprotected against the Saxons, Picts and Irish Goidel tribes. The end of the empire for Rome meant the beginning of a Dark Age for Wales.

Foundations of Roman houses at Caerwent

Caerleon amphitheatre

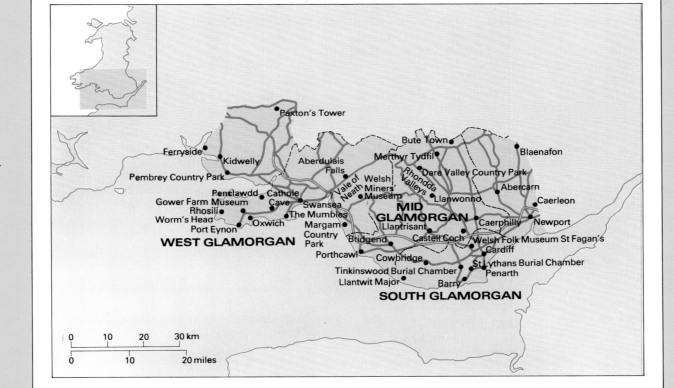

Paxton's Tower
Ferryside
Kidwelly
Aberdulais Falls
Pembrey Country Park
Bute Town
Merthyr Tydfil
Blaenafon
Welsh Miners' Museum
Vale of Neath
Rhondda Valleys
Dare Valley Country Park
Abercarn
Penclawdd
Cathole Cave
Gower Farm Museum
Rhosili
Swansea
Llanwonno
Caerleon
Worm's Head
The Mumbles
MID GLAMORGAN
Caerphilly
Newport
Port Eynon
Oxwich
Margam Country Park
Llantrisant
Castell Coch
Welsh Folk Museum St Fagan's
WEST GLAMORGAN
Bridgend
Cardiff
Porthcawl
Cowbridge
St Lythans Burial Chamber
Penarth
Tinkinswood Burial Chamber
Llantwit Major
Barry
SOUTH GLAMORGAN

0   10   20   30 km
0   10   20 miles

Left: The skeletal, exposed stone framework of St Lythans, a neolithic (New Stone Age) burial chamber in the Vale of Glamorgan

VISITORS WHO WANDER amongst the Neo-Classical buildings of dazzling white Portland stone in Cardiff's Civic Centre may have cause to review their opinions about South Wales. Cardiff, as they will discover, is anything but a lacklustre coal port. Along the cliff-backed Glamorgan coast, Swansea's prestigious new Maritime Quarter is transforming the old waterfront. And the valleys of South Wales, contrary to popular opinion, no longer bristle with pit headgear.

South Wales, misrepresented in the past, should not be ignored in the present. Its powerful personality, a consequence of the dynamic role it played during the Industrial Revolution, demands attention — as do its surprising and dramatic scenic qualities.

Country parks and forests now account for much more landscape than coalmines. Late 20th-century visitors are reminded of the 'good old, bad old days' of the 19th century mainly through sites specially preserved for their industrial heritage. No one claims that all of the old scars have disappeared. Yet it is easier, nowadays, to begin to comprehend the 18th-century, pre-industrial view of the valleys.

Further west, the scenic qualities of the Gower coast are beyond dispute. This stubby peninsula, 20 miles long, was declared Britain's first official 'Area of Outstanding Natural Beauty' in 1956. Its protected shoreline, a succession of towering sea-cliffs and sandy bays in the south, leads to lonely salt-marsh along the Loughor estuary.

ABERDULAIS FALLS
West Glamorgan

Aberdulais is one of those rare sites which manages to marry two apparently irreconcilable bedfellows — great natural beauty and industrial exploitation. The former comes from its setting. Here, in a tree-shrouded gorge, the waters of the Dulais tumble over mossy ledges and through narrow, rocky channels. By the late 18th century, this romantically gloomy spot was attracting artists and writers from far and wide, including the incomparable J.M.W. Turner whose sketchbooks contain a large number of drawings of the falls.

A jumble of ruined masonry, currently being restored by the National Trust, mingles with the woods along the banks of the falls, from which power was harnessed by water-wheel to drive the bellows of a pioneering smelting works. This is an important industrial site, one of the earliest in South Wales, which started life in 1584 as a copper works, later moving to iron and tin.

🚗 ABERDULAIS is at the junction of the A465 and A4109 in the Vale of Neath, about 7 miles north-east of Swansea.

BARRY AND PENARTH
South Glamorgan

This pair of coastal towns, kept apart by the headlands at Lavernock, have little in common even though they share the same Victorian roots.

Barry grew up in the 1880s, a consequence of the increasing number of frustrations and holdups at Cardiff docks. The docklands founded here by coalowner David Davies were soon booming, and in 1913 Barry exported a record-breaking 11 million tons of coal hewn from the neighbouring valleys.

Barry Island, a popular and lively seaside resort, is an island no more, thanks to the dockland developments which bonded it to the mainland. Barry's quieter side resides along The Knap, where a long, steeply-shelving pebble beach leads to a rocky coastline of white limestone cliffs. Porthkerry Country Park, directly landward from these cliffs, is a spacious swathe of grassland, oak and ash wood spanned by an elegant 18-arched railway viaduct.

Penarth was much favoured by Cardiff's prosperous 19th-century coalowners and shipping magnates. Their palatial homes overlook a promenade — complete with ornate pier and sea-front gardens — that still retains the genteel character of a fashionable Victorian watering hole. Penarth's Turner House Art Gallery, part of the National Museum of Wales, exhibits both classical and modern works.

🚗 BARRY AND PENARTH, a few miles south-west of Cardiff, can be reached by the A4055 and A4160 from the city.

BEAUPRE CASTLE
South Glamorgan

Beaupre — pronounced 'Bewper' and also known as Old Beaupre — is a reclusive historic site. Visitors have to embark on a longish, though most pleasant, stroll across rolling river meadows to reach its handsome walls.

The castle is something of a hybrid, an Elizabethan mansion more than a medieval fortress. Its walls, though strong and tall, enclose what is, in essence, a substantial home which displays many stylish features.

Large, mullioned windows add light to the courtyard. Beaupre's outstanding decorative features are at the entrance to, and within, this courtyard. An outer porch, dated 1586, bears the arms of the Bassetts (the family intimately linked with Beaupre's history since medieval times) and their motto (in Welsh), 'Better Death than Shame'. The inner porch is grander still, a three-tiered affair carved in classical style from a sandy stone.

🚗 BEAUPRE CASTLE is approximately 1 mile south-west of St Hillary, a village accessible off the A48 just east of Cowbridge.

BLAENAFON
Gwent

On the face of it, Blaenafon is a most unlikely candidate for inclusion within these pages. Yet thousands of visitors now make their way each year to this rather unkempt old valley town, attracted by the presence of the Big Pit Mining Museum.

The pit headgear on the bare hillside above the town identifies a site that is unique in Britain. Until 1980, Big Pit was a working coalmine. In 1983 it re-opened as a living museum which gives visitors first-hand experience of what life was really like for generations of South Wales miners.

Groups of the public, kitted out in safety helmets, cap lamps and battery belts descend 300 ft by miners' cage to pit bottom for a conducted tour of the old underground workings. On the surface, too, an air of authenticity prevails. Everything has been left very much as it was in the pithead baths, working forge, colliery workshops and engine house.

For anyone professing an understanding of the old South Wales industrial communities, a visit to Blaenafon is obligatory — doubly so, since both iron and coal played their parts here. Blaenafon Ironworks, also open to the public, contains some of

the finest surviving late 18th-century blast furnaces in Europe, an impressive water balance tower and the ruins of ironworkers' cottages.

🚗 BLAENAFON is on the A4043 north of Newport and B4246 south-west of Abergavenny.

At Blaenafon visitors with a strong sense of history can make their way to the Big Pit Mining Museum and descend to pit bottom in a cramped miners' cage, after being kitted out with safety helmets, cap lamps and battery belts

cool tranquillity.

Religious and military influences appear to have been at work here. Parts of the site — the tower in particular — are decidedly robust in their architecture, making this one of the best defended churches in to survive Britain.

Coity Castle, two miles north-east of Bridgend, is military pure and simple. Originally an earth-and-timber Norman stronghold, Coity was later rebuilt in stone. Further remodelling and strengthening in the 14th century was prescient, allowing the castle to withstand a long siege during the Welsh uprising in the early 15th century.

◣ *BRIDGEND, at the junction of the A48, A473, A4061 and A4063 is 20 miles west of Cardiff.*

BRIDGEND
Mid Glamorgan

This large settlement is mentioned on the strength of what can be seen around and about, as opposed to in the town itself.

The priory church at Ewenny, just over one mile to the south, is delightful. The church, which contains fine Norman work, stands on a quiet riverbank amongst the ruins of a Benedictine priory, founded in the 12th century, amid an atmosphere of

BUTE TOWN
Mid Glamorgan

Bute Town is an oddity. For a start, it is a tiny, self-contained village, not a town. More important still, Bute Town defies all the conventions of architecture in the South Wales valleys. The traditional and typical view of terraced housing, one row stacked above the next along the valley slopes, is turned completely on its head at this early model village, built around 1802 by an altruistic local ironmaster to house his workers.

Bute Town's warm-stoned houses — some three storeys high — and wide streets, laid out to an orderly, neat plan, are quite unlike anything else in South Wales. The village remains faithful to its original looks, having benefitted from sympathetic restoration during 1975's European Architectural Heritage Year.

◣ *BUTE TOWN, just north of Rhymney, is accessible off the A465 'Heads of the Valleys' road 4 miles east of Merthyr Tydfil.*

CAERLEON
Gwent

Motorists approaching Newport on the M4 motorway into Wales are mostly unaware that they are speeding past one of the most important Roman sites in Britain. In Roman times, all roads led into Caerleon — or, as it was known then, *Isca*. Together with Chester and York, Caerleon was one of only three fortresses in Britain built to accommodate legionary soldiers, the crack troops of the Roman army.

From A.D. 74, this grassy spot by a bend in the river was the home of the 6000-strong Second Augustan Legion. Caerleon, amongst the largest Roman military sites in northern Europe, was no rough-and-ready army camp. A legionary baths complex has recently been excavated, revealing part of a large, multi-purpose range of buildings — the Roman equivalent to today's sports and leisure centre. Hot and cold baths could be taken here in carefully controlled temperatures. The foundations of an open-air swimming pool are clearly visible next to areas where sporting and non-athletic pastimes (including eating, drinking and gambling) could be pursued or indulged.

Another, darker form of entertainment took place at Caerleon's showpiece Roman site. In its famous, well-preserved amphitheatre thousands of excited spectators once witnessed grim blood sports including gladiatorial combat and animal baiting.

In fields just north of the amphitheatre, the orderly foundations of the soldier's barracks have also been excavated and are on view.

CAERLEON, on the B4236, can be reached from junctions 24 and 25 off the M4 motorway.

CAERPHILLY
Mid Glamorgan

Caerphilly's reputation is in a state of flux. The eponymous cheese, which turned this town into a household name, is no longer made here. Instead, Caerphilly is becoming increasingly well-known on the strength of its quite remarkable castle, now ranked as one of Europe's greatest surviving medieval fortresses.

Probably because of its setting within an unpretentious and otherwise unremarkable valley town, only recently has Caerphilly Castle's true status been generally appreciated. In the hierarchy of British castles, 30-acre Caerphilly stands near the top: only at Dover, and possibly Windsor, is it equalled in size.

The Norman lord, Gilbert de Clare, wary of the native Welsh, commenced serious work on the castle in the 1270s. He created a mighty 'stone and water' system of concentric defences built up, barrier after barrier, from a central core like the layers of an onion. His grey-green walls and powerful gatehouse still stand to their full height above the waters of the moat. The only weak note is struck by a tipsy ruined tower on the site, which manages to out-lean even the world-famous example at Pisa.

CAERPHILLY, on the junction of the A469 and A468, is 8 miles north of Cardiff.

Under its winter skies Caerphilly looks the part as 'the sleeping giant of British castles'. Historians are already aware of its status as one of the great sites of the medieval western world. The castle, strangely unknown, is only now beginning to attract the public attention it rightly deserves

CARDIFF
South Glamorgan

Wales's capital city, population 285,000, began life as a Roman camp, laying the foundations to its present status in the boom-town years of the 19th century. Cardiff's 2000-year history is epitomised in one edifice — its huge castle, standing tall in the busy heart of the city.

The castle is a unique three-in-one historic site, retaining sections of original Roman walls and a well-preserved Norman keep alongside the lavish, no-expense-spared restoration work carried out in Victorian times. As it now stands, the castle is a testament to the phenomenal 19th-century growth of Cardiff from humble sea-town into one of the world's premier coal-exporting ports.

Vast fortunes were made in Cardiff's docklands, largely by the Bute family. The Third Marquess poured much of his wealth into the re-birth of Cardiff Castle, enlisting the services of the outstanding — albeit eccentric — Victorian architect, William Burges.

From 1868, Burges's 'strange genius' was allowed full rein. He created an opulent, extravagant mansion which flaunts an eclectic range of decorative influences ranging from ancient Greece to the Arabian Nights, all executed with a romantic, mock-medieval flourish.

Sobriety and dignity reign a stone's throw away, at the Civic Centre. The 194-ft dome of the City Hall fronts a collection of Neo-Classical official buildings dating from the turn of the century. Built of white Portland stone and set amongst beautiful parklands and wide, tree-lined avenues, Cardiff's Civic Centre has been rated — along with Washington and New Delhi — as one of the world's most elegant examples of civic architecture.

The cavernous Museum of Wales, one of its buildings, contains an encyclopaedic range of exhibits spanning pre-history and the Industrial Revolution, together with a prized collection of French Impressionist paintings. Another familiar landmark is the National Stadium (better known, perhaps, as Cardiff Arms Park), the shrine of Welsh rugby. The stadium stands next to the shopping centre where attractive 19th-century features — canopied arcades and a traditional fresh foods market — integrate well with modern pedestrian precincts and the new St David's Centre.

Llandaff, in the western suburbs, is a 'village within a city'. The old village green, next to the soaring twin towers of Llandaff Cathedral, helps it retain its village atmosphere. The cathedral, standing on the site of an important 6th-century religious community, was badly damaged during

William Burges's ornate decoration in Cardiff Castle

Llandaff Cathedral with its modern sculpture

the last war. Part of its restoration included an uncompromisingly modernistic sculpture by Sir Jacob Epstein, *Christ in Majesty*, which dominates the cathedral interior and is still a source of controversy amongst traditionalists.

🚗 *CARDIFF, accessible off the M4 motorway, is 27 miles from the Severn Bridge.*

CASTELL COCH
South Glamorgan

Castell Coch, 'The Red Castle', leaps straight off the pages of a fairy story or the frames of a Disney movie. Its needle-sharp conical towers prick the skies from their perch on a wooden gorge which guards the northern approach to Cardiff.

A mere 100 years old, this enchanting little castle is a Victorian creation, built as a companion piece to Cardiff Castle for the fabulously wealthy Marquess of Bute. Like its big brother, Castell Coch is a decorative extravaganza. Its rooms are laden with liberal quantities of visual detail depicting Aesop's Fables, figures from Greek mythology, and a Noah's Ark of animals, birds and butterflies.

Purists outraged by Castell Coch's free-ranging excesses can take some comfort in the fact that it at least occupies the site of a genuine medieval stronghold.

🚗 *THE CASTLE, at Tongwynlais off the A470, is 5 miles north-west of Cardiff's city centre.*

Castell Coch — a castle fit for Sleeping Beauty, full of romance

COWBRIDGE
South Glamorgan

This prosperous town — countrified rather than pure country — has become a popular place to live for those who work elsewhere, often in Cardiff, only a short car journey away. Nevertheless, Cowbridge still lives up to its historic status as the 'Capital of the Vale of Glamorgan'.

A long main street, now by-passed by through traffic, is lined with a classy and cosmopolitan collection of shops, inns and restaurants. Cowbridge, possibly of Roman origin, was a fully-fledged market town as long ago as the 11th century. Vestiges of the past can be seen to the south of the main street, where fragmentary remains of the medieval town walls and a well-preserved gateway survive. Other old buildings of note include the Tudor-style school and handsome Town Hall.

🚗 *COWBRIDGE, just off the A48, is 12 miles west of Cardiff.*

CWMCARN SCENIC FOREST DRIVE
Gwent

The conifer-clad hills which loom above the valley community of Abercarn can be explored in a most unorthodox fashion. Under normal circumstances, cars are prohibited from using the loose-surfaced roads which run through Forestry Commission plantations. Not so at Cwmcarn, where a seven-mile route is open to the public as a scenic forest drive.

The drive weaves its way between the trees from valley floor to mountain top, with stopping-off places for picnic sites and waymarked forest walks. In its upper reaches, the road skirts the 1374-ft summit of Twm Barlwm, an ancient hill-fort which preserves its earthwork defences. On a clear day, views from the top are spectacular in the extreme. To the north, the distinctive silhouettes of the Brecon Beacons dominate the horizon. Southwards, Newport spreads itself out between the hills of the South Wales valleys and waters of the Severn estuary.

🚗 *ABERCARN is on the A467, 8 miles north-west of Newport.'*

DARE VALLEY COUNTRY PARK
Mid Glamorgan

Visitors to this country park find it difficult to accept that it stands on the site of old collieries and coal-tips. They have to look long and hard indeed for any tell-tale signs of the Industrial Revolution amongst the swathes of grassland, forests, streams and lakesides which now adorn the valley slopes above the town of Aberdare.

Dare Valley is a prime example of what has been achieved, in terms of environmental improvement, in the South Wales valleys. Established in 1972 as Wales's first country park, the Dare Valley has erased from the 20th century the scars of the 19th. Half-a-dozen old colliery workings and countless coal-tips were completely removed in an ambitious landscaping exercise which involved the planting of 20,000 trees and the creation of a scenic cascade and fishing lake.

🚗 *THE COUNTRY PARK is at Aberdare, on the A4059, about 24 miles north-west of Cardiff.*

DYFFRYN GARDENS
South Glamorgan

These gardens bring a splash of colour to the pervading greenery of the pastoral Vale of Glamorgan. Dyffryn is especially proud of its seasonal bedding displays, rose garden, large herbaceous borders, ponds and individually designed smaller gardens — the Italian Terrace is delightful — all contained within a 50-acre landscaped site.

Various hot houses provide an opportunity to see tropical and subtropical species, including palms, orchids, cacti, banana and pineapple plants. The gardens are laid out around Dyffryn House (not open to the public). Built in 1893 in a grand and affluent style, its regal facade reflects the tremendous fortunes which were made from the coal mining industries of South Wales.

🚗 *DYFFRYN GARDENS are on a minor road south of St Nicholas, a village on the A48 6 miles west of Cardiff.*

FERRYSIDE
Dyfed

The banks of the Tywi estuary are undeservedly unknown. Forgotten Ferryside is a charming village which displays only faint traces of recognition by the outside world — there is a sailing club here, and the small, pebbly beach sometimes sees visitors.

Tregoning Hill, a National Trust property, stands just south of the village. The views from the hillside are splendid, overlooking the silvery junction of three river systems — the Tywi, Taf and Gwendraeth — and the rich green headlands above Llanstephan, topped by dramatic, ragged castle ruins.

Tucked away below Tregoning Hill is the ancient, ivy-covered Church of St Ishmael's and the lost village of Hawton, said to have been drowned in a great storm which occurred in the 17th century.

🚗 *FERRYSIDE, accessible by minor road off the A484, is approximately 10 miles south of Carmarthen.*

GOWER FARM MUSEUM
West Glamorgan

All attention on Gower focusses on the coastline. This museum attempts to redress the balance by introducing visitors to the countryside — specifically, the long history of farming, and farming people, on the Gower peninsula.

The museum's main theme — how people have lived and farmed on Gower in the past 100 years — is told through the eyes of one family, the Watters. Their household goods, farm machinery, butter-making equipment, old documents and family photographs help build up a picture of life on the peninsula before the advent of the tractor and the motor car. Interestingly, the museum also reflects on the relatively recent arrival of visitors from the outside world, for when the Watters were farming here 100 years ago, their peninsula was regarded as a strange, remote backwater.

Most of the exhibits are housed in 17th-century agricultural buildings. This rambling, informal — and informative-museum is one of the surprising number of places to vist away from Gower's magnet-like coast. The pleasant countryside immediately around the museum can be explored via a number of farm trails intended to give walkers an idea of modern methods employed in the surrounding farmlands.

🚗 *THE MUSEUM is just over 1 mile west of Reynoldston on a minor road off the A4118 near the hamlet of Knelston.*

Kidwelly Castle, remarkably intact, is an awesome sight. Its twin-towered gatehouse butts into the sky three storeys tall, dominating the surrounding Dyfed countryside

KIDWELLY
Dyfed

Medieval Wales confronts the Industrial Revolution at this friendly sea-town on the Gwendraeth estuary. Kidwelly is dominated by its old stone castle, an outstanding example of the concentric 'walls within walls' system of defence. The castle stands its ground above the rooftops on a slope commanding the estuary, a strategic site carefully chosen so that it could be supplied with food and ammunition by sea if cut off by land. The fortress's original strength prevails even today, thanks to its remarkable state of preservation — especially the twin-towered Great Gatehouse, which stands, three storeys tall, above everything else.

In the 18th century, Kidwelly was in the forefront of tin-plate production in Britain. A 164 ft-high chimneystack, on the outskirts of town, marks the site of its pioneering tin-plate works, now open to the public as the Kidwelly Industrial Museum.

KIDWELLY, at the junction of the A484 and B4308, is 10 miles south of Carmarthen.

LANGLAND AND CASWELL BAYS
West Glamorgan

This pair of perfectly shaped bays shelter amongst breaks in the cliffs at the southern entrance to the unspoilt Gower Peninsula. The beach at Langland Bay lies beneath rocky headlands in a sunny, south-facing position. One of the many spectacular cliff-walks along the Gower coast links Langland to Caswell Bay.

Caswell, 'the jewel of Gower', is a crescent of sand scooped out beneath profusely wooded hillsides. Footpaths penetrate the dense Bishop's

Wood, a nature reserve in a dry valley leading away from the beach. West of Caswell, another path strikes out over the cliffs to the secluded old smugglers' haunt of Brandy Cove.

🚗 LANGLAND and Caswell Bays can be reached by the B4593, off the A4067 south-west of Swansea.

LLANTRISANT
Mid Glamorgan

Attention here centres on 'old' Llantrisant up on the hill — not the new housing developments which sprawl around the original town — and the iconoclastic figure of Dr William Price. A statue of Dr Price, resplendent in his fox-skin head-dress, stands amongst the streets in the Bull Ring.

Dr Price (1800-1893) was even more provocative in attitude than appearance. Today, the causes he espoused — nudism, vegetarianism, free love and radical politics — are familiar enough. Straight-laced Victorian society was outraged by them.

His greatest *cause célèbre* occurred in 1884, when he attempted to cremate his illegitimate son, Iesu Grist (Jesus Christ), who had died in infancy, on Llantrisant Common. In the ensuing furore, Dr Price was arrested, tried and acquitted of any crime, as a result of which cremation became legal in Britain.

Dr Price's ghostly presence tends to eclipse anything else in Llantrisant, though it should be mentioned that the ancient town has a fine church, Norman in origin, ivy-covered castle remains and — on the outskirts — the modern Royal Mint complex.

🚗 LLANTRISANT, on the junction of the A4119 and A473, is 10 miles north-west of Cardiff.

Left: Caswell, one of the loveliest of Gower's many bays

LLANTWIT MAJOR
South Glamorgan

This pretty little town in the prosperous, pastoral Vale of Glamorgan served as a springboard for Welsh civilization. The sheltered hollow beneath Llantwit Major's narrow, crooked streets was a great religious and educational centre, founded around A.D. 500 by St Illtud, an influential early Christian figure.

St David, Wales's patron saint, studied here in a monastic settlement now occupied by the impressive Church of St Illtud. Like St David's Cathedral, this seminal religious centre stands close to, but invisible from, the sea. St Illtud's grand, cathedral-like dimensions are also reminiscent of St David's. It is, in fact, two churches in one — an earlier Norman and late 13th-century church combined. Painted wall frescos and a fine collection of inscribed Celtic crosses and pillars are amongst its wealth of treasures.

The town's medieval streets are also well endowed with historic buildings, including the Old Swan Inn, Town Hall and stone gabled Ty Mawr ('Great House') on the outskirts.

🚗 LLANTWIT MAJOR, on the junction of the B4265 and B4270, is approximately 15 miles south-west of Cardiff.

LLANWONNO
Mid Glamorgan

An old church, a rambling churchyard, a pub that looks too large for its location and a row of cottages are all that make up the hamlet of Llanwonno, standing over 1000 ft high in the hills between the Rhondda and Cynon Valleys.

Those who are sceptical of the scenic qualities on display within this part of South Wales should visit Llanwonno. Its steep approach roads command wonderful views across and into the severe-sided valleys before entering an extensive conifer woodland — the St Gwynno Forest — which completely surrounds the hamlet.

Llanwonno was the home of Guto Nyth Bran, the 18th-century long-distance runner who, according to legend, ran across the mountain to fetch yeast in the time that it took for his mother to bring a kettle of water to the boil.

🚗 LLANWONNO is accessible by minor roads from Pontypridd (5 miles to the south-east), Ferndale (in the Rhondda Valleys) and Mountain Ash (in the Cynon Valley).

A Celtic wheel-head cross from Llantwit Major's fine collection

MARGAM COUNTRY PARK
West Glamorgan

Although within shouting distance of the M4 motorway and the Port Talbot-Margam industrial sprawl, this country park is a model of peace and tranquillity. The park — all 850 acres of it — shuts itself off most effectively from the outside world. Fallow deer can usually be seen grazing on its open grassland, which rises up into bracken-covered slopes crowned by an Iron Age hill-fort.

The park is based around a ruined 19th-century castle built in haunting Tudor-Gothic style. Margam's great architectural masterpiece is thankfully well preserved. This is the mid-18th-century orangery, an elegant, well-proportioned building with 27 tall windows in its 327-ft length, built to accommodate orange, lemon and citrus trees.

Twentieth-century art is represented here in the form of an imaginative Sculpture Park, featuring work by internationally famous sculptors. The remains of what was once the largest monastic house in Wales can also be seen, together with early Christian memorial stones.

MARGAM COUNTRY PARK is accessible off the A48.

MERTHYR TYDFIL
Mid Glamorgan

In the tumultuous 19th century, Merthyr Tydfil was the iron-and-steel-producing capital of the world. Today, most of old Merthyr has been redeveloped.

Cyfarthfa Castle is the most conspicuous reminder of Merthyr's heyday. This large Gothic mansion, built by the all-powerful Crawshay ironmasters in 1824, stands imperiously on a hillside amongst pleasant, wooded parkland. A more plaintive — and certainly more telling — monument to this stern family can be seen at Vaynor Church, where Robert Thompson Crawshay's grave bears the simple plea 'God Forgive Me'.

The castle houses an immaculate museum filled with a delightful range of exhibits. Particularly intriguing is the model of Richard Trevithick's steam locomotive, which ran along a tramroad from Merthyr a full 20 years before Stephenson's more famous 'Rocket'. Steam power has now returned to Merthyr in the form of the narrow-gauge Brecon Mountain Railway, which follows a scenic route to a lakeside terminus in the foothills of Brecon Beacons.

MERTHYR, at the junction of the A470 and A465, is 25 miles north of Cardiff.

Merthyr's Cyfarthfa Castle, built with the wealth generated by iron and the Industrial Revolution

THE MUMBLES
West Glamorgan

This strangely-titled place — no one seems to know the origin of its name — is also a strange mixture of sailing centre-cum-seaside resort-cum-

suburb of Swansea. The Mumbles is tucked snugly away along the sheltered western shore of Swansea Bay at the gateway to the Gower Peninsula. Hotels, guesthouses, boat parks and pubs — the Antelope Hotel and Mermaid were favourite ports of call for the young Dylan Thomas — line a seafront which leads to Mumbles Head.

The views across Swansea Bay from the pier and lighthouse on this rocky promontory are matched by those from Oystermouth Castle. Dating from 1280, this splendid old fortification stands to its original height on a grassy knoll above the rooftops.

◣ *THE MUMBLES is on the B4433, accessible off the A4067 5 miles south-west of Swansea.*

NEWPORT
Gwent

Modern Newport, the largest town in the county of Gwent, does not look as though it was founded way back in the 6th century. There is, however, a surprising amount of history scattered around the town. The riverside towers of Newport Castle now appear a little lost, marooned amongst busy shops, road systems and a new multi-million pound leisure centre. This medieval castle replaced an earlier one which stood on Stow Hill beside St Woolos's Cathedral.

The hilltop cathedral, occupying a religious site as old as the town itself, is a fine affair noteworthy for its Norman work. Newport's sometimes turbulent history is recalled at the excellent Museum and Art Gallery — though the best paintings of all are in the Civic Centre, decorated by a striking series of heroic murals.

Newport's skyline is dominated by its unusual Edwardian Transporter Bridge (currently closed, alas), a monumental web of girders straddling the waters of the River Usk. Another form of transportation — the inland waterways of the 19th century — is the basis for the exhibitions at the 14 Locks Canal Centre, named after a massive staircase of locks on the outskirts of town.

Fourteen locks stands near to Newport's most significant historic site. The town's rapid expansion as a port serving the 19th-century iron and coal industries of the South Wales valleys is embodied in the fabric of Tredegar House. This magnificent red-bricked Restoration mansion, built between 1664 and 1672, really came of age in the mid 19th century thanks to the wealth of Newport's docklands. Its gilded, opulent interior is complemented by superb surroundings, now a 90-acre country park.

◣ *NEWPORT, accessible off the M4 motorway, is 11 miles from Cardiff.*

OXWICH
West Glamorgan

The variety of landscape and coastline at Oxwich is remarkable. This undeveloped little coastal hamlet's long and accommodating beach is just the start of the story. The beach is backed by the sand dunes of Oxwich Burrows which, in turn, border a large, watery area of marsh and reed beds. This entire low-lying area is protected by a craggy headland, its slopes covered by a thick blanket of oak and ash woods leading to Oxwich Point.

Little wonder, then, that Oxwich, with its unusually wide range of wildlife habitats, has become a nature reserve. Provision is also made for the public, thanks to a helpful information centre and series of waymarked walks.

Oxwich is, quite understandably, mainly popular for its sands. Oxwich Bay sweeps along for well over a mile, ending at the lovely — but somewhat inaccessible — Three Cliffs Bay, a famous Gower beauty spot. The tiny 13th-century Church of St Illtyd, barely visible in the woods beyond the beach, stands beneath a steep slope crowned by Oxwich Castle, a 16th-century manor house currently under restoration. A little way inland, and visible from the surrounding high ground, are two more castles — the 'Old' and 'New' Penrice Castles — in a private estate.

◣ *OXWICH is accessible off the A4118 approximately 13 miles west of Swansea.*

PARC LE BREOS BURIAL CHAMBER AND CATHOLE CAVE
West Glamorgan

The secluded, wooded valley running north-west from Parkmill can only be explored on foot. The walk is well worth it, not only for the tranquil surroundings but also for this pair of prehistoric sites which hide themselves away here.

Gower is dotted with evidence of prehistoric settlement, none more conclusive than Parc le Breos which stands in open grassland encircled by thick woods. This stone tomb — very well preserved considering its age — was used for the communal burial of the dead. Although at least 4000 years old, it is a relative newcomer in comparison to Cathole Cave, located in the hillside further along the valley. Mammoth and woolly rhinocerous bones have been found here, in a cave inhabited by man 10,000 years ago towards the end of the Ice Age.

◣ *PARKMILL, on the A4118, is about 8 miles west of Swansea.*

PAXTON'S TOWER
Dyfed

This tower is pure folly. Put up by Sir William Paxton in the early 19th century, it fulfills no other purpose than to commemorate Lord Nelson.

Its castellated walls, on the crest of a ridge above the Tywi Valley, are a prominent landmark in these parts, visible from miles around. Close examination of the monument itself reveals an imposing, triangular structure, the slender walls of which enclose nothing but thin air.

Any architectural anti-climax is quickly forgotten, for there is nothing disappointing about the siting of Paxton's Tower. From its perch high above the lush Vale of Tywi a great sweep of scenery comes into view, beginning with the verdant farmlands bordering the snaking Tywi and ending in forested hillsides and high mountains.
PAXTON'S TOWER is on a minor road near Llanarthney, a village on the B4300 9 miles east of Carmarthen.

PEMBREY COUNTRY PARK
Dyfed

Pembrey is an unconventional country park by the sea. First impressions of this 520-acre area of open grassland and pine forest are predictable enough, but at the end of the road a different scene comes into view.

A barrier of sand dunes unexpectedly presents itself, guarding the approach to the Cefn Sidan Sands. Notions of size have to be revised upwards at Cefn Sidan. It curves along Carmarthen Bay further than the eye can see — seven miles in all, making it one of the longest beaches in Wales, and an ideal venue for the sport of land yachting.

Pembrey's unorthodox mixture of coast and countryside encourages all kinds of outdoor activities. The conifer woodlands besides the beach — planted to help stabilise an area which suffers from wind erosion — are popular for nature studies, walking and pony trekking.
PEMBREY COUNTRY PARK is accessible off the A484 just west of Burry Port.

PENCLAWDD AND THE LOUGHOR ESTUARY
West Glamorgan

The north Gower coastline is totally unlike that of the rocky, cliff-backed south. In the emptier north, the low-tide sands, salt flats and marsh beds of the Loughor estuary possess a strange and silent beauty.

Few visitors find their way to spectacularly sited Weobley Castle. This old fortified manor house stands on a grassy hillside overlooking Llanrhidian Marsh, a deep-brown expanse of wetlands gripped by a brooding beauty. Fewer still explore the sand dunes and nature reserve at Whiteford Burrows, on the mouth of the estuary.

The sandy wilderness around Penclawdd still yields a living to the traditional cockle pickers, a hardy breed who rely largely on horse-drawn carts and short-handled rakes, the time-honoured tools of the trade.
PENCLAWDD, on the B4295, is 8 miles west of Swansea.

PORT EYNON
West Glamorgan

This little Gower resort, all alone on its sheltered bay bounded by treacherous cliffs, must have been the perfect smugglers' haunt in its time. The pretty beach now attracts a less clandestine clientele, whilst walkers head north-westwards along what is probably the most spectacular coastal path on the Gower Peninsula.

Two interesting diversions beckon near the start of the walk — the strange Culver Hole, a tall, walled-up section of sea-cliff of mysterious origin, and the ruined Salt House, a vulnerably located mansion destroyed, according to legend, during a fierce 18th-century storm.

The walk, six miles long, treads a wary path on top of sheer limestone cliffs all the way to Worm's Head, passing the inaccessible Paviland Cave where the famous 'Red Lady', a prehistoric skeleton, was discovered.
PORT EYNON, on the A4118, is 16 miles west of Swansea.

PORTHCAWL
Mid Glamorgan

Porthcawl, a leading South Wales seaside resort, has two sides to it. Sandy Bay and Trecco Bay, to the east, share the dubious honour of hosting one of Europe's largest caravan parks and a seafront funfair. To the west, beyond the pretty harbour and sturdy breakwater, a quieter, less colourful Porthcawl takes over.

An attractive esplanade leads to a rocky coast bordered by grassy Lock's Common. Further along still are the peaceful sand and rock pools of Rest Bay, culminating in the lonely headland at Sker Point.

The dunes of Merthyr Mawr Warren, two miles away, cover a vast area. A thin strip of woodland near Merthyr Mawr village just manages to keep the sands from swamping the ivy-clad ruin of Candleston Castle.
PORTHCAWL, 6 miles southwest of Bridgend, can be reached by the A4106 or A4229 off the A48.

The Rhigos mountain road, northern gateway to the Rhondda

THE RHONDDA VALLEYS
Mid Glamorgan

In the 19th century, 'King Coal', the 'black diamond', transformed these valleys from a rural backwater to a teeming, tightly-packed — and tightly-knit — series of mining com-

munities. People poured into the Rhondda Fawr ('Big Rhondda') and Fach ('Little Rhondda') Valleys — and coal poured out to fuel the world's Industrial Revolution.

Much has been written about the mining towns — Treorchy, Treherbert and so on — that grew up as layers of long terraces built into the valley sides. *How Green Was My Valley*, the novel by Richard Llewelyn, expresses in its title the typical view, still current, of an area blighted by coalmining. Those deterred by such inaccurate views miss a gauntly beautiful part of Wales.

Mountainsides and open moorlands, untouched by any form of industry, rise abruptly from once-volatile valley floors. Coalmining is no more, and it is not too optimistic to say that the valleys — thanks to far-reaching environmental improvement schemes — are now becoming green again.

🚗 *THE RHONDDA VALLEYS can be approached via Pontypridd and the A4058, Bridgend and Hirwaun (A4061) or Aberdare (B4277).*

RHOSILI AND WORM'S HEAD
West Glamorgan

The Gower Peninsula ends on a high note, a climax of windy cliffs, seemingly endless sands and dizzy viewpoints. To Dylan Thomas, Rhosili beach was 'miles of yellow coldness going away into the distance of the sea'. If he had cared to measure it,

Dylan would have found that the beach is well over three miles long, beginning at the foot of the clifftop village only to end at the faraway Burry Holms headland.

Worm's Head, Rhosili's second spectacular natural feature, is a narrow neck of land pointing bravely into the open seas west of the village. Care should be taken by those venturing on to this wind-scoured, exposed headland, tenuously linked to the mainland by a flooded causeway which is only dry for two-and-a-half hours at low tide.

Petty Officer Edgar Evans, who died on Scott's ill-fated expedition to the Antarctic in 1917, came from this locality. He is remembered by a memorial in Rhosili Church.

🚗 *RHOSILI, reached by the B4247 off the A4118, is 18 miles west of Swansea.*

Gower's end — miles of lonely, windswept sand at Rhosili

SWANSEA
West Glamorgan

Dylan Thomas's much-quoted description of this, his birthplace, as an 'ugly, lovely town' contained a convoluted, poetic truth applicable to the Swansea of the early and mid 20th century. Times change; some towns — Swansea, for one — become cities. Dylan, were he resurrected, would hardly recognise his home town of old.

Swansea, Wales's second city, is busy transforming itself into a fresh and airy 'city-by-the-sea' by making the most of its location on a sandy, sheltered bay. Its historic links with the ocean are being re-defined in the new Maritime Quarter, a far-sighted development that includes a 600-berth marina and waterfront village.

A bronze statue of the young Dylan, looking suitably bemused by it all, stands in a brand-new piazza beside the boat-filled marina. Close by are another two recent additions — the Dylan Thomas Theatre and Maritime and Industrial Museum, the latter containing a fully operational woollen mill, rescued from nearby, which produces traditional Welsh weaves.

This go-ahead city, for all its modernity, retains its links with traditional Wales. It is not at all unusual to hear Welsh spoken in the new shopping complexes or the multi-activity (and multi-million pound) leisure centre. Swansea Market is the city's most endearing meeting place of influences old and new. Despite its functional modern appearance, it houses a market place with bags of local character. The market's stallholders sell a tempting array of home cooking and fresh foods, including cockles handpicked from the Penclawdd beds and that unique Welsh dish, laverbread, a black, gooey concoction made from seaweed with a taste that does justice to its unique appearance.

In the city centre, the scant ruins of Swansea Castle, surrounded by office blocks and shops, present an incongruous sight. Amongst the displays of pottery, glass and porcelain in the Glynn Vivian Art Gallery are superb collections of old Swansea and Nantgarw items. In terms of sheer visual extravaganza, nothing can match the Brangwyn Panels in Swansea's Guildhall, a series of huge, warm-toned murals painted by Sir Frank Brangwyn and originally intended for the House of Lords.

🚗 *SWANSEA is accessible off the M4 and A48, 42 miles west of Cardiff.*

The Penclawdd cockle women continue to set up shop at Swansea's superb fresh foods market. This is *the* place to buy laverbread

Dylan's Wales

Dylan's statue, Swansea, and the tiny shed in which he worked at Laugharne

imaginary sea-town of Llareggub, this 'play for voices' is a lyrical evocation of everything unique about a small Welsh community not a million miles removed from his beloved Laugharne.

Dylan completed the play just one month before his death. His body was brought back from New York and buried in the churchyard at Laugharne. The Boathouse, where Dylan lived, has been converted into a museum dedicated to his memory. No one, though, has thought to improve on the simple white cross, almost lost amongst a forest of grey tombstones, that marks the poet's final resting place.

Never the pious Welshman, Dylan would not have minded. As well as having a certain way with words, he also possessed a sense of humour. Anyone who has spelt Llareggub backwards will know that.

Wales's brilliant national poet, Dylan Marlais Thomas was born at 5 Cwmdonkin Drive, Swansea, on 27 October 1914. He died, aged only 39, in New York on 9 November 1953. During his all too brief life, Dylan's fame — or notoriety — was probably a product more of his image as a boozy Welsh Bohemian than his seductive literary skills.

As stories of his undoubtedly undisciplined and chaotic private life fade, we are left with what really counts — a solid body of work which places him amongst the great writers of the 20th century. Dylan's inspiration sprang from the people and places, landscapes and locations of South and West Wales. His observations, sometimes through the puzzled, innocent eyes of a child, at others through a filter of weary nostalgia, are mostly evocative, always unique.

Young Dylan cut his teeth on the local newspaper at Swansea. The quality of his early poems served as a passport to greater things, and the precocious boy-poet was soon a familiar figure amongst the London literati. Yet no matter how far he strayed, a nagging umbilical ache always drew him back to South Wales.

Some of the happiest years of his life were spent at sleepy Laugharne. He arrived in May 1949, 'got off the bus, and forgot to get on again'. Here, his poetic genius once again flourished, and he began writing *Under Milk Wood*, arguably his greatest work.

The meticulous love of language he brought to his poetry, and the sense of belonging embodied in his short stories are both combined in *Under Milk Wood*. Set in the

TINKINSWOOD AND ST LYTHANS BURIAL CHAMBERS
South Glamorgan

This pair of sturdy and striking prehistoric sites stand no more than a mile apart in the farmlands of the Vale of Glamorgan. Tinkinswood is by far the grander of the two. Apart from the absence of a great earthen mound which would have originally covered it, this burial chamber gives the impression of being almost complete.

The chamber's low stone walls, robust and solid, support an enormous slab of rock — the 24 ft-long, 40-ton capstone — across the roof. When Tinkinswood was excavated in 1914, the bones of at least 50 individuals and items of pottery were unearthed.

Tinkinswood is a megalithic monument dating from around 2500 B.C. St Lythans is of the same period though both taller and smaller than its neighbour — tall enough, in fact, to enter without crouching.

🚗 *BOTH MONUMENTS are off minor roads about 1 mile south of St Nicholas, a village on the A48 6 miles west of Cardiff.*

VALE OF NEATH
West Glamorgan

The A465 'Heads of the Valleys' road skirts the high ground above most of the South Wales valleys before swooping down into the Vale of Neath. The efforts made here to recapture the beauty of the valley whilst preserving its rich industrial heritage are beginning to bear fruit.

At the Aberdulais Falls (see separate entry) the National Trust is involved in a major restoration project. The Aberdulais Basin, nearby, is the meeting place of the Neath and Tennant Canals, 19th-century water-ways used to transport coal, iron and many other goods. Parts of the canal have now been rescued from dereliction — especially around the canal basin itself, where there are pleasant towpath walks, picnic sites and an elegant 10-arched aqueduct.

More visitors are also discovering the waterfalls which tumble down through the thickly wooded valley sides. At Pont-Nedd-Fechan, a foot-path leads past an overgrown and long-abandoned silica mine to a series of falls which rank amongst the loveliest in Wales. There are more waterfalls along the opposite side of the valley at Melyncourt, close to picnic sites and woodland walks in the Rheola Forest above Resolven.

Cilfrew, near Aberdulais, is the home of the Penscynor Wildlife Park, a well designed 16-acre parkland site with an international reputation for its world-wide collection of animals and birds. Just west of Neath itself stand the gloomy ruins of Neath Abbey, a 12th-century Cistercian house used, somewhat sacreligiously, for copper and iron smelting during the Industrial Revolution.

🚗 *NEATH, at the junction of the A465 and A474, is 8 miles east of Swansea.*

WELSH FOLK MUSEUM
South Glamorgan

This museum performs a distance-shrinking trick — with elements of time travel thrown in for good measure — by taking visitors on a trip around the rural Wales of old in one afternoon. At least half a day is needed to do justice to the Welsh Folk Museum, the great fascination of which lies out-of-doors amongst the trees in extensive, grassy parklands where old buildings rescued from all over Wales have been lovingly reconstructed stone-by-stone, timber-by-timber.

The buildings — around 20 in all — include a humble farmworker's cottage, large farmhouse, cruck-built barn, woollen factory, tannery, smithy, cockpit, traditional chapel and tiny toll-house which still displays its list of charges. Domestic and cultural life in the Wales of bygone times is also preserved within a modern, purpose-built museum block where imaginatively presented displays highlight everything from furniture to farming methods, costumes to medical care.

The third side to this multi-faceted site is represented by a fine Elizabethan country house, the 100-acre grounds and gardens of which accommodate the entire museum. The mansion, an imposing, many-gabled affair with a typically opulent Long Gallery (a favourite 16th-century feature) and Flemish tapestries, is also open to the public.
THE MUSEUM, 4½ miles from the centre of Cardiff, is in the village of St Fagan's on the western outskirts of the city.

Left: The Welsh Folk Museum is now the home of this toll-house, which once stood near Aberystwyth

WELSH MINERS' MUSEUM AND AFAN ARGOED COUNTRY PARK
West Glamorgan

The harsh realities of 'coal getting' are neither sensationalised nor treated sentimentally at this thought-provoking little museum. From the outside, it looks rather plain and ordinary. Within the confines of modest dimensions and budgets it manages to accommodate all manner of exhibits and items, putting many a more affluent museum to shame.

Quite deservedly, this museum has attracted a number of awards for the insight it gives into the life and work of the South Wales miner in the unforgiving 19th century. The 'good old, bad old' days of that tumultuous century, which brought catastrophic changes to this part of Wales, are recalled in all manner of ways. Old newspapers tell of terrible mining disasters; miners' lamps and the tools-of-the-trade are displayed; and visitors are taken into the collier's home through a re-created kitchen scene and transported right to the pit face along a reconstructed underground gallery.

The museum stands on the flanks of a tree-lined hillside at the entrance to the Afan Argoed Country Park in the Afan Valley. This vale, known locally as 'Little Switzerland', is one of the most scenic of the South Wales valleys. Evidence of its coal-mining past is now almost exclusively confined to the museum thanks to large-scale landscaping and conifer planting schemes.
THE MUSEUM is on the A4017 near Cymmer, approximately 15 miles east of Swansea.

Right: A claustrophobic coal-face in the Welsh Miners' Museum

West Wales

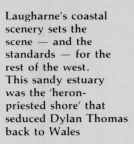

Laugharne's coastal scenery sets the scene — and the standards — for the rest of the west. This sandy estuary was the 'heron-priested shore' that seduced Dylan Thomas back to Wales

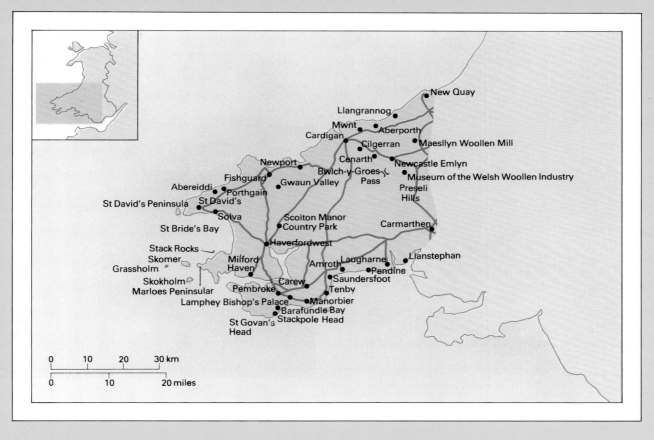

THE SEA HAS ALWAYS been the dominant element here. Iron Age man was drawn to promontory forts overlooking the waves. Celtic saints made perilous journeys across the waters, spreading the Christian message. As the Dark Ages descended, Viking raiders plundered the coast. The Normans, in their turn, built castles such as Pembroke and Kidwelly with sea-borne access.

West Wales's extraordinarily rich coastal heritage — in scenery as well as pure history — manifests itself most strongly within the **Pembrokeshire Coast National Park.** Pembrokeshire is unique as the only one of Britain's ten national parks which is almost entirely coastal-based. At 225 square miles, it is also Britain's smallest: a misleading statistic. The figure that really counts is its 230 miles of seashore.

The park runs from Poppit Sands near Cardigan to Amroth. Pembrokeshire's tide-washed sea-cliffs and sandy bays have tested the pen of many a writer, provoking this 17th-century description of an area 'shaped with divers corners ...... in some places concave, in some convex, but in most .... bending inwards as doth the Moon'.

West Wales also embraces the southern stretch of Cardigan Bay around New Quay and the silent sands near Laugharne, two areas rich in Dylan Thomas associations. Inland, there are the old market and weaving towns and maze of unexplored, leafy lanes around the Teifi Valley, an enchanting, gentle swathe of countryside.

ABERPORTH
Dyfed

Aberporth's twin beaches — each one a neat crescent of sands — today play host to summer visitors. In the 18th and 19th centuries, they provided safe and sheltered anchorage for the coastal traders of Cardigan Bay and the largest fleet of herring boats in Wales.

The old boats, long since departed, have not given way to garish seaside developments. Aberporth, although busy in summer, is largely uncommercialised, retaining the atmosphere of a village-by-the-sea. Its houses fit themselves in as best they can amongst towering cliff scenery, a dominant feature along this stretch of Cardigan Bay. East of Aberporth, a path leads across the blustery headlands for just over a mile to tiny Tresaith, where a waterfall plunges onto sea-rocks next to a small, cliff-backed beach. Beyond Tresaith lies Traeth Penbryn, one of the loveliest stretches of sand on Cardigan Bay.

🚗 *ABERPORTH, accessible by the B4333 off the A487, is 6 miles northeast of Cardigan.*

CARDIGAN
Dyfed

This handsome old town is a meeting place for country and coast, the River Teifi and the sea. Cardigan has led a varied life as a Norman stronghold, sea-port, market town and farming centre.

Each of these different periods is etched on the face of the town. The ruined battlements and round towers of a castle put up in early medieval times to control the river mouth stand on a rise above Cardigan's most picturesque feature, an elegant, five-arched bridge, 17th century in origin.

On the opposite bank, tall wharfside warehouses, now mostly converted, are reminders of Cardigan's role as a busy trading port. The charming covered market, beneath the equally attractive Guildhall, is still going strong, providing for the farming communities from around and about.

Today, this mix of market and sea-town has an added dimension, for Cardigan is now a well-situated holiday centre for those wishing to explore the coves and headlands of both Cardigan Bay and the Pembrokeshire Coast National Park. The national park starts on a high note at nearby St Dogmael's, taking in the sandy Teifi estuary and craggy Cemaes Head.

St Dogmael's itself grew up around its Benedictine abbey, founded in 1115, the remains of which are still visible. At the Cardigan Wildlife Park, a few miles south of the town, many types of animal, including exotic breeds, can be seen at close quarters.

Cardigan enjoys a special status in traditional Welsh circles, for Wales's first eisteddfod (see special feature, page 109) was reputedly held here in 1176.

🚗 *CARDIGAN is accessible by the A487 from Fishguard, A478 from Tenby and A484 from Carmarthen.*

CAREW
Dyfed

Man's early religious preoccupations, his medieval military and social ambitions and more recent exploitation of the mechanical age all put in an appearance at this pretty hamlet, on the upper reaches of the tidal Carew River.

A roadside Celtic cross, slender, tall and heavily decorated with interlacing patterns, bears an inscription which commemorates

Carew, one of Wales's more comfortable, domesticated castles

Maredudd ap Edwin, King of Dyfed, who was killed in battle in 1035. Regarded as one of the finest 11th-century crosses in Britain, it has been adopted as the official symbol of Cadw, the newly created government body responsible for many of Wales's historic monuments.

A splendid castle stands on the grassy riverbanks across the field. Carew Castle, originally a medieval stronghold built here to take advantage of seaborne access via the waters of the Milford Haven, gradually evolved into a handsome Tudor and Elizabethan home. Its purely decorative mullioned windows are a particular visual treat.

Carew Tidal Mill is unique in Wales. As its name implies, this 19th-century mill — which replaced an earlier model — takes advantage of the rise and fall in the river. It stands, three storeys tall, on a dam which traps the high-tide waters, subsequently released to power the waterwheel.

🚗 *CAREW, near the junction of the A4075 and A477, is 4 miles north-east of Pembroke.*

Photographers have been coming to Teifiside's Cenarth Falls since the early days of the camera

CARMARTHEN
Dyfed

The 'capital' of the old county of Carmarthenshire is now the main administrative centre for the huge new 'super-county' of Dyfed, created by local government reorganisation in 1974. The imposing county offices stand on a hill above the River Tywi, sharing a site with the remains of Carmarthen's medieval castle.

Fragments of castle wall and ruined towers appear unexpectedly amongst more modern architecture. The town itself is a pleasant mixture of old and new. Narrow lanes, clearly medieval in origin, lead into wide shopping streets and pedestrianised areas where white-collar office workers mingle with ruddy-faced farming folk.

The best time to visit Carmarthen is on a Wednesday, when the market is in full swing. The animal pens and auction yards behind the covered market are a buzz of activity, as farmers from many miles around haggle over the best prices for their cattle and sheep.

The Romans ventured no further west than Carmarthen. They constructed an amphitheatre here, one of only seven known in Britain, its shape still clearly imprinted in a grassy hollow on the eastern outskirts of town.

Carmarthen Museum, at nearby Abergwili, is based within a lovely old range of buildings, the former Palace of the Bishop of St David's, dating from 1283. Its most talked-about exhibit, a wizened tree stump, recalls Carmarthen's legendary Arthurian connections. This is the famous Merlin's Oak, rescued from its original site during redevelopment presumably to protect the town from the prophecy: 'When Merlin's Oak shall tumble down, then shall fall Carmarthen town.'

🔻 *CARMARTHEN is on the junction of the A40, A48 and A484, approximately 27 miles north-west of Swansea.*

CENARTH
Dyfed

No Victorian Grand Tour of Wales was complete without a visit to the falls at Cenarth. Here, the River Teifi's normally sedate progress is interrupted as it tumbles over rocks before rushing beneath a picturesque old stone bridge.

The Teifi is a river famed for its salmon and sewin (the Welsh name for sea-trout) fishing. It has long been associated with the coracle, a tiny fishing craft made of intertwined laths of hazel and willow, which has been used in Wales for at least 2000 years. These bobbing, precarious looking one-man boats, which resemble an upturned umbrella, are extremely manoeuvrable in skilled hands. They can still sometimes be seen at Cenarth — for a guaranteed siting, come during the coracle races held each August.

The riverbanks here, a repository of fishing lore and traditions, are an appropriate setting for the Cenarth Fishing Museum, where angling enthusiasts can ponder over a huge collection of rods and reels.

🔻 *CENARTH is on the A484 between Cardigan and Newcastle Emlyn.*

CILGERRAN
Dyfed

A Victorian writer, stalking the remains of Cilgerran Castle 'beautiful in its ruins', was overcome by an attack of purple prose, an occupational hazard at that time. His imagination — and pen — ran riot when he wrote: 'Looking from the lofty ruin on the embowered glen below one wonders how the passions of war could rage amid such loveliness. But Teifi's silver flood has been crimsoned with human blood.'

A little over the top, perhaps, but excusable, for Cilgerran sets off the romantically minded. Legend surrounds this Norman stronghold from which, reputedly, Nest, the beautiful wife of Gerald of Wales, was kidnapped by a Welsh prince in 1109. On a sounder historic note, the castle led an active life in the 12th and 13th centuries, when it was captured and recaptured a number of times.

Today, its great attraction lies in its location. Cilgerran's walls and towers, though powerful enough, cannot compete with its setting on a sheer crag above a deep and lushly wooded gorge carved by the River Teifi. When the Victorians came here on their Grand Tour of Wales, coracles (see Cenarth entry for further details) would have been a common sight on these waters. Today, they are mainly confined to a coracle regatta, held every August.

🔻 *CILGERRAN, on a minor road off the A478, is 3 miles south-east of Cardigan.*

DALE PENINSULA
Dyfed

This peninsula is one of the windiest places in Britain, where gusts have been known to exceed 100 m.p.h. In compensation, it is also one of the sunniest, with an annual average of 1800 hours of sunshine.

Dale is a place of extremes. This 'place apart' sits right at the end of the road in a far corner of Pembrokeshire, steadfastly ignoring the comings and goings of the outside world. Although no more than three miles from tip to toe, its largely remote coastline — Dale is the definitive place for walkers and naturalists — is one of the most wildly beautiful in Wales.

Extremes in contrast are also part of Dale's character. Its west-facing cliffs bear the full force of the winds whilst the bays along the east coast look inwards to the calm and sheltered waters of the Milford Haven. The Vikings, when they plundered Wales in the Dark Ages, must have used this sheltered anchorage, for *Dale*, meaning 'valley', is a pure Norse name.

The coastguard and lighthouse station at St Anne's Head, at the entrance to the Haven, keeps a watchful eye on the giant supertankers that glide in and out of this busy waterway. In 1485, a much frailer flotilla landed at nearby Mill Bay, bearing Welshman Harri Tudur and his supporters. From here, Harri marched to victory over Richard III at the Battle of Bosworth, becoming Henry VII, first of the Tudors, initiator of a mighty dynasty.

🚗 *DALE is on the B4327, 12 miles south-west of Haverfordwest.*

The Graham Sutherland Art Gallery, within Picton Castle

FISHGUARD
Dyfed

This is a town of many parts. Goodwick is a commercial port, the end of the line for the Paddington to Fishguard rail link and the embarkation point for the Irish Sea ferries. The town centre and main shopping streets are to be found on the hill, in Upper Fishguard. Call in at the Town Hall, not only for its excellent little covered market but also to see the mementos of Fishguard's seafaring past — including a record of ships rescued by the local lifeboat.

Lower Fishguard, an inlet protected by steep, gorse-covered hillsides, is by far the prettiest part of town. The old harbourside here, lined with its row of gabled cottages, paints the perfect picture of a self-contained and timeless quayside community. Full advantage was taken of the location when it became Llareggub, Dylan Thomas's imaginary, magical seatown, during the filming of *Under Milk Wood* which starred Elizabeth Taylor and the late Richard Burton.

Carreg Wastad Point, a remote headland north of the town, appears in the record books as the scene, in 1797, of the last invasion of Britain. French troops, led by an American colonel, initiated this farcical, half-cocked affair, which ended in ignominious surrender almost before it had begun. An interesting range of invasion memorabilia can be seen in the Royal Oak Inn, opposite the Town Hall.

🚗 *FISHGUARD, on the junction of the A487 and A40, is half-way between Cardigan and St Davids.*

GWAUN VALLEY
Dyfed

Residents of this sheltered, secluded valley deep in the backwoods of north Pembrokeshire are, quite literally, a little behind the times — during the New Year, at least. When Britain adopted changes to the calendar in 1752 which threw everything forward by 11 days, news cannot have filtered through to the Gwaun Valley; either that, or its diehard residents chose to ignore it. As a consequence, its inhabitants still celebrate New Year's Day on 13 January. During the day, folk from the scattered farms and cottages get together for a meal of goose and plum pudding accompanied by traditional celebrations whilst the children collect *calennig*, a New Year's gift of money, apples and oranges.

The valley's ancient, hanging woodlands lend this hideaway a secretive, untouched air. Oakwoods in the main, they clothe steep valley sides above the Gwaun, its waters rushing by on their way to Lower Fishguard and the sea.

🚗 *THE GWAUN VALLEY, a few miles south-east of Fishguard, is accessible by minor road off the B4313.*

HAVERFORDWEST
Dyfed

Before boundary changes in 1974, this was Pembrokeshire's county town. Although the old county, officially at least, no longer exists, Haverfordwest clings to its status as 'capital' of this part of the world. The Pembrokeshire Coast National Park headquarters are located here, together with many administrative and local government offices. Moreover, Haverfordwest's historic pedigree is impeccable.

Haverfordwest has all the characteristics of a river town. It grew up around a hilltop Norman castle which guarded the highest navigable point on the Western Cleddau, a river leading into the mighty Milford Haven waterway. A maze of narrow, steep streets, lined with grand Georgian buildings, points not only to the town's great age but also to its past prosperity as a port. Its trading links with the West of England are perpetuated most strongly in the name of the Bristol Trader Inn which stands in Quay Street next to old warehouses where wool and wine were stored.

Further along the quay, an attractive new riverside shopping complex blends in well with its historic surroundings. The shell of Haverfordwest Castle gazes over the rooftops of an architecturally fascinating town which also contains three interesting churches (St Mary's is particularly lovely). An old gaol, built into the castle, is now the home of the County Museum.

Haverfordwest's central location, roughly equidistant from the coastlines of south, west and north Pembrokeshire (the name lives on despite the politicians) makes it a popular touring centre. The grounds of Picton Castle, a few miles to the south-east, contain the Graham Sutherland Art Gallery, the largest permanent display anywhere in the world of works by this distinguished artist, who found much of his inspiration in Pembrokeshire.

🚗 *HAVERFORDWEST, on the junction of the A40, A4076 and A487, is 15 miles from Fishguard and 10 miles from Pembroke.*

Lamphey Bishop's Palace, used as a country retreat by the medieval churchmen of St David's

LAMPHEY BISHOP'S PALACE
Dyfed

The prelates of the medieval church were no strangers to creature comforts. At Lamphey, the bishops of St David's had a comfortable retreat where they could lead the lives of country gentlemen amongst pleasant surroundings which contained orchards, vegetable gardens and a fishpond.

The former splendour of this large ruin, partly hidden behind low walls, has not entirely vanished. A large grassy enclosure leads to a group of buildings in the far corner of the grounds, decorated with arcaded parapets — an architectural embellishment reminiscent, not surprisingly, of the Bishop's Palace in St David's itself.

The shell of the Great Hall is most impressive, as is the attractive 16th-century chapel, noted for its five-light east window. The gatehouse is a strange sight. Nowadays, this castellated little tower, a mixture of ecclesiastic and military architectural influences, stands isolated in the middle of the enclosure, guarding nothing but grass.

🚗 *THE PALACE is in the village of Lamphey, on the A4139 2 miles east of Pembroke.*

LAUGHARNE
Dyfed

Sleepy Laugharne is indelibly linked with the life and work of poet and writer Dylan Marlais Thomas (see special feature, page **31**). Dylan discovered Laugharne in the 1940s, spending one of the happiest and most productive periods of his life here beside its 'heron-priested shore'.

He lived in the Georgian Boathouse, within sight and sound of the seabirds and lapping waves of the sandy Taf estuary. Laugharne continues to fit Dylan's soothing description of it as a 'timeless, mild, beguiling island of a town'. Increasing numbers of visitors now follow in Dylan's footsteps.

They walk along the narrow cliff path to the Boathouse, which has been converted into a museum dedicated to his life and work, passing on the approach to the house a small hut — no more than a glorified garden shed really — in which he would lock himself away to write. Laugharne appeared everywhere in his work, finally blending with his memories of another sea-town, New Quay, to become imaginary, magical Llareggub in *Under Milk Wood*.

Laugharne Castle ('as brown as owls' according to Dylan) is a sprawling mysterious ruin, part medieval fortification, part Tudor palace. Its romantic, ivy-covered walls and towers (currently under restoration) caught the eye of artist J.M.W. Turner over 250 years ago, when he captured it on canvas.

🚗 *LAUGHARNE is on the A4066, 13 miles south-west of Carmarthen.*

The little resort of Llangrannog shelters beneath some of Cardigan Bay's finest cliff scenery

LLANGRANNOG
Dyfed

A narrow glen winds its way through wooded countryside to open up to the sea at Llangrannog. This picturesque little village of colourfully painted cottages and houses has grown up around a sandy beach on one of the few breaks in the headlands.

Steep steps, cut into the cliff above the beach, mark the start of one of the most spectacular coast paths on Cardigan Bay. The path skirts a hillside crowned by an Iron Age fort before leading to the promontory of Ynys Lochtyn, one mile north-east of Llangrannog. The cliff-backed shoreline suddenly seems tame in comparison to this exposed, sea-washed and wind-scoured promontory, a thin finger of land — its tip often cut off by the waves — pointing into Cardigan Bay.

Appearances at Ynys Lochtyn are not deceptive — caution should be exercised here, and when the winds are high it is best viewed from a secure distance.

🚗 *LLANGRANNOG is on the B4334, accessible off the A487, about 13 miles north-east of Cardigan.*

LLANSTEPHAN
Dyfed

This neat little community, a one-time fishing village, clusters around its church on the sandy banks of the Tywi estuary. The church's 13th-century tower, though sturdy and battlemented, is thoroughly eclipsed by the ruins of Llanstephan Castle, a grey and brooding pile on the bluff above the brightly painted village.

The castle's coarse stone walls and towers spread themselves across a strategic site exploited by man since prehistoric times. Items from the 6th century B.C. have been found here on

Iron Age man and medieval warlord sought security at Llanstephan

the site of an Iron Age promontory fort. When the Normans arrived, they cleared out the prehistoric ditches, incorporating parts of the ancient fort into their plan. The castle gradually grew up over the next few hundred years. Its twin-towered Great Gatehouse, by far its most imposing feature, enjoys expansive views across the mouth of the estuary to Worm's Head on the tip of the Gower Peninsula.

LLANSTEPHAN is on the B4312, 8 miles south-west of Carmarthen.

MAESLLYN WOOLLEN MILL AND MUSEUM OF THE WELSH WOOLLEN INDUSTRY
Dyfed

Until early this century, the banks of the River Teifi and its tributaries around Llandysul echoed to the clatter of many a woollen mill. 'Hardly a spot (remained) on any stream where it would be convenient to build another mill,' so it was said. Some survive, others have been revived, perpetuating a tradition of woollen weaving that stretches back many centuries in Wales (see special feature, page **58**).

Maesllyn's revival came in 1976. Disused and derelict, it has been renovated as a working mill-cum-museum. Early hand-operated looms and 19th-century mechanical weaving frames illustrate the evolution in production methods. Displays also explain the entire production process, from raw wool to finished cloth.

Across the Teifi, a few miles to the south, is the Museum of the Welsh Woollen Industry, part of the National Museum of Wales. Here, old photographs, a 'Factory Trail' and an extensive collection of textile machinery and hand tools tell the story of Wales's most important rural industry from the Middle Ages to the present day.

MAESLLYN is located on a minor road, most easily accessible off the A486 at Croes-lan crossroads 4 miles north-west of Llandysul. The Museum of the Welsh Woollen Industry is at Drefach Felindre, 3 miles south-east of Newcastle Emlyn, by minor road off the A484.

MANORBIER
Dyfed

This select little village-cum-resort boasts the definitive castle-by-the-sea. Manorbier Castle stands on a bluff above the bay, with unbroken views across the sands and surf.

Built by the Norman de Barri family in the 12th and 13th centuries, this fortress is in an excellent state of repair, its baronial character undiminished by the years. The castle was the birthplace, in 1146, of Giraldus Cambrensis, Gerald of Wales, a monk and chronicler to whom we owe much of our knowledge of life in medieval Wales. Both native Welsh and Norman newcomers are subjected to his authoritative and impartial gaze in two classic works, *Itinerary* and *Description*, based on his travels throughout Wales.

Giraldus's objectivity possibly wavered when it came to writing about his birthplace, which he described as 'the pleasantest spot in Wales', though it is often endorsed by those who find Manorbier a more peaceful alternative to busier Tenby.

MANORBIER is on the B4585 (off the A4139) 5 miles south-west of Tenby.

MARLOES PENINSULA
Dyfed

Few people make the long trek west to Marloes; which is good news for those who do, for they have one of Pembrokeshire's finest beaches all to themselves. Marloes Sands, a half-mile walk from the car park, is totally uncommercialised, uninhabited and undeveloped, a rare combination of characteristics even in Pembrokeshire. The beach, a gentle curve of firm sands backed by a low line of rosy-red cliffs, ends at Gateholm Island, accessible at low tide, on which the native Welsh lived during Roman times.

Marloes itself, although landlocked, was once a fishing village. Its harbour was at Martin's Haven, two miles to the west. This tiny inlet, equipped with nothing more than a slipway and winch, is now the embarkation point for summer boat trips to Skomer Island (see separate entry). Martin's Haven is close to the Deer Park headland, a starkly beautiful promontory with exceptional cliff scenery, once inhabited by Iron Age man.

MARLOES is accessible off the B4327, 12 miles south-west of Haverfordwest.

MILFORD HAVEN WATERWAY
Dyfed

The boundary of the Pembrokeshire Coast National Park takes a short detour along the Milford Haven to avoid the oil terminals and petrochemical installations stationed midway along this magnificent deep-water inlet. Admiral Lord Nelson regarded this waterway as one of the finest sheltered harbours in the world. Deserted block-house fortifications, constructed along the Haven in the 19th century to dissuade the French from any thought of attack, are ghostly guardians of the large naval dockyards which were once located here.

The Haven, also busy with deep-sea fishing fleets in the past, continues to keep itself occupied. Judged on tonnage handled, it is Britain's second largest port, a position achieved thanks to the massive oil cargoes transported by the giant supertankers that berth here, beside jetties linked to a steely web of oil storage and processing plants.

The new road bridge north of Pembroke spans a great divide in the Haven. Beyond this point, the national park once again reasserts itself along the Daugleddau, a peaceful backwater of tidal creeks and wooded shores.

➤ *THE MILFORD HAVEN — upstream and downstream — can be explored by boat trips from Hobb's Point, Pembroke Dock, 2 miles north-west of Pembroke.*

MWNT
Dyfed

Everything is in miniature at tiny Mwnt, tucked away on a secluded stretch of Cardigan Bay coastline. Miniature beach, mountain and church are the ingredients of this delightful spot, now in the care of the National Trust.

Mwnt simply means 'mound', a prosaic reference to the headland and viewpoint which towers above the beach. More deservedly, this perfectly formed crescent of sand has also been labelled 'the jewel of Cardigan Bay'.

The Church of the Holy Cross shares the grassy hillside between beach and headland with munching sheep. Whitewashed, austere, solid and very old indeed, with an ancient wood-beamed roof, it has stood here since medieval times, possibly on the site of a religious settlement founded during the 'Age of Saints' in the 5th and 6th centuries.

For all its beauty, Mwnt has its darker side. Up until a few centuries ago, games were held here on the first Sunday in January called *Sul Coch y Mwnt* ('The Bloody Sunday of the Mound') to commemorate the violent defeat of a Flemish landing on the coast here in 1155.

➤ *MWNT, on the coast between the Teifi estuary and Aberporth, is accessible by minor road about 5 miles north-east of Cardigan.*

PEMBROKE
Dyfed

This Norman outpost quickly graduated from its original crude stake and timber stronghold to a mighty fortress, one of the finest in Wales. Pembroke Castle is no tumbledown ruin. It struts, purposeful and well preserved, on a rock above the town and river, its strategic importance and stature plain to see.

The castle is a legacy mostly from the late 12th century and the ambitions of nobleman William Marshall. Later — in 1457 — it was the birthplace of Harri Tudur, the Welshman who became Henry VII, initiator of the mighty Tudor dynasty.

Only from within the walls does the castle reveal its full size and most outstanding feature — the circular Great Keep. For the best view of fortress, river and town, climb to the top of the keep, up a staircase cut into its 20-ft thick walls. From here, the Victorian assessment of Pembroke (akin to 'the skeleton of an ill-conditioned flounder, the castle precinct being the head ...... the only street representing the vertebral bone ......') can be tested for accuracy.

Unflattering though it may sound, the simile does put things into perspective. The town itself occupies a defensive site, its long main street following a narrow spine of high ground which leads away from the castle. But the assessment does not take into account Pembroke's graceful Georgian buildings, nor the pleasant riverside promenade and intact stretches of 14th-century town walls, rare in Britain today.

The hill opposite the castle is occupied by the bulky, and very old, Church of St Nicholas, once part of a medieval Benedictine priory. Pembroke's National Museum of Gypsy Caravans lives up to its rather grand title by containing a marvellous collection of highly decorated, horse-drawn homes, each one a mobile work of art.

➤ *PEMBROKE, at the junction of the A477 and A4139, is 13 miles west of Tenby.*

Within these walls was born Harri Tudur, the Welshman better known as Henry VII, first of the Tudor monarchs. Pembroke Castle made its last historic mark when it was besieged by Oliver Cromwell for seven weeks

NEWCASTLE EMLYN
Dyfed

Livestock marts are held at Newcastle Emlyn every Friday. This old market town, located smack in the midst of the loveliest stretch of the Teifi Valley, has faithfully served the farming communities scattered throughout Teifiside's low hills and wooded vales for many centuries.

Its ruined castle, although intended more as a country seat than military stronghold, makes the most of the protection afforded by a naturally fortified loop in the river. A mile downstream, the Teifi is joined by a tributary, the Ceri. This little river, flowing through a secluded, small and perfectly silent valley just north of Newcastle Emlyn, powers the waterwheel of the Felin Geri Flourmill. Dating from the 17th century, this mill was saved from dereliction in the 1970s and is now open to the public. Its creaking wheels, wooden cogs and grinders are operational once more, producing stoneground wholemeal flour exactly as it was milled 100 years ago.

NEWCASTLE EMLYN, at the Junction of the A484 and A475, is 11 miles south-east of Cardigan.

NEWPORT
Dyfed

Newport typifies the smallish resorts which are strung out irregularly along the rugged north Pembrokeshire coastline. The beach, on the shores of Newport Bay where the River Nevern meets the sea, is a little way from the old town.

Competing with the sands for the visitor's attention are a wealth of historic sites, scattered around the district. The moody Pentre Ifan Cromlech (see Preseli Hills entry) stands nearby. Mynydd Carningli, a 1000-ft outcrop in the Preseli Hills above the town, is littered with remains of a sturdy Iron Age hill-fort. Newport itself, a medieval charter town which still hangs on to its time-honoured ceremonial customs, is full of interest. A group of prehistoric burial chambers can be seen beside the main road, just over one mile west of Newport. And at Cwm yr Eglwys, at the foot of Dinas Head, there are the seashore remains of a church destroyed by a great gale in 1859.

NEWPORT is on the A487 between Fishguard and Cardigan.

NEW QUAY
Dyfed

The quayside here preserves so effectively the look of the last century that it seems as if the old list of 'tolls and dues', displayed on the harbour wall, might still apply. The list is a leftover from the times when the waters of Cardigan Bay were busy with trading vessels.

At New Quay, we learn that they paid three pence to unload soap, six pence for ham, one shilling for bath chairs and two shillings for coffins.

The harbour, completely protected from the westerly winds by New Quay Head, is one of the most sheltered along Cardigan Bay. Crab and lobster boats still work from here, and it is not too difficult — apart from during those peak times in summer when the narrow, steep streets are busy with visitors — to evoke parallels with Llareggub, the imaginary sea-town in *Under Milk Wood*, which Dylan Thomas based on times spent here and at his home at Laugharne.

NEW QUAY, accessible by the A486 and B4342 off the A487, is between Cardigan and Aberystwyth.

Enclosed in a fold of green hills, Cwm Tudu beach at New Quay

PENDINE
Dyfed

A flat, wide corridor of sands stretches into the far distance from the rocky headland above Pendine village to Ginst Point near Laugharne. This served as a battleground for the world land speed record attempts in the 1920s. The two protagonists, Sir Malcolm Campbell in *Bluebird* and Welsh ace J.G. Parry Thomas in *Babs*, sped down this five-mile long beach until, in 1927, the inevitable happened. When attempting to recapture the title by beating Campbell's record-breaking 174.88 m.p.h., Parry Thomas lost control. *Babs* careered into a series of sickening cartwheels, killing its driver. The wreck was buried in the dunes but has since been exhumed.

Pendine Sands can catch out even the most staid and slow driver. A notice at the entrance ramp to the beach says it all: 'Danger. Do not drive or park near the water's edge. On average, ten cars a year are submerged by the sea.' You have been warned.

🚗 *PENDINE is at the junction of the A4066 and B4314, 18 miles south-west of Carmarthen.*

PORTHGAIN AND ABEREIDDI
Dyfed

Porthgain is a great polariser of opinions. Some find the intrusion of 19th-century brickworks into this otherwise idyllic harbourside downright ugly. Others are captivated by the strange beauty of this nautical and industrial site.

No more than a handful of houses and harbour pub — the Sloop Inn, founded, according to the date above the door, in 1743 — Porthgain remained undisturbed as a tiny haven for centuries. Transformation took

place in the mid 19th century. Slate and granite, quarried from the headlands, were exported from here to the burgeoning industrial towns hungry for building materials, and a brickworks grew up along the harbourside.

By the 1930s, it was all over. The abandoned ruins now stand incongruously amongst some of the most silent and serrated coastal scenery in Wales. Across the headland, at Abereiddi, there are more remnants of industrial activity. Beyond the 'black-sand' beach (formed by the action of the waves on the slate and shale cliffs) and ruined workers' cottages is the eerie 'blue lagoon', an abandoned slate quarry flooded by the sea.

Porthgain harbour is a neat little place, transformed in the mid 19th century by the addition of a brickworks

🚗 *PORTHGAIN and Abereiddi are on minor roads off the A487, approximately 6 miles north-east of St David's.*

PRESELI HILLS
Dyfed

The boundary of the Pembrokeshire Coast National Park faithfully hugs the shoreline for the vast majority of its length, venturing inland just once to embrace the smooth, bare flanks of these hills. The Preselis rise to a high point of 1760 ft at Foel Cwm-cerwyn, their rough pastures and moorland presenting a strange contrast to the rocks and headlands of the nearby shoreline.

These hills are a treasure chest for those interested in prehistory. Prehistoric man's preference for high places has left a rich legacy of ancient monuments, hill-forts and standing stones (see Newport, Dyfed entry). The most famous of all is the Pentre Ifan Cromlech, in the northern foothills a few miles south-east of Newport. This striking burial chamber never fails to provoke mystery and speculation. Its huge 16 ft capstone and three upright supports are made from the same Preseli 'blue stone' that found its way — somehow — to Stonehenge on Salisbury Plain, almost 200 miles away.

🚗 *THE PRESELI HILLS lie within a southern arc between Cardigan and Fishguard.*

ST BRIDE'S BAY
Dyfed

The Pembrokeshire coast is a battleground defined by the wildly varying fortunes of sea and land. The waves are winning conclusively along St Bride's Bay, where the pounding surf bites deeply into soft rocks. To the north and south, the tougher underlying rocks of the St David's and Marloes Peninsulas are able to make an effective stand against the tempestuous sea.

South of Solva, cliffs give way to a long, unbroken stretch of sands at Newgale, a west-facing beach popular with surfers and swimmers. Further south still, a succession of 'Havens' — Nolton, Madoc's, Druidston, Broad and Little — dot the shore. Of these, the small resorts of Broad and Little Haven, with their modest selection of holiday accommodation, are the most popular and easily reached.

🚗 *NEWGALE is on the A487. Broad and Little Haven are accessible by the B4341 from Haverfordwest.*

ST DAVID'S
Dyfed

Britain's smallest city stands isolated on its gale-tossed peninsula in the far-flung south-western corner of Wales. The building responsible for St David's city status — its cathedral — is not immediately visible. It squats, low and discreet, in a grassy hollow well below the rooftops.

The full magnitude of this large, cruciform cathedral is only apparent from the top of the Thirty-nine Steps which lead down to a site that has witnessed Christian worship for 1500 years. *Dewi Sant*, St David, Wales's patron saint, founded a monastic community here in the 6th century which became a fountainhead for the Christian message during Britain's Dark Ages.

Welsh leeks and daffodils make a mass appearance every 1 March, St David's Day, to commemorate this Celtic saint's death in A.D. 589. His city has been an important Christian shrine since medieval times when it was declared that two pilgrimages to St David's would equal one to Rome.

The cathedral, built of a purple-hued local stone and dating from 1176 remains in essence a supreme example of medieval religious architecture, though it has inevitably been much restored over the centuries. Its treasures — far too many to list — include an ornately carved 15th-century oak roof and original late-Norman nave.

The shell of the 14th-century Bishop's Palace, in the field opposite, now has the look of a poor relation. In its time, it would have been a grand and desirable residence which proclaimed the worldly wealth of the medieval church. Although in ruin, traces of its original opulence remain, especially in its fine arcades and elaborate windows.

🚗 *ST DAVID'S is on the A487, 16 miles north-west of Haverfordwest.*

ST DAVID'S PENINSULA
Dyfed

This atmospheric and unpopulated peninsula, formed of tough, sea-resistant rocks, is dotted with religious and historic sites. Whitesands Bay, the only large beach along its rock-strewn coastline, lies beneath a 600-ft high headland which bears evidence of prehistoric and Iron Age settlement.

At St Justinian's, a lifeboat station just manages to squeeze itself in amongst the cliffs overlooking the dangerous waters which separate Ramsey Island from the mainland. Non, mother of St David, is

remembered a little further along the coast at the ruined St Non's Chapel and Holy Well, on green slopes overlooking St Non's Bay. The sheltered creek at Porth Clais, west of St Non's Bay, was once the port for St David's when men and goods always travelled by sea instead of by road.

Caerfai and Caerbwdi, further east, are a pair of little bays separated by yet another rugged headland.

ALL THE SITES mentioned are no more than a few miles from St David's. Most are accessible by car. All can be explored by following the relevant section of the long-distance Pembrokeshire Coast Footpath.

SAUNDERSFOOT AND AMROTH
Dyfed

Both places are located along the western arc of Carmarthen Bay on a coastline which alternates between rock, shingle and sand. Saundersfoot, by far the larger of the two, has grown up around its commodious harbour, invariably filled with a bobbing, colourful flotilla of holiday boats. Those who know Saundersfoot only as the premier yachting centre in South Wales are amazed to discover that this pretty resort, with its long, sheltered beach, was once a coal-exporting port.

The Pembrokeshire Coast National Park runs as far as Amroth, a few miles to the north-east of Saundersfoot. This coastal hamlet strings itself out along a thin strip of land between wooded slopes and the sea. From its tall beach-front bank of pebbles, traces of a submerged forest can sometimes be seen at low tide.

SAUNDERSFOOT, on the B4316, is 3 miles north of Tenby.

SCOLTON MANOR COUNTRY PARK
Dyfed

A neat Georgian mansion is the centrepiece of this small but wide-ranging country park. Within a 40-acre estate, Scolton Manor embraces everything from prehistory to the Age of Steam, specimen trees to butterflies.

The house, built in 1840, looks down onto landscaped grounds and spruce and fir plantations, deciduous trees and a 19th-century aboretum with exotic specimens which are only now reaching full maturity. The estate also has a butterfly garden and small pond.

Museum displays and exhibition material are shared amongst a number of buildings. The manor house preserves its period décor, whilst the stables to the rear feature rural crafts. A purpose built exhibition hall, next to these outbuildings, focuses on Pembrokeshire's past from prehistoric to medieval times. Out-of-doors, the old county's 19th-century railway history is represented by *Margaret*, a brightly painted saddle tank steam locomotive.

SCOLTON MANOR is on the B4329, 5 miles north-east of Haverfordwest.

SKOMER, SKOKHOLM AND GRASSHOLM ISLANDS
Dyfed

This foreign-sounding trio of islands remind us of another turbulent chapter in Welsh history. Their Norse-inspired names have been handed down from the Vikings, a brilliant but bellicose sea-faring race who terrorized the shores of Wales between the 9th and 11th centuries.

Today's island invaders are of the feathered, air-borne variety. The islands are now nature reserves of international significance by virtue of their thriving colonies of sea-birds. Skomer, the largest and most accessible of the three (by day trip

St David's Cathedral, its mellow stone exterior and (*above*) wooden roof

from Martin's Haven in summer — see Marloes Peninsula entry) has one of the finest populations of sea-birds in north-west Europe.

The razorbill, adopted as the official symbol of the Pembrokeshire Coast National Park, breeds amongst its rocks and sea-cliffs, one of an ornothological superabundance of species that includes guillemots, puffins, fulmars, shags and Manx shearwaters. The island is also renowned for its wild flowers (try to visit it during the bluebell season), a unique type of vole and the Atlantic grey seals which bask on its reefs.

Skokholm, Britain's first bird observatory (established in 1933) supports similar colonies of birds, though this small island does not normally allow day visitors. Tiny Grassholm, 12 miles out and no more than a lone rock in the sea, is the overcrowded home of over 20,000 pairs of gannets, one of the largest colonies in the world.

THE THREE ISLANDS are off the south-western tip of the Pembrokeshire coast.

SOLVA
Dyfed

The quayside at Solva, snug below steep-sided slopes and a good half-mile from the open seas, is easily the safest anchorage along this part of the coast. Solva Creek, a narrow tidal inlet, completely insulates this placid little natural harbour from, in the words of an old guidebook, 'the violence of the sea' in St Bride's Bay.

In the 18th and 19th centuries, Solva was a thriving port. Limestone was brought in (the old lime kilns still line the harbourside) and agricultural produce was shipped out. People were also an important cargo in the days before good roads and railways — though the prospect of a sea-

journey from Solva to Bristol, for example, paled into insignificance in comparison to the trans-Atlantic crossings to America made from here by 19th-century emigrants for a fare of three pounds and ten shillings. Today's seafaring in Solva is on a slightly less heroic scale, confined mainly to the colourful holiday craft which fill the harbour.

Solva's prosperous shippers and merchants built the grand-looking residences and warehouses which lead from the quay. Some buildings have been tastefully renovated and now participate in Solva's new-found career as a centre for high-quality craft shops, selling such items as handmade clothes and pottery. One old building has become, of all things, a tropical butterfly farm where species from all over the world fly and breed in a cleverly created 'tropical forest' climate.

SOLVA, on the A487, is 12 miles north-west of Haverfordwest.

STACKPOLE HEAD AND BARAFUNDLE BAY
Dyfed

More spectacular south Pembrokeshire coastline displays

Barafundle's cliff-framed beach

itself here — though only to those prepared to use their feet. Stackpole Quay, accessible by narrow minor road, is the footpath's starting point. This well preserved little stone jetty, once a busy limestone-exporting port, lies on the northern doorstep to one of Pembrokeshire's finest beaches.

At one time, the secluded, dune-backed sands at Barafundle Bay were the private preserve of the local gentry. Nowadays, anyone who cares to walk the half-mile across the headland from Stackpole Quay can take pleasure from this lovely beach.

South of the beach, the distinctive square-ended promontory of Stackpole Head comes into view. The Pembrokeshire Coast Path between beach and headland is a must for bird-watchers, for it looks directly down on to the largest congregation of breeding sea-birds — guillemots, razorbills and kittiwakes in particular — on Pembrokeshire's mainland.

STACKPOLE QUAY is accessible by minor road, about 4 miles south of Pembroke.

STACK ROCKS AND ST GOVAN'S HEAD
Dyfed

The coastline south of Pembroke is not recommended for those prone to vertigo. Terra firma ends abruptly in a towering line of limestone cliffs, one of the finest in Britain, populated by teeming colonies of sea-birds.

The strangely-named Elegug Stacks, or Stack Rocks, bear dramatic witness to the action of the waves. This massive pair of limestone pillars, cast adrift from the land by the destructive forces of the sea, are remnants of a collapsed sea-cave. At

Right: **Snug St Govan's Chapel, huddled in the base of the cliffs**

Stack Rocks, land lost to the sea and sea-birds

Georgian elegance in aspic at Tenby harbour

one time, they probably resembled the nearby 'Green Bridge of Wales,' a magnificent natural sea-arch and probably the most celebrated sight on the south Pembrokeshire coast.

Just over three miles to the south east are the magnificent rocks and headlands at St Govan's Head. Huddled in the base of the cliffs, and accessible by 52 stone steps, is the minute St Govan's Chapel. This ancient chapel, almost undetectable in its deep, shady gorge, has been a place of pilgrimage since medieval time.

THIS PART OF THE COAST is accessible by minor roads off the B4319 south of Pembroke (please note that this is a Ministry of Defence area, and public access is sometimes restricted).

TENBY
Dyfed

Not often, hand-on-heart, can a popular seaside resort be described as possessing dignity and understated charm. Tenby is one of those rare exceptions. Its beaches, harbour and town are busy enough — the latter, a maze of narrow medieval streets, seems purpose-built to encourage traffic jams. Yet Tenby manages to take it all in its stride without making any of the garish concessions to change seen all too often along the British coast.

The Victorian description of Tenby (a resort 'whose every view is picturesque in the extreme') is current today. Tenby's harbour, for example, is pure picture-book. Pastel-shaded Georgian houses rise in harmonious ranks above the quayside. Sheer cliffs, lined with hotels, gaze down onto two attractive beaches. The old town is full of interesting nooks and crannies, including the Tudor Merchant's House, a relic of Tenby's prosperous seafaring days. The Five Arches gateway guards an entrance in the well-preserved town walls, Tenby's greatest medieval remains and the most complete circuit in South Wales.

Nowadays, Tenby's fishermen also rely on tourism. In summer, the waters off Tenby are busy with boats carrying visitors the two miles to Caldey Island. *Caldey* is Norse for 'cold', Viking plunderers naming this island possibly after an uncomfortable winter visit when the wind whips wickedly across from the west. On a summer's day, Caldey is balmy and beautiful. Most visitors make for the monastery, where the monks produce a famous range of perfumes made from its island's flower petals.

Caldey has been a sanctuary for religious men since the 6th century. Old priory buildings and a lovely 13th-century church mark the site of the island's original monastic settlement. Today, the monks live in an abbey built early this century, open to the public, or half of it, (men only), on conducted tours.

TENBY is on the A478, 27 miles south-west of Carmarthen.

The Landsker

It is no exaggeration to claim that south and north Pembrokeshire are as different as chalk and cheese. Tenby is the centre of an area known as 'the little England beyond Wales'. South Pembrokeshire is dotted with villages — Templeton, Rosemarket and Cheriton East to name but a few — bearing names which would appear to be more at home on a map of southern England. Only in the north of Pembrokeshire does the 'Welshry' reassert itself with placenames like Maenclochog and Llandysilio.

The reason behind this division is a deep and sometimes disputed one. Its mystique is multiplied by the fact that the line which divides north and south — the landsker or 'land-scar' — is a ghostly barrier which appears on no official map. Although ephemeral in the cartographic sense, its on-the-ground actuality is real enough.

The landsker runs across country from Amroth in the south to Newgale on the west coast, its course marked by a series of castles such as Llawhaden, Narberth and Roch. According to most experts, these castles are the key element in understanding the split between 'Englishry' and 'Welshry'. In the 11th and 12th centuries, the invading Normans established this frontier of castles, behind which the Welsh retreated. In their wake came Anglo-Saxon and Flemish immigrants and a 'little England' of imported ways, customs, farming methods, architecture and alien placenames.

Villages facing each other on either side of the line once had little in common with each other. Welsh-speaking and traditional chapel-going communities would have nothing to do with their English-speaking Anglican neighbours, and vice-versa. Intermarriage was, of course, unthinkable.

In recent times, the landsker's relevance has inevitably declined though its presence can still be felt. This lingering influence may lend credence to the alternative — and altogether more atavistic interpretation placed upon it.

North Pembrokeshire's underlying rocks, rugged and resilient, are amongst the oldest in the British Isles. The rocks in the south, by comparison, are much younger and softer. This immutable difference between north and south prompts romantics to claim that the landsker is some kind of cultural manifestation which reflects man's deep-rooted relationship with the earth on which he stands.

A Norman frontier or mystical measure of man's nature? Take your pick.

Llawhaden Castle, shell-like guardian of the ghostly landsker

Non-Welsh Wales — a Flemish chimney at St Florence

The Welsh Heartlands

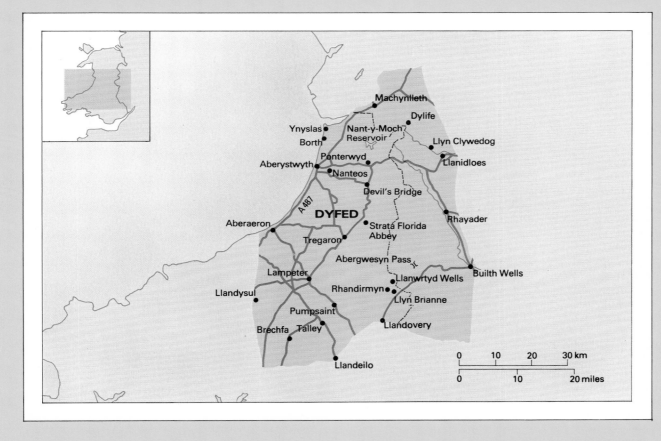

The River Rheidol rushes over falls floodlit on summer nights. Born in the inhospitable Plynlimon Mountains, its waters have been dammed to generate hydro-electricity

EORGE BORROW, a mid-19th-century writer and traveller, recorded his impressions of a journey through Wales in a work which has since become a classic. In naming his book *Wild Wales* he captured, at a stroke, the powerful and sometimes savage personality of the Welsh hills and mountains. Were he to retrace his steps today in search of the 19th-century scenes he wrote so vividly about, he would be drawn to this area, the Wales of his 'wildest solitudes'.

Change continues to be determined by the cycle of the seasons in the Welsh heartlands. Admittedly, the hand of man makes its presence felt — since Borrow's time, for example, massive lakelands and substantial conifer forests have been created. But Mid Wales's tenacious hill-sheep farmers are still here in highlands that remain largely inviolate.

The Cambrian Mountains, the 'backbone of Wales', fill much of these heartlands. There are no great peaks as in the north; rather a large, empty and consistently high upland region of moors, plateaux and rolling mountain crests which reveal their innermost secrets only to those on foot or horseback. Four-wheel exploration is confined to the few narrow mountain roads which gingerly traverse this difficult terrain.

These are the Welsh heartlands in more than a geographic sense. Not surprisingly, they have successfully rebuffed outside influences over the centuries — Roman and Norman invaders made little headway — and survive as a stronghold of Welsh customs and traditions.

ABERAERON
Dyfed

Aberaeron's Georgian harbourside is a gem. The most incompetent of photographers would be hard-pressed to come away with an undistinguished picture of this quayside, lined as it is by buildings which express the essential elements of Georgian architecture in their harmonious proportions, consistency of line and pared-down elegance.

This attractive sea-town owes its good looks to the fact that it was purpose-built to a set plan as a port in the 19th century. Aberaeron flourished as a fishing and trading port and shipbuilding centre during Cardigan Bay's great seafaring days. The death knell was sounded by the coming of the railways, and Aberaeron built its last boat in 1884.

The boats are back now, for Aberaeron has become a popular holiday sailing centre. Aberaeron Sea Aquarium, on the harbourside, gives visitors an insight into the marine life to be found off the west coast of Wales.

🚗 *ABERAERON is at the junction of the A487 and A482, 16 miles south-west of Aberystwyth.*

ABERGWESYN PASS
Dyfed and Powys

George Borrow's classic 19th-century travel book, *Wild Wales*, embodied in its title the uncompromising terrain of the Welsh uplands. He tramped across many a lonely moorland the length and breadth of Wales, so when he found 'some of the wildest solitudes' near Tregaron his assessment deserves to be taken seriously.

So too does the narrow ribbon of tarmac that ventures tenuously into the wilderness from Tregaron. This is the Abergwesyn Pass, one of the few genuinely stimulating motoring experiences left in Britain today. The road follows the course of an old drovers' route across a desolate, uninhabited and unforgettably beautiful landscape of high moorland and rolling mountain crests, passing along the way nothing more than the occasional isolated farmstead and reassuring red telephone box.

For 14 miles and countless curves it weaves its way over an area variously described as the 'roof of Wales' or 'great Welsh desert', descending the hairpinned Devil's Staircase to the hamlet of Abergwesyn and the return of civilization. Just over half-way along, the pass is linked by a new road to the Llyn Brianne reservoir (see separate entry).

🚗 *THE ABERGWESYN PASS can be approached from the west via Tregaron, from the south-east via Llanwrtyd Wells and Abergwesyn.*

ABERYSTWYTH
Dyfed

Although strictly an unofficial title, Aberystwyth is regarded by most as the 'capital' of Mid Wales. This large town, right in the middle of Cardigan Bay, combines three roles with commendable aplomb: those of a seaside resort, university campus and main shopping and administrative centre, with a population of over 12,000, along the bay.

To the Victorian traveller, Aberystwyth was the fashionable 'Biarritz of Wales' which 'seems to scorn the novelties which find favour in the newer and more frivolous watering places'. This description more or less stands today, for Aberystwyth is not a town to move with the times.

Its long, curving promenade, with a ruined medieval castle at one end and a grey-rocked headland at the

Four miles-per-hour mountaineering on Aberystwyth's Cliff Railway

other, is formal and dignified. The ambience of the Victorian Age extends to the 430-ft summit of the headland itself, known as Constitution Hill. It is scaled by a cliff railway, the only one in Wales and a 'conveyance of gentlefolk since 1896'. A camera obscura has recently been installed on the summit to exploit the wide views. This re-creation of a popular Victorian amusement is equipped with a huge 14-inch lens (the biggest in the world, they claim) which captures all of Cardigan Bay and no less than 26 mountain peaks.

The hillsides above the beach are occupied by the large university campus and National Library of Wales, an important Welsh institution which contains many of the oldest documents and books in the Welsh language. The Ceredigion Museum, in the town itself, is well worth a visit. Coastal and rural history and traditions are recalled here, though the star of the show is the museum building itself, an ornate Edwardian music hall. There are more links with the past at Aberystwyth's railway station, the terminus of the Vale of

Rheidol narrow-gauge railway, British Rail's last remaining operational link with the Age of Steam, which chuffs along a 12-mile route to Devil's Bridge.

Llanbadarn Fawr, now a suburb of Aberystwyth, is the home of a grand 12th-century church, one of the largest in Wales, its surprising stature a reflection of the influential role this site has played in religious history since the 6th century.

ABERYSTWYTH is accessible by the A487 from the south and north, the A44 and A4120 from the east.

BORTH AND YNYSLAS
Dyfed

The small stretch of Cardigan Bay between Borth and Ynyslas, its hinterland uncharacteristically as flat as a pancake, is sandy, windswept, and mostly silent. From Borth — a long, straggling and undistinguished little seaside resort — the scenery improves immeasurably.

The dunes and vast expanses of low-tide sands north of Ynyslas command magnificent views across the Dyfi estuary to the mountains around Machynlleth. Aberdovey, on the opposite bank, appears as a brightly-painted dividing line between sandy shore and steep green hillside. The Dyfi estuary's dunes and salt marshes are an important habitat for birds, butterflies and unusual plants. An information centre (open summer only) serves as an introduction to the large area around Ynyslas which is protected as a nature reserve.

BORTH, 6 miles north of Aberystwyth, is accessible by the B4572 or B4353 off the A487 (same directions apply in Ynyslas, 2 miles north of Borth).

BRECHFA
Dyfed

This small village gives its name to one of the largest man-made forests in Wales. The conifers of the Brechfa Forest march in orderly ranks above the village and across a high plateau almost all the way to Llanybydder, nine miles to the north.

Tiny Brechfa is not completely crowded out by all these trees. The views to the south, across the fast-flowing River Marlais, are of open, green and pleasant hill country. The Marlais, and the nearby Cothi into which it flows, help explain Brechfa's popularity, for both rivers are noted for their salmon and sewin (Welsh for sea-trout).

Brechfa, almost sealed off in the back lanes, also attracts those in search of undiluted peace and quiet. Some visitors choose to stay in its 16th-century manor house, Ty Mawr ('The Big House'), which has been converted into an intimate little hotel. The Brechfa Forest to the north is not as inhospitable as it might first sound. Waymarked footpaths and picnic areas sited around its fringes (Brechfa's neighbouring village of Abergorlech is particularly well-endowed) encourage exploration of this vast woodland.

BRECHFA is on the B4310, 12 miles north-east of Carmarthen.

BUILTH WELLS
Powys

Builth's days as a spa resort may be long gone, but its status as a country and farming town is more assured than ever. The markets held here each Monday are important enough locally, though they are put in the shade by the one event entered in the diaries of all countrymen and women: the Royal Welsh Agricultural Show, held

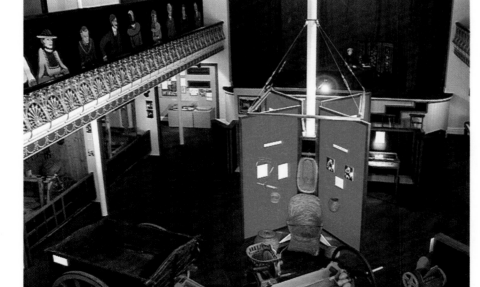

The Ceredigion Museum

here over four days each July, an occasion which attracts farming folk — and urbanites interested in country pursuits — from all over Wales.

Grey-stoned Builth, properly traditional in character, has a fine, six-arched bridge across the River Wye, a pleasant tree-lined riverside promenade, and scant ruins of a medieval castle. The one exuberant touch is provided by the Wyeside Arts Centre, a renovated red-bricked building based around the old cinema and basement market hall.

Cilmeri, three miles west of Builth, is a place familiar to all students of Welsh history. A roadside monument marks the spot where Llywelyn, last of the native Welsh princes, was killed by an English trooper during a chance encounter in 1282.

BUILTH is at the junction of the A470 and A483 between Brecon and Rhayader.

DEVIL'S BRIDGE
Dyfed

The locals living in this dramatically-named mountain village are becoming a little tired of the jokey question: 'Where the devil is the bridge?' In fact, there are three bridges in all, one piled on top of the next, well camouflaged amongst thick woods in a deep and gloomy gorge.

The oldest, *Pont-y-gwr Drwy* ('The Bridge of the Evil One', its name deriving from a devilish folk tale), is the lowest, a simple stone arch across the narrow ravine. A second, wider bridge, put up in 1708, is sandwiched between this original medieval crossing point and a 'new' iron bridge, constructed in 1901, which still carries road traffic.

Devil's Bridge is perched on the flanks of the Plynlimon mountains. Views from the terrace in front of the Hafod Arms (which, thanks to its gabled roof and huge eaves, would look more at home in an alpine ski resort than in the middle of Wales) are splendid.

Most visitors come, though, for what lies down below in William Wordsworth's 'dread chasm', accessible by a precipitious staircase footpath; where the River Mynach plunges 300 ft in a series of torrents on the way to its confluence with the River Rheidol.

The Rheidol has carved a steep and spectacular valley for itself as it winds its way to the sea at Aberystwyth. The Vale of Rheidol narrow-gauge railway, one of the 'Great Little Trains of Wales', gazes down onto the river from a lofty ledge cut into the mountainside. Along its scenic 12-mile route from Aberystwyth to Devil's Bridge, the Rheidol Falls come into view far below, next to the Cwm Rheidol hydro-electric power station (open to visitors in summer).

DEVIL'S BRIDGE, at the junction of the A4120, B4343 and B4574, is 12 miles east of Aberystwyth.

DYLIFE
Powys

High, lonely, desolate Dylife is an eerie sight, especially when it looms unexpectedly into view out of the mists. Mountain moor has been

Amid rugged countryside near Devil's Bridge, the Cwm Rheidol hydro-electric scheme flourishes

scoured away or buried by lead-waste from a great mining settlement, the grey surface remains of which create a lunar-like landscape. Between the 1770s and 1896, when the mines were abandoned, armies of workmen were attracted to this isolated, inhospitable spot. One wonders where they all lived, for Dylife today is nothing more than a few farms and one pub.

Ffrwd Fawr, one of the highest waterfalls in Wales, plunges down a lovely, sheltered valley tucked in below the road on the eastern approach to Dylife. West of the settlement, the mountains proper take over. From Dylife, the road — another of Wales's truly exhilarating mountain passes — climbs to a summit of 1671 ft before beginning its long descent across sharp crests down into the Dulas Valley and Machynlleth.

🚗 DYLIFE is on a minor road, accessible either from Machynlleth or off the B4518, 12 miles north west of Llanidloes.

Inspecting the goods at Llanybydder horse fair

LAMPETER
Dyfed

This town, large by Teifiside standards, is a busy meeting place of routes and an important seat of learning. A pleasant mix of Georgian and Victorian buildings fan out with the roads in all directions from the centre of town. The University College of St David's, one of the seven branches of the University of Wales (Cardiff has three and there are others in Swansea, Aberystwyth and Bangor) stands right in the centre.

The university, the second oldest in Britain after Oxford and Cambridge, was founded in 1822 as a Welsh counterpart to those august colleges. Parallels with Oxford extend to its architecture. The handsome main building, finished in Tudor style, is ranged around a quadrangle with corner towers, a fountain and clocktower.

A scruffy, heather-covered mound at the side of the college disturbs an otherwise orderly campus. It nevertheless commands respect, for it is the remnant of a medieval castle put up to defend a strategic crossing point on the Teifi.

On the last Thursday in each month, Llanybydder, a village five miles south-west of Lampeter, is transformed into an equinine mecca. Buyers from all over Britain and as far afield as the Continent come here for the famous horse fair, where hundreds of ponies and horses are sold off by rapid-fire auctioneers during hectic trading.

🚗 LAMPETER is at the junction of the A482, A485, A475, and B4343, roughly mid-way between Llandovery and Aberaeron.

LLANDYSUL
Dyfed

One way or another, Llandysul's livelihood has always come under the influence of the River Teifi. The river's soft waters, ideal for washing wool, also powered the waterwheels of the woollen mills which, in their heyday, turned Llandysul into the busiest weaving centre in Wales. Modest quantities of this distinctive, traditionally-patterned cloth are still produced locally (see Maesllyn Woollen Mill entry), though the boom years have long since passed.

The Teifi now attracts anglers and canoeists to the town. Fishing for salmon and sea-trout is excellent, whilst white-water canoeists take up the challenge of an exciting slalom course as the Teifi tumbles through a narrow, rocky course beneath the river bridge.

Haste is replaced by repose a short distance upstream. Here, the Teifi charts a slow and gentle course past Llandysul's most imposing historic site. This is the splendid Church of St Tysul, a large 13th-century affair with a fine castellated tower. Llandysul itself, rising in a series of steep terraces above church and river, is a businesslike little country and market town in which sheep and cattle sales are still held once a fortnight.

🚗 LLANDYSUL is at the junction of the A486, B4336 and B4476, 16 miles north of Carmarthen, 12 miles south-west of Lampeter.

LLANIDLOES
Powys

Based on the sole criteria of a central location, Llanidloes would easily qualify as the capital of Wales. Sited right in the middle of Mid Wales, this pretty little town is equidistant from north and south.

Llanidloes is a meeting place of infuences, poised between the traditional stone-built farmsteads of the Welsh hills and the striking black-and-white architecture typical of the border country. The town's old market hall belongs to the latter category. This late-16th-century building, the only one of its kind surviving in Wales, is eye catching in the extreme. Built in half-timbered, black-and-white style, it stands on hefty timber piers above an open market place right in the middle of town, the perfect Elizabethan traffic bottleneck.

Its upper storey now houses the local museum, which reflects Llanidloes's surprisingly rumbustious past as a 19th-century textile town and scene of Chartist riots. The existence in Llanidloes of one of the late Laura Ashley's worldwide chain of fabric shops also comes as something of a surprise to those unaware that the company's factory is located at nearby Carno.

🚗 LLANIDLOES, at the junction of the A470, B4518 and B4569, is 28 miles east of Aberystwyth.

Welsh Woollens

Any traveller passing through the green heartlands of Mid Wales will soon become aware that sheep outnumber people quite conclusively. At one time, the ratio was put even higher than the current three-to-one; little wonder, then, that so much surplus fleece stimulated cloth making in Wales, a tradition almost 2000 years old.

Throughout the centuries, and up to quite recent times, woollen weaving has been one of Wales's most important industries. 'Industry' is perhaps a misleading term to use when describing its early days. Cloth weaving was originally a domestic activity. Most small farmers were growers, spinners and weavers, making their own cloth from spinning wheels and weaving looms.

The transition from hand spinning and weaving to powered machinery came after the Middle Ages. A previously scattered 'cottage industry' became concentrated firstly within small riverbank mills powered by waterwheel and later, with the Industrial Revolution in full swing, highly organised and mechanised factories.

Celtic designs and bold colours are characteristics of Welsh woollens

Woollen mills still produce traditional Welsh weaves

As the industry developed, its focal point shifted around Wales. In the Middle Ages, Pembrokeshire's cottage industries were pre-eminent. By the mid 18th century, Mid Wales had developed as a thriving flannel manufacturing centre, with towns such as Llanidloes and Newtown — the latter known as 'the Leeds of Wales' — almost entirely dependent on textile production. By the late 19th century, the Teifi Valley had taken over. At Drefach Felindre (now the home of the Museum of the Welsh Woollen Industry), for example, there were no less than 52 mills in full production.

A catastrophic decline in the industry since the 1920s has left Wales with only a handful of mills, dispersed throughout the country. Most are fully mechanised, though some retain their old waterwheels in working order. Many of the mills also welcome visitors, and make special efforts to explain the evolution of the industry from the relative simplicity of the domestic spinning wheel to the complexities of the machine age.

Not that the surviving mills should be looked upon as museum pieces. Their distinctively patterned Welsh weaves, a robust interpretation of bold Celtic motifs in strong colours, are much in demand. The characteristic, typically-Welsh product is the heavy tapestry or double-woven cloth, a multi-coloured material used for bedspreads. Flannels, tweeds and blankets are also woven, and a whole range of garments made up from Welsh cloth.

LLANWRTYD WELLS
Powys

Today, it is difficult to envisage this sleepy little town as it must have been in its heyday, when steam trains and charabancs disgorged thousands of summer visitors to 'take the waters'. Llanwrtyd's sulphur, chalybeate and saline springs certainly attracted the crowds when spa holidays were fashionable, though the town's location, on the doorstep of untouched hill country, must also have contributed to its popularity.

Llanwrtyd now relies entirely on its enviable situation. The old well — the aptly named *Y Ffynnon Ddrewllyd* ('The Stinking Well') — is still there and has been partially renovated, so anyone curious enough can once again sample its foul-smelling sulphur water. Most visitors, however, prefer to confine themselves to fishing on the crystal River Irfon or to exploring the hills on horseback.

The town claims to have 'invented' pony trekking — now a popular pastime throughout Britain — in the 1950s. The surrounding terrain, unquestionably ideal for four-legged exploration, has also inspired a challenging 'Man versus Horse' marathon, held here each May. The only hint of industry in this restful place is provided by the Cambrian Woollen Factory, on the outskirts of town, where visitors are welcome to view the weaving process.

LLANWRTYD WELLS is on the A483 between Llandovery and Builth Wells.

LLYN BRIANNE
Dyfed

A helicopter ride is the only way to capture the full enormity of this man-made reservoir. Its watery tentacles extend in many directions into the folds of totally uninhabited highland, one of the last true wildernesses in Wales, north of Llandovery. Motorists have to be content with a new road, cut across previously inaccessible terrain. This follows the eastern shoreline, climbing and swooping roller-coaster fashion alongside drowned valleys before meeting up with the old drovers' route along the Abergwesyn Pass (see separate entry).

Llyn Brianne, opened in 1973, supplies Swansea with its water. A massive, rock-filled dam — the highest of its type in Britain — holds back a 13,500 million gallon lake formed by the headwaters of the Tywi and Camddwr Rivers. A path across the dam leads to the western shores, open to walkers only, where the red kite is sometimes spotted.

LLYN BRIANNE is accessible by minor road about 10 miles north of Llandovery.

LLYN CLYWEDOG
Powys

This sinuous man-made lake fills a steep-sided, six-mile-long fold in silent hill-sheep country above Llanidloes. Llyn Clywedog's 11,000 million gallons do more than supply the Midlands with water, for they also provide recreation in the form of trout fishing and sailing.

Part and parcel of its construction in the 1960s involved a ring road around its lakesides. There are panoramic viewing points along the B4518 which runs close to its eastern shores. Better still is the minor road along the western banks which leads to a viewing area overlooking the 237-ft-high concrete dam. The green hillsides near the dam provide a scenic setting for an incongruous interloper, in the form of a 19th-century industrial site. This is the Bryn Tail Lead Mine, one of the many such mines sunk in Mid Wales during the boom years over a century ago. Extraction and ore crushing took place here, on a site which is now preserved and open to the public.

LLYN CLYWEDOG is accessible by the B4518, approximately 4 miles north-west of Llanidloes.

MACHYNLLETH
Powys

All eyes are unavoidably drawn to Machynlleth's bizarre, over-ornamental clock tower, right in the centre of town, put up in 1873 by the Marquess of Londonderry. Like it or loathe it, it is quite impossible to ignore this horological embellishment which seems at odds with Machynlleth's otherwise harmonious character.

Town planners — or possibly the lack of them — have bestowed upon Machynlleth a wide main thoroughfare lined with architecturally distinguished buildings, some Georgian, others of robust local stone or striking black-and-white half-timbered construction. Such is the length and breadth of this accommodating street that it only really becomes busy when stallholders set up camp here on market day (every Wednesday), perpetuating a tradition that goes back, according to some, over 700 years.

The Owain Glyndwr Institute along the street stirs many a Welshman into historic and mythological speculation over the events of 1404 and what might have been. Owain, Wales's last native leader, held a Welsh parliament at Machynlleth, reputedly on this site. Welsh aspirations for independence disappeared along with Owain, who vanished in 1412, never to be seen again. The life of this mercurial folk-hero is remembered in the Owain Glyndwr Centre, next to the Dyfi Centre which conveys a wide range of information on the locality.

The Marquess of Londonderry lived at Plas Machynlleth, located in parkland just behind the Wynnstay Hotel, the latter's pedigree as an historic coaching inn plainly evident in its arched entrance. The Plas, a fine looking house dating from the 17th century, now serves as a rather grand centre for local government offices.

Furnace, six miles to the south-west, is named after a 17th-century silver refinery, later replaced by an early ironworks (currently under restoration). A picturesque cascade tumbles through the woods before flowing past the old foundry, its waters once turning a wheel which powered the bellows of the furnace. Inland from Furnace, this river — the Einion — rushes through a remote, wooded and lovely vale known as Artist's Valley.

🚗 *MACHYNLLETH, at the junction of the A487, A489 and A493, is 18 miles north-east of Aberystwyth.*

Machynlleth's eccentric clock tower keeps time for the street market

NANTEOS
Dyfed

Devotees of Georgian architecture should make every effort to visit this country house, hidden in the hills east of Aberystwyth. Not that Nanteos is a typical neat-and-tidy Georgian mansion. Its facade cannot be described as immaculate, its interior is shabby rather than showpiece.

Herein lies Nanteos's fascination and unique appeal. The house, dating from 1739, is being slowly restored after a long period of neglect. Unlike other country houses, Nanteos gives the public a sobering insight into the costly, daunting reality behind the rescue and preservation of Britain's architectural heritage. Stately homes never quite seem the same again after a trip around Nanteos.

The house boasts quite a history. The composer Richard Wagner stayed here, and up until the 1950s Nanteos claimed ownership of the Holy Grail, the cup used by Christ in the Last Supper.

🚗 *NANTEOS, about 4 miles south-east of Aberystwyth, can be reached by minor road off the B4340.*

NANT-Y-MOCH RESERVOIR
Dyfed

An elemental landscape of mountain wilderness and water fills the terrain to the north of Ponterwyd. The undisturbed solitudes of the Plynlimon range sweep across the skyline, though unlike conventional mountains this one fails to rise to a climactic, identifiable peak. Its 2468-ft summit is there, somewhere, amongst an outcrop of dark crags that break out from a brooding moorland dome to the east of the Nant-y-Moch reservoir.

Plynlimon, Mid Wales's central core, commands clear-day views as far as North and South Wales. The boggy walk to the top should not be undertaken lightly: most visitors to these uplands are content merely to gaze towards the summit from the mountain road that skirts the western shores of Nant-y-Moch. The inky-black waters of this 7000-million-gallon reservoir, contained by a huge buttressed dam 172-ft high across the River Rheidol, are used to provide hydro-electric power for the Central Electricity Generating Board's Cwm Rheidol scheme (see Devil's Bridge entry).

🚗 *NANT-Y-MOCH is accessible by minor road off the A44 north of Ponterwyd or east off the A487 at Talybont.*

PONTERWYD
Dyfed

Ponterwyd's George Borrow Hotel encapsulates the character of this isolated settlement, high in the mist-shrouded Plynlimon mountains. The hotel, re-named in honour of the 19th-century author of *Wild Wales*, was a welcome refuge to Borrow following his plod across bog and moorland.

Moorland turns into moonscape just west of the village. Grey-green scars in the landscape are the remnants of a metalliferous mining field which, in its heyday, straddled Plynlimon. At the Llywernog Silver-Lead Mine, one mile west of Ponterwyd, the mining boom years of the 1870s have been preserved for posterity. This mine, abandoned like so many others in the late 19th century, has been restored as a museum which recaptures the life and work of the Mid Wales metal miner.

Forestry is now the only 'industry' in these parts. The Bwlch Nant-yr-Arian Forest Visitor Centre, one mile west of Llywernog, gives the public an insight into the work of the Forestry Commission, which has had such a pronounced impact on the landscape in Mid Wales. The spread of the ubiquitous conifer rouses strong feelings in some, though no one can argue that the commission, in the last decade or so, has not made commendable attempts to realise the recreational value of its woodlands. Bwlch Nant-yr-Arian is a good case in point. In addition to its imaginative displays on local history and landscape, the centre — sited on a crest and commanding superb views into the valley below — is surrounded by waymarked walks and picnic areas.

PONTERWYD, at the junction of the A44 and A4120, is 12 miles east of Aberystwyth.

PUMPSAINT
Dyfed

Pumpsaint's name is bound up in a mis-shapen grey stone which stands in a shady knoll in the hills just east of the village. Assiduous visitors will count five indentations in the monolith, said to be the impressions left by the heads of five saints (*pump sant* in Welsh) who used the stone as a communal pillow.

Only the most credulous will persevere with this piece of Welsh hokum on discovering that the stone stands at the entrance to the Dolaucothi Roman Gold Mines. The alternative explanation — that the stone was simply used to pound ore — may be dull, but it has an unavoidable ring of truth about it.

Uncorroborated legend does not surround the gold mines. Dolaucothi is the only site in Britain where it has been definitely established that the Romans mined for gold. Serious mining began here in A.D. 75, Welsh

Lofty views from the Bwlch Nant-yr-Arian Forest Visitor Centre

gold swelling the coffers of the Imperial Mint at Lyons for 100 years.

Thousands of slaves were transported to this remote spot, and a camp was thrown up by the Romans (on the site of the Dolaucothi Arms in the village) to protect their investment. Yet visitors expecting to see overt evidence of this mammoth endeavour are invariably thwarted, for Dolaucothi's Roman interlude has been masked by centuries of disuse (though the site was again mined between the 1870s and 1938).

The sophistication of the Romans' mining operations becomes apparent only to those prepared to look

beyond a thick cloak of wood and bush. Faint traces remain of an incredibly complicated aqueduct system — one stretch no less than seven miles long — in the surrounding hillsides. Overgrown slopes ultimately reveal hidden tunnel entrances and the leftovers from opencast mining.

Waymarked footpaths give a reasonably good understanding of this fascinating and unique National Trust site. Better still are the summer guided tours which take in parts of the underground workings.

PUMPSAINT is on the A482 between Lampeter and Llanwrda.

RHANDIRMWYN
Dyfed

Before the opening of the Llyn Brianne reservoir in the 1970s, Rhandirmwyn was known only to the fortunate few. Up until then, this scattered village, set on a hillside overlooking the wildly beautiful Upper Tywi Valley, was at the end of the road. With the reservoir came new roads, opening up a remote corner of Wales which had previously been accessible only on foot or horseback.

Rhandirmwyn, the last outpost before the wilderness areas of Abergwesyn and the 'roof of Wales', has a surprising history. A veil of trees draws itself over abandoned levels in the mountainsides above the village, keeping secret the fact that Rhandirmwyn was once one of Europe's largest lead mining centres.

There are more secret places just north of the village. Twm Shon Catti, the Welsh Robin Hood, hid from the Sheriff of Carmarthen amongst the boulder-strewn and densely wooded upper slopes of Dinas Hill. This enigmatic 16th-century character — an out-and-out villain according to some — is generally regarded as a local hero who, in an episode reminiscent of a western movie, avoided injuring his enemy by pinning him to his saddle with a carefully placed arrow.

Twm's hiding place was a cave, in the slopes directly above a rocky gorge through which the Tywi flows with some ferocity. Our villainous hero would be gratified to learn that it is still quite difficult to find, even though now partially waymarked off the official footpath around Dinas Hill, an R.S.P.B. nature reserve.

RHANDIRMWYN is on a minor road, approximately 7 miles north of Llandovery. It is also accessible from Tregaron and the Abergwesyn Pass.

RHAYADER AND THE 'LAKELANDS OF MID WALES'
Powys

The market town of Rhayader stands at the gateway to Wales's first, and most famous, collection of man-made lakes. The Birmingham Corporation were responsible for the Elan Valley lakelands, a quartet of reservoirs completed in 1904 and containing over 11,000 million gallons of water between them. The lakes — Caban Coch, Garreg Ddu, Pen-y-garreg and Craig Goch — form a watery chain

Strata Florida's decorative arch frames an utterly peaceful scene

almost nine miles long amongst wooded hillsides and empty moorland west of Rhayader. Unlike many of the reservoirs subsequently constructed in Wales, the Elan Valley dams have a decorative turn-of-the-century elegance, their stonework blending in well with their surroundings.

Craig Goch, the northernmost dam set amongst open mountainsides, is particularly accomplished. It presents an attractive counterpoint to the starkly functional Claerwen dam, built in the 1950s to double the capacity of these lakelands. Unlike its

Elan Valley neighbours, remote, four-mile-long Claerwen locks itself away from motorised traffic, the road venturing no further than its towering dam at the head of the lake.

Rhayader, on the banks of the River Wye, is a friendly country town, architecturally unremarkable apart from a neat little clock tower which presides over its busy crossroads. The town makes the most of its location. Fishermen and pony trekkers are well provided for, as are the farmers who come to town on Wednesdays for the seasonal livestock markets.

🚗 *RHAYADER, at the junction of the A470, A44 and B4518, is mid-way between Builth Wells and Llanidloes. The Elan Valley and Claerwen reservoirs, a few miles west of the town, are accessible via the B4518 and minor roads.*

STRATA FLORIDA ABBEY
Dyfed

White-robed Cistercian monks, sympathetic to Welsh ways and culture, were responsible for creating the 'Westminster Abbey of Wales' in the solitudes east of Pontrhydfendigaid. They arrived c.1200 at Strata Florida, its name a latinized version of the Welsh *Ystrad Fflur* ('The way of the flowers').

Their abbey soon became more than a religious centre. At the height of its importance, Strata Florida exercised great political and educational influence. Evocative fragments are all that remain of a site which has not weathered well. A mosaic tiled floor survives in the chapel, though most impressive of all is the abbey's highly decorated Romanesque arch, miraculously intact. The bleating of sheep is the only noise which disturbs this utterly tranquil spot — a familiar sound at Strata Florida, for amongst

their many talents the enterprising Cistercians were innovative and successful hill-sheep farmers.

In the graveyard, one headstone decorated with an amputated leg inspires a smile. It reads: 'The left leg and part of the thigh of Henry Hughes, cooper, was cut off and intern'd here June 18th 1756.' Whatever became of the rest of Henry is open to speculation. The grave stands close to a gnarled yew tree. According to legend, it marks the resting place of Dafydd ap Gwilym, Wales's most celebrated medieval poet (c. 1320-1380).

Hidden in the lonely hills to the north-east of the abbey are the heather-fringed Teifi Pools, headwaters of one of Wales's loveliest rivers.

🚗 *STRATA FLORIDA is 1 mile east of Pontrhydfendigaid, a village on the B4340 approximately 15 miles south-east of Aberystwyth.*

TALLEY
Dyfed

Twin lakes, a ruined abbey and unusual village church are four good justifications for a visit to Talley. The village's lovely location amongst silent hills and unhurried farming country is a bonus for those who seek out the remains of Talley Abbey, founded here by the Premonstratensian Order in the late 12th century. One or two slender pointed archways and stretches of ruined wall are all that now survive, on an idyllic lakeside site.

The next-door Church of St Michael is thankfully intact. Those brought up on a diet of standard ecclesiastical architecture might consider this 18th-century church to have suffered something of an identity crisis. Its missing central aisle (there are two side aisles instead) and rows of box pews are pure chapel rather than church, more suited to a bastion of Welsh Nonconformity than an Anglican place of worship.

🚗 *TALLEY is just off the B4302, 8 miles north of Llandeilo and about 11 miles south of Lampeter.*

TREGARON
Dyfed

The scene here has not changed substantially since the times when drovers gathered in the town square, in front of the Talbot Hotel and statue of Henry Richard, local M.P. and Victorian 'apostle of peace', before setting off with their sheep and cattle to cross the daunting Abergwesyn Pass on their way to the markets of the Midlands. Grey-stoned Tregaron is not a pretty town. Its charm lies in its location and staunchly traditional character. Welsh is the first language in these parts, and Tregaron is a thoroughly Welsh country and market town.

It lies in a strange no-man's-land on a dividing line between farmlands and barren, unpopulated hill country. The low-lying land to the north presents a most forbidding sight, inundated as it is by the great Bog of Tregaron, the largest in Wales, consisting of mile after mile of reedy marshland.

Tregaron Bog is a prime — and rare — example of a dome-shaped raised peat bog. This watery expanse, now a nature reserve, supports a wide variety of plants and over 40 species of breeding birds. An abandoned section of railway line running parallel to the B4343 along the eastern rim of the bog is open to the public as a nature trail which leads to a bird observation post.

🚗 *TREGARON, at the junction of the A485 and B4343, is 11 miles north-east of Lampeter.*

The remains of 12th-century Talley Abbey, idyllically situated beside twin lakes deep in Dyfed's hills

Undiscovered Border Country

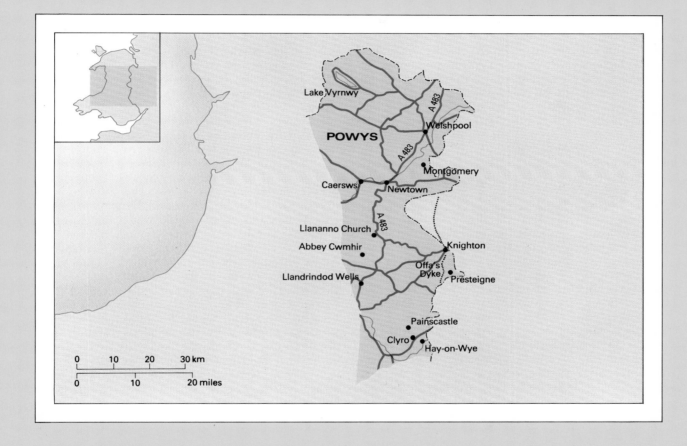

Rood carving at its
most difficult best
is seen on this
exquisite screen in
Llananno Church

TRAVELLERS TEND TO pass across this lush landscape on their comings and goings through Wales, rarely stopping to aquaint themselves with its subtle, secretive charactistics. Mid Wales border country is sleepy and entirely content in its obscurity. There are no tourist honeypots here; the locals remain tight-lipped, in a take-us-or-leave-us way, about its hidden charms.

When they do speak — especially in the old county of Radnorshire (a victim of 1974's government re-organisation) — the accent is hardly Welsh. Cross-border customs and influences play a big part here. The dialect is a hybrid, rustic one, as is the architecture of the borders.

This part of Wales is famous for the half-timbered black-and-white style of building which normally typifies the English country village. Striking 'magpie' farmsteads and cottages stand out against the greenery, in complete contrast to the sturdy, stone-built dwellings of the Welsh heartlands further west.

Historically, this border country was an uneasy interface in the tensions and conflicts between Wales and England. The Offa's Dyke earthwork, a barrier created in the 8th century as the first official demarcation line between Wales and England, lies across the oscillating contours of the land like a giant, slumbering snake. Sentinel-like castles at strategic sites such as Montgomery and Welshpool survey a peaceful patchwork of farmlands that once witnessed bloody conflict.

ABBEY CWMHIR
Powys

Fragments of a Cistercian abbey reveal themselves to those who seek out this remote hamlet, tucked away amongst shady, steep hillsides north of Llandrindod Wells. Abbey Cwmhir makes up in atmosphere for what it lacks in architecture. Crumbling sections of wall and nave, hidden amongst foliage and fields beside the rushing Clywedog Brook, are all that remain of a once-thriving Cistercian house founded in 1143 — sad, really, for Abbey Cwmhir had the largest church in Wales.

Abbey Cwmhir inspires more sad reflections. It is said to be the resting place of Llywelyn, the much-lamented last native prince of Wales, whose body was brought here from Cilmeri for burial following his death in 1282 at the hands of an English trooper (see Builth Wells entry).

Following the Reformation and Dissolution of the Monasteries in 1536 the abbey was dismantled. Some of its pillars were transported to Llanidloes Church where they can still be seen today.

🗨 *ABBEY CWMHIR, 8 miles north of Llandrindod Wells, can be reached by minor road off the A483.*

BWLCH-Y-GROES PASS
Powys and Gwynedd

This spectacular mountain pass could quite as legitimately appear in the Snowdonia section of the book, for it straddles our chosen dividing line between border country and mountain. Intrepid motorists with a penchant for heights, drops and inclines together with a disregard for the narrowness of the road are strongly advised to give this exciting route a try.

Bwlch-y-Groes can be approached from three directions: via mountain-locked Lake Vyrnwy in the east, from Llanuwchllyn in the north and Dinas Mawddwy in the south-west. These three routes eventually meet at the loneliest and quietest Welsh crossroads near a 1790-ft summit which bestows on Bwlch-y-Groes the supreme title of the highest driveable mountain pass in Wales. Views from the top, which visitors share only with bemused Welsh mountain sheep, are predictably panoramic, extending to the North Wales peaks.

🗨 *BWLCH-Y-GROES is accessible off the B4393 (Lake Vyrnwy), A494 (Llanuwchllyn) or A470 (Dinas Mawddwy).*

CAERSWS
Powys

Maesmawr Hall is easy to find. This black-and-white Elizabethan house — one of the finest timber-framed buildings in Wales, and now an hotel — stands out amongst lush greenery on the banks of the meandering River Severn on the outskirts of Caersws.

Caersws's real history is a little more veiled. Almost 2000 years ago, this small village was a place of considerable importance. The Romans sited a seven-acre fort here which became a busy military crossroads, linking their power base in Chester with outposts in Mid Wales. Earthwork defences can still clearly be seen around the railway station.

Llandinam, two miles to the south, is the home of Wales's archetypal local-boy-made-good. A statue of David Davies (1818-90) by Sir Alfred Gilbert, sculptor of Piccadilly's *Eros*, stands in a pretty riverside spot in memory of the deeply religious local farmer's son who made his fortune from South Wales's mines and docks.

🗨 *CAERSWS is close to the junction of the A470 and A492, 5 miles west of Newtown.*

CLYRO
Powys

Readers of Kilvert's Diaries will immediately feel at home in the lush landscape around Clyro. From 1865 to 1872, Francis Kilvert was the curate at Clyro. His best-selling diaries, which start with the last two years of his residence here, paint a marvellous picture of life in rural Wales. Times may have changed; the village, and its surroundings, are little altered.

Peaceful Clyro, which enjoys wide views of the brooding Black Mountains, makes only a few concessions to those in search of Kilvert memorabilia. One house displays a plaque honouring the 'priest and diarist' who lodged there, and the church contains a memorial to its celebrated curate.

The Wye charts a languorous course through a broad river valley south-west of the village, flowing close to a spot with different religious associations. The Anglicanism preached by Kilvert would not have struck a chord with the religious dissenters who, under the cover of darkness, would meet at Maesyronnen, a tiny, secluded chapel tucked away on a country lane in the hillsides above the Wye.

Maesyronnen, a birthplace of the Welsh Nonconformist movement, is one of the earliest chapels in Wales. Built around 1696 and still in regular use, this humble stone house, ordinary enough from the outside, preserves a remarkable interior with original furniture — box pews, pulpit and tables — of the 18th and 19th centuries.

🗨 *CLYRO is at the junction of the A483 and B4351 between Brecon and Hereford. Maesyronnen is accessible by minor road off the A438, 3 miles south-west of Clyro.*

KNIGHTON
Powys

Much is revealed in Knighton's Welsh name, *Tref-y-Clawdd*, 'The town on the Dyke'. The dyke in question is the great north-south earthen barrier, constructed by King Offa of Mercia in the 8th century as the first official border between England and Wales (see special feature, page **71**).

Knighton and the dyke are inexorably linked. The town is the only one to stand squarely on this ancient border, some of the best preserved earthworks of which can be seen in the untravelled hill country a few miles to the north-west of Knighton. Located roughly at the half-way point of the long-distance 170-mile footpath which follows the line of these earthworks, Knighton is also the natural base for the Offa's Dyke Information Centre.

The line of the Wales-England border has not changed too much since Offa's time. Visitors arriving at Knighton by train disembark in England, walking from the railway station across the bridge over the River Teme into Wales and the middle of town. Knighton's centrepiece is a 19th-century clocktower, standing amongst steep streets lined with a jumbled mixture of buildings where black-and-white 'magpie' borderland influences merge with Victorian gables.

🗨 *KNIGHTON, at the junction of the A488, A4113 and B4355, is about 19 miles north-east of Llandrindod Wells.*

LAKE VYRNWY
Powys

Vyrnwy looks like no other Welsh lake. Tall, deep-green pines encircle its shores. High mountains cocoon it from the outside world, shutting out

the sun. A spooky Gothic water tower adds the final forbidding touch to a lake that would be more at home in Switzerland or even Transylvania.

The twin-spired tower along its eastern shore gives the game away. Lake Vyrnwy is man-made, the work of the Liverpool Corporation at the end of the 19th century, a heady time when the creation of reservoirs and the indulgence of architectural eccentricity — such as the ornate water tower — were not viewed as being incompatible by the cost accountants.

Vyrnwy's tall dam holds back over 13,000 million gallons of water, still and black in its mountain shade. The village of Llanddwyn, scattered loosely about the foot of the dam, replaces the original settlement, its 37 dwellings now submerged by the four-mile long lake.

A narrow road curls around the hill immediately to the east of the dam, past the Church of St Wddyn — built to replace the old drowned church — to a wooded glade. Up amongst the trees stands a plain, grey-stoned obelisk, a sombre memorial to the 44 men who died, by accident or natural cause, during the dam's construction.

A mixture of conifer and deciduous woodland surrounds the lake. These forests are noted for their wildlife, especially birds (there is an R.S.P.B. reserve here). The lakeside fauna and the history of the reservoir are both featured at the Vyrnwy Visitor Centre in a converted chapel just west of the dam.

🚗 *LAKE VYRNWY, approximately 19 miles north-west of Welshpool, is accessible by the B4393 and B4396 from the east, and narrow mountain roads from the north and west.*

Lake Vyrnwy brightens its forbidding, gloomy face only when the sun shines directly overhead

LLANANNO CHURCH
Powys

Motorists speeding by on the well-engineered A483 at Llanbister between Llandrindod Wells and Newtown miss a real treat. The roadside church, situated on the banks of the River Ithon in a lovely stretch of the valley, contains what is claimed to be 'the most ornate rood screen in Wales'.

The title is justified. This rich and intricate oak screen, positioned imposingly above aisle and altar, is a supreme example of the skills displayed by the ecclesiastical wood-carver. Dating from the late 15th/early 16th century, with later additions, it embodies a wealth of breathtaking detail. Almost every square inch is redolent of patient and painstaking artistry. Leaf patterns, fruit and vine motifs — vines representing life, pomegranates death — mix and interweave in a complex pattern around a series of 25 biblical figures standing shoulder-to-shoulder.

LLANANNO CHURCH, approximately 11 miles north of Llandrindod Wells and 17 miles south of Newtown, is just over 1 mile north-west of Llanbister.

LLANDRINDOD WELLS
Powys

Unlike the other spa towns of Mid Wales, Llandrindod Wells's *belle époque* lingers quite convincingly and charmingly. Canopied shopping streets and cavernous gabled residences, a subdued riot of red and yellow-bricked Victoriana enlivened by decorative ironwork, are thoroughly busy. There is no hint of disuse or desertion here, thanks largely to the town's twin roles as the main administrative centre for the huge county of Powys and its continued

Llandrindod returns to its roots during its annual Victorian Week

popularity with visitors.

Today's guests come for the surroundings rather than the spa waters. Llandrindod Wells (shortened to a much more convenient 'Llandod' by the locals) nevertheless makes every effort to preserve, and sometimes relive, its past. For seven days each September, the town turns the clock back 100 years during its Victorian Festival. The old pump room in the 18-acre Rock Park has also been re-opened for those partial to 'taking the waters', a taste experience not as innocuous as it might sound.

Llandrindod's wealth of parklands, uniformity of architecture, boating lake and well-planned, spacious streets are no happy accident. Following the coming of the railway in 1865, it was purpose-built as Wales's premier spa resort. An exhibition cen-

tre, also in the refurbished pump rooms, captures Llandrindod's heyday and — to quote an advertisement of the times — its qualities as a 'Famous Spa . . . 750 ft above sea level. Sheltered from east winds. The splendid, bracing air, and the saline, sulphur, magnesian and chalybeate waters are very efficacious in the treatment of gout, rheumatism, anaemia, neurasthemia, dyspepsia, diabetes and liver affections.'

There is another fascinating, albeit unofficial, museum in the flamboyantly-named Automobile Palace, a town-centre garage that houses a collection of old bicycles — including penny-farthings — next to shining new cars.

LLANDRINDOD, on the junction of the A483 and A4081, is 28 miles south of Newtown.

MONTGOMERY
Powys

The gnarled shell of Montgomery Castle, high on its rocky ridge, looks directly down into a most attractive Georgian square. Mangled medieval military architecture and pristine red-bricked Georgian facades somehow sit well together in this strategic border settlement, officially a town thanks to its charter of 1227, though physically no larger than a village.

The castle's ruinous state is attributable more to the destructive forces of man rather than the elements. Much-besieged Montgomery stands guard over the Severn Valley as it enters the Welsh hills, a key position which attracted the attentions of military men for many centuries.

It was built as a front-line fortress by Henry III between 1223 and 1234. In later, more peaceful times, the castle mellowed into a manorial rather than military role, though was back in the wars again — the Civil Wars this time — in the 1640s, after which it was demolished. Thankfully, destruction was not total. A large twin-towered gatehouse, one of the earliest in Britain, massive rock-cut ditch and 220-ft deep well can still be seen, along with far-reaching views into both Wales and England.

MONTGOMERY, at the junction of the B4385, B4386 and B4388, is 8 miles north-east of Newtown.

NEWTOWN
Powys

By Mid Wales standards, this is a large town. It is also something of an odd-man-out, for unlike its neighbours it has a pronounced industrial history. Newtown's last years as a simple market and country town were in the 18th century. By the 19th century, it was known as 'the Leeds of Wales', a reputation based on its thriving flannel industry. Welsh flannel became the basis for the world's first mail-order business, started here in 1859, a profitable diversification which is still going strong. Today, modern estates on the outskirts of town attract new industry, bringing much-needed employment to an essentially rural area.

Newtown sits in a green basin surrounded by low hills, the town centre retaining a pleasant country air. Broad Street, a wide thoroughfare leading to a bridge across the River Severn, is particularly attractive, as are the town's riverside promenades. A former weaving workshop now serves as a textile museum which displays mill machinery, 19th-century handlooms and examples of

Robert Owen is immortalised in stone at Newtown, Powys

the cloth which made Newtown famous.

The old churchyard by the river contains the grave of Newtown's most celebrated son, Robert Owen (1771-1858). Owen, an Utopian Socialist, pioneer of factory reform and founder of the Co-operative movement, was in the vanguard of social reform in Britain. No idealistic dreamer, he put many of his egalitarian theories into practice, most notably at the New Lanark Mills in Scotland. Although he left Newtown when only a boy, he returned here towards the end of his life.

Some of Wales's most enchanting and unexplored border country lies a few miles south-east of Newtown. Around the village of Kerry, hummocky hills and forests, rich in prehistoric earthworks and ancient hill forts, tumble eastwards into England.

NEWTOWN is at the junction of the A483 and A489, 13 miles south-west of Welshpool and 28 miles north of Llandrindod Wells.

PAINSCASTLE
Powys

Aficionados of the contentedly obscure and resolutely rural will find this tiny borderland village enchanting. Do not bring any great expectations to Painscastle. The village's name says it all: castle apart, it lacks almost anything of real note.

In complete character with the place, little is left even of the castle.

Norman nobleman Pain Fitz-John erected the original earthen motte here in 1130, a makeshift stronghold rebuilt in stone by Henry III one century later. This border fort, scene of many a bloody battle, is nowadays devoid of any masonry. All that remains is Fitz-John's earthen mound — not to be dismissed lightly, for this huge motte, surrounded by deep ditches, measures 50 ft from top to bottom.

PAINSCASTLE is on the B4594, accessible off the A470 near Erwood south-east of Builth Wells.

PRESTEIGNE
Powys

When the carriages on the old London to Aberystwyth coaching route decided to stop elsewhere, Presteigne was taken off-the-beaten-track; and there it has remained ever since. Peaceful Presteigne looks out across the River Lugg into England, officially a Welsh settlement — but only just — despite its English-sounding name.

This location is the key to its history. Although nowadays no more than a village, Presteigne was once an important borderland borough town with a charter granted in c. 1225. Welsh forces destroyed its castle in 1262. The church has stood the test of time well. Mainly late 14th century, it incorporates some Saxon work and contains a beautiful Flemish tapestry, early 16th century, depicting the Entry into Jerusalem.

The coaches, when they called, used to stop off at the Radnorshire Arms, a distinguished hostelry dating from 1616 and built in the typical black-and-white half-timbered borderland style.

PRESTEIGNE, which straddles the junction of the B4362 and B4355, is about 21 miles east of Llandrindod Wells.

WELSHPOOL
Powys

Powis Castle, on the southern fringes of the town, captures the limelight here. From relatively common beginnings as a borderland castle, Powis progressed through the ranks to end up as a stately home *par excellence*.

Continuous occupation over the centuries saw its metamorphosis from military stronghold to Elizabethan manor to 19th-century country home. Powis's mellow red limestone stonework reveals its ancestry in the surviving medieval Great Gatehouse and keep. A sumptuous interior also spans the centuries, containing medieval weaponry, an Elizabethan Long Gallery and 1688 gilded State Bedchamber of theatrical proportions.

The gardens, The castle crowns a staircase of four grand terraces, a masterpiece of Italianate design. Created between 1688 and 1722, they are horticulturally and historically important as the only formal gardens of this date which survive in their original form. Powis, a National Trust property, also contains the famous Gold Cup woods, one of Britain's finest old oakwoods.

Welshpool is a prosperous market town and long-established hub of communications. The partially restored Welshpool Canal follows the Severn's broad vale, whilst the narrow-gauge Welshpool and Llanfair Light Railway travels westwards for eight miles through pastoral hill country to Llanfair Caereinion. The town is also noteworthy for its half-timbered and Georgian architecture.

🚗 WELSHPOOL, *at the junction of the A483, A458 and A490, lies between Newtown and Shrewsbury.*

Sumptuous Powis Castle

Offa's Dyke

Offa's Dyke charts a roller-coaster route over undulating country

Speculation surrounds the true purpose behind the construction of *Clawdd Offa*, Offa's Dyke, the first official barrier between Wales and England. It is tempting to look upon it as a military border pure and simple, built to keep the troublesome Welsh within their hill country to the west. Yet it is hardly a serious line of defence, in comparison, for example, to the heavily fortified Hadrian's Wall.

All that can be stated with certainty is that it was constructed in the 8th century at the command of King Offa (757-796), ruler of the Midland Kingdom of Mercia. His great earthen barrier, around 20 ft high with a deep ditch on the Welsh side, ran from north to south, separating Saxon from Celt. Offa's precise motives in undertaking such a monumental task are still obscure, though his dyke did unarguably establish the first demarcation line between Wales and England.

Perhaps it was intended more as an administrative than a military border, a marker line which, once and for all, settled squabbles over disputed territory. By the 10th century it had certainly been accepted as the legitimate border, judging by this piece of Saxon law: 'Neither shall a Welshman cross into English land nor an Englishman cross into Welsh land without the appointed man from that other land who should meet him at the bank and bring him back there again without any offence being committed.' Whether this novel system of chaperoning ever caught on properly is not known.

A quick glance at any map of the border country reveals conclusive evidence of the dyke's effectiveness. To the west, Welsh placenames beginning in 'Llan' or 'Tre' abound. Across the dyke, only a few miles to the east, the English suffixes 'ton' and 'ham' are plentiful.

This 1200-year-old earthworks has long since disappeared in parts. In others, it stands miraculously well preserved almost to its original height. Some of its best stretches traverse the remote hills around Knighton. *Clawdd Offa* drives through this quiet countryside just like a miniature railway cutting, its ditch and high banking an atmospheric reminder that this peaceful landscape was, to our remote ancestors, troubled frontier country.

The present border between Wales and England bears only a rough approximation to the dyke, though the Offa's Dyke path deviates as little as possible from the original. This, the most varied of Britain's long-distance footpaths, takes in everything from pastoral lowlands to high moor in its 170-mile route from Prestatyn in the north to the Severn estuary near Chepstow.

Snowdonia

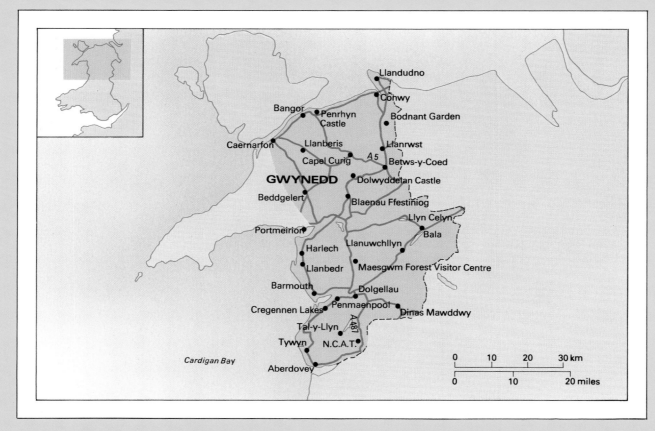

Sunrise from the
summit of Snowdon:
this is the sight
that poet William
Wordsworth aimed for
in his dawn ascent
of the peak, the
highest in England
and Wales

Map labels: Llandudno, Conwy, Bodnant Garden, Bangor, Penrhyn Castle, Llanrwst, Caernarfon, Llanberis, A5, Betws-y-Coed, Capel Curig, GWYNEDD, Dolwyddelan Castle, Beddgelert, Blaenau Ffestiniog, Llyn Celyn, Portmeirion, Bala, Harlech, Llanuwchllyn, Llanbedr, Maesgwm Forest Visitor Centre, Barmouth, Dolgellau, Cregennen Lakes, Penmaenpool, Dinas Mawddwy, Tal-y-Llyn, A481, Tywyn, N.C.A.T., Cardigan Bay, Aberdovey

0 10 20 30 km
0 10 20 miles

WALES, THE LAND OF mountains, reaches its high point here. And Wales, the land of castles, keeps its most powerful for Snowdonia. North Wales's mountains and medieval fortresses are interlinked, for together they help define Welsh history.

Snowdon, at 3560 ft, stands head and shoulders above everything else. This summit gives its name to the Snowdonia National Park — and in doing so creates a degree of confusion. Snowdonia, at 835 square miles the second largest national park in Britain, extends way beyond Snowdon itself down into Mid Wales. The jagged black-and-purple peaks of Mount Snowdon and its neighbours, white-veined with quartz and born in a volcanic turmoil countless thousands of years ago, preside in the north-west corner of the park. This upland terrain culminates at Cader Idris, the mountain which guards the park's southern gateway.

Historically, this part of Wales was a fountainhead of Welsh aspirations. This was once the ancient kingdom of Gwynedd, home of the native Welsh princes. And it was into this mountain fastness that the Welsh retreated after the 13th-century invasion of Wales. Snowdonia is a dramatic stage on which the backdrops are almost overstated, the historic scenario almost too theatrical. Its steely skies and rocky peaks are, in this sense, a perfect accompaniment to the string of mighty castles which testify both to English ambition and Welsh resistance in those troubled bygone times.

ABERDOVEY
Gwynedd

Aberdovey makes the most of the thin strip of land that lies between the steep green hillsides and the sea at the mouth of the Dyfi estuary. Colourfully painted inns and houses run along the front of this classy little seaside resort, also popular with the golfing fraternity due to its excellent 18-hole course.

Aberdovey's salty prospect amidst the inviting sailing waters of Cardigan Bay has also encouraged its role as a popular water sports centre, a natural evolution from the times, a century or so ago, when its quayside was busy with trading schooners. The sea has also contributed to the well-known 'Bells of Aberdovey', composed by Dibdin for the opera *Liberty Hall*. This familiar song is based on the legend of the drowning of *Cantref-y-Gwaelod* ('the Lowland Hundred'), an area of land now submerged beneath the waters of Cardigan Bay.

Directly north of Aberdovey, a scenic little road travels through a pretty mountain vale — unhappily christened 'Happy Valley' by the Victorians, an ugly label that has unfortunately stuck — which contains the isolated tarn of Llyn Barfog (Bearded Lake).

🚗 *ABERDOVEY is on the A493 coast road, 10 miles south-west of Machynlleth and 4 miles south of Tywyn.*

BALA
Gwynedd

The deep fault between the Aran and Arennig Mountains is partially filled by the waters of four-mile-long Llyn Tegid (Bala Lake), the largest natural lake in Wales. Llyn Tegid has an unique occupant: the gwyniad, a white trout, only to be found here, which keeps itself to itself in the deep waters of the lake.

A scenic narrow-guage railway runs along the lakeside from Llanuwchllyn (see separate entry) to Bala. Bala itself is a thoroughly Welsh, and Welsh-speaking, town — and has been for centuries. The celebrated Welsh Nonconformist, Rev. Thomas Charles (1755-1814), preached here. His statue can be seen outside Capel Tegid, Bala's Presbyterian chapel.

One end of the town's long, tree-lined main street is dominated by another figure in a far less humble pose than that of the Bible-bearing Charles. This is the suitably defiant statue of Thomas Edward Ellis, the 19th-century Liberal M.P who advocated home rule for Wales. The rooftops and chimneys behind almost hide the outline of a strange, tall earthen tump, the remains of a Norman fortification known as Tomen-y-Bala.

🚗 *BALA, at the junction of the A494, A4212 and B4391, is 18 miles north-east of Dolgellau.*

BANGOR
Gwynedd

Visitors will not be tempted to tarry long in this large town at the north-eastern end of the Menai Strait. Historically, it is mainly notable as an early centre of Celtic Christianity. Bangor Cathedral was founded c. A.D. 548 by St Deiniol. Although significant as one of the oldest monastic sites in Britain, it is not in the league of great cathedrals, comparing with St David's only in its siting, close to the sea but sheltered by hills. Between 1866 and 1870, the cathedral saw wholesale restoration, though it retains its historic 13th to 16th-century core.

Modern Bangor is a busy university town and — with the Menai and Britannia Bridges so close by — gateway point for the Isle of Anglesey. The town's Museum of Welsh Antiquities boasts a fine collection of prehistoric and Romano-British finds, medieval artefacts, ceramics, old maps and prints.

🚗 *BANGOR, at the junction of the A5 and A4087, is 9 miles north-east of Caernarfon.*

BARMOUTH
Gwynedd

Barmouth's most flattering face is a distant one. On the road down from the Cregennen Lakes (see separate entry), the resort looks like a child's model, a cluster of grey building blocks arranged neatly around the sands below towering mountain slopes at the mouth of the Mawddach estuary.

Take the train or footpath across the beautiful Mawddach estuary

Close-up acquaintance is something of an anti-climax, for Barmouth's confined streets are cluttered with the bric-à-brac of the seaside trade. On the plus side, the resort has a cheerful character, a most attractive old harbourside and, right on the doorstep of magnificent mountain and coastal scenery, must be one of the best sited in Wales.

National Trust buffs will already know as much, for the view from the Trust's cliffland perch of Dinas Oleu is an all-encompassing one, looking out as it does across the estuary to the mountains of Cader Idris. Not only that: this four-and-a-half-acre site will be dear to their hearts as the first property ever to be acquired by the Trust, in 1895.

There are more fine views from the nearby Panorama Walk and an unusual opportunity to see the waters of the Mawddach (William Wordsworth's 'sublime estuary' which might 'compare with the finest in Scotland') at close quarters by following the walkway that accompanies British Rail's bridge across the mouth of the estuary.

🚗 *BARMOUTH, on the A496, is 10 miles west of Dolgellau and 10 miles south of Harlech.*

BEDDGELERT
Gwynedd

Of all the villages in Snowdonia, this one is a personal favourite. Forget the ridiculous story about Gelert, the faithful hound killed in error by his master and buried in a nearby field — the invention of an enterprising 18th-century hotelier — and concentrate instead on Beddgelert's much-praised natural beauty.

Although only seven miles from the sea, stone-built Beddgelert seems to offer no escape from the mountains. It stands at the confluence of

A bird's eye view of the Nant Gwynant valley, near Beddgelert

the Glaslyn and Colwyn Rivers, surrounded by the towering shoulders of Snowdonia where great slabs of exposed rock begin to break through the thin topsoil.

Wordsworth set off on a dawn ascent of Snowdon from here, an episode he later recalled, in inimitable style, within *The Prelude*. Considering such celebrated publicity, and the village's long standing popularity, Beddgelert remains amazingly unspoilt and uncommercialized.

The Nant Gwynant valley slices through the mountains to the north-east, its narrow floor flooded by two idyllic lakes, Llyn Dinas and Llyn Gwynant. The most famous local beauty spot, though, is to be found directly south of the village where the Glaslyn forces a passage through a rocky defile known as the Aberglasyn Pass, its 700-ft-high cliffs and narrow dimensions making sure that the sun rarely penetrates as far as the wooded riverbanks. It comes as something of a surprise to learn that, not so long ago, when the river was tidal, ships were able to sail right up to the picturesque stone bridge at the southern approach to the pass.

🚗 *BEDDGELERT, at the junction of the A4085 and A498, is 13 miles south-east of Caernarfon.*

BETWS-Y-COED
Gwynedd

Inland beauty spots do not come much more famous than this one. Ever since the early 19th century, coaches, trains — and now cars — have deposited visitors at this spot in the wooded foothills of Snowdonia. Yet one cannot help but register a faint tinge of disappointment, for there are certainly prettier and more peaceful places to be found amongst the hills and mountains of North Wales.

Betws-y-coed's charm lies more in its surroundings than the town itself, a long, grey-stoned line of hotels, guesthouses and shops with no identifiable centre. The town stands in a wooded glen where the bare, elemental shoulders of the Snowdon massif have declined into more civilized hill country, dotted with tarns and lakes (Llyn Geirionydd, to the north, is delightful) and criss-crossed by innumerable forest trails.

Betws-y-coed is also close to the meeting place of three rivers, the Conwy, Llugwy and Lledr — which explains this area's plethora of waterfalls. Best known of all, of course, are the Swallow Falls just over a mile west of the town where the Llugwy cascades over great rocks in a wooded gorge. Less famous, but more spectacular, are the Conwy Falls located in the hills a few miles to the east of Betws-y-coed.

Swallow Falls is near the rightly-named Ugly House, a small cottage beside the road made from huge, ill-fitting boulders and looking like something out of a child's nightmare. The old bridge of Pont-y-Pair, in the town itself, is a much more accomplished example of the stonemason's art though it cannot rival the nearby Waterloo Bridge, an ornate iron construction designed by Thomas Telford and erected at the end of the Napoleonic Wars in 1815. True to the spirit of regional equality, it is splendidly decorated with motifs depicting roses, thistles, shamrocks and leeks.

BETWS-Y-COED, at the junction of the A5 and A470, is 20 miles south of Llandudno, 10 miles northeast of Blaenau Ffestiniog.

Telford's Waterloo Bridge at Betwys-y-coed, built in the days before bridges became boring

BLAENAU FFESTINIOG
Gwynedd

Twenty-five years ago, Blaenau Ffestiniog, the former 'slate capital of the world', was a has-been. Its star had ascended and burned brightly in the late 19th century, when thousands of men worked by candlelight in the labyrinthine slate chambers hewn into its mountainsides, producing roofing material for a house-hungry world.

In decline, this tightly packed, terraced town was perceived as the black hole in the middle of Snowdonia. Thanks to the unquenchable inquisitiveness of the modern tourist and the enterprise of a few locals, Blaenau Ffestiniog's star is now on the ascendant again. The town's narrow streets are choked with summer visitors, and a qualified gaeity (North Waleans are not famous for their unbridled sense of fun) has replaced the gloom.

The reasons behind Blaenau Ffestiniog's new lease of life are certainly two, and possibly four-fold. The pyramidal piles of debris and jagged screes of discarded slate waste in the hills around the town mark the sites of two mines, first opened to the public in the early 1970s. Around 200,000 visitors now come to the Llechwedd Slate Caverns each year, to ride by electric tramway through its old chambers or to take the 'Deep Mine' tour. Similar numbers turn up at the rival Gloddfa Ganol Mountain Centre opposite, advertised as 'the largest slate mine in the world'. No one can dispute the size of this vast site, with its underground passageways, exhibitions and working slate mill, which seems to take up the entire mountainside.

The Ffestiniog Railway (see Porthmadog entry) provides the third reason for Blaenau Ffestiniog's renaissance. After years of dedicated work by enthusiasts, this narrow-gauge line now runs again all the way from Porthmadog to Blaenau Ffestiniog, with passengers replacing its original cargoes of slate. The Stwlan Dam, 1000 ft high in the mountains above the town and part of an imaginative hydro-electricity scheme, also attracts visitors — especially since it is possible to drive or take a bus right up to its lofty lakeside.

BLAENAU FFESTINIOG is at the junction of the A470 and A496, 21 miles north of Dolgellau.

BODNANT GARDEN
Gwynedd

The Welsh are not noted for their green fingers. Perhaps it is a case of quality rather than quantity, for the formal gardens at Bodnant — a rare feature in Wales — are amongst Britain's finest.

This 97-acre garden, a National Trust property, has the advantage of a superb location in the Vale of Conwy, along the gentle, pastoral eastern fringe of Snowdonia. The product of three centuries of careful development and grooming, Bodnant is an harmonious blend of natural and decorative influences.

There are fountains and exuberant ballustrading here, complementing a profusion of flowering shrubs and plants. Camelias, azaleas, magnolias and roses grow in colourful abundance, though the outstanding spectacle for many comes in the early summer, when Bodnant's rhododendrons are in full bloom. The garden terraces, part of Bodnant's outstanding landscape modelling — which also include a formal lily pond — command marvellous views across the valley to Snowdonia.

BODNANT GARDEN is accessible off the A470, 8 miles south of Llandudno.

CAERNARFON
Gwynedd

Those unaware of the sensitivities of Welsh history are invariably surprised to discover that not all Welshmen are particularly enamoured of Caernarfon Castle. This imperious medieval fortress, quite easily the best known of all the Welsh castles, strikes an ambivalent chord within Wales. Understand Caernarfon, and you begin to comprehend the complexities of the Welsh character.

Imperious Caernarfon, undimmed by night. Edward I would have appreciated such flattering floodlights

Begun in 1283, Caernarfon put the final stamp of authority on the conquest of North Wales by the English king, Edward I. The castle was designed to serve as more than a mere fortress. This was the palace and official government residence of the English monarch and his successors.

Caernarfon is still almost all that it originally set out to be. Alteration, repair and extensive restoration from the Victorian period onward have not erased its character, a composite of military strength and regal authority. None of Edward's other Welsh castles, for example, boasts Caernarfon's decorative bands of coloured stone, a feature which has been compared to the walls of Constantinople.

The castle's polygonal towers are also exceptional, especially the Eagle Tower, crowned by three tall, slender turrets. With so much in the way of magnificence, it is difficult to single out other architectural features, though the King's and Queen's Gates — the former still serving as the main entrance — are particularly fine.

It was from the ramparts of this palace-castle that, according to legend anyway, Edward is said to have presented his baby son to the Welsh as 'the native-born prince who could speak no English' (sober historians are inclined to think that the venue was Rhuddlan, if it took place at all). Within modern times, the castle has been used for the investitures of the Princes of Wales, the most recent of which was 1969 when Prince Charles was invested.

The foundations of another, earlier stronghold in Caernarfon are overshadowed by the presence of the castle. This is *Segontium*, a Roman fort built on the hill above the town, and dating from around A.D. 78.

🏴 *CAERNARFON, at the junction of the A487, A4085 and A4086 is 9 miles south-west of Bangor.*

CAPEL CURIG
Gwynedd

The highest peaks in England and Wales surround this mountain village. The Snowdonia massif has 13 main summits dominated, of course, by 3560-ft-high Snowdon itself, the highest peak in Britain south of the Scottish Highlands and known in Welsh as *Eryri* ('The abode of the eagle').

Its jagged profile and razor-sharp ridges can be seen emerging out of the cloud and mist from the Pen-y-Pass area at the head of the Llanberis Pass, four miles south-west of Capel Curig. The isolated Pen-y-Gwryd Hotel here is now part of mountaineering folklore. This inn was the original base camp for the first successful attempt on Everest in 1953, the team training in these mountains prior to setting off for the Himalayas — and leaving their names on Pen-y-Gwryd's ceiling to prove it.

Tryfan was their tough testing ground. This 3010-ft mountain is part of the Carneddau, a collective name for Wales's second highest mountain range. Soaring up from the roadside as one towering, unbroken block of exposed rock, Tryfan is just as challenging as neighbouring Snowdon.

The gouging, destructive effects of glaciation are everywhere to be seen in this primeval, boulder-strewn landscape. Huge sheets of ice were responsible for the steep slopes, cwms and mountain lakes around the Nant Ffrancon Pass to the north-west of Capel Curig. Really serious walkers, for whom Snowdon itself is a little *passé*, reckon that North Wales's raw, elemental personality is nowhere stronger than it is here, amongst the peaks of Carnedd Dafydd (3424 ft) and Carnedd Llywelyn (3485 ft), the latter named after the long-lamented Welsh prince who met his death in 1282 fighting the English.

🏴 *CAPEL CURIG is at the junction of the A5 and A4086, 15 miles southeast of Bangor and 5 miles west of Betws-y-coed.*

CONWY
Gwynedd

Photographers in search of the ultimate medieval castle-cummountain shot invariably end up in Conwy. If they are adept enough, they capture even more, for Conwy Castle in its Snowdonia setting is only part of the picture.

Conwy is all about mood and atmosphere — an authentic medieval atmosphere, stronger here than in any other town in Wales. Mighty Caernarfon, Wales's most famous castle, comes a poor second to Conwy in this respect. Well scrubbed and immaculately renovated Caernarfon is not as convincing in its ability to recreate the medieval spirit which pervades the rough, tough, greygreen walls of Conwy.

Comparisons are perhaps unfair, for Conwy's character is aided and abetted by a ring of medieval town walls which are amongst the finest and most complete in Europe. Conwy the military stronghold and Conwy the garrison town are almost as well integrated today as they were at their conception, 800 years ago. The town walls, protected by no less than 22 towers, run for over three-quarters of a mile amongst narrow streets that spill down to the pretty, boat-filled quayside.

The original street plan survives — as do some of the houses. Threestoreyed Aberconwy House (National Trust) dates from the 14th century and is one of the last remaining timber-framed buildings in the town.

Plas Mawr is an imposing 16thcentury town house famous for its inventive, ornamental plasterwork. A little light relief is provided by the tiny dwelling on the quayside, reputedly the smallest house in Britain and furnished as a Welsh cottage.

Every house in Conwy, whatever its size, is well and truly dwarfed by the castle, a masterpiece of late 13thcentury military architecture which makes the most of a confined promontory above the strategic Deganwy estuary where the River Conwy meets the sea. Eight massive round towers and soaring curtain walls tell us, better than any text book, that this was a castle built by Edward I to strike fear into the hearts of the Welsh.

Conwy's cornucopia of architectural heritage goes on and on. The footbridge which spans the estuary is not quite as old as it looks. Put up in the 1820s and the work of Thomas Telford, its mock-military appearance was designed to match the castle. Robert Stephenson's tubular railway bridge, also castellated, was built alongside in 1848. In the late 1950s, all motor traffic was transferred from Telford's sympathetic structure to a modern bridge — devoid, of course, of any such 19th-century niceties — based on an inappropriately functional design.

🏴 *CONWY is on the A55 near Llandudno Junction, 15 miles northeast of Bangor, 4 miles south of Llandudno.*

Thomas Telford's 19th-century approach bridge, built in castellated style, in no way compromises the authentic medieval atmosphere of Conwy's towers and curtain walls. Conwy may not be Wales's greatest castle, but measured by its force of personality, it stands unchallenged

CREGENNEN LAKES
Gwynedd

This pair of lakes are hidden away above the luxuriant Mawddach estuary on the northern slopes of Cader Idris. Their most direct approach, up a narrow, hairpinned road that climbs with alacrity the 1000 ft to Cregennen from sea-level at Arthog, is almost as memorable as the lakes themselves.

In its lower reaches, the road winds upwards along a thickly wooded valley before breaking out onto the bare, exposed shoulders of Cader Idris. The lakes lie in glorious open countryside, Cader's north-facing escarpment sweeping down to their waters. Largely unknown and un-visited 15 years ago, Cregennen Lakes are now becoming an increasingly well-trodden beauty spot. In the care of the National Trust, they remain thankfully devoid of any commercial development.

Motorists wary of the direct ascent can take an easier approach road. They should, though, summon up the will to follow the road back down to Arthog (the descent is always easier) for the panoramic views en route of the swirling waters, sands and woodlands along the lovely Mawd-dach estuary and the resort of Bar-mouth, perched at its entrance.

CREGENNEN LAKES can be approached by minor road off the A493 at Arthog, 5 miles south-west of Dolgellau; alternatively, by an easier minor road running directly to the lakes from Dolgellau.

DINAS MAWDDWY
Gwynedd

This little village nestles, Swiss-fashion, amongst steep, pine-clad slopes in the high, mountainous up-per reaches of the Dyfi Valley. The Meirion Woollen Mill, on the out-skirts, still looks like what it once was: the village's railway station, the end of the line for trains travelling from Machynlleth.

The last train ran in 1951. Disused station site then became woollen mill which, after a few false starts, pro-spered from the late Sixties onwards. The Meirion Woollen Mill is now firmly on the map as one of the best known in Wales. Visitors are welcomed into its workshops, where the noisy weaving frames produce the colourfully patterned cloths and tapestries distinctive to Wales. As an extra attraction, the mill has con-verted the original railway station house into a café rightly renowned for its traditional Welsh teas. Stop off here — as the regulars do — if you are making the north-south journey through Wales on the A470 trunk route.

Pont Minllyn, near the mill, is a picturesque early 17th-century bridge across the Dyfi. The Brigand's Inn at Mallwyd, a little further south, is named after the *Gwylliaid Cochion Mawddwy* ('the wild red brigands of Mawddwy'), red-haired robbers who terrorised this area in the 16th century.

DINAS MAWDDWY is on the A470, 9 miles east of Dolgellau.

DOLGELLAU
Gwynedd

Visitors either love or loathe Dolgellau. Some find its uniformity of character oppressive, built as it is almost entirely of huge blocks of dark local stone which assume a weighty depth of blackness on not-infrequent drizzly days. With no respite from the town's dark slate roofs, Dolgellau is not a place for depressives on a wet Welsh Sunday. Others, in all fairness, are enchanted by the sombre dignity

Dolgellau's classic setting, beneath hill, forest and mountain

of the place, its sense of presence, solidity and robustness of architecture, tall buildings, narrow alleyways and shady nooks and crannies.

Cader Idris is another element in the love-hate equation. This boulder-strewn mountain — lower than Snowdon by 600 ft but no less challenging — looms menacingly above the rooftops. Again, some can live quite happily with this misty, omnipresent Sword of Damocles above their heads. Others find its presence disturbing, their reactions echoing the local legend that those who spend a night on the summit of 'The Chair of Idris' (hence its Welsh name) will awake a poet or madman — or not at all.

Make your own mind up about Dolgellau. On the positive side, it is undisputedly one of the best-located centres from which to tour the Snowdonia National Park. Fans of the town will be pleased to hear that it has now acquired a by-pass, freeing its attractive/gloomy town square from traffic congestion.

DOLGELLAU is at the junction of the A470, A493 and A494, 13 miles north of Machynlleth.

DOLWYDDELAN CASTLE
Gwynedd

This is the real thing. In complete contrast to the Caernarfons and Conwys of this world, castles built by the invading English in the 13th century, Dolwyddelan is a rare surviving example of a fortress put up by the native Welsh.

This proud little castle, of characteristic single tower construction, still stands its ground amongst the rugged mountain country it once commanded. Dolwyddelan dates from the early 13th century, and was probably built by Llywelyn the Great, 'Lord of Snowdon'.

Mighty Harlech, one of the 'top four' of the hundreds of Welsh castles

Llywelyn's castle would have guarded the mountain pass now traversed by the modern road that runs beneath the defences. This strategic consideration, accompanied by some wonderful views, can be appreciated by climbing to the top of the battlements.

DOLWYDDELAN is on the A470 mid-way between Blaenau Ffestiniog and Betws-y-coed.

HARLECH
Gwynedd

Only a handful of the hundreds of castles in Wales are anything approaching household names. Harlech Castle is one of them. This may partly be due to the song *Men of Harlech*, a stirring march inspired by a stout defence of the castle during the Wars of the Roses. Harlech's true celebrity value, though, is a consequence of its stonework and siting.

Academics not noted for their capacity to express natural enthusiasm have been known to rhapsodise over this insolent, grey-stoned fortress, likening it to the military equivalent of a great Gothic cathedral. It was built between 1283 and 1289 and, even today, 700 years on, expresses its original intentions plainly and unequivocally.

This was a castle, one of the so-called 'iron ring' which included Caernarfon and Conwy, built by the English king, Edward I, to contain the native Welsh in their mountain fastness. Harlech's massive twin-towered gatehouse, walls and towers, stand almost to their original height, their stature enhanced by the clever siting of the castle on the summit of a precipitious crag.

From the lofty wall walks, sweeping views encompass not only the distant peaks of Snowdonia into which the Welsh retreated, but also the waters of Tremadog Bay and the long arm of the Lleyn Peninsula. When Harlech was constructed, the sea lapped at its feet. Over the centuries, the sea has receded by over half-a-mile beyond the dunes and sands of Morfa Harlech, leaving the castle high and dry on its landlocked crag. Harlech's 'Way from the Sea', a rocky stairway cut into the cliff, now leads from the castle down to the town's railway station.

Harlech's history reveals an interesting irony which would not have been appreciated by its builder. Constructed by an English king intent on the conquest of Wales, the castle was captured in 1404 by the native leader Owain Glyndwr, who then proceeded to hold a Welsh parliament here.

HARLECH, on the A496, is located between Barmouth and Penrhyndeudraeth.

A Land of Castles

The only Welsh cliché that happens to be true is the one that labels the country 'a land of castles'. No one is quite sure of the precise number here, though experts are happy to quote figures in excess of 400, giving Wales one of the highest concentrations of fortified sites in the world.

This figure encompasses over 1000 years of Welsh history, starting with the first rough-and-ready earth-and-timber defences thrown up hastily by the Normans and ending with the opulent 'sham' castles and follies constructed by *nouveaux riches* 19th-century industrialists. Forget the text books. There is no better way to get to grips with the complexities and contradictions of Wales's tortuous past than through its castles, over 100 of which are open to visitors.

The strongholds built by the Norman invaders had to be both cheap and easy to put up: hence the rash of crude motte-and-bailey castles that appeared throughout Wales from the 11th century. The motte, an earthen mound, overlooked a bailey, or enclosure, the entire site protected by timber defences and ditches.

Remnants of these rudimentary castles are scattered everywhere. Some appear as strangely-shaped tumps, marooned amongst farmers' fields. Others were subsequently strengthened or rebuilt as stone gradually began to replace timber. The coming of these stronger, second-generation sites dates from the construction at Chepstow in c.1070 of Wales's — and Britain's — first stone-built castle.

Medieval fortresses reached a peak of power and sophistication in the great ring of castles built by the English king, Edward I, in his late 13th-century campaigns against Wales. Caernarfon, Conwy, Harlech and Beaumaris are today cited as being amongst the most outstanding examples of medieval military architecture surviving in Europe.

In complete contrast to the mighty Edwardian castles, those built by the native Welsh were much simpler, often single tower affairs (Dolwyddelan in Snowdonia is a classic example), never intended to dominate by force of arms. In the more settled later Middle Ages, castles in Wales became more decorative, less defensive, developing domestic features such as mullioned windows and fine apartments.

From here, it was a short step to the stately home: Chirk Castle, a sumptuously appointed country mansion, is the perfect example, having started life as a medieval fort. The 19th century added the final touch, when mock-medieval and Neo-Norman 'castles' made their appearance, redolent of the wealth and lordly pretensions generated by the Industrial Revolution.

Handsome Raglan marked the end of an era in castle building

LLANBEDR
Gwynedd

The village of Llanbedr stands just inland from a curious stretch of Cardigan Bay coastline known as Mochras. Its alternative name of Shell Island is misleading on one count: the 'island' is a long, narrowing peninsula of sand dunes and peaceful beaches, though the shells are plentiful enough, with over 200 varieties recorded here.

Another curiosity lies landwards of Llanbedr. These are the so-called 'Roman Steps', a well engineered pathway of hundreds of stone steps leading up into the Rhinog Mountains from the remote, romantic lake of Llyn Cwm Bychan. A minor road winds its way up the Artro Valley north-east of the village, ending just past the lakeside. A footpath then takes advantage of the ready-made stone staircase — probably medieval but certainly not Roman in origin — as it climbs into the Rhinogs. These mountains, a shapeless, inhospitable upland mass of exposed rock and heather moor, rise to just under 2500 ft. Few who have tramped this arduous, totally empty terrain will argue with its inclusion amongst Britain's last true wilderness areas, especially in winter.

At Llanfair, just north of Llanbedr, visitors can don miners' helmets for a guided tour of the Old Llanfair Slate Caverns. *Muriau'r Gwyddelod* ('Irishmen's Walls') between Llanfair and Harlech are Iron Age hut circles with well preserved walls four feet high and 18 ft thick in places.

🚗 *LLANBEDR is on the A496, 3 miles south of Harlech.*

An exciting toll road, cut into the cliffside, clings to the Great Orme Headland, Llandudno

LLANDUDNO
Gwynedd

Here we have the regal doyen, the self-appointed but unchallenged 'Queen of the Welsh resorts'. Llandudno is a seaside town redolent of great charm and style. The resort stands aloof from the rest, distanced in character if not geography from its nearby North Wales neighbours and retaining an olde worlde charm.

Like Tenby in the south, Llandudno has not succumbed to the garish excesses that blight so many of Britain's seaside resorts. In Llandudno's case, this is especially commendable, for it has had to deal with the pressures — and put aside the temptations — that come with having the largest selection of hotels in Wales.

Very little has been allowed to compromise its Victorian and Edwardian ambience (in fact, Llandudno is now becoming recognised as one of the most outstanding and best preserved Victorian towns in Britain). Its promenade is particularly splendid. A long row of tall, gabled hotels, painted in muted, pastel tones, stretches into the distance following the gentle curve of the North Beach.

The entire scene is framed between two natural features — the headlands of the Great and Little Ormes. The 679-ft-high Great Orme can be ascended, alpine-style, by cabinlift or on a San Franciscan mode of transport, a cable car tramway. A spectacular coastal toll road has also been cut into its vertical cliffs beneath the tiny headland Church of St Tudno, Llandudno's original place of worship.

This church is much older than the town below, for Llandudno is largely a by-product of the latter part of the 19th century. It represents a coastal equivalent to the inland resort of Llandrindod Wells (see separate entry) as a purpose-built holiday centre. Both share the same uniformity of style, though in Llandudno's case even the street plans are rigidly controlled, conforming to a grid-iron pattern reminiscent of an American town or city. The rule is relaxed only along the pretty shopping centre adorned with decorative iron-and-glass canopies, the streets of which curve in a carefully contrived arc.

Llandudno's North Beach is its busiest, sweeping along the shore from the ornate pier — a prized feature which completes the picture of a Victorian seaside resort in aspic. Along Llandudno's second beach, the West Shore, stands the White Rabbit memorial which commemorates the resort's associations with Charles Dodgson, alias Lewis Carroll, author of *Alice in Wonderland*.

🚗 *LLANDUDNO is on the A546 between Colwyn Bay and Conwy.*

LLANBERIS
Gwynedd

Llanberis stands beside its twin lakes, Llyn Padarn and Peris, at the foot of the Llanberis Pass. This deep cleft, the most famous mountain pass in Snowdonia, was put on the map in the 1950s through the exploits of such pioneering rock climbers as Joe Brown and the late Don Whillans. With little more in the way of equipment than plimsolls and a length of borrowed clothes line, they conquered the fearsome rock slabs and shuddering overhangs that fill this baleful valley.

The little town, at the foot of the highest mountain in England and Wales, has developed into a busy tourist centre. Many are attracted by the Snowdon Mountain Railway, the lazy man's way to reach the top of Snowdon. Weather permitting, the railway's specially designed rack-and-pinion Swiss locomotives climb the four-and-a-half miles from Llanberis to the 3560-ft summit.

Llanberis's second narrow-gauge line — the Llanberis Lake Railway — is pretty enough, though suffers from comparison to its tough big brother. This little line runs along the north-eastern shore of Llyn Padarn for two miles from a terminus near a museum which introduces visitors to a 19th-century industry which dominated these parts. Llanberis's Welsh Slate Museum has a head start in the authenticity stakes for the museum consists of the former workshops of the Dinorwic Quarry. Much of the original machinery has been preserved intact, including a giant water-wheel, over 50 ft in diameter.

Man continues to hew and dig

The twin lakes at the foot of the famous Llanberis Pass

amongst these mountains. Although there is now little external evidence of it, the slopes opposite Llanberis are riddled with giant tunnels and man-made caverns, part of the largest pumped storage hydro-electric scheme in Europe. The Central Electricity Generating Board have joined with the National Museum of Wales in creating *Oriel Eryri* ('The Snowdon Gallery'), an interpretive centre which concentrates on the local environment.

Dolbadarn Castle, on a headland where the two lakes meet, is a single tower fortress, built to a typical design by the Welsh leader Llywelyn the Great in the early 13th century.

LLANBERIS is on the A4086, 8 miles south-east of Caernarfon.

LLANRWST
Gwynedd

This pretty little market town assumes the role of 'capital of the Conwy Valley'. Its delicate, three-arched stone bridge over the river is more robust than it looks. Inigo Jones's most famous Welsh work, it dates from 1636.

At the far end is the 15th-century National Trust property, Tu Hwnt i'r Bont, its location plain to any Welsh-speaker for its name means 'At the other side of the bridge'. The building, once a courthouse, was later split into two cottages.

The riverside Gwydir Chapel ad-joins St Grwst's Church, just off the main square. The church contains a magnificent rood screen, though the real treasure lies within the 17th-century chapel — an ornately carved stone coffin in which was buried Llywelyn ab Iorwerth, Llywelyn the Great, Wales's much-lauded 13th-century leader.

A series of beautiful, little-visited lakes hide themselves away in the pine-clad hills above Llanrwst (Llyn Geirionydd and Llyn Crafnant are particularly attractive). Seekers of obscure religious sites will also want to visit Gwydir Uchaf Chapel (*uchaf* meaning upper), tucked discreetly away amongst the trees. Built in 1673 as a private chapel, it is notable for its carvings and ceiling paintings.

LLANRWST, at the junction of the A470, B5106 and B5427, is 15 miles south of Llandudno.

LLANUWCHLLYN
Gwynedd

This village has grown up around the south-western end of Bala Lake. It is the terminus of the narrow-gauge Bala Lake Railway, one of the 'Great Little Trains of Wales', which runs along the southern shores of the lake for four-and-a-half miles to the out-skirts of Bala.

Llanuwchllyn is also linked to Bala in a cultural sense through shared, deeply felt and continuing associations with the Welsh language. Statues of two famous Welshmen — Sir Owen Morgan Edwards (1858-1920) and Sir Ifan ab Owen Edwards (1895-1970) — stand here. Sir Owen, born on a local farm, championed the survival and spread of the Welsh language. The torch was later carried by his son, Sir Ifan, who founded *Urdd Gobaith Cymru* ('the Welsh League of Youth').

Farming traditions live on at the Cyffdy Farm Park at Parc, in the remote foothills of the Arennig Mountains north of Llanuwchllyn. Visitors are welcome to wander through this typical hill sheep farm ranged around a solid, stone-built farmhouse dating from the early 17th century.

LLANUWCHLLYN is just off the A494, 14 miles north-east of Dolgellau.

LLYN CELYN
Gwynedd

This two-mile-long 16,000 million gallon lake was constructed to supply North-east Wales and Cheshire no more than 20 years ago. Surprise at its relative youth is registered because this man-made lake, unlike others in Wales, looks as though it has been here for much longer, a consequence of sympathetic planning and landscaping.

The eye leads naturally from its wide waters to the Arennig Mountains, rising majestically from Llyn Celyn's southern shore. Along its northern shoreline, a starkly simple and modern stone chapel stands as a replacement to the original place of worship, drowned beneath the waters in the flooded valley below. Capel Celyn Memorial was 'designed to resemble a ship coming in from over the water'. Stones from the lost chapel went into its building, and headstones rescued from the now submerged graveyard have been re-erected alongside. Within the chapel, three magnificently carved slate slabs list those whose bodies lie beneath the lake.

Just east of Llyn Celyn's grass-covered dam, the River Tryweryn rushes along a stretch which has become a white-water canoe slalom course of international repute.

LLYN CELYN, 5 miles north-west of Bala, is accessible by the A4212.

MAESGWM FOREST VISITOR CENTRE
Gwynedd

Coed-y-Brenin, a large Forestry Commission plantation north of Dolgellau, holds many secrets. In medieval times, it was an estate of the Welsh princes. Later, it witnessed Wales's 19th-century gold rush. Today, the blanketing effect that conifers bring fails to disguise this area's inherent natural beauty. Copses of ancient oakwoods and other deciduous trees survive amongst the pines. Waterfalls and crystal rivers rush and tumble through Coed-y-Brenin's dense heart. Regimented greenery has, for once, been unable to swamp the natural lie of the land.

The commission's many enemies consider the conifer, *en masse*, an alien, destructive army, a destroyer of landscapes and vistas. In all fairness, the commission is not unaware of these arguments and within the last 15 years or so has made worthy attempts to explain its position, to open up the forests to visitors, and to increase the amenity and recreational value of woodlands such as Coed-y-Brenin.

Maesgwm is a consequence of all this. Interestingly presented displays tell the history of Coed-y-Brenin's 217,000 acres, also introducing the visitor to the network of over 50 miles of waymarked trails that now run through the forest.

The centre also touches on Coed-y-Brenin's most alluring secret: gold. The Dolgellau gold belt, which stretches from the Mawddach estuary into the forest's cool, green heart, attracted a Klondike-like rush of 19th-century prospectors. Gold is still mined here — somewhere. Of the past endeavours, the ruined mine at Gwynfynydd is undoubtedly the most evocative, with the bonus of a beautiful location. Follow the minor road which leads north-east through the trees from Ganllwyd, a village on the A470 just over two miles south of Maesgwm. When the tarmac ends, walk the rest of the way (about a mile) to two lovely waterfalls, Rhaeadr Mawddach and Pistyll-y-Cain, and the shell of Gwynfynydd, a mine which yielded rich pickings in the mid and late 19th century.

MAESGWM is just off the A470, 7 miles north of Dolgellau, approximately 19 miles south-east of Porthmadog.

NATIONAL CENTRE FOR ALTERNATIVE TECHNOLOGY
Gwynedd

In the early Seventies, a group of committed conservationists moved into a derelict, barren slate quarry in the conifer-clad hills north of Machynlleth — an unpromising environment indeed in which to conduct an experiment in self-sufficiency and alternative living. The success of their 'village of the future', which now produces much of its own energy and food, speaks for itself.

This unique site does not exist just for the dedicated conservationist. Anyone with the faintest interest in the creative management of finite energy resources will be fascinated by the work taking place here. Amongst the ingenious array of devices employed — some simple, others of a Heath Robinson-like complexity — there are aerogenerators (windmills to you and me), water-powered turbines, banks of solar panels, woodgas systems, methane gardens and buildings heavily insulated to minimise heat loss.

The centre has also stumbled on an alternative means of income, thanks to an inquisitive tourist market. Open to visitors throughout the year, it is now Wales's most unconventional tourist attraction. Its brochures, of course, are printed on re-cycled paper.

N.C.A.T. is signposted off the A487 at Pantperthog, about 3 miles north of Machynlleth and 13 miles south of Dolgellau.

PENMAENPOOL
Gwynedd

Start your exploration of the Mawddach estuary's southern shores from this quirky little spot, at the end of a rickety toll bridge which crosses from the northern bank. A ghostly railway signal box, signal gantry and faint remnants of platform mark the eastern end of the Morfa Mawddach walk, a five-mile footpath which follows the waterside course laid by the redundant Great Western Region railway line.

The signal box now serves as a Wildlife Information Centre, and is a perfect place from which to observe cormorants, herons and oystercatchers, some of the many species that frequent the waters of the estuary.

Fairbourne, six miles to the southwest, is the home of a narrow-gauge railway — the smallest of the lot in Wales, with a gauge of only 12 and a quarter inches — that runs for two miles along a sandy spit to the mouth of the estuary.

PENMAENPOOL is on the A493, 2 miles west of Dolgellau.

PENRHYN CASTLE
Gwynedd

This gigantic sham castle expresses the exuberant, over-confident, anything-goes spirit of the 19th century perfectly. Built between 1820 and 1837 for local magnate Lord Penrhyn, it is the North Wales equivalent to the south's Cardiff Castle, the Victorian palace that Lord Bute created for himself from the proceeds of the coal trade.

In the north, the slate quarries and a lucrative sugar trading business allowed Lord Penrhyn to indulge his whimsies. He employed architect Thomas Hopper to create for him a cavernous mock castle that is now regarded as the best example in Britain of the Norman revival.

Penrhyn's enormous four-storeyed Neo-Norman keep is just the beginning. Inside as well as out, the architect's zest was evidently unstoppable. Hardly any surface is left unadorned; nearly every excess is indulged. Quite understandably, Queen Victoria is reputed to have refused to sleep in the enormous bed — made of course from slate — which weighs in at over a ton.

Penrhyn Castle, a National Trust property, stands in magnificent 47-acre grounds and also contains a noteworthy doll collection and railway museum.

PENRHYN, on the eastern approach to Bangor, is accessible from an entrance near the junction of the A5 and A55.

PORTMEIRION
Gwynedd

This is easily the most un-Welsh village in Wales. Portmeirion, a creation of the architect and iconoclast Sir Clough Williams-Ellis (who died in 1978, aged 95), throws convention to the wind. Visitors are advised to expect the unexpected at Portmeirion, his bizarre little kingdom in which renaissance Italy rubs shoulders with 18th-century England, where flights of stone steps lead puzzlingly to nowhere in particular, and whose boat, moored to the harbour wall, is a life-sized model in concrete.

The village, created piecemeal over the years by Sir Clough, is an architectural pot-pourri of styles and influences which reflect his 'gay, light-opera sort of approach'. Humour was an essential element in his repertoire. Architectural jokes and unexpected touches appear around almost every corner; elaborate facades flatter only to

The portal into Portmeirion, a magical, other-worldly village

deceive, fronting absolutely nothing, in the way of flimsy film sets on Hollywood back lots.

Portmeirion's other-worldliness is enhanced by its location at the far end of a secluded, densely wooded little peninsula. The village is now forever identified with actor Patrick McGoohan's cult Sixties television series, *The Prisoner*, in which it became the strange, inexplicable prison-domain. Portmeirion's strong sense of displacement — it should by all rights be located in the sunny south of Italy, not in blustery, damp North Wales — was the perfect architectural complement to McGoohan's surreal storyline.

PORTMEIRION is accessible off the A487 at Minffordd, between Porthmadog and Penrhyndeudraeth.

TAL-Y-LLYN
Gwynedd

This lovely lake, sheltering beneath the green foothills and rocky scree slopes of Cader Idris, gives its name to a long valley, a major geological fault caused by a crack in the earth's crust. The valley, running from the lake south-westwards towards Tywyn, was first fashioned by a river before being scooped into its present deep and emphatic shape by the action of glaciers during the Ice Age.

The B4405 road follows the line of the valley (as does the Talyllyn Railway — see Tywyn entry). At Abergynolwyn, the River Dysynni takes a sharp turn through a narrow defile into a side valley. This detour away from Tal-y-llyn is also worth following by road, for it reveals a trio of fascinating and largely undiscovered places of interest.

Craig-yr-Aderyn, or Bird Rock, is an ornothological oddity. Before the vale silted up, this craggy precipice was a sea-cliff. No one seems to have

Sheep safely graze beneath Bird Rock on meadows once covered by the seas of Cardigan Bay

told the cormorants that the ocean is now four miles away, for these sea-birds continue to nest here well away from the waters of Cardigan Bay.

Further up the valley stand the atmospheric ruins of Castell-y-Bere, a 'proper' Welsh castle in the sense that this mountain fortress was a stronghold of the Welsh native princes as opposed to the invading English. Probably built in 1221, it served as the court of no less a personage than Llywelyn ab Iorwerth, Llywellyn the Great, Prince of Gwynedd.

A ruin of more modest dimensions lies near the end of the tarmac road at the cul-de-sac hamlet of Llanfihangel-y-pennant. A commemorative stone explains its significance as the remains of Mary Jones's cottage. In 1800, 16-year-old Mary walked from here across the mountains, barefoot for part of the way, to collect a Welsh Bible from the great Methodist

preacher, Rev. Thomas Charles. Her arduous 25-mile journey is said to have inspired the foundation, by Charles, of the British and Foreign Bible Society.

TAL-Y-LLYN valley is accessible from the east at Minffordd on the A487. From the west, approach it off the A493 north-east of Tywyn.

TYWYN
Gwynedd

Tywyn is a rather forlorn seaside town which time and fashion seem to have passed by. Today's visitors do better to treat it as a well located touring centre rather than a resort, for Tywyn's hinterland is made up of the spectacular Cader Idris massif.

The Talyllyn Narrow Gauge Railway, one of the 'Great Little Trains of Wales', chuffs inland from Tywyn to a remote mountain terminus near Abergynolwyn, seven

miles distant. En route, passengers can stop off at Dolgoch, a pretty hillside halt shrouded in trees and close to a string of waterfalls. Railway enthusiasts will also want to visit the Narrow Gauge Railway Museum, located at Talyllyn's Tywyn station.

Antiquarian interest in Tywyn centres around a spindly pillar of stone in St Cadfan's Church. Seven feet high, it bears faint traces of what is believed to be the earliest written Welsh, dating probably from the 7th century. This important historic monument is lucky to be here: it was rescued from a farmer's field in which it was reduced to the role of a common gatepost. The little church at Llanegryn, four miles north-east of Tywyn, contains one of Wales's most magnificent rood screens, carved in late medieval times.

TYWYN is on the A493, 19 miles south-west of Dolgellau.

Lleyn & Anglesey

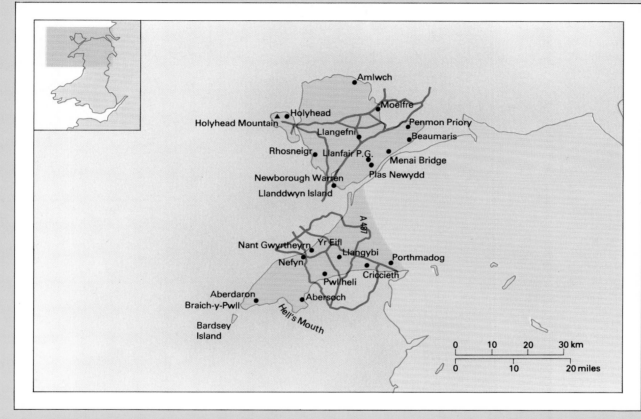

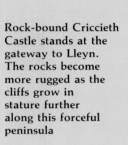

Rock-bound Criccieth Castle stands at the gateway to Lleyn. The rocks become more rugged as the cliffs grow in stature further along this forceful peninsula

ONE IS A RUGGED peninsula, the other a low-lying island. Yet they are the most compatible of neighbours. Both are outposts of North-west Wales, blocked off by Snowdonia. And both are more than grateful to that mountain barrier, for it keeps them away from the mainstream — a distance underlined by Lleyn's isolated, out-on-a-limb location and Anglesey's island status.

The coastlines of both — amounting to around 200 miles in all — are also protected as official 'Areas of Outstanding Natural Beauty'. Lleyn's beauty is a savage, untamed one. Wales's definitive peninsula, it drives dramatically south-westwards into the sea for 24 miles. There is something strongly Celtic about its scattered, whitewashed cottages,

skimpy field-patterns, wind-tangled hedgerows, plunging cliffs and rock-bound shores. In common with Brittany's Finistère and Eire's Kerry, west is the dominant point on the compass.

Anglesey's natural beauty is not nearly as intimidating. This flat island is fringed by a sometimes sandy, sometimes rocky coastline that is positively benign in comparison to its neighbour. The island, known as *Ynys Mon* in Welsh, was a hub of civilization in ancient times and revered as *Mon Mam Cymru* ('The Mother of Wales') because of its fertile farmlands, once the source of so much grain — and also, possibly, due to its importance as a stronghold of Celtic culture before the coming of the Romans.

ABERDARON AND ABERSOCH
Gwynedd

It is possibly provocative, even invidious, to treat these two coastal settlements together, for they are as different as chalk and cheese. Aberdaron, in the remote far west of Lleyn, has until now managed to stand apart from the commercialism and compromises of the outside world.

Overwhelmingly Welsh-speaking and happy to remain so, this little community of stone and lime-washed dwellings crowds into a shallow valley beside a long beach, sheltered from the worst excesses of westerly winds and waves by a cliff-bound headland. Aberdaron, resilient and lonely, almost says something about the Welsh character. The abiding image that lingers in the mind is not of Aberdaron's elemental natural beauty but of its cemetery above the sands which manages to express the Welsh inclination towards bitter-sweet melancholy.

Abersoch is altogether far less weighty and pensive in mood and character. This is where the affluent boating-people congregate. Abersoch harbour, east-facing and sheltered, has developed over the years into a lively sailing and yachting centre as well as a popular little seaside resort.

ABERDARON is at the end of the B4413, approximately 28 miles south-west of Porthmadog. Abersoch, accessible by the A499, is about 19 miles from Porthmadog.

AMLWCH
Gwynedd

This coastal town, in the far north of Anglesey, was the world's busiest copper exporting port in the late 18th century. Amlwch, today a small,

Grey headstones and green headlands gaze down onto the sparse little community at Aberdaron

quite ordinary little place, hardly looks the part. All is explained on its southern approaches, which are dominated by a scarred moonscape. This is Parys Mountain — or, at least, what is left of it after its heyday as Europe's largest copper mining site.

Amlwch, a small-scale seaside and market town, is a good base from which to explore the ruggedly beautiful north Anglesey coast. Neighbouring Bull Bay is popular with cliff walkers and swimmers. Elsewhere, most roads maintain a wary distance from a shoreline which can only properly be explored on foot.

Some of the oldest geological rock formations in the world are to be found along this coast. Evidence of man's influence is scant indeed — apart from one massive exception. Amidst the superb scenic beauty of Wylfa Head, six miles west of Amlwch, a huge nuclear power station has been built. Guided tours are available around a vast, grey complex which is said to be the largest of its kind in the world.

AMLWCH, at the junction of the A5025 and B5111, is 17 miles north-west of Menai Bridge.

BEAUMARIS
Gwynedd

Beaumaris Castle was the final, and in some respects the finest, of the Edwardian fortresses to be built in North Wales. Although the largest of Edward I's castles, it lacks the intimidating presence of its sisters at Conwy and Caernarfon simply because it was never properly finished. Beaumaris comes into its own in pure architectural terms. On the strength of its geometric symmetry, this castle is regarded as the most perfect example of a concentrically planned medieval fortress in Britain.

The castle, dating from 1295, spreads itself out, large, looming and low, in beautiful surroundings at the edge of the town. Those who built it must also have been impressed with its location, giving it the French name of *Beau Marais* ('Beautiful Marsh').

Ring after ring of stone defences radiate outwards from a central core, the whole system presenting a daunting challenge to any would-be attacker. Like most of Edward's castles, Beaumaris was accessible from the sea. The old tidal channel to the Menai Strait has long since disappeared, though the castle's dock — still water-filled, as is part of the moat — survives by the heavily fortified 'Gate Next the Sea', one of the 14 obstacles separating attackers from the inner ward.

Beaumaris itself is a most pleasant seaside town and popular sailing centre, graced with some fine Georgian buildings. There is nothing particularly pleasant about the grimly fascinating Beaumaris Gaol, a Victorian prison, virtually unaltered since its construction in 1829 and now open to visitors.

🚗 *BEAUMARIS, at the junction of the A545 and B5109, is 4 miles northeast of Menai Bridge.*

BRAICH-Y-PWLL AND BARDSEY ISLAND
Gwynedd

Standing on the wind-tossed headland of Braich-y-Pwll contemplating the stormy, dangerous waters of Bardsey Sound, one begins to understand how the medieval pilgrim must have felt. Three pilgrimages to Bardsey, the 'Isle of 20,000 Saints' on which a monastic community had been founded way back in A.D. 615, equalled one to Rome.

The difficulties began when the poor pilgrim, after an undemanding passage along the Lleyn Peninsula, came to face the prospect of crossing the waters to Bardsey, in Welsh *Ynys Enlli*, the 'Isle of the currents' or 'Tide-race island'. Pilgrims braved the hazardous two-mile stretch of Bardsey Sound only after offering prayers for safe passage at the headland Church of St Mary's, the ruins of which can still be made out amongst Braich-y-Pwll's bracken-covered slopes.

Some of the finest coastal views in Britain can be enjoyed from the 524-ft summit of Braich-y-Pwll, the 'Land's End of North Wales'. The land ends very abruptly indeed, plunging down from the viewpoint onto a curtain of jagged sea-cliffs.

Bardsey Sound still causes problems. The island, now privately owned by an environmental trust, is regularly cut off for days.

🚗 *BRAICH-Y-PWLL (a steep road winds its way right to the summit) is accessible by minor road off the B4413, 2½ miles south-west of Aberdaron.*

Beaumaris Castle's stunted, incomplete defences overlook the Menai Strait

CRICCIETH
Gwynedd

Criccieth's castle really looks as though it has been in the wars. Appearances are not deceptive. The castle's ruined walls and ragged towers (there are even scorchmarks to be seen here) testify to an action-packed past. Dating from around 1230, this stronghold has, in its time, been in both Welsh and English hands. The *coup de grâce* was delivered in 1404, when the castle was sacked and burnt by Welsh leader Owain Glyndwr, never to recover.

The castle sits on top of the grassy headland which separates Criccieth's twin beaches. As a seaside resort, Criccieth is deliberately unspectacular, preferring the role of a staid, appealingly traditional Welsh watering place not too concerned with fashion or passing fads.

The village of Llanystumdwy, two miles to the west, was the boyhood home of that charismatic political figure, Liberal M.P. and Prime Minister, David Lloyd George.

The 'Welsh Wizard', although born in Manchester (in 1863), was brought up from 1864 to 1880 in this quiet little village. A slate plaque identifies his humble home, a terraced cottage which stands a few doors from a museum dedicated to his memory. Lloyd George died in 1945 and is buried at Llanystumdwy.

CRICCIETH, at the junction of the A497 and B4411, is 4 miles west of Porthmadog.

HELL'S MOUTH
Gwynedd

Nineteenth-century sailors were in no doubt that this rock-bound bay, between Aberdaron and Abersoch, justified its name. Hell's Mouth (its Welsh name of Porth Neigwl is not a translation) takes a giant-sized bite out of Lleyn's south-western tip. On a sunny, still day, this empty four-mile-long bay looks benign enough. But its exposed waters are deceptive and volatile, with a savage reputation as a graveyard for many a vessel.

One of its most famous wrecks was that of *The Twelve Apostles* in 1898. In keeping with local legends, the ship was drawn siren-like to her doom despite every effort made by the crew to change course.

The densely wooded hillside above the north-western corner of the bay conceals Plas-yn-Rhiw (a National Trust property). This small manor house, medieval in origin with Tudor and Georgian additions, has a wonderfully profuse garden in which shrubs, trees, rhododenrons, azaleas and sub-tropical species flourish in apparent abandon.

HELL'S MOUTH, about 21 miles south-west of Porthmadog, is accessible by minor road between Abersoch and Aberdaron.

HOLYHEAD AND HOLYHEAD MOUNTAIN
Gwynedd

This busy port and holiday centre stands on an island-off-an-island. Holyhead Island is connected to the Isle of Anglesey by two road bridges and a rail link. All routes seem to lead to Holyhead. With the completion of the London to Holyhead road — now the A5 — by Thomas Telford in the early 19th century, a port grew up here serving the Irish cross-channel route (ferries still sail to Dun Laoghaire, near Dublin).

Nineteenth-century engineers were by no means the first to appreciate Holyhead's fine harbour. The Romans constructed a rectangular fort, *Caer Gybi*, here, probably as a base for a small naval flotilla which protected the Welsh coast from Irish raiders.

Caer Gybi ('Cybi's Fort') takes its name from the 6th-century saint who settled within its abandoned walls. These walls, which survive to reasonable height and display the 'herringbone masonry' typical of the late Roman period, now surround the Church of St Cybi in the centre of Holyhead.

The Holyhead Mountain Hut Circles, in the rugged terrain west of the town, are the remnants of a large native farming settlement that existed here in Roman times. The slopes are scattered with circular hut foundations, some of which retain their original hearths and slab beds.

Caer y Twr Hill Fort stands right on the 720-ft summit of the mountain, overlooking Holyhead Bay and the Irish Sea. The climb is well worth it, not only for the views. This Iron Age stronghold was later improved by the Romans, who made good use of the site as a look-out point. Remnants from those far-off days have not entirely disappeared, for Caer y Twr still retains its sentry walk amongst well laid out remains.

On the far west of the island, mountain meets sea at the South Stack lighthouse. Over 400 steps zig-zag down the cliffs to the lighthouse, perched on a rock amongst magnificent coastal scenery. The cliffs here (an R.S.P.B. reserve) are noted for their colonies of sea-birds, especially guillemots, razorbills and puffins, a birdwatcher's paradise.

HOLYHEAD, accessible by the A5 or B4545, is 17 miles north-west of Menai Bridge.

A dizzy staircase leads across to South Stack lighthouse, guardian of the western approach to Holyhead Island

LLANFAIR P.G.
Gwynedd

It is quite impossible for any Welsh travel book to get away without listing Llanfair P.G.'s name in its full glory. So here goes: - Llanfairpwllgwyngyllgogerychwyrn-drobwllllantysiliogogogoch. The locals have long since abbreviated it to a more manageable Llanfair P.G. Those fascinated by this, the longest — and most prosaic — place-name in the world, will want to know that it

means 'St Mary's (Church) by the white aspen over the whirlpool and St Tysilio's (Church) by the red cave'. Visitors flock here to have their photographs taken next to the name (bring a wide-angled camera) which appears in its full unpronounceable glory on the railway station and the frontages of one or two of the local businesses.

In fields just over one mile southwest of the village lies one of Anglesey's — and Britain's — most evocative prehistoric sites. A narrow

stone doorway set into a round, grass-covered mound leads through a cramped underground passage into the central tomb of Bryn Celli Ddu, a burial chamber built as a site of pagan ritual around 3000 to 3500 B.C. Along with Barclodiad y Gawres (see Rhosneigr entry), this tomb is one of the few in Britain that revealed evidence of prehistoric rock art when excavated.

◣ *LLANFAIR P.G., at the junction of the A5, A4080, and B5420 is 1½ miles west of Menai Bridge.*

LLANGEFNI
Gwynedd

Inland Anglesey is at its flattest and most featureless around centrally located Llangefni. The surroundings do little to enhance the appeal of a town with no great deal of character — as one would expect of a place mainly notable as the administrative 'capital' of the island.

Anglesey's farmlands, at one time 'the granary of Wales', have now switched from arable to pastoral use.

A prehistoric graveyard. In the megalithic age, man buried his dead in communal chambers such as Bryn Celli Ddu

Llangefni is at its most animated in its role as a busy market centre when the farmers get together here for the livestock sales every Wednesday and Thursday.

The Bodeilio Weaving Centre at Talwrn, a mile or so north-east of Llangefni, is well worth a detour. Beautifully renovated farm buildings house a museum and crafts gallery that, with the assistance of practical demonstrations, trace the history of early textile production with particular emphasis on handweaving.

LLANGEFNI, at the junction of the A5114, B5109, B5110 and B5111, is approximately 8 miles north-west of Menai Bridge.

LLANGYBI
Gwynedd

Llangybi, in the middle of nowhere in particular, is not the sort of place that immediately catches the eye. The trip along Lleyn's back lanes is justified by the presence here of an enchanting holy well. The claimed curative powers of Ffynnon Gybi, St Cybi's Well, could almost come from the silence and simplicity of this lovely site, traditionally associated with the 6th-century saint who travelled widely throughout Wales.

A short walk past the village church leads down into a secluded little valley and the ruins of a rough stone cottage and walls. The latter enclose the cool waters of the well, an evocative place of pilgrimage for hundreds of years.

LLANGYBI, on a minor road 6 miles north-east of Pwllheli, is most easily accessible off the A499.

Engineer and bridge-builder Thomas Telford excelled himself when faced with the challenge of crossing the Menai Strait

MENAI BRIDGE
Gwynedd

This little Isle of Angelsey town lives under the elegant shadow of its famous road bridge, constructed by that great engineer Thomas Telford in the 1820s. Telford's bridge — the world's first iron suspension bridge — was the last link in the London to Holyhead (and Dublin) route. One thousand feet long, with a main span of 579 ft, it cleverly takes advantage of a narrow channel where the waters of the Menai Strait curl around a wooded promontory.

The symmetrical bridge blends well with the natural beauty of its surroundings. As an exercise in design and decoration, it stands as an interesting comparison to the recent Britannia Road Bridge, built just to the west to relieve the traffic congestion inevitably experienced when the Menai Bridge's narrow portals were the only entry and exit points to the Isle of Anglesey.

MENAI BRIDGE, near the junction of the A5, A545, and A5025, is 8 miles north-east of Caernarfon.

MOELFRE
Gwynedd

On the east coast of Anglesey, this charming little village with its small harbour, pebble beach and lifeboat station looks distinctly Cornish in character. Those in search of a proper beach must journey across the headland to Traeth Lligwy (Lligwy Bay), a beautiful and expansive stretch of sands.

A clutch of memorable historic sites spanning over 4000 years are grouped together amongst fields and woodlands close to the sea. Lligwy Cromlech is colossal. A weather-beaten 28-ton capstone rests on a series of low upright stone supports, the entire framework of this neolithic (New Stone Age) burial chamber exposed to the skies. Originally, the cromlech would have been covered by a large cairn to create an underground vault in which prehistoric farmers laid their dead. Excavations in 1908 unearthed the bones of 30 people, together with examples of Neolithic and early Bronze Age pottery.

A short walk into the woods leads to an extensive collection of stones which, even on first impressions, obviously have a certain order to them. Closer inspection reveals the plan of an ancient village known as Din Lligwy. Visible remains — stout stone walls enclosing a group of huts still standing six feet high in places — probably relate to the Roman period, though the village is thought to date from nearly 3000 years ago.

The story of man's influence on this remote hillside continues at Capel Lligwy, a ruined 12th-century chapel partly restored in the 14th and 16th centuries.

MOELFRE, accessible by the A5025 and A5108, is 10 miles north of Menai Bridge.

NANT GWYRTHEYRN
Gwynedd

According to legend, Vortigen, the 5th-century king said to have invited the Saxons to Britain, paid for his deed by becoming a fugitive and dying in this 'gloomy hollow' of a valley. Nant Gwyrtheyrn, a shadowy, inaccessible vale below the Yr Eifl mountains and just off the saints' route to Bardsey Island, is certainly one of the most eerie places on Lleyn, a location where landscape fits legend perfectly.

Nant Gwyrtheyrn's highly charged atmosphere does not diminish when the valley opens out to the sea and a few rows of cottages come into view. This is the 'ghost village' of Porth-y-nant, finally abandoned in the 1950s after the closure of the quarries that had supplied its lifeblood.

One can understand why the villagers left. Supplies to this isolated settlement had to be brought in by sea. The only way down to this bleak but hauntingly beautiful spot is by foot, along a steep path cut into the slopes of Nant Gwyrtheyrn. New life is now being injected into Porth-y-nant. Some of the derelict dwellings have been renovated for use as a Welsh language studies centre.

NANT GWYRTHEYRN and Porth-y-nant are accessible by foot-path from a car park 1 mile north of Llithfaen, a village on the B4417 16 miles south-west of Caernarfon.

NEFYN
Gwynedd

Nefyn and its neighbouring bays are a classic case of what might have been. This area would have changed beyond recognition had an ambitious 19th-century plan come to fruition. The scheme involved turning Porth Dinllaen — a few miles to the west

A curving bay on the Lleyn Peninsula at Nefyn

and the only safe anchorage on this stretch of coast — into a full-scale cross-channel port serving the London to Dublin route.

Similar plans for Holyhead found greater favour, leaving the bay of Porth Dinllaen untouched and pretty as a picture. A cluster of whitewashed cottages huddle beneath a protective headland at the end of a perfect crescent of sands, a scene made doubly welcoming by its interruption of the stark, forbidding cliff scenery typical of Lleyn's north-facing coastline.

Porth Nefyn, next door, is a smaller version of its neighbour. The excellent beach here has been in-strumental in the development of Nefyn as a popular little seaside resort, the only one along this stretch of the peninsula.

Breaches in the cliffs along northern Lleyn are indeed infrequent. Sandy beaches are something of a rarity, one of the few being Porth Oer, about 12 miles south-west of Nefyn. This little bay is perhaps better known as 'Whistling Sands', thus named because its sand granules are supposed to whistle or squeak underfoot.

NEFYN, where the A497 meets the B4417, is 19 miles south-west of Caernarfon.

Beautiful Llanddwyn on the Isle of Anglesey, capped by a stubby little lighthouse

NEWBOROUGH WARREN AND LLANDDWYN ISLAND
Gwynedd

Anglesey's south-western extremity is a strange combination of dunelands, beaches, pine forests, salt marsh and sea-rocks, capped by an isolated promontory lighthouse. The vast expanses of deserted dunes at the nature reserve of Newborough Warren are a haven for a wide variety of wild flowers and fauna. Newborough Forest, next door, is a large conifer plantation stretching right down to the lonely sands along Llanddwyn Bay.

From the forest car park, a path leads across to Llanddwyn Island, a rocky, narrow promontory cut off only at high tide. Its ruined church is dedicated to St Dwynwen, a 5th-century saint who lived here. A stubby little lighthouse overlooks much more than the western approach to the Menai Strait. It commands truly splendid views down the long arm of the Lleyn Peninsula and up into the gritty purple heights of Snowdonia.

THIS AREA is accessible by minor road leading south-west from Newborough, a village on the A4080 10 miles south-west of Menai Bridge.

PENMON PRIORY
Gwynedd

The Augustinian Priory of Penmon, near the eastern tip of Anglesey and approach to the Menai Strait, is a site of great antiquity. It was probably founded in the 6th century by St Cynlas, who subsequently passed it on to his brother, St Seiriol. As we see it now, Penmon — much raided by the marauding Vikings during the Dark Ages — dates mainly from the 12th and 13th centuries.

A ruined priory range, a large building with cellar, refectory and

Holiday craft in Porthmadog harbour today occupy berths previously used by slate traders

dormitory, stands right next to a medieval place of worship, still in use as the parish church. A holy well and dovecot, both located nearby, complete the scene. The latter, built c.1600 with a domed stone roof which holds nearly 1000 birds, is particularly impressive. From Penmon, it is only a short drive to Penmon Point on the far east of Anglesey which overlooks Puffin Island, another early Christian settlement.

🚗 *PENMON is accessible by the B5109 and minor road, 4 miles northeast of Beaumaris.*

PLAS NEWYDD
Gwynedd

The wooden leg used by the 1st Marquess of Anglesey is one of the more unorthodox relics on view in this splendid house located on the banks of the Menai Strait. 'The Anglesey leg', one of the first articulated artificial limbs to be invented, was used by the Marquess after he was dismembered in the Battle of Waterloo. The replacement now stands, amongst other memorabilia, in the Cavalry Museum.

Plas Newydd, a National Trust property, is more conventionally famous for its Rex Whistler Room which contains a wall painting that puts cinemascope to shame. Painted by Whistler between 1936 and 1940, this 58-ft canvas depicts with great flourish a mountain-backed coastline — in no way representational but surely an echo of the view across the Menai Strait to Snowdonia — on which imaginary buildings straight out of renaissance Italy bask in warm southern sunshine. Whistler's mural is considered to be the finest wall painting in any country house in Britain.

Five-hundred-year-old Plas Newydd ('The New Place') hardly lives up to its name. As it stands now, though, the house — an elegant Georgian Gothick one and largely the work of architect James Wyatt — dates from the late 18th century. It stands amongst grassy slopes, woodlands and gardens in a 169-acre estate leading down to the banks of the Menai Strait.

🚗 *PLAS NEWYDD is accessible off the A4080, 3 miles south-west of Menai Bridge.*

PORTHMADOG
Gwynedd

One hundred years ago, Porthmadog's harbourside would have looked very different. Tall-masted brigs, ketches and schooners then lined its quay, waiting to take on cargoes of fine Welsh slate for shipment to other parts of Britain and overseas.

Sleek yachts and holiday craft have now taken over, and a swish, marina-style housing complex shares the harbour with the old, stone-built wharfside warehouses. Nevertheless, Porthmadog's links with the past largely define the present, especially at the Ffestiniog Railway, arguably the most attractive of the many narrow-gauge 'Great Little Trains of Wales'.

The Ffestiniog was built in 1836 to carry slate from the caverns at Blaenau Ffestiniog to Porthmadog harbour. Nowadays, it transports tourists along a truly delightful and scenic route that begins on the water's edge and ends deep in the mountains, 12 miles distant.

One of the most memorable sections of line comes immediately after the Porthmadog terminus, where the railway crosses the tidal sweep of

Traeth Bach — the confluence of the Glaslyn and Dwyryd estuaries — on a mile-long embankment known locally as The Cob. This was built by William Madocks (1773-1828), a dynamic entrepreneur responsible for shaping much of Porthmadog's past.

Madocks makes an appearance on a huge and heroic wall mural that, as well as depicting the port's history, attracts the summer visitors to the site of Porthmadog Pottery. More history resides along the quay at an unusual maritime museum that is part afloat, part on terra firma. The main 'exhibit' is the *S.S. Garlandstone*, an old sailing ketch moored next to the museum's quayside exhibition hall.

A second enthusiasts' railway is also based at Porthmadog. It is early days yet, though, for the Welsh Highland Railway, which currently runs for only a short distance towards its eventual goal, the Aberglaslyn Pass.

PORTHMADOG is on the A497, 21 miles south-east of Caernarfon.

PWLLHELI
Gwynedd

All that the Victorian guidebooks — not noted for their reticent descriptions — could find to say about Pwllheli was that 'the staple delicacies of the neighbourhood — fried sole and duck — may be most comfortably discussed in its excellent hotels'. Faint praise indeed for a place, admittedly not in the mainstream of Welsh tourism, which boasts an excellent, undeservedly unpatronized beach and fine, sheltered harbour.

Much-mispronounced Pwllheli, the main market town for the area, is also conveniently situated for those wishing to explore the Lleyn Peninsula. Its station is the end of the line for the Cambrian Coast railway, one

Blaenau Ffestiniog slate, transported to Porthmadog, was the original payload on the Ffestiniog Railway

of British Rail's most scenic services, which runs along Tremadog and Cardigan Bays all the way to Aberystwyth.

Pennarth Fawr, on a minor road four miles to the north-east (and signposted off the A497), is a real rarity: an early 15th-century stone-built hall house, one of the few surviving in Wales.

🚗 *PWLLHELI, at the junction of the A497 and A499, is 12 miles west of Porthmadog and 21 miles south-west of Caernarfon on the A499.*

RHOSNEIGR
Gwynedd

A lovely sweep of breezy sands, string of bays and acres of dunes attract visitors to this small resort on Anglesey's west coast. Rhosneigr is almost surrounded by water — saltwater to the west, and the large freshwater lake of Llyn Maelog just inland behind the houses.

The headland of Porth Trecastell, one-and-a-half miles to the south, is a prehistoric graveyard. Barclodiad y Gawres ('The Giantess's Apronful') is one of the most significant of the many ancient burial chambers on the island. Five of its stones are decorated with carved patterns, rare examples of prehistoric tomb art. Unlike most of its stark, bare-stoned contemporaries, Barclodiad y Gawres has been extensively restored and covered over once more. A 20-ft-long passageway leads to a renovated, cross-shaped central chamber which, when excavated in the 1950s, revealed cremated human bones.

Today, one would hardly associate royal splendour and courtly life with the village of Aberffraw, four miles south-east of Rhosneigr. Yet up until the 13th-century conquest of Wales by Edward I, this inconspicuous place served as the seat of government of the Welsh princes.

🚗 *RHOSNEIGR, on the A4080, is approximately 16 miles west of Menai Bridge.*

YR EIFL
Gwynedd

The Yr Eifl mountains (anglicized to 'The Rivals') are a trio of peaks rising to 1850 ft, the highest point on Lleyn. They look as though they should be even higher, for their altitude is magnified by their location, right next to the sea. From the shores around Trefor they soar up almost vertically from the ocean as a massive buttress of land.

Lleyn is littered with prehistoric remains, none finer than those on Yr Eifl. Iron Age man, always drawn to high ground, settled amongst the rock and boulder-strewn eastern summit. His encampment, known as Tre'r Ceiri ('The Town of the Giants'), is very well preserved indeed. This was much more than a simple hill fort. Wall defences — still standing 13 ft high in places — enclose a complete township of around 150 huts which was lived in up until the time of the Roman occupation of Wales.

🚗 *YR EIFL lies between Llanaelhaearn and Llithfaen along Lleyn's north-facing coast, about 16 miles south-west of Caernarfon.*

Seascape at Porth Trecastell, a prehistoric graveyard near Rhosneigr, Anglesey. Many ancient burial chambers can be found on the island

Myths and Legends

Wales's misty mountains, gloomy defiles and haunting hillsides have been a potent breeding ground for myths and legends since the times when tales were passed on, word-of-mouth, from fireside to fireside; aided and abetted, no doubt, by the Welsh gift for storytelling.

Celtic folk tales, their roots thousands of years old, would have been told in the courts of the Welsh princes. They were written for the first time in manuscript form in the early 14th century. The collection became known as the *Mabinogion*, an everyday story of heroism and murder, romance and treachery, magic and the mutation of man to beast in the Celtic Wales of yesterday.

The action in this picaresque collection took place throughout the country, especially in Pembrokeshire, the *Mabinogion's Gwlad hud a lledrith* ('The land of magic and enchantment').

North Wales is evoked powerfully in the 'Dream of Mascen Wledig' who, on coming to Caernarfon, 'could see a great castle, the fairest that mortal had ever seen'. In this case, folklore may well have been founded in fact, for Mascen was Magnus Maximus, the Roman emperor who travelled to his fort at Segontium, alias Caernarfon.

Other tales tax the belief of even the most credulous. Serpents appear from the waves and victims are swallowed by witches to be re-born omniscient babies. Wales, along with the rest of Britain, also claims its cast-iron Arthurian connections. Those in search of the elusive

Devil's Bridge has legendary connections with Satan

Camelot need look no further than Caerleon, quite obviously his court because it was 'the most accessible place in his dominions'. Merlin's Oak in Carmarthen and a pile of 'Arthur's Stones' scattered across Wales either confirm or contradict the legend — depending upon which side of the fence you happen to stand.

Mythology is by no means confined to the *Mabinogion*. Places all over Wales, such as Devil's Bridge, have their own local tales to tell. Lakes have always provided a powerful stimulus to story-telling, typical of which is the tale of the maiden who emerges from the waters to marry the farmer only to vanish after some chance misunderstanding (as at Llyn-y-Fan-Fach in the Brecon Beacons).

Not even Christopher Columbus is safe from such speculations. The Welsh, of course, were responsible for discovering America thanks to Prince Madoc (1150-80) who set sail from North Wales with ten ships. The fact that he was never seen again might confirm or contradict the legend . . .

MAY HEAV'N PROTECT OUR HOME FROM FLAME,
OR HURT OR HARM OF VARIOUS NAME!
AND MAY NO EVIL LUCK BETIDE
TO ANY WHO THEREIN ABIDE!
AS ALSO WHO THEIR HOMES HAVE FOUND
ON ANY ACRE OF IT'S GROUND,
OR WHO FROM HOMES BEYOND IT'S GATE
BESTOW THEIR TOIL ON THIS ESTATE!

—P.Y.

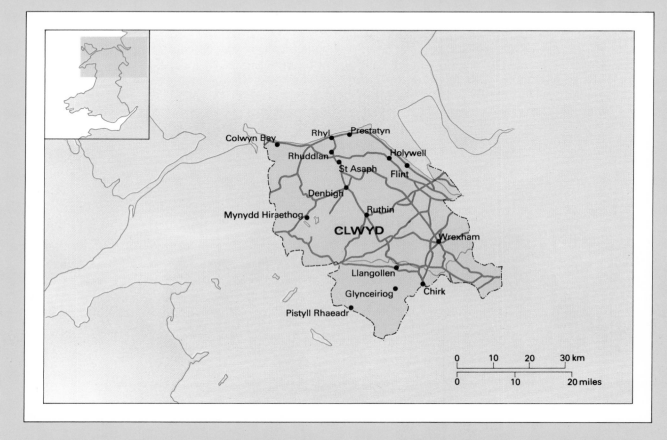

A scene from the
servant's quarters
at Erddig Hall, part
of the social history
of Wales

THE COUNTY OF CLWYD, a geographically convenient entity, fits the north-east corner of Wales like a glove. Two of its main features are the eponymous Vale of Clwyd and Clwydian Hills.

Clwyd is a mixed bag of influences. There are one or two large towns here, a counterpoint to delightful medieval settlements such as Ruthin and Denbigh, full of architectural heritage. Fertile vales, where the farming is rich and productive, shelter beneath inviolate hill country in which sheep farmers maintain a hold that is no more than tenuous. Wild moorland subsides to settled coastline in the north, a sandy strip of seashore which meets the Dee estuary at the Point of Ayr.

The Clwydian Hills, a natural east-west barrier, rise to 1817 ft at Moel Famau above a pastoral valley watered by the River Clwyd. Further west the uplands between the Vales of Clwyd and Conwy are filled with the moody moors, huge lakes and forests of Mynydd Hiraethog.

Mynydd Hiraethog dips down to the sea along a shoreline of familiar resorts which continue to serve as mainstays of the traditional holiday trade. An entirely different seascape resides beyond the Point of Ayr, where many species of wading birds breed amongst empty tidal sands.

South of Hiraethog, the typical Welsh landscape of green valleys and remote mountains once more takes over. Beyond the lovely Vale of Llangollen, the Berwyn Mountains rise to a 2713-ft high point, embracing within their folds Pistyll Rhaeadr, the loftiest waterfall in Wales.

CHIRK
Clwyd

Chirk is the home of a magnificent National Trust property. Chirk Castle, one mile west of the little town, is a rare example of an austere medieval stronghold that has evolved, over the years, into a sumptuous stately home.

The secret of Chirk's success lies in its longevity. Amongst North Wales's many fortresses, this castle is unique in having been occupied continuously from medieval times to the present day. Chirk began life in the late 13th century as a castle put up to consolidate Edward I's hold on Wales. It was bought in 1595 by Sir Thomas Myddleton, a merchant adventurer who sailed with Sir Walter Raleigh, and has been the home of the Myddleton family ever since.

Inevitably, Chirk has seen much alteration — its interiors, for example, are mostly 17th, 18th and 19th century. The incongruity of an erstwhile medieval fort surrounded by landscaped gardens and a splendid 468-acre park is not lost on the visitor.

Within its solid walls, more splendour reigns. Chirk really came of age in the 1760s, when the series of Neo-Classical state rooms were created. Along with the Neo-Gothic additions of the 19th century — the oak panelled entrance hall is particularly fine — these luxuriously furnished and decorated rooms represent Chirk's greatest glories.

Despite such opulence, many visitors come to Chirk just to see the gates. Made by the Davies brothers of Bersham, near Wrexham, in 1719-21, they are an unrivalled achievement, a work of art executed in iron to an impossibly delicate and ornate design, and finished in black and gold.

Castle is separated from town by the Shropshire Union Canal and railway. The former spans the valley

Faint traces of military authority linger as reminders that the stately home of Chirk originated as a border stronghold

at the foot of Chirk on a fine Thomas Telford aqueduct of the late 18th century, an engineering feat imitated in 1848 by its neighbouring railway viaduct.

🚗 CHIRK, at the junction of the A483 and B4500, is 10 miles south of Wrexham.

COLWYN BAY
Clwyd

It is interesting — and often wildly amusing — to read what the old guidebooks have to say about the Welsh seaside resorts. Colwyn Bay's climate, according to one early tome, is 'said to resemble that of the Riviera, without the intense heat, or that of Japan, without the rain'.

Quite how many Victorian tourists were able to travel to the Orient — or the Mediterranean for that matter — to verify this claim is not known. Today's visitors to this cheerful and spacious resort bring with them a less optimistic view of British weather, which assumes tangible form in the shape of the inevitable plastic mac.

Colwyn Bay, along with Llandudno, Rhyl and Prestatyn, make up North Wales's quartet of long-established traditional seaside resorts. Apart from the predictable features of promenade, beach and rorty amusements, it boasts a fine pier — an increasingly cherished piece of seaside architecture, and rightly so — and a well laid out Mountain Zoo in the wooded hillsides high above the resort.

🚗 COLWYN BAY is accessible off the A55 approximately 39 miles west of Chester.

DENBIGH
Clwyd

Denbigh's hilltop castle, conspicuous against its blackcloth of the Clwydian Hills, tends to capture the limelight — to the detriment of another medieval feature, a well preserved but largely ignored series of town walls, which plunge and climb around this hilly, complicated old settlement in an almost complete circuit.

Both castle and walls occupy the centre stage of Welsh history. Denbigh was a nucleus of Welsh resistance to the English invasion of the late 13th century. By 1282 it had fallen into the hands of Henry de Lacy, cohort of the English king, Edward I. Work then began on constructing the castle, on the site of the former Welsh native stronghold.

Denbigh's ruinous state is hardly surprising, considering its turbulent past. Captured by the Welsh in 1294 and later retaken, it was also involved in the Owain Glyndwr uprising of the 15th century, the Wars of the Roses and the Civil War. Its strongest feature is undoubtedly the Great Gatehouse, a huge triangular defence with a trio of interlinked octagonal towers. Look out for the niche which contains a statue, probably that of Edward I.

Denbigh Friary, on the eastern outskirts of town, is a small and simple 14th-century monastic house with a chequered history.

🚗 DENBIGH, between Ruthin and Rhyl, is at the junction of the A525 and A543.

FLINT
Clwyd

Do not avoid this admittedly very ordinary Deeside town. Flint comes to life for the visitor only because of its castle, historically and symbolically most significant as the first of Edward I's chain of mighty 13th-century fortresses built in North Wales to subdue and contain the unruly Welsh.

Urban development has not been kind to Flint Castle. Its once magisterial position has been destroyed by the modern town — indeed, it is quite easy to miss completely. The castle, dating from 1277, is worth seeking out if only for its Great Tower, or donjon, a large, isolated round tower, set apart as a last defence, looking out to sea.

Flint Castle, thanks to William Shakespeare's efforts in his third act of Richard II, is forever remembered as the setting for the final capture of Richard in 1399.

🚗 FLINT, at the junction of the A548 and A5119, is about 15 miles north-west of Wrexham.

Amongst Chirk's most remarkable features are the Davies brothers' wrought iron entrance gates

GLYNCEIRIOG
Clwyd

Off-the-beaten-track Glynceiriog hides itself in a great bend in the Ceiriog Valley. Motorists unafraid of shudderingly steep mountain roads should do as the locals do and take the short cut (as opposed to the long way around via Chirk) to Llangollen: an as-the-crow-flies route which climbs out of the village and across a shoulder of the Berwyn Mountains before dropping into the Vale of Dee.

Before leaving this secluded settlement, visitors should experience something of its industrial past. Records show that slate was quarried here as early as the 9th century, though the heaps of spoil from the old mines are now hidden by trees and wild flowers.

The old Chwarel Wynne slate cavern, evocatively advertised as 'the lost cavern of Glynceiriog', has found a new role for itself since reopening for guided tours in the 1970s. In comparison to the vast underground workings elsewhere in North Wales — especially at Blaenau Ffestiniog, the former 'slate capital' — this cavern is quite small: in its heyday at the turn of the century, it only employed 77 men. Chwarel Wynne's modest size and relative obscurity (Blaenau Ffestiniog's well publicised caverns can become very busy in summer) work to its advantage, visitors benefitting from a more personal conducted tour as they walk down into the first and second-level chambers of the mine.

GLYNCEIRIOG, at the junction of the B4500 and B4579, is 7 miles west of Chirk.

St Winifride's Well. A somewhat sanctimonious Dr Johnson criticised its bathing arrangements

HOLYWELL
Clwyd

This small township owes its name and fame to St Winifride's Well, variously described as one of Wales's 'Seven Wonders' and — more aptly, perhaps — the 'Lourdes of Wales'. Possibly the most famous healing well in Britain, St Winifride's dates from the 7th century when, according to a bloody Celtic folk tale recorded in a book printed by William Caxton in 1485, poor Winifride's head 'was cut off and touchyd the ground (where) sprang up a welle of spryngyng water . . . which heleth al langours . . .'

The shrine has now been a place of pilgrimage for well over 1000 years. Services are still held at the elaborate Well Chapel, built over the waters in perpendicular Gothic style in the late 15th century. A disapproving Dr Johnson noted in 1774 that 'the bath is completely and indecently open: a woman bathed while we all looked on.'

The shallow vale leading for over a mile from the town to the Dee estuary has in recent years been designated the Greenfield Valley Heritage Park. Two hundred years ago, this now tranquil stretch of lakeside and woodland walks was a hive of industrial activity. A number of old buildings survive from the times when textiles, copper and brass were produced here in abundance. The estuary end of the valley is marked by the ruins of Basingwerk Abbey, a monastery founded in 1131 by the French Savignac order and later taken over by the sheep-rearing Cistercians.

The Grange Cavern Military Museum is worth visiting for the setting alone: a chilly, gloomy two-and-a-half acre cavern, hollowed out of the hillside above Holywell, which contains over 70 military vehicles including tanks, jeeps and artillery. With such a distinct dearth of subterranean competitors, no one can possibly doubt its claim to the title of 'the world's largest underground military museum'.

HOLYWELL is at the junction of the A55, A5026 and B5121, approximately 19 miles north-west of Wrexham.

LLANGOLLEN
Clwyd

Llangollen is a little town with a big personality. Its name has been spread worldwide thanks to the prestigious International Musical Eisteddfod held here each July. Unlike other eisteddfodau (see special feature, page 109), Llangollen's looks outside Wales.

First held in 1947 to help heal the wounds of war, the event attracts up to 15,000 musicians and dancers every year from over 30 nations. Performers from countries as disparate as Czechoslovakia, Bangladesh and Japan meet and compete here, their traditional folk costumes bringing a cosmopolitan splash of colour to the streets of this Welsh town.

Exuberant 'magpie' architecture at Llangollen's Plas Newydd, below the ruins of Castell Dinas Bran

Llangollen lies in a deep and protective valley beside the rushing waters of the River Dee, only a few miles from the flat English borderlands but well insulated from them by enveloping mountains. Castell Dinas Bran stands 1000 ft high on one mountain crest, its stumpy ruins casting a weathered eye over the town.

This 13th-century Welsh native stronghold was probably built by Madog, Prince of Powys. Four centuries earlier, Cyngen, another Prince of Powys, erected Eliseg's Pillar in memory of his great-grandfather. The pillar, set on its original mound, is one mile north of Llangollen near the grand loop of the Horseshoe Pass, a road that frequently succumbs to winter snows. Close by are the extensive remains of Valle Crucis Abbey, a Cistercian house founded in 1201 by Prince Madog's father.

A trio of landmarks are located within the town itself. Llangollen grew up around its handsome stone bridge, medieval in origin, and one of the 'Seven Wonders of Wales', an accolade which should not be taken too seriously (see Wrexham entry).

The most talked about inhabitants of the town were undoubtedly the 'Ladies of Llangollen', Lady Eleanor Butler, her companion the Hon. Sarah Ponsonby and their maid Mary Carryll (also known apparently as Molly the Basher). From 1780, they set up a highly eccentric home here which was visited by many luminaries of the time, including Shelley, Byron and Wordsworth. Their black-and-white timbered mansion, its interior displaying a wealth of oak carving, is open to the public. Llangollen Canal, a branch of the Shropshire Union, has inspired the establishment of the Canal Exhibition Centre, an imaginative museum housed beside the town wharf in an

Cruising 120ft above ground on the Llangollen Canal's Pontcysyllte aqueduct, the longest in Britain

early 19th-century warehouse.

☛ *LLANGOLLEN, at the junction of the A5, A539 and A542, is 10 miles south-west of Wrexham.*

MYNYDD HIRAETHOG
Clwyd

The heather covered moorlands west of Ruthin occupy an emotional position in traditional Welsh culture. No equivalent single word exists in the English language which captures the full meaning of *hiraethog*. The nearest approximations are 'homesick' and 'longing', a reflection of the rich seam of history and heritage that underlies Hiraethog's now-empty moorlands.

Where man once lived there are now conifer trees and reservoirs. The Clocaenog Forest, Wales's second largest plantation, clothes much of the southern and eastern moor (at Bod Petrual, just off the B5105, an

old gamekeeper's cottage has been converted into an interesting and attractive Forest Visitor Centre).

The most recent man-made addition is Llyn Brenig, a wide, squat sheet of water — over 13,000 million gallons in all — in the central moor. Completed in 1976, Brenig joins Llyn Alwen, a smaller reservoir built here in the early 1900s. Both are surrounded by Hiraethog's soft, rounded outlines — a deceptive landscape, for this is high, bleak and windy country, consistently over the 1000 ft contour line, and fiercely cold in winter.

Although now unpopulated, Hiraethog was settled for many thousands of years. Mystery surrounds many of the prehistoric sites here, though those excavated around the reservoir reveal definitive evidence of mesolithic (Middle Stone Age) and Bronze Age man. In medieval times, hafodydd were constructed here (a *hafod* is a summer

camp or house, built by those tending flocks of sheep and cattle brought to the moorlands for summer grazing), perpetuating a tradition of transhumance — that is, moving from 'moor to shore' according to the seasons — established by prehistoric man. From these scattered settlements and the shared hardships of living on Mynydd Hiraethog sprang a rich culture, as shepherds met to create their own entertainment at *noson lawen*, evenings of song and poetry.

The history and ecology of this fascinating and unique part of North Wales is told at the excellent Brenig Visitor Centre, located at the dam. This centre is the starting point for a number of lakeside footpaths, one of which leads to the excavated archaeological sites.

☛ *MYNYDD HIRAETHOG is bounded by the towns of Ruthin, Denbigh and Llanrwst, with the A5 running along its southern boundary.*

Eisteddfodau explained – a 2000-year tradition

Bardic ritual at the Royal National Eisteddfod

The International Eisteddfod

The tradition of the eisteddfod — a competitive event in literature, music and the arts, held in the Welsh language — can be traced back to 1176 when the Lord Rhys ap Gruffudd held a Christmastide gathering at Cardigan. Within courtly circles in medieval Wales, the skills of the bard (or poet) were much revered. Events which put those talents to the test soon became popular, most notably at Carmarthen in the early 1450s when the term *eisteddfod* was first coined.

By the 16th century, eisteddfodau had begun to fall into the doldrums. The movement was re-awoken — some would say re-invented — thanks in part to the fertile imagination of one man, Iolo Morgannwg.

Iolo began life, in 1747, as plain and simple Edward Williams. A great self-publicist, he soon transformed his identity into a bardic one. Iolo's romantic obsession with druidic civilization in Britain before the coming of the Romans and Saxons, together with his showmanship and suspect skills as an historian led to the creation of 'The Gorsedd of the Bards'.

Although a pure invention, the idea of the Gorsedd — an association of poets, writers, musicians and artists — soon caught on. The first gathering was held, of all places, at London's Primrose Hill in 1792. By 1819, Iolo had persuaded a Welsh eisteddfod at Carmarthen to adopt the idea.

The Gorsedd has subsequently become an important national institution within Wales. Its rituals and ceremonies, attended by gold, white, blue and green robed druids, reach a peak of symbolic importance during the Chairing of the Bard, the winning poet at the Royal National Eisteddfod. This annual event, held alternately in North and South Wales each August, is Wales's most important festival of traditional culture. The ceremonial side of the proceedings is only one element in a week of competitions which play a valuable — some say crucial — role in the preservation and fostering of the Welsh language (a tongue now spoken by only one-fifth of Wales's two-and-three-quarter-million inhabitants).

However historically spurious the ceremonial side may be, the eisteddfod's cultural importance is enormous, for the Royal National stands at the peak of a pyramid of events large and small, regional and local, formal and informal held throughout Wales. The movement has also spilled over into other, non-traditional areas, most notably at the Llangollen International Eisteddfod which attracts participants from all over the world.

Pistyll Rhaeadr, the highest waterfall in Wales

PISTYLL RHAEADR WATERFALL
Clwyd

The narrow road which ventures north-west into the Berwyn Mountains from Llanrhaeadr-ym-Mochnant travels as far as Pistyll Rhaeadr and no further. The tarmac ends where the valley pinches itself into a block end of near-vertical slopes, a scene pervaded by the sound of water crashing onto rocks.

Pistyll Rhaeadr plunges for 240 ft over its mountain ledge into a gloomy, rocky and tree-shrouded dingle. One of the so-called 'Seven Wonders of Wales', it is the highest Welsh waterfall (and amongst the highest in Britain). The indefatigable George Borrow, 19th-century author of *Wild Wales*, naturally found his way to Pistyll Rhaeadr, recounting 'I never saw water falling so gracefully, so much like thin beautiful threads as here.'

Llanrhaeadr-ym-Mochnant is a peaceful country village on the doorstep of the empty Berwyns, bare-flanked mountains which rise to a summit of 2713 ft at Moel Sych, just over one mile north of Pistyll Rhaeadr. Whilst serving as rector in Llanrhaeadr from 1578 to 1588, William Morgan, later Bishop Morgan, worked on his historic first translation of the whole of the Bible into Welsh.

PISTYLL RHAEADR is 4 miles north-west of Llanrhaeadr-ym-Mochnant, a village on the B4580 approximately 12 miles west of Oswestry.

RHUDDLAN
Clwyd

Two very different historic sites capture the attention here. Rhuddlan Castle stands on a rise above the River Clwyd. Its powerful round towers, part of a clever ring of concentric defences, played their part in the English conquest of North Wales, for Rhuddlan was one of the chain of mighty castles built by Edward I in the late 13th century.

Of particular interest here was the monumental effort required to give the castle access to the sea, an important strategic advantage in Edward's days. The artificial-looking course of the Clwyd here betrays the fact that it first had to be made navigable by digging a deep-water passage over two miles long to the sea.

Bodrhyddan Hall, a mile or so east of the town, belongs to another era. The oldest part of this fine old red-bricked manor house dates from the late 17th century. Inside, Bodrhyddan is noteworthy for its extensive collection of weaponry and armour, two suits of which are believed to date from the Wars of the Roses.

RHUDDLAN is at the junction of the A525, A547, and A5151, 2 miles south-east of Rhyl.

RHYL AND PRESTATYN
Clwyd

There is not a lot that can be said about this pair of straightforward seaside resorts. No such reticence seems to have afflicted our verbose Victorian forbears, besotted as they were by the exaggerations and superlatives of purple prose. This is what an early tourist guidebook had to say about Rhyl: 'Its record of sunshine is known all over the world to be unique. While the big towns and cities are reeking with fog, Rhyl is bathed in warm sunshine, and it is no uncommon thing to see people bathing in the open sea as late as the middle of November.'

This resort still advertises itself as 'Sunny Rhyl', though it no longer

The Clwyd, canalised here to give Rhuddlan Castle sea-borne access

relies on the fickle British climate nor the ambitious claims of copywriters. Rhyl's purpose-built Sun Centre, a multi-leisure complex on the promenade, has its own mini-climate which makes November bathing here a less than chilly prospect.

'The old stigma of lack of amusements has now been entirely removed,' continued the old guidebook. For once, this is something of an understatement, for amusements have taken over well and truly in this unpretentious and uncomplicated resort, cast in the traditional British mould.

It is more of the same a few miles to the east of Prestatyn. A string of

caravan parks and one or two holiday camps — re-christened holiday centres by the image-conscious tourism marketeers of the Eighties — spread themselves out behind the promenade and long sandy beach. With such a preponderance of insubstantial, impermanent development, it is somehow inappropriate that Prestatyn marks the northern end of Offa's Dyke, the great 8th-century earthwork that ran the length of Wales and still survives almost to its original height in parts (see special feature, page 71).

🚗 *RHYL AND PRESTATYN are both on the A548 coast road between Colwyn Bay and Queensferry.*

RUTHIN
Clwyd

The Council for British Archaeology considers Ruthin 'unique in North Wales for its number of timber-framed buildings'. This small market town, one of the prettiest in Wales, provides an architectural feast for those whose appetites incline to the 'magpie' half-timbered style of building.

Clustered around St Peter's Square in the middle of town is a striking array of black-and-white facades, enlivened by a jumble of gables and red-tiled roofs with a profusion of dormer windows. The banks even

enter into the spirit of things. Both the National Westminster and Barclays do business behind timbered frontages, the former occupying Ruthin's old court house and prison. *Maen Huail* ('Huail's Stone'), beside Barclays, has gory Arthurian connections: on this large limestone block, King Arthur is said to have had Huail, his rival in love, beheaded.

The 180-ft spire of St Peter's Church dominates the square. Dating from the 14th century, it boasts a magnificent oak roof decorated with fine carving.

Ruthin, standing at the head of the fertile Vale of Clwyd, has been a prosperous market town for many centuries. The first Tuesday in each month sees a bustling street market, whilst livestock sales are held here twice weekly each Thursday and Friday.

The town's historic ambience has been a springboard for 'medieval Wednesdays', held throughout the summer months, during which period costume is much in evidence and appropriate entertainments are staged. The historic veracity of the so-called 'medieval' banquets, held nightly at the Ruthin Castle Hotel, can also be called into question; though it is perhaps churlish to do so, for these raucous events give pleasure to many. One medieval custom which does survive, authentic to this day, is the ringing at eight o'clock each evening of the Curfew Bell tolls, a practice continuously adhered to since the 11th century.

Little is left of Ruthin's medieval castle. Fragments of original stonework are incorporated into the masonry of a largely Victorian mansion which now serves as the aforementioned hotel.

🚗 *RUTHIN is at the junction of the A525 and A494, about 17 miles north-west of Wrexham.*

ST ASAPH
Clwyd

St Asaph vies with St David's for the title of 'smallest city'. Smallness seems to characterise this city-village. Its cathedral, probably the smallest in Britain, was established in 560 by St Kentigern, St Asaph taking over when the founding missionary returned to his native Scotland.

The cathedral suffers from faint praise. 'Though not large, (it) has something of dignity and grandeur', were Dr Johnson's qualified comments in 1774. Its exterior, admittedly plain and modest, belies the feeling of spaciousness inside and the extensive views that can be enjoyed from the tower (unusually for Welsh cathedrals, this one stands high on a hill).

Outside is an elaborate monument to the important 16th-century religious figure Bishop William Morgan, translator of the Bible into Welsh. He is buried within the cathedral, which also contains a museum displaying an unusual miscellany of artefacts.

ST ASAPH is on the A525, 6 miles south of Rhyl.

WREXHAM
Clwyd

The centre of this large town cannot claim to be well endowed with visitor attractions; apart, that is, from the magnificent early 16th-century tower which adorns the Church of St Giles. This tower is one of the much-quoted 'Seven Wonders of Wales':

'Pistyll Rhaeadr and Wrexham Steeple,
Snowdon's mountain, without its people;
Overton Yewtrees, Saint Winifred Wells,
Llangollen Bridge and Gresford Bells.'

Confidence in this highly contentious list is not inspired by the fact

St Asaph Cathedral, more impressive inside than out

that the 'wonders' are all confined to North Wales. However, this should not detract from the splendour of the tower, and the church which it graces.

The graveyard contains the tomb of Elihu Yale (d.1721) who lived near Wrexham in his later life. Yale is familiar, of course, thanks to the American university named after this generous benefactor (the campus even contains a reproduction of Wrexham tower). Part of the long epitaph on his grave reads:

'Born in America, in Europe bred,
In Africa travell'd, and in Asia wed,
Where long he liv'd and thriv'd;
at London dead.'

Wrexham contains isolated examples of architecture which reflect its former grandeur as a flourishing market, industrial and social centre. Its great treasure, though, lies on the outskirts of town. Erddig is a country house with a difference. Although it has its finery, this late 17th-century house, set in 938 acres, is mainly important for the authentic insight it gives into 'upstairs, downstairs' life on a country estate.

The master-servant relationship is brought to life in a house where the kitchen and working outbuildings are as well preserved — and as full of interest — as, for example, the period furniture in gilt and silver and superb state bed in Chinese silk. We also learn that the relationship at Erddig was, perhaps untypically, not an unhappy one. The Yorkes, owners of Erddig from 1773 to 1973 (when it was handed over to the National Trust), held their staff in high regard, even commissioning paintings of generations of servants which still hang on the walls today.

WREXHAM, near the Wales/England border, is 12 miles south-west of Chester.

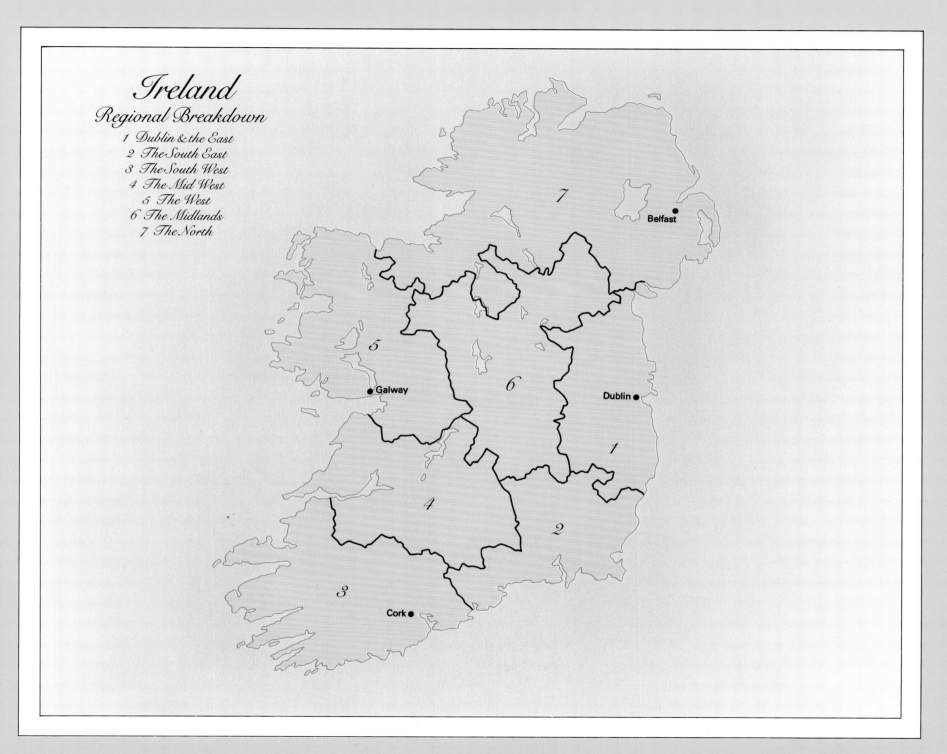

Ireland
Regional Breakdown
1 *Dublin & the East*
2 *The South East*
3 *The South West*
4 *The Mid West*
5 *The West*
6 *The Midlands*
7 *The North*

Belfast

Galway

Dublin

Cork

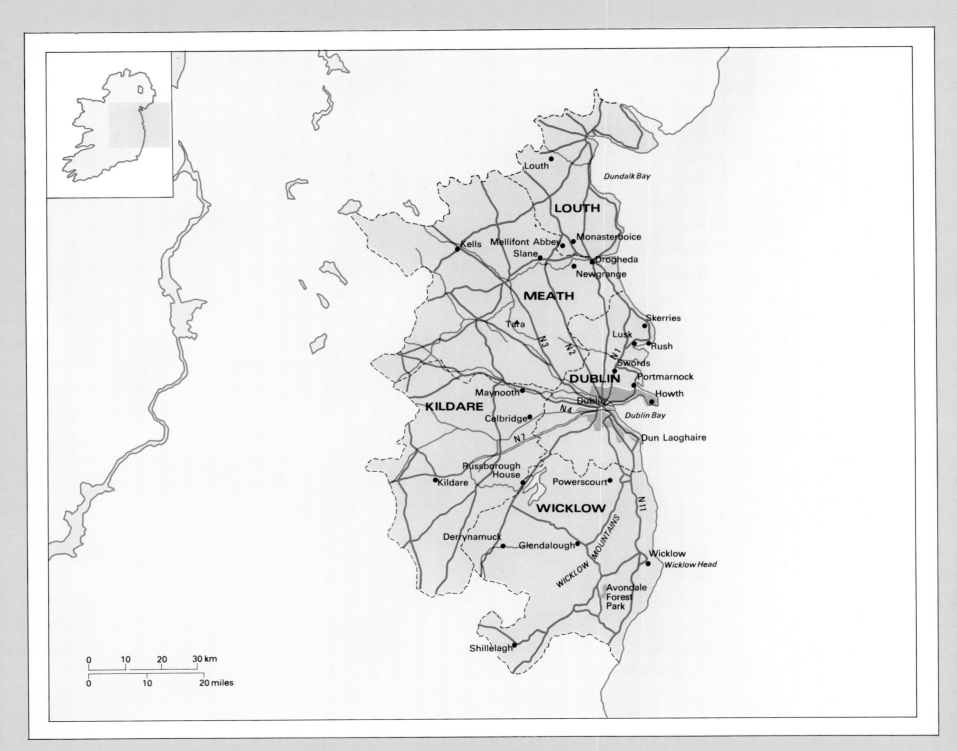

Dundalk Bay

Louth

LOUTH

Monasterboice

Kells   Mellifont Abbey
        Slane   Drogheda
                Newgrange

MEATH

                    Skerries
Tara   Lusk
                            Rush
            N3   N2   N1 Swords
                        Portmarnock
                DUBLIN
Maynooth   Dublin   Howth
KILDARE   N4   Dublin Bay
        Celbridge

                N7   Dun Laoghaire

            Russborough
            House   Powerscourt
Kildare

                    WICKLOW   N11

Derrynamuck
        Glendalough   Wicklow
                    WICKLOW MOUNTAINS   Wicklow Head

                            Avondale
                            Forest
                            Park

Shillelagh

0   10   20   30 km

0   10   20 miles

Once the most elegant and fashionable of Georgian cities, Dublin retains many attractive features from that age. These Georgian doorways, with their distinctive fanlights and pillars, can be seen in many parts of the city

TOLEMY, THE GREEK geographer, referred to Dublin as 'Eblana', and put it on the map of the then-known world in A.D.140. Dublin derives its name from the Irish *Dubhlinn*, literally translated as the 'Dark Pool' (a reference to the Liffey).

Now, Dublin is the attractive and wealthy capital of Ireland, one of Europe's leading partners in trade in the European Common Market and a renowned cultural centre.

Dublin city stands on a bay, with arms of welcome outstretched from the Hill of Howth on the north side of the harbour of Dun Laoghaire, to 'the fort of Leary', formerly Kingstown, on the south side. To the east lies the lovely limestone plateau of Kildare, which produces some of the most valuable bloodstock in the world, and where there has been horseracing since before the time of Christ. To the south of Dublin are the picturesque blue granite-domed hills of Wicklow, with sandy strands and rocky headlands. To the north of Dublin are the rich fat cattle lands, the grasslands of 'Royal' Meath. 'Royal' Meath, because for centuries Tara of the Kings (an iron-age Celtic hill settlement) was the centre of government of Celtic Ireland, and because it is also the land of ancient royal underground graves and tumuli on the banks of the Boyne river and along its valley. Louth, 'the wee county', as it is affectionately known, is adjacent to Meath and is only 317 square miles in area.

AVONDALE FOREST PARK
County Wicklow

This Forestry Department-owned land of some 523 acres was once the estate and home of that celebrated and tragic leader of the Irish people, Charles Stewart Parnell. Here he was taught his Irish nationalism by his Irish-American mother. It lies along the superbly beautiful banks of the River Avondale.

Avondale House, built in 1777 is now the forestry school and its splendid architecture has been well preserved. Open to the public in the summer season, the guide, Mrs O'Connor, will show you the furniture and other articles belonging to Charles Stewart Parnell, and the beautiful hallway, the drawing room and the blue room with its ornamental plaster work of a very high standard.

There are nature trails through the enormous variety of trees.

AVONDALE FOREST PARK is approximately 35 miles south of Dublin city.

CELBRIDGE
County Kildare

Celbridge, a beautiful village on the River Liffey, was, at Celbridge Abbey, the home of Esther Vanhomrigh (1690-1723) immortalised in prose by Jonathan Swift as his ill-fated 'Vanessa'. At the eastern end of the village is what is arguably the most splendid Georgian country house in Ireland, Castletown House, open to the public, and built in 1722 for William Connolly, the speaker of the Irish House of Commons from 1715 to 1719. It is now the headquarters of the Irish Georgian Society. Two miles due north of Castletown House is Connolly's 'Folly',

St Lawrence's Gate, Drogheda — once there were nine others like it

140 ft in height, erected in 1740 by Connolly's widow to provide relief work for famine victimes. It was designed by Richard Castle. Castletown House was the first of the great Palladian houses to be built in Ireland, and Connolly was the richest man of his time in Ireland. It set the pattern for other Palladian houses in Ireland with its central block linked by curved colonnades. The house was designed by the Italian architect Alessandro Galilei, and Bishop Berkeley was consulted about its design. Sir Edward Lovett Pearce, who designed the Irish Parliament House, had a large part in its building. The plasterwork in the house is by the Francini brothers, and the Long Gallery was decorated in the Pompeian manner by Thomas Riley in 1776. It has the only print room in Ireland, created by Lady Louisa Connolly and Lady Sarah Napier in 1775. It has a wealth of Irish Furniture and art treasures.

CELBRIDGE is 13 miles due west of Dublin, a journey which Jonathan Swift so often made on horseback to visit his beloved 'Vanessa'.

DERRYNAMUCK
County Wicklow

The remote, wild beauty of Wicklow County is best seen on the Glen of Imaal road, five miles of hills that rise to more than 1000 ft leading to the thatched cottage at Derrynamuck where Michael Dwyer, rebel leader of 1798, was trapped by Redcoats and saved by his comrade Sam MacAllister, who was killed as he drew the soldiers' fire. The cottage is furnished and restored to its 18th-century appearance.

DERRYNAMUCK is best approached by the Dublin to Hollywood road, via Donard. It is about 38 miles south west of Dublin.

DROGHEDA
County Louth

Drogheda, the 'Bridge of the Ford', is an important and ancient town which spans the River Boyne. It was built by the Norse Sea King Turgesius in 911, and the Normans made it a fortress town. Here Richard II secured the submission of O'Neill, Prince of Ulster and other

The Four Courts at Dublin, designed by James Gandon

Irish chieftains in 1395. In 1649, when Cromwell stormed the town, he personally ordered the butchery of some 2000 of its defenders and sent the rest into slavery in the Barbadoes. The St Lawrence Gate is the only remaining 13th-century one of the original ten.

St Peter's Church, in West Street, was erected in memory of St Oliver Plunkett, (1629-1681), Archbishop of Armagh, who was hanged, drawn and quartered at Tyburn in London in 1681. His embalmed head, blackened by fire, is preserved in a special shrine on an altar in the north transept.

DROGHEDA is 30 miles north of Dublin.

DUBLIN
County Dublin

Dublin has all the pros and cons of a capital city. To the average Dubliner it is one of the most attractive places to live, with two major racecourses in its suburbs, 30 golf courses within half an hour's drive of the city centre and safe bays and beaches only minutes away. It has an east-west axis of the River Liffey and is very definitely divided into a north side and a south side. O'Connell Street is the main street of the city, straddling the river at O'Connell Bridge.

In European or World terms Dublin is a village, and a relatively small village, with one main street.

That is its real attraction, it can be walked, and its treasures of architecture and art visited on foot in a matter of hours. Like all modern cities it has an impossible traffic situation. It is very much a city of the young and a centre of learning, as it boasts two major universities; the modern National University of Ireland, University College Dublin, and the Elizabethan foundation of the College of the Holy and Undivided Trinity.

On the high ground on which the city rose is the magnificent cathedral of Christchurch, founded by the Danes and rebuilt by the Normans under Strongbow in 1172. His tomb and that of his son can be seen to-

day. Dubliners rejoice in the fact that this Norman cathedral was restored by a wealthy whiskey distiller, Henry Roe, while St Patrick's Gothic Cathedral, built in 1190, was restored by a wealthy brewer, Sir Benjamin Lee Guinness.

Down on the quays, near Dublin's Four Courts, in Church Street, is the Church of St Michan, founded in 1096. Handel played the organ there, and in its vaults are the mummified bodies of centuries-old citizens of Dublin, so old that you can, if you so desire, shake hands with a dead Crusader.

The real flavour of Georgian Dublin can be savoured in College Green, where stands the Old Parliament House, now the headquarters of the Bank of Ireland. The work of Lovett Pearce, Surveyor-General of Ireland in 1729, and of James Gandon, who made additions in 1785, its Parliamentary days heard the greatest of Irish orators such as Henry Grattan, and it closed in 1800 when the Act of Union united the British and Irish parliaments in London. Across the road stands Trinity College whose magnificent buildings include the Examination Hall, the Library, the Chapel, and the Printing House, all erected between 1722 and 1732. On the corner of Grafton Street stands one of the most attractive residences in Europe, the Provost's House, built in 1760.

Trinity College Library dates from 1601. By an Act of Parliament in 1801 it has a right to a copy of every book printed in Ireland and in Britain, so its books and manuscripts run into millions. Its greatest treasure, on view to the public, is the 8th-century illuminated manuscript of the gospels, the *Book of Kells*. The most valuable book in the world, it is insured for £10 million. Dublin is a city for book lovers, for the National Library of Ireland in Kildare Street contains over half a million books and hundreds of thousands of prints and Irish newspapers and maps. The Royal Irish Academy Library in Dawson Street houses an extensive collection of rare manuscripts from the 6th to the 16th centuries, and Marsh's Library, adjacent to St Patrick's Cathedral, and open to the public, was founded in 1707 by Archbishop Marsh. The oldest library in the country, it contains tens of thousands of rare volumes and manuscripts. Also open to the public is the Sir Chester Beatty Library, at 20 Shrewsbury Road, with the most valuable collection of Oriental manuscripts in the world.

Trinity College, Dublin, seen from the Bank of Ireland

Despite its Victorian 'glass-case' presentation of antiquities, the National Museum in Kildare Street contains one of the finest collections of Celtic gold objects in Europe. The most famous exhibits are the Tara Brooch, the Ardagh Chalice, the Cross of Cong and St Patrick's Bell and Bell Shrine. In recent times an 8th-century addition has been made in the shape of the Derrynaflan Chalice. There is always some precious antiquity being unearthed in the bog-lands of Ireland. For lovers of the visual arts there are two important Art Galleries. The first is the National Gallery in Merrion Square opened in 1864 and containing over 2000 treasures. The

Irish Room with the works of John Butler Yeats, Hone, Osborne, Lavery, Orpen, Tuohy, Roderick O'Conor, Jack Yeats and Paul Henry gives a cross-section of the works of Ireland's greatest painters. The National Gallery is financed by funds from the estate of George Bernard Shaw in memory of the many happy days of his youth spent there.

Equally important in the world of art is the Municipal Gallery of Modern Art in Parnell Square, founded by Sir Hugh Lane, famous for his collection of French Impressionist paintings. He drowned in the sinking of the *Lusitania*, and his will, leaving his collection of pictures to the Municipal Gallery in

Dublin, was disputed because legally its codicil lacked two witnesses. Due to the efforts of Lord Longford an amicable settlement was reached so that half of his collection is on view in Dublin and the other half in London, changing every five years. The Municipal Gallery is important because its works give a visual glimpse of modern Ireland's history.

Dublin is renowned for its Georgian character, but while many of its wide streets and squares and lovely Georgian doorways remain, a devil-may care attitude in modern times towards things Georgian has left much of it to decay. The steel and glass facades of modern office blocks and hotels now spoil the looks of a once elegant town.

It is understandable that the Irish people of today should have no love for a Georgian age which is associated with deportation and famine, and an alien and absent landlord class. However, much remains from that time that is good. Leinster House is a glorious Georgian mansion in Kildare Street, now the assembly place of the politicians of Ireland, the elected deputies of the Dáil, the Chamber of Deputies, and of the Seanad House, Senate or Upper House. Leinster House, built in 1745, was the town house of the Duke of Leinster. As first Duke, he built it in its solitary state on indifferent marshy land far from the popular north side of Dublin, and boasted that the fashionable would follow him across the Liffey. They did. The style of his building was copied too. The White House in Washington D.C. is modelled on Leinster House.

The Abbey theatre in Abbey Street is one of the most magnificent centres of drama in the world. The old building, built on the unpromising site of the city morgue, was opened in 1904 and burnt to the ground in 1951. The new 1966 building is functional but the glory is in the lobby where hang the portraits in oils of the 'greats' such as Yeats, Synge, O'Casey, Lennox Robinson, George Shiels, Denis Johnston and Lady Gregory.

The world-renowned Royal Dublin Society was founded in 1731 at Ballsbridge. Every year in the first week in August the Dublin Horse-show is staged in its grounds.

In Phoenix Park Dublin can boast the most beautiful enclosed public park in the world, all 1760 acres of it, with its Polo grounds open to the public, its charming Zoological

Gardens and its 200 acres of playing fields, once famous as duelling grounds.

The Shelbourne Hotel has been for well over a century a window on the everyday passing parade of the capital city. It resounds to the talk and the chatter of fashionable people, of politicians on the make, of 'Horse Protestants' up from the country, from their great houses, of hunting men and women, and, in August, the International Show jumping teams of the world.

It is very Irish. It looks down on Iveagh House, the headquarters of the Irish Department of Foreign Affairs. Its rooms have views right

Marsh's Library is full of rare, old volumes

The elegant facade of the Shelbourne Hotel, frequented by Dublin's literati

across the city to the Dublin hills, and to the blue Wicklow mountains. The Dail — the Irish Parliament, meets around the corner. And here too are Government buildings, the National Art Gallery, the National Museum and the National Library. It is a stone's throw from the fashionable walk-about shopping centre that is in Grafton Street, and the Lord Mayor's Mansion House.

As Conrad Hilton said, a successful hotel requires three things; position, position and position. The Shelbourne has all three requirements. Thackeray stayed there in 1842, when it was owned by that splendid Tipperary patriot, Martin Burke. Said William Makepeace of the hotel it is 'much frequented by families from the country . . . majestically conducted by clerks and other officers.' It hasn't changed much. The staff are delightful and helpful Dubliners and the service is superb, although, in Thackeray's day the window of his room was propped open with a broom!

During the 1916 Rising they continued to serve splendid afternoon teas at the Shelbourne, despite the bullets flying from the College of Surgeons, where Countess Markievicz, the former debutante Constance Gore-Booth was in command in a green uniform.

It had great days when it was managed by Captain Peter Jury, always referred to as 'The Captain', who inherited it from his father 'The Colonel', who commanded his regiment, the 18th Royal Hussars, Queen Mary's Own.

Now, after a £4 million face-lift it is one of the best hotels in Ireland with a special Irish flavour and welcome of its very own.

St Patrick's Cathedral contains the death mask, a magnificent bust and the epitaph of Dean Swift, and the

The magnificent interior of St Patrick's Cathedral

altar and the pulpit he used. Made dean in 1713, author Jonathan Swift died in 1745 after terrible mental illness, and lies buried in the south west nave, near his beloved Stella. A brass plate marks the grave.

On the south wall is his bust, and to its right, above the doorway, is the epitaph he wrote. In translation it reads:

"Here lies the body of Jonathan Swift, Doctor of Divinity, Dean of this Cathedral Church, where fierce indignation can no longer rend the heart. Go, traveller, and imitate if you can, this earnest and dedicated champion of liberty. 1745 A.D. Aged 78 years".

To capture the glamour and atmosphere of the eternal calvalcade that is Dublin, a quiet stroll, or a seat in St Stephen's Green, in its centre, off the fashionable promenade of Grafton Street, will provide a glimpse of the passing parade of a young city which James Joyce immortalised and through whose streets strolled men such as Jonathan Swift, George Farquhar, George Berkeley, Edmund Burke, Oliver Goldsmith, Richard Brinsley Sheridan, Thomas Moore, James Clarence Mangan, George Moore, Oscar Wilde, George Bernard Shaw, William Butler Yeats, John Millington Synge, Sean O'Casey and Brendan Behan. Dublin has long been a place of inspiration for writers.

DUBLIN is 160 miles north east of Cork, 104 miles south of Belfast.

James Joyce's Dublin

James Joyce, born in Dublin on 2 February 1882, immortalised the city in *Ulysses*. Said Joyce of this book: 'I want to give a picture of Dublin so complete that if the city one day suddenly disappeared from the earth it could be reconstructed out of my book.' In his *Finnegan's Wake*, the River Liffey was captured forever in splendid prose as 'Anna Livia Plurabelle'. In his *Dubliners*, and his *Portrait of the Artist as a Young Man*, he caught the atmosphere of the pubs of Dublin, the gaiety of Grafton Street, the squalor of the dingy lanes, the 'surly front' of Trinity College, the dignity of the National Library, and recalled the happy times spent at the Martello Tower at Sandycove, now the James Joyce Museum, which he shared with St John Gogarty, the 'Buck Mulligan' of *Ulysses*.

His residences in the Dublin area included 41 Brighton Square, Rathgar, his birthplace; 23 Castlewood Avenue, Rathmines; 1 Martello Terrace, Bray, County Wicklow; 23 Carysfort Avenue, Blackrock, County Dublin; 2 Millbourne Avenue, Drumcondra; 29 Windsor Avenue, Fairview; 8 Royal Terrace, Fairview, 32 Glengariff Parade, off the North Circular Road; and 7 St Peter's Terrace, Cabra.

He attended the Jesuit school of Clongowes Wood and Belvedere College, Dublin, and graduated from the old Royal University in 1898. He died in Zurich in 1941.

James Joyce was a regular in Dublin's pubs

Many streets have hardly changed since Joyce's time

DUN LAOGHAIRE
County Dublin

Formerly named 'Kingstown' in 1821, to commemorate the visit of King George IV to Ireland, the town has reverted to its old Irish name which means the Fort of Laoghaire (pronounced 'Leary'). The great harbour, today the principal sea-link with Britain, was begun in 1817 by John Rennie. It took more than 50 years to build, and covers over 250 acres between its massive granite piers quarried from the nearby Dalkey hills. A major yachting centre, it is the home of several yacht clubs. It is also the base of the Irish Lights Service. The East pier is a delightful promenade. Just one and a quarter miles further south is the James Joyce Martello Tower, which features in *Ulysses*, now a Joycean museum.

Killiney Bay, four miles south of Dun Laoghaire, is popularly known as the Irish Bay of Naples. George Bernard Shaw lived in adjacent Dalkey in Torca cottage, from 1866 to 1874. The Vico road connects Killiney Hill and Dalkey hill and the view from the 500 ft high summit of Killiney affords a magnificent panoramic vista of the sea and the surrounding countryside. At Monkstown, a suburb on the Dublin side of Dun Laoghaire, in Belgrave Square, the Irish Culture Institute, (*Comalthas Ceoltoiri Eireann*) present the most splendid traditional Irish music and dance in summer.

DUN LAOGHAIRE is 8 miles south of Dublin.

GLENDALOUGH
County Wicklow

Glendalough was founded by St Kevin in the 6th century. He came there first to live as a hermit but his sanctity and fame attracted so many people to him that he set up a monastery, and died there at the age of 125 years of age. The monastery became a European university in A.D. 617. Burnt nine times, and pillaged by the Norse raiders three times in the 9th and 10th centuries, it was plundered by the Normans, inundated by a great flood in 1174 and was re-established as a diocese in 1450. It remained beyond the King's Writ in the mountain fortress of Wicklow when the O'Byrne and O'Toole clans held the county against the central government in Dublin. Once a famous centre of pilgrimage it fell silent and deserted, and the wonder is that such a diversity of stone buildings survive.

After St Kevin, Glendalough had one period of glory when St Laurence O'Toole was appointed Abbot in 1153, and became Archbishop of Dublin in 1161. He was a powerful figure and tried to negotiate with the English King Henry II, in France, about his deportation of Roderic O'Connor, high King of Ireland. St Laurence died at Eu, in Normandy and was canonized in 1226.

The monastic settlement and university covers one and a half miles of the valley. Its farthest point is on the Upper Lake, Temple-na-Skellig 'The Church of the Rock', a small, rectangular church standing on a shelf 20ft above the water. It features a twin light east window. On the platform the original wood and mud hut of St Kevin would have stood. St Kevin's Bed, east of Temple-na-Skellig, is a cave 30 ft above the lake level, 4 ft wide, 7 ft deep and 3½ ft high. It was probably a Bronze Age burial place before St Kevin used it.

Reefert Church, — 'The King's Burial Place' — is the burial place of the O'Toole clan, on the south east corner of the Upper Lake, near the Poulanass Waterfall. The ruins of the church date from the 11th century. Near Reefert are the foundations of another church about 35 ft long and with walls 3 ft thick. Along the Upper and Lower Lake are various ancient stone crosses. In the fields west of the graveyard of the monastic university city is Our Lady's Church, the earliest church in the valley with a remarkable west doorway of seven massive blocks of granite. On slightly higher ground, north-west of the cathedral, is the almost perfect Round Tower. Composed of local granite and mica-slate it has six storeys. The doorway is 12 ft above the ground and the whole unique Irish defence tower against hit-and-run Norse raiders has been standing for over 1000 years. The arched gateway to the monastic settlement is the only one of its kind in Ireland. The Priest's House, within the cemetery, was a burial place for local clergy in penal times. Standing between the Priest's House and the Cathedral is the 11 ft high St Kevin's Cross. The largest ruins are of the 11th-century Cathedral. They consist of a nave, chancel and sacristy. St Kevin's Church, popularly known as 'St Kevin's Kitchen', is a perfect example of a barrel-vaulted church with high pitched stone roofs and a miniature Round Tower bell tower. The Church of St Kieran, 12 yards south east of St Kevin's church is a foundation of a nave and a chancel, and commemorates the founder of the monastic university of Clonmacnoise. St Saviour's priory, east of the Round Tower, was founded by St Laurence O'Toole in 1162.

In 1985 eight Benedictine monks from Canada arrived in Glendalough to begin anew its monastic tradition.

Glendalough's almost perfect Round Tower is over 1000 years old and made from local granite

GLENDALOUGH is 32 miles from Dublin.

HOWTH
County Dublin

On the north side of Dublin Bay, Howth derives its name from the Norse name *Höfud*, meaning a head. Its Irish name is *Beann Eadair*, Edar's Peak, 565 ft in height. From its summit is a breathtaking panoramic view, north to the Mountains of Mourne, and south to the Wicklow Mountains. It was originally meant to be the Holyhead-Dublin sea link, built between 1801 and 1810. However, the harbour silted up, the architect committed suicide, and the mail boat station was transferred to Dun Laoghaire. St Mary's Church is on the site of the first church built in 1042 by Sitric, the Norse King of Dublin. The present church is basically 14th century and contains the tomb of the St Lawrence family, the Lords of Howth. Howth Castle and Demesne has been the seat of the St Lawrence family since 1600. The Lords of Howth follow a custom of always setting a place for a stranger at table, even to this day, to avoid a curse placed on the family by Grace O'Malley, the Irish sea queen pirate of Elizabethan days. She was returning from the court of Elizabeth and found the castle gates closed against her at evening meal time. In revenge she kidnapped the St Lawrence heir and only returned him on condition that their gates would never again be locked against the stranger seeking hospitality. The gardens are rich in rhododendra and azaleas and open to the public. Below the Hill of

Howth is the Bailey Lighthouse, erected in 1814, on the site of the Cromlech of King Crimthan who died in the first century A.D. The village is famous for its seafood restaurants and for the best traditional ballad sessions in Ireland at the Abbey Tavern Restaurant. Ireland's Eye, like a sleeping cat, lies two miles north east of Howth, once the settlement of St Nessan. It was plundered time and time again by raiding Norsemen.

HOWTH is 9½ miles north of Dublin city.

KELLS
County Meath

Kells, its ancient name *Ceanannus Mór*, The Great Residence, is a historic market town in the delightfully wooded valley of the River Blackwater. It was the site of one of the most important 16th-century monastic university settlements founded by the great St Colmcille in the 6th century. St Colmcille moved to Iona, and founded a monastic settlement there. In the 8th century his monks returned, driven out by the Viking raiders from Iona. The monastery was pillaged and burnt by the Vikings in 919, in 950 and again in 969. The greatest 9th-century treasure of the monastery was its *Book of Kells*, an illuminated manuscript of the Four Gospels, in Latin, stolen or hidden in the earth in 1007, which is now in the library of Trinity College, Dublin, and valued at £10 million. In the wars between the native Irish and the Normans the monastery was burnt down in 1111 and again in 1156. The Synod of Kells, held there in 1152, set up the provinces of Armagh, Cashel, Dublin and Tuam. It then became a Norman fortress. On top of the hill is the Round Tower

The intricately carved High Cross at Kells

and a collection of Celtic High Crosses. The Round Tower, minus its conical cap, is 100 ft high and has five windows at its top pointing to the five ancient roads that lead to the town. Murchadh Mac Flainn, High King of Ireland, was slain in this tower in 1076. Next to the Round Tower is the Celtic High Cross called the South Cross, erected in the 9th century, and dedicated to St Columba and St Patrick. The Celtic interlacing on the base depicts various animals, including a deer and a chariot procession. The south face depicts Adam and Eve, Cain and Abel, and other biblical scenes, and the arms too are richly carved, as are the ends of the cross. The west side depicts Christ in Judgement and the Crucifixion. There are three other crosses in the graveyard, and the fifth, 9 ft high, richly sculpted, is the Market Cross

standing in the middle of the town. St Colmcille's House was built about 805 to commemorate the return of St Colmcille's monks from Iona. This monastic building is very similar in design to St Kevin's church in Glendalough in County Wicklow. Just six miles from Kells is the Hill of Tailte, at Teltown. On this hill once stood *Rath Dubh*, the Black Fort, which was once the ancient palace of the High King Tuathal.

KELLS is 40 miles north west of Dublin, 10 miles from Navan, and 15 miles from Slane.

KILDARE
County Kildare

Kildare, from the Irish *Cill Dara*, the church of the oak, is forever associated with St Brigid. Tradition says a vast oak tree once stood where the present Cathedral of Kildare now stands. In 490 Brigid, the greatest female saint Ireland has ever produced, built her monastery here and its church became the centre of Christendom in the Kingdom of Leinster. As Abbess St Brigid established the monastery for her nuns, while St Conlaed, as Abbot Bishop, ruled over a separate section for his monks. The whole edifice was divided down the middle, and, continuing an old pagan practice on the site, a perpetual flame was kept burning. The Norsemen plundered the shrines of Brigid and Conlaed in 835, and it was burnt down again in 1050 and in 1067. The Normans built a Franciscan Abbey in 1260, funded by the de Vesci family. By the 1480s the Cathedral had been fully repaired and decorated to be reduced to ruins again in the Confederate wars. In Victorian times the Cathedral was over-restored to its present state. Close to the Cathedral is a magnificently preserved Round Tower, which

The tension mounts as spectators fill the Curragh Racecourse in Kildare

rises to a height of 105 ft.

Kildare is a busy market town with an Irish Army garrison with ornate iron entrance gates, and is a prosperous centre for the Irish horse breeding and training industry with 35 racing stables. The vast limestone grassy plain east of the town of Kildare, 5000 acres of world famous turf, six miles long and two miles wide, has seen classic horseracing there since the time when the gods of Greece were young. In the centre of this domed limestone plain is the Curragh Camp, the West Point or Sandhurst of Ireland, which contains a splendid garrison Church of St Brigid, with works of modern Irish art. All around the Curragh are world famous racing stables and one of the most glorious and poetic sights in Ireland is in the mists of the early morning when the various stable's thoroughbreds are at exercise, at the trot, at the gallop and flat out over the hallowed turf. The Curragh Racecourse is the scene of the Irish Derby, run by the Irish Hospital Sweepstakes with the largest prize money in the world of horseracing, and other Irish Classics such as the Irish 1000 guineas, 2000 guineas, the Irish Oaks and the Irish St Leger. At Tully, a mile south of Kildare town, and open to the public, is the Irish Government's National Stud, where horses worth millions of dollars or pounds are based. There is an excellent museum attached to the National Stud illustrating the history of horseracing in Ireland from earliest times. Adjacent to the National Stud are the Japanese Gardens which symbolise the life of man from birth to death. At the eastern end of the Curragh is Donnelly's Hollow, where a small obelisk commemorates the barefoot boxing victory of the giant Irishman, Dan Donnelly over the English box-

World-class horses are bred at Kildare's National Stud

ing champion George Cooper.

🚗 *KILDARE is 33 miles south west of Dublin.*

LOUTH
County Louth

Now only a tiny village of the 'wee county', as County Louth is affectionately known, (it is Ireland's smallest county, covering only 317 square miles) Louth is nevertheless of great importance, for St Patrick built the original church here and appointed his disciple, St Mochta, who died in 535, as its first bishop. St Mochta's House, beside the village, probably 10th century, is 18 ft long and 10 ft wide with a high-pitched stone roof. It has an upper and lower storey. St Mary's Abbey, once a Dominican friary, and also beside the village, dates from 1148 when the Prince of Oriel Donough O'Carroll endowed it. The 14th-century ruins are all that remain of what was once a church 150 ft long and 50 ft wide.

One mile east of the village at Ardpatrick, St Patrick founded a church, and in Ardpatrick House lived St Oliver Plunkett, to whom it was given by his kinsman, Lord Louth. Two miles north east of

Louth, east of the Dundalk road at Rathneety, is the 12 ft high Clocha-fearmor Standing Stone, which legend associates with the death of Cucchailainn, the mythical hero of old Irish. Cucchailainn 'The Hound of Ulster', mortally wounded, tied himself to this standing stone to face his countless enemies of the army of Queen Maeve of Connacht. Close to death, he stuck to his belief that it is better to have one day of glorious valour than to have a life of mediocrity. His enemies kept their distance and not until the raven of death perched on his shoulder did they dare to approach him. This scene is dramatically captured in the bronze statue of Cucchailainn, by Oliver Sheppard, that stands today in the General Post Office in O'Connell Street in Dublin, as a memorial to the volunteers who fought in the Rising in 1916.

🚗 *LOUTH village is 8 miles south west of Dundalk, which is 52 miles north of Dublin on the main road to Belfast.*

LUSK
County Dublin

This village boasts a well-preserved 8th-century Round Tower, 100ft in height, a classic example of the Irish defence against hit-and-run Norse raiders. Lusk was founded in the 5th century by St Mac Cuilinn who lived a hermit's life in the local cave, the Irish word for cave being *Lusca*. To the Round Tower the Normans added a square tower with round towers at three corners, to which was added a medieval church. The monastic settlement of the 9th century was burnt and pillaged by raiding Norsemen on at least two occasions. The church contains the medieval tomb of the Barnewalls of Turvey, (1589) and of the Berminghams of Ballough, 1527 and 1589. There is a magnificent view of north County Dublin; *Fingal*, the land of the Fair Strangers, from the top of the five-story Round Tower.

The present Catholic church has fine stained-glass windows by the Irish artist Harry Clarke.

🚗 *LUSK is 11 miles north of Dublin City.*

MAYNOOTH
County Kildare

Maynooth stands alongside the old Royal Canal, on the main Dublin to Galway road. At the west end of the

The product of many additions throughout the ages, the church at Lusk

village are the massive ruins and gate of the Geraldine Castle, built by Maurice FitzGerald in 1176, one of Strongbow's original adventurer invaders. The Geraldine Earls of Kildare lived here in considerable style until 1535 when the rebel Silken Thomas was taken after a siege by Sir William Skeffington, Henry VIII's deputy in Ireland, who used siege guns for the very first time in Irish history. Betrayed by his foster mother, Silken Thomas and his entire garrison were given the Tudor 'Pardon of Maynooth', which meant that they were beheaded!

The Gate Tower is now the entrance to the Pontifical University which is St Patrick's College, Maynooth, one of the largest Catholic colleges in the world dedicated to the university education of priests who go out to the missions all over the globe, as well as serving the people of Ireland. The present college dates from 1795 and incorporates the original Stoyte House of the steward to the Duke of Leinster, a magnificent Georgian house. The vast university buildings, sprawling in all directions, include the magnificent college chapel which is the work of Pugin and his pupil J.J. McCarthy. Among its many treasures is an enormous solid silver statue of St George and the Dragon and a cloth-of-gold set of vestments decorated with shamrocks. These were presented to the then all-male establishment in 1878 by Elizabeth, Empress of Austria, who was on a hunting holiday in the neighbourhood and came in, on a horse, over the wall. The nationalist priests, although impressed by her entrance, were not too flattered to be given a statue of the patron saint of England.

Of the many illustrious alumni of the college probably the best known were the rebel Archbishop of Melbourne, Daniel Mannix, president of the college from 1903 to 1912, and the one-time lecturer in mathematics, Eammon De Valera, later to become President of Ireland. Now open to lay students, both men and women, the new campus on the west side of the college is an interesting layout of modern architecture. Visitors are admitted in the holiday times of the students and one of the unusual attractions is the 'Ghost Room', where two students committed suicide in the mid-19th century. The room had to be exorcised, and the corridor wall removed, to make it wide-open to the public. An altar has been placed in the room. Among Maynooth's many artistic treasures is an enormous carved limestone head of St Patrick carved by the Cork sculptor, Seamus Murphy, author of *Stone Mad*.

🚗 *MAYNOOTH is 15 miles west of Dublin, on the main road to Mullingar and Athlone.*

MELLIFONT ABBEY
County Louth

St Malachi of Armagh, student friend of the great St Bernard of Ciairvaux, founded the first Cistercian monastery in Ireland here in 1142. Donogh O'Carroll, King of Uriel granted the land, and St Bernard sent his architect and mastermason, Robert, to assist in building the church. The Gate House, a massive square tower, still stands over 50 ft in height, and four arches of the spectacular 12th-century lavabo also still stand. This was the first of some 35 Cistercian monasteries in Ireland which brought with them a strong continental influence on Irish life.

🚗 *MELLIFONT is 4 miles west of Drogheda.*

Monasterboice's Round Tower was once the tallest in Ireland

MONASTERBOICE
County Louth

Monasterboice's Round Tower, although its top storey is missing, still stands 100 ft high, and was the tallest in Ireland in its heyday. There are the remains of a 9th-century church, the South church, and adjacent to the Round Tower the remains of the North church. The most splendid example of a sculptured 9th-century Celtic cross is Muireadach's Cross, nearly 18 ft high, and still standing at the entrance to the graveyard. It is of superb design and workmanship with a central figure of Christ crucified on the west side and the Last Judgement on the east side. The rest of both faces is a multiplicity of scenes from the scriptures interlaced with animals and hunters. The West Cross is 21½ ft high, highly ornate, and the North Cross, similarly carved, is 16 ft high. There is also a monastic sundial carved in granite.

🚗 *MONASTERBOICE is 6 miles north west of Drogheda, 1 mile west of the main road to Dundalk.*

NEWGRANGE
County Meath

At Newgrange is Ireland's most spectacular and finest prehistoric monument and arguably the best passage grave in Europe. It is a burial mound 42 ft high, 300 ft in diameter, and dating from 2500 B.C. It was once ringed by 38 boulders with an average height of 8 ft, of which a dozen remain. At the base of the underground grave are huge, horizontally lying stones with intricate geometric designs carved on them in triple spiral form, in double circles and semi-circles and diamond shaped carvings. There is more than a hint of an Indian origin in these designs. It is probable that the burial mound served as a primitive observatory as there are carvings of the course of the moon and the stars. The passage into the centre of the burial chamber is 62 ft long, and the central chamber is cruciform in shape. The dead would have been cremated and their ashes placed in the stone basin on the floor. Spirals, zig-zags and lozenges decorate the stones in the passageway which has two burial chambers in addition to the corbelled-roofed, 10 ft-high main burial chamber. Very recently the carved head of what was probably a druidic chieftain's stick or wand was discovered, and archaeologists still have lots to learn about this burial place of Kings. The whole of this historic area of the Boyne Valley is known as *Brugh na Boinne*, 'The Palace of the Boyne', and a mile or two away are the equally fascinating burial mounds of Knowth and of Dowth. Knowth is 40 ft high and 220 ft in diameter, and is a satellite of Newgrange. Dowth is 50 ft high and 280 ft in diameter and also contains ritual stone basins and prehistoric tombs on both sides of the main tomb. The kerb stones all share the mystic spiral carvings of Indian origin.

NEWGRANGE is roughly 30 miles north west of Dublin and a few miles east of Slane.

PORTMARNOCK
County Dublin

Portmarnock has three miles of sandy strand from which the Irish Army Colonel Fitzmaurice and his German companions took off in a Junker's plane to make the first east-west Atlantic crossing.

St Doulagh's Church, two miles west of Portmarnock, is little known, and yet it was the 6th-

Strange carvings decorate stones within fascinating Newgrange passage grave

Quiet and unspoilt, Rush has two sandy beaches and a fishing harbour

century hermit cell of St Doulagh. The old rectangular vaulted church is 13th century and the square tower is presumed to rise above the burial place of the saint. St Doulagh's Well is enclosed by an octagonal stone roof. Adjacent is St Catherine's Well, an underground chamber with a strange sunken bath about 3ft deep. Nearby is St Doulagh's Lodge, once the home of Nathaniel Hone, Ireland's most famous landscape painter of his era, who lived from 1831 to 1917. A Barbizon painter, who had studied with Millet, he was

a distinguished member of the Royal Hibernian Academy.

The town has an 18 hole world championship golf course.
🚗 *PORTMARNOCK is 9 miles north of Dublin.*

POWERSCOURT
County Wicklow

Quite the most beautiful gardens in Ireland are those of the 14,000 acre Powerscourt Demesne on either side of the banks of the lovely Dargle River. The great house, once the

home of Viscount Powerscourt, was badly damaged by fire, but the chief glory are the gardens. As in classical Chinese gardens they blend, deliberately, with the magnificent backdrop of the Sugar Loaf mountain, which looks like a minor Vesuvius. The gardens, complete with formal lake, fountains, trees and shrubs were 30 years in the making and were finished in 1875. The spectacular circular terraces descend to the Triton Lake, which is guarded by winged horses rampant. Daniel Robertson, who originally laid out the formal

gardens, had over 100 gardeners to assist him. Arthur Young, the celebrated 18th-century agriculturalist who frequently stayed at Powerscourt said, quite simply, that it was the most beautiful place in the world. The Japanese gardens were added by the 8th Viscount in 1908 from reclaimed bogland. Many of the trees of the Demesne were planted over 200 years ago and came from all over the world. Some stand over 150 ft high. Roses and rhododendrons, magnolia and azalea grow in great profusion. The famous

Oriental splendour in the gardens of Powerscourt estate. These gardens took 30 years to perfect

Powerscourt Waterfall is one of the highest in Ireland, dropping a spectacular 400 ft. There are herds of deer in the park. Added attractions are an armoury museum, and a gift shop and restaurant, superbly managed by one of Ireland's former leading lady equestrian show jumpers.

🚗 *POWERSCOURT is 4 miles south west of Bray.*

RUSH
County Dublin

Rush has a charming fishing harbour, two beautiful sandy strands and a 9-hole golf links which looks over the island of Lambay and south over Dublin Bay. Its name in Irish, *Ros Eo*, means the peninsular of the yew, and local tradition holds that many of the bows used at Agincourt came from this headland. It is the market garden for Dublin, because its light, sandy soil yields many annual crops. Its people are largely descended from the Norsemen of north Dublin and work with Scandinavian ardour.

The Catholic church of Saint Maur, now being re-built, was originally built by Breton sailors as a thanksgiving for their being saved from a shipwreck off Lambay Island where fierce currents rage.

🚗 *RUSH is 18 miles north of Dublin.*

RUSSBOROUGH HOUSE
County Wicklow

Russborough, at Blessington, is the perfect Palladian style house of two of the most generous supporters of

Inside Russborough House hang the priceless paintings collected by Sir Alfred Beit

the arts in Ireland, Sir Alfred and Lady Beit. A gleaming Wicklow granite mansion, it was built in 1741 for Joseph Leeson by the architect Richard Cassels. Today it stands with almost every detail of its original baroque plasterwork, woodwork, floors and mantels intact. The house is the perfect setting for Sir Alfred Beit's collection of priceless paintings, furniture and objets d'art. The art collection includes Magnacos, Murillos, Velazquez, Gainsboroughs, Raeburns, Guardis, Vermeers, and a superb Goya, his portrait of the dancer Dona Antonia Zarate. The facade of the imposing house embraces a central building joined by curving colonnades to buildings to the east and to the west. The house has the added advantage of overlooking the Poulaphouca reservoir.

RUSSBOROUGH HOUSE is 3 miles south east of the beautiful village of Blessington, which is 18 miles south of Dublin.

SHILLELAGH
County Wicklow

This charming village on the Shillelagh River was once in the midst of the great oak forests of Ireland which supplied the timbers for the roof of the medieval Westminster Hall. It also supplied timbers for the British Navy and for the roof of St Patrick's Cathedral in Dublin.

In the late 19th century the oak cudgel wielded by fighting tinkers was given the name 'Shillelagh', and the word became part of the Irish stage world of Victorian times so that today the distorted sticks of varnished blackthorn wood sold to tourists are called Irish 'Shillelaghs'.

SHILLELAGH is 22 miles south west of Wicklow town.

Skerries is an ideal holiday destination with a good beach. It is also a sea-fishing centre

SKERRIES
County Dublin

From the Irish *Sceiri*, meaning sea rocks, Skerries is a charming seaside resort with a splendid harbour, a popular sailing club, a sandy strand and a good golf course. It was on St Patrick's Island, one and a half miles east of the village that St Patrick

came ashore to get fresh water on his way from Wicklow up to Slemish in A.D. 432. You can see his footprint quite clearly in the rock. According to local legend the inhabitants of Skerries stole the Saint's goat and cooked and ate it while he was seeking fresh water. They became known as the 'skin the goats', and they do not take kindly

to this story, so that when the architect of the local parish church put a statue of St Patrick with a goat at his feet at the entrance door, they had the goat chiselled off!

The other islands off the coast include Colt Island and Shenick's Island, and five miles out to sea stands Rockabill Lighthouse. Because of its historical association

with St Patrick, Skerries was the setting for one of the most important of Synods A.D. 1148 and from this St Malachi was sent to Rome to seek the setting up of the first archbishops of Ireland. Hompatrick, at the southern end of the village, is the site of the monastery built by Sitric, the Norse King of Dublin, in 1120. There is a St Patrick's well in

Irish poet Francis Ledwidge was born in this cottage at Slane

undulating countryside of four counties, and as far as the sea. The monastic settlement and Round Tower of the 9th century was destroyed by Norse raiders. There are the remains of a 16th-century church on the site of the original church founded by St Patrick. From the west tower of these remains are magnificent views. The 9th-century monastic foundation here was associated with St Earc, first bishop of Slane.

Slane Castle, the seat of the Marquis of Conyngham, is a castelated mansion designed by the architect Francis Johnston, and set in a lovely demesne, and with a ballroom akin to the architecture of the Royal Pavilion in Brighton. George IV visited the castle twice, enamoured of the fat, fair, vulgar and avaricious Marchioness of Conyngham. He made her mistress of his household, and her husband was made his Lord Chamberlain.

In the village was born the poet Francis Ledwidge, 1887-1917, killed in action at Flanders.

🚗 *SLANE is 29 miles north west of Dublin, 9 miles west of Drogheda.*

SWORDS
County Dublin

Swords takes its name from the Irish *Sord Colaim Chille* meaning a pure well, blessed by St Columcille. He founded the monastery here which was run by St Finian the Leper. The monastic settlement was burnt and pillaged by the Norsemen on many occasions and the 75 ft high Round Tower would have been the safe refuge of the monastic treasures, books and chalices. A 14th-century square steeple was added to the Round Tower, and the present day ruins are all that remain of what was

the village, and a mile west is St Mobhi's Well, of the 7th-century saint who founded the monastery of Glasnevin in north Dublin. Two miles south are the magnificent ruins of the Norman castle of Baldongan. This was the 13th-century fortress home of the Barnewalls, then the Berminghams and then the St Lawrence family, Earls of Howth. Cromwell destroyed it in 1642 and

butchered the garrison of 200. From the tower there is a fine view north of the Mountains of Mourne, and south to the Bay of Killiney.

🚗 *SKERRIES is 19 miles north of Dublin city.*

SLANE
County Meath

The village of Slane lies in the Boyne

valley just a mile from the 529 ft high hill of Slane, where St Patrick lit the first Paschal Fire in Ireland in A.D. 433. The fire broke the blackout decreed by the pagan King Leary who witnessed it from the neighbouring Hill of Tara. With this fire St Patrick broke the power of the druids in Ireland and introduced Christianity. From the top of the hill are magnificent views of the

once the country palace of the 13th and 14th-century Archbishops of Dublin.

SWORDS *is 8 miles north of Dublin City.*

TARA
County Meath

Tara — *Teamhair na Ríogh* — 'the Royal Acropolis' was the druidic and cultural capital of Ireland from time immemorial, the seat of pagan priest-kings and the centre of the national assembly for law making in peace and war. The pagan goddess Maeve was worshipped here and it became the seat of the High Kings of Tara. The last royal resident was Malachi II, High King of Ireland, who died in 1022. St Patrick came to Tara to confront the druids and convert the High King, Laoire. On the top of the hill is a modern statute of the saint and adjacent is the *Lia Fáil*, the Stone of Destiny, the coronation stone of ancient Kings. Royal palaces no longer stand on the site but there are grassy mounds marking the most historic of sites. The largest is the *Ráth na Ríogh*, the Royal Enclosure, 950 ft by 800 ft, in which stand the mound of King Cormac's House, and of the Royal Seat. Within the Royal Enclosure is the Grave Mound of the Hostages, dating from some 2000 years B.C. Cormac's house has defensive banks and ditches. South of the Royal Enclosure is the Ráth Laoghaire, and to the north is the three-ringed fort, the Ráth of the Synods. The long, deep hollow north of this with its high banks marks the site of the ancient Banqueting Hall which was 700 ft long and 90 ft wide. North west of the Banqueting Hall are the fort of Gráinne, King Cormac's daughter, the tragic lover of Diarmuid, and two other earthen mounds known as

Swords Church and round tower

the Sloping Trenches. On another hill, south of Tara, is the Ráth of Maeve, a hill fort some 750 ft in diameter. The songs of Thomas Moore, such as *The Harp That Once Through Tara's Halls*, have greatly glamourised what are now but mounds of earth, but, undoubtedly Tara is a place of enormous mystery spanning the times from pagan gods to St Patrick and the High Kings of Ireland.

TARA *lies 6 miles south of Navan and 23 miles from Dublin.*

WICKLOW
County Wicklow

The town of Wicklow sits snugly in the slopes of Ballyguile Hill on the mouth of the Vartry river, overlooking a wide crescent-shaped bay. Wicklow derives its name from the Danish *Wykinglo* — it was a Norse pirate station and slaving port. After the Norsemen the Normans took it over in the person of Maurice Fitz-Gerald. Then the local O'Toole and O'Byrne tribes fought over it. Maurice FitzGerald built the Black Castle, the ruins of which stand at the eastern end of the town on a rocky promontory. The Church of Ireland 13th-century church is built on the site of the medieval church of St Patrick and incorporates some of its 12th-century remains.

In the market square is a classic statue of a Wexford Pikeman of the Rebellion of 1798. He commemorates a bare-foot peasantry goaded into rebellion by the excesses of the Redcoats and German mercenaries who put down the Rebels with crack cavalry regiments and heavy artillery. From Wicklow Head, two miles south of the town, are magnificent views.

WICKLOW *is 32 miles south of Dublin.*

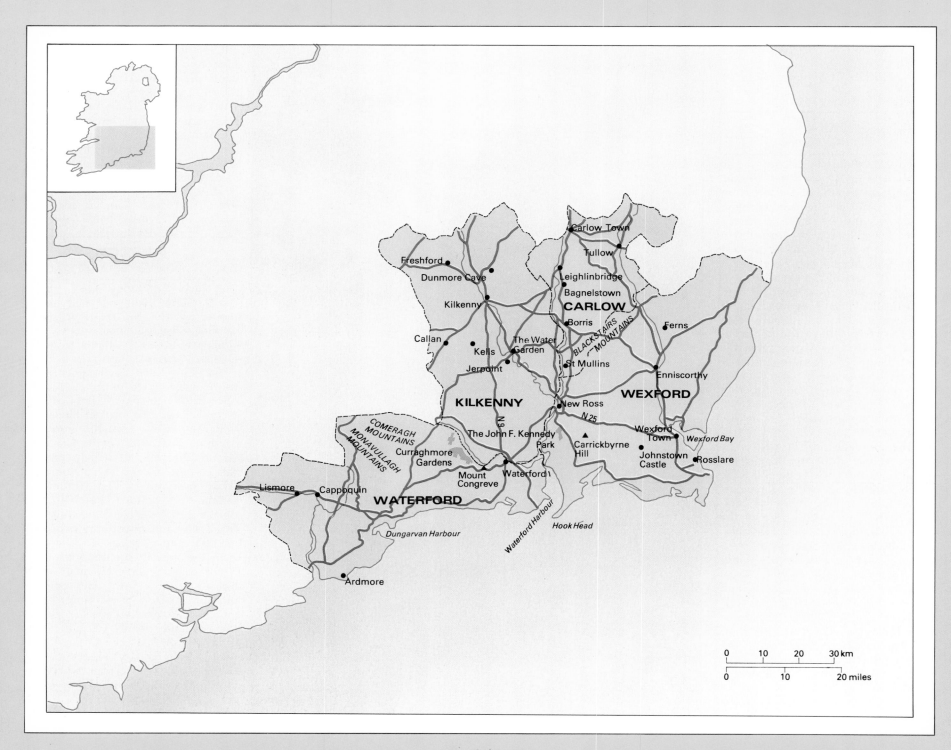

Carlow Town

Tullow

Freshford

Dunmore Cave

Leighlinbridge

Bagnelstown

Kilkenny

CARLOW

Borris

Ferns

Callan

The Water Garden

BLACKSTAIRS MOUNTAINS

Kells

St Mullins

Jerpoint

Enniscorthy

KILKENNY

New Ross

WEXFORD

COMERAGH MOUNTAINS

N 9

N 25

The John F. Kennedy Park

MONAVUILLAGH MOUNTAINS

Carrickbyrne Hill

Wexford Town

Wexford Bay

Curraghmore Gardens

Mount Congreve

Waterford

Johnstown Castle

Rosslare

Lismore

Cappoquin

WATERFORD

Dungarvan Harbour

Waterford Harbour

Hook Head

Ardmore

0   10   20   30 km

0   10   20 miles

The magnificent range of Comeragh mountains are a prominent part of the scenery of south east Ireland and can be seen for miles around

OUNTY CARLOW, COVERING 346 square miles of rich, well watered, fertile farmland is only 29 square miles or so larger than Louth, Ireland's smallest county. This small but wealthy area can boast what is arguably the best provincial weekly newspaper in the country, *The Carlow Nationalist*, European in outlook. The sugar beet industry, flour milling, malting and a rich river, the Barrow, make it a fascinating and prosperous part of the country.

Kilkenny, historically the seat of the Butlers of Ormonde, the royal representatives of English kings, is today best known for its internationally famous Irish design centre, situated in the stables and coach houses of Kilkenny Castle, and the sport of hurling, which is played with a vengeance in this part of the country.

The name of Waterford is, of course, synonymous with cut glass, an ancient Irish craft revived by the McGrath family. Wexford, another county, like Waterford, with a magnificent sea coast, is internationally renowned for its Festival of Opera. This successful annual event, which attracts enthusiasts and critics from all over Europe and America, was the brain-child of Dr Tom Walsh, founder of the festival, and his friend and colleague the late Eugene McCarthy, whose family still run the centuries-old White's Hotel in the town centre. The town, on the River Slaney, is of great antiquity and still bears signs of its Norman heritage.

ARDMORE
County Waterford

Ardmore, in addition to being an attractive seaside resort beautifully located on Ardmore Bay, has the remains of a superb monastic site of the 7th century, founded by St Declan, bishop of Munster before the arrival of St Patrick. These remains include a splendid Round Tower 97 ft high and divided into four storeys. St Declan's Oratory is a tiny church 14 ft long by 9 ft wide, with high pitched gables and a lintelled west door. It was re-roofed in 1716. The Cathedral dates from the 10th century. It has a well-proportioned nave and a chancel. The external wall of the West gable is quite remarkable, a Romanesque arcade of carved figures normally seen on Celtic High Crosses. The ruins also include the Hermitage Church, St Declan's Holy Well, and, on the beach, St Declan's Stone.

Ardmore is some 30 miles south west of Waterford.

BAGNELSTOWN
County Carlow

Bagnelstown, a charming town on the River Barrow, takes its name from Walter Bagnel, who had the grandiose idea of building an Irish version of Versailles on the site. Today the town has reverted to its old Irish name, *Muine Bheag,* 'The Little Shrubbery.' Walter Bagnel lived in Dunleckny Manor, north of the town. His ancestor, Sir Nicholas Bagenal, was a general in the army of Queen Elizabeth and was thus able to purchase vast estates in County Carlow in 1585. Two miles east of the town are the imposing ruins of the 14th-century Ballymoon Castle, a square enclosure with towers, built by the Carew family in

Ardmore church and round tower are sites of great antiquity

the tempestuous 13th century.

BAGNELSTOWN, or Muine Bheag, as it is signposted, is 11 miles from Carlow and 63 from Dublin.

BORRIS
County Carlow

Borris, also known as Borris Idrona, from its name in Irish, is a picturesque Georgian town in the east of the valley of the River Barrow. It is delightfully situated between the foot of the Blackstairs Mountains whose highest point is Mount Leinster, 2610 ft high, and the Hill of Brandon, great walking and climbing country.

Just west of the village itself is Borris House, home of the Mac Murrough Kavanaghs, direct descendants of the King of Leinster, Dermot Mac Murrough Kavanagh, who made possible the Norman occupation of the greater part of Ireland in the 1170s. Some say that due to this a curse was laid on the family, particularly the male heirs.

Be this as it may, the most remarkable and famous of the male Mac Murrough Kavanaghs was the one who lived from 1831 to 1889 and was born without arms or legs. Despite this he learned to ride a horse in a specially constructed saddle-seat, learned to shoot and became a Member of Parliament!

BORRIS is approximately 60 miles from Dublin.

CALLAN
County Kilkenny

Callan, from the Irish *Calainn,* Callan's Tribe, is a busy little town, medieval in origin, and older than Kilkenny as it received its Charter in 1271 from William the Marshal, who established a manor house there. In 1391 it was bought by James Butler, Earl of Ormonde. It

The smooth waters of the River Barrow flow through County Carlow

was a walled town in the 15th century, subject to attack by the local O'Carroll of Ely clan, and in 1650 it was surrendered to Cromwellian forces by Ormonde's governor Sir Robert Talbot. For a small town it has produced some remarkable people. James Hoban, the architect of the White House in Washington D.C. was born near Callan in 1762. Robert Fulton, who designed the first steamship the world ever saw was born in the town in 1765. In the main street is a memorial, a life-size statue, to Brother Edmund Rice, 1762-1844, the founder of the famous Irish educationalists, the Christian Brothers. He was born in the townland of Westcourt, adjacent to the town. The thatched farmhouse in which he was born has been preserved in its 18th-century form, and a chapel and a monastery has been built nearby. In the town are the ruins of the 15th-century Augustian Friary. It was founded by Eamonn MacRisdera Butler of Puttlerath in 1452. His son James built the rectangular church with its central tower. The chancel is near the local Church of Ireland parish church. James was the father of Sir Piaras Rua Butler, Earl of Ossory and Ormonde.

CALLAN *is 6 miles south west of Kilkenny.*

CAPPOQUIN
County Waterford

Cappoquin, *Ceapac Cuinn*, Conn's Plot of Land, is a beautiful and peaceful market town set in wooded countryside, at the foot of the glorious Knockmealdown Mountains, where the Glenshelan River joins the River Blackwater. Across the fine stone bridge, four miles to the north, is the Trappist Monastery of Mount Mellaray, founded by the

Cappoquin — a peaceful market town set in wooded countryside

Cistercians in 1832, who turned a barren mountainside into 800 acres of farmland and built a magnificent Abbey monastery, seminary and guesthouse. Renowned for its traditional hospitality, the guesthouse takes visitors free. The custom is for visitors or pilgrims to make any offering they think fit, although they are not strictly obliged to do so.

CAPPOQUIN is 131 miles south of Dublin and 4 miles from Lismore.

CARLOW TOWN
County Carlow

Carlow Town, from the Irish *Ceatarlac*, meaning the 'Fourfold Lake', beautifully situated on the River Barrow, is a prosperous modern town, once an Anglo-Norman fortress on the edge of the 'Pale', that area around Dublin

which the Normans occupied, and beyond which they could not keep a military presence. In 1361 it was a walled city and remained so until the 1650s. When the peasants of Carlow rose in rebellion in 1798, the Redcoats killed 650 in the fighting, and today a beautiful Celtic Cross marks the grave of 400 rebels buried on one side of the town. Carlow Castle, built in 1200 by William le Mareschal, changed hands many times in many battles and its remains still stand near the bridge on the Barrow, once a rectangular building with a circular Norman tower, now reduced to two towers on the west bank. Cromwell captured it in 1650 and after that it was occupied by Donough, Earl of Thomond.

It became the property of a Dr Middleton, who in order to make room for the erection of a lunatic

asylum, blew up part of the Castle in 1814! The Catholic Cathedral of the Assumption was built in 1833 and has a unique lantern tower 150 ft high. The Cathedral contains a superb marble monument to Bishop Doyle by the Irish sculptor Hogan. The Courthouse has a splendid granite Doric portico modelled on the Parthenon in Athens. Two miles east of Carlow at Browne's Hill, is a dolmen with the largest capstone in Europe. The dolmen dates from 2500 B.C., and its 100 ton capstone is balanced on the earth and three standing stones.

At Killeshin, three miles west of the town, are the ruins of Killeshin Church which include a splendid example of a Hiberno-Romanesque doorway.

CARLOW lies 52 miles south west of Dublin on an old coaching road with little traffic.

CARRICKBYRNE HILL
County Wexford

At over 700 ft high Carrickbyrne Hill offers magnificent panoramic views of the surrounding countryside. It was an Insurgent encampment in the 1798 Rebellion for the period approaching the battle for New Ross. At nearby Carrigadaggin is a granite memorial, erected in 1841, to the memory of a very gallant English soldier, Sir Ralph Abercromby. He was commander-in-chief of the British forces in Ireland just prior to the 1798 Rebellion. He protested again and again in the strongest possible terms about the barbaric behaviour of the Redcoats, and in particular of the brutality of the Hessian forces, the German mercenary troops. Since the Government was bent on goading the peasants into revolt they forced him to resign his command.

CARRICKBYRNE is 8 miles south-east of New Ross.

CURRAGHMORE GARDENS
County Waterford

Curraghmore Gardens are beautifully landscaped grounds next to Curraghmore, the seat of the Marquis of Waterford. There is a shell house decorated in 1754 by Catherine, Countess of Tyrone. The selection of trees is magnificent, and in the months of May and June the rhododrendra, the azaleas and the bluebells are at their very best.

The House is open to groups by advance arrangement. The demesne of the Marquis of Waterford is 10 miles of high hills, deep valleys and rich oak forests through which the River Clodiagh flows.

CURRAGHMORE GARDENS are in the village of Portlaw, 10 miles from the city of Waterford.

Fabulous Clonea Strand at Dungarvan is ideal for seaside holidays

DUNGARVAN
County Waterford

'Dun' is Irish for fortress, so it is hardly surprising that this lively town, with its thriving port, has two castles; Dungarvan Castle and Prince John's Castle in its environs.

Adopted by the Normans, Dungarvan now plays a large part in the great revival of the Gaelic language. People came from all over Europe to learn Gaelic on the nearby peninsula of *An Rinn*.

Dungarvan is ideally situated for those who wish to explore the nearby mountain ranges of Monavullagh and Comeragh.

DUNGARVAN is on the N25, 28 miles south-west of Waterford and 44 miles north-east of Cork.

DUNMORE CAVE
County Kilkenny

At Dunmore are the largest and most accessible limestone caves in the country, specially lit and equipped with a viewing balcony for

Ancient Dunmore Cave has played its part in Irish history. It is now specially lit and open to visitors

visitors. Dunmore comes from the Irish, *Derc Ferna,* the Cave of the Alders. In 928 the raiding Vikings put to death 1000 people who had sheltered there. The cave has a direct historical association with the legendary Kilkenny 'Cats', for it is recorded in the ancient Book of Leinster that a gigantic cat, known in Irish as *Luchthigern,* – the Lord of the Mice – lived in this cave. The interior of the limestone cave is shaped not unlike a recumbent cat with an outstretched tail. Stalagmites and dripstone formations abound.

DUNMORE CAVE is 7 miles north of Kilkenny.

ENNISCORTHY
County Wexford

Enniscorthy is a charming market town, perfectly placed in the middle of the county, in rich, agricultural land in the valley of the River Slaney. It is positioned on both sloping banks of the river, and spanned by a magnificent six-arched bridge. The Norman castle of Raymond le Gros was originally built here in 1235, and rebuilt in the 1590s by Sir Henry Wallop. This four-storey castle has rounded turrets and was associated with the Elizabethan poet, Edmund Spenser. The town is immortalised in the ballads of the 1798 Rebellion, as the rebels held it against the forces of General Lake for several weeks. Long before it went up in flames in 1798, it had been damaged in 1649 by the siege guns of Cromwell. In the market square are the statues of Father Murphy, the patriot priest leader of

This memorial to the 1798 Rebellion stands in Enniscorthy

1798, who was executed, and a pikeman. At the eastern edge of the town lies Vinegar Hill, 390 ft high, equally famous in patriotic songs and ballads, as it was here that the Insurgents made their last desperate stand against the superior forces of General Lake and General Johnson.

One of the most famous ballads, *The Boys of Wexford*, refers to the 'bold Shelmalier', with his long-barrelled gun, which was the duck hunting gun used by the fowlers of this area, who made such expert snipers in the Insurgent forces. Father John Murphy, the Insurgent leader, headed up his peasant forces armed with pikes after the Redcoats had burnt the Catholic church of Boolavogue, just north of Enniscorthy. This burning was the *causus belli* of the 1798 Rebellion. The ballad *Boolavogue* was a special favourite of the late U.S. President John F. Kennedy. The castle of Enniscorthy is now a folk museum.

ENNISCORTHY is 15 miles north west of Wexford.

FERNS
County Wexford

Ferns, *Fearna* – The Alder Trees – now a quiet and pleasant little village, was once the capital of the Province of Leinster and the episcopal see of the 6th century St Maodhóg, better known as St Aidan. The monastery he founded was repeatedly sacked by the Norsemen. Dermot Mac Murrough Kavanagh founded an Abbey here for the Canons Regular of St Augustine. It was burnt down in 1154, rebuilt in 1160 and given to the Augustinians. The ruins of the west tower, the north wall of a church, a sacristy and some of the cloisters remain. The church would have been barrel-vaulted like Cormac's Chapel at Cashel. Parts of the old church are incorporated in the present Church of Ireland building. The sculptured Celtic High Cross in the graveyard marks the grave of King Dermot, the greatest traitor in Irish history. He abducted his neighbour's wife, and then invited Henry II to invade Ireland, blessed by a bull given by Pope Adrian IV, the only English Pope in history. The castle of Ferns occupies the site of the residence of King Dermot. The castle was built in the 12th century by the Earl Marshall family. It is a splendid example of Norman-Irish architecture with three of the four round towers remaining, each 30 ft in diameter. The chapel is circular, covered by a carved vault. Some of the 13th-century trefoil headed windows remain. The Mac Murrough's held the castle in the 14th century and the Cromwellian General Sir Charles Coote captured it in 1649 and butchered the inhabitants of Ferns. Until recently it was in the possession of the O'Donovan family.

FERNS is 68 miles south of Dublin and 21 miles north west of Wexford.

FRESHFORD
County Kilkenny

Freshford, today a busy market town with an attractive square, was once the monastic settlement of the princely St Lachtain who founded his church here in 622. There was a time when his arm was preserved in a 12th-century shrine, and this shrine can now be seen in the National Museum in Kildare Street, Dublin. On the original site of St Lachtain's church a larger church was erected in 1100, and the present church was built in 1730. It incorporates in its west gable the 12th-century Romanesque doorway. There is a steep pointed arch over the ornately carved Hiberno-Romanesque porchway. On the innermost jamb of the door is an inscription which asks for prayers for the builders: *Gill Mu-Cholmóc O Cenncucáin* and for *Mathgamain O Ciarmeic* for whom the church was made.

FRESHFORD is 9 miles north west of Kilkenny.

JERPOINT
County Kilkenny

Jerpoint Abbey is one of the finest examples of a Cistercian monastery in Ireland. It was founded in 1158 for the Benedictine Order by the King of Ossory, Donagh Mac Gillapatrick, and was associated

Jerpoint Abbey — one of the best examples of a Cistercian monastery to be found in Ireland

with Fountains Abbey in Yorkshire. After the suppression of the monasteries the Earl of Ormonde acquired it. A typical Cistercian monastery in lay-out, it would have had a huge choir in the abbey, surmounted by a tower, with an adjacent cloister, chapter house, kitchen, rectory and dormitory. The older portion of the ruins are 12th century with Hiberno-Romanesque chancel and transepts and the square, central 15th-century tower has typical Irish battlements. There is a row of six pointed arches between the nave and the north aisle. Sculptured figures of knights and saints adorn the much-restored cloister. The tombs include those of the Walsh family and one of the Butler family of the 15th and 16th century. The tomb of Bishop Felix O'Dullany who died in 1202, shows him holding a crozier which

has been partly gnawed by a snake. *THE ABBEY is on the banks of the little River Eoir, approximately 11 miles south east of Kilkenny.*

THE JOHN F. KENNEDY PARK
County Wexford

The John F. Kennedy Memorial Park is dedicated to John Fitzgerald Kennedy, who was President of the United States of America from January 1961 to his assassination on 22 November 1963.

It was inspired by the visit he made to the land of his fathers in June 1963. One of the highlights of this visit was his 'home-coming' to the Kennedy homestead in Dunganstown, where his second cousin once removed, the 'Widow Ryan' sat him down to tea and Irish soda bread. The homestead

still stands. The park was opened by the Irish government in May 1968 with the generosity and co-operation of many Irish-Americans who made the project possible.

It is a delightful leisure park, beautifully laid out and landscaped and with facilities for education and research, on the slopes of Slieve Coilte, just behind the ancestral house of the Kennedys in Dunganstown. It embraces 620 acres of land, over a third of which is devoted to the cultivation of specimen plantlife. It is primarily an arboretum, but also has some 6000 specimens of shrubs amid a garden forest of trees from five continents.

From the summit of Slieve Coilte you can view the entire park and the counties of Wexford and Waterford, including the Saltee Islands, the estuary of the Rivers Barrow, Nore

and Suir, and the entire Comeragh range of mountains.

John F. Kennedy had a deep and abiding love of Ireland, and particularly of Wexford. His first visit to Ireland was in 1938, when his father, Joseph P. Kennedy was the United States Ambassador in London. On his second visit to Ireland in 1947 the young John F. Kennedy paid his first visit to the ancestral home in Dunganstown. As Senator Kennedy he visited Ireland in 1955 and was welcomed by the Irish Minister for External Affairs, Liam Cosgrave.

Wexford always retained a special place in his heart and on his inauguration day he had his favourite Irish Ballad of the Rebellion of 1798, *Boolavogue* sung for him.

THE JOHN F. KENNEDY PARK is 8 miles south east of the town of New Ross.

JOHNSTOWN CASTLE
County Wexford

Johnstown Castle was built in the 13th century by the Anglo-Norman family of Esmonde. Cromwell had the castle taken down, and a Cromwellian soldier sold it to John Grogan of Yorkshire in 1683. By coincidence the marriage of a widow, Mrs Grogan-Morgan to Sir Thomas Esmonde brought the castle back to its original owners in the 19th century. It then became the residence of Lady Maurice Fitzgerald who died in 1942, and in 1946 this beautiful 19th-century Gothic castle was presented to the nation by her grandson and is in use today as a State Agricultural College. The castle is used for occasional banquets and the gardens are open to the public.

South of Johnstown Castle are the 'English Baronies' of Forth and Bargy. This title applies to the area from Wexford Harbour to Bannon Bay. This Anglo-Norman country-side has many well-preserved castles, abbeys and churches. Until recently the people of the baronies spoke a dialect in which many early Anglo-Norman words were preserved. In 1169 Robert FitzStephen and Hervey de Marisco landed with 30 men in armour, 60 armoured horses, and 300 bowmen. Dermot MacMurrough, the traitor King of Leinster, joined the Norman freebooters with a force of Danes, and the combined forces took Wexford in the first battle for the Norman Conquest of Ireland.

JOHNSTOWN CASTLE is 5 miles south-west of Wexford town.

The grey turrets and landscaped gardens of Johnstown Castle in County Wexford

KELLS
County Carlow

The Augustinian Priory at Kells was founded in 1193 by Geoffrey de Marisco; Geoffrey FitzRobert de Monte de Marisco to give him his full title, Strongbow's strong-arm man for the Province of Leinster. This was established in the vicinity of an ancient monastic site of St Ciaran, as just two miles south at Kilree is a magnificent 96 ft high Round Tower and a Celtic cross which marks the burial place of Niale Caille, High King of Ireland.

The substantial ruins of the 14th and 15th centuries mark one of the largest collections of medieval buildings in Ireland. Originally the Augustinian Abbey covered five acres of land. The original Abbey or Priory consists of a nave and chancel topped by a huge square tower. There is an aisle to the west of the cruciform church with a Lady Chapel on the east side of the transept. The nave and choir form the cross piece of the cruciform and off the main body of the church is a square cloister and a huge kitchen. The tower at the north west of the main church would have been the residence of the Prior. South of the Priory was fortified by walls and five turrets. The monastery was suppressed in 1540 and granted to the Earl of Ormonde.

KELLS is 6 miles from Callan and 10 miles from Kilkenny.

KILKENNY
County Kilkenny

Kilkenny, a charming cathedral city of considerable prosperity and importance, standing on both banks of the River Nore, has attractive narrow winding medieval streets. Its name in Irish is *Cill Cainnig*, meaning 'Canice's Church', since it was founded by Saint Canice of Aghaboe in the 6th century. It was capital of

St Canice's Cathedral, built in the 13th century

Glowing stonework inside St Canice's Cathedral, Kilkenny

the Irish Kingdom of Ossory. In Anglo-Norman times the freebooter Strongbow built a castle near the monastery of St Canice to command the river crossing of the Nore. His son-in-law, William le Mareschal, inherited it and built it into a solid stone castle in 1204. After being in the hands of the de Clares and the Staffords it was bought by James Butler, 3rd Earl of Ormonde in 1391.

Kilkenny became the seat of many parliaments, and one, in 1366, established the Statutes of Kilkenny. These were enacted because the Anglo-Normans were becoming 'more Irish than the Irish themselves'. Thus the Normans were forbidden to marry the native Irish, adopt their dress or names or language, and all Irish monks and clerics were kept out of Norman monasteries and cathedrals. In the cathedral in 1575, Rory O'Moore, King of Laois, bowed the knee to Elizabeth. The foremost educationalists in Europe, the Jesuits, set up a school in 1619. From 1642 until 1648 the old Irish and the Anglo-Irish Catholics came together in the Assembly known as the Confederation of Kilkenny, which was virtually an Irish parliament. This was a glorious period for the city. Owen Roe O'Neill represented the Old Irish and the Anglo-Normans were represented by the English Viceroy, Ormonde, who in the event, sold the Confederation down the river, and it collapsed. General Owen Roe O'Neill died in 1649, and a year later Kilkenny fell to Cromwell, who, strangely enough, permitted the surrendered garrison to move out with full military honours. His troops 'utterly defaced and ruined' the Cathedral Church of St Canice by taking down the roof, removing all glass from the windows and stealing the doors and the five bells, 'so

that hogs might come and root, and the dogs gnaw the bones of the dead.'

St Canice's Cathedral, a 13th-century building, stands on the site of the 6th-century monastic settlement of St Canice, and the 9th-century Round Tower still stands, 100 ft high, and affords a panoramic view of the city. The cathedral contains the finest collection of tombs of any church in Ireland. It includes the 1285 monument to the son of Henry de Ponto of Lyra, and the 1549 tomb of Edmund Purcell, who was a leader of Ormonde's Gallowglasses, the bodyguards of kings and princes who wielded double-headed axes. Another tomb is of the Franciscan Bishop, de Ledrede, who died in 1360, another to Bishop Rothe, of 1645. There is an altar tomb to the Bishop Hacket dated 1478.

The Black Abbey, in Abbey Street, is a Dominican church incorporating the building of 1225 by William le Mareschal, Earl of Pembroke. Not far away is St Canice's Well, with its stone well house. It has a strange history, for the 13th-century Bishop, Geoffrey de Turville, granted the friars the right to a supply of well water on condition that the water pipe did not exceed the diameter of his episcopal ring. The Black Freren Gate in Abbey Street is the only medieval gate remaining of the once walled city. There are also the ruins of St Francis Abbey of the Grey Friars.

In St Kieran's Street is Kyteler's Inn, Kilkenny's oldest house. Here the witch, Dame Alice Kyteler, was born in 1280, carried on a business as a money lender, became immensely wealthy and dabbled in sorcery. She was suspected of poisoning her four husbands, and in 1324 was tried and convicted of witchcraft. She escaped to England and

Kilkenny's streets retain an old-fashioned atmosphere

left her maid, Petronella, to be burnt at the stake.

The Magdelen Castle, situated in Maudlin Street, was once a medieval leper hospital. It is a square defence tower built to protect the barns and farmyard of the Earls of Ormonde. In Callan Road is St Kieran's College, the diocesan college of the Catholic diocese of Ossory. Among its famous professors were Francis Sheehy-Skeffington, the pacifist, shot in Dublin in 1916 on the orders of Captain Bowen-Colthurst, and the poet leader of the 1916 Insurrection, Thomas McDonagh who was executed by a firing squad.

The 13th-century Kilkenny Castle is the pride of the city. This was the residence of the Butler family, the Dukes of Ormonde. In the old stable of the Castle are the Kilkenny Design Workshops.

These workshops set standards of excellence of design for the whole country in crafts such as weaving, textile-printing, pottery and jewellery making. The original Kilkenny Design Shop has on sale some of the finest hand made crafts in the country. You can see silversmiths, potters and hand weavers at their work. Everything from furniture to candles to hand-blown crystal glass, stonewear and porcelain is on sale to the public, the products of some 35 small craft industries in all.

The Tholsel, now the City Hall, was once the tollhouse of the city, and was built in 1761. The records of the city dating back to 1230 are housed here, along with the city's historic sword and mace. Opposite Kilkenny Castle is Kilkenny College, a Georgian building of 1782. It is built on the site of the old college of St John built in 1616. Kilkenny College educated Swift (1667-1745), Congreve (1670-1729) Berkeley (1685-1753), Farquhar (1678-1707) and the novelist brothers, John Banim (1798-1842) and Michael Banim (1796-1874).

KILKENNY *is 73 miles south of Dublin, 30 miles north of Waterford.*

LEIGHLINBRIDGE
County Carlow

This pleasant village on the River Barrow once guarded a strategic bridge across the river. It is famous for its Black Castle, erected in 1180 by Hugh de Lacey. This was later the site of a 12th-century Carmelite monastery and the present castle was built in 1547 by Sir Edward Bellingham. Sir Peter Carew and the Bagenals also occupied it. The Kavanaghs and the Butlers and the O'Moores fought over it, and Colonel Hewson demolished it on behalf of Oliver Cromwell. Part of the 16th-century tower still remains, as do some defensive walls. The stone bridge over the river still incorporates stones of the original bridge built in 1320 by Maurice Jakis, a Canon of Kildare Cathedral who was a noted bridge builder.

At Cranavonane, in the parish of Leighlinbridge, in 1717 was born Edmund Cullen, the grandfather of Paul Cullen, Ireland's first Cardinal. Hugh Cullen, the Cardinal's father, was born in 1760. For his part in the Rising of 1798 he was imprisoned in Naas jail and other relatives were shot. Not surprisingly as this family was of Irish Jacobite patriot stock and as officers its members had fought in the Confederate army of 1641. Paul Cullen, the future Prince of the Church, was educated at Carlow College which gave sanctuary to 600 rebels in the battle for Carlow in 1798. Paul studied in Rome, became Rector of the Irish

College there and later Primate of All Ireland.

In May 1866 he became Ireland's first Cardinal, a confidant of Pope Pius IX, and revered by John Henry, later Cardinal Newman. He died on 24 October 1878. There is a statue of this lion of a man by Sir Thomas Farrell in the Catholic Pro-Cathedral in Dublin.

LEIGHLINBRIDGE is 7 miles south of Carlow town.

LISMORE
County Waterford

Lismore, sitting pretty on the south bank of the River Blackwater, was originally the site of the 7th-century monastic university city of St Carthach. St Colman, in the 8th century, presided over no less than 20 churches on this site. The Norsemen sacked it frequently and Henry II occupied it to receive the submission of the chiefs of Leinster and of Munster. Raymond le Gros destroyed the monastic city in 1173.

The sheer beauty of the setting of the village is reflected in the delicately poised Lismore Castle overhanging the Blackwater on a cliff. King John built it in 1185 on the site of St Carthach's monastery. It was once in the possession of Sir Walter Raleigh, and Richard Boyle possessed it in 1602, the 'Great' Earl of Cork. His son, Robert Boyle, the famous chemist, who gave his name to 'Boyle's Law' was born in the castle in 1755. It is now the property of the Duke of Devonshire and has the best salmon fishing waters in Ireland.

LISMORE is 134 miles from Dublin and 36 miles from Cork.

Beautiful Lismore Castle looks out over treetops and the dancing progress of the River Blackwater

Such is the reputation of Kilkenny for the generosity and prosperity of its people that a traditional rhyme says:

'Whenever you go to Kilkenny
Just ask for the Hole-in-the-Wall,
You'll get 24 eggs for a penny,
And butter for nothing at all.'

Still prosperous today, the city is internationally known for its Kilkenny Design Workshops which have become the shop-window of Ireland. The studios are in the cleverly re-designed Kilkenny Castle stables and coach houses, built in the late 18th century by the Earl of Ormonde. The workshops are responsible to the government for raising the standards of design in industry and among consumers throughout the country. Behind the little-changed facade are modern workshops for all types of crafts including hand weaving, silverware, hand-thrown stoneware, prototypes of furniture and engineering products, fabrics, jewellery and porcelain. The Kilkenny shops provide VAT-free prices for purchases sent direct to tourist's homes and have a worldwide mail order business.

A panel of experts vigorously assesses and tests products from all over Ireland for value, quality and design. There is also a branch shop in Dublin.

Kilkenny Design Centre

Inside Kilkenny Castle the craftsmen perfect their designs

College and Trinity College, Dublin, his best known drama being the comedy *The Way of the World* (1700). Another William Congreve invented matches, and the first rockets used as weapons, used by the Royal Navy at the battle of Copenhagen, and it was Ambrose Congreve who was responsible for today's woodland garden and vast walled enclosure of lawns and herbaceous borders.

Plants include some hydrangea and buddleia, Oriental poppies, rhododendra, rare plants from South America and Tasmania, and magnolia trees of spectacular beauty. Expert gardeners reckon it to be one of the glories of Ireland, and its high terraces and walks above the beautiful River Suir give it a perfect setting.

➤ *MOUNT CONGREVE demesne is 4 miles west of the town of Portlaw, which is 9 miles west of Waterford.*

NEW ROSS
County Wexford

Delightfully placed on a hillside above the River Barrow, New Ross, one of Wexford's oldest towns, has narrow, winding streets. It was built on the site of the 6th-century monastery of St Abban, a walled town which did not surrender to a fierce siege by the Duke of Ormonde. Cromwell captured it in 1649, and in 1798 it was held briefly by the Insurgent forces under their leader Bagenal Harvey. Today, a trip aboard the *New Ross Galley* offers a splendid opportunity to see the beauty of the surrounding countryside from five miles of river whilst wining and dining.

Five miles from New Ross is the National Memorial Park and Arboretum, dedicated to the memory of U.S. President John F. Kennedy.

MOUNT CONGREVE
County Waterford

The gardens of Mount Congreve, on the south bank of the River Suir, have been described as 'one of the grandest

woodland gardens in Europe' and 'one of the very few Irish gardens in which planting of flowering trees and shrubs still continues on a lavish scale.

The Georgian house on the

demesne was built by John Congreve in 1725. Not only were members of the family world-renowned gardeners but they included the dramatist William Congreve (1670-1729), a contemporary of Swift at Kilkenny

At Dunganstown, near New Ross, is the cottage in which the great-grandfather of President Kennedy was born.

🚗 *NEW ROSS is 27 miles south east of Kilkenny.*

ROSSLARE
County Wexford

Rosslare – the Middle Peninsular – with six miles of curving, sandy beach, has the unique reputation of being the driest and sunniest place in Ireland. The harbour is the terminal for car ferries from Fishguard and Le Havre. Just off the coast is the Tuskar Rock with its famous lighthouse, erected in 1815, and whose beams are visible for more than 20 miles in the busy sea lanes. South of Rosslare harbour is Carnsore Point where there are the remains of an ancient church and the Holy Well of St Vaux, an Irish saint who died in Brittany in A.D. 585. The sandy beach of Carne once appeared on Ptolemy's 2nd-century map of the then-known world as *Hieron Akron*, the Holy Cape. A few miles off the coast are the Saltee Islands, a sanctuary for over three million wild birds in spring and summer.

🚗 *ROSSLARE is 11 miles south east of Wexford.*

ST MULLINS
County Carlow

Carlow's claim to monastic fame lies in St Mullins, the foundation of St Moling who died in 698. Here the Saint achieved the impossible by persuading the men of Leinster to let the men of Munster off the 'Borama', the tribute of cattle which they had been obliged to pay. The McMurrough-Kavanaghs, Kings of

New Ross, on the River Barrow, is one of County Wexford's oldest towns

Leinster, lie buried here. St Moling was Bishop of Glendalough, and of Ferns. His Abbey is medieval with an unusual spiral staircase. There are the remains of what was once a Round Tower, St Jame's Chapel, and a Celtic High Cross of granite featuring the crucifixion. There are also the remains of some Norman buildings. The Norsemen plundered the monastery in 951 and in 1138 almost razed it to the ground. Ancient 7th-century manuscripts describe the original plan of the monastery in considerable detail.

ST MULLINS is 9 miles south of Borris, in the Barrow Valley, and 79 miles south of Dublin.

TRAMORE
County Waterford

This splendid seaside resort counts golden sands, a miniature railway and a boating lake among its many attractions. Those who enjoy a flutter at the races will have heard of Tramore's famous racecourse.

Quite apart from these modern day features, archaeologists will find a great deal to interest them in the vicinity as earthworks, passage graves and castles abound.

TRAMORE is 8½ miles south of Waterford and 23 miles east of Dungarvan on the coast road.

TULLOW
County Carlow

The neat market town of Tullow was once the setting for a Butler castle which commanded the river crossing, and the garrison of a subsequent castle fell to Cromwell's forces in 1650, and were put to the sword. Richard II's hirelings took the surrender of the King of Leinster, Art MacMurrough in 1395 in a meadow near Tullow. By this submission, Art and his followers left the province of Leinster. In the market square is a splendid statue of Father John Murphy, the insurgent leader of the 1798 Rebellion who was hanged in the town.

Tramore's glorious golden sands and good amenities make it an ideal holiday resort

Some four miles east of the town is the traditional burial place of the Kings of Leinster, the ancient four ring stone hillfort of Rathgall. It is 1000 ft in diameter and covers 18 acres. The central fort is 150 ft in diameter with an 18 ft thick rampart. At Aghade, a few miles south of Tullow is the *Cloch and Phoill*, the Holed Stone, a large, flat leaning stone with a hole half a foot wide at one end. In mythology it is the stone to which Niall of the Nine Hostages tied Eochaidh, son of Enna Cinnselach by a chain. He snapped the chain and slew all nine of the men Niall had sent to kill him. This area has a number of grooved standing stones, pre-historic graves and portal dolmens and bronze age cemeteries.
🚗 *TULLOW is 50 miles south of Dublin.*

WATERFORD
County Waterford

The ancient city of Waterford, perched on the south side of the noble River Suir, has a fine harbour on the confluence of the rivers Nore and Barrow. 'Waterford' is a Norse name *Vadrefjord*, which means that the marauding pirates stayed around long enough to name it after they arrived in A.D. 853. The Anglo-Normans under Strongbow and Raymond le Gros then took it. As was the Norman custom, the freebooter Strongbow consolidated his gain by marrying Eva, daughter of Dermot MacMurrough, the treacherous high king of Leinster, who had invited him to Ireland in the first place. Historians differ about the arrival in Waterford in 1171 of King Henry II, armed with a Papal Bull from the first and last ever English Pope, to 'convert' the Irish to Rome. So loyal were the citizens of Waterford to the crown that both King John in 1210

A craftsman at work on Waterford's best known export; beautiful hand-made glass

and Richard II in 1394 visited the city. Henry VII gave it its city arms, which remain today, *Urbs Intacta Manet Waterfordia.*

The Waterford Glass factory, which revived the 18th-century art of glass-blowing, is a mile or so down the road to Cork from Waterford City. The public can see the hand-made glass being created at set times each day. The glass itself is on sale in all the major stores and shops in the city and elsewhere in Ireland. The most striking building in Waterford is Reginald's Tower, a circular fortress with walls 10 ft thick, established by the Danes and taken

over by the Normans. There are still traces of the walls of the old Danish Norman city. Because of its sturdy people and able defences, Waterford is one of the few cities in Ireland which did not succumb to the butchery of Cromwellian troops. Cromwell besieged it, and had to retire, and in August 1650 his son-in-law, General Ireton took it and accepted an honourable surrender. The poet Spenser knew Waterford and wrote:

"...the gentle Shure that making way
By sweet Clonmell, adornes rich Waterford",

Reginald's Tower was erected by the

Danes in 1003 to defend the city, and Strongbow took it in 1171. King John turned it into a mint after he had imprisoned Fitzstephen there.

Near to the tower is the 'French Church' of the Grey Friars, originally a Franciscan church built in A.D. 1240 by Sir Hugh Purcell and much favoured by Henry III. When the monastery was suppressed in the course of the 16th-century Reformation it was bought, in 1545, by Patrick Walsh, who turned it into a hospital for the aged. Later, Huguenot refugees used it as a parish church, hence its name 'The French Church'. The City Hall, near

Reginald's Tower, was built in 1788 by John Roberts (1749-94), Waterford born, and great-grandfather of Field Marshal Lord Roberts. The council chamber boasts a genuine 18th-century chandelier of old Waterford Glass. Christchurch Cathedral, (18th century), was built on the site of a Danish church of A.D. 1050, replaced by architect John Roberts by another church in the 1770s. In Arundel Square are the remains of the Dominican church of 1226. In John's Lane, near the present St John's Catholic Church, are the remains of a Benedictine Priory of St John which was allied to the Benedictine Abbey of Bath. In the comparatively unknown church of the Dominicans in Bridge Street, is a 17th-century oak wood statue of 'Our Lady of Waterford'.

With the exception of Dublin, no other city in Ireland has produced such a variety of famous sons. They include Luke Wadding, the distinguished 16th-century Irish Franciscan historian, the great Shakespearean actor, Charles Kean (1811-1868); Vincent Wallace (1813-1865), composer of the opera *Maritana*; Thomas Francis Meagher, 'Meagher of the Sword' (1823-1867), the Young Ireland leader who led the Irish Brigade at the battle of Fredericksburg in the American Civil War, and who later became Governor of Montana; General Lord Roberts (1832-1914), 'Bobs', the most popular general in the army of Queen Victoria during the Boer War, and John Redmond, who represented the city as an M.P. for 25 years and was the last leader of the Irish Parliamentary Group at Westminster.

◆ *WATERFORD is 103 miles south of Dublin, 30 miles from Kilkenny and 39 miles from Wexford.*

The city of Waterford straddles the banks of the River Suir. There is so much to see and do here visitors are spoilt for choice

THE WATER GARDEN
County Kilkenny

The Water Garden, at Ladywell, Thomastown, open to the public in the summer, is two acres of man-made aquatic heaven, complete with trees, shrubs and blooms which are at their best in the months of June and July. It is a restful place and teas can be taken on the terrace.

🚗 *THE WATER GARDEN in Thomastown is 9 miles south of the city of Kilkenny.*

WEXFORD TOWN
County Wexford

Wexford Town, on the River Slaney, was put on the world map by Ptolemy, the Greek geographer, in the second century A.D. He called it *Menapia*, after the Belgic tribe, the Menapi, who had settled on the site of present day Wexford before the time of Christ. It was captured by the Norsemen in the 9th century, and they called it *Waesfjord*, meaning 'the harbour of the mud flats'. The Norsemen settled down for 200 years and then the Norman free-booters led by Robert Fitzstephen, and with the treacherous connivance of Dermot MacMurrough, King of Leinster, landed and took over in 1169. In 1649 Oliver Cromwell captured the town and butchered all the inhabitants. For one month, in the Rebellion of 1798, it was held by the insurgent peasants against the Red-coats.

While Ptolemy was the first to put this coastal harbour town on the world map, Dr Tom Walsh of the local hospital brought Wexford to the forefront of international song when he established the annual Wexford Festival of Opera in 1951. The 'founding fathers' of this venture

The 'father' of the U.S. navy gazes out to sea at Wexford

were Tom Walsh, Eugene McCarthy, the owner of White's Hotel, Seamus O'Dwyer the local postman, Dr Desmond Ffrench, with Sir Compton Mackenzie as President. The first opera to be performed was *The Rose of Castile*, by the Irish composer, Michael William Balfe, who was born in Dublin in 1808. The present Church of Ireland, the church of St Selskar, occupies the site of the old 12th-century Abbey, of which the ancient tower remains. Early Irish Bishops such as Ó Aodha and Ó Maolaoidh, Bishops of Ferns, and some Norman bishops are buried here. The ruins of the Abbey near the Westgate Tower include the one remaining gateway out of the original five in the town walls. Henry II spent Lent in the Abbey in 1172 doing penance for the murder of Thomas a Becket. In 1175, Raymond le Gros married Strongbow's daughter Basilia there. In the Bull Ring stands a bronze statue of a Wexford Pikeman of 1798, the work of Oliver Sheppard of the Royal Hibernian Academy. No. 29 South Main Street was occupied by Oliver Cromwell. In North Main Street, now part of White's Hotel, was the old rectory where Sir Robert McClure was born, the arctic explorer and discoverer of the North West Passage.

On the seafront at Crescent Quay, is the statue of Commodore John Barry, founder of the American Navy. He was born at Ballysamson, Tacumshane, some ten miles from the town.

Three miles from the town is the Wexford Wildfowl Reserve, where half the population of Greenland's white fronted geese winter each year along with thousands of species of wildfowl.

🚗 *WEXFORD is 88 miles south of Dublin.*

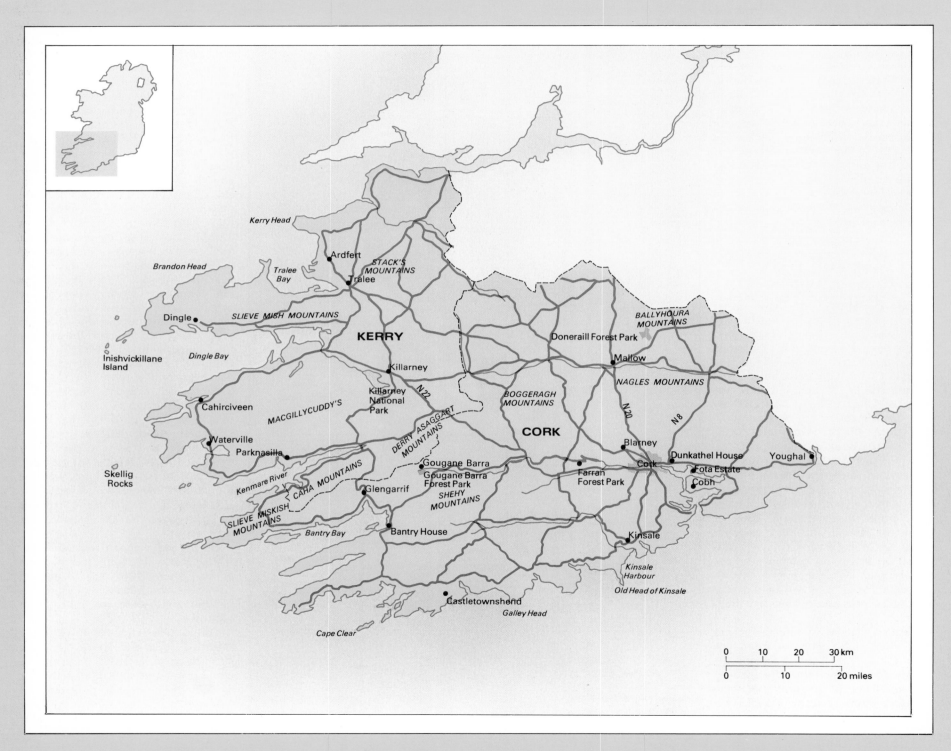

Kerry Head

Brandon Head

Ardfert

STACK'S
MOUNTAINS

Tralee
Bay

Tralee

SLIEVE MISH MOUNTAINS

Dingle

BALLYHOURA
MOUNTAINS

Doneraill Forest Park

KERRY

Mallow

Inishvickillane
Island

Dingle Bay

Killarney

NAGLES MOUNTAINS

Killarney
National
Park

N 22

BOGGERAGH
MOUNTAINS

Cahirciveen

MACGILLYCUDDY'S

N 20

N 8

Waterville
Parknasilla

DERRY ASAGGART
MOUNTAINS

CORK

Blarney

Dunkathel House

Youghal

Skellig
Rocks

Gougane Barra

Cork

Fota Estate

Gougane Barra
Forest Park

Farran
Forest Park

Cobh

Kenmare River

CAHA MOUNTAINS

Glengarrif

SHEHY
MOUNTAINS

SLIEVE MISKISH
MOUNTAINS

Bantry Bay

Bantry House

Kinsale

Kinsale
Harbour

Castletownshend

Old Head of Kinsale

Galley Head

Cape Clear

0   10   20   30 km

0   10   20 miles

The South West

The golden spires of
St Finbarr's
Cathedral rise into
the night sky amid
the twinkling lights
of Cork city

CORK AND KERRY are two counties in Ireland about which writers are prone to speak in superlatives. Cork, all 2880 square miles of it, is most famous for its Blarney Stone and its power of conferring the gift of eloquence on all who kiss it, or kiss it by proxy! To the east of Cork is rich river land with picturesque valleys. To the west, its mountains form mass ranks with the mighty mountain ranges of Kerry. The coast faces Spain, and points long fingers of land into the Atlantic. Around Glengarriff the land is lush, with a mediterranean climate caused by the warm waters of the Gulf Stream. The central valleys of the Blackwater, and of the River Lee are of quiet beauty. The 'Kingdom' of Kerry is a riot of high mountains, including the highest mountain in Ireland, Carrantuohill (3414 ft) and the land which embraces 'Heaven's Reflex', Killarney. Kerry is rugged Atlantic fjord coast, the next parish America. It was from Mount Brandon, 'Brendan's Mountain', that Brendan, the navigator Saint, set off in his frail craft, with his monk companions, and, sailing via Greenland and Iceland discovered America in the 6th century.

Cork is the glamour county, with a capital city which celebrated the 800th anniversary of its charter of foundation in 1985. Kerry is the romantic county, and both are rebels, far removed historically from the constraints of central government run from Dublin. Both retain their Irishry and independence of spirit.

Roofless Ardfert Cathedral stands in County Kerry

ARDFERT
County Kerry

Ardfert was a 6th-century monastic foundation of St Brendan the Navigator, who died in 577. In the 12th century it became the see of the diocese of Ardfert, and the cathedral was built. A 9th-century Round Tower from the original monastic settlement stood in the north-west corner of the church but was demolished by a great storm in 1771. The 12th-century nave and chancel church has a remarkable Hiberno-Romanesque doorway and on the walls of the cathedral ruins is a carving in stone of Bishop Stack who died in 1488. The choir is lit by a high three-light east window. Near the west end of the church are the remains of *Teampall na n-Oigh*, a Romanesque nave cum chancel church, and *Teampall Griffin*, a 15th-century church, which has a carved stone with a dragon and griffin inscribed on it, representing evil devouring itself. Ardfert Abbey, a Franciscan Friary, founded in 1253 by Thomas Fitzmaurice, the first Baron of Kerry, is just half a mile away.

One mile west of Ardfert is an early historic earthen fort where Sir Roger Casement (1864-1916) was captured after landing from a German submarine which had escorted the arms ship the *Aud*, bringing arms for the 1916 Rising. On Banna strand is a memorial commemorating the landing, the scuttling of the arms ship, and the arrest and execution of Casement.

🚗 *ARDFERT is 5½ miles north west of Tralee.*

BANTRY HOUSE
County Cork

The elegant home of the Egerton Shelswell-White family, and once the seat of the Earls of Bantry, from whom the family is descended, Bantry House is a treasure house of furniture, paintings, tapestries and objets d'art collected from all over Europe by the second Earl. It was built in 1750, and the magnificent south front was added to the original Georgian building in 1840. Open to the public it has refreshments and a craft shop.

🚗 *BANTRY HOUSE is 56 miles west of Cork city and overlooks Bantry Bay.*

CAHIRCIVEEN
County Kerry

Cahirciveen is a Y-shaped village nestling at the foot of Bentee Mountain (1245 ft high) beside the River Valentia, and overlooking Valentia harbour. A short distance from the town, on the road to Killorglin, are the ruins of Carhan House, where the Liberator, Daniel O'Connell was born in 1775. In the main street of the town is the massive Daniel O'Connell Memorial Church, built in 1888 from subscriptions by Kerry people from all over the world. On the western edge of the town is the Valentia weather observatory, one of the most important weather stations on the western seaboard of Europe. Across the water is the ancient Stone Fort of Cahergal, enclosed by a circular defence wall 14 ft thick and 79 ft in diameter. A little further north is the 9th-century Fort of Leacanabuaile. Valentia island, at the mouth of the river, was famous as the site of the Western Union Cable Station where the Atlantic cable on the bed of the sea joined telegraphic communications between the Old World and the New before the days of satellite communications. Ten miles south of Cahirciveen is the Stone Fort of Staigue, one of the finest pre-Christian stone forts in Ireland, with a massive stone wall 18 ft high, 13 ft thick and 90 ft in diameter. On the coast road to Staigue Fort from Cahirciveen is Derrynane House and National Park, the home of Daniel O'Connell, and now an excellent museum.

🚗 *CAHIRCIVEEN is 40 miles from Killarney, and 226 miles from Dublin.*

CASTLETOWNSHEND
County Cork

Castletownshend is one of the most attractive, secluded and safe sailing harbours in the county. It was the birthplace of Mrs George Bernard Shaw, and, at the entry to the village in Drishane House, lived Edith Oenone Somerville, (1858-1949), joint author with her cousin Violet Martin (1862-1915) of the classic *Experiences of an Irish R.M.* On the approach to the village is the 420 ft high hill of Knockdrum, an ancient stone ring fort with three finger stones still standing. At the foot of the steeply hilled village is the church of St Barrahane, and in its graveyard are the simple plain single stone graves of Dr Somerville and Violet Martin. The church is a gem with a Harry Clarke (1889-1931) stained glass south window to the memory of Sir Egerton Coghill, and an east window to the memory of the Somervilles. A third Harry Clarke window is to the memory of Colonel Coghill, a veteran of the Indian Mutiny. There is a superb Powell of London window dedicated to Lt. Nevill Coghill V.C. who died saving his regimental colours from the Zulus. The Celtic floor mosaics were designed by Dr Somerville. A mile from the church is the O'Driscoll fortress, Glenbarrahane Castle, occupied by a Spanish naval force in 1601, part of their expeditionary force for Kinsale. The Spanish naval forces successfully fought off the ships of Admiral Sir Richard Leveson.

🚗 *CASTLETOWNSHEND is 5 miles south of Skibbereen.*

COBH
County Cork

Cobh, pronounced 'Cove', was formerly known as Queenstown in honour of Queen Victoria's visit to Ireland in 1849. It stands at the enormous mouth of the River Lee, and was once a famous port of call for transatlantic liners. On the quayside is a memorial to those who died in the sinking of the *Lusitania* in World War I, by the Irish sculptor, Jerome Conor. In the Old Church cemetery are the graves of hundreds of the drowned. The town is dominated by St Colman's Cathedral, built by Pugin in 1868, with its glorious carillon of 47 bells.

It was from the former British naval dockyard at Rushbrooke that the *Sirius*, the first steamer to cross

Young sailors can pursue their hobby in Castletownshend's safe harbour

the Atlantic, sailed in April 1838. The King Alfred Royal Cork Yacht Club at Cobh, founded in 1720, is the oldest yacht club in the world. *COBH is 15 miles south east of Cork city.*

CORK
County Cork

Cork city derives its name from the Irish *Corach,* meaning 'A Marshy Place'. Ireland's third largest city, it was given its first charter by King Henry II of England in 1185. It was founded in the 6th century by St Finbarr, who set up his church and college on the south bank of the River Lee, where the present day University College stands. St Finbarr's small college prospered, and Cork developed into a university city throughout the 8th and 9th centuries. The Norsemen, nosing up the rivers of Ireland in their long boats, on hit and run raids, discovered Cork on the River Lee, and burnt it to the ground in A.D. 820. Eventually they settled, and the Danes lined up with the native Irish under the chieftain, Dermot MacCarthy. The wily Normans gave MacCarthy a Norman wife, and he then submitted to Henry II who granted the city its first charter. Predictably, the Normans soon became more Irish than the Irish themselves, and Cork prospered. In 1492 its people supported the Pretender to the throne of England, Perkin Warbeck. He and his supporters were hung at Tyburn. Then Cork supported Charles I until Cromwell put them down in 1649. Then Winston Churchill's ancestor, John Churchill, later to become the Duke of Marlborough, laid siege to the city for five days, demolished the walls with his artillery, and treated the surrendering citizens with honour. 'Rebel' Cork took a very active part in the War of Independence from 1919 to 1921.

St Colman's Cathedral seen above the serried ranks of houses at Cobh on the River Lee

A distinctly mediterranean atmosphere exists in Cork's attractive streets

This mediterranean style city has a unique pepper pot steeple, 120 ft high, in Shandon church, perched above the historic butter markets. Built in 1722, it has four different faces and chimes of eight bells. About these a local writer, Father Prout, wrote his poem with the opening lines,

"The Bells of Shandon,
that sound so grand on,
The pleasant waters of
the River Lee".

The mortal remains of Father Francis O'Mahoney (Father Prout) lie buried in the cemetery beside the church of St Anne, Shandon.

The Church of Ireland modern 'Gothic' church of St Finbarr ('The Fair Headed'), is on the site of a 6th century church set up by the monk who died in A.D. 623. All that remains of the medieval church on this site is a finely carved doorway. In the medieval church Edmund Spenser, the Elizabethan poet, married Elizabeth Boyle, daughter of the Earl of Cork. Spenser immortalised

The rooftops and spires of Cork, Ireland's third-largest city, rise out of the morning mist

this marriage in his ode, *Epithalamion*. Bishop Lyon, who performed the ceremony, lies buried just behind the high altar of the present church.

A peculiar feature of the modern Gothic St Finbarr's is a cannon ball suspended on a chain in the modern ambulatory. This 24 pound shot was fired from an Elizabethan cannon in the siege of the city in 1690, and was discovered embedded in the steeple of the cathedral when it was being demolished in 1865. A unique brass tablet in the cathedral reads:

"In pious memory of the Honourable Elizabeth Aldworth, wife of Richard Aldworth, of Newmarket Court, County Cork, Esq., daughter of Arthur, first Viscount Doneraile. Her remains lie close to this spot. Born 1695, Died 1775. Initiated into Freemasonry in Lodge No. 44, at Doneraile Court in this County A.D. 1712."

Apparently Elizabeth Aldworth was either hiding behind a screen or up the chimney of Doneraile Court, and overheard the masonic proceedings of Lodge No. 44, so she was made the only female Mason in history!

The city's southern residential suburb boasts a unique modern church, Christ the King, at Turner's Cross, by the Chicago architect, Barry Byrne. The Honan chapel, Donovan's Road, in the grounds of University College Cork, has what is arguably the most beautiful chapel in Ireland. It was built by the late Miss Belle Honan. It has a series of priceless modern Irish stained glass windows by Sarah Purser and Harry Clarke, built in 1916. Cork city has an excellent art gallery in Emmet Place, part of the Crawford Municipal School of Art.

St Patrick's Street is the principal street of the city, adorned by Foley's bronze statue of an apostle of temperance, the Capuchin Father Matthew. Cynics say he is pointing to the pub across the road! The South Mall is the commercial heart of the city and the Grand Parade has pleasant bow windowed houses.

A superb example of 18th-century architecture is Riverstown House, Glanmire, four and a half miles out of the city, on the Dublin road. It was built in 1602, and was the home of Dr Jemmett Browne, Bishop of Cork, who rebuilt it in 1745, and had the Francini brothers do the plaster work. The pleasant environs of Cork city include the Mardyke and Sunday's Well, and Montenotte, and Tivoli. Sir Walter Raleigh resided in Tivoli House, and Woodhill House was the residence of Sarah Curran, betrothed of Ireland's best loved patriot, Robert Emmet, who was hanged in Dublin for his quixotic Rising of 1803. His tragic romance inspired Moore to write one of his haunting melodies, *She is Far from the Land.*

Cork city has the reputation of providing much of the brains of the nation and has produced a number of talented literary figures. One of the best of romantic descriptive writers was D.L. Kelleher, who gave the Irish Tourist Board its slogan, 'Ireland of the Welcomes'. Of the stature of Turgenev and Chekov are the writers 'Frank O'Connor' (Michael O'Donovan) the short story teller, and the novelist and writer Sean O'Faolainn. Both were pupils of the novelist and Professor of Cork University, Daniel Corkery. In the visual arts Cork has produced Royal Academicians such as James Barry (1741-1806) and Daniel Maclise (1806-1870).

CORK city is 161 miles south west of Dublin, 61 miles from Limerick and 54 miles south east of Killarney.

The Blarney Stone

Blarney – *An Blarna* – meaning 'The Plain', is a pretty village north east of Cork, in which stands the massive castle, built in 1446, by Cormac MacCarthy to command the countryside known as Muskerry. It is four storeys high, and set in its topmost battlements is the magical Blarney Stone. With the aid of a guide you lie on your back, grasp iron safety rails, tip yourself, head first, backwards, and slip downwards, to kiss the stone. Legend has it that this will give you the gift of eloquence! The word 'Blarney' was introduced into the English language in 1602, by Queen Elizabeth I. Despite her repeated commands, her Deputy in Ireland, Lord Carew, had failed to bring to heel the wily chieftain of Muskerry, Cormac MacCarthy, who in order not to lose his elected position as clan chieftain, kept putting off his oath of allegiance to the Virgin Queen, by which he would acknowledge the lands belonged to her.

He gave Carew promises and half-promises, but never quite got round to bowing the knee. Finally, Her Majesty exploded with rage at Deputy Lord Carew's ineptitude and declared that the honeyed words and eloquent promises of the Irish Chieftain were all 'Blarney'.

Cormac's ploy paid off, as the castle remained outside the control of the Crown, and successfully withstood successive Cromwellian sieges.

Blarney castle is on the itinerary of most visitors to Ireland

To inherit the 'gift of the gab' you adopt this uncomfortable position

Beautiful Sybil Head on the Dingle Peninsula

Dingle's Gallerus Oratory is a well-preserved early stone building

DINGLE
County Kerry

Dingle – *Daingean ní Cúis* – the Fortress of O'Cush, is the most westerly town in Europe in an Irish-speaking area which has long historic links with Spain and France. It is bounded by hills on three sides, culminating in the north with the 3127 ft high Mount Brandon. A fishing port, it boasts at the corner of Main Street and Green Street the site of what was 'The Highest House in Dingle', once owned by a Colonel Rice of the Irish Brigade in France, who planned to rescue Marie Antoinette and bring her here. She refused to go when she learnt that the King and her children would have had to be left behind.

Across the harbour, is Burnham House, once the home of the local landlord, Lord Ventry. Ventry harbour, a few miles west, was the scene for a romantic 19th-century narrative poem discovered in the Bodlean Library, which relates that Dairre Donn, King of the World, was defeated here by the *Fianna* led by Fiona Mac Cumhaill, when he and his armies attempted to invade Ireland.

Slea Head a few miles to the west, is the nearest point on mainland Ireland to America. Offshore are the seven famous Blasket Islands. West Dingle is an archaeological paradise. The Fahan Group includes 414 clochans, or unmortared beehive-shaped cells, 19 souterrains, 18 standing stones, 2 sculptured crosses, 7 earthen forts and 2 fortified headlands. The forts include Dunbeg fort, Cathair Murphy, Cathair na Mairtineach and Cathair an Da Dhoras.

One of the most remarkable stone dwellings in the Dingle Peninsula is Gallerus Oratory, one of the most perfectly preserved Christian buildings in Ireland. Shaped like an upturned boat it is 22 ft long, 18 ft wide and 12 ft high. The entrance door is of the earliest Irish Christian architecture. It has stood for 1000 years, watertight, built throughout of unmortared stone.

DINGLE can be reached either by the coast road or across the spectacular 1500 ft high Connor Pass. The town is 42 miles west of Killarney and 31 miles south west of Tralee.

DONERAILE FOREST PARK
County Cork

Doneraile Forest Park is one of the latest acquisitions of the nation and is therefore not as widely known as it deserves to be.

It is the walled demesne of the former St Leger estate, 395 acres of rich rolling landscape abounding with deer.

Doneraile Court, a magnificent three-storey mansion, is leased to the Georgian Society of Ireland. It was built in 1725 and reached its present proportions in the early 1900s. The Duke of Atholl planted the first European Larch trees on the lawn in front of the house in 1738.

DONERAILE PARK is 6 miles north-east of Mallow.

DUNKATHEL HOUSE
County Cork

Dunkathel House, little known, is the splendid 18th-century mansion of Mr & Mrs Geoffrey Russell, built in the architectural style of David Ducart.

It is unique, since its collection of antiques and paintings cannot only be viewed but many can be purchased.

DUNKATHEL is 3½ miles from the city of Cork on the Youghal road.

Italianate splendour in the garden island of Garnish, near Glengarriff

FARRAN FOREST PARK
County Cork

The lovely Farran Forest Park came about because of the huge lake formed by the Inniscarra hydro-electric reservoir scheme in conjunction with the River Lee.

It is an enchanting 130 acres with a former shooting lodge in the centre as a tourist information office. The wildlife enclosures embrace a wide variety of birds and deer.

🚗 *FARRAN FOREST PARK is 11 miles from the city of Cork.*

FOTA ESTATE
County Cork

Fota estate, formerly a private property, was acquired by University College Cork, and today a large portion of it is an imaginative national wildlife park open to the public with a unique bee garden, a splendid arboretum containing some of the finest trees and shrubs in the country, and Fota House itself, with its magnificent collection of Irish period furniture and 18th and 19th-century Irish landscape paintings.

Fota estate was originally the home of the celebrated Smith-Barrys of Cork, and they had their family motto carved in stone at the entrance to the estate, 'Boutez en Avant' — Press on Regardless!

🚗 *FOTA ESTATE, on Fota island, is 14 miles from Cork city on the road to Cobh.*

GLENGARRIFF
County Cork

Glengarriff – the 'Rugged Glen' is one of the most beautiful villages in Ireland, by the sea, and surrounded by majestic mountains. It is in a rocky glen abounding with every variety of mediterranean flower and shrub, including Arbutus and fuchsia in profusion. The glen is heavily wooded with oak, elm, pine, yew and holly. At the entrance to this village on Bantry Bay is the Italianate garden island of Garnish. On this sub-tropical island George Bernard Shaw wrote his play *Saint Joan*. Garnish Island or, as it is sometimes known, *Ilnacullin*, – 'The Island of Holly' – is a 37 acre garden

389

paradise which was, until 1910, a barren rock. Annan Bryce commissioned Harold Peto of Somerset to lay out this dream garden on Italian lines. It took 100 gardeners three years to landscape it with rare shrubs from Australia and New Zealand, as well as magnolias, camellias and rhododendrons, their growth made possible by the warm waters of the Gulf Stream. This sub-tropical island paradise was given to the nation in 1953.

GLENGARRIFF is 68 miles west of Cork, Garnish Island is 5 minutes offshore by boat.

GOUGANE BARRA
County Cork

Gougane Barra – 'St Finbarr's Hollow' – is a deep, dark lake, surrounded on three sides by the mountain divide of Cork and Kerry, a mile long, and the source of the River Lee. The fourth side of the Lake is a forested valley of immense beauty. It is set amid a forest park of 1000 acres. On the island, in the middle of the lake, was the hermitage of St Finnbarr, patron saint of Cork. This is marked by a small modern oratory joined to the mainland by a causeway. This is a Gaelic speaking area, and at the adjacent Pass of Keimaneigh – *Céim an Fhiadh* – 'the deers' Pass', after the legend that it was leapt by a hunted deer, the men of Ballingeary fought a pitched battle with the Redcoats of Lord Bantry on 11 January 1822.

GOUGANE BARRA is 43 miles west of Cork.

GOUGANE BARRA FOREST PARK
County Cork

Gougane Barra Forest park is on the lake of the same name, and on the mountainous divide between County Cork and County Kerry.

Nature trails are signposted through the magnificent new forests, there are picnic areas and a ring road for motorists from which they can view the entire park.

GOUGANE BARRA FOREST PARK is 2 miles up the valley off the Macroom to Bantry road at the beautifully named Pass of Keimaneigh — 'The Pass of the Deer' — where legend says a fleeing deer leapt from one ridge of the craggy pass to the other to escape the huntsmen.

INISHVICKILLANE ISLAND
County Kerry

Inishvickillane island is famous for its Eagle's Hollow, where the last of the great eagles of Kerry made their home. It is just 40 years since the last magnificent white-tailed sea eagle of Kerry was observed feeding on gulls and fulmars and puffins on the Great Skellig rock.

If Charles Haughey, the distinguished former Taoiseach of Ireland, has his way, at his private residence and estate on Inishvickillane the Kerry Eagles will one day fly again.

He has commissioned a feasibility study to see if this sea eagle could be encouraged to breed on his private island paradise. Hopes are high, since the white-tailed sea eagle was successfully re-introduced on the island of Rhum in Scotland just 11 years ago. These birds were introduced from Norway, and they are said to have been seen on the Blasket islands.

INISHVICKILLANE ISLAND is a privately-owned island (no visitors), but it can be seen from Slea Head on the Dingle peninsular, on the mainland, a helicopter flight away.

KILLARNEY
County Kerry

Killarney is the principal scenic attraction of Ireland. It has three lakes, luxurious woods and vegetation, waterfalls, mountain ranges, valleys, castles, abbeys and a National Park. No cars are allowed inside the National Park and consequently visitors are obliged to view the scenery on foot or from a horse-drawn Killarney jaunting car, which has been described as 'something you hang down out of'. The jarveys who drive them are real Irish characters, the equivalent of the London Cabbie or the New York taxi driver. They are enormously loquacious, knowledgeable, and thirsty!

Killarney town is, in itself, a tourist trap. Its main claim to fame is its Catholic cathedral, designed by Pugin.

Just one and a half miles out on the road to Kenmare is Ross Castle, (14th-century), belonging to Mac-Carthy Mór, who as Lord Muskerry defended it against Cromwellian forces in 1652. It is perfectly situated on a peninsular which extends into the lower lake of Lough Leane. About a mile from the castle is Innisfallen Island, 20 acres of evergreen and holly, a paradise island with the ruins of the 6th-century abbey of St Fallen.

Two and a half miles from the town of Killarney, on the same road to Kenmare, is the entrance to 'Heaven's Reflex', the Killarney National Park of 11,000 acres presented to the nation by its owners Mr and Mrs Bowers Bourne of California, and their Senator son, Arthur Vin-

The beauty of Killarney's three lakes is almost legendary

cent, in 1932. Three miles along the same road are the ruins of Muckross Abbey, founded in 1448 by the chief of Desmond, Donal McCarthy. Muckross House is a superb stately home, now a splendid folk museum on the shores of the Lake, with gorgeous gardens. Five and a half miles along the Kenmare road the waters of the Upper Lake reach the waters of Muckross Lake and Lough Leane in a delightful weir or rapids. Nearby is the Torc waterfall, 60 ft high. In the luxurious parks are herds of native Irish red deer and Japanese sika deer.

Ladies View, 12 miles from Killarney on the Kenmare road, gives a superb view of the Killarney Valley with a vista of the Upper Lake joining the Middle Lake with Lough Leane in the far distance. The other superlative panoramic view of Killarney is from the 400 ft height of Aghadoe Hill, two and a half miles from the town on the Killarney Tralee road. Seven miles from Killarney town, on the Killorglin road is the Gap of Dunloe and Kate Kearney's Cottage, the entrance point to a seven mile trek by pony up this majestic mountain pass amid the Macgillycuddy Reeks, the Tomies and the aptly-named Purple Mountains. The Macgillycuddy – Pronounced 'Mac-le-Cuddy' Reeks include Carrantuohill (3414 ft), Ireland's highest mountain.

KILLARNEY is 191 miles from Dublin via Limerick and Abbeyfeale, 54 miles from Cork and 68 miles from Limerick.

KILLARNEY NATIONAL PARK
County Kerry

Killarney National Park, the most beautiful park in these islands, was originally known as the Bourn Vin-

cent Memorial Park. This priceless gift to the nation of 19,955 acres of woodlands and mountains on the shores of the famous lakes is one of the most generous American gifts to Ireland ever made. Recently more lakes and woodlands have been added to the national collection from the estate of the late Beatrice Grosvenor. Beatrice served in the British Red Cross in World War II and was a distinguished aide to the late Lady Mountbatten.

Because of the proximity of the sea and the mild influence of the waters of the Gulf Stream, Killarney has the most exotic of shrubs in its sheltered places.

Muckross House, once the 'Big House', is at the centre of the main gardens on the shores of Lake Muckross, the second largest of the three main lakes of Killarney. The formal gardens here are rich in rhododendra and azaleas. The park has four signposted nature trails for visitors to walk. They are also permitted to cycle in the park, or to hire a traditional jaunting car (which is a tourist trap!) and motor cars are absolutely forbidden.

The Grosvenor and McShane estates can be approached through Deenagh Lodge opposite Killarney town's magnificent Pugin Cathedral, the main tourist spot in Killarney town.

Muckross House is fortunate in having a cultured and civilised manager with a sense of history, so there are good information offices throughout the area, and a splendid audio visual show in the house itself. *MUCKROSS HOUSE is 3½ miles from Killarney town, on the road to Kenmare.*

Muckross House lies on the shores of Lake Muckross in the heart of Killarney

Charles fort was built in 1677 to protect Kinsale's strategically-important harbour

KINSALE
County Cork

Kinsale is one of the most attractive seaside towns in the county. It is a Georgian town, with a vast harbour always protected by ancient forts such as Charles fort, built in 1677. It was once one of the most important naval bases in these islands. Here, in 1601, the Elizabethan forces of Carew and Mountjoy smashed the Irish forces of the Earls of Tyrone and Tirconnell and their Spanish Allies. The course of the battle can be followed on maps on the battlefield above Kinsale. In the town is the 12th-century church of St Multose, a Desmond Castle, a 16th-century French prison, and the remains of the Carmelite Friary of 1314. It was off the Old Head of Kinsale, in May 1915, that the liner, the *Lusitania* was torpedoed and sunk by a German submarine.

The founder of the American State of Pennsylvania, William Penn, was clerk of the Admiralty Court of Kinsale, and his father was Governor of Kinsale.

KINSALE is 18 miles south of Cork and 179 miles from Dublin.

MALLOW
County Cork

On the north bank of the River Blackwater, Mallow was made famous by the lilting Irish jig, *The Rakes of Mallow*. It is the hunting centre of the county and has a popular racecourse. Anthony Trollope lived in the town for some time, and among its other celebrated citizens were Thomas Davis, the poet patriot of the Young Ireland movement, Canon Sheehan the novelist, and William O'Brien M.P.

Doneraile, just north of the town, was a haunt of the poet Spenser, who lived at Kilcolman Castle from 1586 to 1598, where he wrote *The Faerie Queen*. Canon Sheehan, was parish priest of Doneraile from 1895 to 1913.

Buttevant, nearby on the River Awbeg was the 12th-century seat of the Barrys of Cork. Just seven miles away, at Killavullen, on a cliff overlooking the river is the ancestral home of the Hennessy family, the original distillers of the world-renowned brand of cognac.

MALLOW is 22 miles north of Cork and 149 miles from Dublin.

PARKNASILLA
County Kerry

Parknasilla – *Pairc an Saileach* – the willow field, is beautifully situated on the north shore of the Kenmare River bay. Renowned for its tropical climate and exotic vegetation, Parknasilla basks in the warm waters of the Gulf Stream. The hotel here was once the home of Charles Graves, protestant bishop of Limerick, father of Alfred Percival Graves, scholar and poet (1846-1931) and grandfather of the poet and novelist Robert Graves. At Sneem, about two miles west on the road to Waterville is the Catholic Church, given by Lord Dunraven, whose parish priest was Father Michael Walsh (1828-1866) the 'Father O'Flynn' of the popular ballad by Alfred Percival Graves. The East window is a memorial to the Limerick born poet Aubrey de Vere (1814-1902), friend of William Wordsworth and Cardinal Newman.
🚗 *PARKNASILLA is about 12 miles west of Kenmare.*

SKELLLIGS ROCKS
County Kerry

Skelligs Rocks – *Na Sceallaga* – the rocks, are three little jagged islands of stone rising out of the Atlantic. Skellig Michael, or Great Skellig, is a massive rocky haunt of puffins, guillemots, petrel and fulmar, 700 ft high, half a mile long, and three quarters of a mile wide. At 540 ft above the landing jetty is the best-preserved and oldest monastic site in Europe. The stone stairs to the site of beehive cells, oratories, cemeteries, holy wells, stone crosses, and the chapel of St Michael are over 1000 years old. The Little Skellig is a bird sanctuary for 20,000 pairs of gannets, the second largest

The Rose of Tralee is a contest for women of typically Irish beauty

gannetry in the North Atlantic. The third island is known as Lemon Rock.
🖕 *THE GREAT SKELLIG is 8 miles west of Bolus head, 12 miles by sea from Portmagee and can be approached by motor boat services from here, and from Reenard, Cahirciveen, or Derrynane.*

TRALEE
County Kerry

Tralee is a thriving town set at the head of the Bay of Tralee and the gateway to the magnificent mountainous peninsular of Dingle. This was the castle home of the Earls of Desmond until it was given over to Sir Edward Denny. The last of the Earls of Desmond finished up with his head on a spike on London Bridge in Elizabethan times.

The town is famous for its International Rose of Tralee Festival, held in September each year. The 'Rose' is in fact a pretty girl, chosen from women of Irish descent all over the world. The festival coincides with the annual four day Tralee horserace meeting. Clogher House, at Ballymullen, near the town, was the home of William Mulchinock (1820-1864), the composer of the world-famous song, *The Rose of Tralee*. In the centre of the town is a garden of roses as a memorial to the composer. The Ashe Theatre, in Denny street, is the leading *Siamsa* or Folk Theatre in Ireland. In St John's Cathedral Church there are magnificent Stations of the Cross by Sean Keating RHA.

About three miles south of the town is the mysterious 'Scotia's Glen'. Historians say that the prehistoric folk of Ireland, the Milesians, landed here in around 3500 B.C. and fought a battle with the mythical Tuatha de Danaan at the foot of the Slieve Mish mountains. The Milesians were victorious but among the dead were Scotia and another princess, Fais. Scotia lies

buried in 'Scotia's Glen', and Fais in the mound at Gleann Fhaise, 10 miles south west of Tralee.
🚗 *TRALEE is 20 miles north west of Killarney and 64 miles south west of Limerick.*

WATERVILLE
County Kerry

Waterville – *An Coireán* – the Little Whirlpool, is a charming resort, nestling between the Atlantic Ocean and the 17-mile circumference of Lough Currane. It was a favourite holiday spot of Charlie Chaplin and his family when they lived in Switzerland. On Lough Currane are the ruins of the oratory of the 6th-century St Fintan. Above the lake the mountains rise 2000 ft and more. Waterville is on the famous Ring of Kerry which starts and ends at Killarney, 110 miles of enchanting scenic road encircling the Iveragh Peninsular.
🚗 *WATERVILLE is 39 miles south west of Kenmare and 241 miles from Dublin.*

YOUGHAL
County Cork

The seaside village of Youghal, pronounced 'Yawl', lies at the mouth of the superbly beautiful River Blackwater. Still standing in the town, and in private ownership, is Sir Walter Raleigh's home 'Myrtle Grove', an Elizabethan manor in which he lived while mayor of Youghal, and where he smoked the first tobacco and grew the first potatoes from the New World.
🚗 *YOUGHAL is 30 miles east of Cork.*

Palm trees grow in Parknasilla. This part of the coast enjoys an exotic climate

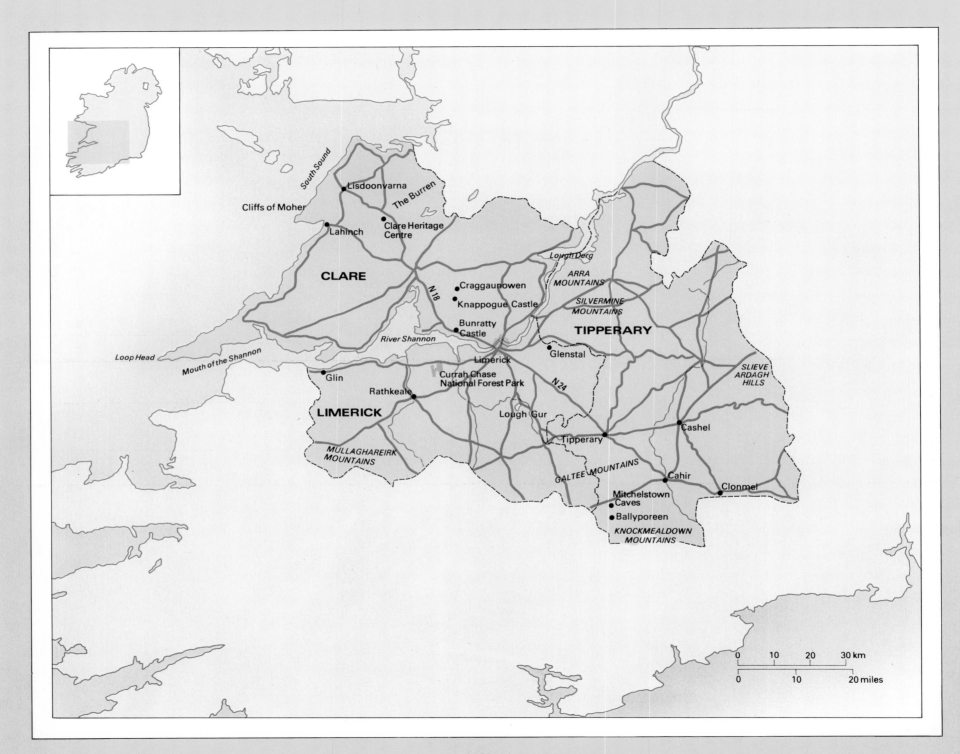

South Sound

Lisdoonvarna

The Burren

Cliffs of Moher

Lahinch

Clare Heritage
Centre

CLARE

Lough Derg

ARRA
MOUNTAINS

Craggaunowen

Knappogue Castle

N18

SILVERMINE
MOUNTAINS

Bunratty
Castle

TIPPERARY

River Shannon

Loop Head

Glenstal

Limerick

Mouth of the Shannon

Glin

Currah Chase
National Forest Park

N24

SLIEVE
ARDAGH
HILLS

Rathkeale

LIMERICK

Lough Gur

Cashel

Tipperary

MULLAGHAREIRK
MOUNTAINS

GALTEE MOUNTAINS

Cahir

Clonmel

Mitchelstown
Caves

Ballyporeen

KNOCKMEALDOWN
MOUNTAINS

0   10   20   30 km

0   10   20 miles

The Mid West

This beautiful thatched cottage with its neat and tidy frontage has an English look about it, but it is situated in Adare in the heart of County Limerick

THE COUNTY OF CLARE lies on the north bank of the mighty estuary of the Shannon, the longest river in these islands, with its west atlantic coast rising to 700 ft in the Cliffs of Moher, looking out over the Aran islands. It is on the world map because of a little-known spot on the river's estuary called *Rineanna*, now known as Shannon International airport, the first duty-free airport in the world, the modern crossroads between the Old World and the New. Limerick, on the other hand, has achieved fame through three of its citizens, Sean Keating, RHA (1889-1978), the distinguished painter, Kate O'Brien (1897-1974), the novelist, and Lola Montez (1818-1861), the famous dancer, born Marie Gilbert, beloved of the insane King Ludwig I of Bavaria. Its name has passed into the English language as the word for a humorous, often ribald rhyme.

The name 'Tipperary' was appropriated for the nostalgic ballad *It's A Long Way To Tipperary* sung by British troops in the 1914-1918 war. It became popular because of the many Irish regiments who fought in this war with distinction, with a loss of over 50,000 volunteers killed in action. To most Irish people, Tipperary is synonymous with the dairy produce which flows from its 'Golden Vale', for the high profile of its patriotic volunteers in the Anglo-Irish war of Independence, and for being the birthplace of the popular novelist and Fenian, Charles Kickham.

BALLYPOREEN
County Tipperary

Ballyporeen is a charming little village at the foot of the Knockmealdown and Kilworth mountains which is famous for three of its sons. The first is Jack O'Brien, local patriot in the War of Independence, and the founder of what is now the highly acclaimed Irish Tourist Board. The second is Pat O'Brien, the veteran Hollywood film star who always played the 'good guy', the lovable Irish-American Parish Priest, or the likeable US Naval officer. The third is Michael Regan, baptised in the local church in 1829, later to emigrate to England, change his name to Reagan, move to America, and who was the great-grandfather of Ronald Reagan, President of the United States of America. On 3 June 1984, President Reagan visited Ballyporeen and saw for himself, in the Parochial House, the register in which his great grandfather's baptism was recorded on 3 September 1829.

BALLYPOREEN *is 8 miles from Mitchelstown and 136 miles from Dublin.*

BUNRATTY CASTLE
County Clare

Bunratty Castle is host to twice-nightly elegant and tastefully-presented medieval banquets in which superb traditional musicians and singers appear in period costume. The castle, thanks to its owner, Lord Gort V.C., who purchased it in 1954, and the Irish Tourist Board, has been fully restored to its 16th-century glory, and is furnished with the best selection of period furniture and furnishings in these islands. The whole

Visitors to Bunratty Folk Park can step back in time as they walk along this quaint old street

area around the castle has been transformed into a magnificent folk-park. Here are examples of every kind of Irish thatched cottage, and traditional craftsmen such as blacksmiths, candle makers, basket-weavers, and bread makers can be seen at work. This is a living folk park in excellent taste with farmhouse teas available.

Originally Bunratty Castle was built on the Ratty river in 1250, by Robert de Muscegros, then held by the de Clare family, and was regularly fought over by the local Irish, the O'Briens and the Macnamaras. The present massive square tower building was erected in

1450 by a Macnamara and taken in 1500 by the O'Brien's, who submitted to Henry VIII. The Shannon Free Airport Development Company Ltd now run the medieval castle enterprise on behalf of the trustees, with any profits from its use by the public going to improvements in the castle. The enormous square building has a huge banqueting hall on the first floor, and another magnificent hall on the second floor with a high 16th-century ceiling, a beautiful chapel (1619) and the living quarters of the great Earl of Bunratty. There are vaulted cellars, and the castle has elegant castellated turrets at its corners.

BUNRATTY CASTLE *is 2½ miles from Shannon Airport and 5½ miles west of Limerick city.*

CAHIR
County Tipperary

Cahir is a charming market town on the beautiful River Suir, at the foot of the Galtee mountains, with a magnificent 15th-century castle. One of the first to be fully restored in Ireland, it has a massive keep, and is enclosed by high walls with a vast courtyard and hall. It was built in 1142 by Conor O'Brien, Prince of Thomond, and was taken over by the Butlers, Earls of Ormonde. The

Cahir Castle, a splendid 15th-century edifice, seen across the tumbling River Suir

Taking its name from the Irish *Caiseal Muman* — the stone fort of Munster — the Rock of Cashel

castle, which is floodlit at night, is open to the public, and was one of the first restored castles to install explanatory visual aids.

CAHIR is 14 miles from Tipperary, and 110 miles from Dublin.

CASHEL
County Tipperary

Cashel is the Irish equivalent to the Acropolis, commonly known as the Rock of Cashel by virtue of its lofty ecclesiastical buildings rising dramatically over the surrounding plain. It was the fortified seat of kings from A.D. 350 to A.D. 1001, when the King of Munster, Murtagh O'Brien, gave the rock to the Church. St Patrick visited it to baptise Aenghus, King of Munster, and gave it a bishop. The most famous Bishop of Cashel was Cormac Mac Cuilleannáin, killed in battle in 908, while attempting to set himself up as High King. Brian Boru was crowned King here in 977. King Cormac Mc-Carthy began the building of Cormac's Chapel in 1127, and it was consecrated in 1134. Domhnall Mór O'Brien founded a cathedral in 1169, which was replaced by the present cathedral whose framework remains. Gerald Fitzgerald burnt the cathedral down in the late 15th century, because as he explained to King Henry VII, he thought the Archbishop was still inside! The 9th-century Round Tower on the Rock is almost 100 ft high with a circumference of 56 ft. Cormac's chapel is a 12th-century Hiberno-Romanesque gem. St Patrick's Cross, inserted into the coronation stone of Munster Kings, is one of the most ancient crosses in Ireland. The cathedral is above Cormac's chapel, cross-shaped with a central tower. The Hall of Vicars Choral was built in 1421. St Mary's Abbey, to the west of the Rock, was once a Benedictine monastery established by monks from Glastonbury. St Dominic's Abbey was the first Dominican church to be built in Ireland, in 1243. Cashel Palace, the Deanery, a Queen Anne style building of 1730, was once the residence of the Protestant Archbishops of Cashel, and is now a first class hotel with a reputation for excellent cuisine.

🚗 *CASHEL is 100 miles from Dublin and 12 miles from Tipperary.*

CLARE HERITAGE CENTRE
County Clare

For visitors to the County of Clare looking for their ancestors there is a 'tracing your ancestor' service in the very original interpretive centre in the village of Corofin, in what was once an old Church of Ireland church. Here, living conditions of the ordinary Irish people for the past hundred years and more are explained with audio-visual aids.

They give an insight into rural Ireland, arts and crafts, culture and famine, land tenure and emigration.

🚗 *COROFIN — 'The Weir of Finne' — lies near the shore of Lough Inchiquin, 13 miles from Lahinch and 13 miles from Lisdoonvarna.*

THE CLIFFS OF MOHER
County Clare

The Cliffs of Moher, the most spectacular cliffs in Ireland, stretch for five miles along the rugged Atlantic coast. Formed from massive beds of yellow Moher Shales looking like coal, and reaching a height of 700 ft, they can be easily approached from the landward side by rolling green meadows which suddenly and fearfully drop precipitously into the Atlantic foam. The rich fishing grounds below the vertical cliffs and the slopes and cliff-sides make ideal homes for thousands of nesting guillemot, razorbill, puffin, kittiwake, herring gulls, fulmar, chough, great blackbacked gulls, and even peregrine. The tourist information centre and observation post, O'Brien's Tower, built in 1835 by Cornelius O'Brien, a notorious landlord and MP for Clare, is the ideal spot from which to view the coastline and the Aran islands to the west. On a clear day the view from the tower stretches as far as the Twelve Pins of Connemara to the north, and the mountains of Kerry, due south. The information office is in the capable hands of local, young and knowledgeable people, who also run an excellent souvenir and craft shop. For the very brave there is an excellent 'platform' of flagstones just below the tower from which there is an awesome and precipitous view vertically downwards of the cliffs and their wild-bird inhabitants. On the road from Liscannor to the cliffs is the phallic O'Brien Monument which the eccentric and prolific landlord ordered his tenants to erect in his honour in 1853.

Three miles from the Cliffs of Moher is the tiny fishing village of Liscannor, and on the north shore of Liscannor Bay, the birthplace of John P. Holland (1841-1914), the inventor of the submarine, who emigrated to America.

The beautiful seaside resort of Lahinch lies nearby, home of the south of Ireland championship golf course and the Aberdeen Arms Hotel, famous for its seafood and 'Liscannor Broth.'

🚗 *THE CLIFFS OF MOHER are 3 miles west of Liscannor.*

CLONMEL
County Tipperary

Clonmel, *Cluain Meala* – the 'Honey Meadow', set against the Comeragh Mountains, is one of the most friendly and attractive towns in the county. Guarding the crossing of the River Suir, it has had the usual turbulent history of Norse raids, Anglo-Norman occupation, and

The precipitous Cliffs of Moher

Re-constructed pre-Christian lake dwellings called 'crannogs' can be seen at Craggaunowen

assault by Cromwellian forces. In fact, in No. 19 Main Street, once a bishop's palace, the 19th-century owner found in the rafters a number of letters signed by Oliver Cromwell during its occupation in 1650.

Laurence Sterne (1713-1768), author of *A Sentimental Journey* – was born in Clonmel, and George Borrow (1803-1881) went to school in the town. In 1766 the parish priest, Father Nicholas Sheehy, was hanged on trumped up charges by the local landlord, and Lord Lismore called out the military to stop a monument being erected over his grave.

Charles Bianconi, the Italian pedlar turned transport magnate, set up his horse-drawn passenger service from Clonmel, 'Bianconi Cars' and established a nationwide fast transport network.

Clonmel is an important horse and greyhound breeding centre. Horseracing takes place at Powerstown Park Racecourse, and greyhound racing takes place at the track at Davis Road. It is also the hunting centre for the Tipperary Foxhounds and the Clonmel Harriers. It is the centre of the greyhound 'Coursing' world.

The Main Guard, once the town house of the Count Palatine of Tipperary, and in which the main guard was once stationed, was designed by Sir Christopher Wren.

CLONMEL is 105 miles from Dublin and 15 miles from Cashel.

CRAGGAUNOWEN
County Clare

Craggaunowen, little known to the visitor because it is difficult to find, boasts a splendid example of an Irish house of the 15th and 16th centuries; a four-storey tower house which was a fortified Irish home and castle. On the ground floor is an excellent museum with items from the celebrated Hunt collection of medieval art. Part of the local scheme for the preservation of the past for the visitor is the reconstructed pre-Christian period crannog or lake dwelling. Within the reconstructed ring fort stands an example of the house an ordinary farmer would have lived in 500 years ago, complete with domestic utensils of the period, and an underground passage or souterrain which would have been used as a storage place for food. Irish afternoon teas are available.

The historic complex also houses a leather boat, the sailing ship the *Brendan*, in which Tim Severin followed the route of the 6th-century St Brendan the Navigator's voyage to America.

🚗 *CRAGGAUNOWEN is just off the Quin to Sixmile bridge road, some 15 miles west of Ennis and just north of Knappogue.*

CURRAH CHASE NATIONAL FOREST PARK
County Limerick

The Forest and Wildlife Service of the Department of Fisheries and Forestry took over the 568 acres of this Forest Park in 1982. The estate has been planted for nearly one hundred years with a wide variety of exotic and unusual trees. The principal trees in this glorious park are sycamore, beech, ash, elm and hornbeam. Within the park is a caravan and camping site and there is a signposted arboretum and nature trails.

This was once the home of the celebrated Irish poet Aubrey de Vere (1814-1902) who was born here, and lived here nearly all his life. Because he was a native of Limerick he was much influenced in his work by his

Glenstal Abbey is a castellated mansion amid grounds of spectacular beauty

quiet life in the magical woods. He was a convert to the religion of the majority of the Irish people, the Roman Catholic faith, and he was to become famous for his English Catholic devotional poetry. In 1897 he published his *Recollections*.

He was much admired, and in the Catholic church of Sneem, in County Kerry, a church built by Lord Dunraven, there is an East window memorial to the poet. Alas, the once splendid and proud 18th-century house of the poet was destroyed by fire in 1941 and only the shell remains. This friend of Tennyson and Wordsworth lies buried in Askeaton in the graveyard of the Protestant

parish church, which was erected on the remains of the Augustinian Pirory of St Mary.

🚗 *CURRAH CHASE PARK is 5 miles from Adare, and 13 miles west of the city of Limerick.*

GLENSTAL
County Limerick

On the hillside north of the village of Murroe – *An Mhá Rua* – the Red Plain, is the Benedictine Abbey of St Columba, with its services open to the public, and a modern centre for the promotion of ecumenism. It is, in its own very quiet way, one of the great civilising influences on the

public and private life of the country through its former students, for it is a school of art and crafts in the liberal tradition.

This magnificent castellated mansion, complete with Black Knight in armour keeping watch from the highest tower of the Windsor Castle-style Norman watch tower and gate, was built in the 19th century by the Barrington family, who founded Barrington's Hospital in Limerick City in 1820. This superb castle, with its surrounding acres of trees and shrubs and artificial lakes was acquired by Benedictine monks from Maredsous, in Belgium in 1926, The hills are alive with colour in rhododendron time, in May and June. The interior includes a library door in stone, a replica of the Hiberno-Romanesque doorway of Killaloe Cathedral. The Abbey church is a riot of colour and contains examples of silver and metal work by the monks.

In the 'Rent an Irish Cottage' scheme in the nearby village of Murroe traditional Irish musical evenings are held during the summer season.

🚗 *GLENSTAL is less than 10 miles east of Limerick City.*

GLIN
County Limerick

Glin is a most attractive village on the southern shores of the Shannon estuary. *An Gleann*, the Glen, takes its name from the Knights of Glin, the Fitzgerald family, whose ancestral home is Glin Castle to the west of the village. They have held land here for over 700 years as the Geraldines of Munster. The present Knight of Glin studied at the Victoria and Albert Museum in London, and is one of the best informed antiquarians in Ireland. The Gothic style lodge of this 1780s castle, on the Tarbert road, is an excellent craft shop and restaurant.

🚗 *GLIN is 8 miles west of Foynes and 31 miles west of Limerick.*

KNAPPOGUE CASTLE
County Clare

Knappogue Castle is one of some 42 castles built by the Clan of McNamara who ruled over Clare from the 5th to the 15th centuries. It was built in 1467 to defend the territory from the advancing Normans. A stout 16th-century tower, it has been fully restored and furnished, and is open to visitors. Twice nightly it is the scene of colourful

Glin Castle, ancestral home of the Fitzgerald family, is set in formal gardens

medieval banquets.

🚗 *KNAPPOGUE is 2¾ miles from Quin, and 8¾ miles east of Ennis.*

LAHINCH
County Clare

Lahinch – *Leacht Ui Chonchubhar* – O'Connor's Cairn, has a magnificent Atlantic sandy beach over one mile in length and perfect for bathing in the huge Atlantic rollers. This is a part of Clare made famous by the novels and stories of Edna O'Brien.

The undulating 18-hole championship golf-links runs all along the spectacular coastline. The barometer in the clubhouse has 'see goats' scrawled on it, as when these gentle tethered animals out on the links seek shelter, it means an Atlantic storm is on its way!

There is a local tradition that a whole village, complete with church and bell-steeple, lies beneath the bay, and you can hear the church bell ringing, very faintly, if you listen hard enough. A lively little resort, it has all amenities such as an entertainment centre, a sea water swimming pool, surfing facilities and a theatre.

Just five miles south, along the coast, is *Rinn na Spainneach*, Spanish Point, named for six huge ships of the Spanish Armada which were wrecked on the rocks in 1588. A thousand sailors perished, and their graves are marked by mounds and boulders in the fields beside the sea. Those who did not perish by drowning were put to the sword on the orders of the Elizabethan Governor of Connacht, Sir Turlough O'Brien, Boetius Clancy, Sheriff of Clare and their men.

🚗 *LAHINCH is 19 miles west of Ennis on a narrow road.*

The Burren — a strange moonscape of grey limestone

The Burren

The Burren – *Boireann* – the Great Rock, is the name given to a 200 square mile lunar landscape of grey limestone forming one of the most unusual natural rock gardens in the world. It is bordered by Galway Bay in the north, the Atlantic Ocean, and its extension, the Aran Islands in the west, and Gort, in County Galway in the north east. The old saying is that in the Burren there is not a tree on which to hang a man, water enough in which to drown him, or earth enough in which to bury him. In the cracks and fissures of the rocks, protected from wind and frost, grow a profusion of exotic wild flowers. They include Mountain Avens, Spring Gentian, Mossy Saxifrages, Maidenhair, Close-flowered Orchids, Bloody Crane's-bill, Hart's tongue, Madder, Hoary Rock-rose, and Pyramidal Bugle, and rare moths and butterflies thrive here. This land of Alpine and other types of rare flowers is not only of interest to the botanist but also to the geologist, speleologist, archaeologist and entomologist. May and June are the months in which to see this natural flower show at its best.

There are over 700 dolmens and stone forts on this lunar landscape and massive underground caves, notably the two million BC Aillwee cave (open to the public). At Kilfenora, a village in the heart of the Burren country, is a Display Centre open to the public for the study and interpretation of this unique natural rock garden.

Many exotic wild flowers grow in the warm climate of the Burren

St John's Castle on the banks of the River Shannon in Limerick

LIMERICK
County Limerick

Limerick City began in the 9th century as a Norse settlement on the River Shannon which was recaptured for the Irish by King Brian Boru. It then became an Anglo-Norman stronghold in 1175, commanding the vital bridge across the River Shannon. The greatest and most tragic years in its history were during the Jacobite-William of Orange wars from 1689 to 1691. In 1691 the Irish garrison surrendered to the Williamite forces of the Dutch general Ginkel, after the signing of the Treaty of Limerick. The garrison of 11,000 marched out with full battle honours to join the armies of King Louis of France, the beginning of an era which was to see half a million Irish soldiers join 'The Wild Geese', to serve in foreign armies.

Modern Limerick has effected many remarkable changes. In Michael Street, for example, an 18th-century Georgian granary has been tastefully transformed to modern usage and houses the Tourist Information Office and shopping, dining and entertainment facilities. Across Matthew Bridge, near the granary, is the Cathedral of St Mary, founded in 1176 by Donal Mor O'Brien, King of Munster, who granted his palace for its building. The carved choir stalls are 15th century. There are numerous 15th-century tombs including that of Murrough O'Brien, the infamous 'O'Brien of the Burnings' who laid waste the Province of Munster as the Earl of Inchiquin (1618-1674). A *Son et Lumiere* presentation tells the story of the cathedral. St John's Castle, in Castle Street, was built by the Normans in 1200. Five sided, it has one complete side on the waters of the Shannon and was established to guard the Thomond Bridge. On the other side of Thomond Bridge, from St John's Castle, on the west side, is a roughly-hewn stone mounted on a pedestal which is said to be the stone on which the surrender treaty of 1691 was signed. On the west side of St John's Square numbers 1 and 2 contain the Limerick Museum with its impressive collection of historical

These mock neolithic dwellings on Lough Gur's shores house an imaginative interpretive centre

material. At the Good Shepherd Convent in Clare Street, on the Dublin road, superb examples of Limerick lace can be seen. The 18th-century craft lives on in Limerick. In the National Institute for Higher Education, not far from the city centre, off the Dublin road, is the modern Hunt Museum housing 1000 items from the collection donated by John Hunt, the art historian and Celtic/Norman archaeologist.

The 'temporary' wooden church on the Ennis road is little known and yet incorporates some magnificent examples of modern Irish ecclesiastical art. These include the teak statue of 'Our Lady of Fatima' by Oisín Kelly, the 'Annunciation' by Imogen Stuart, the 'Deposition' by Andrew O'Connor, the 'Sacred Heart' and 'Our Lady' by Yvonne Jammet, and the baptistry window, the 'Baptism of Christ' by Evie Hone.

The Belltable Arts Centre in O'Connell Street is a venue for theatre and for exhibitions, and at *An Chistin*, in Thomas Street, there is superb traditional Irish music.

🚗 LIMERICK *is 123 miles south west of Dublin, and 65 miles north of Cork.*

LISDOONVARNA
County Clare

Lisdoonvarna – *Lios Duin Bhearna* – the Enclosure of the Gap-Fort, is an amazing spa possessing unique health-giving waters. Its spring waters include sulphur, magnesia and iron, and all the waters contain iodine. The Spa Wells Health Centre has a pump house and baths, and there is a special pump room for the magnesia spring. There are sauna baths, showers, sun lounges, beauty therapy and massage centres, and it is noted for the number of jockeys who undergo fitness courses here.

In the autumn the town is inundated with Irish farmers seeking a wife, after the harvest is in. There is an annual festival of Irish bachelors who dance jigs and swill Guinness all night in the company of the visiting and local women who are hoping to find Mr Right.

🚗 *LISDOONVARNA is 23 miles from Ennis 167 miles from Dublin via Limerick and Ennis.*

LOUGH GUR
County Limerick

Lough Gur is a tiny U-shaped lake on whose shores archaeologists have discovered how people lived some 2-300 years BC and, in modern times, an excellent interpretive centre, designed like neolithic houses, has been built to provide visual aids with commentaries and music. The 'neolithic' thatched houses, one circular and one rectangular, include a tourist information office, and there is an admission charge. There are some 30 monuments around the lake in the form of stone circles, forts, dolmens, megalithic tombs, standing stones and pre-historic dwellings. The principal attraction is the stone circle in the town land of Grange. In diameter it is one of the larger stone circles in Ireland designed for some now-forgotten ritual. It dates from 2000 BC, and pottery of this age has been found inside the circle.

Tempall Nua, the New Church, is 15th century, and has been repaired. The 17th-century harpist, Tomas O Connalláin who composed *Limerick's Lament*, is buried in this churchyard. *Carraig Aille* is a stone fort in an irregular circle, dating from the 8th or 9th centuries. A hoard of Norse silver was discovered on the site, and evidence of iron smelting. The Giants Cave is a wedge-shaped gallery grave divided into two chambers. Near the entrance to the lake stands the 15th-century Bouchier's Geraldine castle. Bolin Island is, in fact, an artificial island as it is a crannog or lake dwelling constructed by man. In the middle of the U-shaped lake is Garret Island, named after Garret Fitzgerald, not the present Irish Taoiseach, but Geroíd, 4th Earl of Desmond. In the Red Cellar Cave the bones of brown bear and other extinct animals such as giant Irish deer and reindeer have been found.

There are many stone age habitations and burial mounds, some of which have yielded up burial urns dating from 1500 BC. 'The Spectacles' are the foundations of the formation of Early Christian huts.

LOUGH GUR is 12 miles south of Limerick City.

MITCHELSTOWN CAVES
County Tipperary

Re-discovered in 1833, these massive caves are a monument to what water can do underground over the centuries to a limestock rock area. They are made up of three gigantic caverns, one is 200 ft by 160 ft and 60 ft high, and feature stalactites, stalagmites, huge columns, one called 'The Tower of Babel'.

The 'Desmond' Cave is the one in which the 'Sugán Earl' of Desmond took refuge in 1601 with a huge price on his hunted head. Arthur Young, the celebrated English traveller, visited the caves in 1777 and Martel, the French speleologist made a sketch plan of them.

THE CAVES are 3½ miles from Ballyporeen in County Tipperary, and about 9 miles from Mitchelstown in County Cork.

RATHKEALE
County Limerick

Rathkeale is a pleasant market town on the River Deel in rich agricultural land. The Earls of Desmond, the Fitzgeralds, owned these lands and their castles, and Sir Walter Raleigh, then Captain Raleigh, commanded the English forces here, who were marched out to massacre the Spanish at Smerwick Harbour in County Kerry in 1580. Castle Matrix, just south-west of Rathkeale, is a Geraldine Castle, built in 1410, and deserves to be more widely known. It has been fully restored by its owner, a military historian, and the splendid library contains the finest collection in existence of documents and weapons relating to the 'Wild Geese', the exiled Irish swordsmen who served with distinction in the Continental armies of the 17th and 18th centuries. It was here that the poet Spenser first met Sir Walter Raleigh, and it is probable that in the rich soil of the Castle grounds the first potato was grown in Ireland.

At the village of Ardagh, just four miles south of Castle Matrix, in an ancient ring fort, the famous 8th-century Ardagh Chalice, brooches and a bronze cup were found.

RATHKEALE is 18 miles south west of Limerick.

TIPPERARY
County Tipperary

Tipperary – *Tiobraid Arann* – The Well of Ara, lays no claim to accidental fame by its inclusion in a popular 1914-1918 British Army marching song, but rests its case for

The fast, exciting game of hurling is Ireland's national sport...

recognition on both being at the very heart of the fertile Golden Vale dairy lands of the county on the River Ara, and as the gathering place of patriots, novelists and writers. It is a straggling town of the people. King John built a castle here, it was laid waste in Elizabethan wars, survived the Land League Agrarian war, when the tenants of local landlord Smith-Barry tried to build a 'New Tipperary' outside the town, and produced military leaders for the New Ireland. Charles James Kickham (1826-1882) has the place of honour in the town, a bronze, seated figure on a limestone base, with the inscription, 'Charles Kickham, poet, novelist, and, above all, patriot,' erected in 1898. Kickham wrote the most popular of all Irish novels *Knocknagow*, into which he put all his love of the country. James O'Neill, father of the Irish-American dramatist Eugene O'Neill, was born on a farm adjacent to the town. John O'Leary, (1830-1907) Fenian patriot and journalist extraordinary, who converted Yeats to Irish nationalism, was a native of the town. Tipperary was also the headquarters of *Muintir na Tire* (the people of the land) founded in 1931 by Canon John Hayes (1888-1957) who was parish priest of the adjacent village of Bansha. Hurling and Gaelic Football are played in the town's Sean Tracy Park. Limerick Junction Racecourse is just two miles away, and the internationally-famous Scarteen Black and Tan Foxhounds hunt across this district.

Tipperary town is beautifully situated at the north of the wooded Slievenamuck Hills, which rise to 1216 ft, and just north of the superb Glen of Aherlow.

TIPPERARY is 112 miles from Dubin and 25 miles from Limerick.

Here Tipperary take on Cork

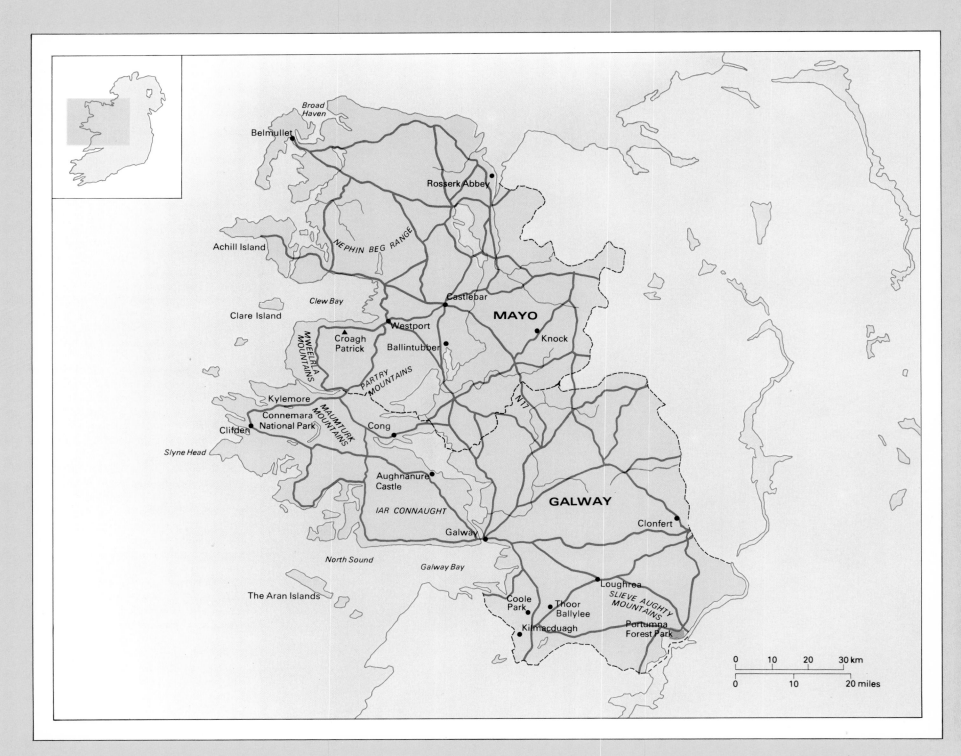

Broad
Haven

Belmullet

Rosserk Abbey

NEPHIN BEG RANGE

Achill Island

Clew Bay

Clare Island

Castlebar

MAYO

Westport

Croagh
Patrick

Knock

Ballintubber

MWEELREA MOUNTAINS

PARTRY
MOUNTAINS

N17

Kylemore

MAUMTURK MOUNTAINS

Connemara
National Park

Cong

Clifden

Slyne Head

Aughnanure
Castle

GALWAY

IAR CONNAUGHT

Clonfert

Galway

North Sound

Galway Bay

Loughrea

The Aran Islands

Coole
Park

Thoor
Ballylee

SLIEVE AUGHTY
MOUNTAINS

Kilmacduagh

Portumna
Forest Park

| 0 | 10 | 20 | 30 km |
| 0 | 10 | | 20 miles |

The West of Ireland

The tranquil waters
of picturesque Lough
Corrib, in County
Galway, its surface
still as a pond

TRADITION HOLDS THAT in Galway City, at the Collegiate Church of St Nicholas, set up by the Anglo Normans in 1320 and enlarged in the 16th century, Christopher Columbus heard mass, and took with him a Galway man, Rice de Culvy, as his navigator to assist him in his voyage of discovery to the New World. Many of the houses of Galway city today retain their Spanish appearance, reflecting the centuries-old trading links between Galway and Spain. Behind the city lies the wild hinterland of Connacht, largely Irish-speaking. The Atlantic rollers pound the indented coastline. The 12 blue Bens, or Pins, of Connemara dominate the lakelands and the skyline. Here the traditions and customs of old Ireland are preserved in a scenic wonderland which includes the most western tip of Celtic Europe, the Aran islands.

Mayo, adjacent, and to the north, is majestic fjord coast with massive bays from Killary to Killala, in which many giant ships of the Spanish Armada foundered in violent storms. Mayo is dominated by Croagh Patrick, St Patrick's holy mountain, rising to a spectacular cone, over 2500 ft high, still easily climbable today. Thousands of pilgrims ascend it annually, striving to reach its sparkling quartzite peak. From the summit is a God's eye view of the west coast of Ireland from the mountains of Kerry in the deep south, to the mountains of Donegal in the far north.

Achill Island is crowned by heather-topped mountains

ACHILL ISLAND
County Mayo

Achill Island, the largest of Irish islands, at over 36,000 acres, 15 miles long and 12 miles wide, is an isle of magnificently wild Atlantic beauty. Crowned by a heather covered mountain range over 2000 ft high, including Slievemore (2204 ft), Croaghaun (2192 ft), Minaun (1530 ft) and gigantic cliffs 800 ft high, the island is joined to the mainland by the slim Michael Davitt Bridge. An ideal centre for hang-gliding and deep sea angling there are beautiful beaches, lake-ringed settlements,

cloud-capped mountains, and sun drenched villages. Achill Sound has four excellent trout lakes. Dugort is a magnificent strand, above which towers Slievemore mountain. The area abounds in pre-Christian tombs and cairns. Keem Bay is the haunt of basking sharks. Dooagh bay is famous for its salmon netting.

Corrymore House, near Dooagh, on the slopes of Croaghaun mountain, was once the home of Captain Boycott, who was shunned by the people during the Land League days of the 1880s, and thus gave a new word to the English language.

Keel village has a three mile sandy

strand, and the 800 ft high Minaun Cliffs, at low tide, provide a breathtaking view of the Cathedral Rocks. This is the island of Atlantic fishermen, with their haunting ballad sessions.

ACHILL ISLAND is 17 miles west of Newport.

THE ARAN ISLANDS
County Galway

The three islands of Aran lie in Galway Bay; Inishmore, (7635 acres), Inishmaan (2252 acres) and Inisheer (1400 acres). They are Irish-speaking islands made famous by

J.M. Synge (1871-1909) in his classic play *Riders to the Sea*, set on Inishmaan, and by Robert Flaherty who made his film *Man of Aran* in 1934. Liam O'Flaherty, the short story writer and author of *The Informer*, was born on Inishmore in 1896. The fishermen of the islands are famous for their frail lath and tarred canvas boats known as 'currachs', their homespun oiled wool 'bawneen' coats, shoes of rough hide, 'pampooties', and colourful woollen belts, the 'crios'. Kilronan, on Inishmore, is capital of the islands. Inishmore has the most westerly prehistoric fort in Europe, Dun Aengus, semi-circular, with its back to the sheer 300 ft cliff drop into the Atlantic Ocean. The fort was composed of ring after ring of stone defence walls, of which the inner court wall remains, 150 ft in diameter with a wall 20 ft high and 18 ft thick. The islands abound in pre-Christian stone forts, early Christian hermitages and tiny monastic churches.

THE ARAN ISLANDS are 30 miles from Galway and can be reached by steamer service from Galway city, motor-boat from Rossaveal, or by frequent twin-engined Aer Arann planes from Galway's Carnmore airport.

AUGHNANURE CASTLE
County Galway

On the western shore of Lough Corrib, on the River Drimneen, stands the beautifully-preserved castle of Aughnanure. Originally it was erected as a stark, stone, square fortress some four storeys high by the 'ferocious O'Flahertys' in the 16th century. It has stout inner and outer

The ruins of St Enda's Church on Inishmore in the Aran Islands

Castlebar's tree-lined Mall is a pleasant place to while away a summer's afternoon

walls and the O'Flaherty's took good care of the inner man with an enormous banqueting hall, most of which remains, but some of which vanished into the River Drimneen.

🚗 *THE CASTLE stands 2 miles south east of Oughterard.*

BALLINTUBBER
County Mayo

Ballintubber – *'Baile Tobair Phádraig'* – the townland of the well of Patrick, as its name implies, is the name of a well spring in which St Patrick baptised the pagan Mayo men and women in 441 and where

he built a church. It was closely associated with Croagh Patrick, and there was at one time a pilgrim road known as Tóchar Phádraig, 20 miles long, to the 'Reek'. Ballintubber Abbey is known as 'The Abbey that refused to die', as mass has been celebrated there for over 760 years without a break. The Abbey is cruciform in shape with transepts, nave and choir. The main doorway is Early Gothic with a high gable, and there are eight early pointed windows. The windows above the altar are Norman, and at the end of the south transept are monastic buildings. The Abbey was founded

in 1216 by the King of Connacht, Cathal More of the wine red hand, for the Canons Regular of St Augustine. The Viscounts Mayo are buried here, and there is a tomb to the son of Grace O'Malley the Pirate Queen, *Tiobód na Long,* Theobald of the Ships. He was a Bourke, son of her second husband, and died in 1629, having been made Viscount Mayo in 1627. Despite being burnt twice, supressed in 1542, and unroofed in Penal times, the Abbey was never abandoned by priest and people.

Just two miles to the south east are the remains of Castle Bourke,

fortress of Myles Bourke, the 4th Viscount Mayo. Nine miles south are the remains of Moore Hall, on the east shore of Lough Carra, birthplace of the novelist George Moore. His remains are buried in a cairn of solid rock on Castle island, at the north end of Lough Carra. One of his ancestors was John Moore (1763-1799), who was President of the Republic of Connacht, set up in Castlebar, when the forces of Napoleon landed at Killala in 1798.

🚗 *BALLINTUBBER is 9½ miles north of Ballinrove, 1 mile off the Ballinrobe to Westport road.*

BELMULLET
County Galway

Belmullet, shaped like a sea-urchin, with Broad Haven Bay at its head and Blacksod Bay at its tail, is a neck of land embracing magnificent sandy beaches, wild headlands and cliff-top forts. It is as serenely wild and beautiful today as the day in September 1588, when one of the Spanish Armada's proudest ships, *La Rata Santa Maria Encoronada*, 820 tons, with 35 guns, ran aground in Blacksod Bay and was fired by her Captain, Don Alonso de Leira.

🚗 *BELMULLET is 39 miles west of Ballina.*

CASTLEBAR
County Mayo

Castlebar – *Caislean an barraig* – Barry's Castle, is the capital of Mayo county, with a pleasant tree-lined Mall. It was founded by the de Barra family, then taken over by John Bingham, the ancestor of the Earls of Lucan in the 17th century. The present-day holder of the title is an infamous Missing Person. The Green in the centre of the town was once a cricket pitch when the Lord Lucans were in residence. It achieved fame curing the 1798 Rebellion when the joint Irish-French forces took over the area and the French troops landed in Killala. The Humbert Inn is named after the French General who won the battle known as the 'Races of Castlebar', as, initially the Redcoats ran. John Moore, the 'President' of the short-lived Republic of Connacht is buried in the Mall. The Linen Hall, now the Town Hall, recalls the days when the town was the centre of the linen industry. The Education Centre was once a chapel whose foundation stone was laid by John Wesley.

The lush greenery of Clare Island is broken only by tiny whitewashed cottages

Michael Davitt founded the Land League in the town in 1879. A commemorative plaque in the Mall marks the house in which Margaret Burke Sheridan (1889-1958), the Prima Donna of La Scala, Milan, and the greatest interpreter of the role of Madame Butterfly, was born.

Louis Brennan, (1852-1932), the inventor of the torpedo, and of the gyroscopic monorail, was born in Main Street, Castlebar. Ernie O'Malley, (1898-1957) revolutionary and author, was born in the town. He is best remembered for his saga, *On Another Man's Wound*.

🚗 *CASTLEBAR is 11 miles north west of Westpoint and 12 miles from Newport.*

CLARE ISLAND
County Mayo

Clare Island, roughly 4000 acres in area, lies at the south of the many-islanded Clew Bay, an isle of tranquillity connected to the mainland by a daily boat service from Roonagh Point, near Louisberg. The island was the headquarters of the Elizabethan Pirate Queen, Grace O'Malley (1530-1600). When her father, Owen O'Malley, chieftain of the barony of Murrisk died, she took over power, and at the age of 16 married Donal O'Flaherty of Bunowen Castle. She attacked rich merchant ships on their way to Galway, and traded with Spain and Portugal. She later married the chief of the Mayo Burkes, Sir Richard Burke and took over his Rockfleet castle. She visited Queen Elizabeth at Hampton Court in 1593 and declined to be made a countess on the grounds that she was already an Irish Queen!

Her O'Malley three storey castle still stands above the harbour on the east coast of the island. She died in 1600 and lies buried in the Carmelite

415

Thackeray praised the incomparable beauty of Clifden and its environs

Clare Abbey, one and a half miles south west of the harbour. The south coast of the island is extremely beautiful, with a range of precipitous cliffs. Knock Mountain drops 1550 ft into the sea. Her fortress home on the mainland, at Carraigahowley Castle, near Newport, was restored by Sir Owen O'Malley in recent years, and is now a national monument.

CLARE ISLAND is roughly 4 miles by sea from Roonagh Quay on the mainland.

CLIFDEN
County Galway

Accepted as the 'capital' of Connemara, Clifden is an attractive village made famous by Ethel Mannin in her novel *Late Have I Loved Thee*, which she wrote in her cottage on Mannin Bay. Perched on the white strands of the Atlantic and set against a backdrop of mountains of incomparable beauty, Thackeray described it as 'one of the most beautiful districts that it is ever the fortune of a traveller to examine'. It is the centre for the annual Connemara Pony Show, held in August. A few miles south of the town, at Derrygimlagh Bog, there is a stone cairn in the shape of the tail of an aeroplane which marks the spot where those intrepid airmen, Alcock and Brown landed their old World War I converted Vickers bomber, to conclude the first non-stop transAtlantic flight in June 1919.

CLIFDEN is 49 miles north west of Galway.

CLONFERT
County Galway

Clonfert, almost on the banks of the Shannon river, has the remains of a renowned monastic settlement

Ashford Castle, an 18th-century castellated mansion, is now a superb hotel

established in 558 by St Brendan the Navigator. The remains of the 11th-century cathedral are incorporated in the present Church of Ireland building. The chief glory is the west doorway, superbly Hiberno-Romanesque, incorporating a high triangular pediment above the eight pillars and rounded recesses of the semi-circular doorway. In this triangular area are a series, one above the other, of five layers of carved heads peaking finally in a single carved head. This has direct symbolic links with the old Celtic pagan custom of the cult of the severed human head. By this the severed heads of enemies were placed on carved niches of pagan temples, in the belief that to possess the skull of an enemy meant the possession of power, since the head was deemed the dwelling place of the soul.

CLONFERT is 1 mile north of Ballinasloe, 43 miles of Galway.

CONG
County Mayo

Cong – *Cunga* – a neck, gets its name from being on the isthmus between the Lakes of Mask and Corrib which are the finest free trout fishing waters in Europe. Cong achieved international fame in 1951 when the Irish-American film director, John Ford, filmed *The Quiet Man* in the area, featuring Maureen O'Hara, John Wayne and Barry Fitzgerald. Cong Abbey was founded in the 12th century by the King of Connacht, Turlough Moore O'Connor. It was rebuilt by another King of Connacht, and in 1203 Rory O'Connor, the last High King of Ireland, died there in retirement. An east window and four doorways are all that remain of the Augustinian monastery which was built on the site of the 7th-century monastic settlement of St Feichin. In the tiny village is the medieval Market Cross erected in the 14th century. The modern Catholic church adjacent to the Abbey has superb Irish stained glass windows by Harry Clarke. The priceless processional Cross of Cong, now in the National Museum in Dublin, was made in Roscommon in 1123 for the Cathedral of Tuam, on the orders of King Turlough O'Connor, to enshrine a relic of the True Cross sent to him from Rome.

His son, Roderick, brought it to Cong, a reliquary of great beauty of oak and copper and decorated with Celtic designs in gold filigree work.

Ashford Castle, recently voted the best hotel in Europe, an 18th-century castellated mansion, was built by the Browne family, and then purchased from the Lord Oranmore and Browne by Sir Benjamin Guinness, who in 1905 entertained the Prince of Wales, later to become King George V. The hotel reached its greatest days of *haute cuisine* and service when it was first run as a hotel by Noel Huggard and his wife. It was then bought by the Irish American millionaire John A Mulcahy, who entertained his friend President Nixon of the United States there on his Irish-American vote-catching visit to the 'Auld Sod'. It is now owned by Tony 'Heinz' O'Reilly and his fellow directors. The lakeside setting is perfection, the interior is elegant and the grounds are beautiful. Cong is also famous for its unique Dry Canal, four miles long. It was built in the 1840s as famine relief work.

The Irish Viceroy himself performed the opening ceremony, and when the lock gates opened, the waters which were to link Loughs Mask and Corrib disappeared through the porous limestone bed!

President Reagan and his wife Nancy spent a relaxing evening in Ashford Castle on their visit to Ireland on 1 June 1984.

There are some 40 underground caves to be explored in Cong.

CONG is 28 miles north of Galway.

CONNEMARA
County Galway

Connemara is the name given to what is generally accepted as the most beautiful part of Galway, the western area between the vast Lake Corrib and the Atlantic ocean. It is dominated by the blue ridge mountains of the 'Twelve Pins' or 'Twelve Bens' of Connemara, which have been captured on canvas in the oil paintings of Paul Henry (1876-1958) the celebrated Irish landscape painter. Largely Irish-speaking, the local people are renowned for their skill at May fly fishing for trout on Lough Corrib, which is also famous for salmon angling. The touring road of Connemara is roughly a figure eight over an area of 30 square miles to the north west of Galway city. It runs west along the Corrib to Oughterard, through Maam Cross, Recess and Ballynahinch to Clifden, returning through Letterfrack and Kylemore to Galway. Ballynahinch Castle was once the home of the Martin family whose most famous member was 'Humanity Dick' Martin, the founder of the Royal Society for the Prevention of Cruelty to Animals.

CONNEMARA lies to the north west of Galway city.

The Blue Ridge Mountains of Connemara are known as The Twelve Bens or Pins

Knock Shrine

Knock – *Cnoc Mhuire* – Mary's Hill, in the middle of the plain of Mayo, 37 miles north of Galway city, is the Irish 'Lourdes', attracting 750,000 visitors every year. This is where Pope John Paul II made his historic visit to Ireland in 1979, visiting the shrine by helicopter on 30 September.

The story of Knock began at 7pm on the evening of Thursday 21 August 1879, when a girl called Mary Beirne, and her companion, Mary McLoughlin, were walking past the gable end of the old parish church, and on the wall, in a globe of light,

they saw the figures of the Virgin Mary, St Joseph and St John the Evangelist, the latter bearing in his arms a lamb. They gathered 15 friends to see these silent figures, which appeared dry in the midst of the driving rain. Mgr. James Horan, the parish priest of the vast modern basilica which stands in the prosperous village today, sees in this alleged vision a parallel with contemporary Ireland, as the Virgin Mary appeared at a time of violence. To the hundreds of thousands of present-day visitors to the village of Knock the main attraction is

to see the 'Wall of Apparitions', now portrayed by figures in stone on the glass-enclosed gable end of the old parish church. The huge new basilica of 'Our Lady, Queen of Ireland', has an encircling ambulatory supported by 40 pillars of stone from every county in Ireland, and has accommodation for 20,000 people. The Basilica is set amid a landscaped parkland where impressive candlelight processions are held in honour of 'Our Lady of Silence', so named because she said nothing when she appeared. She gave no message.

Worshippers at the Shrine of Our Lady in the village of Knock

CONNEMARA NATIONAL PARK
County Galway

Unknown to many visitors, Connemara National Park covers 5000 acres of land south of the Leenane to Clifden main road. There are superb nature trails, signposted long walks and signposted short walks, all amid glorious scenery embracing sea, mountain and lake. A helpful and informative visitor centre is located at Letterfrack, in a splendidly-converted farmhouse and outhouses. These converted farm buildings have flagged floors of Liscannor slate and traditional Irish style furnishings, including the famous 'sugán' chairs. There are audio visual presentations about the area.

LETTERFRACK is 9 miles north east of Clifden on the T71.

COOLE PARK
County Galway

Although Coole Park, the former home of Lady Augusta Gregory (1859-1932) no longer exists, as it was vandalised during World War II, the outline of where the house once stood remains and the long avenue of overhanging yew trees leading up to it. On one of the copper beeches are the initials, beautifully preserved, of some of Lady Gregory's famous guests and visitors, such as George Bernard Shaw, John Masefield, Sean O'Casey, Douglas Hyde, Oliver St John Gogarty, Augustus John, W.B. Yeats, J.M. Synge, Violet Martin and Katharine Tynan. Next to Coole House, in the National Forest and Wildlife Park, is the beloved lake of W.B. Yeats whose poem on the swans of Coole immortalised it, and swans are still there today.

There is, in the fields beside this

Croagh Patrick is Ireland's Holy Mountain. St Patrick fasted on its summit for 40 days and 40 nights

lake an almost physical presence of the greatest revival in Irish literature ever begun, and in which the little Old Lady of Coole Park played such a huge part. Near Coole is the national school house at Kiltartan, and its 15th-century church. Listening to the accents of the children of Galway attending this school gave Lady Gregory the idea of a uniform Irish dialect for the actors in her plays. This has been described as 'Kiltartanese'.

COOLE PARK is about 2 miles from the village of Ardrahan, on the Galway to Limerick road, 18 miles south of Galway and 8 miles north of Gort.

CROAGH PATRICK
County Mayo

Croagh Patrick, (2510 ft) Ireland's Holy Mountain, stands out sharply, the white path to the summit clearly visible all the way from the shores of Clew Bay. St Patrick fasted on the small summit of this mighty mountain for 40 days and 40 nights, and every year, on the last Sunday of July, thousands of pilgrims, many in their bare feet, climb the holy mountain to hear mass in the passing clouds. There is a chapel on the summit. The view from the top is most rewarding with the many-islanded Clew Bay at the foot, Clare Island, Achill Island, and, on a clear day as far as the blue mountains of Donegal in the north, and the towering ranges of the Kerry mountains in the deep south. The pilgrim path is a fairly arduous and steady climb, and only very near the summit, where the quartzite shale is broken up into sharp pieces, is the steady walk reduced to a scramble on all fours!

The locals refer to the mountain as 'The Reek' The legend is that it was from this mountain St Patrick banished all the snakes in Ireland, and, after successfully wrestling with the Devil, was promised by the Good Lord that he would be allowed to sit with him on Judgement Day to judge the Irish people, who would never lose the Christian faith.

🚗 *CROAGH PATRICK is 6 miles west of Westport.*

GALWAY
County Galway

Galway gets its name from the River Corrib, on which it stands. Ptolemy put it on his world map as 'Magnata', and the local O'Halloran clan included it in their territories until the Anglo-Norman, Richard de Burgh, took it in 1232. It was a walled city, and the prevailing winds made it easy for an enormous sea trade to grow up between Spain and Galway, so much so that Spanish traders had homes in Galway and Irish traders had them in Spain, and there was much inter-marriage between the two countries. Richard II granted the city a charter in 1484. The Anglo-Norman families who ran the city were known as the 'Tribes of Galway', and they included the Blakes, Bodkins, Brownes, D'Arcy's, ffrenches, Kirwans, Joyces, Lynches, Morrisses, Martins, and Skerrets. These settlers kept themsleves pure from the native Irish, and a bye-law of 1518 declared that 'neither O nor Mac shall strutte ne swagger thro the streets of Galway'.

The native Irish made regular raids, so much so that over the West Gate of the city an inscription read 'From the fury of the O'Flahertys, good Lord deliver us'. Such was the inter-trade over the centuries with Spain, particularly in the smuggling of wines and brandies, silks, laces and tobacco, that there is a strong Iberian influence on the people, the architecture and the manners of to-

Hundreds of salmon can be seen leaping to the spawning grounds upstream at Galway salmon weir

day's Galwegians. So many young Irishmen were smuggled to the Continent and returned as expert swordsmen that in Williamite times the rules of duelling by pistol were drawn up. This was necessary because the young Catholic expert swordsmen, trained in Europe and returned home to Ireland, were challenging their Protestant Ascendancy landowning heirs and decimating them in sword play, so that the 'back-to-back' and shots at twenty paces was agreed as a new form of duelling to make things more equal in affairs of honour.

There is much to be seen in this Spanish-style city. The Collegiate Church of St Nicholas in Lombard Street, erected by the Anglo-Normans in 1320, is remarkable for its unique triple nave. The modern Cathedral of St Nicholas and Our Lady of the Assumption, built on the site of the old city jail, beside the famous salmon weir, is of cut limestone with Connemara marble flooring. Cardinal Cushing of Boston dedicated it in August 1965, and a chapel commemorates the late President John F. Kennedy of the United States. The salmon weir is

one of the most unusual and popular of sights, as in season huge shoals of salmon can be seen queueing up to leap their way upstream to their mysterious spawning grounds. The nearby Franciscan Abbey, in Francis Street, is built on the site of the friary founded in 1296 by William Liath de Burgo.

The Lynch Memorial, near the Church of St Nicholas, is a built-up Gothic door, above which, set in the black marble, is the inscripton, 'This memorial of the stern and unbending justice of the chief magistrate of this City, James Lynch FitzStephen,

Padraic O'Conaire atop his throne of rubble in Eyre Square

The Spanish Arch was built in Galway in 1594

elected Mayor A.D. 1493 who condemned and executed his own guilty son, Walter on this spot.' Beneath this, on a stone dated 1624, is the inscription, 'Remember Death. Vanite of Vanites, Al is Vanite.' Tradition says that Walter ran his sword through a young Spanish visitor who was 'on their Keeping', in a duel over a girl, and as nobody else in the city would carry out the sentence of death, Judge Lynch hanged his own son from a window of the house.

The Allied Irish Bank in Shop Street occupies the fine old building of Lynch's Castle, a family mansion dating from 1320. The walls are beautifully decorated with coats of arms and carved stone work, and the fireplaces date from Henry VIII's time. Similar buildings and shops are to be found in Shop Street, Abbeygate Street, St Augustine Street and Middle Street. In the centre of the city is the John Fitzgerald Kennedy Memorial Park, in honour of the late President of the United States, who spoke to the people of Galway in June 1983 from the spot now marked with a memorial plaque. In the Square stands the

Browne doorway, and the charmingly playful stone statue to the Irish scholar and short-story writer, Padraic O'Conaire (1883-1928). The statue is by Albert Power R.H.A.

In the Bank of Ireland, at 19 Eyre Square, the 17th-century Galway Silver Sword and the Great Mace of 1710 are on display.

The Spanish Arch, and Spanish Parade, are all that remain of the 1594 wall of arches to protect the Spanish ships unloading their cargoes.

The Galway City Museum at the Spanish Arch covers all aspects of life and the city's history. The Claddagh, on the West bank of the River Corrib, was for many years an Irish speaking fishing village of thatched cottages with its own first citizen or 'King'. The Claddagh ring, the traditional wedding ring of Galway, a heart held between two hands, is a popular souvenir of the city.

University College Galway, an old 'Queen's University', built in 1845, in Tudor style, is now very much a Gaelic University and much used by American student summer schools. Millions of pounds exchange hands through the bookies at the celebrated annual Galway Races held July/August at Ballybrit Race track.

🚗 GALWAY CITY is 135 miles west of Dublin.

KILMACDUAGH
County Galway

Because it is very much off the map, visitors making the effort to see this monastic settlement of the 6th-century St Colman will probably find themselves sharing the view with only a flock of sheep. It has a collection

Kylemore Abbey delights the eye, a fairytale mansion above a lake

of assorted churches and a round tower, 112 ft high, known as the Irish 'Leaning Tower of Pisa' as it is really leaning over two feet off its perpendicular line! The cathedral building is 14th century, 98 ft long, and contains the altar-tomb of the O'Shaughnessys.

🚗 KILMACDUAGH is 3 miles south west of Gort.

KYLEMORE
County Galway

Kylemore Abbey, north of Clifden, and on one of the most beautiful scenic routes through the 12 Bens of Connemara, is a glorious castellated mansion standing on the shores of Kylemore Lake. Once the home of Mitchell Henry, an M.P. of the 1860s, it is now a convent and school of the Irish Benedictine nuns of Ypres. It has charming tea rooms and an excellent souvenir shop with first class pottery. The Gothic chapel is beautifully furnished with Connemara marble.

🚗 KYLEMORE is less than 10 miles north west of Clifden.

LOUGHREA
County Galway

Loughrea – Baile Locha Riach – Grey Lough Town, is an attractive market town, beautifully situated on the north side of a lake, famous for its coarse fish angling. The town was founded by the Norman, Richard de Burg, in 1300. He established the Carmelite Priory, the remains of which are still to be seen in the middle of the town, but its main attraction is St Brendan's Cathedral, not because of its dull exterior, but because of the exciting, artistic content of its interior. There are superb examples of Irish stained glass work of the incomparable Evie Hone, A.E.

Exquisite stained glass in the cathedral at Loughrea

Child, Michael Healy, Hubert McGoldrick, Sarah Purser, Patrick Pye and Ethel Rhind. There are embroideries by Jack Yeats and sculptures by John Hughes, notably in the Lady Chapel. The artworks span the period from around 1900-1950, and were greatly inspired and assisted by Edward Martyn (1859-1923) of Galway, who was the inspiration behind the Irish stained glass revival movement.

Just two miles north of Loughrea is the Turoe Stone, the finest example in Ireland of La Tene Celtic art. It is a phallic symbol, connected with some ancient pagan ritual, 3 ft high, and covered in a profusion of Celtic curvilinear designs and a Greek step outline. It is related to similar stones in Ireland and in Brittany, and dates from 100 BC.

LOUGHREA is 22 miles east of Galway and 19 miles west of Ballinasloe.

PORTUMNA FOREST PARK
County Galway

The old town of Portumna — 'The Oak Harbour' — looks out over Lough Derg, and makes a bridge across the River Shannon. Just outside the town are the impressive ruins of Portumna Castle, once the home of Lord Clanricarde, one of the lesser-loved landlords of the area.

Adjacent to the town is Portumna Forest Park, 1403 superb acres of recreational and amenity land all along the edge of Lough Derg. Complete with a wildlife sanctuary, with hides for birdwatching, and a herd of fallow deer, it has fine nature trails.

The large harbour is a haven for mooring boats and cruisers on the mighty River Shannon.

PORTUMNA FOREST PARK is 20 miles from Ballinashoe and 24 miles by river from Killaloe.

ROSSERK ABBEY
County Mayo

Founded around 1400 by one of the Joyce Clan, Rosserk Abbey is a Franciscan friary, and one of the best preserved typical friary churches in the country. Look closely at the double piscina and you will see the carving of an early Celtic round tower.

ROSSERK ABBEY is 4 miles north of Ballina.

THOOR BALLYLEE
County Galway

Thoor Ballylee, a Norman square tower, was originally the home of Richard de Burg in the 16th century. William Butler Yeats purchased it for £35, fully restored it, and used it on and off as his ivory tower during the early 1920s. When the castle fell back into ruins after he moved to Dublin, the Irish Tourist Board fully restored it as a four-storey precious national monument, open to the public, and with a erudite and cultured guide in charge. The original oak furniture, designed by W.A. Scott, the china, some first editions of Yeats, and all the colourful broadsheets of his brother, Jack, are on view. Yeats' 'Winding stair, a chamber arched with stone. A grey stone fireplace with an open hearth,' are still there, in situ, and there is a marvellous view from the flat roof of the tower. Splendid teas and conversation are to be had in the adjacent Yeatsian thatched cottage.

THOOR BALLYLEE is 3 miles north east of Gort on the Galway-Ennis road.

WESTPORT
County Mayo

Westport, on the edge of the vastness that is Clew Bay, 15 miles

long and six miles wide, has the unique distinction of being a town that was designed by James Wyatt. Westport House, designed in 1731 by Richard Castle with additions by James Wyatt, was the first stately home in Ireland to open its doors to the public. It is run by Jeremy Ulick, 12th Earl of Altamont and his wife Jennifer. Richard Castle built it for the 1st Earl, and it has remained in the family ever since. A family of engaging eccentrics, the Lord Sligo of 1812, friend of Byron, excavated and brought back to Westport from his 'Grand Tour' the 3000 year old columns that guarded the Treasury of Atreus at Mycenae, the tomb of Agamemnon. They were later presented to the British museum, the concrete substitute columns now adorn the home. There is a magnificent entrance hall with a Sicilian marble staircase. To the left of the entrance is the library designed by James Wyatt. The drawing room to the right incorporates wood from the Lord Sligo estates in Jamaica. The house is full of panelled walls, magnificent plaster ceilings, old Irish silver, Waterford glass and rare furniture. There are statues by Antonio Rossetti and John Gibson, and, notably a Mother and Child by Dalou. There is a Chinese room, a gallery of landscapes, and family protraits by Kneller, Reynolds and Copley. The dining room is by James Wyatt's son, Benjamin. On the premises are tea rooms, caravan and camping parks, a zoo park and a children's playground.

WESTPORT is 162 miles from Dublin, and 52 miles north west of Galway.

Each room in Westport House is furnished in elegant style

427

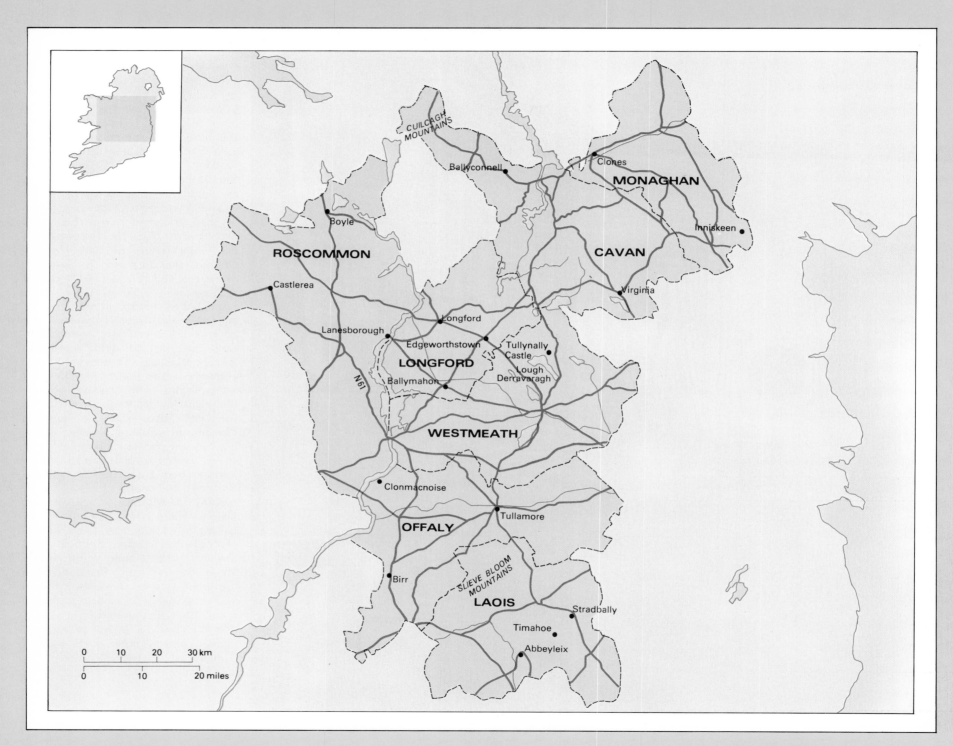

CUILCAGH
MOUNTAINS

Ballyconnell

Clones

MONAGHAN

Boyle

Inniskeen

ROSCOMMON

CAVAN

Castlerea

Virginia

Longford

Lanesborough

Edgeworthstown

Tullynally
Castle

LONGFORD

Lough
Derravaragh

N 61

Ballymahon

WESTMEATH

Clonmacnoise

Tullamore

OFFALY

SLIEVE BLOOM
MOUNTAINS

Birr

LAOIS

Stradbally

Timahoe

Abbeyleix

0   10   20   30 km

0   10   20 miles

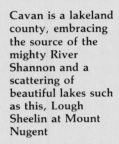

Cavan is a lakeland county, embracing the source of the mighty River Shannon and a scattering of beautiful lakes such as this, Lough Sheelin at Mount Nugent

A GULL'S EYE VIEW of the Midlands shows Athlone, County Westmeath, right in the middle of Ireland, on the River Shannon, which divides the Province of Leinster from Connacht. Offaly is famous for the home of the Earl and Countess of Rosse, Birr Castle, with its superb gardens, open to the public, incorporating 100 acres of 1000 different species of trees and shrubs. To the south is Laois, formerly Queen's County, named after Queen Mary in the reign of Philip and Mary. Westmeath, to the north of Offaly is fat cattle pasture land. It is Goldsmith country, as he was born at Pallas or Elphin in 1730. Edgeworthstown is famous as the home, still standing today, of the novelist, Maria Edgeworth (1768-1849) whose writings inspired Turgenev and Sir Walter Scott. Roscommon, north west of Athlone, is lakeland country, embracing the vast waters of the beautiful Lough Ree. Longford is forever associated with the late Lord Longford, patron of the Gate Theatre in Dublin, and Frank Pakenham, now Lord Longford. The family mansion, (open to the public) Tullynally Castle, is actually in County Westmeath. It is a remarkable 'gothic' castle, once the home of Kitty Pakenham who married the Duke of Wellington. Cavan, the most southerly of the nine counties of Ulster, is a lakeland of amazing beauty, and the Shannon 'Pot' has its source at Cuilcagh. Its source is so small that you can almost leap across it!

Abbeyleix House stands in woodland gardens laid down by Emma, wife of the third Viscount de Vesci

ABBEYLEIX
County Laois

Abbeyleix – *Mainistear Laoighse* – the Abbey of Laoighis, takes its name from the now long-since vanished Cistercian monastery founded in 1183 by Conor O'More. Today the attractive, tree-lined town is dominated by the Viscount de Vesci stately home designed by James Wyatt in 1773, and built by William Chambers for Thomas, the first Viscount de Vesci. While the house is not open to the public the magnificent woodland gardens which surround the house are. They contain a superb collection of giant oaks, natives of the woods, supplemented by rare and exotic specimens of ornamental trees, shrubs and flowers. Within the walls, in the King's Garden, is the tomb of the Prince of Laois, Malachy O'More, who died in 1486, and the 13th-century monk's bridge over the River Nore is still in use, all that is left of the original 12th-century Cistercian monastery.

ABBEYLEIX is 60 miles south west of Dublin and 9 miles south of Port Laoise.

BALLYCONNELL
County Cavan

Ballyconnell, a pretty town on the Cavan-Fermanagh border, has twice won the coveted National Tidy Towns Award. It lies at the foot of Slieve Russell (1331 ft) and the Cuilcagh Mountain (2188 ft). It is a superb coarse fishing centre, and gets its name from Conal Cearnach, the 1st-century Red Branch Knight who slew the King of Connacht, and was slain in revenge by the King's men. On the western slope of Cuilcagh Mountain is the little-known 'Shannon Pot', the source of the mightiest and longest river in these islands. It is a marshy spot on the mountainside, and the temptation is to leap across the welling waters and their surrounding shrubs, to boast that you have leapt across the Shannon. However, common sense should prevail as you would really need to be an Olympic Gold Medalist to succeed. The views from this spot on the Cavan-Fermanagh border are extremely beautiful. At Killycluggin, just three miles to the south west of Ballyconnell, is a phallic stone with Celtic designs, similar to the Turoe Stone of County Galway. This is pagan country, as it was in this neighbourhood that

St Patrick overthrew the druidic idol of Crom Crúaich, on the 'Plain of Adoration'.

BALLYCONNELL is 8 miles north of Killeshandra and 7 miles west of Belturbet.

BALLYMAHON
County Longford

Ballymahon – literally 'Mahon's Town' – is named after Mahon, King of Thomond, who defeated Fergal, son of Ruarc, High King of Bréifne and Connacht here in 960. Beautifully situated on the charming River Inny, the river is spanned here by a five arch bridge from which you can

see the brown trout in the river below.

This is the very heart of the Goldsmith country as the essayist, poet and playwright was born near here, at Pallas, five miles north of the town. A statue to him was unveiled in Pallas in 1974 to mark his bi-centenary year. Goldsmith (1728-1774), fully earned his epitaph that 'nothing touched that he did not adorn'. His novel *The Vicar of Wakefield* was widely aclaimed, his poem *The Deserted Village* established him, and his play *She Stoops to Conquer* immortalised him.

Auburn, just six miles from Pallas, where Goldsmith went to

school, and his father was rector, (its real name is Lissoy) is referred to as 'Sweet Auburn' in his *Deserted Village*. A little to the north-east is the Three Jolly Pigeons pub, named after the Inn in *She Stoops To Conquer*. Its doorstep is the mill stone from the 'Busy Mill' with its 'never failing brook'. The ruins of the Ale house, 'where village statesmen talked and looked profound', still remain. The front wall and the end walls of the original Lissoy Parsonage still stand.

Ardagh, a sweet little village three miles south-west of Edgeworthstown, is where Goldsmith mistook Ardagh House for an inn and used the incident in the plot of *She Stoops To Conquer*. His statue by John Henry Foley, stands in College Green outside the College of the Holy and Undivided Trinity, where he was educated. All the places associated with Goldsmith are well signposted.

BALLYMAHON is 69 miles from Dublin and 13 miles from Longford.

BIRR
County Offaly

Birr Castle, home of the Earl and Countess of Rosse, is famous for its beautiful demesne gardens, open to the public. The 100-acre grounds cover 1000 different species of shrubs and trees. In spring the formal gardens are a mass of flowering magnolia, and in autumn the maples and hedges are magnificent. There are hornbeam walks, and the box hedges are the tallest in the world. In the grounds are the remains of the Great Telescope invented by the 3rd Earl of Rosse (1800-1867) with which he mapped the milky way and discovered the spiral nebulae. Another exhibition commemorates

Twice winner of the Tidy Towns Award, Ballyconnell also boasts the mysterious Tomregon Stone

Sir Charles Parsons (1854-1931) the youngest son of the 3rd Earl of Rosse, who invented the steam turbine. He put the fear of God into the entire coal-burning British Navy, assembled before the King for review at Spithead, when he darted in and out of the fleet in his fast steam turbine powered boat.

Anthony Armstrong Jones and Princess Margaret were frequent visitors to Birr Castle, as the Countess of Rosse is the mother of Princess Margaret's former husband. *BIRR is 27 miles south of Athlone and 80 miles south west of Dublin.*

BOYLE
County Roscommon

Boyle – 'The Monastery of the Pasture River' – lies at the foot of the Curlew Mountains on the north bank of the River Boyle which links Lough Gara with Lough Key.

Two miles to the north east of Boyle is Lough Key Forest Park, a lovely wild park where the Departments of Fisheries, Tourism and Forest and Wildlife have combined to make a natural wonderland of forest walks, boating and swimming. There is an excellent lakeside restaurant. Lough Gara, just west of Boyle, is an area rich in antiquities dating from 2500 BC, with over 300 crannogs, over 30 dug-out boats, and one of the largest dolmens in Ireland, 15 ft long and 11 ft wide on five standing stones. *BOYLE is 117 miles from Dublin and 27 miles north of Roscommon.*

BOYLE ABBEY
County Roscommon

The Cistercian Abbey of Boyle was established in 1161 by Abbot Maurice O'Duffy and was closely linked with

The stately grey pile of Birr Castle is surrounded by glorious grounds

the great Abbey of Mellifont in County Louth. It was partially destroyed in 1569, but retains its massive and picturesque ruins of a cruciform church, a lofty central tower, and a large nave, choir, kitchen and cloisters.

BOYLE ABBEY is in the town of Boyle, 25 miles from Sligo and 117 from Dublin.

CASTLE LESLIE
County Monaghan

Castle Leslie, originally a medieval fortress, is today the 1870s stately home of the distinguished Leslie family. In its grounds there is one of the finest equestrian cross-country courses in these islands.

One branch of the family was connected with the mother of Sir Winston Churchill, and they still have his baby dress! Charles Powell Leslie paid for the upbringing of his brother-in-law, Lord Mornington, who was without means, and who later became Duke of Wellington. His Waterloo bridle and death mask are preserved in the castle.

CASTLE LESLIE is at Glaslough, 7 miles north east of the town of Monaghan.

CASTLEREA
County Roscommon

Castlerea – 'The Grey Castle' – is a pretty wooden village on the River Suck, which was the birthplace of Sir William Wilde (1815-1876), an eminent Dublin eye specialist and antiquarian and father of Oscar Wilde (1854-1900), dramatist and wit. Sir William's wife, Lady Wilde (1826-1896) wrote patriotic verse and articles for the *Nation*, the newspaper voice of the Young Ireland Movement, under the pen name of 'Speranza'.

Just west of the town is Clonalis

Boyle Abbey is magnificent even in its ruined state

House, the ancestral home of the Clan of Connacht, who ruled the province and produced the High Kings of Ireland, notably Turlough Mor who died in 1156. Arguably the oldest documented family in Europe, their genealogical papers go back over 1500 years. This Victorian House, set in parkland, is a treasure house of ancient Irish manuscripts, books, documents, regalia, costume, furniture and paintings, open to the public. The portraits include the pictures of Major Owen O'Connor, Count and Countess O'Rourke, and Don Carlos O'Connor. Count O'Rourke, father of Bishop O'Rourke, was killed fighting the red-coats of Marlborough at the Bat-

tle of Luzzara. His wife was Maid-of-Honour at the Court of King James, in France. The O'Connors fought as brigadiers and high ranking officers in the 'Wild Geese' Irish regiments in the service of France, and in the Regiment of Dillon. In the dining room is a portrait of Don Carlos O'Connor, Spanish Diplomat. The portrait of Charles O'Connor of New York shows the man who was the first Catholic ever to have been nominated to the Presidency of the United States. He was defeated by Ulysses Grant in 1872. Clonalis House is open to the public.

CASTLEREA is 19 miles north of Roscommon.

CLONES
County Monaghan

Clones was the site of a monastery founded by St Tighearnach who died in AD 548. The 10th-century Celtic Cross of the Scriptures, 15 ft high, formally stood near the Round Tower, and now stands in the town square. The Round Tower in the graveyard is 75 ft in height with a square headed doorway. The adjacent shrine of St Tighearnach is in the shape of a house carved out of a single stone. All around this area are superb coarse fishing lakes. The town is famous for its lace making.

CLONES is 13 miles south west of Monaghan town.

CLONMACNOISE
County Offaly

"In a quiet watered land, a land
of roses,
Stands Saint Kieran's city fair;
And the warriors of Erin in their
famous generations
Slumber there ...
There they laid to rest the seven
Kings of Tara
There the sons of Cairbre sleep
Battle-banners of the Gael that
in Kieran's plain of crosses
Now their final hosting keep..."

Thus wrote the poet T.W. Rolleston (1857-1920), translating the Irish of Angus O'Gillan, about the mighty monastic city of Clonmacnoise on the banks of the Shannon, city of churches, high crosses and round towers, founded by St Kieran in AD 548 and which flourished for over 1000 years. Entering the monastic

Clonmacnoise (seen from the air, *left*) is full of ancient monastic remains like the ones below

enclosure from the car park there are ten churches, two round towers, a castle, three high crosses, including the superb 10th-century 'Cross of the Scriptures' and over 400 historic gravestones and tomb stones.

◄ *CLONMACNOISE is 4 miles north of Shannonbridge. The ideal approach is 9 miles by river from Athlone.*

DÚN A RÍ FOREST PARK
County Cavan

Dún a Rí Forest Park covers 588 acres and part of the famous Kingscourt Forest. It is noted for its mixed hardwoods and conifers. It has an excellent selection of nature trails.

◄ *DÚN A RÍ PARK is 1 mile north of Kingscourt on the road to Carrickmacross.*

EDGEWORTHSTOWN
County Longford

Edgeworthstown is a delightful market town. It takes its name from the Edgeworth family, formerly of Edgeworthstown House, a Georgian house, later a convent, and now a nursing home, built by Richard Lovell Edgeworth (1744-1817) author, inventor and father of the novelist Maria Edgeworth (1767-1849). Maria achieved fame with her novel *Castle Rackrent*, first published in 1800. She influenced the writings of Turgenev and entertained Sir Walter Scott, whose novels she also influenced, and also William Wordsworth, in her Longford home. Their family vault is in the local Protestant church, in which the delightful Maria Edgeworth Museum is housed. Her novels were published in 12 volumes. Another famous Edgeworth was the Abbé Edgeworth

de Firmont, (Firmont is a village three miles north of Edgeworthstown), son of Essex Edgeworth, who was confessor to Louis XVI at his death on the scaffold.

◄ *EDGEWORTHSTOWN is 69 miles north west of Dublin and 19 miles north west of Mullingar.*

EMO COURT
County Laois

Emo Court, a private residence, is a glorious house designed in 1790 by James Gandon, who also designed the Church of Ireland church in Coolbanagher, two and a half miles south of Emo. Formerly a Jesuit Novitiate, Emo Court has magnificent gardens with fine specimens of trees and shrubs, open to the public by special arrangement.

◄ *EMO COURT is 45 miles from Dublin off the main Dublin to Cork and Limerick road.*

INNISKEEN
County Monaghan

In the local Folk Museum in this charming village, is a section devoted to the poet Patrick Kavanagh (1904-1967), who was born in the vicinity and worked as a cobbler and small farmer. While working here he published his first collection of poems *The Ploughman and Other Poems* in 1936. In his two light semi-autobiographical novels *The Green Fool* and *Tarry Flynn* he described life during the 'thirties in the tiny village. His actual birthplace was the adjacent townland of Muckner, and he lies buried in the local cemetery. The remains of a Round Tower in Inniskeen show that it was once the monastic settlement of the 6th-century St Dega.

◄ *INNISKEEN is 7 miles north east of Carrickmacross.*

Patrick Kavanagh

The seven counties, roughly grouped together into their collective 'Midlands', have in their midst a major poet who binds them together, Patrick Kavanagh, the 'ploughman poet' (1904-1967) who was born and farmed for 30 years in Iniskeen in the 'hungry hills' of Monaghan. Arguably the greatest Irish poet since W.B. Yeats, he caught the spirit of childhood as he looked back from his adult days of quiet desperation. The poet who is,

"...astonished
At a stick carried down a stream
Or at the undying difference in the corner of a field"

and who remembers so vividly

"...the newness that was in every stale thing
When we looked at it as children;"

Or the prophetic astonishment in the tedious talking

"Of an old fool ...
... the bog-holes, cart tracks, old stables where time begins."

In his poem, *Shancoduff*, the midland counties share in this image,

"My hills hoard the bright shillings of March
While the sun searches in every pocket."

And the bog-lands shared by these regions are reflected thus;

"That beautiful, beautiful beautiful God
Was breathing his love by a cut-away bog."

In his poem, *Peace* he asks:

"Out of that childhood country what fools climb
To fight with tyrants Love and Life and Time?"

Lake Derravaragh — Kavanagh was inspired by melancholy Midland beauty such as this

KILLY KEEN FOREST PARK
County Cavan

Killy Keen Forest Park comprises 600 acres of spectacular beauty. Its Devinish nature trail takes in a number of crannogs, or ancient lakeside dwelling places, the most notable being that of Cloughoughter. There are four excellent fishing locations beside the lake, and a car park.

Cloughoughter Castle, the remains of which still stand on a small island in Lough Oughter, was once the 13th-century fortress of the O'Reilly's.

KILLY KEEN FOREST PARK is 8 miles west of the town of Cavan.

LANESBOROUGH
County Longford

Lanesborough, a delightful town spanning the River Shannon, with a nine arch bridge at the tip of the northern end of Lough Ree, is a Shannon River cruising centre. Lough Ree is a coarse fish angler's paradise, and the Shannon at this point is a trout fisherman's heaven. A glimpse of modern Ireland can be seen near the town on the east bank in the form of a turf-fired electricity generating power station. On the island of Lough Ree is the 6th-century monastery founded by St Diarmuid, who taught St Kieran of Clonmacnoise. The history of the island is much older than this as there are great Ogham stones and a small circular mound said to have been the Palace of Queen Maeve. The legend concerning her is unkind to the men of Ulster, as it claims that one of their number took a shot at her with a stone from a sling, and killed her while she was bathing!

LANESBOROUGH is 19 miles by boat or 27 miles by road from Athlone.

LONGFORD
County Longford

The town of Longford – from the Irish word for 'fortress', lies on the southern bank of the charming River Camlin, east of the mighty River Shannon. Nothing is left of the original ancient O'Farrell Fortress, princes of Annaly, after which the town was named. The enormous St Mel's Cathedral dominates the town. At the rear of the cathedral is the Diocesan Museum, open to the public, (admission free), which houses the crozier of St Mel, the shrine of St Manchan and much of the library from Edgeworthstown House, the former home of the novelist, Maria Edgeworth. At Clondra, seven miles west of the handsome town, is the village's *Teach Cheoil* or Irish Music House, where the best of old-fashioned Irish music can be heard in traditional kitchen-like surroundings.

LONGFORD is 8¼ miles north west of Edgeworthstown.

LOUGH DERRAVARAGH
County Westmeath

County Westmeath boasts three beautiful lakes; the picturesque Lough Ennell, six miles long and three miles wide, Lough Owel, 2200 acres of brown trout fishing, and Lough Derravaragh – 'The Lake of the Oaks' – with its well wooded shores and waters teeming with trout, pike and perch. However, the greatest attraction of its shining waters is that it is the scene of the most tragic of all Irish romantic legends, 'The Fate of the Children of Lir'. Lir was the Tuatha Dé Danann Chief whose second wife, Aoife, a witch, was so jealous of her four step-children that she changed them into swans, and decreed that they would remain so until the sound of the first Mass bell in Ireland. The whole Irish saga is a metaphor for the freeing of Ireland from the pagan bondage of the Druids. And so it was, after 900 years of suffering, that the magic spell ceased at the sound of St Patrick's Mass bell, and the children Finola, Aedh, Fiachra and Conn returned to their human form, and were converted and baptised by St Mochaomhog.

LOUGH DERRAVARAGH is approximately 4 miles south west of Castlepollard.

ROSSMORE FOREST PARK
County Monaghan

Rossmore Forest Park is 691 acres of woodland set among pleasant hills and tiny lakes just south and adjacent to the town of Monaghan.

Formerly it was the estate of the Cunningham family, the first holder of the Rossmore baronetcy title being General Robert Cunningham, MP for Monaghan from 1769 to 1796.

It has a number of nature trails and carefully laid out forest walks.

ROSSMORE FOREST PARK is next door to Monaghan town which is 17 miles from Armagh, and 75 from Dublin.

STRADBALLY
County Laois

Stradbally is a charming little 17th-century town which is historically the centre of the Clan O'More, the O'Mores of Noughaval who, for centuries, had in their possession the precious 'Book of Leinster'. The town boasts the Stradbally Steam Museum, open to the public, and dedicated to the part played by steam in the social history of Ireland. A Steam Rally is held every August. Also open to the public is the Pony Stud, at Stradbally Hall. The 18th-century gardens of Stradbally Hall are well worth visiting for their unique herbaceous borders and 90 species of perennials.

Near Stradbally, on the road to Portlaoise, is the Rock of Dunamase.

STRADBALLY is 9 miles from Athy and 7 miles from Portlaoise.

The Rock of Dunamase is a Celtic fortress symbolising the struggle for territorial possession in the Midlands

TIMAHOE
County Laois

Timahoe – *Teach Mo-Chúa* – the House of Mo-Chua, named after St Mochua who died in 657, boasts a fine 11th-century Round Tower 96 ft high, and with a base circumference of 57 ft, the largest of any Round Tower in Ireland. It is made from local limestone and sandstone and is divided into a basement and five storeys. One of the unique features is the fine Romanesque doorway, 17 ft above the ground. It is splendidly ornamented with little bearded heads.

The Catholic church in Timahoe has two magnificent stained glass windows by Michael Healy (1873-1941) who was one of the original stained glass artists of *An Túr Gloine*, which he joined in 1903.

TIMAHOE is 7½ miles south east of Portlaoise.

TULLAMORE
County Offaly

The town of Tullamore – *Tulac Mór* the Great Assembly Hill, was once the mound of ancient formal assemblies but is now famous as the home of the Irish Mist Liqueur Company, the leading liqueur made in Ireland with 100 years of history. The factory welcomes visitors. Admission is free.

TULLAMORE is 60 miles west of Dublin.

TULLYNALLY CASTLE
County Westmeath

Tullynally Castle, formerly Pakenham Hall, is the residence of the celebrated literary family, the Longfords, and is open to the public. Lord Longford's son, Tom Pakenham, is the present owner. Edmund Pakenham came to Ireland as secretary to Sir Henry Sidney, Queen Elizabeth's Lord Deputy. Henry, his grandson, purchased Tullynally in 1655. Neighbour Richard Lovell Edgeworth, the inventor, installed gas-fired, underfloor central heating around 1794, the first in these islands! The house was made into a 'Gothic' castle between 1801 and 1806 by Francis Johnson, to make it look like an Irish version of Inveraray Castle in Scotland. It was a fortress during the 1798 insurrection. The ground plan of this romantic castle shows it to be nearly 400 ft long. There is a huge front hall, complete with organ, a vast bow-windowed drawing room, a charming library, a family wing, and a huge Victorian kitchen installed by the bachelor third Earl, who obviously enjoyed his food and being waited on by masses of servants. The latest addition to the castle is the 1860 Gothic tower by the architect of the late Lord Mountbatten's Castle, Classiebawn in County Sligo. Kitty Pakenham married the Duke of Wellington and the house is full of fascinating family history. The present Lord Longford, under the name of Frank Pakenham, wrote the definitive book on the Irish Troubles, *Peace by Ordeal*. Lady Elizabeth Longford is famous as a writer of historical biographies, notably her life of the Duke of Wellington. Tom Pakenham is the author of a history of the 1798 Rebellion, *The Year of Liberty*, and a study of the Boer War. The 6th Earl of Longford (1902-1961) was a director of the Gate Theatre and founder of Longford Productions.

TULLYNALLY CASTLE is 1½ miles west of Castlepollard.

Tullynally Castle's sturdy facade

VIRGINIA
County Cavan

Virginia, a market town on the banks of lovely Lough Ramor, five miles of beautiful wooded shores and waters, is named after the 'Virgin Queen', Elizabeth I. Three miles north of the town is Cuilcagh Lough, on whose banks once stood Cuilcagh House, the home of schoolmaster the Reverend Thomas Sheridan (1687-1738) friend of Dean Jonathan Swift who began writing *Gulliver's Travels* here. Thomas Sheridan was the father of another Thomas Sheridan, actor-manager of Smock Alley Theatre, Dublin, and grandfather of Richard Brinsley Sheridan (1751-1816) playwright, immortalised by his works *The Rivals* and *The School for Scandal*.

Ballyjamesduff, a town just six miles north west of Virginia, was made famous in a song by Percy French, *Come Back Paddy Reilly*. It was also the birthplace of William James, who emigrated to America in 1789 and was the grandfather of William James the philosopher, and of the novelist, Henry James.

VIRGINIA is 52 miles from Dublin.

Virginia is beautifully laid out on the banks of Lough Ramor

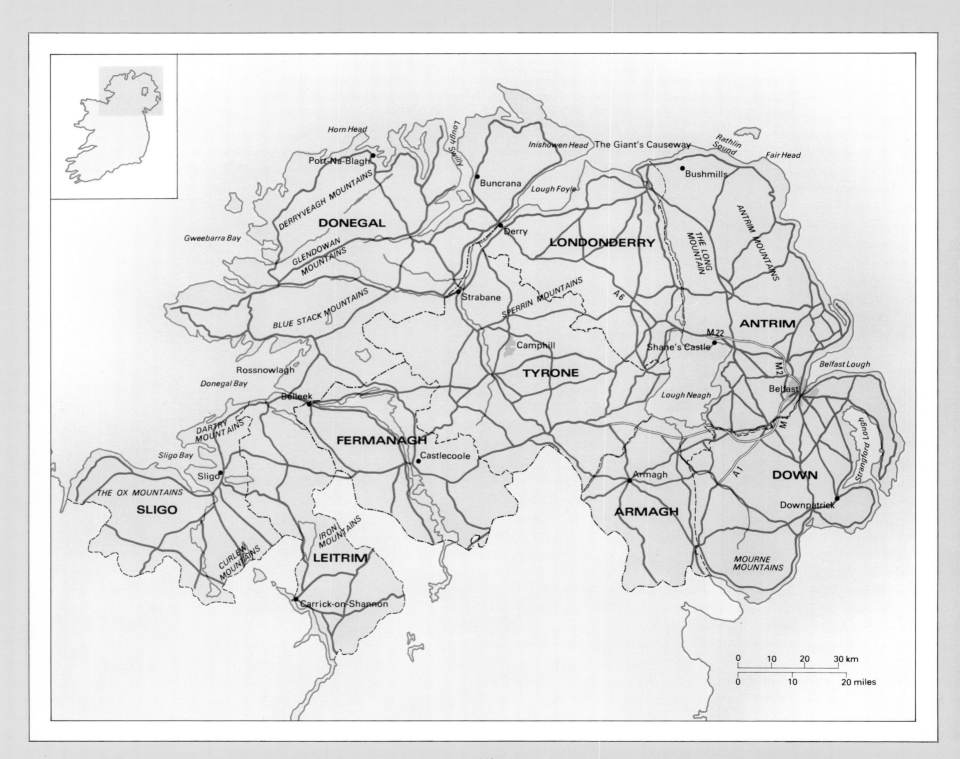

Horn Head

Lough Swilly

Inishowen Head   The Giant's Causeway

Rathlin Sound

Fair Head

Port-Na-Blagh

Buncrana

Bushmills

DERRYVEAGH MOUNTAINS

Lough Foyle

DONEGAL

Gweebarra Bay

Derry

LONDONDERRY

ANTRIM MOUNTAINS

THE LONG MOUNTAIN

GLENDOWAN MOUNTAINS

Strabane

SPERRIN MOUNTAINS

A6

ANTRIM

BLUE STACK MOUNTAINS

M 22

Camphill

Shane's Castle

Rossnowlagh

TYRONE

M 2

Belfast Lough

Donegal Bay

Belleek

Lough Neagh

Belfast

DARTRY MOUNTAINS

FERMANAGH

Strangford Lough

Sligo Bay

Castlecoole

Sligo

M 1

THE OX MOUNTAINS

Armagh

A 1

DOWN

SLIGO

Downpatrick

IRON MOUNTAINS

ARMAGH

CURLEW MOUNTAINS

LEITRIM

MOURNE MOUNTAINS

Carrick-on-Shannon

0   10   20   30 km

0   10   20 miles

The North

The ancient Irish were convinced that County Antrim's Giant's Causeway was the work of Ulster warrior-giant Finn McCool. In fact, this mass of basalt columns, mostly hexagonal, is the result of volcanic action

THE REGION WE CALL 'The North' transcends all man-made political lines, and flows fully and naturally across the Atlantic coastline of Sligo, Leitrim and Donegal, swinging around the stepping stones to Scotland of Derry, Antrim and Down, embracing the vast lakeland that is Fermanagh and the glory of the O'Neill territories of Tyrone. A tidy people these Northerners, they have gathered together all their industrial might in one place, Belfast, leaving the unspoilt countryside and the clean sandy beaches, the massive lakes and rivers free. The countryside and new forests are as neat and tidy as the kit of an Irish guardsman laid out for inspection! The Northern Irish are largely made up of hard working small farmers, with a scattering of great 'garrison' houses of the old Etonian guardsmen, who kept the British army supplied with leaders, men such as Alexander of Tunis, Governor General of Canada. Irish soldiers such as Lord Terence O'Neill of Shane's Castle, Prime Minister of Northern Ireland from 1963 to 1969. The 'Micks', the Irish Guards, where would they be without them? Some dozen great houses remain, run by the National Trust, and open to the public. Ardress and the Argory and Derrymore, in Armagh, Castlecoole and the Florence Court in Fermanagh, Castle Ward, Mount Stewart House and Rowallane Gardens in Down, Hazlett House, Springhill, and Mussenden Temple in Derry. Here, too, are the 'Northern Lights' of Irish literature and poetry.

ARMAGH
County Armagh

Armagh – *Ara Maca* – Macha's Height, was named after the fabulous warrior Queen, Macha, who founded the enormous fort of *Eamhain Macha* just two miles west of Armagh. Her burial place here dates from 300 BC, and *Eamhain Macha* was the seat of the Kings of Ulster from then until A.D. 332. Then King Conor MacNessa made it the training camp for his Red Branch Knights. The Church of Ireland Cathedral occupies the site of the original church of St Patrick. The Catholic Cathedral, twin towered, atop the hill, is 1840s Gothic, and here resides the Catholic Cardinal Archbishop of Armagh 'Primate of all Ireland.' Armagh, amid its seven hills, dated as an episcopal see from A.D. 445.

🚗 *ARMAGH is 85 miles from Dublin.*

BELFAST
County Antrim

Belfast, capital of Northern Ireland, lies on the River Lagan. Industrial centre of the North, well known for its huge ship-building yards and the manufacture of aircraft, the city has a noble 19th-century City Hall, a beautifully-restored Opera House, and its own Queen's University, established in 1849. The Ulster Museum, in the Botanic Gardens, near the University, houses a fine collection of Irish antiquities, including the Downpatrick Gold Hoards, historic Irish silver, and a magnificent Art Gallery which includes the works of Sickert, Steer, Stanley Spencer and Francis Bacon. Of particular interest is the dazzling collection of treasures recovered by underwater divers from the wreck of the largest ship in the Spanish Armada, the *Gerona*, which was wrecked off the Giant's Causeway in 1588. The treasures were recovered in 1968.

The annual Belfast Festival, the biggest in Britain after Edinburgh, takes place at The Queen's University and its environs. An exhilarating mixture of music, theatre, satire, dance, comedy and mime, the autumn festival draws international performers such as Yehudi Menuhin, actors Anthony Quayle and Ian McKellen and musicians such as Cleo Laine and Johnny Dankworth.

🚗 *BELFAST is 103 miles north of Dublin and 75 miles from Derry.*

This aerial view of Belfast (*right*) shows the blue dome of the city hall, seen from Windsor House

Queen's University (*below*) has mullioned windows and a fine Tudor cloister

BELLEEK
County Fermanagh

Belleek china, the internationally famous white lustre finished pottery, is named after the town where it has been manufactured by hand since 1863. Originally local clays and water power were used. The highly ornamental glazed earthenware covers a wide range, from fragile translucent teacups and saucers to intricate designs for pots, plates and teapots, with platted, inter-woven basket-like exteriors. Statues too, and ornate candelabra are all part of the tradition. Early Belleek pottery is particularly valuable, and much sought after by American collectors. There are many elegant modern Celtic designs with the shamrock motif. You can see the master potters at work on the porcelain, and the 'Fettlers', the men who assemble the pieces for the fiery furnaces.

BELLEEK is on the Donegal-Fermanagh border 23 miles from Enniskillen.

BUNCRANA
County Donegal

Buncrana, perched on the east side of the Inishowen Peninsular, on the shores of Lough Foyle, is sheltered by high mountains such as Slieve Snacht (2019 ft), and is a charming seaside resort. Just 11 miles south is the most impressive and awesome stone fortress in Ireland, the Grianan of Aileach. A unique circular stone fort standing over 800 ft high above Loughs Swilly and Foyle on Greenan Mountain, it is 77 ft in diameter, with walls 17 ft high and 13 ft thick. Built in 1700 BC, it was once the residence of the O'Neills, Kings of Ulster.

BUNCRANA is 161 miles from Dublin and 13 from Derry.

This intricate 'basket weave' design characterises Belleek pottery

Carrick-on-Shannon has a popular marina

CAMPHILL
County Tyrone

The Ulster-American Folk Park at Camphill, made possible by the generosity of the descendants of Thomas Mellon, founder of the Pittsburg, Pennsylvania banking family, recreates the old world and the new world in an imaginative presentation of buildings and their contents which tell the story of the emigration of Ulster people to the United States of America. The Dr Mathew T. Mellon Building at the entrance to the Folk Park shows audio-visual representations of the mass migration. There is a Pine Walk from there to the splendidly re-created forge, to the Weaver's Cottage, the Meeting House, and the *pièce de resistance*, the actual Mellon homestead, the cottage in which Thomas Mellon was born on 3 February 1813. His family emigrated with him to America in 1818, but he never forgot his humble cottage birthplace, and he returned to see it in 1882. There is a magnificent viewpoint atop the hill above the Mellon Homestead. Back to the Schoolhouse, moved from its original site in Castletown, it was founded in 1790 and renewed in 1845, retaining its name as the local 'National School'.

Then there is the 'New World' of the Log Cabin, based on the Mellon family farmhouse in Pennsylvania, the Log Barn, the Smoke House for hickory chip or corn cob, curing of bacon and of venison, the Spring-house or Dairy, the Corncob or Granary, the Camp Meeting Site, the Poultry Exhibit and, to cap it all, a magnificent Conestoga Wagon of 1790, the type of wagon in which the Mellon family and hundreds of thousands of Ulster emigrants moved West. The Ulster-American Folk

Irish whiskey — created not made

The Old Bushmills Distillery, where whiskey is 'created'

At Bushmills, in County Antrim, is the world's first licensed distillery, founded in 1608. Here, they make 'Old Bushmills', a deluxe Irish whiskey of superb quality, set apart and unique because it is a blend of a single malt and a single grain. The malt whiskey comes from the Bushmills distillery, the grain from the sister distillery in Coleraine. The barley is grown locally, and the water comes from the distillery's own privately owned tributary of the River Bush, St Columb's Rill. Bushmills whiskey has always been made with this special water which rises in peaty ground and flows over basalt. The Irish word for whiskey (always spelt with an 'e'), is *Uisce Beatha*, meaning, 'the water of life.' They say that Bushmills whiskey is not made, it is 'created.' The three raw materials in the creation are malted barley, yeast and water.

The first stage is milling, the malt being screened to ensure purity and quality, and then milled, or ground. The next stage is mashing, the 'grist', or ground malt, being mashed or mixed with hot water, and allowed to settle in a cylindrical cast-iron vessel called a 'Mash Tun.' The starch in the ground malt becomes sugar. The 'Wort', or sugar and water, are drained through the perforated base of the Mash Tun into a vessel called the 'underback'. The Wort is cooled on its way to the fermenting vessel known as the 'washback', where yeast is fed to the sugar producing the 'wash' which is non alcoholic. Ten gallons of wash make one gallon of alcohol at proof strength. Then comes the distillation process in pot stills. The wash is heated in the first still. The alcohol vapour is collected as a distillate which is heated in the second still. Then come the 'feints', the distillate is separated into two parts, the heads and the tails, the stronger heads being distilled in a third still, the 'Spirit' still, the tails recycled.

The third distillate is sampled by the stillman and from the pure spirit running he selects only that portion with the desired character and flavour, which goes into the Spirit Receiver at a collecting strength of 45° proof. Oak casks receive the spirits reduced in strength by the addition of purified water, and maturing takes place, the best being up to 12 years old, Bushmills famous 'Black Label''.

Park is a major tourist attraction in the north of Ireland.

🚗 *CAMPHILL is a 26-acre site, on the River Strule midway between Newtonstewart to its north, and 4 miles from Omagh to its south. It is approximately 73 miles from Belfast, 34 from Derry and 119 from Dublin.*

CARRICK-ON-SHANNON
County Leitrim

Carrick-on-Shannon, on the mighty River Shannon, is the centre for marinas and flotillas of cruisers who come to explore the most beautiful and navigable stretch of the river. It is also the coarse-fishing angling centre of the county and is equally famous for trout fishing. They say 'Leitrim, God help us!' is the poorest county in Ireland, but its little known mountains and lakes, with Lough Allen seven miles long and three miles wide, is every bit as beautiful as the better-known landscape of its neighbouring Sligo. Its Lough Melvin is famous for its salmon and trout angling.

🚗 *CARRICK-ON-SHANNON is 101 miles from Dublin and 23 from Longford.*

CASTLECOOLE
County Fermanagh

Bordering the town of Enniskillen, in a 1500-acre wooded demesne is Castlecoole, once the seat of the Earls of Belmore, now in the care of the National Trust, and open to the public. It has been described as the perfect Georgian house in Grecian Style, built of imported Portland Stone. Designed by James Wyatt, it was built in the 1790s. The plaster work is by Joseph Rose. The six mantels are by the English sculptor Westmacott and there is an excellent collection of period furniture. In the parklands, on the lake, are a famous flock of greylag geese.

🚗 *CASTLECOOLE is approximately 112 miles from Dublin and 86 from Belfast.*

DERRY
County Derry

Derry – *Doire* – The Oak Wood, dates from the year 546 when St Colmcille, or Columba as he was more generally known, founded a monastery here. Tradition ascribes an ancient Irish verse to Colmcille, who expressed his love for his favourite monastery thus, 'Derry, my own grove, Little cell, my home, my love.' The Protestant Cathedral stands on the site of his monastery. It is a walled city, famous for its siege of 1689, and these walls today are a delightful promenade. Situated on the estuary of the River Foyle, it is the gateway to the romantic county of Donegal, which lies on its western side.

🚗 *DERRY is 152 miles from Dublin, 75 miles from Belfast, and 25 from Letterkenny.*

DOWNPATRICK
County Down

Downpatrick – *Dun Padraig* – St Patrick's Fort, is where St Patrick founded his first or second church, after his return to Ireland. The Church of Ireland Cathedral, standing at the western edge of the town, was built in the 1800s to include part of the 12th-century cathedral in its nave and transepts. Outside the east end of the cathedral is a re-assembled 10th-century Celtic cross. There is a large granite boulder in the churchyard on the south side of this cathedral, marked 'Patric', placed there in 1900, and, without any evidence, the reputed burial place of St Patrick. Excavations on this hill site in 1985 have simply uncovered evidence of a large medieval building and a very early Christian cemetery. Defensive ditches, and bronze age pottery 2500 years old have also been found.

Perfectly situated on the River Quoile, just three miles from Downpatrick, are the remains of Inch Abbey, a Cistercian foundation of John de Courcy in 1180, who brought over monks from Furness Abbey in Lancashire. Saul – *Sabhall* – a barn, just two miles north east

A pair of white oxen are said to have carried St Patrick to his grave, marked by this stone in the churchyard of Down Cathedral, Downpatrick

of Downpatrick, where St Patrick landed, has the ruins of the 12th-century Abbey founded by St Malachi on the site of a barn in which St Patrick celebrated his first mass in Ireland. At Struell, two miles east of Downpatrick, are St Patrick's Wells, originally Druidic waters, and blessed by the saint. Some hold that the blessed well waters will cure pilgrims suffering from eye ailments.

🚗 *DOWNPATRICK is 22 miles from Belfast and 96 from Dublin.*

THE GIANT'S CAUSEWAY
County Antrim

The rock formation of the Giant's Causeway ranks it as a geological structure of world interest. It is divided into the Honeycomb Causeway and the Little Causeway, a series of thousands of hexagonal vertical basalt columns assaulted by the sea. Bands of iron ore abound, and the causeway was formed by molten lava cooling as it burst through the earth's crust in the Cainozoic period. The various spectacular formations have been given fanciful names such as the Wishing Chair, My Lady's Fan, the Giant's Organ, the Giant's Loom and the Giant's Coffin. Fortunately Bushmills and its Distillery is only three miles south of the Causeway, which is not as 'Giant' as it is made out to be.

🚗 *THE GIANT'S CAUSEWAY is*

the property of the National Trust and is 8 miles from Portrush, which is 60 miles from Belfast.

PORT-NA-BLAGH
County Donegal

Sheltered in Sheephaven Bay, this romantic and cosy little seaside resort has a splendid sandy beach and is an ideal centre from which to explore the exciting Atlantic Coast of the Rosguill Peninsular. Horn Head (600 ft of cliff), and Bloody Foreland, with Mount Errigal, the shining white and blue cone-shaped mountain (2466 ft) can be seen dominating the glorious landscape in the background like an Irish Fujiyama.

🚗 *PORT-NA-BLAGH is just over 20 miles north west of Letterkenny and approximately 176 miles from Dublin, via Strabane.*

ROSSNOWLAGH
County Donegal

Rossnowlagh has one of the finest and most beautiful strands and surfing beaches in the country. It has an excellent Museum of the County Donegal Historical Society, housed in the modern Franciscan Friary, which has lovely gardens and a beautiful church. The attractive Sand House Hotel is right on the water's edge, and the proprietress is Margaret Thatcher's double!

🚗 *ROSSNOWLAGH is 133 miles from Dublin and 11 miles from Donegal town.*

SHANE'S CASTLE
County Antrim

Shane's Castle has the unique distinction of having the only steam locomotive railway in regular service in Northern Ireland. The most popular amateur engine driver is the Lord Raymond O'Neill of Clannaboy. The railway runs all the way through his superb Nature Reserve, from Shane's Castle Station.

🚗 *SHANE'S CASTLE is about 3 miles north of Antrim town, and about 17 miles from Belfast.*

SLIGO
County Sligo

Sligo – *Sligeac* – The Shelley River, is a charming town on the south bank of the broad Garavogue River

Lord O'Neill with his gleaming steam train on the Shane's Castle Railway

Lough Gill, its waters smooth as glass, contains Yeats' magical Island of Innisfree

which links Lough Gill with the Atlantic ocean. Historically, it guarded the north-south main route on the west coast. It lies between the mountains of Benbulben and Knocknarea. The splendid ruins of Sligo Abbey date from 1641. The Sligo County Museum and Art Gallery has a special section of Yeats manuscripts, broadsheets and paintings, and is open to the public.

Lough Gill, just two miles from the town, contains the magical island of Innisfree which inspired Yeats' most famous poem *The Lake*
Isle of Innisfree. On the south shore, near Cottage Island, is Dooney rock, made famous in Yeats' poem *The Fiddler of Dooney.* West of Sligo is Knocknarea (1078 ft), also featured in his poetry, on the summit of which is the huge burial cairn of Queen Maeve of Connacht. Five miles along the road from Sligo to Bundoran is Drumcliff. In its churchyard is the burial place of W.B. Yeats, with his own epitaph, 'Cast a cold Eye on Life, on Death. Horseman, pass by'. Two miles north of Drumcliff is Lissadell
House, open to the public, the home of the Gore-Booth family whose illustrious daughters were the poetess, Eva Gore-Booth, and Constance, Countess Markievicz, a leader of the 1916 Rising.

🚗 *SLIGO is 135 miles from Dublin.*

STRABANE
County Tyrone

Strabane, on the River Mourne, was the birthplace of John Dunlap, in 1747. He emigrated to Philadelphia
in 1771 and founded the first daily newspaper in America, the *Pennsylvania Packet.* He printed the Declaration of Independence, served as a member of General Washington's bodyguard, and gave £4000 to his army. He served his time in Gray's printing press in Strabane, which is still in existence. James Wilson, grandfather of President Woodrow Wilson, also worked in Gray's printing works before emigrating to America in 1807.

🚗 *STRABANE is 81 miles from Belfast, 18 miles from Letterkenny.*

Index · England

Page numbers in **bold** denote illustrations.

Acknowledgements
AA Picture Library: endpapers, contents, 6, 12/3, 19, 20, 21, 24, 28, 29, 33, 37(l,r), 38, 44, 45, 50/1, 52, 53, 54, 56, 57, 58, 59, 60, 61, 65, 66, 67, 69(l,r), 70/1, 71, 72, 73, 76/7, 78, 79, 80(l,r), 81, 83, 84, 85, 86, 87, 89, 92, 94/5, 96, 97, 98, 99, 104, 105, 106, 108, 110, 112.
Janet and Colin Bord: 14, 63, 68.
Britain on view: 32, 35, 42/3, 49, 91, 93, 95, 101, 102, 103, 107, 111.
John Heseltine: title page, 9, 17, 22(t,b), 23, 25, 26.
Neil Menneer: 31, 39, 41.
Colin Molyneux: 8, 10.
John Sims: 2/3, 4, 4/5, 7, 11.
Harry Smith Collection: 27.
Richard Surman: opener.

Acknowledgements
AA Picture Library: 123, 130, 149(t,b), 150(t,b), 151, 152, 162, 175, 176(t,b), 177, 180, 182(r), 188(t,b), 191, 192, 201, 202, 204, 208/9.
Mary Evans Picture Library: 52(tl).
Gleneagles Hotel Group: 205.
Bill Howes/Angling Photo Service: 122(t,b).
Anthony Lambert: 193.
Cameron McNeish: 116, 117, 119, 132/3, 134(t,b), 218(t,b).
Colin Molyneux: 215(t,b).
National Trust for Scotland: 118, 120/1, 126, 131, 206, 217, 219, 222, 223.
Scottish Tourist Board: contents, 115, 124, 125(l,r), 127, 129, 133, 135, 136, 137, 138, 139, 140/1, 143, 144, 145, 146, 147, 148, 153, 154/5, 155, 157, 158, 159, 160, 160/1, 163, 164 (tr,b), 165, 166/7, 169, 171, 172, 173, 174, 178, 179, 181, 182(l), 183, 185, 186, 187, 189, 190, 194/5, 196, 197, 199, 200, 203, 210, 211, 213, 216, 220/1.
Sotheby's: 168.

Acknowledgements
AA Picture Library: 230, 235, 256, 266/7, 303, 305, 306.
Janet and Colin Bord: contents, 237(r), 238, 247, 249, 324, 325.
Wales Tourist Board: 227, 228, 229, 232, 234, 236, 237(1), 240/1, 242/3, 244(1,r), 245, 248, 250/1, 252/3, 253, 254, 255(1,r), 257, 258, 260, 261, 262, 264, 265, 268, 269, 270/1, 271, 272, 273, 274(1,r), 275(1,r), 276, 277, 278, 279, 280, 281, 282(1,r), 284, 285, 286, 288, 291, 292, 293, 294, 295, 296, 298, 299, 300, 301, 304, 307, 308, 310, 311, 312, 314, 315, 316/7, 318, 319, 320, 321, 322, 323, 326, 328, 329, 330, 331, 332, 333(1,r), 334, 335, 336.

Acknowledgements
Borde Fáilte: contents, 339, 340, 341, 342, 343(l,r), 344, 345(l), 347, 348, 349, 350, 351, 352, 353, 354, 355, 356, 357, 358, 359, 361, 362, 363, 364, 365, 366, 367, 368, 369, 370(l,r), 371, 372/3, 374, 375, 376, 377, 378, 379, 381, 382, 383, 384, 385, 386, 387(t,b), 388(t,b), 389, 390/1, 392, 393, 394, 395, 397, 398, 399, 400, 401, 402, 403, 404, 405(l,r), 406, 407, 408/9, 411, 412, 413, 414, 415, 416, 417, 418/9, 420, 421, 422, 423(l,r), 425, 426/7, 429, 430, 431, 432, 433, 434, 435, 436, 437, 438, 439, 444(b), 448, 449.
John Freeman: 424.
Northern Ireland Tourist Board: 441, 442, 443, 444(t), 445, 446, 447.
Edward Pitcher: 345(l).